LAW OF Medical Negligence and Compensation

NEGLIGENCE is the failure to exercise the standard of care that a reasonably prudent person would have exercised in a similar situation. Negligence is a tort which involves a person's breach of duty that is imposed upon him to take care, resulting in damage to the complainant. Like other professionals, the medical personnels are liable to pay damages for their negligence under the law of torts.

The present work provides clear, detailed and in-depth analysis of the principles of medical negligence under general, penal and consumer laws. It deals with the concept of reasonable care, standard of skill and competence, criteria of informed consent in treatment, difference between wrong and negligent diagnosis, duty towards foetus, wrongful birth, obligation for gratuitous service, etc. The work comprehends both general and consumer law with regard to the rights to claim for, and individual as well as vicarious liability to pay compensation.

In the instant edition the author has discussed various issues such as variation of consent in elective and emergency surgery, sterilization failure and unwanted child, liability of hospital, deficiency in service, mode of assessment of compensation, expert evidence and its evaluation, guidelines for prosecution of doctor for causing death of the patient by rash and negligent treatment. It throws light on the procedure, pleading and proof for claiming compensation under general law and consumer laws. The present edition has incorporated almost all the important case laws of both India and abroad including the cases decided by the apex court and different High Courts on testing and treatment of Covid-19 patients and disposal of dead body of the patients infected therewith.

Kolkata

Eastern Law House Private Ltd.

54 Ganesh Chunder Avenue

Kolkata 700 013

New Delhi

Eastern Law House Private Ltd.

36 Netaji Subhash Marg, Daryaganj

New Delhi 110 002

LAW OF
Medical Negligence
and
Compensation

Covering the Rights and Liabilities under
THE LAW OF CONSUMER PROTECTION

by

R.K. Bag MA, LLB
Former Judge
High Court at Calcutta

THIRD EDITION

Kolkata New Delhi
EASTERN LAW HOUSE

Published and processed by
EASTERN LAW HOUSE PRIVATE LTD.
54 Ganesh Chunder Avenue
Kolkata 700 013
Tel: (033) 2215-1989
Email: mail@elh.co.in
www.elh.co.in

First Edition 1996
Second Edition 2001
Third Edition 2021

ISBN 978-81-7177-363-3

Printed at
Dey's Offset, Kolkata

Dedicated to

my beloved younger brother Babul
who belonging to my generation,
has become my ancestor.

Preface to the Third Edition

This edition comes after long interval and the volume has considerably increased. The law has developed at an ever increasing pace due to enormous growth in the number of claims for medical negligence. The Supreme Court of India has not only enunciated new juristic principles to meet various aspects of negligence of the doctors and the hospitals, but has also evolved new mode and method of assessment of compensation. I have radically revised the erstwhile materials by incorporating all important case-laws and by deleting obsolete case-laws in order to meet the current demand of both legal and medical profession of the country.

As in the first and second editions, I have attempted to summarise neatly the entire law of medical negligence and compensation on the basis of judicial pronouncements of India and abroad. I have also sought to provide clear, detailed and in-depth analysis of the principles of medical negligence and compensation under general, penal and consumer laws. Like the previous editions, I have tried my best to expound and demonstrate, *inter alia*, the concept of reasonable care, standard of knowledge and skill, difference between wrong and negligent diagnosis, criteria for informed consent, variation of consent in elective and emergency surgery, unwanted child and failure of sterilization, delegation of duty, liability of the hospital, criteria of consumer, concept of deficiency in service, evaluation of expert evidence, individual and vicarious liability to pay compensation, standard of proof of negligence in Civil Court as well as Consumer Court, mode of assessment and apportionment of compensation and text of important statutes connected with medical profession. I have thoroughly revised and updated the voluminous chapter on "Judicial Pronouncement" with various headings and sub-headings to illustrate what may or may not amount to negligence. The last chapter is also improved and updated by giving examples of how the compensation was assessed and awarded by the Civil Court, Constitutional Court and the Consumer Courts of India.

With increasing availability of case reports through law journals of India and abroad, I have had to restructure the entire book by giving more headings and sub-headings to facilitate easy handling by members of legal and medical professions. Some important decisions incorporated in this edition are worth mentioning. The criteria for fixing liability of the doctor under penal law are discussed in detail in *Malay Kumar Ganguly* v *Dr. Sukumar Mukherjee*. In *Jacob Mathew* v *State of Punjab* the Supreme Court has given guidelines that a doctor accused of causing death of the patient by rash and negligent treatment, cannot be prosecuted and arrested arbitrarily by the police without obtaining expert medical opinion. While the House of Lords evolved the criteria for condemning the expert evidence in *Bolitho* v *City and Hackney Health Authority*, the Supreme Court has laid down in *Arun Kumar Manglik* v *Chirayu Health and Medicare Private Ltd* that the medical man cannot escape liability merely by relying on a body of professional opinion, unless the course of treatment adopted is established as reasonable, when there exists genuine difference between two bodies of professional opinion. The Apex Court of India has elucidated in *Dr. Tokugha Yepthomi* v *Appollo Hospital Enterprises* when disclosure of HIV of the patient is permissible in public interest as an exception to the rule of confidentiality under the Code of Medical Ethics. By discarding the traditional mode of assessment of compensation by multiplier method, the Apex Court has spelt out, in *Nizam's Institute of Medical Sciences* v *Prasanth S. Dhananka* and *Balaram Prasad* v *Kunal Saha*, the criteria for assessment of compensation in cases of medical negligence to the tune of Rupees one crore and Rupees six crore respectively and the manner of apportionment of the amount of compensation between the hospital and the doctors. I have updated all available case-laws of India and abroad till the month of July, 2020 including the cases decided by the High Courts and the Supreme Court on testing and treatment of Covid-19 patients and disposal of dead body of the persons infected therewith.

I take this opportunity to express my gratitude to all my benevolent readers whose continuing support kept me on the job. I am grateful to Hon'ble Justice Soumen Sen for providing me the foreign law journals from the library of the High Court. I am also thankful to my son, Pranit Bag, Advocate, High Court, Calcutta for assisting me to revise and update the book. I place on record my indebtedness to my wife, Tapasi Bag for her encouragement in completion of my task. I am deeply obliged to Mr. Asok De, Director of Eastern Law House Pvt. Ltd. for his active assistance, encouragement and whole-hearted support in completing the work.

Suggestion for improvement of quality of the book is solicited from all those who may have a chance to browse through it.

Kolkata
28th January 2021

R.K. Bag

Peface to the First Edition

The classical concept of doctor-patient relationship born in the golden days of family physicians has undergone drastic change due to dramatic advancement in medical technology, availability of sophisticated imaging system, high-tech electronics and preponderance of new diseases. With the immense strides in technology health care has emerged as a profitable sector attracting investors from varied background in our country and the doctors get to spend less and less time with their patients. Owing to lack of time of the doctors to communicate adequately with the patients, the patient-dissatisfaction is on the rise. Naturally, the disgruntled patients are resorting to legal remedy.

Like other professionals the medical men are liable to pay damages for their negligence under the law of torts. There are instances where doctors were convicted and sentenced to imprisonment for causing death by negligence. Unlike foreign countries the instances of award of damages in India are few and far between. The reason is obviously the low level of awareness of rights, the exorbitant court fees and the unending court procedures. However, the accountability of the doctors under the law of professional negligence has emerged as a debatable issue among the medical fraternity all over the country after the enactment of the Consumer Protection Act 1986, which has not changed the law of medical negligence, but created an inexpensive and speedy remedy against medical malpractice. A glance at the emerging scenario of the country indicates that our consumer courts are doing justice by giving adequate compensation to the genuinely affected patients and by dismissing the false and frivolous complaints with exemplary costs against committed doctors. The recent judgment of the Supreme Court in *V.P. Shantha's* case has also given a new dimension to the law of medical negligence and compensation by transforming the law from "a sealed book to a living letter" and by making the law as "inheritance of the poor from the patrimony of the rich". The dictum of the Apex Court has been greeted with mixed feelings by common people on the one side and medical profession on the other. I have endeavoured to analyse and arrange the available materials to demonstrate that the judgment of the Apex Court provides no reason either for the common people to indulge in euphoria or the medical profession to sink into deep depression.

Within the short compass of this book I have sought to provide clear, detailed and in-depth analysis of the principles of medical negligence under general, penal and consumer law. I have made effort to expose, *inter alia*, the concept of reasonable care, standard of skill and competence, criteria of informed consent in treatment, difference between wrong and negligent diagnosis, duty towards foetus, wrongful birth, obligation for gratuitous service, patient as consumer, concept of deficiency of medical service and contract of personal service. The book comprehends both general and consumer law with regard to rights to claim for, and individual as well as vicarious liability to pay for compensation. The manner of proof of negligence in Civil Court as well as consumer forum, mode of assessment of compensation and text of important Statutes connected with medical profession, such as, code of medical ethics, termination of pregnancy, pre-natal sex diagnosis and transplantation of human organs are discussed in detail. For the benefit of lawyers and laymen, patients and professionals, one chapter of the book is wholly devoted to the common errors of surgeons as well as physicians and remedies thereof.

The principles of medical negligence and compensation developed mainly by way of judicial pronouncements in U.K.

are followed, modified or enlarged by courts of Canada, U.S.A., Australia, New Zealand and India. With a wide spectrum of case laws of India and abroad I have tried to extract and demonstrate the underlying principles covering the entire range of the subject. I have incorporated all the available reported decisions of the Consumer Courts of India. The cases are gleaned from multitude of sources—some from medical journals also. With examples of cases where negligence is established and compensation paid and where negligence is not established and complaints dismissed, I hope, the book will be helpful in illustrating how the existing law may be applied to totally new situations.

I have made my best effort to deal with the classic problem of doing justice to both patients and professionals by taking into consideration the fears of the medical profession without ignoring the legitimate claims of the patients against medical malpractice. I have had principally in mind the members of legal and medical profession—both those who deny justice and those who are denied justice. I have had next in mind the patients and public who often fumble for help and guidance to deal with the medical accidents. I would feel amply rewarded if the book is found useful by legal and medical professions alike.

I take this opportunity to express my deep gratitude to all my colleagues of judicial service of West Bengal and the faculty members of S.V.P. National Police Academy, Hyderabad, whose continuing support and encouragement kept me on the job. I record my gratitude to the Hon'ble Justice M. Sengupta, Judge, Sikkim High Court, Shri A.P. Durai, Director, S.V.P. National Police Academy, Hyderabad, Shri D. Banerjee, Professor and Head, Faculty of Law, L.B.S. National Academy of Administration, Mussoorie, Shri S.N. Bhattacharjee, Registrar, High Court, Calcutta and Shri P.K. Sen, Additional Registrar, High Court, Calcutta, for their help and warm affection. I must place on record my indebtedness to my wife, Smt. T. Bag for her constant help and encouragement in completing my task. I am also grateful to my elder brother, Shri R.N. Bag, Advocate, High Court,

Calcutta, my younger brother, Dr. Gautam Bag, a dermatologist and member of West Bengal Health Service and my sister's husband, Shri K. Palmal, Advocate, who inspired and helped me in various ways to complete my work. I owe special thanks to Shri Asok De, Director, Eastern Law House, whose active assistance made it possible for me to complete the work. My thanks are also due to the staff of National Police Academy and Eastern Law House in general and to Shri Somnath Chakraborty in particular. I also put on record my deep appreciation for the assistance rendered by my stenographer, Shri E. Gopi Reddy.

Suggestions for removal of flaws and for improvement of quality of the work are solicited from all those who may have a chance to browse through the book.

Hyderabad
1st July 1996 R.K. BAG

Contents

CHAPTER PAGE

CHAPTER PAGE

Contents

Appendix

Table of Cases

Table of Abbreviations

AC	Appeal Cases (Law Reports)
ACC	Accidents Compensation Cases
ACJ	Accidents Claims Journal
All ER	All England Law Reports
AIR	All India Reporter
ALR	Australian Law Reports
ALR	American Law Reports
ALJ	Australian Law Journal
APLJ	Andhra Pradesh Law Journal
BMLR	Butterworths Medico-Legal Reports
Bom LR	Bombay Law Reporter
BLR	Business Law Review
BCCA	British Columbia Court of Appeal
BCSC	British Columbia Supreme Court
CA	Court of Appeal
Ch	Chancery Division (Law Reports)
CD	Chancery Division
CLR	Commonwealth Law Reports
CLY	Current Law Year Book
Cr LJ	Criminal Law Journal
Cur C C	Current Civil Cases
CANB	New Brunswick Court of Appeal
Can SC	Canadian Supreme Court
CWN	Calcutta Weekly Notes
Cr App R	Criminal Appeal Reporter
CCJ	Consumer Claims Journal
CPR	Consumer Protection Reporter

CPJ .... Consumer Protection Judgment
CS (OH).................. Court of Services (Outer Home)
CTJ .... Consumer Protection and Trade Practices Journal
DLR .... Dominion Law Reports
DC .... Divisional Court
EWCA .... England and Wales Court of Appeal (UK)
EWHC .... High Court of Justice in England and Wales
Fam .... Family Division (Law Reports)
FC .... Federal Court
FD .... Family Division
HL .... House of Lords
Ill .... Illinois Case
ILR........................... Indian Law Reporter
IRLR .... Industrial Relations Law Reports
IA .... Indian Appeals
IR .... Irish Reports
ICR .... Industrial Case Reports
JIMA........................ Journal of the Indian Medical Association
Jab LJ .... Jabbalpur Law Journal
JPIL......................... Journal of Personal Injury Litigation
KB .... King's Bench
Ker LT..................... Kerala Law Times
L Ed 2d .... United States Supreme Court Reports (Lawyers' Ed., 2nd Series)
LJ .... Law Journal Newspaper
LJR .... Law Journal Reports
LT .... Law Times
Lloyd's Rep .... Lloyd's List Reports
Lloyd's Rep Med .... Medical Law Reports (Published by Lloyds of London Press)
LGR .... Local Government Reports
Lab IC .... Labour and Industrial Cases
Minn .... Minnesota Case
MLJ .... Malayan Law Journal
Mad LJ.................... Madras Law Journal
Mad LW .... Madras Law Weekly
Mah LJ.................... Maharashtra Law Journal
Med LR .... Medical Law Reports
MPLJ .... Madhya Pradesh Law Journal

Mys LJ	Mysore Law Journal
N–J & B	Medical Negligence Case Law (By Nelson-Jones and Burton, 2nd Edition)
NZLR	New Zealand Law Reports
NZCA	New Zealand Court of Appeal
NC	National Consumer Disputes Redressal Commission
New LJ	New Law Journal
OC of Appeal	Ontario Court of Appeal
PC	Privy Council
PILR	Butterworths' Personal Injury Litigation Service
PMILL	Personal and Medical Injuries Law Letter
Pun LR	Punjab Law Reports
QB	Queen's Bench (Law Reports)
QBB	Queen's Bench Division
RCS	Supreme Court Reports (Canada)
SC	Supreme Court
SCC	Supreme Court Cases
SCC (Cr)	Supreme Court Cases (Criminal)
SCDRC	State Consumer Disputes Redressal Commission
SCJ	Supreme Court Journal
SCR	Supreme Court Reports (Canada)
SCA	Supreme Court Appeals
SCD	Supreme Court Decision
SCWR	Supreme Court Weekly Reporter
Sol.Jo.	Solicitor's Journal
SLT	Scots Law Times
State Commission	State Consumer Disputes Redressal Commission
TAC	Transport and Accident Cases
UKHL	United Kingdom House of Lords
UKSC	United Kingdom Supreme Court
WN	Weekly Notes (Law Reports)
WLR	Weekly Law Reports
WWR	Western Weekly Reports

Table of Statutes

Bibliography

A.M. Dugdale and K.M. Stanton, *Professional Negligence* (Ed. 1989)

Avtar Singh, *Law of Contract* (7th Ed. 1999)

Bennion, *Professional Ethics*

Black's Law Dictionary (9th Ed.)

Charles J. Lewis, *Medical Negligence* (4th Ed. 1998)

Code of Medical Ethics framed under s. 33 of the Indian Medical Council Act, 1956

Durga Das Basu, *Shorter Constitution of India* (12th Ed., Reprint 1999)

D.F. Mulla, *Principles of Mahomedan Law* (19th Ed. 1990, Reprint 2000)

Fowler, *Concise Oxford Dictionary* (7th Ed. 1983)

H.M. Seervai, *Constitutional Law of India* (4th Ed.)

Halsbury's *Laws of England* (4th Ed.)

Harrison, *Principles of Internal Medicine* (Vols. 1 & 2) (12th Ed.)

Ian Kennedy & Andrew Grubb, *Medical Law, Text with Materials* (2nd Ed. 1994)

John J. Fleming, *Law of Torts* (8th Ed. 1992)

J.M. Shelat, *Mulla on the Code of Civil Procedure* (19th Ed. 1990, Reprint 2000)

Michael A. Jones, *Medical Negligence* (5th Ed. 2018)

Michael J. Powers and Nigel H. Harris, *Medical Negligence* (Ed. 1990)

Nelson, *Text Book of Paediatrics* (13th Ed. 1991)

O.P. Ghai, *Essential Paediatrics* (Second Revised and Enlarged Ed. 1990)

Pollock, *Torts* (15th Ed.)

P.M. Bakshi, *Mulla on the Code of Civil Procedure* (Vol. I to III) (15th Ed. 1995-97, Reprint 1997)

R.A. Percy and C.T. Walton, *Charlesworth and Percy on Negligence* (9th Ed. 1997)

Ramaswamy Ayer, *Law of Torts* (8th Ed.)

R.M. Jackson and J.L. Powell, *Professional Negligence* (2nd Ed.)

Rupert Cross and Philip Asterley Jones, *An Introduction to Criminal Law* (7th Ed.)

Ratanlal and Dhirajlal, *The Code of Criminal Procedure* (15th Ed. 1997, Reprint 1999)

Salmond and Heuston, *Law of Torts* (20th Ed. 1992; 3rd Indian Reprint 1997)

Shorter Oxford English Dictionary, Vol. I & II (3rd Ed. 1944; Reprinted with corrections and Revised addenda 1959)

Trikamlal R. Desai and Ratilal K. Desai, *Limitation Act* (8th Ed.)

W.V.H. Rogers, *Winfield and Jolowicz on Tort* (13th Ed. 1989)

Part A

NEGLIGENCE

CHAPTER 1

Ambit of Negligence

1 Meaning of negligence Negligence is not susceptible of any precise definition. Various meanings may be attributed to negligence. First, negligence connotes careless state of mind which may amount to recklessness or indifference. A physician prescribing drugs with dangerous side effects without informing the patient of risk of those side effects and without carrying out the recommended tests in order to discover whether such side effects are happening, is guilty of carelessness in exposing the patient to the risk of suffering from those side effects of the drugs. Secondly, negligence is a careless conduct without reference to any duty to take care. The best illustration of such careless conduct is found in cases of contributory negligence. A patient undergoing medical treatment under the care of a quack, exhibits such careless conduct. This meaning of negligence is also found in performance of contractual duty. Lastly, negligence refers to a breach of legal duty to take care. Lord Wright points out: "Negligence means more than heedless or careless conduct, whether in omission or commission; it properly connotes the complex concept of duty, breach and damage thereby suffered by the person to whom the duty was owing".[1]

1 *Lochgelly Iron and Coal Co.* v *M. Mullan* [1934] AC 1; 77 Sol Jo 539.

It is pointed out by Chagla, ACJ and Bhagwati, J[2] that actions for negligence in India are to be determined according to the principles of English Common Law.

2 Components of negligence The definition of negligence given by Alderson B in *Blyth* v *Birmingham Water Works Co.*[3] has been modified by Charlesworth[4] in the following ways: "Negligence is a tort which involves a person's breach of duty that is imposed upon him to take care, resulting in damage to the complainant". The essential components of the modern tort of negligence propounded by Percy and Charlesworth[5] are as follows:

(*a*) the existence of a duty to take care, which is owed by the defendant to the complainant;

(*b*) the failure to attain that standard of care, prescribed by the law, thereby committing a breach of such duty; and

(*c*) damage, which is both causally connected with such breach and recognised by the law, has been suffered by the complainant.

If the plaintiff proves that the doctor was negligent, but fails to establish that any loss or injury was caused thereby, then he will not be entitled to claim any compensation.[6] The general test for causation requires the plaintiff to establish that the injury would not have occurred, but for the negligence of the defendant.[7]

3 Negligence as tort

(i) *Tortious liability* "Tortious liability arises from the breach of a duty primarily fixed by law; this duty is towards persons generally and its breach is redressible by an action for

2 *Amelia Flounders* v *Dr. Clement Perreira* (1947) OCJ Appeal No. 27 of 1947 (unreported).

3 *Blyth* v *Birmingham Water Works Co.* (1856)11 Ex 781; 25 LJ Ex 212.

4 Charlesworth & Percy on *Negligence*, 9th Ed., p. 16 (1·26).

5 Supra, p. 16 (1·25).

6 *Sidhraj Dhadda* v *State of Rajasthan* AIR 1994 Raj 68; 1993(1) Raj LW 532.

7 *Athey* v *Leonati* [1996]3 RCS 458.

unliquidated damages".[8] This definition of negligence as tort involves the following constituents:

(*a*) a legal duty to exercise due care;

(*b*) breach of the duty;

(*c*) consequential damages.[9]

Moreover, the above definition of Winfield enables one to distinguish tortious liability from other liabilities of the professionals. The duty in tort is owed to persons in general, whereas the duty in contract is owed to specific persons. The duty in tort is imposed by law whereas the duty in contract is fixed by agreement between the parties. The unliquidated damages awarded in tortious claim is distinguishable from predetermined liquidated damages of contract.

Greer, LJ has put the distinction between contract and tort in the following way: "Where the breach of duty alleged arises out of a liability independently of the personal obligation undertaken by contract, it is tort and it may be tort even though there may happen to be a contract between the parties, if the duty in fact arises independently of that contract".[10] In spite of these basic differences the concurrent liability in tort and contract may co-exist in practice in the field of negligence of the professionals in general and the medical profession in particular.

(ii) ***Concurrent liability in tort and contract*** The courts of England did not recognise the concurrent contractual and tortious liability for professional services before 1976. Lord Denning pointed out that a professional is liable in both tort and contract for his negligence.[11] The Court of Appeal[12] in

8 Winfield and Jolowicz on *Tort,* 19th Ed., p. 3, para 1-003.

9 *Poonam Verma* v *Aswin Patel* AIR 1996 SC 2111; (1996)4 SCC 332; 1996(3) CPR 205 (SC); II(1996) CPJ 1 (SC); (1996)4 CTJ 465 (SC) (CP).

10 *Jarvis* v *Moy, Davies, Smith, Vandervell & Co.* [1936]1 KB 399; 105 LJKB 309; 154 LT 365 (CA).

11 *Esso Petroleum Co. Ltd.* v *Mardon* [1976] QB 801; [1976] 2 All ER 5; [1976]2 WLR 583; 120 Sol Jo 131.

12 *Forsikrings Aktieselskapet Vesta* v *Butcher* [1986]2 All ER 488; [1986]2 Lloyd's Rep 179 affirmed [1988]2 All ER 43; [1988]1 Lloyd's Rep 19 (CA).

England is in favour of concurrent liability in tort and contract, though Lord Scarman[13] opines that the existence of a contractual nexus excludes the possibility of a claim in tort. In Australia the decision of the Supreme Court of Victoria[14] is in favour of the concurrent liability in tort and contract. Similarly, the Canadian Supreme Court[15] has held that out of concurrent tortious and contractual liability the plaintiff has a right to assess the cause of action that appears to be most advantageous in respect of any particular legal consequence, but the concurrent liability will not be permissible where liability in tort enables the plaintiff to circumvent a contractual exclusion of liability. The law laid down by the Supreme Court of India,[16] is as follows: "If the claim depends upon proof of contract, action does not lie in tort. If the claim arises, from the relationship between the parties, independent of the contract, an action would lie in tort at the election of the plaintiff, although he might alternatively have pleaded in contract".

4 Negligence under contract

(i) ***Contractual liability*** It is trite law that an agreement supported by consideration is contract. The terms of contract may be explicit or implied. The express terms are incorporated in the form of a single memorandum or formal exchange of letters. The terms of implied contract can be gathered from the circumstances reflected in the custom of the profession and the conduct of the parties. The House of Lords[17] is reluctant to allow implied contracts to be used as a device to extend professional duties beyond general tortious liability.

Liability in contract depends on the express or implied terms agreed upon by the patient and the medical man.

13 *Tai Hing Cotton Mill Ltd.* v *Liu Chong Hing Bank Ltd* [1986] AC 80; [1985]2 All ER 947; [1985]3 WLR 317.

14 *Macpherson and Kelley* v *Kevin J Prunty & Associates* [1983]1 VR 573.

15 *Central Trust Co.* v *Rafuse* (1983)147 DLR (3d) 260 affirmed (1986)31 DLR (4th) 481.

16 *Rajkot Municipal Corporation* v *Manjulaben Jayantilal Nakum* (1997)9 SCC 552.

17 *Independent Broadcasting Authority* v *EMI Electronics Ltd. and BICC Construction Ltd.* [1980]14 BLR 1 (HL).

Consent for treatment on payment of fees on the part of a patient can be treated as an implied contract with the doctor who by undertaking treatment on acceptance of fees, impliedly promises to exercise proper care and skill.[18] The contractual duties are generally more onerous in nature than those imposed by tort. Tortious duties in the professional context are limited to taking reasonable care. They do not impose any continuing duty requiring advice or action to be reviewed as may be the case with a contractual duty.[19]

(ii) *Liability of retainer* Professionals often act as agents and contractual relationship may be established through agency. A doctor retained by a poor law infirmary was held to have impliedly contracted with a patient who submitted to treatment in return for the doctor's implied undertaking to use reasonable care.[18]

The retainer problem of medical profession is reflected in a few reported decisions in England. A doctor retained by a patient for treatment is not recorded in writing, except where the patient-party has to sign the consent form before undergoing surgery in the hospital or nursing home. The object of obtaining consent form is to protect the surgeon and the hospital authority from liability in assault and trespass. It does not provide any basis on which a patient may settle his legal claim in respect of damages resulting from negligence. However, it was held by Tucker, J that "Where a surgeon is retained to perform an operation, he will perform the operation personally and that he would pay such visits as were necessary in the ordinary case".[20]

5 Negligence as crime

(i) *Criminal liability* The extent of liability in tort depends on the amount of damages done, but the extent of liability in

18 *Everett* v *Griffiths* [1920]3 KB 163; 89 LJKB 929; 123 LT 280; 64 Sol Jo 445 affirmed [1921]1 AC 631; 90 LJKB 737; 125 LT 230; 65 Sol Jo 395.

19 A.M. Dugdale and K.M. Stanton, *Professional Negligence,* 1989 Ed., p. 43 [4.01].

20 *Morris* v *Winsbury White* [1937]4 All ER 494 (500).

criminal law depends on the amount and degree of negligence. The unliquidated damages awarded in tortious action is distinguishable from the mode of punishment imposed in criminal liability. This distinction between tort and crime has been reduced in England by giving power to the criminal courts to pay compensation to the victim.[1] In India s. 357 of the Code of Criminal Procedure 1973 empowers the criminal courts to award compensation to the victims while passing judgment of conviction. By way of interpretation of s. 357 of the Code of Criminal Procedure 1973, the Supreme Court has observed that the criminal court may order the convict to pay compensation to the victim who has suffered by his action.[2] It may be noted that this power of criminal courts to award compensation is not ancillary to other sentences, but it is in addition thereto. The Supreme Court[3] has directed all criminal courts to exercise the power of awarding compensation to victims of offences in such liberal way, that the victims or their legal heirs may not have to rush to the civil court for compensation. By authorising the criminal courts to award compensation on consideration of the nature of the crime, justness of claim of the victim, and ability of the accused to pay, the distinction between tort and crime has been reduced to the extent that the degree of negligence in criminal liability is higher than that of negligence in tortious liability.

The action or omission of a medical man can be termed as criminal only when he exhibits gross lack of competence and wanton indifference to the patient's safety, which is found to have arisen from gross ignorance or gross negligence. When a patient's death results merely from error of judgment or accident, no criminal liability should be attached to it. Mere inadvertance or some degree of want of adequate care and caution may create civil liability, but will not be

1 The Powers of Criminal Courts Act 1973.

2 *Hari Kishan and State of Haryana* v *Sukhbir Singh* AIR 1988 SC 2127; 1989 CrLJ 116.

3 Supra.

suffice to hold any member of medical profession criminally liable.[4]

The medical officer of a Government hospital, who is prosecuted on the allegation of medical negligence in the hospital, is entitled to get protection under s. 197 of the Code of Criminal Procedure. In other words, the prosecution of Government doctor on the allegation of committing offence under Indian Penal Code is not maintainable without sanction of the Government.[5]

(ii) *Mens rea in negligence* The expression *mens rea* is used to mean the mental state expressly or impliedly mentioned in the definition of crime charged.[6] An act does not make a person guilty unless his mind is guilty. The *mens rea* in criminal negligence is defined by Lord Diplock[7] in the following way: "Without having given any thought to the possibility of there being such risk or having recognised that there was some risk involved, had nevertheless gone on to take it". In order to amount to criminal rashness or criminal negligence one must find out that the rashness has been of such a degree as to amount to taking a hazard knowing that the hazard was of such a degree that injury was most likely to be occasioned thereby. The criminality lies in running the risk or doing such an act with recklessness and indifference to the consequences.[8]

Thus, it is recklessness that constitutes *mens rea* in criminal negligence. The recklessness is not the desire to cause harm, but total disregard for the possible consequences. To establish the existence of criminal rashness or criminal negligence, the rashness would amount to taking a hazard

4 *Dr. Suresh Gupta* v *Government of NCT of Delhi* (2004)6 SCC 422; AIR 2004 SC 4091.

5 *Manorama Tiwari (Dr.)* v *Surendra Nath Rai* (2015)9 Scale 747; JT 2015(8) SC 512; 2015 AIR SCW 6802; (2016)1 SCC 594; 2016 CrLJ 367 (SC).

6 Rupert Cross and Philip Asterley Jones, *An Introduction to Criminal Law,* 7th Ed., p. 41.

7 *R.* v *Lawrence* [1981]1 All ER 974; [1982] AC 510; [1981]2 WLR 524 (HL).

8 *Krishna Prasad (Dr.)* v *State of Karnataka* 1989(1) ACJ 393.

knowing fully well that the hazard was of such a degree that injury was most likely imminent.[9]

It is held by the Supreme Court of India that for negligence to amount to an offence the element of *mens rea* must be shown to exist, because the jurisprudential concept of negligence differs in civil and criminal law.[10]

6 Negligence under consumer law

(i) *Consumer law to medical profession* The Consumer Protection Act 1986* was enacted by Parliament to provide for better protection of the interests of consumers in the background of the guidelines contained in the Consumer Protection Resolution passed by the United Nations General Assembly on 9th April 1985. Accordingly, the Consumer Protection Act 1986* provides protection and relief to persons who have hired any service for consideration when the service provided is found to be suffering from deficiency in any respect.[11] According to our Apex Court, a determination about deficiency in medical service is to be made by applying the same test as is applied in an action for damages for medical negligence.[12] Since the very purpose for which the statute was enacted is to provide a cheap and speedy remedy to the aggrieved consumers by way of an alternative to the time consuming and expensive process of civil litigation, the Consumer Forum cannot refuse to adjudicate the dispute regarding deficiency in service rendered by medical practitioners for consideration.[13] Naturally, the complaint for deficiency in service rendered by medical man is not liable to be dismissed, merely because the complaint involves complicated questions

9 *Jacob Mathew* v *State of Punjab* (2005)6 SCC 1; 2005 ACJ 1840; AIR 2005 SC 3180; 2005(3) CPR 70; 2005 CrLJ 3710; JT 2005(6) SC 584.

10 *Malay Kumar Ganguly* v *Dr. Sukumar Mukherjee* (2009)7 SCJ 124; (2009)9 SCC 221; AIR 2010 SC 1162; (2009)10 Scale 675; III(2009) CPJ 17; 2009(3) CCR 558; 2010 AIR SCW 769.

* Now replaced by the Consumer Protection Act 2019 w.e.f. 9.8.2019.

11 *Consumer Unity and Trust Society, Jaipur* v *State of Rajasthan* 1991(1) CPR 241 (NC); I(1992) CPJ 259 (NC); (1993)1 CTJ 89 (NCDRC).

12 *Indian Medical Association* v *V.P. Shantha* AIR 1996 SC 550; (1995)6 SCC 651; III(1995) CPJ 1 (SC); 1995(3) CPR 412 (SC); (1995)3 CTJ 969 (SC) (CP); 1996 CCJ 1 (SC).

13 *S.K. Abdul Sukur* v *State of Orissa* II(1991) CPJ 202 (NC).

of law and facts requiring detailed investigations.[14] The order of dismissal of the complaint passed by the National Commission was set aside by the Supreme Court by holding that the National Consumer Forum should have taken the complaint to its logical conclusion by asking the parties to adduce evidence and rendered its findings on merit.[15] However, it is observed by the Supreme Court of India[16] that in complaints involving complicated issues requiring recording of evidence of experts, the complainant can be asked to approach the Civil Court for necessary relief. As a matter of policy and principle where subject-matter of a complaint is *sub judice* before ordinary court, a concurrent adjudication in respect of the same should not be conducted under the Consumer Protection Act 1986* by a Redressal Agency.[17]

The National Commission[18] is of the view that the consumer forum cannot come to the conclusion whether the hospital and the operating surgeon were negligent without the evidence of the experts as well as extracts of medical literature and without cross-examination of the experts giving evidence on affidavit. However, the dispute whether the professional fee charged by a doctor is reasonable or exorbitant cannot be determined by the consumer courts,[19] because the amount of professional fee charged by a medical practitioner depends on number of factors, viz. qualification, experience and nature and quality of service rendered by him.

14 *R. Gopinathan* v *Eskeycee Medical Foundation* I(1994) CPJ 147 (NC); (1994)2 CTJ 97 (CP) (NCDRC); 1994(2) CPR 488 (NC) affirming decision of State Commission, Madras 1993(1) CPR 456 (Mad).

15 *Charan Singh* v *Healing Touch Hospital* (2000)7 SCC 668; AIR 2000 SC 3138; 2000(3) CPR 1; (2000)6 Scale 431.

16 *Indian Medical Association* v *V.P. Shantha* AIR 1996 SC 550; (1995)6 SCC 651; III(1995) CPJ 1 (SC); 1995(3) CPR 412 (SC); (1995)3 CTJ 969 (SC) (CP); 1996 CCJ 1 (SC).

* Replaced by the Consumer Protection Act 2019 w.e.f. 9.8.2019.

17 *Jitendra Nath* v *Dr. (Mrs.) Manju Geeta Mishra* 1994(3) CPR 551 (Bihar); I(1995) CPJ 96 (Bihar).

18 *Baburao Satappa Irrannanavar* v *Kle Society's Hospital & Research Centre* 2006(3) CPR 92; IV(2006) CPJ 71.

19 *Dr. K.B. Kapoor* v *Phool Dev Parshad* III(1996) CPJ 477 (Chandigarh); *B.S. Hegde* v *Dr. Sudhensu Bhattacharya* (1994)2 CTJ 10 (CP) (NCDRC); 1993(3) CPR 414 (NC); III(1993) CPJ 388 (NC) reversing II(1992) CPJ 449 (Bom); (1993)1 CTJ 523 (SCDRC).

It is well-settled by various decisions of the National Commission[20] that the activity of providing medical assistance for payment carried on by private hospitals and members of the medical profession falls within the scope of the expression "service" as defined in s. 2(1)(*o*)* of the Consumer Protection Act 1986 (since repealed) and in the event of any deficiency in the performance of such service, the aggrieved party can invoke the remedies provided before the Consumer Forum having jurisdiction. The principle enunciated by the National Commission is elaborated by the Supreme Court[21] by categorising the medical practitioners, government hospitals, private hospitals and nursing homes as follows:

(*i*) Where services are rendered free of charge to everybody availing of the said services;

(*ii*) Where charges are required to be paid by everybody availing of the services; and

(*iii*) Where charges are required to be paid by persons availing of services, but certain categories of persons who cannot afford to pay are rendered service free of charges.

The service rendered by the first category of doctors and hospitals would not fall within the ambit of "service" under s. 2(1)(*o*)* of the Consumer Protection Act 1986. On the other hand, the service rendered by the second and third category of doctors and hospitals would fall within the ambit of "service" defined in s. 2(1)(*o*)* of the Consumer Protection Act 1986. The All India Institute of Medical Sciences is covered under s. 2(1)(*o*)* of the Consumer Protection Act 1986, as the Institute recovers various charges, like hospital

20 *Consumer Education and Research Society* v *Dr. Ratilal B. Patel* III(1992) CPJ 25 (NC) reversing decision of State Commission, Gujarat, reported in 1991(2) CPR 204; *M/s. Cosmopolitan Hospital* v *Smt. Vasantha P. Nair* 1992(1) CPR 820 (NC); I(1992) CPJ 302 (NC) affirming decision of State Commission, Kerala, reported in 1991(2) CPR 155; II(1991) CPJ 444.

* Replaced by s. 2(42) of the Consumer Protection Act 2019 w.e.f. 9.8.2019.

21 *Indian Medical Association* v *V.P. Shantha* AIR 1996 SC 550; (1995)6 SCC 651; III(1995) CPJ 1 (SC); 1995(3) CPR 412 (SC); (1995)3 CTJ 969 (SC) (CP); 1996 CCJ 1 (SC).

charges, diagnostic charges from the patients, apart from registration.[1]

It is, thus, well-settled that the Consumer Protection Act 1986* is applicable to persons engaged in the medical profession either as private practitioners or as Government doctors working in hospitals or Government dispensaries and that a patient who is a "consumer' within the meaning of the Act, has to be awarded compensation for loss or injury suffered by him due to negligence of the doctor by applying the same tests as are applied in an action for damages for negligence.[2]

Relying on *V.P. Shantha*[3] wherein the Apex Court expounded the proposition that where medical service was rendered as part of terms and conditions of service, the same would not amount to free service and would constitute "service" for the purpose of the Consumer Protection Act, it is held by the National Commission that the doctors who have given treatment under the Central Government Health Service Scheme in a Government hospital free of charge, would be covered under the Consumer Protection Act.[4] The National Commission is of the view that the employee of the Indian Railways availing of medical treatment in a hospital funded by the Railways is a consumer for the purpose of the Consumer Protection Act 1986.[5] The Apex Court is of the view that the service rendered by the medical practitioners in the hospitals & dispensaries run by the E.S.I. Corporation to a member of the E.S.I. Scheme or members of his family is covered under the Consumer Protection Act 1986,* as the

1 *Sailesh Manjul* v *All India Institute of Medical Sciences* 2004(3) CPR 27; 2004(3) CLT 269; 2004(2) CPC 514; III(2004) CPJ 93.

* Now replaced by the Consumer Protection Act 2019 w.e.f. 9.8.2019.

2 *Poonam Verma* v *Aswin Patel* AIR 1996 SC 2111; (1996)4 SCC 332; (1996(3) CPR 205 (SC); II(1996) CPJ 1 (SC); (1996)4 CTJ 465 (SC) (CP).

3 *Indian Medical Association* v *V.P. Shantha* (1995)6 SCC 651; AIR 1996 SC 550; III(1995) CPJ 1; 1995(3) CPR 412 (SC).

4 *Arvind Pandey* v *Dr. (Mrs.) Sulekha Saran* 2012(3) CPR 142; III(2012) CPJ 357.

5 *K. Kotaiah* v *T. Anjaiah (Dr.)* 2017(1) CPR 707; IV(2014) CPJ 225 (NCDRC).

insurance scheme contributes to the service rendered by the E.S.I. hospitals/dispensaries.[6]

(ii) *Deficiency of medical service* Deficiency means any fault, imperfection, shortcoming or inadequacy in the quality, nature and manner of performance which is required to be maintained by or under any law for the time being in force or has been undertaken to be performed by a person in pursuance of a contract or otherwise in relation to any service.[7] According to the Supreme Court,[8] the determination about deficiency in service is to be made by applying the same test as is applied in an action for damages for negligence.

Medical professionals are expected to exercise and provide reasonable degree of skill and knowledge and also exercise reasonable degree of care in treating the patients. A medical man rendering professional service for consideration is liable under Consumer Forum if he falls short of the standard of a reasonably skilful medical person in his field.[9] For establishing negligence in diagnosis or treatment on the part of the doctor before Consumer Forum, the test is whether the doctor has been proved to be guilty of such failure as no doctor of ordinary skill could be guilty of it acting with reasonable care.[10] It is the duty of the redressal agencies to safeguard the interest of the patients against malpractices by medical professionals. However, the inexpensive nature of consumer jurisdiction should not be allowed to become a vicious weapon in the hands of unscrupulous patients to

6 *Kishore Lal* v *Chairman, Employees' State Insurance Corporation* AIR 2007 SC 1819; (2007)4 SCC 579; II(2007) CPJ 25; JT 2007(6) SC 541; (2007)4 Supreme 775.

7 Section 2(1)(*g*) of the Consumer Protection Act 1986 which is replaced by s. 2(11) of the Consumer Protection Act 2019 w.e.f. 9.8.2019; *Yasmin Sultana* v *Dr. Rupaben D. Patel* 1994(1) CPR 407.

8 *Indian Medical Association* v *V.P. Shantha* AIR 1996 SC 550; (1995)6 SCC 651; III(1995) CPJ 1 (SC); 1995(3) CPR 412 (SC); (1995)3 CTJ 969 (SC) (CP); 1996 CCJ 1 (SC).

9 *Ganga Ram Hospital* v *D.P. Bhandari* 1992(1) CPR 796 (NC); II(1992) CPJ 397 (NC) reversing decision of State Commission, II(1991) CPJ 409 (Del).

10 *Dr. Sr. Louie* v *Smt. Kannolil Pathumma* 1993(1) CPR 422; I(1993) CPJ 30 (NC); (1993)1 CTJ 32 (NCDRC).

harass the medical professionals without good and adequate reasons.[11] The consumer courts faced with the classic problem of doing justice to both parties, have taken into account the fears of the medical profession without ignoring the legitimate claims of the patients.

(iii) *Ambit of deficiency in service* Failure on the part of the hospital authority to accede to the request of the complainant to furnish all the papers relating to his operation and treatment, cannot amount to "deficiency in service" within the meaning of the Consumer Protection Act 1986.[12] However, it is now well-settled that there is deficiency of service on the part of the hospital by not providing medical record disclosing the fact of little chance of recovery of the patient, which is obligatory under Regulations 2.3 and 3.6 framed by the Medical Council of India in consultation with the Central Government under s. 33 of the Indian Medical Council Act 1956.[13] The National Commission has laid down that failure on the part of the hospital and the doctor to supply the record of medical treatment on demand by the patient within 72 hours from the date of demand, amounts to deficiency in service.[14]

When the patient suffered post injection nerve palsy consequent upon injection administered by the doctor, it is deficiency in service on the part of the doctor.[15] The hospital is held liable for refusal to admit the patient in the hospital for treatment of acute pain in abdomen and for not giving timely medical treatment to the patient by the attending doctor of the hospital.[16] The fact of leaving critically ill patient

11 *Sachin Aggarwal* alias *Vicky* v *Dr. Ashok Arora* I(1993) CPJ 113 (Haryana).

12 *Poona Medical Foundation Ruby Hall Clinic* v *Marutirao L. Titkare* I(1995) CPJ 232 (NC); 1995(1) CPR 661 (NC).

13 *T. Rama Rao* v *Vijay Hospital* I(2008) CPJ 170; CDJ 2007 (Cons) Case No. 481.

14 *Inscol Hospital* v *Inderjit Arora* 2017(2) CLT 108; 2017(2) CPR 34; II(2017) CPJ 402 (NCDRC).

15 *Rajender Lal* v *Dr. Rudra Singh* 1996(2) CPR 364 (Chandigarh); (1996)4 CTJ 649 (CP) (SCDRC).

16 *Ranjit Kumar Das* v *Medical Officer, ESI Hospital, Manicktala* 1998(1) CPR 165 (Cal); III(1997) CPJ 336 (Cal); 1999 CCJ 70 (WB).

under the care of an unqualified compounder, particularly when the situation demands constant monitoring of the patient, amounts to deficiency in service on the part of the doctor.[17] Similarly, deficiency in service was attributed to the doctor for leaving the patient under care of a compounder who caused death of the patient by administering "nivaquine" injection.[18] Failure to record previous case history of the patient viz., number of past antenatal visits, medical case history, important parameters pertaining to height, wait gain, abdominal and pelvic assessment and information about screening of gestational diabetes etc. before conducting caesarian section amounts to deficiency in service. This lapse on the part of the doctor led the National Commission[19] to award compensation of rupees five lakh, although no negligence was attributed to the doctor in providing treatment.

17 *Pravinbhai Khubchandbhai Soni* v *Dr. Rajendra R. Shah* 1997(3) CPR 224 (Guj); II(1998) CPJ 627 (Guj); 1998 CTJ 797 (CP) (SCDRC); 1999 CCJ 1323 (Guj).

18 *Nivrutti G. More* v *Dr. Vinayak Deshmukh* (1994)4 CTJ 614 (CP) (SCDRC) (Bom).

19 *K.K. Kakkar (Dr.)* v *Neetu Singh* III(2014) CPJ 642 (NCDRC).

CHAPTER 2

Duty of Care

1 Duty to take care—need of Law imposes a duty on everyone to conform to a certain standard of conduct for protection of others. To establish liability in negligence, the defendant must owe a duty to take care of the plaintiff. The need for existence of duty of care is illustrated by Lord Wright[1] as follows:

> "All that is necessary as a step to establish the tort of actionable negligence is to define the precise relationship from which the duty to take care to be deduced. It is, however, essential in English law that the duty should be established, the mere fact that a man is injured by another's act gives in itself no cause of action, if the act is deliberate, the party injured will have no claim in law even though the injury is intentional, so long as the other party is merely exercising a legal right; if the act involves lack of due care, again no case of actionable negligence will arise unless the duty to be careful exists."

To paraphrase the words of Charlesworth and Percy,[2] "the word duty connotes the relationship between one person and another, imposing on the one an obligation, for the benefit

1 *Grant* v *Australian Knitting Mills Ltd.* [1936] AC 85 (103); 154 LT 18; 79 Sol Jo 815.

2 Charlesworth & Percy on *Negligence*, 9th Ed., p. 19 (2·02).

of that other, to take reasonable care in all the circumstances". The duty of a medical practitioner arises from the fact that he does something to a human being which is likely to cause physical damage unless it is done with proper care and skill.[3] The duty of a medical man starts from the time of accepting the patient for treatment, irrespective of financial considerations. This duty commences from taking the history of the patient and covers all aspects of treatment like writing proper case note, performing proper clinical examination, advising necessary tests and investigations, making proper diagnosis and carrying out careful treatment.[4]

The breach of duty may be occasioned either by not doing something which a reasonable man, under a given set of circumstances would do, or, by doing some acts which a reasonable and prudent man would not do.[5] A medical practitioner has various duties towards his patient and he must act with a reasonable degree of skill and knowledge, which he is to exercise with a reasonable degree of care. This is the least which a patient expects from a doctor.[6] When the patient developed complications after surgery for removal of appendix, the Privy Council is of the view that sepsis from ruptured appendix developed incrementally over a period of six hours and thereby progressively causing myocardial ischaemia. This development is a continuous process which contributed materially to the injury suffered by the patient. Lord Toulson giving the judgment for Privy Council held that the breach of duty of the doctor contributed materially to the complications after surgery.[7]

3 *Philips India Ltd.* v *Kanju Punnu* AIR 1975 Bom 306; 1975 ACJ 311; 77 Bom LR 337; 1975 Mah LJ 792.

4 *P.D. Hinduja National Hospital & Medical Research Centre, Dr. Sanjay Agarwala* v *Veera Rohinton Kotwal* II(2018) CPJ 342 (NCDRC).

5 *Poonam Verma* v *Aswin Patel* AIR 1996 SC 2111; (1996)4 SCC 332; 1996(3) CPR 205 (SC); II(1996) CPJ 1 (SC); (1996)4 CTJ 465 (SC) (CP).

6 *Achutrao Haribhau Khodwa* v *State of Maharashtra* (1996)2 SCC 634; 1996 ACJ 505; (1996)4 CTJ 950 (SC) (CP).

7 *Williams* v *The Bermuda Hospitals Board* [2016] UKPC 4; [2016] AC 888.

2 Neighbour principle—liability under

(i) ***Obligation under neighbour principle*** The general principle forming the basis of duty to take care enunciated by Lord Atkin[8] is known as neighbour test expanding the scope of tortious liability. The circumstances explained by Lord Atkin for deducing the existence of duty to take care are as follows:

> "The liability for negligence.... is no doubt based upon a general public sentiment of moral wrongdoing for which the offender must pay. But acts or omissions which any moral code would censure cannot in a practical world be treated so as to give a right to any person injured by them to demand relief. In this way rules of law arise which limit the range of complainants and the extent of their remedy. The rule that you are to love your neighbour becomes in law, you must not injure your neighbour; and the lawyer's question, 'who is my neighbour?' receives a restricted reply. You must take reasonable care to avoid acts or omissions which you can reasonably foresee would be likely to injure your neighbour, who, then, in law, is my neighbour? The answer seems to be—persons who are so closely and directly affected by my act that I ought reasonably to have them in contemplation as being so affected when I am directing my mind to the acts or omissions which are called in question."

This classic speech of Lord Atkin is regarded as shining milestone on the upward path of development of the principle of negligence in tort. This "neighbour test" is not invoked in contractual duty of care owed to persons in privity of contract with the professionals.

The House of Lords did not decide the issue whether rejection of claim for the cost of raising a child applies when the child happens to be disable.[9] This issue is decided by the Court of Appeal in *Parkinson* v *St. James and Seacroft*

8 *Donoghue* v *Stevenson* [1932] AC 562; 147 LT 281; [1932] All ER Rep 1; 1932 SLT 317 (HL).

9 *McFarlane* v *Tayside Health Board* [2000]2 AC 59.

University Hospital NHS Trust[10] by holding that the parents of a disabled child born following a negligently performed sterilization operation, are entitled to the additional costs of raising that child, i.e. the costs attributable to the disability of the child.

The 'neighbour test' has been reinforced by Lord Wilberforce[11] in the following words:

> "To establish that a duty of care arises in a particular situation, it is not necessary to bring the facts of that situation within those of previous situations in which a duty of care has been held to exist. Rather the question has to be approached in two stages. First, one has to ask whether, as between the alleged wrong-doer and the person who has suffered damage there is sufficient relationship of proximity or neighbourhood so that, in the reasonable contemplation of the former, carelessness on his part may be likely to cause damage to the latter—in which case a *prima facie* duty of care arises. Secondly, if the first question is answered affirmatively, it is necessary to consider whether there are any considerations which ought to negative, or to reduce or limit the scope of the duty or the class of persons to whom it is owed or the damages to which breach of it may give rise."

This two-stage test formulated by Lord Wilberforce has guided the courts not only to consider the imposition of duty of care, but also to consider the duty of care in the light of public policy. There has been a steady trend towards depending on principle so that, when a new point emerges, one should not ask whether it is covered by authority but whether recognised principles apply to it.[12]

(ii) *Limitation of neighbour principle* The high-water mark of the trend in imposition of duty of care developed in *Donoghue*

10 [2001] EWCA Civ 530; [2002] QB 266.

11 *Anns* v *Merton London Borough Council* [1978] AC 728; [1977]2 All ER 492 (HL); [1977]2 WLR 1024; 121 Sol Jo 377.

12 *Dorset Yacht Co.* v *Home Office* [1970] AC 1004; [1970]2 All ER 294; [1970]2 WLR 1140; [1970]1 Lloyd's Rep 453.

v *Stevenson*[13] and culminated in *Anns* v *Merton London Borough Council*[14] was criticised in England and other Commonwealth countries. Foreseeability of an act is to be considered by the court not only for imposition of duty to take care, but also for limiting the liability of the persons to whom the duty is owed. Duty can be inferred from the circumstances where the law recognises the wrongful act and consequential damage. The Australian High Court[15] accepted the Anns' two-stage test as appropriate in cases involving physical injury to person or property, but considered the same as inappropriate in cases involving economic loss caused by negligent statement. On the other hand, Lord Roskill[16] criticised as artificial the distinction between physical damage and economic loss and imposed a duty in relation to economic loss flowing from defective work. Accordingly, to impose liability the courts will be guided by the dictates of good conscience and what is considered as reasonable and fair, and not by mere foreseeability and proximity necessary to establish a duty of care.

3 Damage and reasonable foresight

(i) *Chain of causation* A causative link has to be established between the act of negligence and the injury suffered in order to be successful in any claim of negligence. The plaintiff has to show that as a result of the defendant's negligence, i.e. breach of duty of care owed to him, he has suffered damage. The damage may be physical (to person or property), mental or financial, but it must be:

(A) CAUSED BY THE BREACH OF DUTY. A patient who cannot show that an admitted act of negligence contributed to his present condition has not proved a causative link between the negligence and his injury;

13 [1932] AC 562; [1932] All ER Rep 1; [1932] SLT 317 (HL); 147 LT 281.

14 [1978] AC 728; [1977]2 All ER 492 (HL); [1977]2 WLR 1024; 121 Sol Jo 377.

15 *Sutherland Shire Council* v *Heymen* [1985]60 ALR 1; 59 ALJR 564; *San Sebastian Pty. Ltd.* v *Minister Administering the Environmental Planning and Assessment Act 1979* [1986]68 ALR 161 (HC).

16 *Junior Books Ltd.* v *Veitchi Co. Ltd.* [1983]1 AC 520; [1982]3 All ER 201; [1982]3 WLR 477; 126 Sol Jo 538; 21 BLR 66;1982 SLT 492 (HL).

(B) A TYPE OF DAMAGE RECOGNISED BY LAW. Certain types of damages are not recognised by the law, at any rate if they stand alone, e.g. distress and disappointment, mental strain or nervous shock not amounting to a psychiatric disorder or illness, and financial loss not accompanied by any physical injury to person or property and did not arise in the context of a fiduciary or proximate relationship between the parties; and

(C) IT MUST COME WITHIN THE FORESEEABLE AREA OF RISK CREATED BY THE BREACH OF DUTY. The damage will not be subject of compensation, even if directly caused by the breach of duty, if it was not reasonably foreseeable.[17]

Death caused by failure to treat a patient does not amount to negligence if the patient would have died even after giving treatment. When the doctor is alleged to be negligent for not treating a night watchman who complained of vomiting after drinking tea and died of arsenic poisoning, the claim of his widow failed on the ground that the workman would have died even if he had received all due care, because the judge is of opinion that there was no chance of administering any effective antidote in time.[18] Similarly, the doctor was not found to be negligent in not administering a test dose of an anti-tetanus serum before injecting it in a patient who developed encephalitis leading to brain damage and paralysis, because the judge concluded from the evidence that even if the test dose had been administered there would have been no observable reaction in the patient and as such the doctor would have administered the injection.[19] When the plaintiff alleged that the consultant obstetrician had been negligent by not telling her that the sample from her amniocentesis had not produced sufficient cultures to determine whether

17 Charles J. Lewis, *Medical Negligence*, 4th Ed., pp. 195-196.

18 *Barnett* v *Chelsea and Kensington Hospital Management Committee* [1969]1 QB 428; [1968]2 WLR 422; [1968]1 All ER 1068; (1968)111 Sol Jo 912.

19 *Robinson* v *Post Office* [1974]1 WLR 1176; [1974]2 All ER 737; (1973)117 Sol Jo 915.

her child would suffer from Down's syndrome, the claim of the plaintiff was dismissed as the court concluded that the plaintiff would not have proceeded to a second amniocentesis which always carries risk to the foetus, and the outcome would have been the same had the obstetrician not been negligent.[20]

The defendant health authority was not negligent for delay of about two hours in taking decision to conduct caesarean operation for delivery of the child who suffered brain damage, because the same could not have been prevented even by early delivery of the child by caesarean section.[21] Similarly, the claim of the plaintiff failed, when the judge held that earlier admission to hospital would not have affected the outcome and that the plaintiff would still have been admitted for observation only and the unavoidable and unpredictable onset of septicaemia resulting in brain damage would have occurred in hospital at the same time and with the same results.[22] The plaintiff must establish that the delay in treatment was "at least a material contributory cause" of his injury.[23] It is not sufficient to show that delay materially increased the risk of injury or that delay could cause injury, because the plaintiff had to go further and prove that damage was actually caused.[1] The delay in diagnosing breast cancer may not substantially alter the outcome, but there is a degree of injury as the plaintiff would probably have lived longer.[2]

An intervening act or event occurring after the original act of negligence may operate to break the chain of causation, with the result that the wrong-doer is not liable for loss caused by that event. The surgeon was not held negligent for unwanted pregnancy of the plaintiff due to failure of

20 *Gregory* v *Pembrokeshire Health Authority* [1989]1 Med LR 81.

21 *Robertson (an infant)* v *Nottingham Health Authority* 22 BMLR 49 (QBD); [1996]7 Med LR 421 affirmed by [1997]8 Med LR 1 (CA).

22 *Stockdale* v *Nicholls* [1993]4 Med LR 190.

23 *Hotson* v *East Berkshire Area Health Authority* [1987] AC 750 (HL); [1987]1 All ER 210; [1987]2 WLR 287; 130 Sol Jo 925; [1987]3 WLR 232; (1987)131 Sol Jo 975; [1987]2 All ER 909.

1 *Tahir* v *Haringey Health Authority* [1998] Lloyd's Rep Med 104.

2 *Taylor* v *West Kent Health Authority* [1997]8 Med LR 251.

sterilization operation, as the plaintiff's decision to have unprotected sexual intercourse with the knowledge that she was not sterile, was a *novus actus interveniens* (an independent supervening act) breaking the chain of causation.[3] However, the Court of Appeal observed that the conduct of refusal of abortion by a woman who had become pregnant after negligently performed sterilization was not so unreasonable as to eclipse the original negligence by breaking the chain of causation.[4]

The Supreme Court of Canada[5] has laid down the principle for fixation of liability when there is more than one potential cause for the damage suffered by the patient. The basic test for determining causation in multi-cause injuries is that the claimant must prove that the injury would not have occurred, but for the negligent act or omission of each of the defendants. The recognised contribution to the above principle is material contribution test, which involves two requirements: first, when it is impossible for the claimant to prove defendant's negligence due to lack of knowledge, and secondly, when the defendant breached duty of care exposing the claimant to the unreasonable risk of injury and the claimant ultimately suffered from the injury.

(ii) *Remoteness and foreseeability* The neighbour test of Lord Atkin has established the general concept of reasonable foresight as the criterion of negligence. Every reasonable man has a duty to take care to avoid foreseeable harm to his neighbour. To put in the words of Charlesworth,[6] "The reasonable man is only bound to foresee the probable consequences of his act and not also the possible consequences, because in the simplest and apparently least harmful acts there are always possibilities of damage, improbable though that damage may be". Naturally, to

3 *Sabri Tabrizi* v *Lothian Health Board* 43 BMLR 190 CS (OH).

4 *Emeh* v *Kensington and Chelsea and Westminster Area Health Authority* [1985] QB 1012; [1984]3 All ER 1044; [1985]2 WLR 233; 128 Sol Jo 705 (CA); (1985)11 ACC (BJ) 1.

5 *Hanke* v *Resurfice Corp.* 2007 SCC 7; [2007]4 WWR 1; (2007)278 DLR (4th) 463.

6 Charlesworth & Percy on *Negligence*, 9th Ed., p. 23 (2·10).

establish negligence the mere possibility of accident is not enough. Lord Russell of Kollowen[7] observed that "in considering whether a person owes to another a duty, a breach of which will render him liable to the other in damages for negligence, it is material to consider what the defendant ought to have contemplated as a reasonable man".

Even if the plaintiff has established a duty of care, a breach of that duty, and loss of a type recognised by the law and caused by the breach, the defendant will only be liable to compensate for that loss if it was reasonably foreseeable at the time of the breach that it could arise. In other words, the basic principle is that the plaintiff cannot recover for an injury that was not foreseeable, and not natural and probable consequences of his actions.[8] The Court of Appeal[9] dealt with a case where the plaintiff, a trained nurse, married and of child-bearing age, had to undergo a medical check up with a view to taking employment with the defendants. The defendants' radiologist who interpreted her chest x-ray, had failed to report the presence of a significant abnormality, which if reported, would have been diagnosed as primary pulmonary hypertension (PPH). The plaintiff became pregnant and thereafter PPH was diagnosed. She gave birth of a healthy baby and after six months of delivery of the child she had to undergo hysterectomy and cardiac catheterisation. The Court of Appeal concluded that the domestic life of the plaintiff and consequently the decision to become pregnant fell outside the area of foreseeability of the radiologist of the defendants.

A doctor retained by a company for the purpose of examining a potential employee for his medical fitness to do a job, has been held to owe a duty of care to the potential employee in carrying out his examination and in interpreting the results of that examination when reporting to the company.[10] Negligence is not attributed to an orthopaedic surgeon for his wrong

7 *Bourhill* v *Young* [1943] AC 92; [1942]2 All ER 396; 167 LT 261.

8 Charles J. Lewis, *Medical Negligence*, 4th Ed., pp. 219-220.

9 *R.* v *Croydon Health Authority* [1998] Lloyd's Rep Med 44; 40 BMLR 40 (CA).

10 *Baker* v *Kaye* [1997] IRLR 219.

advice in a personal injury action, when the report was given by the surgeon for the purpose of assisting lawyers to conduct the case in court and not for the purpose of advising the patient about medical treatment.[11]

A psychiatric patient, who was released from the hospital along with his friend after consultation with the mother and friends of the patient, killed his friend during the journey. The relatives of the deceased brought an action against the health authority responsible for the hospital and its staff. The High Court of Australia[12] held that the hospital authority did not owe any duty of care to the patient's friend to protect him from the harm caused by the patient.

One nursing auxiliary sustained injury to back while lifting one spastic male patient with student nurse. As a result of the accident the nurse suffered a prolapsed disc for which she underwent surgical treatment leaving her with a scarring of nerve route which caused constant pain. It was alleged that the defendant health authority was negligent in failing to provide the nurse with a safe system of work and protect her from a foreseeable risk of injury. The Queen's Bench of U.K.[13] held the defendant health authority negligent for adopting the method of lifting the spastic patient by employing two nurses, because the method presented a foreseeable risk of injury to the auxiliary nurse. The view expressed by the Federal Court of Australia[14] is that to establish actionable negligence it must be proved that an individual contracted cancer due to exposure to radiation without relying on usual causes of cancer.

The foresight of reasonable man in medical profession is discussed in detail in *Roe* v *Minister of Health*[15] wherein the

11 *Landall* v *Dennis Faulkner and Alsop* [1994]5 Mad LR 268.

12 *Hunter and New England Local Health District* v *McKenna* [2014] HCA 44; (2014)314 ALR 505.

13 *Fitzsimmons* v *Northumberland Health Authority* [1989]5 BMLR 48 (QBD).

14 *Merck Sharp & Dohme (Australia) Pvt. Ltd.* v *Peterson* [2011] FCA FC 128; (2011)284 ALR 1.

15 [1954]2 QB 66; [1954]2 All ER 131; [1954]2 WLR 915; 98 Sol Jo 319 (CA).

Court of Appeal in England decided the problem of using a particular spinal anaesthetic kept in sealed glass ampoules which were stored in solution of phenol for avoiding infection. The ampoules were washed and examined visually to ensure that there was no crack by which the phenol might have contaminated the anaesthetic as per standard practice prevalent in 1947. The patient who underwent operation developed paraplegia as a result of injection of spinal anaesthetic containing phenol. The subsequent investigation revealed that the visual examination of the ampoules was inadequate to detect the microscopic crack whereby the phenol contaminated the anaesthetic. The subsequent development of medical knowledge would have pointed out the act of the anaesthetist as negligent had the accident occurred in 1954. The anaesthetist was held not negligent as the standard medical practice approved the visual examination of the ampoules and as the wisdom of exclusion of hindsight pointed out the accident as unforeseeable. To put in the words of Lord Denning[16] "we must not look at a 1947 accident with 1954 spectacles".

It is held by the Supreme Court of India that the standard of care for establishing negligence has to be judged in the light of knowledge available at the time of the incident and not at the time of the trial.[17]

(iii) ***Obligation for economic loss*** The negligent conduct of a medical man may cause physical damage or economic loss to the patient. The extent of imposing liability for damage is of particular importance to the medical profession, because the law of tort provides compensation for injuries to person or property and for financial loss flowing from such damage. The pure economic loss which is not consequential upon physical damage was regarded as beyond the scope of the tort of negligence till the decision of the House of

16 *Roe* v *Minister of Health* [1954]2 QB 66; [1954]2 All ER 131; [1954]2 WLR 915; 98 Sol Jo 319 (CA).

17 *Martin F. D'Souza* v *Mohd Ishfaq* (2009)3 SCC 1; 2009 ACJ 1695; AIR 2009 SC 2049; JT 2009(2) SC 486; (2009)2 Scale 620.

Lords[18] which decided that the professional giving advice is liable to a person who suffers economic loss following such advice, so long as there is a special relationship between the professional and the said person. In other words, economic loss can be claimed when it accompanies physical injury or arises out of a particular relationship between the parties.

The epoch making decision of House of Lords in *Hedley Byrne*[19] enjoins that a professional making negligent statements owes a duty of care to a person who suffers economic loss through reliance upon the statements containing information, advice, opinion and warning. To invoke the principle of *Hedley Byrne* there must be a special relationship between the person suffers and the person who causes to suffer. Lord Reid pointed out in *Hedley Byrne* that a special relationship would arise where the party seeking information and advice was trusting the other to exercise such a degree of care as the circumstances required, where it was reasonable for him to do that, and where the other gave the information or advice when he knew or ought to have known that the inquirer was relying on him. Thus, the duty of the doctor will arise when the information or advice is given to the patient with the intention that he would rely on it. The professional liability will no doubt arise from inaccurate information or incorrect advice. The meaning of any statement should be considered in the sense in which the maker intended it, or in which he knew or ought to have known that the recipient would understand it.[20]

Lord Devlin points out in *Hedley Byrne* that if the doctor negligently advises the patient to abandon his work when that course of action is unnecessary, the loss would be

18 *Hedley Byrne & Co. Ltd.* v *Heller and Partners Ltd.* [1962]1 QB 396; [1961]3 All ER 891; [1961]3 WLR 1225; 105 Sol Jo 910 (CA) affirmed by [1964] AC 465; [1963]2 All ER 575; [1963]3 WLR 101; 107 Sol Jo 454; [1963]1 Lloyd's Rep 485 (HL).

19 *Hedley Byrne & Co. Ltd.* v *Heller & Partners Ltd.* [1962]1 QB 396; [1961]3 All ER 891; [1961]3 WLR 1225; 105 Sol Jo 910 (CA) affirmed by [1964] AC 465; [1963]2 All ER 575; [1963]3 WLR 101; 107 Sol Jo 454; [1963]1 Lloyd's Rep 485 (HL).

20 *McInerny* v *Lloyd's Bank* [1973]2 Lloyd's Rep 389 affirmed by [1947]1 Lloyd's Rep 246 (CA).

recovered.[21] The House of Lords is of the view that economic loss which was foreseeable would be recoverable, as any other loss, unless there were policy considerations in the particular case militating against such recovery.[22] Public policy does not stand on the way of awarding compensation for economic loss caused by wrongful birth of a child due to failure of the surgeon to perform sterilization successfully.[1]

To have a sustainable case in negligence against a defendant in respect of financial loss arising from reliance on advice given by the defendant, the plaintiff must establish, *inter alia*, that the defendant knew, either actually or inferentially, that the advice communicated by him was likely to be acted upon by the plaintiff, without *independent inquiry*, for a purpose, whether particularly specified or generally described, which was made known either actually or inferentially, to the defendant at the time when the advice was given, and that it had been so acted upon by the plaintiff to his detriment.[2]

(iv) *Obligation for nervous shock* Nervous shock amounting to psychiatric disorder can be subject of compensation in a claim of negligence. Lord Keith[3] indicated that "nervous shock" meant a reaction to an immediate and horrifying impact, resulting in some recognisable psychiatric illness. There had to be some serious mental disturbance outside the range of normal human experience, not merely the ordinary emotions of anxiety, grief or fear. Accordingly, shock, anxiety,

21 *Hedley Byrne & Co. Ltd.* v *Heller & Partners Ltd.* [1962]1 QB 396; [1961]3 All ER 891; [1961]3 WLR 1225; 105 Sol Jo 910 (CA) affirmed by [1964] AC 465; [1963]2 All ER 575; [1963]3 WLR 101; 107 Sol Jo 454; [1963]1 Lloyd's Rep 485 (HL).

22 *Anns* v *Merton London Borough Council* [1978] AC 728; [1977]2 All ER 492; [1977]2 WLR 1024; 121 Sol Jo 377.

1 *Emeh* v *Kensington and Chelsea and Westminster Area Health Authority* [1984]3 All ER 1044 (CA); [1985] QB 1012; [1985]11 ACC (BJ) 1; [1985]2 WLR 233; 128 Sol Jo 705 (CA).

2 *Goodwill* v *British Pregnancy Advisory Service* [1996]2 All ER 161 (CA); [1996]1 WLR 1397 (CA); 31 BMLR 83 (CA); [1996] Fam Law 471; [1996] NLJR 173; 140 Sol Jo LB 37 (CA).

3 *Page* v *Smith* [1996] AC 155; [1995]2 All ER 736; [1995]2 WLR 644; [1995]2 Lloyd's Rep 95; 28 BMLR 133 (HL).

depression, disappointment or grief, not amounting to psychiatric disorder, is not compensable when it stands alone, but it may be taken into account to increase the award when it accompanies other recognised injuries.[4]

The Court of Appeal[5] dismissed a claim by a father who suffered psychiatric injury by remaining in the hospital for about two weeks near the bed of his 23-year-old son who had been injured in a traffic accident and fatally deteriorated in hospital due to allegedly negligent medical treatment. The Court of Appeal observed that the psychiatric damage said to have been suffered by a child as a result of allegedly incompetent diagnosis of sexual abuse was not recognised as compensable injury.[6] The court awarded damages to the mother of a still born child for shock when the still birth of one of the twins was caused by a horrendous and agonising piece of obstetric management.[7] Similarly, the court awarded compensation to a woman for psychological damage caused by still birth of the child.[8]

4 Contractual duty

(i) *Liability under implied contract* The relationship between the doctor and the patient is mostly contractual, even if the payment for professional services is not paid by the patient himself. The duty of the doctor undertaking the treatment of the patient is to advise or act for the betterment of the patient, until the patient terminates the contract by accepting the service of another professional without the consent of the previous one or until further performance of the duty becomes impossible for the negligent conduct of the patient. The implied contractual relation between the medical practitioner and the patient imposes continuing duty on the medical practitioner requiring his advice or action to be reviewed in the light of changed circumstances.

4 Charles, J. Lewis, *Medical Negligence*, 4th Ed. 1998, p. 227.

5 *Sion* v *Hampstead Health Authority* [1994]5 Med LR 170 (CA); *The Times*, 10th June 1994 (CA).

6 *M (a minor)* v *Newham London Borough Council* [1995]2 AC 633.

7 *Kralj* v *McGrath and St. Theresa's Hospital* [1986]1 All ER 54; [1985] NLJ Rep 913; (1985)135 New LJ 913.

8 *Grieve* v *Salford Health Authority* [1991]2 Med LR 295.

The law does not usually imply a warranty that the professional will achieve the desired result, but only a term that he will use reasonable care and skill.[9] The House of Lords[10] dictates that the court must be reluctant to allow implied contracts to be used as a device to extend professional duties beyond express terms or general tortious principles. However, the existence of a contract for medical treatment does not preclude an action for breach of the implied duties of care and skill being regarded as tortious in nature.[11] Tucker, J. considered the evidence of agreement reached between the surgeon and the patient at the initial interview and observed that a surgeon agreed to perform an operation on his patient in the hospital, impliedly undertook the responsibility to perform the operation personally and to pay such visits as were necessary for proper supervision of the patient's progress.[12]

(ii) ***Liability on express undertaking*** The contractual duties are generally more onerous in nature and extent than those imposed by tort. Tortious duties do not impose the extent of personal responsibility and strict liability that may be attached to contractual duties. The strict liability is expected from those professionals who give an express undertaking.

Generally surgeons are unlikely to guarantee the success of an operation, but cosmetic surgery, dental surgery and sterilization are exceptional areas where the surgeons may agree to give guarantee of success. For example, a dentist who undertakes to remove a tooth by painless process may be strictly liable if pain is caused in the process of extraction of tooth.[13] In an American decision[14] a cosmetic surgeon was

9 *Greaves & Co. (Contractors) Ltd.* v *Baynham, Meikle & Partners* [1974]3 All ER 666; [1974]1 WLR 1261; 118 Sol Jo 595; [1975]1 Lloyd's Rep 31 affirmed by [1975]3 All ER 99; [1975]1 WLR 1095; 119 Sol Jo 372; [1975]2 Lloyd's Rep 325 (CA).

10 *Independent Broadcasting Authority* v *E.M.I. Electronics Ltd. and BICC Construction Ltd.* [1980]14 BLR 1 (HL).

11 *Edwards* v *Mallan* [1908]1 KB 1002; 77 LJKB 608; 98 LT 824; 52 Sol Jo 316 (CA).

12 *Morris* v *Winsburry-White* [1937]4 All ER 494.

13 *Edwards* v *Mallan* [1908]1 KB 1002; 77 LJKB 608; 98 LT 824; 52 Sol Jo 316 (CA).

14 *Bailey* v *Harman* [1924]74 Colo 390.

held liable for failure to achieve the success guaranteed by him. To infer strict liability there must be clear and cogent evidence of an express undertaking on the part of the professional. The plaintiff's allegation that the surgeon guaranteed the permanency of sterilization was negated in a Canadian decision,[15] as there was no evidence of the clear meeting of minds. The argument that the professional contracts should contain implied duties guaranteeing success was put forward in *Eyre* v *Measday*[16] and *Thake* v *Maurice*[17] as an alternative to the claim that an express term warranting success could be found in a contract to perform sterilization. The Court of Appeal could see no scope for an implied term beyond the normal one to perform the operation with reasonable care and skill. The reason behind this dictum of the Court of Appeal is that there cannot be any express undertaking in a matter which depends on the healing of human tissue. Slade, LJ[18] adopting the conventional approach echoed the words of Lord Denning, "In the absence of any express warranty, the court should be slow to imply against a medical man an unqualified warranty as to the results of an intended operation, for the very simple reason that, objectively speaking, it was most unlikely that a responsible medical man would intend to give a warranty of this nature."[19]

5 Tortious duty

(i) *Liability for failure to act* The tort of negligence applicable to the medical practitioner indicates that a medical practitioner is liable for failure to show due care or skill in treatment resulting in pain, injury or consequential death of the patient. Where a person holds himself out to be competent

15 *Dendaas* v *Yackel* (1980)109 DLR (3d) 455.

16 *Eyre* v *Measday* [1986]1 All ER 488 (CA).

17 *Thake* v *Maurice* [1986] QB 644; [1986]1 All ER 497; [1986]2 WLR 337; 129 Sol Jo 894 (CA).

18 *Eyre* v *Measday* [1986]1 All ER 488 (CA).

19 *Greaves & Co. (Contractors) Ltd.* v *Baynham, Meikle & Partners* [1974]3 All ER 666; [1974]1 WLR 1261; 118 Sol Jo 595; [1975]1 Lloyd's Rep 31 affirmed by [1975]3 All ER 99; [1975]1 WLR 1095; 119 Sol Jo 372; [1975]2 Lloyd's Rep 325 (CA).

to do some special kind of job, an action for negligence will lie for damage which has been caused by the failure to exercise due care and skill either by proving that the defendant did not possess the requisite skill or by showing that, although he possessed it, he did not exercise it in the particular case.[20] The duty of a medical man is stated elaborately by Lord Hewart, CJ[1] in the following way:

> "If a person holds himself out as possessing special skill and knowledge and he is consulted, as possessing such skill and knowledge, by or on behalf of a patient, he owes a duty to the patient to use due caution in undertaking the treatment. If he accepts the responsibility and undertakes the treatment and the patient submits to his direction and treatment accordingly, he owes a duty to the patient to use diligence, care, knowledge, skill and caution in administering the treatment. No contractual relation is necessary, nor is it necessary that service be rendered for reward...... The law requires a fair and reasonable standard of care and competence ..... in all the matters above mentioned. If the patient's death has been caused by the defendant's indolence or carelessness, it will not avail to show that he had sufficient knowledge; nor will it avail to prove that he was diligent in attendance, if the patient had been killed by his gross ignorance and unskilfulness. As regards cases where incompetence is alleged, it is only necessary to say that the unqualified practitioner cannot claim to be measured by any lower standard than that which is applied to a qualified man. As regards cases of alleged recklessness, juries are likely to distinguish between the qualified and the unqualified man. There may be recklessness in undertaking the treatment and recklessness in the conduct of it. It is, no doubt, conceivable that a qualified man may be held liable for recklessly undertaking a case which he knew, or should

20 Charlesworth & Percy on *Negligence*, 9th Ed., p. 536 (8·02).

1 *R.* v *Bateman* [1925]94 LJKB 791; 133 LT 730; 69 Sol Jo 622 followed in *Akerele* v *The King* [1943] AC 255; 168 LT 102; [1943]1 All ER 367.

have known, to be beyond his powers, or for making his patient the subject of reckless experiment."

(ii) *Liability for omission* Omission to inform the patient of the risks involved in course of treatment is actionable negligence, if it is established that the patient suffers damage due to such failure of the medical man. In the absence of express terms and conditions to the contrary, the liability of a medical practitioner is limited to the sphere of his profession only. A medical man called upon to advise partly on medical matters and partly on administrative matters, is liable for medical aspect only.[2]

A doctor owes a duty of care to a patient in making the report to the Board of Guardians for the purpose of deciding whether to commit the patient to an asylum.[3] Failure on the part of the doctor to record clinical parameters of the patient on the prescription does not amount to negligence when proper and adequate treatment is given by the doctor.[4] The Privy Council held the doctor negligent for omission to make appropriate enquiry or to carry out any test before administering penicillin injection to the deceased.[5] The High Court of Australia[6] held an Ophthalmic Surgeon negligent for omission to warn the patient of the risk of developing a condition known as sympathetic ophthalmia in her left eye as a result of surgery on her right eye.

The Supreme Court of California[7] held a psychiatrist liable to a third person attacked by one of his patients on the ground that the patient had confided his intention to attack the third party and the psychiatrist omitted to take proper

2 *Stokes* v *Guest, Keen & Nettlefold (Bolts and Nuts) Ltd.* [1968]1 WLR 1776; 112 Sol Jo 821.

3 *Everett* v *Griffiths* [1920]3 KB 163; 89 LJKB 929; 123 LT 280; 64 Sol Jo 445 (CA) affirmed by [1921]1 AC 631; 90 LJKB 737; 125 LT 230; 65 Sol Jo 395 (HL).

4 *Mihir Banerjee* v *Dr. Abhijit Roy* II(2015) CPJ 102 (NCDRC).

5 *Chin Keow* v *Government of Malaysia* 1967 ACJ 379; [1967]1 WLR 813; 111 Sol Jo 333 (PC).

6 *Rogers* v *Whitaker* 109 ALR 625; 16 BMLR 148 (H.C. of Australia).

7 *Tarasoff* v *Regents of the University of California* 551 P (2d) 334 [1976]; 17 Cal (3d) 425; 529 P (2d) 55 [1974].

steps for protection of third party. However, the courts may treat the consequences of any omission as being too remote to justify imposition of liability. Lord Denning, MR.[8] dismissed the claim by stating that the attempt to commit suicide was far too remote a consequence to be the subject of damages. The doctor is not liable for negligent advice on the basis of which a patient may settle a legal claim in respect of his injuries.[9]

(iii) *Manufacturers' duty towards patient* A manufacturer of a product has a duty in tort to warn consumers of damages it knows or ought to know are inherent in the product's use. This duty is a continuing one, requiring manufacturers to warn not only of dangers known at the time of sale, but also of dangers discovered after the product has been sold and delivered. The principles underlying the doctrine of informed consent apply to the relationship between manufacturers of medical products and consumers. The manufacturer-consumer relationship, unlike the doctor-patient relationship, is characterised primarily by a lack of direct communication which creates a relationship of complete dependency between manufacturer and patient. Accordingly, manufacturers are reasonably required to make clear, complete and current disclosure of information to the consumers concerning the risks inherent in the ordinary use of their products.[10] The Supreme Court of Ireland[11] is of the view that the manufacturers of a vaccine has a duty to exercise all reasonable care to avoid exposing recipients to danger and harm from the use of their products. Failure to meet this standard of reasonable care will subject the manufacturer to liability for any resulting injury. None the less, the fact that the injuries were proximately caused by the manufacturer's product would not of itself establish liability in negligence

8 *Hyde* v *Tameside Area Health Authority* [1981]2 PN 26; [1981] CLY 1854 (CA).

9 *Stevens* v *Bermondsey and Southwark Group Hospital Management Committee* (1963)107 Sol Jo 478.

10 *Hollis* v *Dow Corning Corporation* [1995]4 SCR 634.

11 *Best (an infant)* v *Wellcome Foundation Ltd.* 17 BMLR 11 (SC of Ir); [1994]5 Med LR 81.

on the part of the manufacturer, provided that the proper standards of care have been exercised in the production and testing of the vaccine. When the capsules prescribed by an Ayurvedic doctor for treatment of diabetes were found to contain lead more than permissible limit, the State Commission, Tamil Nadu[12] gave direction for withdrawal of capsules from the market for stopping of unfair trade indulged by the advertisement claiming guaranteed care of diabetes.

(iv) ***Obligation for gratuitous service*** The members of medical profession often provide service gratuitously. The professionals cannot escape their liability in tort for negligent performance of duty, even if he does the work free of cost or for goodwill reasons.[13] An eye camp was organised for extending expert ophthalmic surgical service to the cataract patients of a particular area. Unfortunately, the operated eyes of the patients were irreversibly damaged due to post-operative infection of the "intra ocular" cavities of the eyes caused by common contaminating source, *viz.* normal saline used at the time of surgery. A public interest litigation was filed before the Supreme Court, praying, *inter alia*, for compensation to the victims for the negligence in arranging the eye-operation camp. The Supreme Court directed the State Government to pay ₹12,500 to each of the victims in addition to ₹5,000 already paid by way of compensation.[14]

6 Duty under penal law

(i) ***Criteria of criminal negligence*** To establish negligence under criminal law, the prosecution must prove (*a*) the existence of duty, (*b*) a breach of duty causing death, and (*c*) the breach of duty must be characterised as gross negligence.[15]

12 *K.M. Balakrishnan* alias *Premnath* v *Padma Ayurveda Vaidyasala & Research Centre* III(2003) CPJ 645.

13 *Hedley Byrne & Co. Ltd.* v *Heller & Partners Ltd.* [1962]1 QB 396; [1961]3 All ER 891; [1961]3 WLR 1225; 105 Sol Jo 910 (CA) affirmed by [1964] AC 465; [1963]2 All ER 575; [1963]3 WLR 101; 107 Sol Jo 454 (HL).

14 *A.S. Mittal* v *State of U.P.* (1989)3 SCC 223.

15 *R.* v *Prentice* and *R.* v *Adomako* [1993]4 All ER 935; 15 BMLR 13 (CA) affirmed by [1994]3 All ER 79 (HL).

The concept of gross negligence for the purpose of criminal liability was developed by Lord Atkin,[16] as follows:

> "For the purposes of criminal law there are degrees of negligence; and a very high degree of negligence is required to be proved before the felony is established. Probably of all the epithets that can be applied 'reckless' most nearly covers the care. It is difficult to visualise a case of death caused by reckless driving in the connotation of that term in ordinary speech which would not justify a conviction for manslaughter, but it is probably not all-embracing for 'reckless' suggests an indifference to risk, whereas the accused may have appreciated the risk and intended to avoid it and yet shown sign of high degree of negligence in the means adopted to avoid the risk as would justify a conviction."

The test for recklessness formulated by Lord Diplock[17] is that the defendant having recognised the risk, had nevertheless gone on to take it. This criterion of recklessness is based upon the premise that the defendant himself created the obvious and serious risk. Often the risk of danger to health is not created by the doctor, but pre-exists in the doctor's assuming a duty of care to the patient. In Lord Diplock's formulation the "obvious risk" meant obvious to "the ordinary prudent individual". Where duty is undertaken by the professional, the criterion of the ordinary individual's appreciation cannot be applied. Naturally the definition of "recklessness" given by Lord Diplock, excludes the person who recognises the risk, who does not go to take it, and who seeks to remove it, but does so in a grossly negligent way. The formulation of "gross negligence" of Lord Atkin is capable of embracing such behaviour. It is, thus, clear that the professional must be proved to have been indifferent to an obvious risk of injury to health, or has actually foreseen the risk, but has determined nevertheless to run it.

16 *Andrews* v *D.P.P.* [1937]2 All ER 552; [1937] AC 576 (PC).

17 *R.* v *Lawrence* [1981]1 All ER 974; [1982] AC 510; [1981]2 WLR 524 (HL).

The Supreme Court of India is of the opinion that the negligence must be of a gross degree or of a very high degree for an act to amount to criminal negligence. To prosecute a medical professional for negligence under criminal law, it must be shown that the accused did something or failed to do something, which in the given facts and circumstances no medical professional in his ordinary senses and prudence would have done or failed to do.[18]

The following is the test to bring home the charge of criminal negligence in medical accidents:[19]

(*a*) indifference to an obvious risk of injury to health;

(*b*) actual foresight of the risk coupled with the determination nevertheless to run it;

(*c*) an appreciation of the risk coupled with an intention to avoid it, but the attempted avoidance involved such a high degree of negligence as the jury may consider justifies conviction; and

(*d*) inattention or failure to advert to a serious risk which goes beyond "mere inadvertence" in respect of an obvious and important matter which the defendant's duty demanded, he should address.

The Gujarat High Court[20] has laid down the following criteria for consideration whether any doctor is liable for criminal action:

(*i*) Is it a case of gross lack of competence on the part of the doctor or is it a case of total indifference shown by the doctor to the patient's safety?

(*ii*) Is it a case of mere error of judgment or accident?

(*iii*) Is it possible to infer that the doctor has to gain something by showing indifference in the facts and circumstances of the case?

18 *Malay Kumar Ganguly* v *Dr. Sukumar Mukherjee* 2009(7) SCJ 124; (2009)9 SCC 221; AIR 2010 SC 1162; (2009)10 Scale 675; III(2009) CPJ 17; 2009(3) CCR 558; 2010 AIR SCW 769.

19 *R.* v *Adomako* [1993]4 All ER 935 (CA) affirmed by [1994]3 All ER 79 (HL).

20 *Hemaben Sanjeev Kumar Kanadiya* v *Dr. D.N. Nanavati* 2013 CrLJ 2472.

The Supreme Court of India refused to quash the criminal proceedings against the doctor on the ground that the materials disclosed by the complainant for causing death of the patient do not rule out the offence under s. 304A of the Indian Penal Code. According to the Supreme Court, the issue whether the medical opinion other than cancer was possible on the basis of first blood report requires deeper consideration after thorough examination of the opinion of the experts and only the trial court can take up the issue whether the same falls within the ambit of medical negligence.[1]

A doctor registered as a homeopathic practitioner is guilty of negligence in prescribing allopathic medicines to the patient without being qualified in that system of medicine. According to the Supreme Court of India,[2] a homeopathic practitioner practising allopathic system of medicine without possessing requisite qualification and without being registered under Indian Medical Council Act or the State Medical Council Act, is liable to be prosecuted under s. 15(3) of the Indian Medical Council Act. However, it is observed by the Supreme Court that if any State law relating to registration of medical practitioners permits practice of allopathic medicines on the basis of degree in integrated medicines, the bar under s. 15(2) of the Indian Medical Council Act will not apply.[3]

The Magistrate was held not justified in issuing summons against the accused doctor under s. 304 of the Indian Penal Code for causing death of the patient by administering three injections within half an hour, although summons could have been issued by the Magistrate against the accused doctor for an offence punishable under s. 304A of the Indian Penal Code.[4]

1 *B. Jagdish* v *State of Andhra Pradesh* (2009)1 SCC 681; AIR 2009 SC 19; 2009 CrLJ 828 (SC); (2008)15 Scale 599.

2 *Poonam Verma* v *Aswin Patel* AIR 1996 SC 2111; (1996)4 SCC 332; 1996(3) CPR 205 (SC); II(1996) CPJ 1 (SC); (1996)4 CTJ 465 (SC) (CP).

3 *Dr. Mukhtiar Chand* v *State of Punjab* 1998 CTJ 813 (SC) (CP).

4 *Mahadev Prasad Kaushik* v *State of Uttar Pradesh* (2008)14 SCC 479; (2008)13 Scale 356; AIR 2009 SC 125.

(ii) ***Criminal negligence—not established*** A criminal proceeding against the medical practitioner for causing death due to negligence was quashed by High Court of J&K[5] on the ground that mere carelessness is not sufficient for conviction under s. 304A of IPC. The criminal proceeding against the medical practitioner for committing an offence under s. 304A of IPC was quashed by Punjab and Haryana High Court[6] on the ground that the action of the medical practitioner was not even proximately the cause of death of the baby which was born as a result of induced delivery. The doctor was prosecuted under s. 304A of IPC for death of the patient aged about 26 years as sequel to planned surgery for repair of right inguinal scrotal hernia. The Bombay High Court[7] quashed the criminal proceeding on the ground that the non-attendance of the patient by the surgeon in the night on being told by the Medical Officer on duty about the bleeding from the operation site, cannot be the direct or proximate cause of death of the patient.

The deceased was an old patient of bronchial asthama. The doctor injected Coramine and thereafter patient expired. In the absence of any evidence to establish direct nexus between the death of the patient and the rash act of injecting Coramine by the doctor, the criminal liability of the doctor was not established.[8] The patient was admitted for child delivery in the nursing home. The doctors decided caesarean operation under local anaesthesia. The blood pressure began to fall soon after administering local anaesthesia and ultimately the patient died. The criminal proceeding against the anaesthetist was started on the allegation that he was not an expert anaesthetist and that the test dose of spinal xylocaine injection was not given to the patient. The Karnataka High Court quashed the criminal proceeding on the grounds that the doctor holding degrees like MBBS,

5 *Dr. Ved Khuller* v *State* 1988(1) ACJ 328.
6 *Dr. Ajit Kaur* v *State of Punjab* 1986(2) ACJ 696.
7 *Dr. Sujay Das* v *State* CDJ 2006 BHC 38; 2006 CrLJ 1148; 2006(1) AIR (Bom) R 488.
8 *Ghanshyamdas Bhagwandas* v *State of M.P.* 1977 ACJ 182.

FRCS, DGO is qualified to administer anaesthesia and that the omission to give test dose of spinal xylocaine does not amount to rashness or negligence.[9] The reasons given by the High Court may not appear to be sound to a prudent person.

The deceased went to the clinic of the doctor for treatment, as she had a compliant of sinusitis and hypertension. The doctor gave S.P. test dose to the patient and then she was given injection bistrepen half gram I.M. After administration of the injection the patient immediately complained of giddiness, pain in chest, perspiration and her pulses were fast. When reaction was noticed by the doctor, she immediately gave a number of injections for anti-reaction treatment. The trial court held the doctor guilty of charge under s. 304A, IPC and awarded simple imprisonment for seven days and a fine of ₹1000, in default simple imprisonment for seven days. The High Court of Gujarat acquitted the doctor of the charge under s. 304A, IPC on appeal on the grounds that the deceased did not react to test dose of procaine penicillin injection, and that the doctor after noticing reaction of regular dose of injection, gave immediately a number of injections for anti-reaction treatment.[10]

Where it appears from the medical opinion that the death was caused during performance of operation for nasal deformity for not introducing a cuffed endotracheal tube of proper size as to prevent aspiration of blood from the wound in the respiratory passage, the act of the doctor cannot be termed as gross negligence liable to be prosecuted under s. 304A of the Indian Penal Code. As a result, the criminal proceedings initiated against the doctor was quashed by the Supreme Court of India.[11]

The patient suffering from cancer for about 10 years was treated by doctor in US. She was hospitalised due to vaginal

9 *Dr. Krishna Prasad* v *State of Karnataka* 1989(1) ACJ 393.
10 *State of Gujarat* v *Dr. Maltiben Valjibhai Shah* 1994(1) ACJ 375.
11 *Dr. Suresh Gupta* v *Govt. of N.C.T. of Delhi* (2004)6 SCC 422.

bleeding. During exploratory laparotomy the doctor found plastering of intestine and the abdomen was closed under advice of the appellant surgeon, but ultimately the patient died. The surgeon was prosecuted on the allegations that he conducted surgery against the advice of the doctor of USA, that he did not conduct or supervise the operation and that he did not treat the patient during post operative period after formation of fistula. The conviction and sentence of the appellant surgeon under ss. 338 and 109 of the Indian Penal Code imposed by the trial court was affirmed by the Sessions Court and the High Court. By setting aside the conviction and sentence of the appellant surgeon, the Supreme Court has laid down that the appellant surgeon being an expert in the field can take decision to go for surgery against the advice of the doctor of US who was not an expert in the field and that the decision of the appellant surgeon to go for surgical procedure was not an act of wanton negligence.[12] The surgeon on call was not found guilty of criminal negligence when she attended the patient suffering from haemophilia in the hospital and referred the case to the physician, but left the hospital without waiting for the arrival of the physician.[13]

The doctors were prosecuted on the allegation of committing offence under s. 304A of the Indian Penal Code on the ground that the patient died of infection, immune suppression and sepsis which were adverse effect of administration of excessive high dose of long acting steroid by all the doctors at the initial stage of the treatment of the patient suffering from T.E.N., i.e. Toxic Epidermal Nircolysis. It was established from evidence that the doctors did not recommend for supportive therapy like iv fluids/electrolyte replacement, dressing of skin wounds and close monitoring of the infection which were mandatory for treatment of T.E.N. patients. The Supreme Court of India observed that the negligence on the part of each of the treating doctors and the also the hospital may have contributed to the ultimate death of the patient. Since the doctrine of cumulative effect is not

12 *P.B. Desai* v *State of Maharashtra* (2013)15 SCC 481.

13 *Sou Jayshree Ujwal Ingole* v *State of Maharashtra* (2017)14 SCC 571; (2018)1 SCC (Cri) 145; AIR 2017 SC 2078; 2017 SCC Online SC 354.

available in criminal law, it is very difficult to distil the extent of individual negligence with respect to each of the doctors. Accordingly, the Supreme Court did not hold the doctors guilty of criminal negligence in causing death of the patient, which is punishable under s. 304A of the Indian Penal Code.[14]

The cardiologist conducted angiogram on the patient and finding three blocks in the coronary arteries conducted angioplasty. The bypass surgery was conducted due to failure of angioplasty after long gap, but the patient died. The cardiologist was prosecuted for committing gross negligence under s. 304A of the Indian Penal Code. The criminal proceeding was quashed by the Supreme Court on the ground that the expert has opined that the time gap between failure of angioplasty and bypass surgery was not a factor for causing death of the patient and thereby gross medical negligence was not established.[15]

(iii) ***Criminal negligence—established*** A registered homoeopath administered to the patient suffering from guinea worm, 24 drops of stramonium and a leaf of dhatura without studying its effect and the patient died of poisoning. This rash and negligent act of the doctor to prescribe poisonous medicines without studying their probable effect was of such a degree as to amount to taking a hazard whereby injury was most likely to be occasioned. The criminality lies in running the risk of doing such an act with recklessness or indifference to the consequences. The homoeopath doctor was held guilty under s. 304A of the Indian Penal Code by the Apex Court.[16]

The Indore Bench of Madhya Pradesh[17] High Court held a registered Hakim guilty for committing an offence under s. 304A, IPC. The fact that a person totally ignorant of the

14 *Malay Kumar Ganguly* v *Dr. Sukumar Mukherjee* (2009)9 SCC 221; (2009)7 SCJ 124; AIR 2010 SC 1162; 2010 AIR SCW 769; (2009)10 Scale 675; III(2009) CPJ 17; 2009(3) CCR 558.

15 *A.S.V. Narayanan Rao* v *Ratnamala* (2013)10 SCC 741.

16 *Juggankhan* v *State of M.P.* AIR 1965 SC 831; (1965)1 CrLJ 763; (1965)2 SCJ 119; (1965)1 SCWR 796.

17 *Dr. Khusaldas Pammandas* v *State of M.P.* AIR 1960 MP 50; 1960 CrLJ 234; 1959 MPLJ 966.

science of medicine or practice of surgery undertakes a treatment or performs an operation is very material in showing his gross ignorance from which an inference about his gross rashness and negligence can be inferred.

A person projecting himself as a doctor administered glucose to a nine month old child intravenously leading to anaphylax reaction to I.V. fluid and thereby the child expired. The conviction of the person under s. 304 of Indian Penal Code was upheld by Delhi High Court.[18]

The doctor, who gave inadequate blood transfusion after delay of one and half hours of severe postpartum haemorrhage resulting in death of the patient, was found to be grossly negligent and reckless in treating the deceased and thereby he was convicted under s. 304A of the Indian Penal Code. The Kerala High Court[19] upheld the judgment and order of the trial court and the appellate court, by which the accused doctor would serve the sentence of imprisonment for one day and pay compensation of ₹1,00,000 to the husband of the deceased.

(iv) *Guidelines for prosecution of doctor under s. 304A, IPC*

The Supreme Court of India[20] has given the following guidelines for prosecution of the doctors on the allegation of committing offences under s. 304A of the Indian Penal Code. "A private complaint may not be entertained unless the complainant has produced *prima facie* evidence before the court in the form of a credible opinion given by another competent doctor to support the charge of rashness or negligence on the part of the accused doctor. The investigating officer should, before proceeding against the doctor accused of rash or negligent act or omission, obtain an independent and competent medical opinion preferably from a doctor in Government service, qualified in that branch of medical practice, who can normally be expected to give an impartial

18 *Ravinder Ram Chander Banshi* v *State of NCT of Delhi* 2015(5) RCR (Criminal) 783; 2014(213) DLT 259; 2014(4) Cri CC 457 (Del).

19 *Vasumathy* v *State of Kerala* Cri Rev. Pet. No. 696 of 2011 decided on 23.06.2020.

20 *Jacob Mathew* v *State of Punjab* (2005)6 SCC 1; 2005 ACJ 1840; AIR 2005 SC 3180; III(2005) CPJ 9; 2005(3) CPR 70; 2005 CrLJ 3710; JT 2005(6) SC 584.

and unbiased opinion to the facts collected during investigation. A doctor accused of causing death of the patient by rashness or negligence should not be arrested in a routine manner unless it is necessary for collection of evidence or if the investigating officer thinks that the accused doctor would not face the prosecution without arrest".

7 Duty under consumer law

(i) ***Service rendered free of cost*** A medical practitioner rendering professional service free of charge has no obligation under the Consumer Protection Act 1986. A gratuitous patient is not a consumer for availing of medical services free of cost. The patient undergoing medical treatment in a hospital providing the service of doctor free of cost is not a consumer within the meaning of s. 2(1)(*d*)(*ii*)* of the Consumer Protection Act 1986.

It has been categorically laid down by the National Commission[21] that the persons who avail themselves of the facility of medical treatment in government hospitals are not consumers, because the medical practitioners render professional service in government hospital free of cost, and as such the said professional service of the doctor in government hospital is not service for the purpose of the Consumer Protection Act. However, it is now well-settled by the decision of the Supreme Court[22] that the service rendered by a medical practitioner attached to government hospital or non-government hospital or nursing home or health centre or dispensary where such services are rendered free of charge to everybody, would not be service for the purpose of the Consumer Protection Act. The payment of a token amount for registration purpose only at the hospital or nursing home would not alter the position. It is clear from the above decision of the Supreme Court that service rendered at a government hospital or non-government hospital or nursing home where services are rendered on payment of charges to some persons

* Replaced by s. 2(7)(*ii*) of the Consumer Protection Act 2019 w.e.f. 9.8.2019.

21 *Consumer Unity & Trust Society, Jaipur* v *State of Rajasthan* 1991(1) CPR 241 (NC); I(1992) CPJ 259 (NC); (1993)1 CTJ 89 (NCDRC); *Mrs. Mable Roosevelt* v *State of Kerala* 1991(1) CPR 330 (NC).

22 *Indian Medical Association* v *V.P. Shantha* AIR 1996 SC 550; (1995)6 SCC 651; III(1995) CPJ 1 (SC); 1995(3) CPR 412 (SC); (1995)3 CTJ 969 (SC) (CP); 1996 CCJ 1 (SC).

and rendered free of charge to other persons availing of such services would fall within the ambit of the expression "service", irrespective of the fact that the service is rendered free of charge to persons who are not in a position to pay for such services. Accordingly, free service rendered by a medical practitioner may be "service" and the recipient a "consumer". By following the decision of the Supreme Court it is held by the National Commission[1] that "service" rendered gratuitously by a doctor to the relation of colleague doctor in the nursing home where patients are treated on payment of charges, falls within the ambit of "service". Where services of government hospital are rendered on payment of charges to some patients and free of charges to others, such services would fall within the ambit of "service".[2]

By following the decision of the Supreme Court it is also laid down by the National Commission that a Government Servant under Central Government Health Scheme is not a consumer and the service rendered to him under CGHS does not constitute "service".[3] The payment of a token amount for registration or a token contribution made cannot be classified as consideration for availing the services falling within the ambit of "service".[4] It is held by the State Commission, W.B.,[5] that an employee governed under ESI Scheme is "consumer" for availing of medical service from the ESI hospitals. This view is upheld by the Supreme Court in *Kishore Lal* case.[6]

The service rendered by the medical practitioner to his patient under the contract of personal service is not covered by the exclusionary part of the definition of service. The

1 *Vijay H. Mankar* v *Dr. (Mrs.) Mangla Bansod* 2000 CTJ 101 (CP) (NCDRC); I(2000) CPJ 37 (NC); 2000 CCJ 610.

2 *Sukhwarsha Rani* v *General Hospital, through its Medical Superintendent* 2000(1) CPR 337 (Chandigarh).

3 *Additional Director, CGHS, Pune* v *Dr. R.L. Butani* 1996(1) CPR 136 (NC); I(1996) CPJ 255 (NC); 1996 CCJ 1017 (NC).

4 *Anthony Dass* v *Ex Engineer, Earth Movers Division, BEML* III(1997) CPJ 224 (Bangalore); 1998 CCJ 1301 (Kant).

5 *Ranjit Kumar Das* v *Medical Officer, ESI Hospital, Manicktala* 1998(1) CPR 165 (Cal); III(1998) CPJ 336 (Cal); 1999 CCJ 70 (WB).

6 *Kishore Lal* v *Chairman, Employees' State Insurance Corporation* AIR 2007 SC 1819; (2007)4 SCC 579; II(2007) CPJ 25; JT 2007(6) SC 541; (2007)4 Supreme 775.

Supreme Court has clearly laid down that the service rendered by the medical practitioners in the hospitals/dispensaries run by the E.S.I. Corporation to a member of the E.S.I. Scheme or members of his family is covered under the Consumer Protection Act as the insurance scheme contributes to the service rendered by the E.S.I. hospitals/dispensaries.[7]

According to the dictum of the Apex Court,[8] service rendered by a medical practitioner or hospital or nursing home cannot be regarded as service rendered free of charge, if the person availing of the service has taken an insurance policy for medical care whereunder the charges will be reimbursed by the insurance company. Similarly, where, as a part of the condition of service, the employer bears the expenses of medical treatment of an employee and his family members, the medical service rendered to such an employee and his family members, would not be considered free of charge.

(ii) ***Service rendered on payment*** By enactment of the Consumer Protection Act 1986, the intention of the Parliament is to provide protection and relief to persons who have hired any services for consideration when the services provided are found to suffer from deficiency in any respect.[9] The professional service of medical man is not specifically mentioned in s. 2(1)(*o*)* of the Consumer Protection Act 1986, but the facilities of services mentioned therein are merely illustrative of the definition of service which is wide enough to include medical service available on payment of consideration. The exclusionary part of the definition of service excludes any service rendered free of charge or a contract of personal service.

The professional service rendered by medical practitioner for consideration falls within the scope of the expression

7 *Kishore Lal* v *Chairman, Employees' State Insurance Corporation* AIR 2007 SC 1819; (2007)4 SCC 579; II(2007) CPJ 25; JT 2007(6) SC 541; (2007)4 Supreme 775.

8 *Indian Medical Association* v *V.P. Shantha* AIR 1996 SC 550; (1995)6 SCC 651; III(1995) CPJ 1 (SC); 1995(3) CPR 412 (SC); (1995)3 CTJ 969 (SC) (CP); 1996 CCJ 1 (SC).

9 *Consumer Unity & Trust Society, Jaipur* v *State of Rajasthan* 1991(1) CPR 241 (NC); I(1992) CPJ 259 (NC); (1993)1 CTJ 89 (NCDRC).

* Replaced by s. 2(42) of the Consumer Protection Act 2019 w.e.f. 9.8.2019.

"service".[10] According to the National Commission, the activity of providing medical assistance for payment carried on by the hospitals and members of the medical profession falls within the scope of the expression "service" and in the event of any deficiency in the performance of such service the aggrieved party can invoke the remedies provided under the Consumer Protection Act by filing a complaint before the Consumer Forum having jurisdiction.[11]

"Deficiency" means, "any fault, imperfection, shortcoming or inadequacy in the quality, nature and manner of performance which is required to be maintained by or under any law for the time being in force or has been undertaken to be performed by a person in pursuance of a contract or otherwise in relation to any service".[12] It is now well-settled by the Supreme Court[13] that service rendered to a patient by a medical practitioner (except where the doctor renders service free of charge to every patient or under a contract of personal service) by way of consultation, diagnosis, and treatment both medicinal and surgical, would fall within the ambit of "service".

There is no distinction between medical negligence in the law of torts and deficiency in the medical service rendered within the consumer jurisdiction. The concept of medical negligence in tort and deficiency in medical service in consumer jurisdiction overlaps in a very large field. The deficiency of service under consumer jurisdiction undoubtedly includes what is negligence in the law of torts, but is somewhat wider.[14] According to our Apex Court,[15] a

10 *Dr. Sr. Louie* v *Smt. Kannolil Pathumma* 1993(1) CPR 422 (NC); I(1993) CPJ 30 (NC); (1993)1 CTJ 32 (NCDRC).

11 *Consumer Education and Research Society* v *Dr. Ratilal B. Patel* III(1992) CPJ 25 (NC); (1993)1 CTJ 89 (NCDRC); *M/s. Cosmopolitan Hospital* v *Smt. Vasantha P. Nair* (1992)1 CPR 820 (NC); I(1992) CPJ 302 (NC).

12 Section 2(1)(*g*) of the Consumer Protection Act 1986 replaced to s. 2(11) of the Consumer Protection Act 2019 w.e.f. 9.8.2019.

13 *Indian Medical Association* v *V.P. Shantha* AIR 1996 SC 550; (1995)6 SCC 651; III(1995) CPJ 1 (SC); 1995(3) CPR 412 (SC); (1995)3 CTJ 969 (SC) (CP); 1996 CCJ 1 (SC).

14 *Dr. Ravinder Gupta* v *Ganga Devi* 1993(3) CPR 255 (Haryana); (1993)1 CTJ 1004 (SCDRC).

15 *Indian Medical Association* v *V.P. Shantha* AIR 1996 SC 550; (1995)6 SCC 651; III(1995) CPJ 1 (SC); 1995(3) CPR 412 (SC); (1995)3 CTJ 969 (SC) (CP); 1996 CCJ 1 (SC).

determination about deficiency in service is to be made by applying the same test as is applied in an action for damages for negligence. For example, in a case in which there was choice of treatment, various possibilities should be explained to the patient with specific risks and advantages, and failure on the part of the doctor to do so, amounts to deficiency in service.[16]

Medical professionals are expected to exercise and provide reasonable degree of skill and knowledge and also exercise reasonable degree of care in treating patients. A medical man can be held guilty of negligence when he falls short of the standard of a reasonably skilful medical person in his field.[17] The Supreme Court is of the view that to establish negligence in administering treatment by committing mistake, the complainant must prove (*i*) that the doctor made a mistake, and (*ii*) that the mistake was such which a reasonably careful and skilful medical practitioner would not have made.[18] For establishing negligence in diagnosis and treatment on the part of the doctor, the test is whether the doctor has been proved to be guilty of such failure as no doctor of ordinary skill could be guilty of it acting with reasonable care.[19] The opinion of the State Commission, Maharashtra that the doctor undertaking surgery has the duty to take care of postoperative complications, has been turned down by the National Commission[20] which has held that the private doctor performing operation for a fee in the private hospital, cannot be expected to undertake and provide

16 *V. Vassanda Conmary* v *Dr. T. Ramachandrudu* 1998(3) CPR 227 (Pondicherry).

17 *D.P. Bhandari* v *Sri Ganga Ram Hospital* II(1991) CPJ 409 (Del) reversed by National Commission in *Sri Ganga Ram Hospital* v *D.P. Bhandari* 1992(1) CPR 796 (NC); II(1992) CPJ 397 (NC).

18 *Post-Graduate Institute of Medical Education and Research, Chandigarh* v *Jaspal Singh* (2009)7 SCC 330; JT 2009(7) SC 527; 2009 ACJ 2672.

19 *Dr. Sr. Louie* v *Smt. Kannolil Pathumma* 1993(1) CPR 422 (NC); I(1993) CPJ 30 (NC); (1993)1 CTJ 32 (NCDRC).

20 *B. Sekhar Hegde* v *Dr. Sudhansu Bhattacharya* 1993(3) CPR 414 (NC); (1994)2 CTJ 10 (CP) (NCDRC); III(1993) CPJ 388 (NC) reversing State Commission, Bombay II(1992) CPJ 449 (Bom); (1993)2 CTJ 523 (SCDRC).

postoperative treatment and care to the hospital's patient. It is the duty of the institution, i.e. the hospital to render postoperative care and treatment to the patient undergoing operation in the said hospital.

The State Commission, Maharashtra, did not award any compensation against an anaesthetist, because there was no privity of contract between the patient and the anaesthetist whose service was hired by the surgeon for the patient. By reversing the decision of the State Commission on appeal, it is held by the National Commission[21] that the anaesthetist who participated in the process of delivery of medical services to the beneficiary is as much liable as the main surgeon if negligence is established, and that a privity of contract need not be established for a claim to be made under Consumer Protection Act 1986 which is replaced by the Consumer Protection Act 2019, so long as there is hiring or availing of services for consideration.

Whenever a complaint is received against a doctor or hospital by the Consumer Forum or by the criminal court, then before issuing notice to the doctor or hospital against whom the complaint was made, the consumer forum or the criminal court should first refer the matter to a competent doctor or committee of doctors specialised in the field relating to which the medical negligence is attributed and only after obtaining expert opinion that there is a *prima facie* case of medical negligence, should notice be then issued to the doctor or the hospital concerned.[22] However, the above view expressed in *Martin F. D'Souza*,[1] is declared as *per incuriam* by the Supreme Court of India in *V. Kishan Rao* v *Nikhil Super Speciality Hospital*.[2]

21 *Mumbai Grahak Panchayat* v *Dr. (Mrs.) Rashmi B. Fadnavis* 1996(1) CPR 137 (NC); (1996)4 CTJ 286 (CP) (NCDRC) confirmed by NC in *Dr. (Mrs.) Rashmi B. Fadnavis* v *Mumbai Grahak Panchayat* III(1998) CPJ 21 (NC); 1998(3) CPR 34 (NC); 1998 CTJ 742 (CP) (NCDRC); 1999 CCJ 391 (NC).

22 *Martin F. D'Souza* v *Mohd. Ishfaq* (2009)3 SCC 1; 2009 ACJ 1695; AIR 2009 SC 2049; JT 2009(2) SC 486; (2009)2 Scale 620.

1 *Martin F. D'Souza* v *Mohd. Ishfaq (supra).*

2 *V. Kishan Rao* v *Nikhil Super Speciality Hospital* (2010)5 SCC 513 followed in *A. Srimannarayana* v *Dasari Santa Kumari* (2013)9 SCC 496.

8 Duty towards foetus A legal duty is the counterpart of legal right. An unborn child lacks the status to be the subject of a legal duty, but a newly born child enjoys that status. If injury is done to an unborn child, no duty is broken. If injury is negligently caused to a newly born baby, liability in negligence arises.[3]

There is no liability until *damnum* and *injuria* concur. Doctors engaged in the delivery of a foetus owe a duty of care to avoid injury to that foetus and once the foetus ceases on birth to be a foetus and becomes a person, there is a concurrence of *injuria* and *damnum* with the result that the newly born child has a right to sue the person whose breach of duty has resulted in the child's loss.[4]

The question whether the minor plaintiff had a cause of action for injury to her mother's womb before birth came up for consideration before the Court of Appeal in U.K.[5] The unanimous opinion of the Court of Appeal is that the infant plaintiff's claim for what has been called "Wrongful life" discloses no cause of action.

Stephenson, LJ[6] delivering the judgment observed as follows:

> "The law recognises a difference between the life of a foetus and the life of those who have been born. It does not follow that the doctor is under a legal obligation to a foetus to terminate its life, or that the foetus has a legal duty to die. The defendant doctor has had no duty to the child to give the child's mother an opportunity to terminate the child's life. That duty may be owed to the

3 *de Martell* v *Merton and Sutton Health Authority* [1992]3 All ER 820 affirmed by Court of Appeal in [1992]3 All ER 833 (CA); 10 BMLR 63 (CA); *Burton* v *Islington Health Authority* 10 BMLR 63 (CA).

4 *Hamilton* v *Fife Health Board* 13 BMLR 156; [1993]4 Med LR 201.

5 *McKay* v *Essex Area Health Authority* [1984]1 ACC (BJ) 159; [1982] QB 1166; [1982]2 All ER 771; [1982]2 WLR 890; 126 Sol Jo 261 (CA); 1983 ACJ 374.

6 *McKay* v *Essex Area Health Authority* [1984]1 ACC (BJ) 159; [1982] QB 1166; [1982]2 All ER 771; [1982]2 WLR 890; 126 Sol Jo 261 (CA); 1983 ACJ 374.

> mother, but it cannot be owed to the child. To impose such a duty towards the child would make a further inroad on the sanctity of human life which would be contrary to public policy."

The majority view of the Supreme Court of Canada[7] is that when a child not actually born at the time of an accident is subsequently born alive and viable, it is clothed with all the rights of action which it would have had in existence at the date of the accident to the mother. The Supreme Court of Victoria (Australia)[8] also rejected the contention that a careless act can never give rise to a cause of action in negligence unless there is in existence at the time of the act a legal person affected by it who can sue. The changed view that the child can sue is adopted by the United States in the year 1946.[9] On consideration of the above decision of Canada, Australia and United States, the Court of Appeal in England[10] changed its earlier view and held that a child born started suffering from disabilities caused as a result of medical negligence before birth could maintain an action for damages for negligence in respect of a breach of duty of care, since, although not a person in the eye of law at the time when the injury took place, an unborn child is deemed for the purpose of such action to be born whenever its interests required and was therefore clothed with all rights of action when born which it would have had if actually in existence at the date of the accident to its mother.

Accordingly, the breach of duty of care would be established if at the time the wrongful act was committed there was merely a potential or contingent duty of care which crystallised into an actual duty when the person injured suffered the injury, and it was irrelevant that at the time the wrongful act was committed there was no specific person towards whom the duty could be said to exist. The plaintiff

7 *Montreal Tramway* v *Leveille* (1933)4 DLR 337.

8 *Watt* v *Rama* (1972) VR 353.

9 *Bonbrest* v *Kotz* (1946)65 F-Supp 138.

10 *de Martell* v *Merton and Sutton Health Authority* [1992]3 All ER 820 affirmed by [1992]3 All ER 833 (CA); 10 BMLR 63 (CA).

born with numerous abnormalities, brought an action against the health authority alleging that her condition had been caused by carrying out the operation on her mother while the plaintiff was *in utero*, that the operation should not have been performed on a pregnant woman and that the medical staff had been negligent in carrying out the operation without first ascertaining whether the plaintiff's mother was pregnant. It was held by Queen's Bench Division[11] that since the medical staff ought reasonably to have foreseen that the operation carried out on the plaintiff's mother was liable to damage any embryo being carried in her womb and since on birth the plaintiff not only suffered damage by being born with physical deformities but also acquired legal status and legal rights to sue in respect of that damage, she had a cause of action in respect of the injury caused to her by the negligence of the medical staff before she was born.

The baby born with severe brain damage claimed compensation through his father on the ground that the obstetrician of the defendant health authority first attempted to deliver him using a ventouse extractor, and after failure of this attempt, a forceps delivery was carried out and thereby he suffered brain damage. The Queen's Bench Division[12] held the obstetrician negligent in using untoward force to deliver the baby, resulting in intermittent hypoxia and thereby brain damage of the baby. Similarly, the defendant health authority was held negligent for cerebral palsy of the female baby caused by delay of six hours in conducting caesarean section of her mother.[13] The obstetrician was negligent for brain damage of the child due to foetal distress, as there was delay in carrying out caesarean section by mismanagement.[14] The negligence was attributed to the defendant health authority as the plaintiff succeeded in establishing a causative link between the cerebral palsy she had suffered as a result of

11 *Burton* v *Islington Health Authority* 6 BMLR 13 (QBD) affirmed by 10 BMLR 63 (CA); [1992]3 All ER 833.

12 *Townsend* v *Worcester and District Health Authority* (1994)23 BMLR 31 (QBD).

13 *Re, R* (a minor) (No. 2) 33 BMLR 178 (CA).

14 *Wiszniewski* v *Central Manchester H.A.* [1996]7 Med LR 248.

oxygen starvation at birth and midwives' negligence in failing to carry out an examination that would have revealed a secondary arrest of labour.[15] The hospital could not escape liability when there was medically unacceptable delay of one hour in securing the attendance of a suitably qualified doctor to deal with an emergency arising in delivery of a second twin, resulting in brain damage of the child.[16]

The defendant health authority was not held negligent for delay of about 50 minutes in conducting caesarean section after failure to deliver the baby by forceps and thereby causing severe hypoxic distress for about 50 minutes, resulting in cerebral palsy of the baby, as there are conflicting medical opinions about the procedure adopted by the obstetrician of the defendant health authority and it is difficult to dismiss the opinion of the defendant doctor as untenable.[17]

9 Obligation in medico-legal cases There can be no second opinion that preservation of human life is of paramount importance. Every doctor whether at a government hospital or otherwise has the professional obligation to extend his services with due expertise for protecting life. No law or State action can intervene to avoid or delay the discharge of paramount obligation cast upon members of the medical profession. Many a time the members of the medical profession avoid their duty to help a person when he is facing death, only because it is a medico-legal case. The Supreme Court of India[18] has laid down that whenever a member of the medical profession is approached and if he finds that whatever assistance he could give is not sufficient to save the life of the patient, but some better assistance is necessary it is the duty of the medical man so approached to provide primary medical aid to the patient and then to

15 *Murphy* v *Wirral Health Authority* [1996]7 Med LR 99.

16 *Bull* v *Devon Area Health Authority* [1993]4 Med LR 117; 22 BMLR 79 (CA).

17 *Nash* v *Kingston and Richmond Health Authority* 36 BMLR 123 (QBD).

18 *Pt. Parmanand Katara* v *Union of India* (Cr. Writ Petition No. 270 of 1988) AIR 1989 SC 2039.

refer the patient to the hospital where the expert facilities required for the treatment are available. The practice of the doctors and certain Government institutions to refuse even the primary medical aid to the patient and referring them to other hospitals simply because they are medico-legal cases is deprecated by the Apex Court.

A physician is free to choose whom he will serve. He should, however, respond to any request for his assistance in an emergency or whenever temperate public opinion expects the service. No medical practitioner shall commit an act of negligence that may deprive his patient from necessary medical care.[19]

10 Duty of the hospital The duty of the hospital is not limited to diagnosis and treatment only, but extends to looking after safety and security of the patients, particularly those who are sick or under medication and therefore can become delirious and incoherent.[20] The hospital owes duty to a voluntary psychiatric patient to detain in the hospital when the patient is under real and immediate risk of committing suicide.[21] Very often the claim of medical negligence is based on availability of evidence furnished by medical records kept and maintained in the hospital. In UK the right of a patient to access to his medical record is determined by the statute enacted by British Parliament. It is held by the Court of Appeal in UK[1] that a patient does have a right of access to his medical records at common law, but it is qualified at least to the same extent as the statutory right is qualified by s. 5(1)(2) of the Access to Health Records Act 1990. A health authority, as the owner of a patient's medical records, may deny the patient access to them if it is in his best interest to do so, for example, if their disclosure

19 Clause 13 of the Code of Medical Ethics drawn up with the approval of the Central Government under s. 33 of the Indian Medical Council Act.

20 *Ashish Kumar Mazumdar* v *Aishi Ram Batra Charitable Hospital Trust* (2014)9 SCC 256.

21 *Rabone* v *Pennine Care NHS Trust* [2012]2 WLR 381; [2012] UKSC 2.

1 *R.* v *Mid Glamorgan Family Health Services Authority and South Glamorgan Health Authority* 21 BMLR 1 (CA); [1995]1 All ER 356; [1995]1 WLR 110; [1994]5 Med LR 383; 138 Sol Jo LB 195 (CA).

would be detrimental to his health. The circumstances in which a patient or former patient is entitled to demand access to his medical records will be infinitely various and it would be neither desirable nor possible to attempt to set out the scope of the duty to afford access or, its obverse, the scope of the patient's right to demand access. Accordingly each case must depend on its own facts.

The hospital is vicariously liable for the acts of negligence committed by the paediatrician and ophthalmologist by not screening pre-term baby for Retinopathy of Prematurity (RoP) during his stay in the hospital for four weeks and even during review and routine check up on two different dates in OPD of the hospital after discharge from the hospital, and thereby the child became blind.[2]

It is the bounden duty of the nursing home to record the previous case history of the patient, summary of laboratory reports, sensitive test reports relating to drugs to be given to the patient.[3] However, failure on the part of the hospital authority to accede to the request of the complainant to furnish all the papers relating to his operation and treatment cannot amount to "deficiency in service" within the meaning of the expression used in the Consumer Protection Act 1986 (replaced by the Consumer Protection Act 2019 w.e.f. 9.8.2019).[4] The hospital was held negligent for not administering insulin to the patient for two days after admission when the patient was diagnosed as diabetes mellitus with blood sugar ranging from 580 mg to 734 mg. The National Commission held the hospital and the doctor guilty of deficiency in service for not maintaining the record of treatment given to the deceased for abortion and D&C operation.[5]

2 *Maharaja Agrasen Hospital* v *Master Rishabh Sharma* 2019 SCC Online SC 1658.

3 *Force* v *Dr. M. Ganeswara Rao* 1998(3) CPR 251 (Hyderabad); I(1998) CPJ 413 (Hyderabad); III(1997) CPJ 228 (Hyderabad); 1998 CTJ 314 (CP) (SCDRC); 1999 CCJ 163 (AP).

4 *Poona Medical Foundation Ruby Hall Clinic* v *Marutirao L. Titkare* I(1995) CPJ 232 (NC); 1995(1) CPR 661 (NC).

5 *Dr. (Smt.) Prabha Agarwal* v *Kanakhya Singh* IV(2011) CPJ 380.

The maintenance of medical record is important for proper management of the patient. The proper medical record will help the doctor and the hospital in scientific evaluation of their patient profile, in analysing the treatment result and in planning the treatment protocol. It will help in establishing that the treatment was carried out properly. The National Commission[6] has reminded that "poor records mean poor defence" and "no record means no defence". The view of the National Commission[7] is that there is deficiency of service on the part of the hospital by not providing medical record disclosing the fact of little chance of recovery of the patient which is obligatory under Regulations 2.3 and 3.6 framed by the Medical Council of India with the previous approval of the Central Government in exercise of powers conferred by s. 20A read with s. 33 of the Indian Medical Council Act 1956.

The ambulance service is part of the health service provided by the hospital, because its function includes transportation of patients to and from hospital. The Court of Appeal in U.K.[8] held the defendant ambulance service negligent for delay of 40 minutes in providing ambulance, which resulted in respiratory-arrest of the patient. The hospital is duty bound to ensure transportation of collected sample of biopsy to the laboratory for test and to collect the test report and hand over the same to the patient, when the hospital has charged the patient for the same.[9] However, the hospital cannot be held liable in negligence for not releasing the dead body from the hospital before settling the bills.[10]

There was delay of six hours in conducting caesarean section due to break down of the communicating system in the hospital, resulting in birth of a baby with an Apgar

6 *Indu Sharma (Dr.)* v *Indraprastha Apollo Hospital* III(2015) CPJ 248; 2015(2) CLT 454 (NCDRC); *Venkati* v *Dr. Prakash M. Bhandari* 2015(4) CLT 371 (NCDRC).

7 *T. Rama Rao* v *Vijay Hospital* I(2008) CPJ 170; CDJ 2007 (Cons) Case No. 481.

8 *Kent* v *Griffiths* [2000]2 All ER 474 (CA); [2000]2 WLR 1158.

9 *Mayo Hospital* v *Sunil Tiwari* 1997(3) CPR 574 (Bhopal); III(1997) CPJ 387 (Bhopal); 1998 CTJ 156 (CP) (SCDRC); 1999 CCJ 51 (MP).

10 *Mrs. Usha Mehrotra* v *Apollo Hospitals Enterprises Ltd.* 1999(2) CPR 453 (Chennai).

Score of 4. The baby suffered from severe spastic quadriplegic cerebral palsy with developmental retardation. The Court of Appeal[11] held the defendant health authority liable in negligence for catastrophic injury to the baby by delay in conducting caesarean section of the mother. Similarly, the hospital was held liable in negligence where significant breakdown in communication system of the defendant health authority in respect of obstetric care was proved and shown to constitute breaches of standard of care.[12] The defendant health authority could not escape liability when there was medically unacceptable delay of one hour in securing the attendance of a suitably qualified doctor to deal with an emergency arising in the delivery of a second twin, resulting in brain damage of the child.[13] The patient developed bilateral pulmonary embolism after two months of discharge from the hospital where he had undergone surgery for inguinal hernia. He was asked to contact general practitioner without disclosing the risk of developing deep vein thrombosis or pulmonary embolism as a consequence of surgery. The defendant health authority was held negligent for not providing adequate information to the patient about post operative risks.[14] On the other hand, the defendant health authority was held not liable in negligence for delay in shifting the patient to intensive therapy unit resulting in cardiac arrest and consequent permanent brain damage, as it was established from evidence that the patient would not have been transferred to intensive therapy unit earlier had Senior Registrar been called in time and that the patient would have suffered cardiac arrest had he been transferred to intensive therapy unit earlier.[15]

11 *Re, R* (a minor) (No. 2) 33 BMLR 178 (CA).

12 *Robertson* v *Nottingham Health Authority* [1996]7 Med LR 421; 22 BMLR 49 affirmed [1997]8 Med LR 1 (CA).

13 *Bull* v *Devon Area Health Authority* [1993]4 Med LR 117; 22 BMLR 79 (CA).

14 *Spencer* v *Hillingdon Hospital NHS Trust* [2015] EWHC 1058 (QB).

15 *Sherlock* v *North Birmingham Health Authority* 40 BMLR 103 (CA).

The Supreme Court of India has laid down that once the initial burden is discharged by the complainant by making out a case of negligence on the part of the hospital or the doctor concerned, the onus shifts on to the hospital or to the attending doctors to satisfy the court that there was diligence and no lack of care.[16] The hospital is in a better position to disclose what care was taken or what medicine was administered to the patient. It is, therefore, the duty of the hospital to satisfy that there was no lack of care or diligence.[17]

The patient had undergone a cosmetic procedure intended to rejuvinate skin by relying on the treatment disclosed in the brochure of the clinic. The procedure indicated that the skin sample of each patient would be sent to the company for culture of a bovine product and the cultured materials would be sent back to the clinic for administering injection to the patient. The brochure of the clinic was prepared on the basis of the brochure of the company, which indicated that the injectate would contain only patient's cells, but in practice injectate contained 0% to 0.2% bovine product, which caused allergic reaction in 3% to 10% of the patients. The Court of Appeal in UK[18] held that in the absence of any disclaimer on the part of the clinic, the clinic will be liable for providing inaccurate statement in the brochure, which would amount to misrepresentation on the part of the clinic. A two years old baby girl suffering from pneumonia was given intravenous fluids by inserting needle into artery instead of vein resulting in blockage of blood supply to the right forearm. The patient had to undergo amputation of

16 *Nizam Institute of Medical Sciences* v *Prasanth S. Dhananka* (2009)7 Scale 407; *Malay Kumar Ganguly* v *Dr. Sukumar Mukherjee* (2009)9 SCC 221; AIR 2010 SC 1162; (2009)10 Scale 675; III(2009) CPJ 17; 2010 AIR SCW 769.

17 *Savita Garg (Smt.)* v *Director, National Heart Institute* (2004)8 Scale 694; (2004)8 SCC 56; *Malay Kumar Ganguly* v *Dr. Sukumar Mukherjee* (2009)9 SCC 221; AIR 2010 SC 1162; (2009)10 Scale 675; III(2009) CPJ 17; 2010 AIR SCW 769.

18 *Webster* v *Liddington* [2014] EWCA Civ 560; [2014] PNLR 26.

right hand due to inadvertent intra-arterial injection in the radial artery resulting in gangrene of the right hand. The hospital was held liable for negligence of the doctor.[19]

11 Duty of the State for treatment of patients during pandemic of Covid-19 The mismanagement in providing treatment to the patients in the civil hospital at Ahmedabad was brought to the notice of the Gujarat High Court by way of Public Interest Litigation. The Division Bench of Gujarat High Court[20] directed the State Government to improve the working conditions of the resident doctors, increase the number of ventilators and oxygen beds, take punitive action against negligent ward boys and fix responsibility of senior officers who have failed to improve the health care in the civil hospital leading to massive loss of human lives. The media report of the plight of an expecting lady who was refused admission in the hospital for not having Covid-19 negative report was brought to the notice of Bombay High Court by filing one Public Interest Litigation. The Division Bench of Bombay High Court[21] directed the State Government and local bodies to ensure proper health care of the expecting ladies in the testing time of pandemic due to out break of Covid-19. The Supreme Court took *suo motu* cognizance of mismanagement of the hospitals dedicated to Covid-19 patients in Delhi, Maharashtra, Tamil Nadu, West Bengal and Gujarat and issued notice to all these States for filing affidavits about patient's management and infrastructure in the Government hospitals.[22]

The sufferings and harassment of the common people for test of Covid-19 went upto the Supreme Court. The Supreme

19 *Alfred Benedict* v *Manipal Hospital, Bangalore* (2015)11 SCC 423; 2014 SCC Online SC 1089.

20 *State of Gujarat* v *Suo Motu* Civil Application No. 14 of 2020 in connection with WP (PIL) No. 42 of 2020 decided on 25.05.2020.

21 *Mohiuddin Vaid* v *State of Maharashtra* LD-VC 50 of 2020 decided on 22.05.2020.

22 Proper treatment of Covid-19 patients and dignified handling of dead bodies in the hospitals (2020)5 SCC 304.

Court[23] gave the following guidelines for testing of Covid-19 in Government hospitals and private laboratories:

(*i*) Free testing for Covid-19 shall be available to persons eligible under "Ayushman Bharat Pradhan Mantri Jan Aarogya Yojana" implemented by the Government of India and any other category of weaker sections of the Society notified by the Government for free testing of Covid-19;

(*ii*) The Government of India may consider for providing the benefit of free testing of Covid-19 to the persons belonging to other weaker sections of the Society e.g. workers having low income in informal sector, beneficiaries of Direct Benefit Transfer etc.;

(*iii*) The private laboratories may charge the patient for testing of Covid-19 at the rate to be fixed by ICMR;

(*iv*) The Government of India may issue necessary guidelines for reimbursement of cost of free testing of Covid-19 undertaken by the private laboratories for persons who are unable to pay the cost of testing for belonging to lower strata of the Society.

The undignified manner of disposal of the dead body of the persons infected with Covid-19 was brought to the notice of Calcutta High Court by way of Public Interest Litigation. The Division Bench of Calcutta High Court[24] ruled in favour of dignified disposal of the mortal remains of the persons who died of Covid-19 by way of burial or burning. It is held that the relatives and friends of the deceased must be given the opportunity to pay respect to the deceased and perform the last rites as per religions practice, faith and conscience of the individuals. On consideration of the guidelines given by the Ministry of Health and Family Welfare, Government of India on March 15, 2020 and in addition to the procedure laid down by Government of West Bengal in notification

23 *Shashank Deo Sudhi* v *Union of India* Writ Petition (Civil) Diary No. 10816 of 2020 IA No. 48265 of 2020 decided on 13.04.2020.

24 *Vineet Ruia* v *Principal Secretary* 2020 SCC Online Cal 1664.

dated June 6, 2020, the Calcutta High Court has laid down the following guidelines for disposal of dead body of the persons infected with Covid-19:

(*i*) When the post-mortem of the dead body is not required, the dead body shall be handed over to the immediate next of kin of the deceased, i.e. the parents/surviving spouse/children etc. after completion of hospital formalities. The body should be secured in a body bag, the face end of which should preferably be transparent and the exterior of which will be appropriately sanitized/decontaminated, so as to eliminate/minimise the risk to the people transporting the dead body.

(*ii*) The people handling the dead body shall take standard precautions by using surgical mask, gloves etc. If available and possible, PPE should be used.

(*iii*) The vehicle carrying the dead body to the crematorium/burial ground will be suitably decontaminated.

(*iv*) The staff of the crematorium/burial ground should be sensitized to practise standard precautions, so that Covid-19 does not pose additional risk.

(*v*) The face end of the body bag may be unzipped by the staff at the crematorium/burial ground to allow the relatives to see the body for the last time. At this time, religious rituals, such as reading from religious scripts, sprinkling holy water, offering grains and such other last rites that do not require touching of the body, should be allowed.

(*vi*) After the cremation/burial the family members and the staff of the crematorium/burial ground should appropriately sanitize themselves.

(*vii*) As a social distancing measure, large gathering at the crematorium/burial ground should be avoided.

(*viii*) The persons handling the dead body shall go directly from the hospital to the crematorium/burial ground, as the case may be, without going to the home of the deceased or any where else.

(*ix*) If the body of a Covid-19 infected deceased remains unclaimed, the same shall be cremated/buried as the case may be with due dignity at the State expenses.

CHAPTER 3

Nature of Professional Duty

1 Professional duty—ambit of The doctors owe a duty of care to their patients. Failure to show due care or skill in medical treatment resulting in death, injury or pain of the patient, gives rise to a cause of action in negligence. Shelat, J delivering the judgment of the Supreme Court of India[1] lays down the criteria for determination of the professional duty of a medical man in the following way:

> "A person who holds himself out ready to give medical advice and treatment impliedly undertakes that he is possessed of skill and knowledge for the purpose. Such a person when consulted by a patient owes him certain duties, viz., a duty of care in deciding whether to undertake the case, a duty of care in deciding what treatment to give, or a duty of care in the administration of that treatment. A breach of any of those duties gives a right of action for negligence to the patient. The practitioner must bring to his task a reasonable degree of skill and knowledge and must exercise a reasonable degree of care."

A charge of professional negligence against a medical man is serious. It stands on a different footing than a charge of

1 *Dr. Laxman Balkrishna Joshi* v *Dr. Trimbak Bapu Godbole* AIR 1969 SC 128; 1968 ACJ 183 (SC); 1968 SCD 866; (1968)2 SCWR 73.

negligence against the driver of a motor car. The consequences are far more serious. It affects his professional status and reputation. With the best will in the world, things sometimes go amiss in surgical procedure or medical treatment. A doctor is not to be held negligent simply because something goes wrong. He is not liable for mischance or misadventure, or for an error of judgment. He is not liable for taking one choice out of two or for favouring one school rather than another. He is only liable when he falls below the standard of a reasonably competent practitioner in his field so much so that his conduct may be deserving of censure or inexcusable.[2] A surgeon or an anaesthetist will be judged by the standard of an average practitioner of the class to which he belongs or holds himself out to belong.[3]

The likelihood of injury or damage caused is the criterion for determination what degree of care needs to be taken in a particular case. To paraphrase Lord Dunedin,[4] "People must guard against reasonable probabilities, but they are not bound to guard against fantastic possibilities." Lord Macmillan[5] opined that the degree of care for the safety of others which the law requires human beings to observe in the conduct of their affairs varies according to the circumstances. There is no absolute standard, but it may be said generally that the degree of care required varies directly with the risk involved. Those who engage in operations inherently dangerous must take precautions which are not required of persons engaged in the ordinary routine of daily life. To be precise, the degree of care must be commensurate with the degree of risk involved in an action. To establish the liability of a doctor for medical negligence, it must be established (*i*) that the doctor deviated or departed from accepted standard of practice and (*ii*) that

2 Per Lord Denning, M.R. in *Hucks* v *Cole* [1968]118 New LJ 469; 112 Sol Jo 483.

3 *Dr. P. Narasimha Rao* v *Gundavarapu Jaya Prakash* AIR 1990 AP 207; (1990)1 ACC 468; 1990(1) ACJ 350; (1989)3 Andh LT 564; (1989)2 APLJ (HC) 491.

4 *Fardon* v *Harcourt Rivington* (1932)146 LT 391; 76 Sol Jo 61.

5 *Glasgow Corporation* v *Muir* [1943] AC 448; [1943]2 All ER 44; 169 LT 53.

such departure was proximate cause of the injuries suffered by the patient.[6]

A person having studied one particular system of medicine cannot possibly claim deep and complete knowledge about the other system of medicine. A doctor registered as homeopathic practitioner cannot prescribe allopathic medicines to the patient without being qualified in that system of medicine and without being registered under the Indian Medical Council Act or the State Medical Council Act. One homeopathic practitioner is held guilty of negligence for prescribing allopathic medicines to the patient without being qualified in that system of medicines by the Supreme Court of India,[7] which enunciates the following principle of negligence:

> "When the law, under which a person was registered as a medical practitioner, required him to practise in homeopathy only, he was under a statutory duty not to enter the field of any other system of medicine and when he trespassed into a prohibited field, without being qualified in that system, his conduct amounted to actionable negligence."

It is held by the Supreme Court of India,[8] that for establishing medical negligence or deficiency in service, the court would consider the following points:

(*i*) No guarantee is given by any doctor or surgeon that the patient would be cured;

(*ii*) The doctor must undertake a fair, reasonable and competent degree of skill, which may not be the highest skill;

(*iii*) Adoption of one of the modes of treatment, if there are many, and treating the patient with due care and caution would not constitute any negligence;

6 *Manika Roy* v *B.L. Chitlangra* 2016(1) CLT 374; 2016(1) CPR 380; II(2016) CPJ 348 (NCDRC).

7 *Poonam Verma* v *Aswin Patel* AIR 1996 SC 2111; (1996)4 SCC 332; 1996(3) CPR 205 (SC); II(1996) CPJ 1 (SC); (1996)4 CTJ 465 (SC) (CP).

8 *Malay Kumar Ganguly* v *Dr. Sukumar Mukherjee* 2009(7) SCJ 124; (2009)9 SCC 221; AIR 2010 SC 1162; (2009)10 Scale 675; III(2009) CPJ 17; 2009(3) CCR 558; 2010 AIR SCW 769.

(*iv*) A medical practitioner must exercise the reasonable degree of care, skill and knowledge which he possesses. However, failure to use due skill in diagnosis with the result that wrong treatment is given would be negligence.

(*v*) In a complicated case the court would be slow in attributing negligence on the part of the doctor, if he is performing his duties to the best of his ability.

2 Standard of reasonable care Every person has a duty to take reasonable care to avoid foreseeable harm to his neighbour.[9] The professional has no duty to guard against the risk which is beyond the ambit of the professional's contemplation and as such truly unforeseeable. The question whether the risk involved in medical treatment is foreseeable, is to be judged according to the knowledge possessed by the profession at the time of accident, and not by wisdom of hindsight. The subsequent development of medical knowledge cannot be taken into consideration to hold the professional negligent. An anaesthetist acquitted of the charge of negligence for administering an anaesthetic kept in a manner thought to be safe in 1947, though the subsequent development of medical knowledge proved the manner of keeping the anaesthetic as dangerous. To paraphrase Lord Denning,[10] "We must not look at a 1947 accident with 1954 Spectacles".

The standard of reasonable care is a flexible criterion capable of setting the boundaries of legal liability of the professionals depending on duties founded on tort or contract. The standard can be assessed in an objective manner according to the nature of the task undertaken by the professional, irrespective of his qualifications or job title. Inexperience is no defence for a person who holds himself out as a specialist,[11] though inexperienced medical

9 *Donoghue* v *Stevenson* [1932] AC 562; 147 LT 281; [1932] All ER Rep 1; 1932 SLT 317 (HL).

10 *Roe* v *Minister of Health* [1954]2 QB 66; [1954]2 All ER 131; [1954]2 WLR 915; 98 Sol Jo 319 (CA).

11 *Poole* v *Morgan* [1987]3 WWR 217.

practitioner may protect himself by seeking the advice and assistance from his experienced colleagues.[12]

The professional may take reasonable risk for obtaining desired advantages of treatment in many areas of medical practice. Emergencies may force a medical practitioner to act without taking all the precautions required in ideal circumstances, and in such cases it may be reasonable to run the risks of a high degree of probability. Similarly, a medical practitioner cannot provide same level of care to all patients undergoing treatment, as particular individual may pose particular risk.[13] But a uniform standard is expected to be applied to all persons subject to a particular duty of care. Accordingly the standard of care is to be judged as to what ought to have been done and the standard of foresight is to be assessed as to what ought to have been foreseen in the particular circumstances. The obstetrician was not held negligent for premature delivery of baby by caesarian section when the mother was suffering from deteriorating pre-eclamperia.[14]

The test of reasonable care in medical profession is to be judged by the standard of the ordinary skilled man exercising and professing to have that special skill at that time.[15] The view adopted by the Canadian courts[16] is that the work of a specialised nature calls for a higher standard of care. The English law does not demand higher standard of care and skill for highly specialised kind of work within a particular profession. It is sufficient if the professional exercises the ordinary skill of an ordinary competent man exercising that

12 *Wilsher* v *Essex Area Health Authority* [1987] QB 730; [1986]3 All ER 801; [1987]2 WLR 425; 130 Sol Jo 749 (CA) reversed [1988]1 All ER 871; [1988]2 WLR 557; 132 Sol Jo 418; 3 BMLR 37 (HL).

13 *Selfe* v *Ilford and District Hospital Management Committee* (1970) *The Times*, 25th November, 114 Sol Jo 935 (CA); *Hyde* v *Tameside Area Health Authority* (1981) CLY 1854; 2 PN 26 (CA).

14 *French* v *Thames Valley Strategic Health Authority* [2005] EWHC 459 (QB).

15 *Bolam* v *Friern Hospital Management Committee* [1957]2 All ER 118; [1957]1 WLR 582; 101 Sol Jo 357; 1 BMLR 1.

16 *Baills* v *Boulanger* [1924]4 DLR 1083; *Poole* v *Morgan* [1987]3 WWR 217.

particular art. The English law contemplates medical negligence as the failure to act in accordance with the standards of reasonably competent medical man of the time.[17] The National Commission is of the view that the conduct of a general practitioner is to be judged on the touchstone of the conduct of a general practitioner, whereas the conduct of a professed specialist has to be at par with the conduct of a similarly skilled specialist. If a doctor professes that he is a specialist, possessing some special skills to deal with a particular ailment or condition, he is expected to exercise a higher degree of case than a general practitioner, whose conduct is to be judged on a different parameter.[18]

The High Court of Australia[19] is of the view that the law imposes on a medical practitioner a duty to exercise reasonable care and skill in the context of professional advice and treatment. That duty is a single comprehensive duty covering all the ways in which a doctor is called upon to exercise his skill and judgment; it extends to the examination, diagnosis and treatment of the patient and the provision of information in an appropriate case. For example, the court expects that the general physicians would properly advise the patients of the risks of taking oral contraceptives with high blood pressure.[20] The general practitioner who failed to refer a patient with a lump in her breast for specialist investigation was held to be negligent,[21] but the Court of Appeal[1] did not hold the doctor negligent for failure to refer a woman who repeatedly complained of pain and lump in her breast, when no lump was palpable on clinical examination. A general practitioner was held to be negligent for failure to consider diagnosis of pulmonary embolism and refer the patient to the hospital for further

17 *Bolam* v *Friern Hospital Management Committee* [1957]2 All ER 118; [1957]1 WLR 582; 101 Sol Jo 357; 1 BMLR 1.

18 *Baidyanath Chakraborty (Dr.)* v *Chandi Bhattacharjee* 2014(2) CPR 490; II(2014) CPJ 601; 2014(4) Andh LD 1 (NCDRC).

19 *Rogers* v *Whitaker* 109 ALR 625; 16 BMLR 148 (H.C. of Australia).

20 *Coker* v *Richmond, Twickenham and Roehampton Area Health Authority* [1996]7 Med LR 58.

21 *Official Solicitor* v *Allinson* [2004] EWHC 923 (QB).

1 *Ministry of Justice* v *Carter* [2010] EWCA Civ 694.

investigation.[2] A surgeon was guilty of medical negligence for carrying out major surgery on the patient without the help of an anaesthetist.[3] The doctor who is unwilling to provide medical treatment such as termination of pregnancy on ethical ground, has the duty to refer the patient to another doctor.[4]

3 Criteria for deciding reasonable care The test of reasonable care is applicable not only to the members of medical profession, but also to the hospital authority. The hospital authority can be held liable, if it fails to provide sufficient or properly qualified and competent medical staff for a unit.[5] To diagnose and to prescribe treatment over telephone in the circumstances in which the doctor could have called on the patient personally, may suggest want of reasonable care on the part of the doctor.[6] Illegible prescriptions may also lead to suggest lack of reasonable care.[7] Failure of the nursing staff to ensure that adequate supervision was maintained in a ward of psychiatric patients may prove negligence of the hospital authority.[8] Want of reasonable care may be inferred from the facts where the doctor has omitted to ensure that adequate information as to the treatment given or not given was supplied to the patient's general practitioner or to another hospital authority that would treat him,[9] or where the doctor has failed to use the procedure designed to ensure that surgical instruments were not left inside the patients.[10] An orthopaedician has failed to take reasonable care of the patient, as he noticed fracture of bone of the leg of the patient

2 *Wardlaw* v *Farrar* [2003] EWCA Civ 1719; [2003]4 All ER 1358; [2004] Lloyd's Rep Med 98.

3 *R.M. Gautam (Dr.)* v *Master Nav Kshitij* III(2015) CPJ 351; 2015(3) CPR 496 (NCDRC).

4 *Doogan* v *Greater Glasgow and Clyde Health Board* [2015] AC 640.

5 *Jones* v *Manchester Corporation* [1952]2 QB 852; [1952]2 All ER 125 (CA).

6 *Barnett* v *Chelsea and Kensington Hospital Management Committee* [1969]1 QB 428; [1968]1 All ER 1068; [1968]2 WLR 422; 111 Sol Jo 912.

7 *Prendergast* v *Sam & Dee Ltd.*, *The Times*, 24th March 1988.

8 *Selfe* v *Ilford and District Hospital Management Committee* 114 Sol Jo 935; (1970) *The Times*, 25th November (CA).

9 *Coles* v *Reading and District Hospital Management Committee* (1963)107 Sol Jo 115.

10 *Urry* v *Bierer, The Times*, 15th July 1955.

after two weeks of admission in the hospital and advised for x-ray of the leg after two weeks of admission.[11] Failure on the part of the doctor and the hospital to refer the patient to better equipped hospital in spite of inability to diagnose leptospirosis (rat fever) and thereby causing death of the patient amounts to negligence.[12]

The National Commission held the hospital and the doctor negligent for discharging the patient from the hospital in spite of infected surgical wound and high fever due to lack of proper care during post operative period.[13] The operation on the healthy side of brain of the mother of one film actress, leaving an untreated malignant tumour on the opposite temporal lobe was considered to be the result of miscommunication and misidentification of the patient, and thereby the chief Neurosurgeon of Sloan-Kettering Cancer Centre, Washington was dismissed from service for botching up the operation in the world's finest hospital on the ground that the proper identification of the patient by the senior attending physician is part of reasonable care and fundamental to the practice of medicine.[14] A child suffering from vomiting over 30 hour period, was not referred to the hospital for better treatment by recognising the risk of dehydration in the child. The child suffered cardiac arrest and the delay in referring the child to the hospital was attributed to the negligence of the doctor by the court of U.K.[15] The damage to the ureter during a hysterectomy was caused due to want of reasonable care.[16] The sciatic nerve damage resulting from a hip replacement operation was caused by a degree of stretching of the nerve that was incompatible with the exercise of due care.[17] The hospital, paediatrician

11 *Akhilesh Chandra Gaur (Dr.)* v *Manik Chand* 2016(4) CPR 182 (NCDRC).
12 *Sir Dorabji Tata Trust Aided Hospital* v *Rajeswari* 2014(2) CPR 412; II(2014) CPJ 644 (NCDRC).
13 *Phool Chand Soni* v *Dr. Maya Pathak through Pathak Nursing Home* IV(2011) CPJ 361.
14 *The Times of India*, 3rd September 1995.
15 *Fisher* v *McKenzie* (1994)26 BMLR 98 CS (OH).
16 *Bouchta* v *Swindon Health Authority* [1996]7 Med LR 62.
17 *Bentley* v *Bristol and Weston Health Authority (No. 2)* [1992]3 Med LR 1.

and ophthalmologist were held guilty of medical negligency by the Supreme Court of India for their failure to carry out mandatory check up of Retinopathy of Prematurity (RoP) on a pre-term baby (32 weeks gestation and weight of 1.49 kg at the time of birth), which ultimately led to his blindness.[18]

4 Skill, knowledge and competence—standard of A person holding himself out to be competent to do some special kind of job, is liable to pay compensation for negligence which has been caused by the failure to exercise due care and skill, either by proving that he did not possess the requisite skill or by showing that although he possessed it, he did not exercise it in the particular case.[19] Thus, a professional may be held liable for negligence on one of two findings (*i*) either he was not possessed of the requisite skill which he professed to have possessed (*ii*) or he did not exercise, with reasonable competence in the given case, the skill which he did possess.[20]

The true test for establishing negligence in diagnosis or treatment on the part of a doctor is whether he has been proved to be guilty of such failure as no doctor of ordinary skill would be guilty of, if acting with ordinary care.[1] The standard of care and skill to satisfy the duty in tort is that of the ordinary competent medical practitioner exercising the ordinary degree of professional skill.[2] It is true that a doctor does not undertake that he will positively cure a patient, nor does he undertake to use the highest possible degree of skill, as there may be persons more learned and skilled than himself, but he definitely undertakes to use a fair, reasonable and competent degree of skill.[3] The standard

18 *Maharaja Agrasen Hospital* v *Master Rishab Sharma* 2019 SCC Online SC 1658.

19 Paying for Mistakes—Professional Negligence and Economic Loss (Keeler) 53 ALJ 412; Charlesworth & Percy on *Negligence,* 9th Ed., p. 536 (8·02).

20 *Jacob Mathew* v *State of Punjab* (2005)6 SCC 1; 2005 ACJ 1840; AIR 2005 SC 3180; III(2005) CPJ 9; 2005(3) CPR 70; 2005 CrLJ 3710; JT 2005(6) SC 584.

1 *Hunter* v *Hanley* 1955 SLT 213.

2 *Philips India Ltd.* v *Kanju Punnu* AIR 1975 Bom 306; 1975 ACJ 311; 77 Bom LR 337; 1975 Mah LJ 792.

3 *Poonam Verma* v *Aswin Patel* AIR 1996 SC 2111; (1996)4 SCC 332; 1996(3) CPR 205 (SC); II(1996) CPJ 1 (SC); (1996)4 CTJ 465 (SC) (CP).

of skill and competence expected from a medical man is illustrated by Mc Nair, J[4] as follows:

> "In the ordinary case which does not involve any special skill, negligence in law means this: Some failure to do some act which a reasonable man in the circumstances would do; and if that failure or doing of that act results in injury, then there is a cause of action. How do you test whether this act or failure is negligent? In an ordinary case it is generally said, that you judge that by the action of the man in the street. He is the ordinary man. In one case it has been said that you judge it by the conduct of the man on the top of a Clapham omnibus. He is the ordinary man. But where you get a situation which involves the use of some special skill or competence, then the test whether there has been negligence or not is not the test of the man on the top of a Clapham omnibus, because he has not got this special skill. The test is the standard of the ordinary skilled man exercising and professing to have that special skill. A man need not possess the highest expert skill at the risk of being found negligent. It is well-established law that it is sufficient if he exercises the ordinary skill of an ordinary competent man exercising that particular art. A doctor is not guilty of negligence if he has acted in accordance with a practice accepted as proper by a responsible body of medical men skilled in that particular art. Putting it the other way round, a doctor is not negligent, if he is acting in accordance with such a practice, merely because there is a body of opinion that takes a contrary view. At the same time, that does not mean that a medical man can obstinately and pig-headedly carry on with some old technique if it has been proved to be contrary to what is really substantially the whole of informed medical opinion."

It is held by the Privy Council[5] that the standard of care and skill, to be attained, is that of the ordinary competent

4 *Bolam* v *Friern Hospital Management Committee* [1957]2 All ER 118; [1957]1 WLR 582; 101 Sol Jo 357; 1 BMLR 1.

5 *Chin Keow* v *Government of Malayasia* [1967]1 WLR 813; 111 Sol Jo 333 PC; 1967 ACJ 379.

medical practitioner who is exercising the ordinary degree of professional skill. The House of Lords[6] did not infer want of skill and care where a baby sustained severe brain damage at birth, allegedly caused by the defendant obstetrician's pulling too hard and over too long a period, during a difficult forceps delivery. Similarly, a house surgeon was not liable for the wrong treatment of a child, since the prescribed treatment was being given under the instructions of a responsible consultant.[7] Failure to detect foetal deformity in ultrasound scans when mother was more than 27 weeks pregnant, was not considered negligence by the Queen's Bench of U.K., because it was too late to carry out a lawful termination of pregnancy.[8] In the absence of any evidence to prove the causative link between the doctor's failure to prevent excess oxygen being given to the patient and the injury suffered by the patient from an incurable condition of the retina resulting in near blindness, the doctor could not be held liable in negligence by the House of Lords.[9] The law laid down by the Supreme Court of Canada[10] is that a physician is not liable for a mere error of judgment that does not amount to professional fault.

The patient had undergone colposuspension operation in order to cure urinary leakage arising from genuine stress incontinence. The operation was performed by a specialist Registrar in obstetrics and gynaecology under supervision of an Associate specialist of the same field. The patient suffered huge blood loss due to damage to an artery in course of the operation. The Court of Appeal in UK[11] held that arterial bleed is not a recognised complication of the operation and as such the specialist Registrar is negligent in carrying out

6 *Whitehouse* v *Jordan* [1980]1 All ER 650 (CA) affirmed [1981]1 All ER 267; [1981]1 WLR 246; 125 Sol Jo 167 (HL).

7 *Junor* v *Mc Nichol, The Times*, 26th March 1959.

8 *Rance* v *Mid Downs Health Authority* (1990)5 BMLR 75 (QBD).

9 *Wilsher* v *Essex Area Health Authority* [1987] QB 730; [1986]3 All ER 801; [1987]2 WLR 425; 130 Sol Jo 749 (CA) reversed by [1988]1 All ER 871; [1988]2 WLR 557; 132 Sol Jo 418; 3 BMLR 37 (HL).

10 *Lapointe et al* v *Chevrette* 90 DLR (4th) 7.

11 *Greenhorn* v *South Glasgow University Hospital NHS Trust* (2008)104 BMLR 50.

the surgery and specialist Associate is negligent in supervising the performance of the operation.

Very often in a claim for compensation arising out of medical negligence a plea is taken that it is a case of *bona fide* mistake which under certain circumstances may be excusable, but a mistake which would tantamount to negligence cannot be pardoned. In the former case the court can accept that ordinary human fallibility precludes the liability while in the latter the conduct of the medical man is considered to have gone beyond the bounds of what is expected of the skill of a reasonably competent doctor.[12] The patient was suffering from ulcer on the heel which required a small excision only, whereas the operation which was effected was flap cover and skin grafting and also contour of the bone projection. It is established from the medical literature that there were strong proposition of the course of treatment adopted by the doctor and also those who suggest a less invasive course. Since the surgical world is divided on this point, the treatment given by the doctor was not considered as deficiency in service by the Consumer Court.[13] The doctor was not held negligent by the National Commission for giving chemotherapy and radiotherapy followed by modified radical mastectomy without resorting to surgery for the treatment of cancer of right breast, because the doctor had the discretion to follow one of the two lines of accepted treatment.[14]

The National Commission also did not hold the gynaecologist and the hospital guilty of deficiency in service for the death of the baby after 12 days of delivery due to administration of contramal injection instead of oxytocin injection, merely because one set of medical literature does not recommend contramal injection for relief of labour pain, when

12 *Spring Meadows Hospital (Noida)* v *Harjot Ahluwalia through K.S. Ahluwalia* AIR 1998 SC 1801; (1998)4 SCC 39; 1998(1) CPR 1 (SC); I(1998) CPJ 1 (SC); 1998 CTJ 81 (SC) (CP); 1998 CCJ 521 (SC); JT 1998(2) SC 620; III(1998) SLT 684.

13 *V. Vassanda Coumary* v *Dr. T. Ramachandrudu* 1998(3) CPR 227 (Pondicherry).

14 *S.K. Sharma* v *Dr. Praful B. Desai* II(2003) CPJ 90 (NC).

another body of expert opinion is that the administration of this analgesic is unlikely to have caused respiratory distress in the neonate leading to birth asphyxia.[15]

The Supreme Court of India[16] did not hold the orthopaedician guilty of negligence for adopting the procedure of hemiarthoplasty, i.e. partial hip joint replacement operation for treatment of fracture of neck of right femur of leg of a patient aged 42 years, because existence of divergence of opinion as to the choice of procedure of treatment between internal fixation and hemiarthoplasty. However, the contrary view is expressed by the Court of U.K.[17] when the mother admitted to the hospital for the birth of child had spontaneous rupture of the membrances and the baby's head was $^3/_5$th palpable. The foreseeable risk of cord prolapse resulting in hypoxia could have been avoided by immediate vaginal examination. The doctor was held negligent on the basis of expert evidence, even when there was existence of professional opinion of responsible body for not conducting vaginal examination of the low risk of cord prolapse. The doctor was liable for negligence for not conducting caesarian section to avoid damage to and possible birth asphyxia to the new born, when administration of oxytocin did not yield result of normal delivery.[18] Similarly, the pathologist who gave wrong report of ultrasonography (USG) of lower abdomen of the patient, was held to be negligent by the National Commission.[19]

A doctor registered as homoeopathic practitioner treated the patient for eight days with strong antibiotics without making any diagnosis by any pathological test and also

15 *Radhika Rakesh Nigam* v *Dr. (Mrs.) Swaraj Naik of Naik Nursing Home* 2012(1) CPR 341; IV(2011) CPJ 486.

16 *C.P. Sreekumar (Dr.)* v *S. Ramanujam* JT 2009(6) SC 221; 2009 ACJ 2305; (2009)7 SCC 130; 2009 AIR SCW 3878; (2009)6 Scale 613.

17 *Reynolds* v *North Tyneside Health Authority* [2002] Lloyd's Rep Med 459.

18 *Indu Sharma (Dr.)* v *Indraprastha Apollo Hospital* III(2015) CPJ 248; 2015(2) CLT 454 (NCDRC).

19 *Madaan Surgical and Maternity Hospital* v *Santosh* 2014(2) CPR 351; 2014(2) CLT 318; II(2014) CPJ 368 (NCDRC).

prescribed intra-muscular injections of sodium compound to relieve the patient of pain without ascertaining the cause of pain. Ultimately the patient died in a hospital without any positive diagnosis. The Supreme Court of India[20] held the homoeopathic doctor guilty of negligence in giving allopathic medicines to the patient without being qualified in that system of medicine. However, it is held by the Supreme Court[1] that the notification issued by the Government of Punjab under r. 2(*cc*)(*iii*) of the Drugs and Cosmetics Rules 1945, declaring the categories of Vaids and Hakims who were practising modern system of medicine (allopathic) and were registered in the State Medical Registers, is valid in law. As a result, if any State law relating to registration of medical practitioners permits practice of allopathic medicines on the basis of degree in integrated medicines, such registered medical practitioners shall have the right to practise allopathic medicines within the boundary of the said State and the prohibition contained in s. 15(2) of the Indian Medical Council Act will not apply. The State Commission, Karnataka,[2] held the homoeopathic doctor guilty of negligence for prescribing, allopathic drugs to the patient who lost eye-sight due to adverse reaction of the drugs. Similarly the State Commission, Punjab,[3] held one unqualified doctor negligent for giving treatment in allopathic system of medicines to the patient whose left arm was amputated due to unskilled treatment of fracture of the bone. The doctors registered under Mysore Ayurvedic and Unani Practitioner Registration and Medical Practitioner Miscellaneous Provisions Act 1961, were held liable in negligence by the State Commission, Kerala,[4] for conducting Medical Termination of Pregnancy and for practising modern scientific medicines beyond the State of Karnataka.

20 *Poonam Verma* v *Aswin Patel* AIR 1996 SC 2111; (1996)4 SCC 332; 1996(3) CPR 205 (SC); II(1996) CPJ 1 (SC); (1996)4 CTJ 465 (SC) (CP).

1 *Dr. Mukhtiar Chand* v *State of Punjab* 1998 CTJ 813 (SC) (CP).

2 *Dr. A.M. Mulla* v *Mashaksab Ismailsab Nonawada* 1999(2) CPR 353 (Bangalore); 1999 CTJ 504 (CP) (SCDRC).

3 *Dr. Ali Mohammad Shahi* v *Harbans Lal* alias *Bansi through natural guardian (father) Kuldip Singh* 2000 CTJ 62 (CP) (SCDRC).

4 *Dr. K. Mahabala Bhat* v *K. Krishna* 2000(1) CPR 369 (Ker).

5 Diagnosis and treatment

(i) ***Error of judgment—when may amount to negligence*** An error of clinical judgment does not always amount to negligence. Whether an error of clinical judgment amounts to negligence depends on the circumstances of each case. Lord Fraser of Tullybelton delivering the judgment of House of Lords[5] has observed: "Merely to describe something as an error of judgment tells us nothing about whether it is negligent or not. The true position is that an error of judgment may, or may not, be negligent; it depends on the nature of the error. If it is one that would have been made by a reasonably competent professional man professing to have the standard and type of skill that the defendant held himself out as having and acting with ordinary care, then it is negligence. If, on the other hand, it is an error that a man, acting with ordinary care, might have made, then it is not negligence." Lord Edmund Davies[6] pointed out as follows:

> "To say that a surgeon committed an error of clinical judgment is wholly ambiguous, for, while some such errors may be completely consistent with the due exercise of professional skill, other acts or omissions in the course of exercising clinical judgment may be so glaringly below proper standards as to make a finding of negligence inevitable."

Lord Clyde[7] has observed: "In the realm of diagnosis and treatment, there is ample scope for genuine difference of opinion, and one man clearly is not negligent merely because his conclusion differs from that of other professional men, not because he has displayed less skill or knowledge than others would have shown. The true test for establishing negligence in diagnosis or treatment on the part of a doctor is whether he has been proved to be guilty of such failure as

5 *Whitehouse* v *Jordan* [1980]1 All ER 650 (CA) affirmed by [1981]1 All ER 267; [1981]1 WLR 246; 1982 ACJ 107; 125 Sol Jo 167 (HL); 1 BMLR 14 (HL).

6 *Whitehouse* v *Jordon* [1980]1 All ER 650 (CA) affirmed by [1981]1 All ER 267; [1981]1 WLR 246; 1982 ACJ 107; 125 Sol Jo 167 (HL); 1 BMLR 14 (HL).

7 *Hunter* v *Hanley* 1955 SLT 213.

no doctor of ordinary skill would be guilty of, if acting with ordinary care."

The National Commission[8] divided the professional duty of a doctor into three phases: (*i*) diagnosis, (*ii*) advice and (*iii*) treatment. An error in diagnosis may result in denial of timely effective therapy or administration of potentially toxic and incorrect medicines, which may lead to devastating consequences. On the contrary, right diagnosis will ensure timeliness and accuracy. Delay in diagnosis and treatment may become fatal in a few situations. As proper and timely diagnosis is the key deciding paradigm for the line treatment of a patient, anything going amiss at that stage is a critical circumstance to determine the question whether or not an error of judgment in treatment of a patient tantamounts to negligence.

The National Commission,[9] is also of the view that a doctor cannot be found to be negligent merely because in a matter of opinion he made an error of judgment. A medical practitioner is not liable to be held negligent simply because things went wrong from mischance or misadventure or through an error of judgment in choosing one reasonable course of treatment in preference to another.[10] The Consumer Court[11] did not hold the doctor negligent for giving treatment to the patient for about ten months by making wrong diagnosis of gastric ulcer, because the ultrasound report of pelvic area disclosed in the investigations and symptoms narrated by the patient were not indicative of diagnosis of recurrent appendicitis from which the patient was really suffering.

The Supreme Court[12] affirmed the decision of the National Commission by not holding the doctor negligent for not

8 *Hardwari Lal* v *A.K. Aggarwal (Dr.)* 2017(3) CLT 295; IV(2017) CPJ 218; 2017(4) CPR 295 (NCDRC).

9 *Dr. N.T. Subrahmanyam* v *Dr. B. Krishna Rao* 1996(2) CPR 247 (NC); II(1996) CPJ 233 (NC); (1996)4 CTJ 785 (CP) (NCDRC); 1997 CCJ 1138 (NC).

10 *Matin F. D'Souza* v *Mahd. Ishfaq* (2009)3 SCC 1; 2009 ACJ 1695; AIR 2009 SC 2049; JT 2009(2) SC 486; (2009)2 Scale 620.

11 *Shri Rajeev Kumar* v *Dr. U.K. Biswas* 1998(2) CPR 149 (Pat); II(1998) CPJ 494 (Pat).

12 *Vinitha Ashok (Smt.)* v *Lakshmi Hospital* (2001)8 SCC 731; AIR 2001 SC 3914; JT 2001(8) SC 142; (2001)6 Scale 476; I(2002) CPJ 4 (SC).

detecting ectopic pregnancy in the cervical canal before dilation and curettage for medical termination of pregnancy, because there is difference of opinion among the experts about efficacy of ultrasonography in establishing ectopic pregnancy and adoption of prevailing practice in the area by not recommending ultrasonography before medical termination of pregnancy and by administering the treatment of hysterectomy on account of heavy bleeding. The Supreme Court of India held the doctor negligent without any expert evidence for treating the patient by making wrong diagnosis of typhoid when the smear for malaria parasite was found to be positive and widal test for typhoid was found to be negative, and this wrong treatment ultimately led to the death of the patient.[13]

The law laid down by the Supreme Court of India,[14] is that medical opinion may differ with regard to the course of action to be taken by a doctor treating a patient and it would be difficult to hold the doctor guilty of negligence, as long as the doctor acts in the manner acceptable to the medical profession and the court finds that he has attended on the patient with due care, skill and diligence. A psychiatrist is not held negligent by the Court of Appeal,[15] when there is evidence to conclude that the diagnosis, even if wrong, was not an opinion that no reasonable doctor within the specialisation would have reached, based on the clinical features presented to the psychiatrist. A consultant obstetrician is not found negligent for delivery of a baby weighing 11 lb 2az by using Keillands forceps during long period and thereby causing damage to perineum resulting in persistent rectal and abdominal pain, which were diagnosed as irritable bowel syndrome and vaginal prolapse, because the consultant having considerable experience, skill and clinical judgment, has the liberty to exercise his option of using forceps instead

13 *V. Kishan Rao* v *Nikhil Super Speciality Hospital* (2010)5 SCC 513; 2010(4) SCJ 690; 2010 AIR SCW 4252; III(2010) CPJ 1; CDJ 2010 SC 428.

14 *Achutrao Haribhau Khodwa* v *State of Maharashtra* (1996)2 SCC 634; 1996 ACJ 505; (1996)4 CTJ 950 (SC) (CP).

15 *Adderly* v *North Manchester Health Authority* (1995)25 BMLR 42 (CA).

of caesarean section, particularly when the baby was healthy and normal.[16]

Two consultants thought that the cause of chest complaint of the patient was due to tuberculosis or Hodgkin's disease. The consultants decided to perform an exploratory operation to determine whether she was suffering from Hodgkin's disease before obtaining the result of test to determine tuberculosis. As a result of the operation, the patient suffered damage to a nerve affecting her vocal cord which caused her speech to be impaired. The diagnosis of tuberculosis was confirmed subsequently. The allegation against the consultants was that they had been negligent in deciding to carry out the operation before obtaining the result of the tuberculosis test. The House of Lords[17] did not hold the consultants negligent for committing error of judgment in taking the decision to operate on the patient, because the decision to undertake the operation of the patient was in accordance with the responsible body of medical opinion. Where a case is based on an allegation that a fully considered decision of two consultants in the field of their special skill was negligent, it is not enough to show that there is a body of competent professional opinion which considers that there was a wrong decision, if there also exists a body of professional opinion, equally competent, which supports the decision as reasonable in the circumstances.

(ii) ***Various aspects of diagnosis and treatment amounting to negligence*** A medical practitioner owes a duty to diagnose his patient's condition.[18] The duty of a doctor is not only to make inquiries in ascertaining the necessary data, but also to exercise reasonable professional skill in forming a conclusion from such data.[19] Failure to exercise due skill in

16 *Knight* v *West Kent Health Authority* 40 BMLR 61 (CA); [1998] Lloyd's Rep Med 18 (CA).

17 *Maynard* v *West Midlands Regional Health Authority* (1983)1 BMLR 122; [1984]1 WLR 634; [1985]1 All ER 635 (HL).

18 *Gibbons* v *Harris* [1924]1 DLR 923.

19 *Everett* v *Griffiths* [1920]3 KB 163; 89 LJKB 929; 123 LT 280; 64 Sol Jo 445 (CA) affirmed by [1921]1 AC 631; 90 LJKB 737; 125 LT 230; 65 Sol Jo 395 (HL).

diagnosis, as a result of which wrong treatment was given, would amount to negligence.[20] A competent medical practitioner must know when a case is beyond his skill. It is the bounden duty of the doctor either to call in a more skilful person or to advise removal of the patient to a place where skilled treatment is available. A doctor was held negligent in failing to diagnose a broken patella after the patient had fallen from a height of twelve feet on to a concrete floor.[1] A casualty medical officer at a hospital was negligent when he allowed a patient who had been struck on the head with a spanner to go home without proper examination being made that would have disclosed a depressed fracture of the skull.[2] General practitioner who was informed that a child had ingested hot tea from the spout of a teapot, was negligent in failing to appreciate the potential consequences and to visit and to refer the child to the hospital.[3] When the patient's bowel was perforated during the course of gynaecological surgery, the doctor was held liable not for perforating the bowel, but for failing to identify and repair the hole in the bowel.[4] In a Canadian case[5] a doctor who wrongly diagnosed influenza, instead of meningitis, was held to be negligent in failing to arrange for pathological tests to determine the correct diagnosis. A doctor is liable for negligence when he gives his patient a hypodermic injection for malaria and thereby piercing the sciatic nerve and causing foot-drop;[6] when he injected cocaine instead of procaine;[7] when he failed to suspect and prescribe proper tests for malaria;[8] when penthol was injected to the patient under an anaesthetic and

20 *Pudney* v *Union Castle Mail S.S. Ltd.* [1953]1 Lloyd's Rep 73.
1 *Newton* v *Newton's Model Laundry, The Times*, 3rd November 1959.
2 *McCormack* v *Redpath Brown & Co., The Times*, 24th March 1961; N-J&B (2nd Ed.) 445.
3 *Sa'd* v *Robinson* [1989]1 Med LR 41.
4 *Tagg* v *Countess of Chester Hospital Foundation Trust* [2007] EWHC 509 (QB); (2007)95 BMLR 76.
5 *Dale* v *Munthali* (1976)78 DLR 588.
6 *Caldeira* v *Gray, The Times*, 15th February 1936.
7 *Collins* v *Hertfordshire C.C.* [1947] KB 598; [1947]1 All ER 633.
8 *Langley* v *Campbell, The Times,* 6th November 1975; N-J&B (2nd Ed.) 425.

thereby causing his death,[9] when he failed to administer penicillin for a condition of fulminating septicaemia of a finger after completion of a five-day course of tetracycline,[10] and when a consultant paediatrician failed to refer a hydrocephalic baby suffering symptoms consistent with blockage of its venticular peritoneal shunt, for CT scan.[11] The paediatrician, who made initial diagnosis of dehydration of a child due to flu failed to monitor the changes in the condition of the child by properly assessing the symptoms. He was found to be negligent, as the reasonableness of the initial diagnosis was undermined and ultimately the child died of acute peritonitis resulting from ruptured appendix.[12]

The health authority was held liable in negligence for reduced life expectancy of the patient due to failure to diagnose primary pulmonary hypertension (PPH) before pregnancy of the patient.[13] A doctor was held negligent not only for his failure to terminate the pregnancy of the patient, in spite of performance on her spinster a legal abortion, but also for his failure to inform that another such operation could have been performed as a result of which she gave birth to a child.[14] The doctor performed an abortion to terminate the pregnancy of the patient. Owing to miscalculation of the date of conception the doctor used a curette of wrong size, with the result that pregnancy was not terminated. The doctor examined the patient two weeks later, but did not recommend any test to determine whether abortion had been successful. The doctor was held liable in negligence for failure to diagnose the continuing pregnancy during postoperative check up of the patient and to ensure

9 *Jones* v *Manchester Corporation* [1952]2 QB 852; [1952]2 All ER 125 (CA).

10 *Hucks* v *Cole* (1968)118 New LJ 469; 112 Sol Jo 483.

11 *Robinson* v *Jacklin* [1996]7 Med LR 83; *Rhodes* v *Spokes and Farbridge* [1996]7 Med LR 135.

12 *Gemeto* v *Calgary Regional Health Authority* 2006 ABQB 740; [2007]2 WWR 243.

13 *R.* v *Crydon Health Authority* 40 BMLR 40 (CA); [1998] Lloyd's Rep Med 44.

14 *Scuriaga* v *Powell* (1979)123 Sol Jo 406 affirmed by (1980) unreported (CA).

that all foetal materials had been removed during abortion to terminate the pregnancy.[15] The doctor who performed a smear test, but failed to examine the cytology report showing evidence of abnormality is found to be negligent when the patient subsequently died of cervical cancer.[16] The doctor who treated the patient suffering from suspected cancer, did not conduct biopsy in order to ascertain the stage of cancer and plan the treatment in a better way and thereby reduced the span of life of the patient. The National Commission[17] held the doctor guilty of negligence for not conducting biopsy of suspected cancer.

Liability was admitted where an obstetrician attempted to rotate internally a second twin by inserting his arm per vaginam—a procedure characterised as horrific and totally unacceptable.[18] It was negligence of an obstetrician to rely upon a midwife to make a clinical judgment as to whether caesarean section should be carried out and thereby delaying caesarean section, resulting in foetal distress and consequent brain damage of the child.[19] The General Physician was found to have been negligent for not suspecting the correct diagnosis for the plaintiff's neurological symptoms and so failing to refer her in proper time to a neurologist.[20] The general practitioner diagnosed gastroenteritis due to failure on his part to take full medical history from the members of family of the child and thereby he was held liable to negligence for failing to refer the child suffering from meningitis to the hospital.[1]

The general practitioner was held to be negligent for failure to obtain full and accurate history of the child and to

15 *Cherry et al* v *Borsman* 94 DLR (4th) 487; 75 DLR (4th) 668.

16 *Braun Estate* v *Vaughan* [2000]3 WWR 465.

17 *R.M. Gautam (Dr.)* v *Master NAV Kshitij* III(2015) CPJ 351; 2015(3) CPR 496 (NCDRC).

18 *Kralj* v *McGrath* [1986]1 All ER 54.

19 *Wiszniewski* v *Central Manchester H.A.* [1996]7 Med LR 248; *Murphy* v *Wirral Health Authority* [1996]7 Med LR 99.

20 *Rhodes* v *Stokes and Farbridge* [1996]7 Med LR 135.

1 *McDonnell* v *Holwerda* [2005] EWHC 1081 (QB); [2005] Lloyd's Rep Med 423.

carry out proper examination of the child by measuring the temperature and testing for photophobia resulting in failure to refer the child to the hospital, though the child was in fact suffering from meningococcal septicaemia.[2]

However, the doctor cannot be blamed for failure to make correct diagnosis when the symptoms do not indicate the disease from which the patient has been suffering. The general practitioner, who failed to diagnose a subarachnoid haemorrhage and thereby failed to refer the patient to the hospital for further investigation following a fall, was not found to be negligent, when there was absence of symptoms of pounding headache and vomiting shortly after the fall.[3]

The consultant gynaecologist examined the patient who was suffering from an abnormal absence of menstruation over the previous two months. Without recommending any test to determine pregnancy, the gynaecologist ruled out the possibility of pregnancy on the basis of clinical signs. The patient was found to be pregnant after six months, which was too late to terminate the pregnancy. The Queen's Bench of U.K.[4] held the gynaecologist negligent for failure to diagnose pregnancy of the patient. The Queen's Bench Division[5] also held one general surgeon negligent for failure to detect the lump in left breast of the patient and thereby to diagnose breast cancer at initial stage, particularly when the patient asserted that there was a lump and the letter of referral from the general practitioner also indicated lump in left breast.

The Judicial Committee[6] held a surgeon liable for leaving an abdominal swab in a patient's body having regard to his departure from the normal routine. Lord Denning expressed the view that if the swab were a mopping pack it was negligent to lose control of it, whilst if it were a restraining

2 *Large* v *Waldron* [2008] EWHC 1937 (QB).
3 *Holt* v *Edge* [2007] EWCA Civ 602; (2007)97 BMLR 74.
4 *Gardinar* v *Mounfield* (1989)5 BMLR 1 (QBD); [1990]1 Med LR 205.
5 *Judge* v *Huntingdon Health Authority* 27 BMLR 107 (QBD); [1995]6 Med LR 223.
6 *Cooper* v *Nevill*, *The Times*, 24th March 1961.

pack, then having regard to the small number used, their obvious position, the absence of movement and the lack of any particular need for haste at the end of the operation, it was negligence on the part of the surgeon not to remove it, since the responsibility for doing so was admittedly his. In some cases[7] the surgeon is held not negligent where the operation is a piece of team work, because the surgeon is entitled to leave part of the work, e.g. counting of the swabs taken from the patient's body, to some other competent member of the team. The National Commission,[8] held the doctors negligent for leaving artery forceps inside the abdomen of the patient during caesarean operation. Similarly, the State Commission, Bangalore,[9] held the doctor negligent for leaving a metallic tip of suction tube in the abdomen of the patient during caesarean operation. The State Commission, Kerala,[10] held the hospital negligent for leaving sponge in the abdomen of the patient during caesarean operation. The Supreme Court of India[11] held the State of Maharashtra liable for negligence of Government doctors who left a mop (towel) inside the peritoneal cavity of the patient during sterilization operation, resulting in death of the patient.

There was a mass lesion in the left upper chest of the patient with erosion of ribs and vertebrae. The patient had undergone excision biopsy under one cardiothoracic surgeon to determine the nature of mass after failure to detect the same by several attempts of fine needle aspiration cytology under ultrasound guidance and under C.T. guidance. The

7 *Mahon* v *Osborne* [1939]2 KB 14; 108 LJKB 567; 160 LT 329; [1939]1 All ER 535; *Chasney* v *Anderson* [1950]4 DLR 223; *White* v *Westminster Hospital Board of Governors, The Times*, 26th October 1961.

8 *Ms. Sau Madhuri* v *Dr. Rajendra* 1996(3) CPR 174 (NC); III(1996) CPJ 75 (NC); (1997)5 CTJ 43 (CP) (NCDRC); 1997 CCJ 1499 (NC).

9 *Smt. Rohini Pritam Kabadi* v *Dr. R.T. Kulkarni* 1998(1) CPR 142 (Bangalore); III(1996) CPJ 441 (Bangalore); (1997)5 CTJ 83 (CP) (SCDRC); 1998 CCJ 910 (Kant).

10 *Aleyamma Varghese* v *Dewan Bahadur Dr. V. Varghese* 1996 CTJ 911; 1997(1) CPR 310 (Ker); III(1997) CPJ 165 (Ker); 1998 CCJ 1310 (Ker).

11 *Achutrao Haribhau Khodwa* v *State of Maharashtra* (1996)2 SCC 634; 1996 ACJ 505; (1996)4 CTJ 950 (SC) (CP).

surgeon carried out complete excision of the mass without obtaining consent and without involving any neuro-surgeon with the operation, resulting in complete paralysis of lower limbs of the patient and other associated complications. It is held by the Supreme Court that had MRI or myelography been performed, the intraspinal extension of the mass could have been revealed during pre-operative stage, leading to the intervention of neuro-surgeon during the operation and paraplegia could have been avoided. According to the Supreme Court,[12] the attending doctors were seriously remiss in not associating a neuro-surgeon at the pre-operative as well as at the stage of the operation and in not making complete investigation during pre-operative stage.

The surgeon did not explain the hazards of chloroform anaesthesia before taking consent of the patient for operation of appendicitis. Finding appendix to be normal, he proceeded to remove the gall-bladder without further investigation and without preparing the patient for the second operation. The surgeon was held negligent for acting rashly in removing the gall-bladder and without caring for the ill-effects of keeping the patient under chloroform for two hours especially when the patient's kidney was affected.[13] The Privy Council[14] held the doctor negligent for prescribing an injection of procaine penicillin without making appropriate enquiry about the history of the patient, because such enquiry was essential as per prevailing professional practice. The surgeon was held negligent by the Consumer Court[15] for failure to drain out bile liquid after cholecystectomy, resulting in biliary peritonitis of the patient. The surgeon was also held guilty of negligence for cutting common bile duct in the process of

12 *Nizam's Institute of Medical Sciences* v *Prasanth S. Dhananka* (2009)6 SCC 1; JT 2009(2) SC 385; 2009 AIR SCW 3563; 2010 ACJ 38; (2009)4 Supreme 165.

13 *Ram Bihari Lal* v *Dr. J.N. Shrivastava* AIR 1985 MP 150; 1985 ACJ 424; 1985 Jab LJ 259; (1985)1 Cur Civ Cas 987; 1985 MPLJ 288; 1985 Cur Civ LJ 149.

14 *Chin Keow* v *Government of Malaysia* 1967 ACJ 379; [1967]1WLR 813; 111 Sol Jo 333 (PC).

15 *Altaf Hussain Farooqui* v *Dr. Ashok Mathure* 1998(1) CPR 427 (Bom).

removal of gall-bladder by way of laparoscopic surgery, because only cystic duct was required to be cut in the said surgery known as laparoscopic cholecystectomy.[16] The doctor was found to be negligent for failure to diagnose glaucoma and give effective treatment for glaucoma before undertaking cataract operation.[17] The National Commission held the opthalmologist negligent for prescribing Mitomycine-C without mentioning the duration for which the drug should be used and thereby caused damage to the eye of the patient who continued the medicine for several months.[18]

A surgeon escaped liability in treating a child whose arm was amputated for lack of giving sufficient penicillin on the ground that the prescribed treatment was being given under the instructions of a responsible consultant.[19] The doctor put the plaster cast on the fractured leg of the injured patient, which resulted in the infection of the affected part as a consequence of which traumatic gas gangrene had set in necessitating the amputation of the leg. The doctor was not held negligent even when the swollen immobile and anaesthetic leg was the result of plaster cast put by the doctor, because expert witness admitted that the plaster cast would become tight if there was swelling after the plaster.[20] The National Commission[1] did not hold the surgeon negligent for adopting conservative treatment by deferring cholecystectomy when the patient was suffering severe abdominal pain and vomiting due to multiple stones in the gall bladder, as the treatment adopted by the surgeon is in accordance with accepted professional practice. The National

16 *Smt. Gurmit Mahal* v *Chauhan Nursing Home* 1998(3) CPR 405 (Chandigarh); 1999 CTJ 55 (CP) (SCDRC); *N.K. Kohli* v *Bajaj Nursing Home through Dr. Nilam Bajaj* 1999(2) CPR 79 (Bhopal); II(2000) CPJ 308.

17 *K.N. Lal* v *R.K. Akhaury* III(1997) CPJ 112 (Pat); 1998 CCJ 1223 (Bihar).

18 *Devinder Singh Gupta* v *Dr. Vivek Pal Navjyoti Eye Centre* 2013(1) CPR 229; I(2013) CPJ 442.

19 *Junor* v *Mc Nichol, The Times*, 26th March 1959.

20 *Usha* v *Dr. G.P. Namboodiri* 1986(1) ACJ 141.

1 *Dr. Devendra Madan* v *Shakuntala Devi* I(2003) CPJ 57 (NC).

Commission,[2] is of the view that the doctor should not be held guilty of giving wrong treatment without some medical evidence to that effect.

The Supreme Court[3] is of the view that the doctor is often called upon to adopt a procedure which involves higher element of risk, but which he honestly believes as providing greater chances of success for the patient rather than a procedure involving lesser risk, but higher chances of failure. A doctor cannot be penalised if he adopts the former procedure, even if it results in a failure.

The Court of Appeal[4] did not hold the doctor negligent for prescribing oral contraceptive, as there was no evidence to establish that the patient was suffering from hypertension or migraine, and that a single recording of high blood pressure was insufficient to establish hypertension. The parents of a child claimed compensation on the ground that the child had suffered encephalopathy, i.e. impairment of brain function after receiving vaccination against diphtheria, pertussis, and tetanus (DPT). The claim was ultimately dismissed by the United States Supreme Court[5] on the ground that the child experienced symptoms of injury after receiving vaccination, but the claimants failed to establish that the child had no symptoms of that injury before the vaccination.

(iii) *Diagnosis and treatment by unqualified persons* The doctor registered as homeopathic practitioner, treated the patient for eight days by administering strong antibiotics initially for treatment of viral fever and subsequently for typhoid fever without confirming the diagnosis by any pathological test. The doctor also prescribed intramuscular injection of sodium compound to relieve the patient of pain without ascertaining the cause for the pain. The Supreme Court of

2 *Subhashish Dhar (Dhir)* v *Smt. Sanjukta Sengupta* III(1999) CPJ 29 (NC); 1999(3) CPR 13 (NC); 1999 CTJ 573 (CP) (NCDRC).

3 *Martin F. D'Souza* v *Mohd. Ishfaq* (2009)3 SCC 1; 2009 ACJ 1695; AIR 2009 SC 2049; JT 2009(2) SC 486; (2009)2 Scale 620; *Kusum Sharma* v *Batra Hospital and Medical Research Centre* AIR 2010 SC 1050.

4 *Vadera* v *Shaw* 45 BMLR 162 (CA).

5 *Donna E. Shalala* v *Margaret Whitecotton* (1995)131 L Ed 2d 374; 115 S Ct 1477.

India,[6] held the doctor guilty of negligence in giving medicine without confirming his diagnosis by pathological tests. Similarly, the State Commission, Karnataka,[7] held the homeopathic doctor guilty of negligence for prescribing allopathic medicines to the patient whose eyesight was lost due to adverse reaction of those medicines. The State Commission, Punjab,[8] also held one unqualified doctor negligent for giving treatment in allopathic system of medicines to the patient whose left arm was amputated due to unskilled treatment of fracture of the bone. However, in the absence of expert evidence the majority of the State Commission, Tamil Nadu,[9] did not hold one para-medical personnel guilty of negligence for conducting medical termination of pregnancy and for prescribing allopathic medicines.

6 Advice, information and warning A doctor's duty of reasonable care involves giving the patient a description of his condition and advice as to the appropriate courses of treatment including the risks involved. A doctor's professional functions may be divided into three phases: diagnosis, advice and treatment. The objectives, sometimes conflicting, sometimes unattainable, of the doctor's services are the prolongation of life, the restoration of the patient to full physical and mental health and the alleviation of pain. Where there are dangers that treatment may produce results, direct or indirect, which are harmful to the patient, those dangers must be weighed by the doctor before he recommends the treatment. The patient is entitled to consider and reject the recommended treatment and for that purpose to understand the doctor's advice and the possibility of harm resulting from

6 *Poonam Verma* v *Aswin Patel* AIR 1996 SC 2111; (1996)4 SCC 332; 1996(3) CPR 205 (SC); II(1996) CPJ 1 (SC); (1996)4 CTJ 465 (SC) (CP).

7 *Dr. A.M. Mulla* v *Mashaksab Ismailsab Nonawada* 1999(2) CPR 353 (Bangalore); 1993 CTJ 504 (CP) (SCDRC).

8 *Dr. Ali Mohammad Shahi* v *Harbans Lal* alias *Bansi through natural guardian (father) Kuldip Singh* 2000 CTJ 62 (CP) (SCDRC).

9 *TMT Panjali* v *Dr. (Mrs.) S. Jamuna Lokanathan* II(1999) CPJ 555 (Chennai); 1992(2) CPR 408 (Chennai).

the treatment.[10] This entitlement is the foundation of the doctrine of "informed consent" enunciated by the courts of United States of America.

The doctrine of "informed consent to medical treatment" is based on the landmark case of *Canterbury* v *Spence*[11] wherein the United States Court of Appeal, District of Columbia circuit, laid down the following propositions:

(*i*) Every human being of adult years and of sound mind has right to determine what shall be done with his own body;

(*ii*) the consent is the informed exercise of a choice which entails an opportunity to evaluate knowledgeably the options available and the risks attended on each;

(*iii*) the doctor must disclose all material risks to which a reasonable man would attach significance in deciding whether or not to forgo the proposed therapy;

(*iv*) the "therapeutic privilege" enables the doctor to withhold from his patient information as to risk if it can be shown that disclosure would have posed a serious threat of psychological detriment to the patient. The above propositions set a standard and formulate a test of doctor's duty, the effect of which is that the court determines the scope of the duty and decides whether the doctor has acted in breach of his duty. The doctor is liable if he omits to warn where the risk is such that in the court's view a prudent person in the patient's situation would have regarded it as significant.

Laskin, CJ[12] of Canadian Supreme Court expressed broad approval of the doctrine enunciated in *Canterbury* v *Spence*.[13] There is no rule in English law comparable with the doctrine

10 *Sidaway* v *Bethlem Royal Hospital Governors* [1985] AC 871; [1985]1 All ER 643; [1985]2 WLR 480; 129 Sol Jo 154; 1 BMLR 132 (HL).

11 (1972)464 F (2d) 772, approved by District of Columbia Appeal Court in *Crain* v *Allison* (1982)443 A (3d) 558.

12 *Reibl* v *Hughes* (1980)114 DLR (3d) 1 Can (SC); (1980)2 SCR 880.

13 *Canterbury* v *Spence* (1972)464 F (2d) 772.

of "informed consent". However, Bristow, J[14] held that a doctor ought to warn of what may happen by misfortune however well the operation may be carried out "if there is a real risk of a misfortune inherent in the procedure". The duty of a doctor to warn was considered in "Bolam",[15] where the plaintiff claimed damages alleging negligence (*i*) in failing to administer a relaxant drug prior to the treatment, (*ii*) in failing to provide some form of manual restraint during the passing of electric current through his brain, and (*iii*) in failing to warn him of the risks involved in the treatment. McNair, J[16] laid down (*i*) that a doctor was not negligent, if he was acting in accordance with a practice accepted as proper by a responsible body of medical men skilled in that particular art, merely because there is a body of such opinion that takes a contrary view; (*ii*) that when a doctor was dealing with a mentally sick man and had a strong belief that his only hope of cure was submission to electro-convulsive therapy, the doctor could not be criticised if, believing the dangers involved in the treatment to be minimal, he did not stress them to the patient; and (*iii*) that in order to recover damages for failure to give warning the plaintiff must show not only that the failure was negligent but also that if he had been warned he would not have consented to the treatment. Accordingly, the "Bolam" principle has formulated the rule that a doctor is not negligent if he acts in accordance with a practice accepted at the time as proper by a responsible body of medical opinion, even though other doctors adopt a different practice.

The majority of the House of Lords,[17] held that the test of liability in respect of a doctor's duty to warn his patient of risks inherent in treatment recommended by him was the same as the test applicable to diagnosis and treatment,

14 *Chatterton* v *Gerson* (1980)1 BMLR 80; [1981]1 All ER 257; [1981]3 WLR 1003.

15 *Bolam* v *Friern Hospital Management Committee* (1957)1 BMLR 1; [1957]1 WLR 582; [1957]2 All ER 118 (QBD).

16 *Bolam* v *Friern Hospital Management Committee* (1957)1 BMLR 1; [1957]1 WLR 582; [1957]2 All ER 118 (QBD).

17 *Sidaway* v *Bethlem Royal Hospital Governors* [1985] AC 871; [1985]1 All ER 643; [1985]2 WLR 480; 129 Sol Jo 154; 1 BMLR 132 (HL).

namely that the doctor was required to act in accordance with a practice accepted at the time as proper by a responsible body of medical opinion. Lord Scarman[18] has laid down the following proposition:

> "The English law must recognise a duty of the doctor to warn his patient of risk inherent in the treatment which he is proposing; and especially so if the treatment be surgery. The critical limitation is that the duty is confined to material risk. The test of materiality is whether in the circumstances of the particular case the court is satisfied that a reasonable person in the patient's position would be likely to attach significance to the risk. Even if the risk be material, the doctor will not be liable if on a reasonable assessment of his patient's condition he takes the view that a warning would be detrimental to his patient's health."

The dictum of the House of Lords[18] with regard to duty of the doctor to warn is that although a decision on what risks should be disclosed for the particular patient to be able to make a rational choice whether to undergo the particular treatment recommended by a doctor is primarily a matter of clinical judgment, the disclosure of a particular risk of serious adverse consequences might be so obviously necessary for the patient to make an informed choice that no reasonably prudent doctor would fail to disclose that risk. Moreover, when questioned specifically by a patient of apparently sound mind about the risks involved in a particular treatment proposed, the doctor's duty is to answer both truthfully and as fully as the questioner requires. The neuro-surgeon failed to warn the patient about the risk of nerve injury resulting in paralysis during surgery for removal of three intra-vertebral discs, and the risk materialised causing nerve damage resulting in paralysis, the Court of Appeal in UK[19] held that the causal connection between negligence and damage was not broken, even if the patient had failed to

18 *Sidaway* v *Bethlem Royal Hospital Governors* [1985] AC 871; [1985]1 All ER 643; [1985]2 WLR 480; 129 Sol Jo 154; 1 BMLR 132 (HL).
19 *Chester* v *Afshar* [2002] EWCA Civ 724; [2002]3 All ER 552.

establish that she would not have undergone surgery had the risk been disclosed to her.

The view expressed by the UK[20] Supreme Court is that a doctor has a duty to take reasonable care to ensure that the patient was informed of any material risk involved in the recommended treatment and of any reasonable alternative treatment. The test of materiality was whether a reasonable person in the given situation would have regarded a particular risk as significant or the doctor would have been aware that the patient would be likely to attach significance to it. It is observed that the high risk pregnant mother with diabetic carrying a larger than usual baby should have been advised of the risk of "shoulder dystocia" in course of vaginal delivery and informed of alternative elective caesarian section.

The Court of Appeal[1] did not hold the doctor negligent for failure to advise in favour of vaccination resulting in child contracting measles, as the mother of the child came to know about the alternative form of immunization by using immunoglobulin, but did not avail of the same. The principle enunciated by the Court of Appeal is as follows:

> "The doctor's duty is to take reasonable care to ensure that the parents of the minor patient are in a position to make an informed choice in the best interest of the patient. Where advice is given by a skilled adviser, to enable the adviser to reach an informed decision, it must be shown that the adviser could foresee, from its nature and circumstances in which it is given, that the advice might have a significant influence on the advisee when taking a decision."

Lindel, J[2] has observed that the cooperation of the medical profession will be vital to the task of defining the scope of duty of disclosure. The courts should accept as reasonable

20 *Montgomery* v *Lanarkshire Health Board (General Medical Council Intervening)* [2015]2 All ER 1031; [2015] UKSC 11.

1 *Thomson* v *James* 31 BMLR 1 (QBD) reversed by 41 BMLR 144 (CA).

2 *White* v *Turner* (1981)120 DLR (3d) 269.

the customary practices of the profession as to disclosure, as they are, after all, based on experience, common sense and what doctors perceive their patients wish to know. The choice of accepted professional practice as the criterion governing disclosure of risks supports the view that a medical practitioner owes no duty to warn of normal risks, such as infection and those created by anaesthesia which are inherent in any surgical procedure.[3] However, failure to disclose of low risks was considered as negligent in a few Canadian cases.[4] The view of the Queen's Bench of UK[5] is that the obligation to warn the patient is not limited to treatment, but the same can extend to his life-style. Failure to warn the patient against drinking alcohol is negligent, when the patient is at the risk of developing fatal cirrhosis of liver unless stopped from drinking alcohol.

The patient sued her physician for costs associated with rearing her daughter, who was congenitally injured by chickenpox, the patient had contracted during her pregnancy. It is alleged that the patient would have terminated the pregnancy, had she been properly warned of the risk of injury to her foetus during pregnancy. By reversing the decision of the trial judge and by directing a new trial it is held by the Canadian Supreme Court[6] that the trial judge must look at all the evidence and determine whether the patient would have taken the suggested course on a balance of probabilities. The test enunciated relies on a combination of objective and subjective factors in order to determine whether failure to disclose the risks actually caused the harm of which the patient complained.

The view of the Apex Court of Australia[7] is that the question whether the patient has been given all the relevant

3 *Kenny* v *Lockwood* [1932]1 DLR 507.

4 *Considine* v *Camp Hill Hospital* [1982]133 DLR (3d) 11; *Ferguson* v *Hamilton Civic Hospitals* (1983)144 DLR (3d) 214; *Casey* v *Provan* (1984)11 DLR (4th) 708.

5 *Hutchinson* v *Epson and St. Helier NHS Trust* [2002] EWHC 2363 (QB).

6 *Arndt* v *Smith* [1997]2 RCS 539; [1996]7 Med LR 35 Sup CT (BC).

7 *Rogers* v *Whitaker* 109 ALR 625; 16 BMLR 148 (H.C. of Australia).

information to choose between undergoing and not undergoing the treatment, does not depend upon medical standards or practices. That is a question for the court to decide, and the duty of deciding it cannot be delegated to any profession or group in the community. A doctor has a duty to warn a patient of a material risk inherent in the proposed treatment. A risk is material if, in the circumstances of the particular case, a reasonable person in the patient's position, if warned of the risk, would be likely to attach significance to it or if the medical practitioner is or should reasonably be aware that the particular patient, if warned of the risk, would be likely to attach significance to it. This duty is subject to the therapeutic privilege, i.e. an opportunity afforded to the doctor to prove that he or she reasonably believed that disclosure of a risk would prove damaging to a patient. The High Court of Australia[8] held an ophthalmic surgeon liable in negligence for failure to warn of the risk of developing a condition known as sympathetic ophthalmia in left eye as a result of surgery on right eye and the surgeon had to pay damages to the patient who lost in her left eye sight due to sympathetic ophthalmia following operation in her right eye.

It is held by the UK Supreme Court[9] that the standard of duty to disclose material risks of the treatment is measured with reference to the risks which a reasonably prudent patient would have wanted to be informed for taking a decision about the course of treatment.

Failure of the surgeon to inform the patient who had undergone an operation for sterilization of the fact that there was a slight risk of her further pregnancy or advise her to use contraceptive, falls within the ambit of accepted standard of professional practice.[10] The surgeon was not held to be in breach of duty by failing to warn the patient of less than 1% risk, because the surgeon's non-disclosure of the risk of damage to the patient's spinal cord accorded with a practice

8 *Rogers* v *Whitaker* 109 ALR 625; 16 BMLR 148 (H.C. of Australia).

9 *Montgomery* v *Lanarkshire Health Board* [2015] UKSC 11; [2015] AC 1430.

10 *Waters* v *Park, The Times*, 15th July 1961.

accepted as proper by a responsible body of neurosurgical opinion.[11] The Supreme Court of Canada[12] did not hold the physician liable for failure to inform the patient of the diagnosis of cancer, because the patient's chances of survival would not have been greater if she had been informed of the diagnosis. However, the court awarded compensation to the patient for psychological sufferings and lack of comfort which were directly attributed to the failure to inform the patient of the diagnosis. The surgeon was not held negligent for failure to warn of the risk of less than 1% brain damage in heart transplant surgery of a baby of 15 months old, as the parents of the baby would not have withheld consent to the transplant surgery, had the information of small risk of serious brain damage been given to the parents of the baby.[13]

The New Brunswick Court of Appeal[14] did not hold the doctor negligent for failure to disclose the material risk of contracting hepatitis associated with the use of "Hemofil", a blood product containing high level of blood clotting factor, because a reasonable person in patient's position would have consented to the infusion of blood products, particularly "Hemofil" to stop the bleeding in the mouth, had he been informed of the risk of contracting hepatitis.

Woodhouse, J[15] has laid down that a disclosure is essential if the course of treatment being recommended will inevitably produce damaging side-effects. Similarly non-disclosure of risks is wholly unwarranted when medical experimentation is being proposed on a healthy volunteer.[16] Failure to warn a patient of the high risk of visible scarring as a result of a breast reduction operation is negligence.[17]

11 *Sidaway* v *Bethlem Royal Hospital Governors* [1985] AC 871; [1985]1 All ER 643; [1985]2 WLR 480; 129 Sol Jo 154; 1 BMLR 132 (HL).

12 *Lawson* v *Laferriere* 78 DLR (4th) 609 (SC of Canada).

13 *Poynter* v *Hillington Health Authority* 37 BMLR 192 (QBD).

14 *Kitchen* v *McMullen* (1989)5 BMLR 59 (CA).

15 *Smith* v *Auckland Hospital Board* [1964] NZLR 241 reversed by [1965] NZLR 191 (NZCA).

16 *Haluskhka* v *University of Saskatchewan* (1965)53 DLR (2d) 436; 52 WWR 608.

17 *White* v *Turner* (1981)120 DLR (3d) 269.

The doctor was held to be in breach of duty to warn of the risks associated with contraceptive pill.[18] The patient or legal representative of the deceased patient has the right to be informed of the nature of injury sustained by the patient in an accident and as such, failure to deliver x-ray films to the patient party amounts to negligence.[19]

The obstretician failed to detect anomaly in report of ultrasound scan when foetus was small for gaestational age. The child was delivered after 11 days of due date and sustained brain damage. The Court of Appeal[20] held that the mother of the child would have opted to deliver the child on due date by induction of labour and thereby damage to the child would have been avoided, had the obstetrician disclosed both the options and the risks associated with conservative treatment and induction of labour.

The surgeon advised an operation on the brain to avoid a threatened stroke. The surgeon knew or ought to have known that there was 4% chance that the operation might cause death and 10% chance that the operation might precipitate the very stroke which the operation was designed to prevent. The surgeon was held negligent for not giving information of these specific risks in order to form a balanced judgment in deciding whether or not to submit to the operation.[1] A physiotherapist has a duty to give warning to the patient to enable him to avoid the dangers inherent in certain treatment.[2] The doctor was held to be negligent in leaving his patient with the false impression that an abortion had been successful.[3] The neuro-surgeon was held negligent in failing to mention the risks arising from the surgery of congenital cervical fusion with atlantoaxial subluxation and

18 *Buchan* v *Ortho Pharmaceutical (Canada) Ltd.* (1986)25 DLR (4th) 658 (CA).

19 *V.P. Shanta* v *Cosmopolitan Hospitals (P) Ltd.* 1997(1) CPR 377 (Ker); (1997)5 CTJ 172 (CP) (SCDRC).

20 *Webster* v *Burton Hospitals NHS Foundation Trust* [2017] EWCA Civ 62; [2017] Med LR 113; (2017)154 BMLR 129.

1 *Reibl* v *Hughes* (1978)89 DLR (3d) 112 (Ont CA) reversed by (1980)114 DLR (3d) 1 (S C Canada); (1980)2 SCR 880.

2 *Clarke* v *Adams* (1950)94 Sol Jo 599.

3 *Scuriaga* v *Powell* (1979)123 Sol Jo 406.

for not informing the patient of alternative conservative treatment, nature of operation and risk of damage to spinal cord.[4] One surgeon was held negligent for not giving adequate information and advice to the patient during pre-operative consultations on breast augmentation surgery and for inadequate assessment of the need of the patient during pre-operative consultations.[5]

The advice of unnecessary and inappropriate investigations by reference to the standard of reasonably competent doctor exercising or professing the same skill, may be held to be actionable negligence if the patient suffers injury as a consequence.[6] The patient was referred to the cardiologist for examination and opinion whether the patient can go for surgery. The cardiologist noted the blood pressure of the patient as 150/100 mm and STT changes in anterolateral leads in ECG, and treated the blood pressure as high without recognising the condition as hypertension. The patient was declared fit for the operation without making adequate diagnosis of condition of heart and cardio-vascular system by advising proper investigation and treatment of the patient. The patient developed cardio-respiratory arrest and collapsed in the midst of the operation. The cardiologist was held guilty of negligence by the Consumer Court of India.[7]

The duty of disclosure is subject to therapeutic privilege enabling the doctor to withhold information where disclosure would have posed a serious threat of psychological detriment to the patient. The clinical assessment of the patient's condition may justify the withholding of information in the interest of the patient. The doctors are justified in withholding of information in cases where the patient is too ill to assess the information properly[8] and where the information may

4 *Smith* v *Salford Health Authority* 23 BMLR 137 (QBD).
5 *O'Keefe* v *Harvey-Kemble* 45 BMLR 74 (CA).
6 *Mellor* v *Sheffield Teaching Hospitals NHS Trust* [2004] EWHC 780 (QB); [2004] All ER (D) 195.
7 *Arunaben D. Kothari* v *Navdeep Clinic* 1996(3) CPR 20 (Guj); III(1996) CPJ 605 (Guj); (1997)5 CTJ 533 (CP) (SCDRC); 1998 CCJ 972 (Guj).
8 *Male* v *Hopmans* (1965)54 DLR (2d) 592 on appeal (1967)64 DLR (2d) 105 (CA).

unduly alarm the patient and create a risk of refusal to accept beneficial treatment.[9] The contrary view expressed by Ontario Court of Appeal in Canada[10] is that there is no exception to the principle of informed consent to treatment by way of therapeutic privilege. In an Irish case[11] the doctor succeeded in establishing that it was reasonable to withhold knowledge of breaking the tip of a syringe in the patient's body in view of her emotional condition and the fact that she was under the supervision of the nursing staff.

7 Accepted professional practice The true test for establishing negligence in diagnosis or treatment on the part of a doctor is whether he has been proved to be guilty of such failure as no doctor of ordinary skill would be guilty of, if acting with ordinary care.[12] The test of liability in respect of a doctor's duty to warn his patient of risks inherent in treatment recommended by him is the same as the test applicable to diagnosis and treatment, namely that the doctor is required to act in accordance with a practice accepted at the time as proper by a responsible body of medical opinion.[13] Accordingly, a doctor charged with negligence can clear himself if he shows that he acted in accordance with the prevailing professional practice. McNair, J[14] has laid down that a doctor is not negligent if he is acting in accordance with a practice accepted as proper by a responsible body of medical men skilled in that particular art, merely because there is a body of such opinion that takes a contrary view. The "Bolam" principle that a doctor is not negligent if he acts in accordance with a practice accepted at the time as proper by a responsible body of medical opinion even though

9 *Smith* v *Auckland Hospital Board* [1964] NZLR 241 reversed [1965] NZLR 191.

10 *Meyer et al* v *Rogers et al* 78 DLR (4th) 307 (O.C. of Appeal).

11 *Daniels* v *Heskin* [1954] IR 73.

12 *Hunter* v *Hanley* 1955 SLT 213 (217).

13 *Sidaway* v *Bethlem Royal Hospital Governors* [1984] QB 493; [1984]1 All ER 1018; [1984]2 WLR 778; 128 Sol Jo 301 (CA) affirmed by [1985] AC 871; [1985]1 All ER 643; [1985]2 WLR 480; 129 Sol Jo 154; 1 BMLR 132 (HL).

14 *Bolam* v *Friern Hospital Management Committee* [1957]2 All ER 118; [1957]1 WLR 582; 101 Sol Jo 357; 1 BMLR 1 (QBD).

other doctors adopt a different practice, has been accepted by House of Lords as applicable not only to diagnosis and treatment,[15] but also to advice and warning.[16] Lord Denning[17] points out that a doctor is not liable for taking one choice out of two or for favouring one school rather than another. He is only liable when he falls below the standard of a reasonably competent practitioner in his field, so much so that his conduct might be deserving of censure or inexcusable.

To establish liability on the basis of deviation from normal practice, it must be shown and established (*i*) that there is a usual or normal practice; (*ii*) that the defendant has not adopted it, and (*iii*) that the course in fact adopted is one which no professional man of ordinary skill would have taken had he been acting with ordinary care.[18] However, two things are to be noted: first, the standard of care, when assessing the practice as adopted, is judged in the light of knowledge available at the time of the incident and not on the date of trial, and secondly, when the charge of negligence arises out of failure to use any particular equipment, the charge would fail if the equipment was not generally available at that point of time on which it is suggested as should have been used.[19]

A two-year-old boy was treated for breathing difficulties in a hospital. Owing to failure of the doctor to attend the patient in response to urgent summons of the ward sister,

15 *Whitehouse* v *Jordan* (1980)1 BMLR 14; [1981]1 WLR 246; [1981]1 All ER 267; 125 Sol Jo 167 (HL); 1982 ACJ 107; *Maynard* v *West Midlands Regional Health Authority* (1983)1 BMLR 122; [1985]1 All ER 635 (HL); [1984]1 WLR 634 (HL).

16 *Sidaway* v *Board of Governors of Bethlem Royal Hospital* [1984] QB 493; [1984]1 All ER 1018; [1984]2 WLR 778; 128 Sol Jo 301 (CA).

17 *Hucks* v *Cole* [1968]118 New LJ 469; 112 Sol Jo 483.

18 Charlesworth & Percy on *Negligence*, 9th Ed., p. 576 (8-91); Halsbury's *Laws of England*, 4th Ed., vol 30, paras 34 & 35 followed by the Supreme Court of India in *Jacob Mathew* v *State of Punjab* (2005)6 SCC 1; 2005 ACJ 1840; AIR 2005 SC 3180; III(2005) CPJ 9; 2005(3) CPR 70; 2005 CrLJ 3710; JT 2005(6) SC 584.

19 *Kusum Sharma* v *Batra Hospital and Medical Research Centre* 2010(1) CPR 167; I(2010) CPJ 29; (2010)3 SCC 480; AIR 2010 SC 1050; 2010 ACJ 1444, followed in *Arun Kumar Manglik* v *Chirayu Health and Medicare Private Ltd.* (2019)3 Scale 333; 2019(2) CPR 27; JT 2019(5) SC 379; III(2019) CPJ 1 (SC).

the patient suffered a respiratory and cardiac arrest. He was resuscitated, but sustained severe brain damage. The allegation of negligence against the doctor could not be established due to division of expert medical opinion as to the necessity of intubation.[20] The law in this regard is well-settled by the House of Lords[1] as follows:

> "A case which is based on an allegation that a fully considered decision of two consultants in the field of their special skill was negligent clearly presents certain difficulties of proof. It is not enough to show that there is a body of competent professional opinion which considers that there was a wrong decision, if there also exists a body of professional opinion, equally competent, which supports the decision as reasonable in the circumstances. A judge's preference to one body of distinguished professional opinion to another also professionally distinguished is not sufficient to establish negligence in a practitioner whose actions have received the seal of approval of those whose opinions, truthfully expressed, honestly held, were not preferred."

The principle of law propounded by House of Lords[2] in subsequent decision is that the court is not bound to hold that a doctor escapes liability for negligent treatment or diagnosis just because he leads evidence from a number of medical experts who are genuinely of opinion that the doctor's treatment or diagnosis accorded with sound medical practice. The court has to be satisfied that the exponents of the body of opinion relied on can demonstrate that such opinion has a logical basis. In particular, in cases involving, as they so often do, the weighing of risks against benefits, the judge

20 *Bolitho* v *City and Hackney Health Authority* 13 BMLR 111 (CA); (1993)4 Med LR 381 affirmed by House of Lords [1997]4 All ER 771 (HL); [1998] AC 232 (HL); [1997]3 WLR 1151 (HL); 39 BMLR 1 (HL); 141 Sol Jo LB 238 (HL).

1 *Maynard* v *West Midlands Regional Health Authority* (1983)1 BMLR 122; [1984]1 WLR 634; [1985]1 All ER 635 (HL).

2 *Bolitho* v *City and Hackney Health Authority* [1997]4 All ER 771 (HL); [1998] AC 232 (HL); [1997]3 WLR 1151 (HL); 39 BMLR 1 (HL); 141 Sol Jo LB 238 (HL).

before accepting a body of opinion as being responsible, reasonable or respectable, will need to be satisfied that in forming their views, the experts have directed their minds to the question of comparative risks and benefits and have reached a defensible conclusion on the matter. A judge has the right to come to the conclusion that views genuinely held by a competent medical expert are unreasonable, when he is satisfied that the body of expert opinion cannot be logically supported at all, and that such opinion will not provide the bench mark by reference to which the doctor's conduct falls to be assessed. The Court of Appeal has observed that the defendant doctor would be guilty of negligence, even if his acts or omissions were in accordance with accepted clinical practice, because the court is duty bound to see whether "that general practice stood up to analysis and was not unreasonable in the light of the state of medical knowledge of the time."[3]

The doctor is not negligent in his choice of a particular anti-tetanus serum to administer to his patient, as he had followed an accepted school of thought within the profession as to whether the said serum or a more modern one was appropriate to the facts of the case.[4] In *Bolam*[5] the doctor was held not negligent in failing to administer a relaxant drug prior to the treatment and in failing to provide some form of manual restraint during the passing of electric current through the brain of the patient, as there were two views in the profession about the mode of treatment. In *Sidaway*[6] the surgeon did not disclose the risk of damage to the spinal cord of the patient, which was less than 1%, but if the risk materialised the resulting injury could range from mild to the very severe. Since the surgeon's non-disclosure of the

3 *Joyce* v *Merton Sutton and Wandsworth Health Authority* [1996]7 Med LR 1.

4 *Robinson* v *Post Office* [1974]2 All ER 737; [1974]1 WLR 1176; 117 Sol Jo 915 (CA).

5 *Bolam* v *Friern Hospital Management Committee* [1957]2 All ER 118; [1957]1 WLR 582; 101 Sol Jo 357; 1 BMLR 1 (QBD).

6 *Sidaway* v *Bethlem Royal Hospital Governors* [1984] QB 493; [1984]1 All ER 1018; [1984]2 WLR 778; 128 Sol Jo 301 (CA).

risk of damage to the plaintiff's spinal cord accorded with a practice accepted as proper by a responsible body of neuro-surgical opinion, and since the plaintiff failed to prove from evidence that the surgeon had been in breach of duty by failing to warn of the risk, the doctor was held not negligent.

The doctor charged with negligence can clear himself of the charge by keeping the following three points in mind. First, the standard of care, when assessing the practice as adopted, is judged in the light of knowledge available at the time of the incident and not at the date of trial. Secondly, when the charge of negligence arises out of failure to use particular equipment, the charge would fail, if the equipment was not generally available at that point of time, i.e. the time of the incident on which it is suggested as should have been used. Thirdly, when it comes to the failure of taking precautions, what has to be seen is whether those precautions were taken which the ordinary experience of a man has found to be sufficient; a failure to use special or extra-ordinary precautions which might have prevented the particular happening cannot be the standard for judging the alleged negligence.[7]

The majority of the Court of Appeal held that if the course of treatment adopted by the doctor gets support of a responsible body of medical opinion, then the doctor cannot be held to be negligent.[8] The surgeon was not held negligent for undertaking surgery to alleviate suspected nerve root compression of the patient even in the absence of radicular, although normal medical opinion would not have countenanced surgery in that situation, because the decision to operate was one which a responsible body of surgeons practising in that specialisation would not have considered it unreasonable.[9] A neuro-surgeon was not negligent in adopting a method of performing decompression of the spine to correct a prolapsed thoracic disc which was unique in its

7 *Jacob Mathew* v *State of Punjab* (2005)6 SCC 1; 2005 ACJ 1840; AIR 2005 SC 3180; III(2005) CPJ 9; 2005(3) CPR 70; 2005 CrLJ 3710; JT 2005(6) SC 584.

8 *Adams* v *Rhymney Valley District Council* [2000] Lloyd's Rep 777.

9 *De Freitas* v *O'Brien* 25 BMLR 51 (CA); [1993]4 Med LR 281 affirmed [1995]6 Med LR 108.

combination of procedures, particularly when a body of professional opinion supported that method.[10]

Thus, it is not enough to show that there is a body of competent professional opinion which considers that the decision of the medical practitioner was wrong, provided there also exists a body of professional opinion, equally competent, which supports the decision as reasonable in the circumstances.[11]

The anaesthetist was held negligent in adopting a new hypotensive anaesthetic technique which had never been attempted routinely before by anyone else. The anaesthetist had never attempted to make any proper scientific validation of it, although he had practised the technique previously on some 1,500 patients to a greater or lesser extent.[12] The ophthalmologist was held negligent for performing keratotomy on a young boy aged 14 years resulting in loss of his eyesight, as performing keratotomy on a teenager is in violation of accepted professional practice.[13]

The question arose whether the anaesthetist was negligent for causing injury to a patient due to positioning of his arm in course of an operation in a manner which was condemned six months ago in the article of a journal. The Court of Appeal[14] held that a professional person is not required to read every article appearing in the professional literature and is not negligent merely by failing to adopt immediately suggestions made in such literature. The individual professional person will be at fault in failing to adopt it only when the new technique has been proved and accepted as an invariable part of the accepted practice in the profession.

10 *Waters* v *West Sussex Health Authority* [1995]6 Med LR 362.

11 *Martin F. D'Souza* v *Mohd. Ishfaq* (2009)3 SCC 1; 2009 ACJ 1695; AIR 2009 SC 2049; JT 2009(2) SC 486; (2009)2 Scale 620; *Jacob Mathew* v *State of Punjab* (2005)6 SCC 1; 2005 ACJ 1840; AIR 2005 SC 3180; III(2005) CPJ 9; 2005(3) CPR 70; JT 2005(6) SC 584.

12 *Hepworth* v *Kerr* [1995]6 Med LR 139.

13 *Smt. Adarsh Bararia* v *Dr. P.S. Hardia* 2000(2) CPR 188 (Bhopal).

14 *Crawford* v *Board of Governors of Charing Cross Hospital, The Times*, 8th December 1953 (CA).

The patient suffered permanent damage to the lingual nerve during surgery to remove three wisdom teeth. This resulted in pain and loss of taste. It is alleged that the patient had not been warned about the possibility of an alteration in sensation as a result of the operation and that had she been so warned, she would not have undergone such treatment. It is established from the evidence that damage to the nerve was not caused by unavoidable manipulation of the retractor, but by lack of due care and skill on the part of the dental surgeon who allowed the drill to cut into the lingual nerve. The surgeon was held not negligent for not giving warning of loss of taste, because a responsible body of professional opinion would not have warned of the 1 in 200 risk of the symptoms involving partial loss of taste and unpleasant sensation in the mouth following the operation and even if the patient had been warned, she would probably still have consented to the operation.[15]

The plaintiff participated in the defendant obstetrician and gynaecologist's artificial insemination (Al) programme for about four years and ultimately became infected by HIV. The defendant did not warn her of risk of HIV infection. There was no test available for the detection of HIV in semen or blood in Canada when the plaintiff got infected by HIV. There was expert evidence during trial that the defendant's Al practice was in keeping with general practice across Canada. The trial judge instructed the jury that it was open to find the defendant negligent on the basis that he failed to comply with the standard medical practice at that time. Alternatively, they could find that the approved practice itself was negligent. On appeal, it is held by the Supreme Court of Canada[16] that while conformity with common practice will generally exonerate physicians of any complaint of negligence, there are certain situations where the standard practice itself may be found to be negligent. It is further held that the question whether the standard practice itself

15 *Heath* v *Berkshire Health Authority* (1991)8 BMLR 98 (QBD).
16 *Ter Neuzen* v *Korn* [1995]3 SCR 674.

was negligent is a question of law to be determined by the judge not by the jury.

The orthopaedic surgeon prescribed Heparin (a drug to thin the blood) following surgery on patient's leg. One blood platelet count was done and another prescribed for two days later was not done. The patient developed deep vein thrombosis and was treated aggressively with Heparin resulting in amputation of both the legs. The trial judge found the orthopaedic surgeon liable for prescribing Heparin without monitoring platelet count of the patient, in spite of the fact that the surgeon followed the standard orthopaedic practice. Ultimately, the majority of the Court of Appeal held that the issue in this case was not what was standard practice among the orthopaedicians but the doctors prescribing medicines with dangerous side effects should have taken precautions of monitoring the side effects, for preventing dangerous risk of causing harm to the patient.[17]

A doctor will be liable for negligence in respect of diagnosis and treatment in spite of a body of professional opinion approving his conduct where it has been established to the satisfaction of the court that such opinion is not reasonable or responsible. The Supreme Court of India did not hold the doctor negligent for not recommending ultrasonography for detection of ectopic pregnancy in cervical canal before dilation and curettage for medical termination of pregnancy, as there is difference of opinion among experts about efficacy of ultrasonography in establishing ectopic pregnancy and adoption of the prevailing practice of not recommending for ultrasonography and administering treatment of hysterectomy for heavy bleeding.[18]

Streatfield, J[19] opined that a doctor was entitled to use his common sense and experience and judgment in the

17 *Nattrass* v *Weber* 2010 ABCA 64; (2010)316 DLR (4th) 666; [2010]12 WWR 36.

18 *Vinitha Ashok (Smt.)* v *Lakshmi Hospital* (2001)8 SCC 731; AIR 2001 SC 3914; JT 2001(8) SC 142; (2001)6 Scale 476.

19 *Holland* v *Devitt and Moore Nautical College*, *The Times*, 4th March 1960.

treatment of each particular case, and a slight departure from the textbook would not of itself establish negligence. The defence of accepted professional practice may not absolutely protect the professional, because the court is the final authority to determine what is reasonable. The judiciary has retained the power to declare any recognised practice of the professional as negligent. The accepted professional practice was condemned as negligent in a few cases in New Zealand.[20] The criteria for evaluation of accepted professional practice are laid down by Lord Browne Wilkinson[1] as follows:

> "A doctor could be liable for negligence in respect of diagnosis and treatment despite a body of professional opinion sanctioning his conduct where it had not been demonstrated to the judge's satisfaction that body of opinion relied on was reasonable or responsible. In the vast majority of cases the fact that distinguished experts in the field were of a particular opinion would demonstrate the reasonableness of that opinion. However, in a rare case, if it could be demonstrated that the professional opinion was not capable of withstanding logical analysis, the judge would be entitled to hold that the body of opinion was not reasonable or responsible."

According to the Supreme Court of India,[2] there can be genuine difference of opinion in diagnosis and treatment. The medical professional adopting a course of treatment must ensure that it is reasonable. The threshold to prove unreasonableness is set with due regard to the risks associated with medical treatment and the conditions under which medical professionals function. This is to avoid a situation where doctors may resort to defensive medicine to avoid claim of negligence, often to the detriment of the patient. So, in specific cases where unreasonableness of

20 *Bowen* v *Paramount Builders (Hamilton) Ltd.* [1977]1 NZLR 394.

1 *Bolitho* v *City and Hackney Health Authority* [1997]4 All ER 771 (HL); [1998] AC 232 (HL); [1997]3 WLR 1151 (HL); 39 BMLR 1 (HL); 141 Sol Jo LB 238 (HL).

2 *Arun Kumar Manglik* v *Chirayu Health and Medicare Private Ltd.* (2019)3 Scale 333; 2019(2) CPR 27; JT 2019(5) SC 379; III(2019) CPJ 1 (SC).

professional conduct is proved with regard to the circumstances of that case, a doctor cannot escape liability merely by relying on a body of professional opinion.

8 Delegation of duty

(i) ***Delegation of duty and fixation of liability*** A medical practitioner undertaking the treatment of patient is personally liable for the diagnosis and treatment. A surgeon retained to perform an operation will be liable if he delegates his duty to a colleague who fails to use reasonable care.[3] A medical practitioner retained to act for a patient may delegate part of his work to another doctor, but he remains responsible for any lack of care in the performance of the delegated work. The contractual duties of care and skill are non-delegable, in the sense that performance of some works of the retainer may in practice be delegated, but the responsibility for it cannot. The general tortious duty which cannot be assimilated to the contractual one, is that a person is not liable when another to whom he has delegated a duty, performs it negligently, unless that person acted without reasonable care in selecting the person to whom performance was delegated.[4]

The English law does not recognise the team standard. Accordingly the responsibility of a nurse in the course of an operation is different from that of a surgeon.[5] Mustill, LJ[6] rejected the notion of a team standard of care "whereby each of the persons who formed the staff of the unit held themselves out as capable of undertaking the specialised procedures which that unit set out to perform" on the ground that it would expose a student nurse to an action of negligence for failure to possess the skill and experience of a consultant.

3 *Morris* v *Winsbury-White* [1937]4 All ER 494; *Stewart* v *Rayner* (1957)84 NW (2nd) 816.

4 *D and F Estates* v *Church Comrs. for England* (1987)36 BLR 72 (CA) affirmed 132 Sol Jo 1092; [1988]2 All ER 992; [1988]3 WLR 368 (HL).

5 *Gold* v *Essex County Council* [1942]2 KB 293; [1942]2 All ER 237; 167 LT 166; 86 Sol Jo 295 (CA).

6 *Wilsher* v *Essex Area Health Authority* [1987] QB 730; [1986]3 All ER 801; [1987]2 WLR 425; 130 Sol Jo 749 (CA) reversed [1988]1 All ER 871; [1988]2 WLR 557; 132 Sol Jo 418; 3 BMLR 37 (HL).

The duty towards patient is owed not only by the radiographers,[7] anaesthetists,[8] pathologists,[9] physiotherapists,[10] dentists,[11] and nurses,[12] but also by the hospital staff.[13] The hospital authority is not responsible for the negligence of the physicians, surgeons, and nurses in course of their professional duties, but the hospital authority is legally responsible to the patient for due performance of ministerial or administrative duties of its servants.[14] The distinction drawn by Kennedy, LJ[15] between professional duties and ministerial or administrative duties has been disapproved by the Court of Appeal in *Cassidy* v *Ministry of Health*[16] wherein it is laid down that the hospitals are liable for negligence of the members of their staff including nurses and doctors. The nursing home and the private hospital are not responsible for the negligence of the physicians and surgeons who are not appointed by the nursing home and the private hospital.[17] Lord Denning[18] has summarised the proposition by expressing the view that the hospital is liable if it provides the specialist, but not if the patient obtains him. In India the Government is a necessary party in a suit instituted

7 *Gold* v *Essex County Council* [1942]2 KB 293; [1942]2 All ER 237; 167 LT 166; 86 Sol Jo 295 (CA).
8 *Jones* v *Manchester Corporation* [1952]2 QB 852; [1952]2 All ER 125 (CA).
9 *Crivon* v *Barnet Group Hospital Management Committee* [1958] CLY 2283 (CA).
10 *Clarke* v *Adams* (1950)94 Sol Jo 599.
11 *Edwards* v *Mallan* [1908]1 KB 1002; 98 LT 824; 52 Sol Jo 316 (CA).
12 *Cassidy* v *Ministry of Health* [1951]2 KB 343; [1951]1 All ER 574; 95 Sol Jo 253 (CA).
13 *Morris* v *Winsbury-White* [1937]4 All ER 494.
14 *Hillyer* v *St. Bartholomew's Hospital* [1909]2 KB 820; 78 LJKB 958; 101 LT 38; 53 Sol Jo 714; *Lindsey C.C.* v *Marshall* [1937] AC 97; 105 LJKB 614; 155 LT 297; 80 Sol Jo 702; [1936]2 All ER 1076.
15 *Hillyer* v *St. Bartholomew's Hospital* [1909]2 KB 820; 78 LJKB 958; 101 LT 38; 53 Sol Jo 714.
16 [1942]2 KB 293; [1942]2 All ER 237; 112 LJKB 1; 167 LT 166; 86 Sol Jo 295 (CA).
17 *Gold* v *Essex County Council* [1942]2 KB 293; [1942]2 All ER 237; 112 LJKB 1; 167 lT 166; 86 Sol Jo 295 (CA).
18 *Roe* v *Minister of Health* [1954]2 QB 66; [1954]2 All ER 131; [1954] WLR 915; 98 Sol Jo 319 (CA).

against a doctor attached to the government hospital for damages or other reliefs in respect of any act alleged to have been done by the doctor in his official capacity.[19]

(ii) ***Delegation of duty and liability of the hospital and government***

The hospital is liable when an unqualified surgeon negligently injects a patient with cocaine in mistake for procaine,[20] when the medical staff were negligent in the post-operational treatment of a patient,[1] when an anaesthetic was negligently administered by a physician,[2] and when a radiographer was negligent in providing adequate screening material during the use of x-rays.[3] The hospital authority is held liable for its failure to warn the patient of the danger of infection of puerperal fever—a risk within the knowledge of the medical superintendent.[4] The hospital is guilty of negligence in failing to provide continuous supervision of a psychiatric patient and a known suicide risk who left his bed by ground floor window, climbed to a roof and threw himself off and thereby sustained severe injuries.[5] Similarly, in a Canadian case[6] the hospital was liable for negligence when, in the absence of nurse, a seven-year-old boy fell out of the window and suffered personal injuries. Even the hospital could not escape its liability for negligence of part time medical man attached to the hospital.[7]

19 Order 27, r. 5A of the Code of Civil Procedure 1908.

20 *Collins* v *Hertfordshire C.C.* [1947] KB 598; [1947]1 All ER 633; [1947] LJR 798.

1 *Cassidy* v *Ministry of Health* [1951]2 KB 343; [1951]1 All ER 574; 95 Sol Jo 253 (CA).

2 *Jones* v *Manchester Corporation* [1952]2 QB 852; [1952]2 All ER 125 (CA).

3 *Gold* v *Essex County Council* [1942]2 KB 293; [1942]2 All ER 237; 112 LJKB 1; 167 LT 166; 86 Sol Jo 295 (CA).

4 *Lindsey C.C.* v *Marshall* [1937] AC 97; 105 LJKB 614; 155 LT 297; 80 Sol Jo 702; [1936]2 All ER 1076; *Heafield* v *Crane*, *The Times*, 31st July 1937.

5 *Selfe* v *Ilford and District Hospital Management Committee* (1970)114 Sol Jo 935; *The Times,* 25th November 1970 (CA).

6 *Lepine* v *University Hospital Board* (1964)5 DLR (2d) 225 affirmed (1965)54 DLR (2d) 340.

7 *Roe* v *Minister of Health* [1954]2 QB 66; [1954]2 All ER 131; [1954]2 WLR 915; 98 Sol Jo 319 (CA).

The attending doctor allowed the unqualified nurse to give lariago injection intravenously to the patient, though the consultant doctor advised that the lariago injection must be given by the doctor. The minor patient had suffered irreparable brain damage due to negligence on the part of the nurse and the attending doctor who were employees of the hospital. The Supreme Court of India[8] held the hospital was liable to pay compensation for the negligence of its staff. The principle enunciated by the Supreme Court of India[9] is that the delegation of duty to another may amount to negligence in certain circumstances. A consultant could be negligent where he delegates the responsibility to his junior with the knowledge that the junior was incapable of performing his duties properly. The fact of leaving critically ill patient under the care of unqualified compounder particularly when the situation demands constant monitoring of the patient, amounts to deficiency-in-service.[10] Similarly, negligence is attributed to the doctor for leaving the patient under the care of a compounder who caused death of the patient by administering "Nivaquine" injection.[11] The ESI hospital was held liable for not giving proper timely medical treatment to the patient and for refusal to admit the patient in the hospital for treatment of acute pain in abdomen by the attending doctor of the hospital.[12] The hospital was

8 *Harjot Ahluwalia (minor) through parents* v *Spring Meadows Hospital* 1997(3) CPR 1 (NC); II(1997) CPJ 98 (NC); (1997)5 CTJ 734 (CP) (NCDRC); 1998 CCJ 405 (NC) confirmed by Supreme Court in *Spring Meadows Hospital (Noida)* v *Harjot Ahluwalia through K.S. Ahluwalia* AIR 1998 SC 1801; (1998)4 SCC 39; 1998(1) CPR 1 (SC); I(1998) CPJ 1 (SC); 1998 CTJ 81 (SC) (CP); 1998 CCJ 521 (SC); JT 1998(2) SC 620; III(1998) SLT 684.

9 *Spring Meadows Hospital (Noida)* v *Harjot Ahluwalia* AIR 1998 SC 1801; (1998)4 SCC 39; 1998(1) CPR 1 (SC); I(1998) CPJ 1 (SC); 1998 CTJ 81 (SC) (CP); 1998 CCJ 521 (SC); JT 1998(2) SC 620; III(1998) SLT 684.

10 *Pravinbhai Khubchandbhai Soni* v *Dr. Rajendra R. Shah* 1997(3) CPR 224 (Ahmedabad); II(1998) CPJ 627 (Ahmedabad); 1998 CTJ 797 (CP) (SCDRC); 1999 CCJ 1323 (Guj).

11 *Nivrutti G. More* v *Dr. Vinayak Desmukh* (1994)2 CTJ 614 (CP) (SCDRC) (Bom).

12 *Ranjit Kumar Das* v *Medical Officer, ESI Hospital, Manicktala* 1998(1) CPR 165 (Cal); III(1997) CPJ 336 (Cal); 1999 CCJ 70 (WB).

directed to pay compensation to the father of the minor patient for causing injury to the sciatic nerve of the patient by the unqualified nurse of the hospital.[13] Similarly, the hospital was directed to pay compensation to the patient for sufferings caused by leaving sponge in the abdomen of the patient during caesarian operation.[14]

The Supreme Court of India[15] directed the State of Maharashtra to pay compensation to the legal representatives of a deceased patient who died after sterilization operation in a Government hospital due to negligence of the Government doctor who left a mop (towel) inside the peritoneal cavity of the patient during the operation. The High Court of Rajasthan[16] also directed the State Government to pay compensation to the husband of the deceased patient whose death was caused by insertion of pneumoperitoneal needle during laparoscopic tubectomy in a Government hospital.

The hospital authority was not liable for placing a patient suffering from diphtheria in a room on the same floor where the patients suffering from small pox were placed, because this system of practice was approved by medical science at the relevant time.[17] The hospital authority has been held not liable where a patient who had been operated in a hospital was discharged with a wad of surgical gauze in her body due to negligence of the surgeon and nurses conducting the operation.[18] The hospital authority is not liable when a mental patient receiving electro-convulsive therapy, sustained fractures of the pelvis on each side, due to driving of the head of the femur through the acetabulum.[19]

13 *A.M. Mathew* v *Director, Karuna Hospital* 1998(1) CPR 39 (Ker); I(1998) CPJ 476 (Ker); 1999 CCJ 960 (Ker).

14 *Aleyamma Varghese* v *Dewan Bahadur Dr. V. Varghese* 1996 CTJ 911; 1997(1) CPR 310 (Ker); III(1997) CPJ 165 (Ker); 1998 CCJ 1310 (Ker).

15 *Achutrao Haribhau Khodwa* v *State of Maharashtra* (1996)2 SCC 634; 1996 ACJ 505; (1996)4 CTJ 950 (SC) (CP).

16 *Rajmal* v *State of Rajasthan* 1996 ACJ 1166.

17 *Vancouver General Hospital* v *Mc Daniel* [1934] WN 171; 152 LT 56.

18 *Dryden* v *Surrey C.C. & Stewart* [1936]2 All ER 535; (1936)80 Sol Jo 656.

19 *Bolam* v *Friern Hospital Management Committee* [1957]1 WLR 582; [1957]2 All ER 118; 101 Sol Jo 357; 1 BMLR 1 (QBD).

9 Wrongful birth Sterilization is a form of birth control or family planning. Pregnancy after sterilization does not by itself establish negligence. Omission to warn the risk of failure of such operation is actionable negligence. Public policy in India professed by the Government is to control the population and that is why various programmes have been launched to implement the State sponsored family planning programmes and policies.[20]

The action may be brought to recover damages for unsuccessful sterilization followed by pregnancy and sometimes wrongful birth of a child, healthy or handicapped, who would not have been born had the gynaecologist not been negligent. The claim arises not only from a failed sterilization followed by a birth, but also where, for example, there has been a negligent failure to terminate a pregnancy, or a failure to diagnose a pregnancy in time after termination, or, more complex, a failure to advise that the foetus, due to hereditary factors or exposure to disease, was likely to be deformed, thus denying the mother the chance of a termination.[1] It may be the result of a failed sterilization procedure or failure to give appropriate advice for abortion or termination of pregnancy or failure to inform the patient about the risks of a sterilization operation not achieving complete sterility.[2]

There is conflict of judicial opinion on whether the doctor is liable to pay for all expenses which might reasonably be incurred in the education and upkeep of the unplanned child born due to negligence of the doctor. In *Udale* v *Bloomsbury Area Health Authority*[3] the plaintiff had undergone operation for laparoscopic sterilization by the doctor of the health authority. Owing to negligence of the doctor the operation was not successful and the plaintiff became pregnant. The

20 *State of Haryana* v *Smt. Santra* 2000 CTJ 481 (SC) (CP); I(2000) CPJ 53 (SC).

1 Charles J. Lewis, *Medical Negligence,* 4th Ed. 1998, p. 314.

2 Michael A. Jones, *Medical Negligence,* 5th Ed. 2018, p. 103.

3 [1983]2 All ER 522; [1983]1 WLR 1098; (1984)1 ACC (SN) (BJ) 46; 127 Sol Jo 510.

plaintiff claimed damages for (*i*) pain and suffering, (*ii*) loss of earnings, (*iii*) cost of enlarging family home, and (*iv*) cost of bringing up the child upto the age of 16 years. Jupp, J rejected the claim of damages on last two heads, i.e. for enlarging the family house and for bringing up the child, by giving careful consideration to the question of public policy. The Judge held that it was contrary to public policy that damages should be recoverable arising from the cost of coming into the world of a healthy normal child. In *McKay* v *Essex Area Health Authority*[4] the unanimous opinion of the Court of Appeal is that the infant plaintiff's claim for what has been called "Wrongful life" discloses no cause of action.

The judicial opinion expressed in various American decisions[5] can be summarised as follows:

(*i*) though what gives rise to the cause of action is not just life, but life with defects, the real cause of action is negligence in causing life;

(*ii*) negligent advice or failure to advise is the proximate cause of the child's life;

(*iii*) a child has no right to be born as a whole, functional being (without defect);

(*iv*) it is contrary to public policy to give a child a right not to be born except as a whole functional being and to impose on another a corresponding duty to cause death of an unborn child with defects;

(*v*) it is impossible to measure the damages for being born with defects, because the life of a child born with defects cannot be compared with his non-existence as human being; and

(*vi*) accordingly by being born with defects a child suffers no injury cognizable by law.

4 (1984)1 ACC (BJ) 159; [1982] QB 1166; [1982]2 All ER 771; [1982]2 WLR 890; 126 Sol Jo 261 (CA); 1983 ACJ 374.

5 *Gleitman* v *Cosgroove* 227 A (2d) 689; *Becker* v *Schwartz, Park* v *Chessin* (1978)413 NYS (2d) 895; *Phillips* v *U.S.A.* (1980)508 F Supp 537.

The contrary view is expressed by Peter Pain, J in *Thake* v *Maurice*[6] wherein the plaintiff who had four children, had undergone an operation of vasectomy. Owing to negligence of the doctor the operation was unsuccessful and the wife of the plaintiff became pregnant again. The judge considered very carefully the matters referred to by Jupp, J in "Udale" and came to the conclusion that he was not prepared to lay down any public policy objections to the claim which was being made, in spite of the fact that the parents were absolutely delighted and were very happy with the unwanted normal healthy child.

Forced with the conflict of decision between "Udale" and "Thake" the Court of Appeal[7] preferred the approach of Peter Pain, J as more reasonable and awarded damage for pain, suffering and loss of amenity which will have to be given to the congenitally abnormal child over the years. Slade, J[8] delivering the judgment in the Court of Appeal held as follows:

> "If a woman wishes to be sterilized and in a legal way causes herself to be operated on for that purpose, I can, for my part, see no reason why, under public policy, she should not recover such financial damage as she can prove she has sustained by the surgeon's negligent failure to perform the operation properly, whether or not the child is healthy."

So, the changed view of the Court of Appeal is that if as a result of a doctor's negligence, an unplanned child is born, the doctor is liable to pay for all expenses which might reasonably be incurred in the education and upkeep of the child, having regard to the child's condition in life. However, the parents of a child suffering from congenital rubella

6 [1984]2 All ER 513; [1986] QB 644; [1985]2 WLR 215; 129 Sol Jo 86 on appeal [1986]1 All ER 497; [1986]2 WLR 337; 129 Sol Jo 894.

7 *Emeh* v *Kensington and Chelsea and Westminster Area Health Authority* [1984]3 All ER 1044 (CA); [1985] QB 1012; (1985)11 ACC (BJ) 1; [1985]2 WLR 233; 128 Sol Jo 705 (CA).

8 *Emeh* v *Kensington and Chelsea and Westminster Area Health Authority* [1984]3 All ER 1044 (CA); [1985] QB 1012; (1985)11 ACC (BJ) 1; [1985]2 WLR 233; 128 Sol Jo 705 (CA).

syndrome, brought an action for damages against the health authority alleging that the birth of the child resulted from the failure of the health authority to diagnose and warn the mother that the child she was carrying might be affected by rubella syndrome, with the result that she was unable to have the pregnancy terminated. The health authority admitted liability for its negligent failure to diagnose and warn the mother that the child may be infected with rubella. The court ultimately did not allow damages for the basic cost of maintaining the handicapped child.[9]

The plaintiff suffered miscarriage and the foetus was found to be anencephalic (i.e. without brain) and suffered from exomphalus which means that any future pregnancies might be attended by certain risks of congenital deformity. The plaintiff was never informed of any abnormalities in the foetus. Subsequently the plaintiff gave birth to a child who suffered from spina bifida. The doctor was negligent by not disclosing the abnormalities of the earlier foetus when the patient suffered miscarriage. The court awarded a substantial sum in addition to the actual loss of earnings.[10]

The claim of the plaintiff for compensation for unwanted pregnancy of wife due to failure of vasectomy operation, was dismissed by the Queen's Bench Division,[11] as the health authority explained to the plaintiff about the small risk of failure of vasectomy operation at the time of counselling before the operation. The Court of Appeal[12] awarded damages in favour of the plaintiff who became pregnant after 15 months of sterilization operation on the ground that the doctor of the health authority did not give proper warning to the plaintiff about the risk of failure of sterilization operation. The patient, mother of three children, suffering from ectopic

9 *Salith* v *Enfield Health Authority* 7 BMLR 1 (CA); [1991]3 All ER 400; [1990]1 Med LR 333.

10 *Fish* v *Wilcox and Gwent Health Authority* 13 BMLR 134 (CA); [1994]5 Med LR 230 (CA).

11 *Stobie* v *Central Birmingham Health Authority* (1994)22 BMLR 135 (QBD).

12 *Lybert* v *Warrington Health Authority* 25 BMLR 91 (CA); [1996]7 Med LR 71.

pregnancy had undergone laparoscopic sterilization and dilation and curettage operation, in order to remove fertilized egg from uterus, but her pregnancy survived and she refused to undergo termination of pregnancy after 15 weeks gestation. The consultant gynaecologist was held negligent for not communicating adequately with the patient before undertaking the operation, particularly when the patient disclosed about her late menstruation period.[13]

The plaintiff underwent an operation for dilation and curettage (D&C) and sterilization at a hospital managed by the health authority. After three months of operation the plaintiff discovered that at the time of operation she had been four weeks pregnant and that her pregnancy had survived the operation. The court[14] enunciated the following principles:

(*i*) If a doctor fails to act towards his patient with the standard of care reasonably to be expected of him, and as a foreseeable result of the doctor's breach of duty a child is born whose potential for life would have been lawfully terminated but for the doctor's negligence, the law entitles the mother to recover damages for the foreseeable loss and damage she suffers in consequence of the doctor's negligence.

(*ii*) The mother is entitled to damages for the financial loss incurred in the upkeep of the child althrough adulthood and for the financial loss suffered, because of loss of earnings or the incurring of expenses as a result of her obligation to the child which she would otherwise have sought to avoid.

(*iii*) The mother is entitled to recover general damages for the discomfort and pain associated with the continuance of her unwanted pregnancy and delivery of her unplanned child, although the benefit of not having to undergo an abortion had to be set off against the quantum of general damages. In appropriate cases, the mother is also entitled to general damages for the foreseeable additional

13 *Cronchman* v *Burke* 40 BMLR 163 (QBD).
14 *Allen* v *Bloomsbury Health Authority* 13 BMLR 47.

anxiety, stress and burden involved in bringing up a handicapped child.

It is held by the Court of Appeal in UK.[15] that if a disabled woman gives birth to a healthy child due to negligent performance of sterilization operation by the surgeon, she is entitled to recover as damages the extra costs of bringing up the child that were attributable to her disability.

The Supreme Court of India[16] is of the view that the principles on the basis of which damages have not been allowed on account of failed sterilization operation either on account of public policy or on account of pleasure in having a child being offset against the claim for damages cannot be strictly applied to Indian conditions. The public policy proposed by the Government of India is to control the population and as such, the claim for compensation for giving birth of an unwanted child due to medical negligence cannot be denied. However, the view expressed by the House of Lords[17] is that the mother of the unwanted child is entitled to general damages for pain, suffering, inconvenience of pregnancy and child birth and special damages for extra medical expenses, clothing and loss of earnings associated therewith. However, the claim for upbringing the healthy, unwanted child is not sustainable in law, as the benefits would out weigh the loss and the parents would not be entitled to recover the cost of caring for and bringing up the child.

The doctor can be held liable for child birth in spite of sterilization operation if the failure of the surgery is attributable to the negligence of the doctor in performance of the operation. The Kerala High Court[18] affirmed the order of trial court for payment of compensation to the parents of unwanted child after failure of sterilization operation, as the State of Kerala did not adduce evidence to rebut the allegation

15 *Rees* v *Darlington Memorial Hospital NHS Trust* [2002]2 All ER 177; [2002] EWCA Civ 88.

16 *State of Haryana* v *Santra (Smt.)* (2000)3 Scale 417; (2000)5 SCC 182; I(2000) CPJ 53; AIR 2000 SC 1888; 2000 ACJ 1188; JT 2000(5) SC 34.

17 *Tayside Health Board* v *Mcfarlane* [1999]3 WLR 1301.

18 *State of Kerala* v *P.G. Kumarimma* 2011(1) KLT 64 (SN); AIR 2011 NOC 250; 2011(1) KLJ 174.

of child birth due to negligent sterilization operation. The Supreme Court of India[19] did not hold the doctor liable for negligence for unwanted pregnancy due to failure of sterilization operation, as it is established from medical literature that failure of sterilization operation due to natural causes varies from 0.3% to 7% depending on the techniques or method chosen for performing the sterilization operation. The law laid down by the Supreme Court of India[20] is that the operating surgeon or his employer cannot be held liable for compensation on account of unwanted pregnancy or unwanted child, merely because a woman became pregnant and delivered a child after sterilization operation. The claim for compensation in such cases can be sustained only if there was negligence on the part of the surgeon in performing the surgery and not on account of child birth. The Madras High Court[1] refused to award compensation for unwanted child on the ground of negligence of the doctor in performing sterilization operation as the High Court was of the view that the claim for damages could be granted only in appropriate civil proceedings or in a proceeding before Consumer Forum by adducing relevant evidence to prove negligence on the part of the doctor conducting the operation. However, the contrary view expressed by the Punjab and Haryana High Court[2] is that the birth of a female child after tubectomy operation is *per se* proof of negligence unless contrary is proved that the doctor has performed his duty with reasonable care and skill.

10 Role of conduct and ethics "A recognised standard of conduct contained in statutory codes and official literature may be used as a practical guide to the standard of care to be aimed for, as well as to the nature and extent of any

19 *State of Haryana* v *Raj Rani* (2005)7 SCC 22; 2005 ACJ 2116; AIR 2005 SC 3279; IV(2005) CPJ 28; 2005(4) CTC 703; JT 2005(8) SC 56; (2005)7 Scale 1.

20 *State of Punjab* v *Shiv Ram* (2005)7 SCC 1; AIR 2005 SC 3280; IV(2005) CPJ 14; JT 2005(7) SC 606; 2005(3) ACC 717.

1 *Rukmani* v *State of Tamil Nadu* 2003(3) ACJ 1748; 2003(3) CTC 47.

2 *Fulla Devi* alias *Fullo Devi* v *State of Haryana* 2005 ACJ 51; IV(2004) CPJ 593.

particular damage, which is likely to be encountered. A code may appear to be exhaustive but there is always space left for discerning the common law duty of care. Where there has been compliance with a statutory regulation, it might well constitute valuable evidence that the defendants were not guilty of negligence, but there could be no presumption that such was sufficient. This is because statutory codes cannot be expected to cover every known eventuality and possible kind of danger. Accordingly, it is still left to the court to decide what is required to constitute a reasonably safe system of work".[3] The code of conduct applicable to medical profession is in substance no more than codified accepted professional practice. The value of this code of conduct is assessed by Beattie, J in a New Zealand case[4] in relation to the engineers in the following way:

> "I am of the view that bearing in mind the function of codes, a design which departs substantially from them is *prima facie* a faulty design, unless it can be demonstrated that it conforms to accepted engineering practice by rational analysis."

Barrowclough, CJ[5] strongly suggested that the prevailing professional codes of ethics dealing with confidentiality would set the standard of legal liability. In a New Zealand case[6] the doctor was held negligent for providing his patient's husband with a written report diagnosing the patient as suffering from paranoia which was disclosed by the husband in course of subsequent divorce proceeding. It is pertinent to point out that the law of confidentiality and misuse of private information are two separate and distinct causes of action. The law of confidentiality protects secret or confidential information which focuses on the duty of good faith, whereas

3 Charlesworth & Percy on *Negligence*, 9th Ed., pp. 452-453 (6·31 and 6·32).
4 *Bevan Investments Ltd.* v *Black-hall and Struthers* [1973]2 NZLR 45 on appeal [1978]2 NZLR 97 (CA).
5 *Furniss* v *Fitchett* [1958] NZLR 396.
6 *Furniss* v *Fitchett* (supra).

the misuse of private information focuses on privacy and protection of human autonomy and dignity.[7]

A member of medical profession acquires confidential information about his patient. The doctor is duty bound to keep such information confidential. All professions treat deliberate breach of confidence by a member as serious professional misconduct.[8] The British Medical Association in its *Handbook of Medical Ethics,*[9] has laid down the following five situations when the duty of confidentiality is overridden by other considerations:

(*i*) the patient gives consent;

(*ii*) when it is undesirable on medical grounds to seek a patient's consent but it is in the patient's own interest that confidentiality should be broken;

(*iii*) the doctor's overriding duty to society, e.g. a doctor should surely reveal information which would show his patient to have been guilty of a serious crime, for he is under the ordinary duty imposed on every citizen not to protect offenders;

(*iv*) for the purposes of medical research when approved by a local clinical research ethical committee;

(*v*) when the information is required by due legal process.

The right to confidentiality is impliedly waived when the patient brings an action of medical negligence against the doctor.[10] The duty of confidentiality owed by a doctor to a patient detained in a hospital is subordinate to his public duty to disclose the results of his examination to the authorities responsible for the welfare of the patient.[11] The patient was treated by various physicians over a period of years before being treated by the defendant physician. The patient demanded the contents of her complete medical file

7 *Vidal Hall* v *Google Inc.* [2015] EWCA Civ 311; [2016] QB 1003.
8 Bennion, *Professional Ethics*, pp. 72 & 73.
9 Charles J Lewis, *Medical Negligence* (4th Ed. 1998), pp. 174-175.
10 *Hay* v *University of Alberta Hospital* [1991]2 Med LR 204.
11 *W.* v *Egdell* [1989]1 All ER 1089 affirmed by [1990]1 All ER 835 (CA); 4 BMLR 96 (CA).

from the defendant physician who refused to hand over copies of the reports and records that she had received from other physicians. The Supreme Court of Canada[12] affirming the decision of the lower courts directed the physician to provide copy of the entire medical file to the patient. The principle enunciated by the Supreme Court of Canada is that the patient has a vital interest in information contained in his medical records. The relationship between physician and patient gives rise to the duty of the doctor to hold information received from patients in confidence. The relationship also gives rise to the physician's duty to make proper disclosure of information to the patient. The patient is entitled to reasonable access to examine and copy the records, provided the patient pays a legitimate fee for the preparation and reproduction of the information. Access is limited to the information the physician obtained in providing treatment. It does not extend to information arising outside the doctor patient relationship. Accordingly, the patient is entitled on demand to inspect and copy all information in the patient's medical file which the physician considered in administering advice or treatment. This general rule of access is subject to superintending jurisdiction of the court.

A doctor was charged before the Professional Conduct Committee of the General Medical Council with serious professional misconduct in relation to the errors he had made in his diagnosis of three patients and failure to refer them to the hospital. The Committee found most of the facts alleged in the charges proved and found the doctor guilty of serious professional misconduct. The committee directed that the doctor's name be erased from the medical registers in accordance with s. 36(1) of the Medical Act 1983. On appeal it is held that serious professional misconduct was not restricted to conduct which was morally blameworthy, but could include seriously negligent treatment measured by objective professional standards; and that, accordingly, there were no grounds for interfering with the conclusion of the committee that the doctor was guilty of serious professional

12 *McInserney* v *MacDonald* (1992)93 DLR (4th) 415 (SC of Canada).

misconduct and that such misconduct warranted the penalty of his name being erased from the registers.[13]

One complaint was filed against the surgeon before Maharashtra Medical Council on the following allegations: (*i*) that the surgeon conducted surgery against the advice of the doctor of US; (*ii*) that the surgeon did not conduct or supervise the operation, but asked his colleague surgeon conducting the operation to close the abdomen without proceeding further with the operation, and (*iii*) that the surgeon did not treat the patient during post operative period after formation of fistula. The patient suffering from cancer for about ten years and treated by the doctor in US, was admitted to the hospital for exploratory laparotomy due to vaginal bleeding. The Maharashtra Medical Council found the surgeon guilty of professional misconduct, which resulted in issuance of warning against the surgeon under s. 22(1) of the Maharashtra Medical Council Act 1965.[14]

It is held by the Privy Council[15] that professional misconduct is not simply misconduct in carrying out of medical work. There may be cases of serious failure to meet the necessary standards of practice, such as gross neglect of patients or culpable carelessness in their treatment, or taking advantage of a professional relationship for personal gratification. Certain behaviour may constitute professional misconduct even though it is not within the actual course of carrying on the professional practice, such as abuse of the patient's confidence or making of some dishonest private financial gain. The act of doing private practice on acceptance of professional fees by the doctor of primary health centre of the Government amounts to misconduct.[16] Lord Esher, MR[17] has observed:

13 *David Noel McCondles* v *General Medical Council* [1996]1 WLR 167 (PC).

14 *P.B. Desai* v *State of Maharashtra* (2013)15 SCC 481.

15 *John Roylance* v *General Medical Council (No. 2)* [1999]3 WLR 541 (PC); [2000]1 AC 311.

16 *Dr. Ranjit Singh Buttar* v *Sewa Singh* II(2000) CPJ 180 (Chandigarh).

17 *Allinson* v *General Council of Medical Education and Registration* [1894]1 QB 750.

"If it is shown that a medical man, in the pursuit of his profession, has done something with regard to it, which would be reasonably regarded as disgraceful or dishonourable by his professional brethren of good repute and competency."

The Code of Medical Ethics framed under s. 33 of the Indian Medical Council Act 1956, may be used as a practical guide to the standard of care to be aimed for, as well as to the nature and extent of any particular danger, which is likely to be encountered. Since power of judicial review is the basic structure of the Constitution of India, the court is the ultimate authority to decide what constitutes reasonable conduct of the medical practitioners.

The Code of Professional Conduct made by the Medical Council of India under s. 33 read with s. 20A of the Indian Medical Council Act 1956, protects medical information from disclosure. The provisions of the Code of Medical Ethics contain an exception to the general rule of confidentiality, inasmuch as it provides that the information may be disclosed in a court of law under the orders of the presiding judge. The Code of Medical Ethics carves out an exception to the rule of confidentiality and permits the disclosure in the circumstances enumerated above under which public interest would override the duty of confidentiality, particularly where there is an immediate or future health risk to others.[18]

The petitioner was found to be HIV(+) after conducting several tests in the hospital. The marriage of the petitioner was called off, as the doctors of the hospital disclosed the HIV(+) status of the petitioner to his fiancee. The petitioner moved the court for damages against the doctor on the ground that the information which was required to be kept secret under medical ethics was disclosed illegally and, therefore, the doctor and the hospital are liable to pay damages. It is held by the Supreme Court of India[19] that the woman with

18 *Dr. Tokugha Yepthomi* v *Appollo Hospital Enterprises* III(1998) CPJ 12 (SC); 1999 CCJ 467 (SC); *Mr. "X"* v *Hospital "Z"* 1999 CTJ 1 (SC) (CP).

19 *Dr. Tokugha Yepthomi* v *Appollo Hospital Enterprises* (supra).

whom the marriage of the petitioner was settled, was saved in time by the disclosure of the vital information that the petitioner was HIV(+). It is also held by the Supreme Court that when there is a clash of two fundamental rights, viz, petitioner's right to privacy and his fiancee's right to lead a healthy life, the court would enforce the right which would advance the public morality or public interest. The law laid down by the Supreme Court is that the disclosure of HIV(+) status of the petitioner would not be violative of either the rule of confidentiality or petitioner's right to privacy, as this is an exception to the general rule that a doctor cannot disclose to a person information regarding his patient, which he has gathered in course of treatment or regarding mode of treatment and advice given to the patient.

CHAPTER 4

Consent to Treatment

1 Object of consent All kinds of medical treatment and surgical procedure involve interference with human body. The interference may be done by assault, battery and false imprisonment. The tort of battery is defined as "the application of force to the person of another without lawful justification".[1] "Assault is an act of the defendant which causes to the plaintiff reasonable apprehension of the infliction of a battery on him by the defendant".[2] False imprisonment is the infliction of bodily restraint which is not expressly or impliedly authorised by the law.[3] The tort of battery is an important weapon for protection of a patient's right of self-determination. In the words of Justice Cardozo,[4] "Every human being of adult years and sound mind has a right to determine what should be done with his body; and a surgeon who performs an operation without his patient's consent commits an assault for which he is liable in damages". In one Canadian case,[5] the anaesthetist administered the anaesthetic by injection into a vein in the patient's left arm. The anaesthetic leaked into the tissue of the arm, as the

1 Salmond & Heuston on *The Law of Torts*, 20th Ed., p. 125.
2 Winfield and Jolowicz on *Tort*, 15th Ed., p. 63.
3 Winfield and Jolowicz on *Tort*, 15th Ed., p. 69.
4 *Schloendorff* v *Society of New York Hospital* (1914)103 NE 92.
5 *Allan* v *New Mount Sinai Hospital* (1980)109 DLR (3d) 634 reversed (1981)125 DLR (3d) 276.

needle slipped during the course of the operation. The patient suffered severe and unexpected reaction, but the doctor was not held liable in negligence on the ground that the occurrence of leakage of anaesthetic into the tissue of the arm was recognised risk, and the form of administration of anaesthetic was the accepted professional practice. However, the doctor was held liable in battery on the basis of the evidence that the patient expressly prohibited the doctor from administering the anaesthetic to her left arm. The principle enunciated in *Allan*[6] is that a doctor who proceeds to disregard the requirement of obtaining consent, is strictly liable for any untoward consequences resulting from the procedure of treatment, even if he conforms to the accepted medical practice. However, the decision of *Allan* was reversed by the Ontario Court of Appeal on the ground that the plaintiff had not pleaded battery. The patient's right of self-determination suggests that a competent adult is entitled to reject a specific treatment or all treatment or to select an alternative form of treatment even if the decision may entail risk as serious as death and may appear to be erroneous in the eyes of the medical profession or of the community.[7]

2 Necessity for consent A doctor is required, as part of his duty of care to his patient, to explain what he intends to do, and the implication involved, in the way in which a responsible doctor in similar circumstances would have done, and if there is a real risk of misfortune inherent in the procedure, however well it is carried out, the doctor's duty is to warn of the risk of such misfortune.[8] To warn of common risks involved in an operation which is essential for continued good health and welfare of the patient, may not be necessary, but the same may be necessary where the operation is totally elective, e.g. sterilization operation.[9] The obligation to disclose

6 *Supra* (1980)109 DLR (3d) 634 reversed (1981)125 DLR (3d) 276.

7 *Malette* v *Shulman et al* (1990)67 DLR (4th) 321 (Ontario Court of Appeal).

8 *Chatterton* v *Gerson* (1980)1 BMLR 80 (QBD); [1981] QB 432; [1981]1 All ER 257; [1981]3 WLR 1003; 124 Sol Jo 885.

9 *Videto* v *Kennedy* (1980)107 DLR (3d) 612 on appeal (1981)125 DLR (3d) 127 (CA); *Zamparo* v *Brisson* (1981)120 DLR (3d) 545.

risks of elective medical procedures such as sterilization and cosmetic surgery depends on the normal negligence principles of accepted professional practice.[10] The Supreme Court of India held the gynaecologist negligent for conducting hysterectomy and bilateral salpingo-oopherectomy, i.e. removal of uterus, ovaries and fallopian tubes without obtaining consent during laparoscopy test under general anaesthesia for affirmative diagnosis.[11]

A patient approaching a medical practitioner for treatment impliedly gives his consent for medical procedures undertaken by the said doctor. Naturally, the consent to medical procedure may be implied from the circumstances.[12] The question may arise as to whether such hypothetical consent is to be judged objectively or subjectively. The subjective approach may expose the doctor to the danger of being bogged down by the allegation of the patient who by using the benefit of hindsight, would deny the fact of giving consent, even when full disclosure had been made. On the other hand, the objective approach has the advantage for the medical practitioner who may rely on the common reaction of the patient to the news of their suffering from a particular condition, but it fails to account for the individual patient's right of self-determination. The American[13] and Canadian Courts[14] favour the objective approach, whereas the English Courts[15] tend to adopt the subjective approach to the question of determining hypothetical consent. In India the individual patient's right of self-determination will flow from the fundamental right enshrined in Art. 21 of the Constitution of India.

10 *Gold* v *Haringey Health Authority* [1988] QB 481; [1987]2 All ER 888; [1987]3 WLR 649; 131 Sol Jo 843 (CA).

11 *Samira Kohli* v *Dr. Prabha Manchanda* (2008)2 SCC 1; 2008 ACJ 747; AIR 2008 SC 1385; JT 2008(1) SC 399; (2008)1 Scale 442.

12 *Schweizer* v *Central Hospital* (1974)53 DLR (3d) 494.

13 *Canterbury* v *Spence* (1972)464 F (2d) 772.

14 *Reibl* v *Hughes* (1977)89 DLR (3d) 112 (Ont CA) reversed (1980)114 DLR (3d) 1; [1980]2 SCR 880.

15 *Sidaway* v *Board of Governors of Bethlem Royal Hospital and the Maudsley Hospital* [1984] QB 493; [1984]1 All ER 1018; [1984]2 WLR 778; 128 Sol Jo 301 (CA) affirmed [1985] AC 871; [1985]1 All ER 643; [1985]2 WLR 480; 129 Sol Jo 154; (1985)1 BMLR 132 (HL).

3 Informed consent—criteria for The English law recognises a duty of the doctor to warn his patient of the risk inherent in the treatment which he is proposing; and especially so if the treatment is surgery. The clinical limitation is that the duty is confined to material risk. The test of materiality is whether in the circumstances of the particular case the court is satisfied that a reasonable person in the patient's position would be likely to attach significance to the risk. The question whether or not the omission to warn constitutes a breach of the doctor's duty of care towards his patient is to be determined not exclusively by reference to the current state of responsible and competent professional opinion and practice at the time, though both are, of course, relevant consideration, but by the court's view whether the doctor in advising his patient gave the consideration which the law requires him to give to the patient or make up his own mind in the light of the relevant information whether or not he will accept the proposed treatment.[16]

It goes without saying that a conscious adult patient of sound mind is entitled to decide for himself whether or not he will submit to a particular course of treatment proposed by the doctor. This entitlement is the foundation of the doctrine of informed consent, which originated in United States of America[17] and found favour by the Supreme Court of Canada.[18] The North American concept of "informed consent" implies an objective test of a doctor's duty to advise the patient of the advantages and disadvantages of undergoing the treatment proposed and more particularly to advise the patient of the risks involved.

16 Lord Scarman in *Sidaway* v *Board of Governors of Bethlem Royal Hospital and the Maudsley Hospital* [1984] QB 493; [1984]1 All ER 1018; [1984]2 WLR 778; 128 Sol Jo 301 (CA); affirmed [1985] AC 871; [1985]1 All ER 643; [1985]2 WLR 480; 129 Sol Jo 154; (1985)1 BMLR 132 (HL).

17 *Conterbury* v *Spence* (1972)464 F (2d) 772.

18 *Reibl* v *Hughes* (1977)89 DLR (3d) 112 (Ont CA) reversed (1980)114 DLR (3d) 1; [1980]2 SCR 880.

According to the majority decision of the House of Lords in *Sidaway*[19] the English law does not recognise the doctrine of informed consent. The test of liability in respect of a doctor's duty to warn his patient of risks inherent in treatment recommended by him is the same as the test applicable to diagnosis and treatment, namely that the doctor is required to act in accordance with a practice accepted at the time as proper by a responsible body of medical opinion. When questioned specifically by a patient of apparently sound mind about the risks involved in a particular treatment proposed, the doctor's duty is to answer both truthfully and as fully as the questioner requires.[20]

The question of disclosure of risks tested by the tenets of "accepted professional practice" may vary from patient to patient depending on the needs of the particular patient. A risk is material when the reasonable person, in what the physician knows or should know to be the patient's position, would be likely to attach significance to the risk or cluster of risks in deciding whether or not to undergo the proposed therapy.[1] The disclosure is essential when the course of treatment being recommended will inevitably produce damaging side-effects[2] and when medical experiment is being proposed on a healthy volunteer.[3]

The obligation to disclose risks of elective medical procedures such as sterilization operation or cosmetic surgery depends on the principles of accepted professional

19 *Sidaway* v *Board of Governors of Bethlem Royal Hospital and the Maudsley Hospital* [1984] QB 493; [1984]1 All ER 1018; [1984]2 WLR 778; 128 Sol Jo 301 (CA) affirmed [1985] AC 871; [1985]1 All ER 643; [1985]2 WLR 480; 129 Sol Jo 154; (1985)1 BMLR 132 (HL).

20 *Sidaway* v *Board of Governors of Bethlem Royal Hospital and the Maudsley Hospital* [1984] QB 493; [1984]1 All ER 1018; [1984]2 WLR 778; 128 Sol Jo 301 (CA) affirmed [1985] AC 871; [1985]1 All ER 643; [1985]2 WLR 480; 129 Sol Jo 154; (1985)1 BMLR 132 (HL).

1 *Canterbury* v *Spence* (1972)464 F (2d) 772; *Hopp* v *Lepp* (1979)98 DLR (3d) 464 reversed (1980)112 DLR (3d) 67 (CA).

2 *Smith* v *Auckland Hospital Board* [1964] NZLR 241 reversed [1965] NZLR 191.

3 *Halushka* v *University of Saskalchewan* (1965)53 DLR (2d) 436; 52 WWR 608.

practice.[4] Where the doctor had carried out his duty to inform the patient of the implications of the operation, he was not liable for failure to warn the patient of the possibility of loss of muscle power and numbness in the leg of the patient, which was not foreseeable risk of the operation.[5] The majority of the House of Lords did not hold the surgeon negligent for failure to warn of the risk of damage to the spinal cord of the patient, because the surgeon's non-disclosure of the risk of damage to the patient's spinal cord accorded with a practice accepted as proper by a responsible body of neuro-surgical.[6]

A neuro-surgeon formed the opinion that his patient required surgery in order to clear blocked artery and to prevent a stroke in later part of life. The patient was kept in complete ignorance of the high risks involved in the operation. The patient was paralysed for stroke suffered during surgery. The surgeon was held negligent for his failure to obtain proper consent from the patient after giving full information of risks involved in the operation.[7]

The criteria for informed consent with regard to abortion of a pregnant woman laid down in Pennsylvania abortion legislation were upheld as constitutionally valid by the United States Supreme Court[8] by holding "that except in a medical emergency: (*i*) at least 24 hours before performing an abortion, a physician must inform the woman of the nature of the abortion procedure, the health risks of the abortion and of child birth, and the probable gestational age of the unborn child; (*ii*) the physician or a qualified non-physician must inform the woman of the availability of printed materials published by the State describing the foetus and providing

4 *Gold* v *Haringey Health Authority* [1988] QB 481; [1987]2 All ER 888; [1987]3 WLR 649; 131 Sol Jo 843 (CA).

5 *Chatterton* v *Gerson* (1980)1 BMLR 80; [1981]1 All ER 257; [1981] QB 432; [1981]3 WLR 1003.

6 *Sidaway* v *Bethlem Royal Hospital Governors* [1985] AC 871; [1985]1 All ER 643; [1985]2 WLR 480; 129 Sol Jo 154; (1985)1 BMLR 132 (HL).

7 *Reibl* v *Hughes* (1977)89 DLR (3d) 112, (Ont CA) reversed (1980)114 DLR (3d) 1 (SC of Canada); [1980]2 SCR 880.

8 *Planned Parenthood of South Eastern Pennsylvania* v *Robert P. Casey* 505 US 674; (1992)120 L Ed 2d 674; 112 Sct 2791.

information about medical assistance for child birth, information about child support from father, and a list of agencies which provide adoption and other services as alternatives to abortion; and (*iii*) the woman must certify in writing that she has been informed of the availability of these materials".

The surgeon did not explain the hazards of chloroform anaesthesia before taking consent of the patient for operation of appendicitis. On finding appendix to be normal, he proceeded to remove the gall-bladder without consent and without caring for the ill-effects of keeping the patient under chloroform especially when her kidneys were affected. Accordingly, the surgeon was held negligent.[9] A patient died of an allergic reaction to a dye used in a diagnostic medical test (I.V.P.). Severe reaction was known to occur in about one in 2000 cases and death in between one in 40000 and 100000. The radiologist acted in accordance with the advice of the Canadian Association of Radiologists by not giving any warning to the patient of these risks. The Ontario Court of Appeal in Canada held the radiologist liable for not obtaining informed consent to treatment.[10]

The patient gave consent for excision biopsy and the cardiothoracic surgeon carried out the operation for complete excision of the tumour and thereby caused damage to the nervous system resulting in complete paralysis of lower limbs of the patient and other associated complications. The hospital withheld the production of the document of consent given by the patient before the operation. It is held by the Supreme Court of India[11] that the consent given by the patient for excision biopsy cannot, by inference, be taken as an implied consent for surgery of excision of tumour, which resulted in paralysis of lower limbs of the patient.

9 *Ram Bihari Lal* v *Dr. J.N. Shrivastava* AIR 1985 MP 150; 1985 ACJ 424; 1985 Jab LJ 259; (1985)1 Cur CC 987; 1985 MPLJ 288; 1985 Cur Civ LJ 149.

10 *Meyer et al* v *Rogers et al* 78 DLR (4th) 307 (OC of Appeal).

11 *Nizam's Institute of Medical Sciences* v *Prasnath S. Dhananka* (2009)6 SCC 1; JT 2009(2) SC 385; 2009 AIR SCW 3563; 2010 ACJ 38; (2009)4 Supreme 165.

The law laid down by the Supreme Court of India[12] for obtaining consent before surgical procedure is as follows: (*i*) A doctor must seek and secure the real and valid consent of the patient before commencing treatment including surgery. The consent will be real and valid (*a*) if the patient has the capacity and competence to give consent, (*b*) if his consent is voluntary, and (*c*) if he gives consent on the basis of adequate information about the nature and procedure of treatment. (*ii*) The adequate information furnished by the doctor or any member of his team, should enable the patient to make a balanced decision whether he should submit himself to the particular treatment or not. The doctor must disclose (*a*) nature and procedure of treatment and its purpose, benefits and effect, (*b*) alternatives if any available, (*c*) an outline of the substantial risks, and (*d*) adverse consequences of refusing treatment. (*iii*) The consent given only for a diagnostic procedure cannot be considered as consent for therapeutic treatment. Similarly, consent given for a specific treatment procedure will not be valid for conducting some other treatment procedure. The unauthorised additional surgery is necessary only to save the life or preserve the health of the patient and it would be unreasonable to delay such unauthorised procedure until patient regains consciousness and takes a decision. (*iv*) There can be a common consent for diagnostic and operative procedures where they are contemplated. There can also be a common consent for a particular surgical procedure and an additional or further procedure that may become necessary during the course of surgery. (*v*) The nature and extent of information to be furnished by the doctor to the patient to secure the consent need not be of the stringent and high degree mentioned in "Canterbury", but should be of the extent, which is accepted as normal and proper by a body of medical men skilled and experienced in the particular field.

4 Validity of consent To be valid the consent must be real. Once the patient had been informed in broad terms of the

12 *Samira Kohli* v *Dr. Prabha Manchanda* (2008)2 SCC 1; 2008 ACJ 747; AIR 2008 SC 1385; JT 2008(1) SC 399; (2008)1 Scale 442.

nature of the intended treatment and gave his consent, the patient could not say that there had been lack of real consent.[13] Consent is not valid if it is obtained by fraud or misrepresentation as to the nature of the procedure. Consent is also vitiated by undue influence or threat of violence. A consent obtained when the patient is under sedation may be held invalid on the ground that the consent given by the patient is not voluntary.[14] The court of law may test the validity of a consent critically if the doctor stands in a position of authority over the patient, as in the case of a prisoner and prison medical officer.[15] The husband of the patient gave consent to create embryo for implantation into his wife in a fertility clinic. By mistake the clinic used the sperm of another person to create an embryo for implantation. The consent given by the husband of the patient is vitiated by the error of the clinic, as the consent was given on belief that the sperm of the husband will be used for creation of embryo.[16]

The consent for treatment may be vitiated by fraud, coercion or undue influence. While considering the effect of outside influence, the court will take into account the mental condition of the patient and the relationship of the persons who influenced the patient in making the decision. It is held by the Court of Appeal in UK[17] that the threat held out by a nurse in IVF clinic that the IVF treatment of the patient and her husband may be stopped for not giving consent for storage and use of the sperm after the death of the husband was not vitiated by undue influence.

It is now well-settled that a consent which is not properly informed, is not a real consent. An apparent consent may be

13 *Chatterton* v *Gerson* (1980)1 BMLR 80; [1981]1 All ER 257; [1981] QB 432; [1981]3 WLR 1003.

14 *Kelly* v *Hazlett* (1976)75 DLR (3d) 536.

15 *Freeman* v *Home Office* [1984] QB 524; [1983]3 All ER 589; [1984]2 WLR 130; 127 Sol Jo 825 affirmed [1984]1 All ER 1036; [1984]2 WLR 802; 128 Sol Jo 298 (CA).

16 *Leeds Teaching Hospitals NHS Trust* v *A.* [2003] EWHC 259 (QB); [2003] Lloyd's Rep Med 151; [2003]1 FLR 1091.

17 *Mrs. U.* v *Centre for Reproductive Medicine* [2002] EWCA Civ 565; [2002] Lloyd's Rep Med 259.

vitiated due to failure of the doctor to make proper disclosure of risks inherent in the procedure consented to. There is no obligation on the doctor to canvass with the patient anything other than the inherent implications of the particular operation he intends to carry out. Once the patient had been informed in broad terms of the nature of intended treatment and had given his consent, the patient could not say that there had been a lack of real consent.[18] The legality of what the doctor ought or ought not to tell his patient about the risks of the proposed procedure of treatment, will be judged by the tenets of accepted professional practice. Failure to make adequate disclosure of the proposed risks should not be the ground to hold the doctor liable for committing unlawful battery. Bristow, J[19] dictates, "when the claim is based on negligence the plaintiff must prove not only the breach of duty to inform but also that she would not have chosen to undergo the operation had the duty not been broken". This principle has been consistently followed in later cases[20] where the doctor may be held liable to pay damages for negligence if he did not make adequate disclosure and the patient satisfies the court that he has suffered harm as a consequence of non-disclosure of risks of proposed treatment.

The hospital obtained signature of the patient and her son on blank consent form without filling up necessary blanks and without striking off the unwanted columns for critical and delicate surgery. There was no negligence during surgery, but the National Commission[1] held that obtaining of consent for surgery was improper and defective and for which cost of ₹50,000 was imposed on the hospital. The National

18 *Chatterton* v *Gerson* (1980)1 BMLR 80; [1981]1 All ER 257; [1981] QB 432; [1981]3 WLR 1003; 124 Sol Jo 885 (QBD).

19 *Chatterton* v *Gerson* (1980)1 BMLR 80; [1981]1 All ER 257; [1981] QB 432; [1981]3 WLR 1003; 124 Sol Jo 885 (QBD).

20 *Sidaway* v *Bethlem Royal Hospital Governors* [1984] QB 493; [1984]1 All ER 1018; [1984]2 WLR 778; 128 Sol Jo 301 (CA) affirmed [1985] AC 871; [1985]1 All ER 643; [1985]2 WLR 480; 129 Sol Jo 154; 1 BMLR 132 (HL).

1 *Vimhans Hospital* v *Anand Kumar Jha* III(2015) CPJ 316 (NCDRC).

Commission[2] also held that the consent given by the relative of the deceased patient for delivery of the child at the time of admission in the hospital, cannot be construed as consent for tubectomy operation of the patient after two days of her admission. The consent of the patient was not obtained for undertaking invasive procedure by inserting central venous line under general anaesthesia by the doctors, who were not found to be negligent for conducting the procedure. The State Commission directed the hospital to pay compensation of ₹7 lakh for conducting invasive procedure without obtaining informed consent of the patient which was upheld by the National Commission.[3]

The patient had undergone dilation and evacuation operation for termination of 13 week's pregnancy. The surgeon who conducted the operation, removed uterus of the patient to save her life, as she was suffering from excessive bleeding per vagina. On the allegation of removal of uterus by emergency hysterectomy without consent, it is held by the State Commission that the doctor had obtained opinion of two senior consultants of the field on the need of emergency hysterectomy. According to the surgeon, the written consent was obtained, but the document was lost. To substantiate the claim of loss of paper, the surgeon informed the police, and the police conducted investigation and recorded the statement of the patient and her husband, wherein they admitted to have given their consent. The State Commission,[4] Gujarat, believed the version of the surgeon that the consent was obtained before emergency hysterectomy.

The patient gave consent for diagnostic operative laparoscopy with contingent for laparotomy, if needed. The gynaecologist obtained the consent of the mother in the midst of operation and removed the uterus, ovaries and fallopian

2 *G. Rajendra* v *City Hospital* III(2014) CPJ 598 (NCDRC).

3 *Sitaram Bhartia Institute of Science and Research* v *Vidya Bhushan Jain* 2017(3) CLT 17; 2017(4) Andh LD 19; II(2017) CPJ 580; 2017(2) CPR 609 (NCDRC).

4 *Mrs. Manjulaben Vinodbhai Patel* v *Dr. Harshida K. Patel* 1997(3) CPR 264 (Guj); II(1998) CPJ 660 (Guj); 1999 CTJ 257 (CP) (SCDRC).

tubes of an unmarried woman of 44 years of age on the ground that the patient was suffering from endometriosis. It is held by the Supreme Court of India[5] that the consent for diagnostic operative laparoscopy and laparatomy if needed, does not amount to consent for AH-BSO surgery for removal of uterus, ovaries and fallopian tubes. The Supreme Court also held that the consent of the mother of an adult patient for performing hysterectomy would not be considered as valid consent for hysterectomy and salpingo-oophorectomy when there was no emergency and the matter was still at the stage of investigation.

A young lady suffering from cancer gave consent for preservation of her eggs, so that embryo can be created with anonymous donor sperm and implant the same in her mother's womb for having a child after her death, but did not fill up all the forms before Human Fertilization and Embryology Authority (HFEA). The eggs were not provided by HFEA for creation of embryo after the death of the lady. The Court of Appeal in UK[6] held that HFEA was not justified in refusing consent to provide donor's eggs for creation of embryo for giving birth to a child by the mother of the lady, when there was enough evidence to indicate the will of the donor.

The Queen's Bench of UK[7] did not hold the surgeon liable in negligence in carrying out total pelvic clearance without consent of the patient, as the surgeon explained to the patient and her mother that the standard treatment for ovarian cancer was total pelvic clearance and the patient was aware that her reproductive organs would be removed if the cancer had spread. However, one cosmetic surgeon was held negligent by the Queen's Bench Division[8] for not conveying her intention as to the full nature and extent of breast

5 *Samira Kohli* v *Dr. Prabha Manchanda* (2008)2 SCC 1; AIR 2008 SC 1385; 2008 ACJ 747; JT 2008(1) SC 399; (2008)1 Scale 442.

6 *R. (M)* v *HFEA* [2017]3 All ER 77; [2016] EWCA Civ 611.

7 *Abbas* v *Kenney* 31 BMLR 157 (QBD); [1996]7 Med LR 47.

8 *Williamson* v *East London and City Health Authority* 41 BMLR 85 (QBD).

augmentation surgery with sufficient clarity before obtaining consent of the patient, although the operation to remove most of the breast tissue and underlying muscle was necessary to resist the adverse effect of breast augmentation surgery.

5 Refusal of treatment—consent to The patient has a right to control his own body. The tort of battery protects the interest in bodily security from unwanted physical interference. Any non-conscientious touch which is harmful or offensive to a person's reasonable sense of dignity is actionable. A competent adult is entitled to reject a specific treatment or all treatment or to select an alternative form of treatment even if the decision may entail risk as serious as death and may appear to be mistaken in the eyes of the medical profession or of the community. The doctor cannot disregard a patient's advance instructions, though in an emergency the doctrine of necessity may protect the physician who acts without consent of the patient. The interest of the State in protecting and preserving the lives and health of its citizens may override the individual's right to self-determination in order to eliminate a health threat to the community, but it does not prevent a competent adult from refusing life-preserving medical treatment.[9] The view expressed by the Court of Family Division in England[10] is that the right of an adult of sound mind to self-determination would prevail over any countervailing interest of the State and, as a result, the prison officials, physicians and nursing staff responsible for the care of a prisoner of sound mind, who went on hunger strike could lawfully observe and abide by his refusal to receive nutrition and could lawfully abstain from providing hydration and nutrition, whether by artificial means or otherwise, so long as he retained the capacity to refuse the same.

9 *Malette* v *Shulman et al* (1990)67 DLR (4th) 321 (Ontario Court of Appeal).

10 *Secretary of State for the Home Department* v *Robb* 22 BMLR 43 (Fam D); [1995] Fam 127; [1995]1 All ER 677; [1995]2 WLR 722; [1994] NLJR 1695.

Consent is implicit in the case of a patient who submits to the doctor and the absence of consent must be made out by the person alleging it. When a surgeon or medical man advances a plea that the patient did not give his consent for the surgery or the course of treatment advised by him, the burden is on him to prove that the non-performance of the surgery or the non-administration of the treatment was on account of the refusal of the patient to give consent thereto.[11]

One young woman suffering from incurable paralyzing neurological disorder, could breathe only with the assistance of a respirator. She commenced an action for an injunction against the hospital to establish her right to refuse further treatment. The Quebec Supreme Court[12] granted injunction with direction to the physician to cease treatment with the respirator at a time chosen by the patient. It was held by the House of Lords[13] that a doctor could lawfully withdraw life-prolonging medical treatment and care from an insensate patient with no hope of recovery, provided that it was in the best interest of the patient not to prolong life and that such a course of action was in accordance with a responsible and competent body of medical opinion.

A woman suffered severe brain damage in a car accident. When the woman had virtually no chance of regaining her mental faculties, the parents of the woman asked the hospital authority to terminate the artificial nutrition and hydration procedures. The hospital authority refused to honour the request without court approval. The Missouri trial court directed the hospital authority to cause the parent's request to be carried out. On appeal, the Supreme Court of Missouri, reversed the decision of the trial court by holding (*i*) that although the woman was in "persistent vegetative state", she was neither dead, nor terminally ill; (*ii*) that the woman's

11 *Dr. T.T. Thomas* v *Elisa* AIR 1987 Ker 52; 1987(1) ACJ 192; 1987(1) ACC 461; 1986 Ker LT 1026; (1987)2 TAC 50.

12 *Nancy B.* v *Hotel-Dieu de Quebec et al* (1992)86 DLR (4th) 385; 15 BMLR 95.

13 *Airedale NHS Trust* v *Bland* [1993]1 All ER 821 affirmed by House of Lords (1993)12 BMLR 64 (HL).

right to refuse treatment—whether such right proceeded from a constitutional right of privacy or a common law right to refuse treatment—did not outweigh Missouri's strong policy favouring the preservation of life; (*iii*) that the woman's conversation with her housemaid was unreliable for the purpose of determining her intent, and thus insufficient to support the parents' claim to exercise substituted judgment on the woman's behalf, and that (*iv*) no person could assume the choice of terminating medical treatment for an incompetent person in the absence of clear, convincing and inherently reliable evidence, which was absent in the case at hand. The US Supreme Court[14] confirmed the decision of the Supreme Court of Missouri.

The question arose before the Ontario Court of Appeal in Canada[15] as to whether or not the medical test will continue for withholding of consent by the patient in the midst of an angiogram. It was held that the burden of decision as to whether to commence the test was properly placed on the patient, but, once initiated, the analysis of risks inherent in proceedings, as opposed to terminating the test, became a matter of medical judgment. The doctor is not duty-bound to stop the medical test for withholding of consent by the patient before completion of the test.

A lady with 36 weeks pregnancy, was suffering from pre-eclampsia and so she was advised of the need of bed rest with an induced delivery. She rejected the advice after knowing the risk of her life and the life of her unborn child. The lady was shifted to a hospital against her will and the court granted a declaration dispensing with the lady's consent to caesarian section. The hospital carried out a caesarian section and the lady delivered a baby girl. On appeal against the order of the trial court it is held that an adult of sound mind is entitled to refuse medical treatment, even when his or her own life depended on receiving medical treatment.[16]

14 *Nancy Beth Cruzan* v *Director, Missouri Department of Health* (1990)497 US 261; (1989)111 L Ed 2d 224; 110 Sct 2841.

15 *Ciarlariello et al* v *Schacter et al* (1991)76 DLR (4th) 449.

16 *St. George's Healthcare N.H.S. Trust* v *S*. [1998]3 WLR 936 (CA); [1998]3 All ER 673 (CA); 44 BMLR 160 (CA); [1999] Fam 26.

A 30-year-old woman was admitted to the hospital with ruptured membrances, having begun spontaneous labour with her third pregnancy. The child was in a position of "transverse lie" and there was risk of rupture of uterus if a caesarean section was not performed as a matter of urgency. The woman supported by her husband refused to undergo caesarean operation on religious ground. It was held that the operation of caesarean section and necessary consequential treatment which the doctor proposed to perform on the patient in the hospital was in the vital interest of the patient and the unborn child and could lawfully be performed despite the patient's refusal to give her consent.[17] Lord Donaldson[18] gave guidance to the hospital authorities and to the medical profession in situations involving a refusal to consent to treatment in the following way:

> "A patient's interest consists of his right to self-determination. Society's interest is in upholding the concept that human life is sacred and should be preserved if possible. In a situation where these two interests conflict, the right of the individual is paramount. But where there is doubt, the doubt falls to be resolved in favour of the preservation of life."

6 Duty of court The doctrine of informed consent to therapeutic medical treatment is developing in England, while in American medical law it is the most controversial issue for last two decades. In Canada, Linden, J,[19] observed as follows:

> "The exercise of defining the scope of the duty of disclosure is now a complex one for the court, requiring much time, effort, thought and evidence. The cooperation of the medical profession will be vital to the task. The courts will, as always, move very cautiously in this area. In most cases, the courts will probably accept as

17 *Re, S (*adult: refusal of medical treatment) (1992)9 BMLR 69; [1992]4 All ER 671.

18 *Re, T.* (adult: refusal of medical treatment) (1992)9 BMLR 46 (CA); [1992]4 All ER 649.

19 *White* v *Turner* (1981)120 DLR (3d) 269.

reasonable the customary practices of the profession as to disclosure, since they are, after all, based on experience, common sense, and what doctors perceive their patients wish to know."

The Canadian Courts[20] are of the view that the onus of proving informed consent rests with the defendant. On the other hand, the view of the courts in UK[1] is that the burden of proof of lack of real consent for failure to disclose risks of treatment lies with the plaintiff. However, the court has jurisdiction at common law to authorise the use of reasonable force in medical procedures where there was a necessity to act. The court can grant permission to the doctor to deliver foetus by forceps or by caesarian section, even when the patient refuses to give consent for delivery by those means.[2] It is held by UK Supreme Court[3] that the court has the power to take decision on behalf of the person suffering from mental illness or disability, as the said person is unable to take decision in his best interest.

Consent is rendered invalid in cases where there was misrepresentation of the surgery or treatment for which consent was elicited and a different surgical procedure or treatment was carried out. The doctor cannot remove patient's left testicle, when consent is given to operation to cure hernia.[4] The allegation that the surgeon removed the left testicle along with its blood vessel without consent during operation of left inguinal hernia of the patient was not believed by the State Commission, Gujarat.[5] A patient suffering from an injured knee, gave consent to general treatment for it. The doctor being afraid of serious infection

20 *Videto* v *Kennedy* (1980)107 DLR (3d) 612 on appeal (1981)125 DLR (3d) 127 (CA).

1 *Chatterton* v *Gerson* [1981] QB 432; [1981]1 All ER 257; [1981]3 WLR 1003; 124 Sol Jo 885; (1980)1 BMLR 80.

2 *Norfolk and Norwich Health Care (NHS) Trust* v *W.* 34 BMLR 16 (Fam D).

3 *N* v *A Clinical Commissioning Group* [2017]3 All ER 719; [2017] UK SC 22.

4 *Marshall* v *Curry* [1993]3 DLR 260.

5 *Harjivanbhai Khodabhai Gohil* v *Dr. Yogendra D. Shah* 1997(3) CPR 517 (Guj).

resulting fatal results, decided to use a drug with side-effects without obtaining specific consent of the patient, and without carrying out the recommended tests in order to discover the side-effects of the drug. The doctor was held to be negligent in failing to carry out the recommended tests to discover the side-effects of the drug, but he having obtained incipient consent to general treatment, was not liable for exercising his discretion to use the drug. A doctor, thus, may be liable in negligence if he fails to follow proper professional standard of care when obtaining his patient's consent.[6] The colonoscopic procedure was undertaken by the doctor without apprising the patient of the risks and benefits of the procedure. The National Commission[7] held the hospital and the doctor liable for deficiency in service by conducting colonoscopy procedure on the patient without obtaining valid consent and awarded compensation of ₹10 lakh in favour of the patient.

A child who is a ward of court should be treated medically in exactly the same way as one who is not, the only difference being that the doctors will be looking to the court rather than the parents for any necessary consent. In deciding in any given case what is in the best interests of a ward, the court must adopt the same attitude as the responsible parent would do in the case of his or her child.[8]

The allegation that the patient was not informed of the chances of impairment of vocal cord due to surgery, was negated from the detailed written consent of the patient.[9] Similarly, the allegation that the uterus was removed without consent during surgery for removal of lump in the left breast was turned down, as the patient and her husband gave written consent for removal of uterus and lump in the left

6 *Male* v *Hopmans* (1965) 54 DLR (2d) 592 on appeal (1967)64 DLR (2d) 105 (CA).

7 *Manmohan Kaur* v *Fortis Hospital* 2018(4) CPR 121; I(2019) CPJ 175 (NCDRC).

8 *Re, J* (a minor) (wardship: Medical treatment) 6 BMLR 25 (CA).

9 *C. Anjani Kumar* v *Madras Medical Mission* 1998(2) CPR 308 (Chennai); I(1998) CPJ 533 (Chennai); 1998 CTJ 504 (CP) (SCDRC); 1999 CCJ 915 (TN).

breast.[10] However, merely signing the consent form does not exclude doctor's responsibility if he is negligent in carrying out his duties.[11]

It is held by the Court of Family Division in UK[12] that where the patient has been suffering from incurable disease without having any recognised effective treatment for prolonging life and arresting deterioration, the court should grant permission to the patient for giving consent to undergo experimental treatment with unknown benefits and risks, but without significant risks of increased suffering and with some chances of benefit to the patient.

7 **Treatment of children** Section 3 of the Indian Majority Act 1875, speaks of attainment of majority on completion of the age of 18 years. A person who has not completed the age of 18 years is a minor.[13] The intention of the legislature to be gathered from s. 3 of the Indian Majority Act 1875 is to extend the age of minority upto 21 years when the minor's person or property was in the hands of the guardian before attaining the age of 18 years by the minor.

In England, s. 8(1) of the Family Law Reform Act 1969 provides that the consent of a minor who has attained the age of sixteen to any surgical, medical or dental treatment which, in the absence of consent would constitute a trespass to his person, shall be as effective as it would be if he was of full age, and where a minor has by virtue of this section given an effective consent to any treatment, it shall not be necessary to obtain any consent to it from his parent or guardian. There is no analogous provision of law in India.

10 *Lakshmi Rajan* v *Malar Hospitals Ltd.* 1999 CCJ 221; 1997(3) CPR 90 (Chennai).

11 *Rajan S. Parab* v *Dr. Kalpana Desai* 1998(3) CPR 398 (Mumbai); *Nirmala R. Parab* v *Dr. Kalpana Desai* III(1998) CPJ 66, 527, 692 (Mumbai); 1998 CTJ 807 (CP) (SCDRC); 1999 CCJ 1296 (Mah).

12 *Simms* v *Simms* [2003] All ER 669; [2002] EWHC 2734 (Fam).

13 Section 4(1) of the Guardians and Wards Act 1890; s. 4(*a*) of the Hindu Minority and Guardianship Act 1956; s. 348 of the *Principles of Mohammedan Law* by D.F. Mulla 19th Ed. 1990, Reprint 2000.

However, under the common law the natural guardian[14] has power to do all acts which are necessary or reasonable and proper for the benefit of the minor. In the absence of the natural guardian the District Court[15] is authorised to appoint the guardian for the welfare of the minor in accordance with the law to which the minor is subject, and such guardian must look after the health of the minor.[16] The natural guardian and in his absence the guardian appointed by the court has the legal authority to give consent for medical or surgical treatment on behalf of the minor child. The principle is derived from the trite law that the guardian has control over the person, health and education of the ward during his minority.[17]

In India, the pregnancy of a minor or mentally ill woman cannot be terminated except with the consent in writing of her guardian.[18] The unanimous opinion of the House of Lords[19] is that a minor can give a valid consent to medical treatment without the knowledge and consent of the parents, if the minor is capable of sufficient intelligence and power of understanding about the procedure of proposed treatment and the risks which may be entailed. So, a minor can also give valid consent to treatment if he is of such an age and intelligence as to be fully aware of the risks and benefits of the proposed treatment. It is pertinent to point out that a child witness is competent to testify if he is capable of understanding the questions put to him, and giving rational answers to those questions.[20] The natural corollary is that the extent and duration of the parental right to control the

14 Section 6 of the Hindu Minority and Guardianship Act 1956; ss. 352, 356 and 357 of the *Principles of Mahomedan Law* by D.F. Mulla, 19th Ed. 1990, Reprint 2000.

15 Section 4 of the Guardians and Wards Act 1890.

16 Section 24 of the Guardians and Wards Act 1890.

17 Section 24 of the Guardians and Wards Act 1890; s. 8 of the Hindu Minority and Guardianship Act 1956.

18 Section 3(4) of the Medical Termination of Pregnancy Act 1971.

19 *Gillick* v *West Norfolk and Wisbech Area Health Authority* [1986] AC 112; [1985]3 All ER 402; [1985]3 WLR 830; 129 Sol Jo 738; (1985)2 BMLR 11 (HL).

20 Section 118 of the Indian Evidence Act 1872.

minor child depend on the degree of intelligence and understanding of the particular child, not on his fixed age. This capacity to understand is a question of fact to be determined by the court on the basis of evidence adduced during trial.

The court exercising wardship jurisdiction may assume the common law right of the parents and give consent to treatment for the benefit and welfare of the minor. It is held by the Court of Appeal in U.K.[1] that no minor of whatever age has power by refusing consent to treatment to override a consent to treatment by someone who has parental responsibility for the minor and a fortiori consent by the court. Lord Templeman[2] is of the view that sterilization of a minor girl should be carried out with the consent of the court exercising wardship jurisdiction: a doctor performing a sterilization operation with the consent of the parents alone may still be liable in criminal, civil or disciplinary proceedings. The paramount consideration for the exercise of the wardship jurisdiction was the welfare and best interest of the ward in question and accordingly where it was for the welfare and in the best interests of the ward that he or she be sterilised, the court had jurisdiction to authorise the operation.[3] A 15-year-old boy suffering from leukaemia required blood transfusion as a life saving measure. As devout Jehovah's witnesses, the parents of the boy refused consent to blood transfusion. The court under wardship jurisdiction granted leave to the hospital authority to carry out the treatment by overriding the decision of the parents.[4]

A child was born with a life threatening liver defect. The paediatricians expressed the view that the child would be likely to have many years of normal life by liver transplant. The mother refused to give her consent to the operation.

1 *Re, W* (a minor: medical treatment) [1992]4 All ER 627 (CA).
2 *Re, B* (a minor) (wardship: sterilization) [1988] AC 199; [1987]2 All ER 206; (1987)2 BMLR 126 (HL); [1987]2 WLR 1213; 131 Sol Jo 625 (HL).
3 *Re, B* (a minor) (wardship: sterilization) (1987)2 BMLR 126 (HL).
4 *Re, E* (a minor) (1990)9 BMLR 1 (FD); *Devon County Council* v *S* (1992)11 BMLR 105 (FD).

Under wardship jurisdiction the judge granted permission for the operation in the best interest of the child. By reversing the decision it is held by the Court of Appeal[5] that the welfare of the child depended on the mother, who would be expected to care for him through surgery and for many years after, her views were relevant and the trial judge had erred in deciding that mother's decision was unreasonable in the light of the unchallenged clinical opinion in favour of the operation.

8 Treatment of mentally ill persons Any person who needs mental health care due to suffering from mental illness may be called a mentally ill person. "Mental illness" means "a substantial disorder of thinking, mood, perception, orientation or memory that grossly impairs judgment, behaviour, capacity to recognise reality or ability to meet the ordinary demands of life, mental conditions associated with the abuse of alcohol and drugs, but does not include mental retardation which is a condition of arrested or incomplete development of mind of a person, specially characterised by sub-normality of intelligence."[6] Any person whose ability to comprehend ordinary things and reality of life or whose judgment and behaviour are impaired due to various aspects of mental disorder, but the suffering is not due to mental retardation has right to access mental health care and treatment or mental health services run by the appropriate Government.[7] The person suffering from mental illness has the right to confidentiality in respect of his mental health, mental health care and treatment and physical health care.[8] Such person has the right to access to medical records, except when the mental health professional in charge of the record would like to withhold specific information in the record on the ground that the disclosure of the information may cause serious mental harm to the person or that there is likelihood of causing harm to other persons by disclosure of the

5 *Re, T.* (a minor) (wardship: Medical treatment) [1997]1 All ER 906 (CA); [1997]1 WLR 242 (CA); (1996)35 BMLR 63 (CA); 1996 NLJR 1577; 140 Sol Jo LB 237 (CA).

6 Section 2(s) of the Mental Health Care Act 2017.

7 Section 18 of the Mental Health Care Act 2017.

8 Section 23 of the Mental Health Care Act 2017.

information. However, if any information is withheld from the record of medical treatment by the mental health care professional, he has the duty to inform the mentally ill person to apply to the concerned Board constituted under the Mental Health Care Act 2017 for release of such information.[9]

It is held by the Court of Appeal in UK[10] that where a mentally ill person refused to eat and the doctor gave treatment in the form of forced tube feeding to alleviate the symptoms of mental disorder, as feeding by nasogastic tube constitutes medical treatment. McCullough, J[11] declared unlawful the treatment given by the psychiatrist in good faith, but without consent of the patient suffering from chronic schizophrenia. It is observed that in the absence of clear statutory authority to the contrary no one is to be detained in a hospital, or to undergo medical treatment, or to be submitted to medical examination without his consent—this is as true of a mentally disordered person as any one else. So, the medical treatment of patients suffering from mental disorder is governed by the normal rules of consent. These rules serve to prevent the doctor from giving treatment against the will of the patients suffering from mental illness, but the medical practitioners may be in a predicament where the patient is incapable of understanding the nature of the procedure of proposed treatment. The House of Lords[12] considered what is the legal basis on which a doctor or surgeon may lawfully treat someone who is unconscious or mentally ill to give a valid consent when surrogate decision maker is not available. At common law, a doctor can lawfully operate on or give other treatment to adult patients who are incapable of consenting to his doing so, provided that the operation or treatment is in the best interest of such patients. The operation or the treatment will be in their best interests

9 Section 25 of the Mental Health Care Act 2017.

10 *B.* v *Croydon Health Authority* [1995]1 All ER 863 (CA).

11 *R.* v *Hallstrom, ex parte W* [1986] QB 1090; [1986]2 All ER 306; [1986]2 WLR 883; 130 Sol Jo 204; 2 BMLR 54 (CA).

12 *F.* v *West Berkshire Health Authority* [1989]2 All ER 545; [1989]2 WLR 1025; 133 Sol Jo 785; (1989)4 BMLR 1 (HL).

only if it is carried out in order either to save their lives or to ensure improvement or prevent deterioration in their physical or mental health. In a case decided by the Court of Family Division,[13] the patient's sister needed bone marrow transplant. The patient was the most suitable donor, but unable to give consent to operation due to mental disorder. There was medical evidence in favour of bone marrow transplantation from the patient and as such the court granted permission in the best interest of the patient and her family. When impairment of mind prevents a patient from weighing information relevant for appropriate course of treatment, it is lawful for the doctor to take necessary, reasonable and appropriate measures in the best interest of the patient.[14]

A 19 years' old woman suffering from severe mental handicap became pregnant, and her medical advisers recommended termination of her pregnancy and sterilization. The judge granted the declaration sought for relying on the principle that in these exceptional circumstances where there is no provision in law for consent to be given and therefore there is no one who can give consent, and where the patient is suffering from such mental abnormality as never to be able to give such consent, a medical adviser is justified in taking such steps as good medical practice demands.[15] Where there are no two opinions about the course of treatment, the approval of the court should not be a condition precedent to carry out termination of pregnancy of a severely mentally handicapped patient.[16]

The mother of a 29 year old mentally retarded woman was distressed by her menstrual periods. The mother of the woman moved the court for declaration that it would be lawful to perform an operation of hysterectomy or

13 *In re, Y* (mental patient: Bone Marrow Donation) [1997] Fam 110; [1997]2 WLR 556; 35 BMLR 111 (Fam D); [1997] Fam Law 91.

14 *Mental Health Trust* v *D.D.* [2014] EWCOP 11; [2015]1 FLR 1430; (2014)140 BMLR 118.

15 *T.* v *T.* [1988]1 All ER 613; [1988]2 WLR 189; 131 Sol Jo 1286.

16 *Re, S.G.* (a patient) (1990)6 BMLR 95 (FD).

sterilization. The doctors were in favour of insertion of contraceptive coil which would not only prevent pregnancy but would reduce the patient's menstrual flow. On consideration of merits and demerits of both sides the trial judge held that hysterectomy might lawfully be performed on the patient. The order of the trial judge was set aside by the Court of Appeal which declared in favour of insertion of contraceptive coil in the best interest of the patient.[17]

9 Emergency treatment A doctor can lawfully operate on or give other treatment to adult patients who are incapable of consenting to his doing so, provided that the operation or treatment is in the best interest of such patients. The operation or treatment will be in their best interests only if it is carried out in order either to save their lives or to ensure improvement or prevent deterioration in their physical or mental health.[18] It is clear that in cases of emergency or unconsciousness all considerations regarding consent will be set aside and doctors will do whatever is necessary to save the life of a patient-infant or adult, to save him from permanent disability or from unnecessary pain and suffering. Accordingly, in life-threatening situations, doctors would not be required to consult with parents of minor patient, though in normal course of events they would be required to make consultation and consider any reasonable alternative to the proposed treatment.[19]

The Nova Scotia Supreme Court[20] has settled the law by stating that in the ordinary case where there is an opportunity to obtain the consent of the patient, consent must be obtained. If there is no consent—express or implied, and the conditions which have been discovered make it imperative on the part of the surgeon to operate, then he will be entitled to act without consent. Scott, J[1] observes

17 *In re, S* (Adult patient: Sterilization) [2000]3 WLR 1288 (CA).

18 *F.* v *West Berkshire Health Authority* [1989]2 All ER 545; [1989]2 WLR 1025; 133 Sol Jo 785; (1989)4 BMLR 1 (HL).

19 *Re, R* (minor) 15 BMLR 72 (FD).

20 *Marshall* v *Curry* (1993)3 DLR 260.

1 *Pratt* v *Davis* Ill 300 (1906).

that when emergency arises and a surgeon finds that some action must be taken immediately for the preservation of the life or health of the patient, it is impracticable to obtain the consent of the ailing or injured one or anyone authorised to speak for him. In such cases it is the duty of the surgeon to perform such operation as good surgery demands, without such consent. The principle of law enunciated by the courts in America[2] is that the discretion to be exercised by the physician for welfare of his patient in a case of emergency should not be interfered with. If a person is injured to the extent of rendering him unconscious and his injuries require prompt surgical attention, a medical man called to attend him will be justified in applying such medical or surgical treatment as may reasonably be necessary for the preservation of his life or limb, and the consent on the part of the patient will be implied in such circumstances. The upshot of the above discussion is that the doctor has authority to give such treatment as is necessary for the best interest of the patient in an emergency without his consent, whether this authority is based on the principles of "implied consent" or "agency of necessity". According to the National Commission,[3] when the patient suffered crush injuries on his leg and was in a state of shock, consent for surgical intervention taken from the persons who accompanied the patient in emergent situation to save the life of the patient, was valid.

10 Life support treatment The Supreme Court of India[4] upheld the constitutional validity of abetment to commit suicide by observing that the right to live with human dignity cannot be construed to include within its ambit the right to terminate natural life. However, the issue of euthanasia was subsequently considered by the Supreme Court,[5] when the court was called upon to decide whether sixty-year old staff

2 *Mohr* v *Williams* 95 Minn 261 (1905).

3 *Ram Gopal Yadav* v *Dr. Pushkar Anand* 2015(2) CLT 310; 2015(2) CPR 571 (NCDRC).

4 *Gian Kaur* v *State of Punjab* (1996)2 SCC 648; 1996 SCC (Cri) 374.

5 *Aruna Ramachandra Shanbaug* v *Union of India* (2011)4 SCC 454; (2011)2 SCC (Cri) 294.

nurse of a private hospital in Mumbai who was in persistent vegetative state (PVS) for last 37 years should be subjected to passive euthanasia by denying her food and nursing aid. By negating the claim of the next friend of the patient for granting permission to allow her to die it is held by the Supreme Court that passive euthanasia is permissible under certain situations. The law laid down for withdrawal of life support treatment in *Aruna Ramachandra Shanbaug*[6] is as follows: (*i*) A decision has to be taken to discontinue life support either by the parents or the spouse or other close relatives, or in the absence of any of them, such a decision can be taken even by a person or a body of persons acting as a next friend. It can also be taken by the doctors attending the patient. (*ii*) The decision requires approval from the High Court even if the decision is taken by the near relative or doctor or next friend of the terminally ill patient.

The five Judge Constitution Bench of the Supreme Court[7] enumerated the concept of active euthanasia and passive euthanasia and unanimously held that passive euthanasia is permissible and "Advance Directive" of the terminally ill patient unable to give consent for withholding or withdrawing life prolonging medical treatment can be executed for ending natural life with dignity. Even passive euthanasia has been categorised into (*a*) voluntary passive euthanasia, and (*b*) non-voluntary passive euthanasia. The voluntary passive euthanasia has been described as a situation where a person who is capable of deciding for himself decides to die for various reasons, whereas non-voluntary passive euthanasia has been construed to mean that a person is not in a position to decide for himself, e.g. when he is in persistent vegetative state (PVS). The procedure of execution of Advance Medical Directive for withdrawal of life support treatment to expedite the process of natural death of terminally ill patient or patients of permanent vegetative state (PVS) is laid down in

6 (2011)4 SCC 454; (2011)2 SCC (Cri) 294.

7 *Common Cause* v *Union of India* (2018)5 SCC 1; AIR 2018 SC 1665.

Common Cause.[8] Even the procedure for review or revocation of such Advance Medical Directive has been laid down by the Supreme Court.[9]

The hospital sought for declaration for withdrawing artificial nutrition and hydration from two patients in a permanent vegetative state. The issue for consideration was whether discontinuance of such nutrition and hydration would contravene the right to life in Art. 2 of the European Convention for Protection of Human Rights and Fundamental Freedoms (as set out in Schedule 1 to the Human Rights Act 1998). The Family Division of UK[10] held that it was lawful for the hospital to withdrew artificial nutrition and hydration from the patient suffering from permanent vegetative state in the best interest of the patient. It is also held that where a responsible clinical decision was made to withhold treatment on the ground that it was not in the best interest of the patient and that clinical decision was made in accordance with a respectable body of medical opinion, the State's positive obligation for protection of dignity of life is discharged.

8 *Common Cause* v *Union of India* (2018)5 SCC 1; AIR 2018 SC 1665.
9 *Supra.*
10 *NHS Trust A.* v *M.* [2001]1 All ER 801.

CHAPTER

5

Limitation of Action

1 Limitation—object of A statute of limitation does not confer a right of action on the defendant; it is enacted to restrict the period within which the plaintiff must assert his right. The expiry of the period of limitation does not extinguish the right of the plaintiff, but it bars his remedy. The existence of time-limit helps to expedite the commencement of legal action. Similarly, brevity of time-limit may lead to denial of justice where the claim was barred by statute before the plaintiff could realise about his right.

2 Limitation—provisions of statute

(i) ***Tortious claim*** The Limitation Act 1963 contains no provision specific to actions for negligence as tort, though Arts. 72 to 91 enshrined in Part VII of the Schedule annexed to the said Act deal with suits relating to torts. In the absence of any specific provision in the Limitation Act 1963, an action for damages based on medical negligence will be governed by Art. 113 of the said Act.

It is held by Calcutta,[1] Allahabad[2] and Bombay[3] High Courts that Art. 36 of the Limitation Act 1908 (since repealed

1 *Jadu Nath* v *Hari Kar* 36 Cal 141; *Pannalal* v *Adjai Coal Co. Ltd.* 31 CWN 92; *Surat* v *Umar* 22 Cal 877.

2 *Ram Narain* v *Umrao* 29 All 615; *Kripa Ram* v *Kunwar Bahadur* AIR 1932 All 256.

3 *Esso* v *Steamship "Savitri"* 11 Bom 133.

by the Limitation Act 1963) is a general or residuary Article governing suits for compensation founded on torts to which no specific Article applies. Article 113 of the Limitation Act 1963 has replaced Art. 36 of the Limitation Act 1908. Naturally a suit for damage based on medical negligence must be instituted within three years from the date when the right to sue accrues as per provision of Art. 113 of the Limitation Act 1963. The right to sue accrues only when a cause of action arises.

Lord Diplock[4] has defined the "cause of action" as simply a factual situation the existence of which entitles one person to obtain from the court a remedy against another person. To be precise, the expression means every fact which, if traversed, would be necessary for the plaintiff to prove in order to support his right to the judgment of the court.[5] It is pertinent to point out that damage is an essential element of a tortious cause of action. If a suit is for compensation for any malfeasance or misfeasance, independent of contract, time will run not from the date of malfeasance, but from the time when the injury results.[6] The period of limitation against the State in respect of actions founded on tortious liability is the same as that of actions against private persons.

It goes without saying that the person suffering injury often dies before commencement of any action against the negligent defendant. The legal representatives of the deceased may institute any suit for damage founded on negligence against the defendant within one year from the date of death of the person wronged, as per provision of Art. 81 of Limitation Act 1963.

The legal representatives of the deceased filed suit claiming damages against the doctor after more than three years of death in violation of Arts. 72 and 79 of Limitation Act which prescribe period of limitation of one year and

4 *Letang* v *Cooper* [1964]2 All ER 929; [1965]1 QB 232; [1964]3 WLR 573; 108 Sol Jo 519 (CA).

5 *W.W. Joshi* v *State of Bombay* AIR 1959 Bom 363.

6 *Jagannath* v *Kalidas* AIR 1929 Pat 245; *Kothari & Sons* v *Krishna Rao* AIR 1953 Mad 726.

residuary Art. 113 thereof which provides for a period of limitation of three years. The Panaji Bench of Bombay High Court[7] held that the liability sought to be established against the doctor was essentially based on a tortious act alleged to be committed by him as contemplated in Art. 2361 of the Portuguese Civil Code which is considered as special law under s. 29(1) of the Limitation Act 1963. As the suit was governed under Portuguese Civil Code where the period of limitation is 20 years, the suit was not barred by limitation.

(ii) ***Contractual claim*** A tortious cause of action in negligence differs from one for breach of contract. In contractual liability the cause of action is complete as soon as the contract is broken, even if the plaintiff suffers no loss as a result of the breach. The duty of a doctor to perform a particular act at a particular time may be contractual—the contract being implied between doctor and patient. For example, any adult, sane, pregnant woman or the guardian of a minor or lunatic pregnant woman may contract with any registered medical practitioner for termination of pregnancy as per provisions of s. 3 of the Medical Termination of Pregnancy Act 1971, and hence the liability of the doctor is both contractual and tortious.

An aggrieved party may institute the suit for compensation against the negligent defendant for breach of contract—express or implied—within a period of three years from the date when the breach takes place, as per provision of Article 55 of the Limitation Act 1963. The expression "implied contract" is used in this Article in the sense in which it is understood in English Law. Article 55 is not confined to cases of what would be implied contracts as per definition given in s. 9 of the Indian Contract Act.[8] A suit by the doctor to recover his fees is also governed by Art. 55 of the Limitation Act 1963.[9]

7 *Dr. Sharad Vaidya* v *Paulo Joel Vales* (deceased by LRs.) 1994(2) ACJ 835.

8 *Vairavan* v *Avicha* 38 Mad 275.

9 *Baroda Kant* v *Court of Wards* AIR 1931 All 752.

(iii) ***Consumer claim*** The Consumer Court—District Forum (now District Commission), State Commission or National Commission—shall not admit a complaint, unless it is filed within two years from the date on which the cause of action has arisen.[10]

The cause of action for filing the complainant arose on 21st January 1992 when the patient finally came to know that he had permanently lost his eyesight. The claim of the complainant was not barred by limitation, because the period of limitation for two years prescribed in s. 24A* of the Consumer Protection Act 1986 came into force with effect from 18th June 1993.[11]

The appeal was presented before the State Commission after delay of 46 days. The delay of 46 days in filing the appeal was sought to be explained by the fact that the order of the District Forum was studied at various levels by different persons and in the process delay was caused. By dismissing the application for condonation of delay it is held by the State Commission, Andhra Pradesh,[12] that leisurely deliberation cannot be a ground for condonation of delay. By setting aside the order of the National Commission, the Supreme Court of India dismissed the complaint filed after nine years of the cholecystectomy on the ground that several gauze pieces left in the abdomen during the operation were recovered by way of surgery after lapse of nine years.[13]

3 Limitation—computation of Negligence as a tort is the breach of a legal duty to take care which results in damage, undesired by the defendant, to the plaintiff.[14] Negligence as such is not actionable. "The right to sue accrues"[15] when the

10 Section 24A of the Consumer Protection Act 1986 (now replaced by s. 69 of the Consumer Protection Act 2019 w.e.f. 9.8.2019).

* Replaced by s. 69 of the Consumer Protection Act 2019 w.e.f. 9.8.2019.

11 *Mukunda Lal Ganguly* v *Dr. Abhijit Ghosh* I(1995) CPJ 453 (Cal); III(1995) CPJ 64 (Cal).

12 *Christian Medical Centre* v *A. Shajahan* III(1998) CPJ 242 (Hyderabad); 2000 CCJ 554.

13 *Dr. V.N. Shrikhande* v *Anita Sena Fernandes* AIR 2011 SC 212; 2011(2) SCJ 238; (2011)1 SCC 53; 2011 AIR SCW 6630; 2010(7) SLJ 648; 2013(2) CPR 294.

14 Winfield and Jolowicz on *Tort,* 15th Ed., p. 90.

15 Article 113 of the Limitation Act 1963.

plaintiff suffers damage or specific injury resulting from the negligence of the defendant, and the period of limitation will be computed from the time when the injury results.[16] In other words, the running of the limitation period depends on the accrual of the cause of action,[17] and the cause of action arises at the time when the plaintiff actually suffers the injury. If the effect of negligence on the part of the doctor is patent, the cause of action will be deemed to have arisen on the date when the act of negligence was done. On the other hand, if the effect of negligence is latent, the cause of action will arise on the date when the patient or his representative discovers the injury caused due to such act or the date when the patient or his representative could have by exercise of due diligence discovered the act constituting negligence.[18]

Under the (English) Limitation Act 1980,[19] the date of computation of the period is either from accrual of cause of action or from date of knowledge, but the date of knowledge is not the starting point of limitation in an action for negligence based on torts under the (Indian) Limitation Act 1963.[20] It is well-settled that limitation period can run against a person who does not know, and could not have discovered the existence of damage.[1] It may take time to realise the consequences of defective treatment or the causes of symptoms to be attributed to medical negligence. For example, a patient came to know after three years of operation about the negligent treatment of the doctor who left the patient with the false impression that failure to terminate the pregnancy was due to her physical difficulties.[2] It is held by the Court of Appeal in UK[3] that where a plaintiff expected

16 Section 23 of the Limitation Act 1963.

17 *Letang* v *Cooper* [1965]1 QB 232; [1964]2 All ER 929; [1964]3 WLR 573; 108 Sol Jo 519 (CA).

18 *V.N. Shrikhande (Dr.)* v *Anita Sena Fernandes* AIR 2011 SC 212; (2011)1 SCC 53; IV(2010) CPJ 27 (SC) followed in *S. Ashok (Dr.)* v *K. Shanthi* 2015(4) CPR 401; 2015(4) CLT 368 (NCDRC).

19 Sections 11-14 of the (English) Limitation Act 1980.

20 Article 113 and s. 23 of the Limitation Act 1963.

1 *Pirelli General Cable Works Ltd.* v *Oscar Faber & Partners* [1983]2 AC 1; [1983]1 All ER 65; [1983]2 WLR 6; 127 Sol Jo 16.

2 *Scuriaga* v *Powell* (1979)123 Sol Jo 406.

3 *Forbes* v *Wandsworth Health Authority* [1996]4 All ER 881 (CA).

that an operation would be successful and it was not, with the result that he sustained a major injury, a reasonable man would take advice promptly if he was minded to make a claim, and if he did not, he would be fixed with constructive knowledge of the matter for the purpose of computation of the period of limitation.

The majority of cases of medical negligence are claims for compensation for personal injury. "Personal injury" is defined in s. 2(*c*) of the Personal Injuries (Compensation Insurance) Act 1962 as "physical or mental injury or a disease whether manifesting itself immediately or subsequently". Damages claimed by a male plaintiff for failure of vasectomy would not include damages in respect of personal injury, but compensation claimed by a female plaintiff for failure of vasectomy of her husband or for failure of her own sterilization would include damages for personal injury if she suffered the pain of pregnancy. The female plaintiff will get three years period from the date of pregnancy for commencement of legal action.[4] The period of limitation for filing complaint on the ground of unsuccessful sterilization operation will be counted from the time of knowledge of conception by the spouse.[5]

Computation of the period of limitation in contractual liability will start when the contract is broken. The contractual professional obligation may be of a continuing nature and in these cases the plaintiff can rely on the breach latest in time. For example, failure to advise a private patient of the risk of drinking alcohol during the period of taking some drugs prescribed by general physician is a continuing wrong to be rectified by the doctor by giving proper advice till the termination of contractual relationship. The contracting doctor is under an implied duty to inform the patient party that he has committed a mistake for which

4 *Thake* v *Maurice* [1986] QB 644; [1984]2 All ER 513; [1985]2 WLR 215;129 Sol Jo 86 on appeal [1986] QB 644; [1986]1 All ER 497; [1986]2 WLR 337; 129 Sol Jo 894 (CA).

5 *Walkin* v *South Manchester Health Authority* 25 BMLR 108 (CA); [1995]4 All ER 132; [1995]1 WLR 1543 (CA).

further treatment is necessary.[6] In case of continuing breach of contract or tort, a fresh period of limitation begins to run at every moment of the time during which such breach, or tort, as the case may be, continues.[7] The complainant was under the treatment of the orthopaedician till 1989. Thereafter he suffered a heart attack and consulted other orthopaedician and had undergone surgery in November 1992. The complaint filed in August 1993 was not held to be barred by limitation, as the cause of action continued upto November 1992.[8]

The period of limitation prescribed in the schedule annexed to the Limitation Act 1963, lapses not on the expiry of the definite number of years prescribed therein, but on the expiry of that number of years together with the time which is excluded from the calculation.[9] The day on which the cause of action arose is excluded in computing the period of limitation, but the day on which the action is started is included.[10] The period of service of notice under s. 80 of the Code of Civil Procedure, time required for obtaining sanction of the Government and the period during which the legal action is stayed by the court, will be excluded in computation of the period of limitation.[11] Similarly, time spent for prosecuting the defendant with due diligence and in good faith in a court having no jurisdiction to entertain the suit, will be excluded in counting the period of limitation.[12] The

6 *Naylor* v *Preston Area Health Authority* [1987]2 All ER 353; [1987]1 WLR 958; 131 Sol Jo 596 (CA); *Lee* v *South West Thames Regional Health Authority* [1985]2 All ER 385; [1985]1 WLR 845; 128 Sol Jo 333 (CA).

7 Section 22 of the Limitation Act 1963.

8 *Mohd. Ubaid Siddiqui* v *Dr. Ramesh Kumar Upadhaya* 2000 CTJ 284 (CP) (SCDRC); 2000(1) CPR 77 (Lucknow).

9 *Chheda* v *Baldeo* AIR 1949 All 764; *Dhonessur* v *Ray Gooder* 2 Cal 336 (FB).

10 Section 12(1) of the Limitation Act 1963.

11 Section 15 of the Limitation Act 1963; *Shri Bhagwan* v *Secretary of State* AIR 1939 All 277; *I.S.P. Trading Co.* v *Union of India* AIR 1973 Cal 74.

12 Section 14 of the Limitation Act 1963; *Satyanarayanamurthi* v *Maharaja of Pithapur* AIR 1939 Mad 724; *Shiv Shiv Tewari* v *Ganesh Prasad* AIR 1978 All 117.

prayer to exclude the period spent in pursuing the wrong jurisdiction, *viz*., by filing application under Art. 226 of the Constitution before the High Court instead of preferring appeal before National Commission, in computation of the period of limitation was rejected by the National Commission.[13] Due care is to be exercised when the prescribed period for any suit expires on a day when court is closed because in that case the prescribed period must be extended till the day of reopening of the court.[14] When the patient died of medical negligence on 3rd October 1958 and the suit was instituted on 3rd October 1959, the High Court found the suit to be well within the period of limitation.[15] The insured took overseas medi-claim policy on 10th June 1991. The agent of the Insurance Company refused to make payment in USA on 4th November 1991. The Insurance Company finally disclaimed liability by giving reply on 15th October 1994. The complaint filed on 10th October 1995 was held to be within the period of limitation.[16] Similarly, the complaint filed on 25th June 1998 on the allegation of negligence in carrying out the operation on 26th June 1996, was held well within the period of limitation of two years.[17]

The statute of limitation cannot begin to run in the absence of either the party capable of suing or the party liable to be sued. This well-known maxim is incorporated in s. 16 of the Limitation Act 1963 which relates to the rights of action accruing either simultaneously on death or thereafter of the person suing or sued. The law of limitation will not begin to run where the knowledge of the right on which the suit is founded is concealed by the fraud of the defendant or his agent, and the period of limitation will be computed from

13 *Mumbai Grahak Panchayat* v *Dr. (Mrs.) Rashmi B. Fadnavis* 1996(1) CPR 137 (NC); (1996)4 CTJ 284 (CP) (NCDRC); 1998 CCJ 766 (NC).

14 Section 4 of the Limitation Act 1963; *Maqbul Ahmed* v *Onkar Pratap* AIR 1935 PC 85.

15 *Ram Bihari Lal* v *J.N. Shrivastava* 1985 ACJ 424; AIR 1985 MP 150; 1985 Jab LJ 259; (1985)1 Cur CC 987; 1985 MPLJ 288; 1985 Cur Civ LJ 149.

16 *Iswar Chandra Gangrade* v *New India Assurance Co. Ltd.* II(2000) CPJ 254 (Bhopal).

17 *Jaswinder Singh* v *Dr. J.S. Saini* II(2000) CPJ 262 (Chandigarh).

the time when the plaintiff has discovered the fraud or could have discovered the same with due diligence.[18]

Like a regular suit for compensation on the ground of medical negligence, the period of limitation under Consumer Protection Act will be computed from the date when the cause of action arises.[19] The operation was performed without consent of the patient on 10th December 1990. The patient died on 22nd January 1993 after surgery for removal of cancerous growth in vagina. It was not established from the evidence that the patient died due to negligence in performance of the operation. The cause of action did not continue from the date of operation till the death of the patient. The complaint filed on 12th January 1994 was held to be barred by limitation.[20] However, it is held by the National Commission[1] that the period of limitation for filing complaint before Consumer Forum will start not from the date of the operation, but from the date of discharge of the patient from the hospital. The National Commission also held that the cause of action in a case of medical negligence will continue till the patient or the complainant comes to know about the real injury and the period of limitation will be reckoned from that date.[2]

4 Claim under legal disability It is well settled that the statute of limitation does not run against a person under legal disability, and time will run against him as soon as he ceased to be under disability.[3] The effect of s. 6 of the Limitation Act 1963 is that notwithstanding the expiry of the normal period of limitation, the person under legal disability like minority, insanity or idiocy may bring his claim for tortious or contractual liability within three years from

18 Section 17 of the Limitation Act 1963.

19 Section 24A(1) of the Consumer Protection Act 1986.

20 *Dr. R.N. Sethi* v *Hardial Singh* 2000 CCJ 732 (Chandigarh); I(1999) CPJ 33 (Chandigarh).

1 *Smt. Saroj Chandhoke* v *Sir Ganga Ram Hospital* 2007(3) CPR 209; III(2007) CPJ 189.

2 *Indu Sharma (Dr.)* v *Indraprastha Apollo Hospital* III(2015) CPJ 248; 2015(2) CLT 454 (NCDRC).

3 Section 6 of the Limitation Act 1963.

the date when he ceases to be under the disability. Even the legal representatives of the deceased person suffering injury due to negligence of the defendant will get extension of time for commencement of any legal action during the period of their disability.[4] A child in the womb is also entitled to get the benefit of legal disability.[5] Once time begins to run, no subsequent disability or inability can stop it.[6]

5 Limitation—pleading of The defendant must plead that the action is barred by limitation. This trite principle is recognised in Or. 6, r. 2 of the Code of Civil Procedure wherein it is laid down that every pleading must contain a brief statement of material facts on which the party pleading relies for his defence, though the matter of fact which the law presumes in his favour need not be pleaded.[7] Addition or substitution of new party to a suit which was omitted due to mistake made in good faith, will relate back to the date of institution of the suit.[8] Where the plaintiff consented to biopsy, and not full surgery, the court allowed to add the allegation of assault along with allegation of negligence in performance of surgical operation on the ground that it is difficult to distinguish what happened in the ward and in the operation theatre.[9]

6 Burden of proof The dictum of English law is that if the defendant pleads limitation as a defence, the plaintiff bears the burden of proving that his cause of action arose within the period of limitation.[10] In our country the plaintiff is under an obligation, as a matter of pleading, to show the grounds on which the exemption from limitation is claimed.[11] Lord

4 Section 6 read with s. 16 of the Limitation Act 1963.
5 Section 6 of the Limitation Act 1963.
6 Section 9 of the Limitation Act 1963.
7 Order 6, r. 13 of the Code of Civil Procedure.
8 Section 21 of the Limitation Act 1963.
9 Section 6 of the Limitation Act 1963.
10 Halsbury's *Laws of England*, 4th Ed., vol. 28, paras 648-652; *London Congregational Union Inc.* v *Harris and Harris* [1988]1 All ER 15 (CA); *Cartledge* v *E. Jopling and Sons Ltd.* [1962]1 QB 189; [1961]3 All ER 482 (CA).
11 Order 7, r. 6 of the Code of Civil Procedure.

Parkar[12] has laid down that where the limitation period running from the accrual of the cause of action had lapsed, the onus is on the plaintiff at the first instance to assert and give evidence that he had knowledge of the relevant facts on a date later than the accrual of the cause of action. If the defendant wishes to rebut the same by asserting earlier knowledge, the onus is on the defendant to prove such earlier knowledge.

7 Limitation—discretion to override The court, in exercising its discretion, will give weight to the consideration that action for professional negligence is a serious matter for a medical practitioner, and that such action ought to be dealt with expeditiously.[13] Section 5 of the Limitation Act 1963 confers wide discretion on the court for extension of prescribed period of limitation in certain cases. The words "Suit" and "Plaint" are conspicuously absent from s. 5 of the Limitation Act. As the legislature has omitted to mention the word "Suit" or "Plaint" at the time of enactment of s. 5 of the Limitation Act 1963, the plaintiff cannot invoke the discretion of the court for extension of the period of limitation at the time of institution of the suit. The clear dictum of the Calcutta High Court is that s. 5 of the Limitation Act is not applicable to a suit.[14]

Unlike the plaint the complaint can be admitted by the District Forum, State Commission or National Commission after expiry of limitation, if the complainant makes out sufficient cause for not filing the complaint within two years from the date on which the cause of action has arisen.[15] It may be noted that the words "sufficient cause" and "satisfied" used in s. 24A* of the Consumer Protection Act 1986 are in *pari materia* with the words used in s. 5 of the Limitation Act 1963. Naturally, the principles laid down in s. 5 of the

12 *Fowell* v *National Coal Board* (1986) CILL 294; *The Times*, 28th May 1986 (CA).

13 R.M. Jackson and J.L. Powell, *Professional Negligence*, 2nd Ed., para 1·79.

14 *S.K. Md. Ismail* v *S.K. Anwar Ali* AIR 1991 Cal 391.

15 Section 24A of the Consumer Protection Act 1986 (now replaced by s. 69 of the Consumer Protection Act 2019 w.e.f. 9.8.2019).

* Replaced by s. 69 of the Consumer Protection Act 2019 w.e.f. 9.8.2019.

Limitation Act 1963 can be invoked for condonation of delay in filing a complaint in Consumer Courts. The Consumer Court exercising discretion to condone the delay, must record reasons for condonation of delay. The delay of 28 days in filing appeal before the National Commission was not condoned on the ground that the appellant filed writ petition in the High Court of Bombay on wrong legal advice.[16] The National Commission did not condone the delay of 207 days in preferring revision challenging the order passed by the State Commission due to negligence, deliberate inaction and lack of *bona fide* on the part of the petitioner.[17] The National Commission did not condone delay of 50 days in preferring revision when the delay was attributed to the failure to translate the documents into English in a cosmopolitan city like Delhi.[18]

16 *Mumbai Grahak Panchayat* v *Dr. (Mrs.) Rashmi B. Fadnavis* 1996(1) CPR 137 (NC); (1996)4 CTJ 284 (CP) (NCDRC); 1998 CCJ 766 (NC).

17 *St. Joseph's Hospital* v *P.K. Jimmy* 2012(4) CPR 259.

18 *M. Perumal* v *Salem Poly Clinic Represented by Dr. K.N. Rao* III(2012) CPJ 337; 2013(1) CPR 45.

CHAPTER

6

Common Complaints—Rights and Obligations

1 Anaesthesia[1]

(i) *Disclosure of information* Anaesthesia is a potent source of allegation of negligence. Except the cases of emergency, pre-operative discussion with the patient about the choice of suitable anaesthetic is mandatory. The patients should be informed of the possibility of damage or displacement of loose teeth, crowns and bridge work during anaesthesia. The possibility of postoperative headache should be discussed with the patient pre-operatively during spinal and epidural block. The anaesthetist must take care to avoid regional blocks of all types in patients with neurological disease. It is not only obligatory on the part of the anaesthetist to explain the anaesthetics administered, the technique used, and the pathological investigations recommended, but also to document the same clearly, precisely and accurately in order to repudiate the future allegation of negligence.

(ii) *Vigilance and monitoring* The constant vigilance during anaesthesia falls within the ambit of duty of the anaesthetist. Delegation of duty to inexperienced anaesthetist is not

1 *Anaesthesia*, Professor M. Rosen, MB, FRCOG and Dr. J.N. Horton, MBBS, FC Anaes referred to *Medical Negligence* by Michael J. Powers and Nigel H. Harris, Chapter 27, Edition 1990.

permissible in law. It is the duty of the anaesthetist to check the equipments including gas cylinder and anaesthetic machine prior to operation and to ensure that the equipments will function correctly throughout the period when the patient was dependent on it. The standard of monitoring is to be judged by the tenets of accepted professional practice prevailing in the country.

The anaesthetist is liable for not assessing the patient's condition for anaesthesia in view of blood pressure of 150/100 mm and STT changes in anterolateral leads in ECG and for not ensuring the existence of defibrillator in the operation theatre before starting anaesthesia. It is the duty of the anaesthetist to maintain proper oxygenation, when lack of oxygen may be the cause of cardiac arrest of a patient suffering from hypertension.[2] The anaesthetist was held negligent in adopting a relatively idiosyncratic anaesthetic procedure, reducing the patient's blood pressure to an unacceptably low level for an unacceptably long period, with the result that he suffered anterior spinal artery syndrome.[3] The anaesthetist was held negligent for cardiorespiratory failure of the patient due to administration of heavy dose of anaesthesia within five hours of first examination of the patient and without taking proper precautions.[4]

(iii) ***Accident in intubation*** Intubation of the trachea carried out under general anaesthesia, carries its own risks. By careful and gentle manipulation of the endotracheal tube, the experienced anaesthetist may prevent damage to the soft tissues of the lips, mouth, tongue, pharynx and larynx. Misplacement of the endotracheal tube by itself cannot constitute negligence, but failure to detect and recognise that the tube is misplaced before hypoxic damage occurs is negligence on the part of the anaesthetist. It is obligatory on the part of the anaesthetist to verify the correct placement

2 *Arunaben D. Kothari* v *Navdeep Clinic* 1996(3) CPR 20 (Guj); III(1996) CPJ 605 (Guj); (1997)5 CTJ 533 (CP) (SCDRC); 1998 CCJ 972 (Guj).
3 *Hepworth* v *Kerr* [1995]6 Med LR 139.
4 *Smt. Bhanupal* v *Dr. Prakash Padode* II(2000) CPJ 384 (Bhopal).

of the tube by some means of post-intubation check preferably by auscultation of both sides of the chest. The anaesthetist was held negligent by Andhra Pradesh High Court for removal of endotracheal tube from the mouth of the patient without giving fresh breaths of oxygen and failure to resuscitate the patient with mask and bag or by mouth to mouth ventilation before inserting the tube for the second time, which led to cerebral anoxia and ultimately permanent brain damage of the patient.[5]

Barring emergency intubation the duty of the anaesthetist is to inspect the patient's dentition pre-operatively and to make note of loose teeth, crowns, bridge work, and missing teeth. The displacement of a tooth may be defensible under certain circumstances, but failure to search for and retrieve the missing tooth will be indefensible. The careful use of laryngoscope and the use of plastic protector over the upper anterior teeth in anticipation of difficulty are advisable.

(iv) ***Accident in regional anaesthesia*** Intravenous block may cause severe systemic toxicity if the local anaesthetic agent is allowed to escape in large quantity into the circulation. The result may be convulsions, cardiac depression and even death. It is obligatory on the part of the anaesthetist to ensure that the block carried out is safe, effective and useful. It is pertinent to point out that abscess drainage, small cutaneous tumours, circumcision, some eye and ENT operations can be done under local anaesthesia by the surgeon himself.

The spinal and epidural block are used both for analgesia during surgery and for pain relief in labour. The possibility of headache due to spinal anaesthesia cannot be ruled out, when large-bore needle is used. The anaesthetists must avoid regional blocks of all types in patients with neurological disease.

5 *Dr. P. Narasimha Rao* v *Gundavarapu Jaya Prakash* AIR 1990 AP 207; 1990(1) ACJ 350; (1990)1 ACC 468; (1989)3 Andh LT 564; (1989)2 APLJ (HC) 491.

Meningitis may occur if lumber puncture is carried out without observing a septic precaution.[6] However, negligence was not attributed to the anaesthetist, when an epidural anaesthetic needle had accidentally penetrated the dura and led to a leak of cerebrospinal fluid.[7]

(v) *Brain damage* Failure of oxygen delivery to the brain results in cerebral hypoxia which not only stops the brain machinery, but also wrecks the same. The result of cerebral hypoxia is profound viz. impairment of intellect, permanent disability and at worst death. The anaesthetist was held negligent for causing brain damage to a patient due to faulty method of induction of anaesthetics.[8]

(vi) *Awareness during anaesthesia* There are number of causes for awareness during anaesthesia, e.g. inadequate doses of anaesthetic drug, entrainment of air into the gas mixture and abnormal resistance to anaesthetic agents. The prime duty of the anaesthetist is to administer anaesthesia for unconsciousness and relief of pain. It is difficult to defend the allegation of awareness on the part of the anaesthetist (*a*) where faulty equipments were not detected prior to operation, (*b*) where there was a failure to make constant vigil and minimum monitoring during the period of anaesthesia, (*c*) where there was a failure to keep adequate record of anaesthetic procedure, and (*d*) where there was a failure to adhere to generally accepted clinical practice in the choice of anaesthetic technique. The anaesthetist was held negligent when a woman remained conscious for over an hour under anaesthetic and suffered therefrom enduring nervous shock.[9] To avoid the allegation of awareness during anaesthesia, the anaesthetist is required to keep constant vigil on the following clinical signs: (*a*) the appearance of sweating and lacrimation, (*b*) the reaction of the pupil to

6 *Shrimati Kulwinder Kaur* v *Dr. Kiranpreet Kaur Makkar* II(1997) CPJ 354 (Chandigarh); 1999 CCJ 143 (Punj).

7 *Muzio* v *North West Herts Health Authority* [1995]6 Med LR 184.

8 *Dr. P. Narasimha Rao* v *Gundavarapu Jaya Prakash* AIR 1990 AP 207; 1990(1) ACJ 350; (1990)1 ACC 468; (1989)3 Andh LT 564; (1989)2 APLJ (HC) 491.

9 *Ackers* v *Wigan Health Authority* [1991]2 Med LR 232.

light, and (*c*) a rise in pulse or blood pressure which cannot be accounted for any other physiological event. Negligence was not attributed to the anaesthetist who had followed a procedure that was acceptable at the relevant time and particularly when the awareness arose after the operation at the reversal stage of the anaesthetic.[10]

2 Cardiology[11]

(i) *Disclosure of information* Operations for heart disease are palliative and not curative. Patients must be made aware of the need for continuing medical treatment after surgery. Operations on the heart may be carried out as 'closed' or 'open' procedures. A closed cardiac operation is performed while the heart continues to beat and support the circulation of blood. By open procedure of operation the heart is stopped temporarily and the circulation is supported artificially by means of cardiopulmonary by-pass using a heart lung machine. Prolonged periods of cardiopulmonary by-pass may lead to death. Brain damage is the most significant hazard and complication of open heart surgery. The risks and benefits of the procedures, and the complications of the surgery must be explained to the patients very carefully.

(ii) *Accepted professional practice* The following precautions should be taken to reduce the chances of infection during cardio thoracic surgery: (*a*) the patient should not undergo operation if there is known source of sepsis in the body; (*b*) the patient should take bath with dilute antiseptic solution to remove as many organisms from the skin as possible; and (*c*) antibiotics should be given prophylactically to the patient during the operative period. Failure to take these precautions may amount to negligence.

If the cardiologist notes down the blood pressure of the patient as 150/100mm and STT changes in anterolateral leads in ECG, and treats the blood pressure as high without

10 *Taylor* v *Worcester and District Health Authority* [1991]2 Med LR 215.

11 Professor G.H. Smith, MB, FRCS referred to *Medical Negligence* by Michael J. Powers and Nigel H. Harris, Chapter 32, Edition 1990.

recognising the condition of the patient as hypertension, and declares the patient fit for the operation, the cardiologist is liable for negligence for not making adequate diagnosis of the condition of heart and cardiovascular system by advising proper investigation and treatment of the patient.[12]

3 Dental surgery[13]

(i) *Disclosure of information* The duty of the dentist is to warn the patient of the possible damage to the sensory nerve supply to soft tissues of lip, tongue and cheek due to difficult extraction of teeth. Omission to inform the patient of the accidental fracture of teeth, or jaw, or breaking of root during extraction of teeth is negligence on the part of the dental surgeon. It is obligatory on the part of the dentist to remove the broken root of teeth if it is considered necessary, or to explain the patient about the risk of complications if the removal of broken root is considered to be greater risk of damage to the patient.

Prior consultation with the patient about the matching of colour and shape of the restored teeth is mandatory, where crowns, veneers, or bridges are to be constructed. Failure to warn the patient of the stark reality that replacement by dentures of natural teeth can never recreate the chewing and masticating ability of the patient's natural teeth, may be considered negligence. Omission to advise the patient adequately of the scope of treatment—the likely outcome and risks of failure may also amount to negligence.

(ii) *Common allegations against dentists* Patients attend the dentists for pain or discomfort in teeth, gums, jaws, face, or temporoman-dibular joints. Pain may be caused due to damaged pulp of tooth, dental caries, trauma, loss of protective enamel or inflammation or abscess formation. Failure to recognise obvious lesions and to treat the patient

12 *Arunaben D. Kothari* v *Navdeep Clinic* 1996(3) CPR 20 (Guj); III(1996) CPJ 605 (Guj); (1997)5 CTJ 533 (CP) (SCDRC); 1998 CCJ 972 (Guj).

13 *Dental Surgery*, Professor Keith Mortimer, BDS (Hon) Ph.D., referred to *Medical Negligence* by Michael J. Powers and Nigel H. Harris, Chapter 37, Edition 1990.

is considered negligence. Similarly, failure to identify the causes of pain amounts to negligence if appropriate investigation is not prescribed.

The extraction of wrong tooth by the dental surgeon is always considered negligence. Omission to obtain satisfactory medical history and record of drug therapy before commencing treatment may be considered negligence, if complications due to treatment, which would have been evaded had precautions been taken in time, occur subsequently.

The duty of the dentist is to examine carefully ulcers, swellings or other lesions of the soft tissues of the mouth and to refer to consultant for assessment of any condition or symptom which persists despite diagnosis and treatment or for which no diagnosis can be made. The prime duty of the dentist is to avoid damage to the pulp during cavity preparation. The dentist may invite potential litigation by cementing permanently the bridges or crowns on teeth displaying symptoms of pulp damage. The object of treatment during root canal therapy is to remove the pulp from within the tooth and eliminate infection and to seal the canal to prevent any further risk of infection. Failure to place an adequate root filling which seals the cavity of the root canal can lead to infection or cyst formation which is considered negligence when it results in failure of crowns and bridges placed on a tooth with defective root filling.

Liability was established in respect of permanent damage to the lingual nerve during the removal of the lower left wisdom tooth.[1] Similarly, an orthodontist was held to be negligent during extraction of a wisdom tooth when the burr of the drill severed the lingual nerve of the patient.[2]

4 Dermatology[3]

(i) *Disclosure of information* Informations regarding the probable and possible diagnoses, course and prognosis of the

1 *Health* v *West Berkshire Health Authority* [1992]3 Med LR 57.
2 *Tomkins* v *Bexley Health Authority* [1993]4 Med LR 235.
3 Views expressed by Dr. G. Bag, MBBS, MD (Skin).

disease, probable aetiological agents related to it, if possible the pathogenesis of the disorder in most comprehensible terms, options of treatments available, side effects of the treatment regimens and the chances of success should be properly explained to the patient, preferably in writing. In case of cosmetic management and dermatosurgery informed consent from the patient, a thorough operation report and wound care instructions along with the probable result and prognosis (with pre and postoperative photographs) of the disorders should be communicated to the patients to rule out the misgivings about the treatment and prognosis.

(ii) ***Common skin disorders***

(A) GENODERMATOSES. Mere diagnosing a case of genodermatoses (tuberous sclerosis, neurofibromatosis, xeroderma pigmentosa, ectodermal dysplasia etc.) is not the end of the duty of a dermatologist. The patient should be informed about the prognosis of the disorder and should be referred to neurologist, opthalmologist and surgeons for proper management of the case. Furthermore advice regarding genetic counselling is a must in cases of genodermatoses. Failure to refer the patient to the specialists for counselling may amount to negligence.

(B) NAEVI AND OTHER DEVELOPMENTAL DEFECTS. The patients should be informed of the course and nature of the disorders. Few lesions may not require treatment (angiomatous naevus) as they involute spontaneously. Few required topical therapy, few surgical and others LASER treatment. Few lesions (congenital melanocytic naevus, junctional naevus) have malignant potential and should be removed as early as possible. LASER therapy has its complication too, like scarring, disfigurement and pigmentary changes. Patients should be informed of all these complications to rule out the future allegation of negligence.

(iii) ***Infective skin disorder*** It is the largest group of skin disorder seen in day to day practice.

(A) BACTERIA. Every effort should be given to find out the possible causative agent by culture, skin scraping or by serology and intradermal antigen sensitivity test, radiography or by biopsy and proper staining.

Proper chemotherapy for required duration should be prescribed with explanation of probable side effect of the agents used. Regarding management of skin tuberculosis (lupus vulgaris, TVC, scrofuloderma) every effort should be made to identify M. tuberculosis.

(B) VIRUS. To identify the causative agent in our setup is almost impossible except in a few cases (herpes, AIDS). Patients should be explained about the nature of herpes infections which follow a recurrent course and the outcome of pregnancy in herpes infected women. Recurrent course is seen in human papilloma virus infection (HPV) also. Female patients with HPV infection should be advised for regular gynaecological check up to exclude cervical malignancy at its earliest stage. Patients with herpes zoster should be warned before-hand about the possibility of post herpetic neuralgia and accordingly advised to contact neurologist.

(C) FUNGAL INFECTIONS. Proper duration of treatment should be advised clearly alongwith confirmation of diagnosis with KOH preparation and culture when necessary. Failure rate to detect the organism, (50% with T. unguium) also to be explained. Persistence of altered skin colour (pityriasis versicolor) should be explained to the patient, though the disease may be cured.

(D) INFESTATION WITH PROTOZOA AND ARTHROPODS. Persistence of itching for 2-3 weeks in a case of scabies patient should be informed after successful treatment and cure of the patients. Advise should be given regarding method of application, duration, clothings and management of household contact in treating cases of scabies and pediculosis.

(iv) ***Eczematous disorder*** To reach to the aetiological factor is the cornerstone of treating a case of eczematous disorder. There are a battery of tests including patch test, prick test, etc. each having its own limitation and advantage. The significance of these tests should be clearly explained to the patients. Prognosis of eczema should always be guarded, because if the aetiological factor cannot be delineated properly it will usually follow a chronic and recurrent course. Side effects of systemic and topical steroids which are almost as a routine used here, should be properly explained.

Contact dermatitis which is the commonest form of occupational dermatosis need special mention. The doctor should have a clear idea which of the disorders are notifiable and compensable to avoid medico-legal problems.

(v) *Cutaneous vascular responses* Predicting the prognosis of crythema multiforma should be guarded. Effort should be given to identify the causative factor and the role of steroid should be explained to the patient.

Managing a case of urticaria is very difficult. Proper inquiry has to be made about drugs, food, inhalants, infection, food additives, emotional factors etc. The patient should be informed that the disorder will follow a chronic and recurrent course if aetiology cannot be identified. The side effects of antihistaminics should also be explained to the patient.

(vi) *Pigmentary disorders* A patient of vitiligo should be informed about the nature of the disease, type, prognosis, response of treatment with photochemo therapy and its side effects. While receiving PUVA or PUVASOL therapy advice should be given about eye protection and sun screen application. In case of managing vitiligo with punch grafting, consent, pre and postoperative photograph should be taken always.

(vii) *Disorders of hair and nail* Different modes of treatment available for management of androgenetic alopecia should be explained clearly. The response, side-effect and continuous use of minoxidil should be stressed. The antiandrogenic side-effect of fenesteride acetate when used, should be informed and cosmetic outcome of hair transplantation should also be explained. Prognosis of alopecia areata also to be explained.

The nail changes associated with disorder like psoriasis, lichen planus, alopecia areata may persist though the skin lesion may subside and it should be informed to patient well in advance.

(viii) ***Disorders of keratinization*** Chronic and relapsing nature of psoriasis should be informed to the patient before starting treatment. The patient should have his say in choosing the mode of treatment. While managing cases of difficult psoriasis with drugs like methotraxate, retinoids, PUVA or cyclosporine, the side-effects of the drugs should be properly explained. The need of contraception while under methotrexate and retinoids, teratogenicity, liver disorders, skeletal disorders, immunosuppression should be properly explained to the patient to avoid medico-legal problems.

(ix) ***Vesiculo-bullous disorder*** Without going through detail investigation it is often very difficult to reach to proper diagnosis. Options for histopathological, immunofluorescence (direct and indirect) and immuno electron microscopy should always be given to the patients. Prognosis of pemphigus vulgaris is always grave and almost always need high dose cortico steroids or immunosuppressive drugs. The side-effects of steroids and others drugs should be explained to the patient.

In managing a case of Dermatitis herpeteformis, dietary restriction of gluten has to be explained to patient, in default a case of medical negligence can be made out.

In managing cases of Epidermolysis bullosa, the role of genetic counselling and prognosis should be explained to the parents of the patients.

The grave prognosis of toxic epidermal necrosis and Stevens-Johnson syndrome should be properly informed and patients are preferably managed in dermatological intensive care unit or in a specialised centre to avoid and counter acute skin failure.

(x) ***Systemic collagen disorders*** The prognosis of disorders like progressive systemic sclerosis and systemic lupus erythematosus are always grave. The mode of treatment, side-effect of drugs and the course of the disorder should be explained to the patient to avoid future allegation of negligence.

(xi) *Metabolic disorders* Investigations should be always advised in managing a case of xanthelasma or other xanthomas and patients should have thorough check up of lipid profile etc. and get advice from a cardiologist.

(xii) *Skin tumours and malignant disorder* Biopsy should always be advised in a suspected case of benign or malignant skin disorder. Advice from surgeon, oncologist and radiologist should be sought for. Different forms of treatment options to be placed before the patient to choose and advantages and disadvantages of it should be properly explained. Prognosis of different premalignant skin disorder and malignancies should be properly explained alongwith the side-effects related to each form of treatment.

(xiii) *Dermatosurgery and cosmetology* The prognosis, outcome, side effect of therapeutic modalities, pre and postoperative photograph and consent of the patient in writing are the prerequisites in dermatosurgical management. The same is applicable to cosmetic management also.

(xiv) *Veneral diseases* Secrecy should be maintained in dealing with veneral diseases. Investigations should be advised (VDRL, DGI, FTA-ABS) for proper diagnosis of a case of syphilis. The patients should be advised not to be engaged in sexual relation with others while the lesions are active. Sexual partner or partners should be identified and should get the treatment alongwith the patient. The children of the infected couple should be examined. Vaginal speculum should be used to detect cervical lesion which are often missed. The side effect of penicillin therapy should be kept in mind and resuscitation kit should be ready in hand while giving or testing penicillin. No management of a veneral disease is complete without advice of using condom to avoid further exposure.

The course of herpes genitalia should be explained and made it clear that in spite of complete cure of the existing lesions, the disease will follow a chronic and recurrent course throughout life. The risk of being pregnant in female patient and severe degree of disease in neonate should also be explained to patient. Option of using prophylactic acyclovir should be placed before the patient.

While managing a case of AIDS, investigations like ELISA and Western blot assay should be done by strictly following the guidelines prescribed by NACO and anonymity of the patient should be maintained. Pre and post test counselling is a must. Every aspect of the disease, the aetiology, pathogenesis, prognosis, nature of transmission and importance of using condom should be properly explained to patient.

(xv) ***Management of leprosy*** Every effort should be made to properly diagnose a case of leprosy by doing clinical, slit skin smear, histopathology and immuno pathological investigations before declaring it to the patient. Therapeutic or immunological subclass should be detected and therapy prescribed for the stipulated period and drugs by strictly following the National Leprosy Eradication Programme (NLEP) guidelines. The significance of reactions in leprosy should be properly explained to the patient and side effects of drugs used in leprosy should be given. The patient should also be informed that sensory loss and motor or other disabilities may not be fully corrected by the drug therapy alone, because nerve damage associated with leprosy is an irreversible process.

(xvi) ***Drugs and skin disorders*** Different drugs are used in the treatment of different disorders and all of them have some side effects and a few of them may produce or may simulate different skin disorders.

Fixed drug eruption is one of them. The list of offending drugs should be supplied to the patient to avoid the recurrence of the disorder.

Exfoliative dermatitis, Stevens-Johnson syndrome, toxic epidermal necrolysis like dreaded disorder may be precipitated by drugs, and as such enquiry should be made to establish the diagnosis and stopping the offending drug is of utmost importance.

5 Gynaecology and obstetrics[4]

(i) *Disclosure of information* The duty of the doctor is to explain the risk of the procedure for sterilization, legally induced abortion, laparoscopy, hysterectomy etc., because those relate to family planning, future child-bearing capacity and sexual enjoyment. Omission to explain the side-effects of oral contraceptives and intra-uterine contraceptive devices may constitute negligence. The doctor must inform the patient of the risks and complications associated with the use of steroidal contraceptives and intra-uterine contraceptive device. There are four types of hysterectomy, viz. total, sub-total, pan and radical. Pre-operative discussion with the patient is mandatory about the particular type of hysterectomy to be performed, because the surgeon will be guilty of trespass to body, if consent is given for one type of hysterectomy and surgery is done for another type of hysterectomy. It is incumbent on the part of the gynaecologist to give warning about all complications of hysterectomy. The known complications of hysterectomy, viz. VVF (Vesico Vaginal Fistula) which may result from injury to the bladder during surgery, should be disclosed to the patient before the operation.[5]

The accepted professional practice is to obtain informed consent for obstetric procedure like termination of pregnancy under general anaesthesia irrespective of whether for social or medical reasons. Consent obtained to a procedure of treatment at the height of labour when the women are distressed by pain or under the influence of narcotic drugs, has no validity in the eye of law.

(ii) *Common allegations against gynaecologists and obstetricians* A ten year study on maternal death in the Department of Obstetrics and Gynaecology, R.G. Kar Medical College and

4 *Obstetrics and Gynaecology*, Peter J. Huntingford, MD, FRCOG referred to *Medical Negligence* by Michael J. Powers and Nigel H. Harris, Chapter 31, Edition 1990; Dr. (Mrs.) Ilorasri Chakrabarti, MBBS, MD, DGO, FICMH.

5 *Dr. Rameshwar Prasad Agarwal* v *Md. Abas Ansari* 1999(2) CPR 386 (Pat); 1999 CTJ 664 (CP) (SCDRC); I(2000) CPJ 433 (Pat).

Hospital, Calcutta, revealed that the medical professionals were responsible for 8.14% of maternal deaths.[6] The common allegation against gynaecologists is their failure to detect internal haemorrhage following major vaginal operations or hysterectomy or injuries to urinary bladder and ureters. Hysterectomy is an important gynaecological operation for several pathological conditions of the female genital tract. Vaginal hysterectomy with adequate and good repair and suspension of vault gives lasting results as compared to abdominal hysterectomy or less conservative operations.[7]

It is the duty of the gynaecologist to explain the risk and benefit of the procedure before undertaking laparoscopy for therapeutic reasons, e.g. occlusion of uterine tubes, recovery of eggs for in vitro fertilisation and also for diagnostic purposes e.g. to find out blockage of uterine tubes in infertile woman, to elucidate abdominal pain by examination of the pelvic organs, or to confirm intra-uterine pregnancy.

The common causes of complaint against the obstetrician are based on the disordered intra-uterine growth of foetus, placental insufficiency, acute pre-partum hypoxia due to placental separation, acute intra-partum hypoxia due to prolapse of the umbilical cord, intracranial haemorrhage and delay in delivery in breech presentation, post-partum hypoxia due to administration of narcotic analgesics to the mother, and inadequate resuscitation of the baby without calling paediatrician to the delivery room. Failure to diagnose and treat abnormalities in the foetus or to detect congenital or inherited defect of the foetus by ultrasound, bio-chemical analysis of amniotic fluid, amounts to negligence, though technical facilities are limited in India. Omission to remove swabs from the vagina or abdominal cavity or to monitor post-partum haemorrhage also amounts to negligence. The obstetrician may be negligent for lack of sexual enjoyment resulting from damage to the perineum and vagina caused by episiotomy.

6 JIMA, vol. 91, p. 56.
7 JIMA, vol. 90, p. 294.

(iii) ***Drugs during pregnancy*** The adverse effects of the drugs depends on several factors such as the drug itself, maternal age, maternal disease, genetic make up, nutritional status, state of the embryonic/foetal development and the foetal organ susceptibility. While prescribing drugs to a pregnant woman or during lactation one should be very careful to prevent the occurrence of foetal malformation and to provide a safeguard for both mother and the foetus.

For any infection during pregnancy some form of antibacterial agents are necessary. The safe antibiotics during pregnancy are: Ampicillin, Penicillin, amoxycillin, erythromycin and cephalosporins. The following antibiotics are not safe during pregnancy: Tetracycline, chloramphenicol, aminoglycosides (streptomycin, gentamicin, kanamycin). Chloroquine sulphate has been reported to cause congenital cataract occasionally. The problems like intra-uterine growth retardation, thrombocytopenia, premature closure of ductus arteriosus and persistent pulmonary hypertension in the foetus may be caused due to anti-inflammatory and analgesic drugs such as indomethacin, naproxen and aspirin in high doses. Diuretics can cause more harm than good in treatment of common pregnancy oedema.

Propranolol and other beta-blockers when gain access to foetus will interfere with regulation of foetal circulation and cause hypoxia. Increased foetal malformations had been reported when mothers took anticonvulsants during pregnancy. The use of insulin for the treatment of diabetic mothers should proceed with caution as it may cause foetal skeletal defects. Heavy dose of oestrogen progestogen when used in early pregnancy can cause multiple congenital anomalies in the foetus. The use of progestogen can cause virilisation of female foetus. The female foetus may develop primary carcinoma of vagina and vaginal adenosis in later life when diethylstilboestrol (DES) is given to the mother. However, during pregnancy diazepam and nitrazepam are commonly used as sedatives/tranquillizers without any risk to both mother and the foetus.[8]

8 JIMA, vol. 88, p. 207.

(iv) ***Delivery of child*** Vaginal delivery is the normal way of extricating the baby in the labour room. Labour is said to be in active phase when the cervix is 2 to 3 cm. dilated. The active phase of labour should not last more than 8 to 11 hours. Various agents are in wild clinical use for the purpose of inducing or accelerating labour. The most commonly used drug is oxytocin. The known complications associated with the use of oxytocin is rupture of uterus which results from failure to observe where exactly the oxytocin and the uterine response overstep the physiological limits. The only contra-indication is grossly contracted pelvis.[9]

Brain damage of the child was attributed to the delay of 68 minutes in delivery of the child.[10] The brain damage of the child was attributed to intermittent hypoxia caused by inappropriate amount of force during forceps delivery after failure to deliver the child by using ventouse extractor.[11]

Delivery of the baby is the only treatment in toxaemia of pregnancy described as pre-eclampsia or eclampsia when chronic renal disease or high blood pressure is preceded by excessive water retention, weight gain and albuminuria. Induction of labour is the common treatment for conditions like post-maturity of the baby, repeated antepartum bleeding of undetermined origin, in case of suspected intra-uterine growth retardation and hypertension of mother with high diastolic blood pressure. However, with introduction of calcium channel blockers such as nifedipine, its use for suppression of pre-mature labour is considered to be significantly effective.[12]

Trial of forceps is permissible in the second stage of labour by skilled and experienced obstetrician in an operating theatre made ready to proceed to caesarian section in case of failure of trial. Trial of forceps can be undertaken with

9 JIMA, vol. 91, p. 40.

10 *Bull* v *Devon Area Health Authority* 22 BMLR 79 (CA); [1993]4 Med LR 117.

11 *Townsend* v *Worcester and District Health Authority* (1994)23 BMLR 31 (QBD).

12 JIMA, vol. 91, p. 8.

adequate pain relief for the mother either under general anaesthesia or complete epidural block, if the cervix is fully dilated, the fetal head is engaged and at the level of or below ischial spines and the pelvis is thought to be of adequate dimensions.

Caesarian section may be an elective procedure carried out before the onset of labour for conditions such as breech presentation, absolute cephalopelvic disproportion, premature baby, and major degree of placenta praevia. Caesarian sections are also undertaken for emergencies that arise during labour such as foetal distress, prolapse of the umbilical cord, placental abruption, transverse lie, and failure of trial by forceps. The best treatment of cord entanglements associated with signs of foetal distress is delivery of the baby as soon as possible by caesarian section, if the cervix is not fully dilated. The presence of paediatrician and anaesthetist along with obstetrician in the delivery room is mandatory not only for delivery of premature baby, but also for any high risk pregnancy.

The doctors were held negligent for leaving "artery forceps" in the abdomen of the patient during caesarean operation.[13] Similarly, the doctor is negligent for leaving a metallic tip of suction tube in the abdomen of the patient during caesarian operation.[14] The negligence was attributed to the hospital for leaving sponge in the abdomen of the patient during caesarian operation.[15]

(A) PRECAUTIONS IN THE PREMATURE DELIVERIES

(I) FOETAL

(*a*) DURING PREGNANCY. There is a chance of foetal hypoxia, due to placental insufficiency as the pregnancy overruns the expected date. As placental

13 *Ms Sau Madhuri* v *Dr. Rajendra* 1996(3) CPR 174 (NC); III(1996) CPJ 75 (NC); (1997)5 CTJ 43 (CP) (NCDRC); 1997 CCJ 1499 (NC).

14 *Rohini Pritam Kabadi* v *Dr. R.T. Kulkarni* 1998(1) CPR 142 (Bangalore); III(1996) CPJ 441 (Bangalore); (1997)5 CTJ 83 (CP) (SCDRC); 1998 CCJ 910 (Kant).

15 *Aleyamma Varghese* v *Dewan Bahadur Dr. V. Varghese* 1996 CTJ 911; 1997(1) CPR 310 (Ker); III(1997) CPJ 165 (Ker); 1998 CCJ 1310 (Ker).

ageing leads to diminished placental function with resultant foetal asphyxia, the hypoxic state is aggravated by the associated factors such as elderly patients, hypertensive disorders in pregnancy and history of bleeding during pregnancy.

(*b*) DURING LABOUR. There is increased incidence of asphyxia and intracranial damage due to: (1) aggravation of pre-existing hypoxia leading to increased foetal distress; (2) increased incidence of difficult labour due to big size baby, non-moulding of the head due to hardening of skull bones and occasional shoulder dystocia; (3) increased incidence of operative delivery; (4) scanty liquor amnii and less Wharton's jelly in the cord favours cord compression.

(*c*) FOLLOWING BIRTH. (1) Meconium aspiration syndrome and atelectasis are the result of premature attempt at respiratory effects due to intrauterine anoxia with consequent inhalation of meconium containing liquor amnii; (2) hypoglycaemia and polycythemia specially occurs in growth retarded post term babies.

All these factors lead to increased perinatal loss, the magnitude of which is increased in between 43 weeks and 44 weeks.

(II) MATERNAL. There is increased morbidity, incidental to hazards of induction and operative delivery. Post-maturity *per se* does not put the mother at risk.

(B) ADVERSE EFFECT OF PROLONGED LABOUR

(A) DEFINITION. The labour is said to be prolonged when the combined duration of the 1st stage and second stage is more than the arbitrary time limit of 18 hours.

(B) DANGERS

(I) FOETAL. The foetal risk is increased due to the combined effects of:

(1) Hypoxia due to diminished uteroplacental circulation specially after rupture of the membranes.

(2) Intra uterine infection.

(3) Intracranial stress or haemorrhage following prolonged stay in the perinium and/or supermoulding of the head.

(4) Increased operative delivery.

All these result in increased perinatal loss due to asphyxia, intracranial haemorrhage and neonatal sepsis.

(II) MATERNAL. There is increased incidence of:

(1) Distress—like—excessive foetal movement, meconium stained liquor, alteration of foetal heart rate pattern.

(2) Postpartum haemorrhage.

(3) Trauma to the genital tract—concealed (undue stretching of the perineal muscles which may be the cause of prolapse at a later period) or revealed such as cervical tear, rupture uterus.

(4) Increased operative delivery.

(5) Puerperal sepsis.

(6) Subinvolution.

The sum effects of all these lead to increased maternal morbidity and also increased maternal deaths.

(C) DANGERS OF FORCEPS OPERATION

The hazards of the forceps operation are mostly related to the faulty technique and to the indication for which the forceps are applied rather than the instrument. The hazards are grouped into: (*i*) Maternal, (*ii*) Foetal–*(a) Immediate (b) Remote*

(I) MATERNAL. (*a*) Immediate (*b*) Remote

(A) *IMMEDIATE.* The immediate complications are:

(1) Injury: (1) Extension of injury even to involve the rectum or its upward extension upto the vault of the vagina; (2) Vaginal laceration; (3) Cervical tear specially when forceps applied through an incompletely dilated cervix.

(2) Postpartum haemorrhage—due to (*a*) trauma or (*b*) atonic uterus due to prolonged labour or effect of anaesthesia.

(3) Shock—due to (*a*) blood loss (*b*) prolonged labour and dehydration.

(4) Sepsis—due to improper asepsis and devitalisation of the local tissue.

(5) Anaesthetic hazards.

(B) *REMOTE:*

(1) Chronic low backache—due to tension imposed on the soften ligaments guarding the lumbosacral or sacroiliac joints during lithotomy position.

(2) Genital prolapse or stress incontenence—this may occur specially when the head is dragged down through incompletely dilated cervix or in unrotated position or due to faulty repair of perineal laceration.

(II) FOETAL. (*a*) Immediate (*b*) Remote

(A) *IMMEDIATE*

(1) Asphyxia due to intracranial stress out of prolonged compression.

(2) Intracranial haemorrhage due to malapplication of the blades (occipito-frontal plane) leading to over compression.

(3) Cephal haematoma.

(4) Facial palsy.

(5) Abrasions on the soft tissues of face and forehead by the forceps blades.

(B) *REMOTE.* Cerebral and spastic palsy due to residual cerebral injury.

(v) *Sterilization* Most of the gynaecologists would accept that failure rate in sterilization is higher with laparoscopic techniques than the techniques of dividing the tubes and removing a portion at laparotomy. Failure rate is higher in sterilization carried out at the time of caesarean section.

Medical termination of pregnancy has been accepted as one of the methods of reducing population in developing countries like India. It is the duty of the doctor to explain the chances of failure in sterilization operation before obtaining consent for the operation. Omission to warn the patient of the risk of failure of the sterilization operation amounts to negligence. The Supreme Court of India,[16] held the State of Maharashtra liable for negligence of Government doctors who left a mop (towel) inside the peritoneal cavity of the patient during sterilization operation, resulting in death of the patient. There is possibility of missing the product when MTP is performed at early stage of the pregnancy, i.e. before six weeks of pregnancy. Failure to warn this risk of failure amounts to negligence.

The complications of incomplete abortion, bleeding, perforation of uterus may happen after D&C operation conducted by the specialists. Failure to diagnose the cause of complications during postoperative management of the patient and to give effective treatment, amounts to negligence.[17]

The cause of failure of sterilization operation may be obtained from laparoscopic inspection of the uterine tubes, or by x-ray examination, or by pathological examination of the materials removed at a subsequent operation of re-sterilization. The discrepancy between operation notes and the result of x-ray films in respect of the number of rings or clips or nylon sutures used for occlusion of the tubes, will lead to logical inference of negligence on the part of the gynaecologist in case of failure of sterilization operation.

(A) COMPLICATIONS OF PUERPERAL LIGATION

Complication of tubal ligation depend on several factors such as method of sterilization, method of anaesthesia, routes of ligation (abdominal or vaginal), association of MTP or delivery, age of patient, place of operation, selection of patient and technical capability of the operator.

16 *Achutrao Haribhau Khodwa* v *State of Maharashtra* (1996)2 SCC 634; (1996)4 CTJ 950 (SC) (CP); 1996 ACJ 505.

17 *Dr. C.V. Mathew* v *P. Babu* 1999(3) CPR 461 (Ker); I(2000) CPJ 134 (Ker).

Operative complications included anaesthetic hazards, bladder and bowel injuries, injuries of tubes and ovaries, broad ligament hematomas. Post-operative complications include wound infection (commonest), wound haematoma and dehiscence, pelvic infection, peritonitis, urinary infection, pelvic haematoma, intraperitoneal haemorrhage, bladder and bowel fistula.

The mortality rate following tubal ligation is very low. Three major causes of death are: anaesthetic hazards, infection (particularly tetanus in developing countries) and haemorrhage if the tying sutures on the tubes are too loose. Most of the deaths are preventable. Complications are more frequent with vaginal than with abdominal ligations, and following delivery, C.S. and MTPs, than after interval ligations.

The sequel or remote complications are loss of weight, occasional obesity, psychological upset, loss of libido etc. The gynaecological complications are chronic pelvic pain, congestive dysmenorrhoea, menstrual abnormalities, like menorrhagia hypomenorrhoea or irregular periods, hydrosalpinx, incisional hernia etc. Pelvic pain, menorrhagia along with cystic ovaries constitute a post ligation syndrome. It may be vascular in origin. However, the incidence can be minimised if the blood vessels adjacent to the mesosalpinx are not unduly disturbed.

The overall failure rate in tubal sterilization is 0·1% to 0·7%. (Failure rate is lowest with Pomeroy's technique 0·1 to 0·3%). The failure rate of minilap is less (0·1 to 0·3 HWY) compared to failure rate of Laparoscopic tubal ligation (0·2 to 0·6 HWY). Failure rate is more with vaginal route compared to abdominal route.

(B) COMPLICATIONS OF IUCD (INTRA UTERINE CONTRACEPTIVE DEVICE)

(A) IMMEDIATE AFTER INSERTION OF CUT

(1) CRAMP LIKE PAIN. Sometime pain does occur. It is transient but it may be occasionally severe and usually lasts for $^1/_2$ to 1 hour.

(2) SYNCOPAL ATTACKS. It may be associated with pain.

(3) PARTIAL OR COMPLETE PERFORATION OF UTERUS. It is due to faulty technique of insertion but liable to be met with lactational period when the uterus remains small and soft.

(b) REMOTE COMPLICATIONS

(1) PAIN. Persistent pelvic pain may be due to abnormal position of IUD, uterine perforation, beginning of its expulsion, disparity between cavity size and IUD size, associated pelvic inflammatory disease (PID) or ectopic pregnancy. However, persistent pain should be investigated and often needs removal of the IUCD.

(2) ABNORMAL MENSTRUAL BLEEDING. The excessive bleeding involved increased menstrual loss, prolongation of duration of period and intermenstrual bleeding. The exact cause of blood loss is not definitely known but thought to be due to various other reasons. The effect of bleeding is almost nil in healthy women but can lead to increased anemia of women of developing countries. Removal of IUCD may be indicated due to persistent heavy bleeding.

(3) SPONTANEOUS EXPULSION. The expulsion rate is about 5%. The rate is however, more following post-abortal and puerperal. Spontaneous expulsion usually occurs within a few months of insertion, more commonly during periods, at times unnoticed by the patient. Failure to palpate the thread is an urgent ground to report to the doctor.

(4) PERFORATION OF UTERUS. It occurs very rarely but most perforation occurs during insertion and migration may also occur following initial partial perforation with subsequent myometrial contraction. Proper technique may reduce the chance of perforation during insertion.

(5) MISSING THREAD. The thread may not be visible through the cervical Os due to (*i*) thread coiled inside; (*ii*) thread torn through; (*iii*) device expelled unnoticed; (*iv*) device perforated the uterine wall and lying in the peritoneal cavity; (*v*) device pulled up by the growing uterus of pregnancy. After ruling out pregnancy straight X-ray abdomen USG may diagnose the problem and it is to be managed accordingly.

(6) PID. The chance of pelvic inflammation disease is 2-10 times higher in IUCD users. Infection with actinomycoses is more. Failure rate is 1·5 to 3 HWY though the incidence of ectopic pregnancy is high.

(C) ADVERSE EFFECT OF OCP (ORAL CONTRACEPTIVE PILLS)

Oral contraceptives produce several metabolic, functional and organic changes which are responsible for side-effects and certain diseases in pill users.

The side-effects are broadly divided into two groups: (1) Minor side-effects which are by and large temporary. (2) Major side-effects and changes of serious nature.

(1) MINOR SIDE-EFFECTS

(*a*) Nausea, vomiting, headache (E) and leg cramps (P)—transient, sometimes subside following in for 2–3 cycles.

(*b*) Mastalgia—transient heaviness and tenderness of breast

(*c*) Weight gain (P)– Progestagens have got anabolic effect.
– Edema legs sometimes due to retention of sodium and increased cortisol.

(*d*) Chloasma (E) and Acne (P)—Annoying cosmetic problems.

(*e*) Menstrual problems—

- Breakthrough bleeding—sometimes occur with low-dose estrogen preparations.

- Hypomenorrhoea—local effect on endometrium.
- Menorrhagia—usually pre-existing and subsides with progestagens.
- Amenorrhoea—post-pill amenorrhoea of more than 6 months duration occurs in less than 1% of cases. Resumption of menstruation occurs on withdrawal of pills.
- Libido—sometimes low due to dryness of vagina and sometimes increased due to loss of fear of pregnancy.
- Leucorrhoea—Estrogen may produce excessive cervical secretion, sometimes due to monilial infection.

(2) MAJOR SIDE-EFFECTS

(*a*) DEPRESSION. Changes of mood, sleep disturbances and psychotic manifestations. Depression is thought to be due to alteration of tryptophan metabolism.

(*b*) HYPERTENSION. May occur in less than 1% of cases after 1 year of use. Pre-existing hypertension may get aggravated. It may reverse back to normal after stoppage of medicine for 3–6 months.

(*c*) VASCULAR COMPLICATIONS (E):

- Thrombo-embolic phenomenon. The overall risk is to the extent of 4-6 times more than the non-users. Previous history of thrombo-embolism, pre-existing hypertension, obesity diabetes, smoking etc. are risk factors. Low-dose estrogen in pills has reduced the incidence to a great extent.
- Incidence of coronary thrombosis 6 times, cerebral hemorrhege 2 times, and thrombosis is 9 times higher than non-users.

(*d*) CHOLESTATIC JAUNDICE. Susceptibility is more with women who have suffered with idiopathic jaundice in pregnancy or hepatitis.

(*e*) NEOPLASIA. It has got protective effect against neoplasia of breast, endometrium fibrocystic diseases of breast and cystic ovaries.

(*f*) METABOLIC EFFECT

- CHO-metabolism is depressed. Both plasma level of insulin and blood sugar elevated. Sometimes altered glucose tolerance test is obvious.
- Proteins (E) thyroxine, PBI and sometimes cortisol may be increased.
- Lipids. Low dose Estrogen increases HDL Cholesterol and decreases LDL and triglycerides —thus protective effect Progestagens decreases HDL cholesterol and increases LDL thereby promotes heart disease.

(*g*) REPRODUCTION. OCP acts by anovulation but ovulation returns within 3 months of withdrawal of drugs in 90% of cases.

(*h*) LACTATION. (E + P) Lactation is probably hampered qualitatively and quantitatively.

(*i*) Failure rate is on 0.5 HWY (Hundred Women Years).

(vi) *Medical termination of pregnancy (MTP)* There is no universally safe and effective method which is applicable to all cases. However, the complications are much less (5%) if termination is done before 8 weeks by S/E. The complications are about 5 times more in mid-trimester termination irrespective of the methods employed.

Complications of S/E and D+E depend a lot upon several factors of which the most important ones are operator's skill, available facilities and gestational age; others are type of anaesthesia and instrumentation, patient's age, parity, socio-economic status and pre-existing disease.

Compared to other surgical operations legally induced first trimester pregnancy terminations are remarkably safe, the major complication rate being less than 1 in 100 pregnancies.

(A) IMMEDIATE COMPLICATIONS

(1) **Uterine haemorrhage.** It usually occurs in 0·2% to 3·4% of cases. Haemorrhage happens more often with advanced gestational age, when D+E is performed instead of S/E.

(2) **Pelvic infection.** It ranges from 0·5% to 1·5%. It is due to incomplete evacuation and improper aseptic technique. The incidence can be reduced to a great extent by prophylactic use of antibiotics.

(3) **Cervical injury.** It occurs in 0·01% to 1% of cases. It also happens more often D+E than S/E, in advanced gestational age and in nulliparous women.

(4) **Uterine perforation.** Though it is a very dangerous complication but fortunately it rarely happens. The incidence of perforation can be minimized by using proper technique. With strong clinical suspicion and investigations when actual diagnosis of intestinal injury, haemorrhage etc. is made, laparotomy followed by necessary steps should be made.

(5) **Retained products.** Incomplete abortion happens in 0·9% to 3·3% of cases. The incidence can be reduced by performing check curettage following S/E.

(6) **Continuation of pregnancy.** S/E fails in less than 1% of cases. By routine check up and continuation of pregnancy symptoms may help in diagnosis—further MTP may be necessary. Usually patient comes late in 2nd trimester then decision may be taken as per discussion, clinical examination and USG test. If the uterine growth and USG findings corresponds with the period of amenorrhoea it is quite unlikely to have any ill effect on foetus, yet it depends.

(7) **Maternal deaths.** The maternal death is lowest in first trimester but the figure varies widely. The mortality rate increases with advancing gestational age as the mortality is 5-6 times higher in mid-trimester MTP compared to the MTP in first trimester. The common causes of death are usually haemorrhage, infection, anaesthetic hazards, embolic events etc.

(8) COMPLICATIONS OF METHOD APPLIED. Complications of mid-trimester MTP's may be related to the methods employed.

(*a*) Hypertonic saline—hypernatrimia, endotoxic shock, DIC, cerebral haemorrhage.

(*b*) Prostaglandins—intractable vomiting, diarrhoea, cervico-uterine injury.

(*c*) Syntocinon—water intonixtions, convulsions etc.

(*d*) Hysterectomy—haemorrhage and shock, Peritonitis, anaesthetic complications and intestinal obstruction, etc.

(B) LATE/REMOTE COMPLICATION

(1) GYNAECOLOGICAL. Menstrual disturbances, chronic pelvic infection, infertility due to tubal block, scar endometriosis, incisional hernia, uterine synechac leading to secondary amenorrhoea.

(2) OBSTETRIC COMPLICATION. Recurrent mid-trimester abortion due to cervical incompetence, ectopic pregnancy, premature labour, increased perinatal loss, rupture uterus, etc.

The immediate complications can be diagnosed at the earliest even during the procedures and can be managed accordingly.

At the time of discharge even with all routine advice patient should be specially instructed to visit at the earliest if she develops: (*i*) acute pain in lower abdomen; (*ii*) rise of temperature; (*iii*) persistent pain for more than 7 days; (*iv*) heavy or persistent fresh bleeding; (*v*) persistent pregnancy symptoms.

Before venturing for MTP, patient and her guardian should be made alert about the risk factors though the complications are rare and the procedures are technically not very difficult. If any complication crops up, that should be identified, diagnosed and if managed properly without delay, many serious hazard may be avoided.

(vii) *Intrauterine growth retardation*

(1) **Definition.** Dysmaturity is said to be present in those babies whose birth weight is below the tenth percentile of the average for the gestational age. The growth retardation can occur in preterm, term or post-term babies.

(2) **Incidence.** Dysmaturity comprises about one-third of low birth weight babies. In advanced countries, its overall incidence is 2–8%. The incidence among the term babies is about 5% and that among the post-term babies is about 15%.

(3) **Types.** The clinical types are grouped into—

(*a*) Constitutional

(*b*) Growth retarded—(I) SYMMETRICAL (II) ASYMMETRICAL

(4) **Aetiology.** The causes of foetal growth retardation can be divided into four groups—

(*a*) *MATERNAL*, (*b*) *FOETAL*, (*c*) *PLACENTAL*, (*d*) *UNKNOWN*

(*a*) *MATERNAL*

- Constitutional. Small women, maternal genetic and racial factor may be associated with small babies and is not necessarily an undesirable event.
- Maternal malnutrition before and during pregnancy. As most of the foetal weight gain ($^2/_3$) occurs beyond 24th week of pregnancy, malnutrition and anaemia in the 2nd half of pregnancy play a significant role in the reduction of the birth weight.
- Poor weight gain during pregnancy.
- Low blood oxygen as in cyanotic heart disease.
- Inadequate substrate level–malabsorption syndrome.
- Toxins. Alcohol intake, chronic renal failure, chronic urinary tract infection etc.

(*b*) *FOETAL*. There is enough substrate in maternal blood and also crosses the placenta but is not utilised by the foetus. For example, congenital anomalies, chromosomal, TORCH infection, multiple pregnancy etc.

(c) *PLACENTAL.* Chronic placental insufficiency as it occurs in conditions such as preeclamptic toxaemia, essential hypertension, chronic nephritis, decompensated organic heart disease, placental and cord abnormalities such as chronic placental abruption, infraction, small placenta, circumvallate placenta, vellamentous insertion of cord etc.

(d) *UNKNOWN.* The causes remain unknown in about 40% cases.

(5) **DIAGNOSIS.** Precise prenatal diagnosis of IUGR poses a problem, though it is made—

(I) *CLINICALLY*

(a) by identification of high risk factors;

(b) by periodical clinical examination as in routine ante-natal care.

(II) *BIOPHYSICALLY*

(a) by ultrasonography;

(b) by doppler blood flow velocimetry.

It is to be borne in mind that accurate prediction of foetal growth retardation using sonography has not been achieved as yet. However, the high rate of negative predictive value proves the value of the test.

(6) **MANAGEMENT.** As there is no specific treatment to improve the placental function, the following may be tried with occasional success: (1) Avoidance of smoking and alcohol. (2) To correct malnutrition by an adequately balanced diet, 300 extra calories to be taken per day. (3) Strenuous work and physical activity to be avoided. (4) Adequate bed rest specially in left lateral position (2 hrs. following lunch and 8 hrs. at night). (5) To institute appropriate therapy for the associated complicating factors likely to produce growth retardation. (6) Administration of folic acid tablets 5mg thrice daily may be given but of doubtful value. However, if the foetus is symmetrically growth retarded, a meticulous search

should be made for foetal anomalies—structural or chromosonal with the available gadgets.

(7) TERMINATION OF PREGNANCY. The crucial decision in the management of IUGR is the timing of termination. The factors to be considered are: (*a*) duration of pregnancy; (*b*) degree of growth retardation; (*c*) associated complicating factors; (*d*) previous obstretric history; and (*e*) environment of the place of delivery.

(I) Beyond 38 weeks termination of pregnancy should be done.

(II) Before 38 weeks:

(1) Uncomplicated slight degree of IUGR.

Usual treatment as outlined above to improve the placental function may be employed. The pregnancy is allowed to continue but the tendency to overrun the expected date is to be curtailed by termination.

(2) Severe degree of IUGR.

Termination is better than further procrastination if facilities permit to assess the lung maturation.

(8) METHODS OF TERMINATION

(*a*) Low rupture of the membranes followed by oxytocin is employed in cases such as pregnancy beyond 36 weeks with favourable cervix and the head is deep in the pelvis. The colour of the liquor could be a guide for further management.

(*b*) Caesarean section is preferred in unfavourable conditions.

(9) CARE DURING VAGINAL DELIVERY. The delivery should be in an equipped institution where intensive intranatal monitoring (clinical or electronic) is possible and having facilities for intensive neonatal care unit.

(10) IMMEDIATE CARE OF THE BABY AFTER BIRTH

(*a*) A paediatrician should be available at the time of delivery.

(*b*) The precautions like premature delivery are to be taken.

(*c*) The baby should be placed preferably in the intensive neonatal care unit.

(viii) *Multiple congenital anomaly of foetus—steps for detection*

(A) INCIDENCE

The incidence of significant congenital malformations is about 2–5% at birth; a lower incidence of 1 in 500 is however reported from the hospital statistics of India.

(B) DIAGNOSIS

(I) ANTE-NATAL

GENETIC COUNSELLING. Genetic counselling is the screening procedure designed to identify the individual having a greater risk of producing an offspring with genetic abnormalities. Identification of the cases at risk is done by meticulous family and reproductive history, as well as the possible effects of the environmental factors. Birth of a congenitally malformed baby increases the chance of repetition to the extent of 6 folds and that following the two consecutive babies increases the chance to 70% as compared to normal woman. The aim is to allow the patient and her husband to make a unified decision regarding future management of pregnancy. Its objectives are to provide information, assist in counselling and help the couple to adjust to the problem and hereby to decrease the incidence of births of genetically defective babies.

(II) POSTNATAL

(*a*) CLINICAL EVALUATION AT BIRTH. While gross palpable congenital malformations are easily evident at birth, concealed abnormalities of grave magnitude are more often missed unless conscious of their entity. These include malformations like imperforated anus or tracheo oesophageal fistula.

(*b*) RADIOGRAPHY. It helps to detect the abnormalities in the gastro-intestinal tract like oesophageal or duodend atresia and the extent of atresia in imperforate anus, etc.

C. INVESTIGATION PROTOCOL (CURRENTLY AVAILABLE METHODS)

(A) *DIAGNOSIS IN EARLY PREGNANCY.* The groups of disorders that can be detected early enough in pregnancy so as to consider termination are (1) chromosonal abnormalities (Down's Syndrome); (2) open neural tube defects; (3) inborn error of metabolism; (4) X-linked recessive disorders. The following diagnostic procedures are available for their early detection:

- Amniocentesis
- Sonography
- Estimation of alpha foetoprotein in the amniotic fluid
- Foetoscopy
- Chorionic villus biopsy
- Chordocentesis

(B) *DIAGNOSIS IN LATE MONTHS OF PREGNANCY.* It is of limited value in the screening programme. For diagnostic purpose, it is used only in the later months of pregnancy.

(1) Simple radiography to diagnose gross skeletal abnormalities such as anencephaly, marked hydrocephaly, open spinabifida etc.

(2) Angiography to detect atresia of gastrointestinal tract, tracheo-oesophageal fistula or diaphragmatic hernia.

(3) Feotography to detect soft tissue anomalies like meningocele, extrophy of bladder or certaneous oedema hydrops foetalis etc.

(4) Sonography replaces all the methods employed in later months of pregnancy.

(D) SCREENING IN PREGNANCY TO DETECT CONGENITAL ABNORMALITY OF THE FOETUS

Nature of investigation	*Period of gestation*	*Maternal study*	*Abnormality detected*
Examination of maternal blood	14 weeks	Estimation of Alphafoeto-protein	Open nural tube defects
Non-invasive remote examination ultrasonography	16–22 weeks	Foetal visualisation, skeleton and visceral echoes	To detect skeletal or visceral abnormalities
Invasive direct exam (under Sonar guidance) Amniotic fluid study (Amniocentesis)	14–16 weeks	Desquamated foetal cell study Culture/chromosomal study Biochemical/Enzyme study	Barr bodies for foetal sex to determine x-linked diseases Down's syndrome Open neural tube defect To defect inborn error of metabolism Tay-sachs disease
Chorion villus biopsy	6–11 weeks	Culture/chromosomal/enzyme study	Same as above, as such mostly replacing amniocentesis
Foetoscopy	17–20 weeks	Foetal blood/ tissues	To detect haemoglobinopathies on haemophilia Enzyme study for certain inborn error of metabolism Congenital skin disease Foetal infection specially —TORCH
Cordocentesis	18 weeks	Foetal blood	Same as above as such replacing foetoscopy

(ix) *Various causes of Asphyxia—steps for early detection*

(A) DEFINITION. In common clinical practice, asphyxia neonatorum means non-establishment of satisfactory pulmonary respiration at birth. Its literal meaning is absence of pulse.

(B) AETIOLOGY. The aetiology of asphyxia can be classified broadly into the following groups:

– Continuation of intrauterine hypoxia.

- Birth trauma to the neonate.
- Prenatal and intranatal medication to the mother.

These often overlap making isolation of a single causative factor difficult.

Continuation of intrauterine hypoxia:

- Premature placental separation, extensive infarcts with or without postdatism, retroplacental haemorrhage, thin small placenta, circum vallate placenta, hypertensive disorders in pregnancy, supine hypotensive syndrome, cord compression, true knot in cord, vascular anomalies in cord—are some of the important causes.
- MATERNAL HYPOXIC STATES. The maternal diseases such as anaemia, eclampsia, cyanotic cardio vascular disorders, status asthmaticus, emphysema, shock and hypotension etc.

(C) BIRTH TRAUMA. It may occur in vaginal delivery as in breech, occipito posterior requiring manipulative and operative procedure. Premature attempt of the foetus to initiate respiratory efforts in utero results in:

(1) Increased venous pressure;

(2) Aspiration of amniotic fluid. The end result is either:

(*i*) Intrauterine foetal death due to cardiac failure or

(*ii*) Delivery of an asphyxiated baby, the degree of which is dependent upon the intensity and duration of noxious effects.

(D) MEDICATIONS. Morphine, pethidine and anaesthetic agents depress the respiratory centres directly and the chance of development of asphyxia is increased.

(E) CLINICAL FEATURES. According to the parameters denoted by Apgar, a scoring procedure has been designed for better understanding of the clinical state. The Apgar score is related to the status of oxygenation of the foetus at or immediately after birth. In case where the score remains significantly depressed at 5 minutes it should be evaluated again after 15 minutes. This scoring is done in a new born baby at 1 minute, 5 minutes and 15 minutes and can be tabulated as follows:

(F) APGAR SCORING

Signs	*0*	*1*	*2*
Respiratory effort	Absent	Slow, irregular	Good, crying
Heart rate	Absent	Slow (below 100)	Over 100
Muscle tone	Flaccid	Flexion of extremities	Active body movements
Reflex irritability	No response	Grimace	Cry
Colour	Blue, pale	Body pink, extremities blue	complete pink
Total score = 10	No depression = 7–10	Mild depression = 4–6	Severe depression = 0–3

6 Medicine[1]

(i) ***Disclosure of information*** The duty of the physician is to examine the patient, record the findings, diagnose the disease, prescribe investigations, if necessary, and to explain the possible treatment and its natural outcome. The male doctors examining female patients especially rectally or vaginally, are duty bound to do so in presence or hearing of a female relative or nurse or receptionist or any member of the practising team. The neurologist[2] has a duty to explain the patient that anti-convulsant drugs have risks of inducing foetal abnormalities and can reduce the efficiency of oral contraceptive pills.

Many patients with malignant disease are happy to continue in blissful ignorance of the true nature of the disease.

1 *General Practice*, Professor Brian Jarman, PhD, FRCP referred to *Medical Negligence* by Michael J. Powers and Nigel H. Harris, Chapter 20, Edition 1990; Dr. A.G. Ghoshal, MD, DNB, FCCP, WHO Fellow.

2 *Neurology*, Dr. F.B. Gibberd, MD, FRCP referred to *Medical Negligence* by Michael J. Powers and Nigel H. Harris, Chapter 24, Edition 1990.

It is important that the majority of the patients suffering from cancer or the members of their family must be informed of the disease and possible complications of recommended treatment, e.g. radiotherapy, chemotherapy etc.[3] Negligence was attributed to the doctor when a mother suffered post-traumatic shock on being wrongly and negligently informed that her newborn child had died.[4]

The physician must explain about invasive procedure which can be therapeutic or diagnostic. The risks of therapeutic procedures can be judged against the possible advantages. The risks of diagnostic procedures are not directly related with benefit. The patients must know about the possible findings of the procedure and subsequent probable treatment. For example, exploratory arthrotomy and synovial biopsy are recognised procedures for early diagnosis of joint tuberculosis, particularly when clinical and radiological findings are inconclusive.[5]

(ii) *Precaution in use of drugs* The prescription of a doctor needs to be legibly written, so that the pharmacist can understand the statement of the doctor.[6] It is expected that the doctor will take proper care not to cause injury to the sciatic nerve at the time of administration of injection on the buttock of the patient.[7]

Injection of penicillin (intramuscular or intravenous) should always be preceded by skin test for hypersensitivity. Absence of the latter may be attributed to negligence. Side-effects of drugs should be explained to the patients before administration. For example, tremor with oral salbutamol, extrapyramidal rigidity with drugs like metoclopramide. All

3 *Medico-legal Problems in the Non-surgical Management of Cancer*: Dr. A.M. Jelliffe, MD, FRCP referred to *Medical Negligence* by Michael J. Powers and Nigel H. Harris (Chapter 25), Edition 1990.

4 *Allin* v *City and Hackney Health Authority* [1996]7 Med LR 167.

5 JIMA, vol. 90, p. 263.

6 *Prendergast* v *Sam & Dee Ltd.* [1989]1 Med LR 36.

7 *A.M. Mathew* v *Director, Karuna Hospital* 1998(1) CPR 39 (Ker); I(1998) CPJ 476 (Ker); 1999 CCJ 960 (Ker); *Kanaiyalal Ramanlal Trivedi* v *Dr. Satyanarayan Vishwakarm*a 1996(3) CPR 24 (Guj); I(1997) CPJ 332 (Guj); 1998 CCJ 690 (Guj).

analgesics may cause gastric irritation, vomiting and even gastric bleeding—patients should be cautioned against overdose.

(iii) *Common advice to the patients* Important advices like salt restriction, bed rest, cessation of addiction should be prescribed in writing. Epileptics should be cautioned in writing against fire, high places and occupational hazards. Diabetic patients should be advised to carry their prescriptions indicating disease and doses of drugs least they fall in coma (diabetic or hypoglycemic) in unknown circumstances.

(iv) *Treatment of some common diseases*

(A) DYSENTERY. The disease spectrum of shigellosis or bacillary dysentery can change from mild diarrhoea to severe dysenteric syndrome leading to mortality. Appropriate antibiotic therapy decreases the duration of fever, diarrhoea and excretion of the pathogen in Shigella infection. Shigella strains are resistant to commonly used antibiotics, but are susceptible to nalidixic acid, gentamycin, and furazolidone. Ciprofloxacin and norfloxacin are effective in treatment of Shigellosis.

(B) DYSPEPSIA. It may be an early symptom of serious illness, such as peptic ulcer, cholelithiasis or gastric carcinoma, but often no organic lesion is found. Before carrying out special investigations like endoscopy, sonography, mucosal biopsy, barium X-ray series of gastrointenstinal tract etc, the patient must be advised for routine stool examination by concentration method at least for three consecutive days in order to exclude parasitic infestation.[8] Persistent dyspepsia should be investigated with upper gastrointestinal endoscopy.

(C) URTICARIA. It is a vascular reaction pattern characterised by transient, erythematous swellings of the skin and/or mucous membranes. An endeavour to establish the cause of urticaria must be made by eliciting the history of correlating urticaria to season, environment, food, drugs, physical

8 JIMA, vol. 90, p. 128.

activity, heat and cold. A thorough interrogation into the environment, food-habit and the history of drug intake like aspirin and related non-steroidal anti-inflammatory drugs, oral contraceptives, anti-diarrhoeal, laxatives and cough mixtures, is mandatory. Avoiding precipitating cause, if identifiable, is essential for treatment. The mainstay of treatment is anti-histamines.[9]

(D) ENTERIC FEVER.[10] Typhoid fever is acute systemic febrile infection caused by a group of organism of the genus salmonella. The complications with typhoid fever are more common in children than in adults. Intestinal perforation, severe haemorrhage coupled with peritonitis and toxic encephalopathy are life threatening complications of this disease. The chronic carrier state even after full course of treatment is a known complication of typhoid.

To diagnose typhoid fever total count of W.B.C. (shows leucopenia) along with culture of blood (in the first week) is advisable followed by Widal test (in the 2nd week) which is mandatory. Stool and urine culture in the 2nd and 3rd week of the disease is also important. Though chloramphenicol is the mainstay of treatment, the more potent antibiotics like ciprofloxacin and other conventional drugs like amoxicillin, ampicillin and cotrimoxazole have come into play for treatment of typhoid due to more and more resistance to chloramphenicol.

Drug resistant typhoid is on the rise and lack of response to other drugs like ciprofloxacin should prompt the physician to go for culture and sensitivity (blood & urine) test. Third generation cephalosporins like ceftriaxone are now the recommended drugs in this situation.

(E) ANIMAL BITES. No vaccine gives hundred per cent protection against rabies. Presently two types of tissue culture vaccine (TCV) are freely available in India, i.e. human diploid cell strain vaccine (HDCSV) and purified chick embryo cell vaccine

9 JIMA, vol. 90, p. 21.
10 Harrison's *Principles of Internal Medicine* (vols. 1 & 2), 12th Edition.

(PCECV). Another vaccine called purified vero cell rabies vaccine (PVCRV) produced at Pasteur Institute, Coonoor in Tamil Nadu will be released shortly for public use. Though tissue culture vaccines (TCV) are more potent than nerve tissue vaccines (NTV), the outcome of the treatment depends on factors like severity of exposure, how soon the treatment was started, whether proper wound treatment was given, and whether timely administration of anti-rabies serum (ARS) was done. The dosage schedule for TCV like HDCSV and PCECV is 1 ml of reconstitued vaccine administered by either intramuscular or deep subcutaneous route over the deltoid on days 0, 3, 7, 14, 28 and 30. This dosage is applicable to both class II and class III exposure cases, but in class III cases, ARS should be administered in proper dose. According to the recommendation of WHO, class I exposure cases need not be given any treatment, but if the patient is apprehensive 3 doses of TCV can be advocated on days, 0, 7, and 21. All immunosuppressive drugs and anti-malarials like chloroquine should be avoided during the course of treatment.[11]

(F) HEADACHE. The commonest causes of chronic headache are sinusitis, migraine, tension-headache (muscular) and hypertension. However, any intracerebral event like vascular malformation, tumour, viral or bacterial infection—may cause chronic headache. Diagnosis rests primarily on good history taking, general and neurological examination including measurement of blood pressure, and ophthalmoscopy.

Treatment should be based on specific diagnosis as far as possible. X-ray skull is frequently non-contributory. CT Scan of brain is invaluable for diagnosis, but not mandatory as the first investigation. CT brain may be recommended if there is any doubt in diagnosis or if the treatment is not effective initially. If headache is associated with other symptoms like vomiting or diplopia, intracerebral events will be high in the list.

(G) MALARIA. Intermittent fever coming with chill and rigor and subsiding with sweating is the commonest symptom of

11 JIMA, vol. 91, p. 20.

malaria. Malaria Parasites should be searched in blood (thick and thin films) within the first few days. However, other fevers like viral, typhoid and septicaemia may present with these symptoms. Malaria itself may present atypically with continuous or irregular fever. Malaria Parasite is not always detectable in peripheral blood; repeated examinations are necessary. One may look for falciparum antigen in blood if falciparum malaria is suspected. Empirical anti-malarial (chloroquine) may be started on clinical grounds after subjecting blood for malaria parasites test. Doses of anti-malarials have been suggested in national guidelines. It is the duty of the doctor to abide by the national guidelines.

(H) **CHEST PAIN.** Chest pain is a very common symptom. Mid-sternal chest pain may be due to cardiac or gastro-esophagial origin. Belching or flatulence may accompany both. Cardiac pain is usually aggravated on exertion and relieved on rest. Non-cardiac chest pain (neurocirculatory asthenia) is very common, more so in anxious and nervous patients. Resting ECG may be normal in all. Relation to exertion is the most important clue in cardiac pain. Other chest pain may be in chest wall (costo chondritis) or pleural (sharp localised pain). Differentiation can be done clinically. Whenever suspected ECG and cardiac enzyme estimation in serum should be ordered to exclude myocardial ischemia/infarction.

(I) **JAUNDICE.** Jaundice may be hemolytic (due to destruction of blood), hepatocellular (liver disease) or obstructive (obstruction in excretion of bile). Drug history and test for viral infection (Hepatitis B) are mandatory in all cases of hepatocellular jaundice. Ultrasonography of the liver and biliary tract should be done in all cases of obstructive jaundice.

(J) **ASTHMA.** Acute severe asthma is a medical emergency and the patient should be hospitalised. Sedating the patient without arrangements for resuscitation or ventilator in the event of probable respiratory arrest is contraindicated. Oxygen, nebulisers and cortico steroids (oral or parenteral) are the cornerstones of therapy.

(K) **BLOOD TRANSFUSION.** Mismatched blood transfusion is frequently a fatal event. All the particulars including patient's name, bed and ward number, batch number of the bottle, blood group and date of expiry should be checked and noted with date, time and doctor's signature before transfusing the blood. Lack of proper documentation may be attributed to negligence.

7 Paediatrics[12]

(i) ***Disclosure of information*** The duty of the paediatricians is to inform the parents or guardians of the details of diagnosis, treatment and prognosis known from time to time. Explanation of complicated investigations, and laboratory tests are expected from the caring doctors. Parents should be kept informed of the change in treatment and the likely outcome of the treatment. Particular care is required at the time of prescribing dose and volume of the drug with damaging side effects. The doctors have an obligation to give factual information to the parents and respond to their questions. To avoid future allegation of negligence the paediatrician must take care to prepare the clinical note reflecting the condition of deterioration or improvement of the child, diagnosis, advice for investigations, treatment including change in treatment, prognosis, and important points discussed with parents. The clinical note must be prepared contemporaneously and if necessary, a retrospective clarifying note with proper signature, date and explanation may be added to the original clinical note.

A good physician is the person who treats well his patient and satisfies the parents avoiding any misunderstanding that lead to litigation. He should be readily available to give information and condition of the patient as developed from time to time. Any change of treatment if necessary should be conveyed to the parents and also its likely outcomes. There should be no excessive optimism that raises false hope or excessive pessimism that destroys all hope.

The conservative treatment given to a premature baby of 29 weeks was upheld by the Consumer Court,[13] as the

12 *The Paediatrician and Medical Negligence*, Professor A.G.M. Campbell, FRCP, DCH referred to *Medical Negligence* by Michael J. Powers and Nigel H. Harris, Chapter 22, Edition 1990; Dr. R. Jana, MBBS, DCH.

13 *Anup Kumar Jana* v *Dr. Pabitra Chatterjee* 1998(1) CPR 693 (Cal).

treatment was supported by the medical authority. The allegation that the baby of 29 weeks pregnancy was fully matured is contrary to the established medical opinion, as a full grown baby requires 37 weeks for normal maturity.

(ii) ***Birth asphyxia and development of cerebral palsy*** Failure of establishment of spontaneous breathing at one minute or presence of unsatisfactory ventilation as evidenced by slow gasping breathing are suggestive of birth asphyxia. Spontaneous breathing with smooth change over from foetal to neonatal life is the rule in most of the cases. Only a few, about 3·5-7·5 per cent of babies require active resuscitation. These cases only require continuous watch, observations and prompt intervention by obstetrician. Obstetrician should alert paediatrician of high risk pregnancies in advance as in the cases of placental insufficiency, hypertension, toxaemia, diabetes mellitus, malpresentation, bleeding in the second or third trimester, drug therapy, premature labour, ante-partem haemorrhage etc. Understanding and co-operation between obstetricians and paediatrician is desirable for a healthy outcome in all the above mentioned critical situations. High risk deliveries should be attended by a physician well trained in the art of cardiorespiratory resuscitation. Delivery room should be well-equipped for resuscitation of an asphyxiated baby. Resuscitation kit must be checked by the physician before each delivery. It must include straight blade baby laryngoscope with its light source, oxygen cylinder, press type rubber bulb or oral suction Dee Lee mucus trap, ambu bag and mask, endotracheal tube of different sizes. All electrical points should be checked before hand. The kit should also contain syringes, needle 7·5 per cent sodium bicarbonate, epinephrine one in 10,000, nalorphine, naloxone hydrochloride, ampoules of distilled water, physiological saline .5% dextrose. Resuscitation of newborn is not cost effective but is highly skill oriented.

Brain damage causes cerebral palsy which is a non-progressive neuromuscular disorder of cerebral origins, factors lying in the prenatal, intranatal or postnatal period. Mentally handicapped child is a personal and family tragedy. Medico legal help is sought in many cases in causation of mentally handicapped child due to negligence of obstetrician as well as paediatrician. Failure of obstetrician to diagnose foetal asphyxia and of paediatrician for not doing intubation timely may cause invariable trauma to brain leading to hypoxic ischaemic encephalopathy. Foetal hypoxia can be diagnosed by abnormalities of foetal heart-rate (slow foetal heart-rate without any variability in response to foetal movements or uterine contractions), passage of meconium into the amniotic fluid and by foetus scalp blood sampling for acidosis.

(iii) ***Intrauterine hypoxia*** Intrauterine hypoxia as identified by obstetrician does not inevitably lead either to neonatal symptoms or to evidences of later damage. Some neonates tolerate anoxia better than others. Babies who have suffered intrapartum hypoxia are likely to be asphyxiated and have difficulties in establishing independent respiration and circulation. The conventional method of assessing neonatal status is by means of Apgar Score and there are significant correlations between very low Apgar Scores of less than 3 at birth and moderately low Apgar Scores of less than 8 continuing beyond first 20 minutes of life and later neurological dysfunctions. Absence of significant neonatal asphyxia as evidenced by Apgar Score and other clinical criteria is a strong pointer against intrapartum asphyxia. Many severely asphyxiated newborns do not develop cerebral palsy and many infants with cerebral palsy have no history of perinatal asphyxia. Clinical notes should be given in every case. It should contain all details of the patient and the action taken. Causes should be mentioned if any action is not taken.

There are some limitations of Apgar Score. Recently action oriented assessment (depicted by presence or absence of foetal distress, pethidine or morphine given, first cry, respirations and heart beat) offers immediate therapeutic guideline for managing an asphyxiated baby. Most babies can be resuscitated by bag and mask ventilation. However if cardiac status fails to improve or heart rate falls below 60 per minute infant should be ventilated with intermittent positive pressure after endotracheal intubation. It should not be delayed beyond 2 to 3 minutes to ensure effective oxygenation within 5 minutes after birth. In meconium stained liquor, oral cavity, oropharynx and hypopharynx should be sucked as soon as head is delivered before baby takes its first breath to avoid meconium aspiration. Apparently still born baby should be immediately intubated and ventilated with intermittent positive pressure with simultaneous external cardiac massage.

(iv) ***Resuscitation*** Failure to breathe spontaneously within one minute of birth is an indication for resuscitation.[14] The duration between return of heart beat and the commencement of regular rhythmic respiration as the possible cause of brain damage is still a bone of contention. There are instances of permanent brain damage where regular respiration is not established within 90 seconds, and there are instances of no brain damage in spite of failure of starting regular respiration within 30 minutes of return of heart-beat. Resuscitation of severely asphyxiated infants of any gestation age, weight and apparent abnormality is the prime duty of the paediatrician. It may be done by mouth to mouth respiration and mild stimulation followed by bag and mask ventilation, failing which intubation is indicated and expected. Owing to congenital abnormality, neonatal intubation is sometimes extremely difficult. Failure of the heart rate to respond to intubation within seconds indicates that the indotracheal tube has slipped into the oesophagus instead of the trachea, and the error must be corrected by immediate re-intubation. The decision to defer intubation or for not intubating must be documented by describing the clinical condition of the infant, especially heart-rate, respiratory effort, peripheral perfusion and tone.

(v) ***Immunisation*** One effective way of controlling the spread of infection is to strengthen the host defences. Under certain circumstances this may be accomplished by active immunization which is one of the most powerful and cost effective weapon of modern science. There are some infectious diseases whose control is solely based on active immunization e.g. polio, tetanus, diphtheria, measles. Every country has its immunization schedule. The following is the table of National Immunization Schedule of India:

14 Nelson, *Text Book of Paediatrics*, Chapter 8, 15th Ed. 1996.

NATIONAL IMMUNIZATION SCHEDULE[15]

Vaccine	*When to give*	*Dose*
FOR INFANTS		
BCG	At birth or as early as possible till one year of age	0.1 ml (0.05 ml until 1 month age)
Hepatitis B–Birth Dose	At birth or as early as possible within 24 hours	0.5 ml
OPV-0	At birth or as early as possible within the first 15 days	2 drops
OPV 1, 2 & 3	At 6 weeks, 10 weeks & 14 weeks (OPV can be given till 5 years of age)	2 drops
Pentavalent 1, 2 & 3	At 6 weeks, 10 weeks & 14 weeks (can be given till one year of age)	0.5 ml
Rotavirus#	At 6 weeks, 10 weeks & 14 weeks (can be given till one year of age)	5 drops
IPV	Two fractional dose at 6 and 14 weeks of age	0.1 ml
Measles /MR 1st Dose$	9 completed months-12 months (can be given till 5 years of age)	0.5 ml
JE - 1*	9 completed months-12 months	0.5 ml
Vitamin A (1st dose)	At 9 completed months with measles —Rubella	1 ml (1 lakh IU)
FOR CHILDREN		
DPT booster-1	16-24 months	0.5 ml
Measles/MR 2nd dose$	16-24 months	0.5 ml
OPV Booster	16-24 months	2 drops
JE-2	16-24 months	0.5 ml
Vitamin A** (2nd to 9th dose)	16-18 months. Then one dose every 6 months up to the age of 5 years	2 ml (2 lakh IU)
DPT Booster-2	5-6 years	0.5 ml
TT	10 years & 16 years	0.5 ml

\# Phased introduction, at present in Andhra Pradesh, Haryana, Himachal Pradesh and Orissa from 2016 & expanded in Madhya Pradesh, Assam, Rajasthan and Tripura in February 2017 and planned in Tamil Nadu & Uttar Pradesh in 2017.

$ Phased introduction, at present in five states namely Karnataka, Tamil Nadu, Goa, Lakshadweep and Puducherry. (As of February 2017).

* JE Vaccine is introduced in select endemic districts after the campaign.

** The 2nd to 9th doses of Vitamin A can be administered to children 1-5 years old during biannual rounds, in collaboration with ICDS.

15 Collected from <https://main.mohfw.gov.in/sites/default/files/245453521061489663873.pdf>, last visited on 8.12.2020.

Care should be taken during immunization, as the vaccines are not inert. The risks and benefits of immunization must be discussed with the parents or guardians. Personal or strong family history of epilepsy, convulsions, any febrile upset until fully recovered or reaction to previous doses of DPT, are the contraindications of DPT. Reactions include collapse or shock-like state, persistent screaming episodes, temperature above 40°C. Subsequent immunization with DT only is recommended. Patients with history of systemic anaplylaxis after eating egg may rarely be a special risk for anaplylaxis after administration of vaccines that contain egg proteins. Measles, mumps, and measles-mumps-rubella vaccine have been included among vaccines with such precautions. Administration of vaccines should be supervised carefully with preparations of 1:1000 Epinephrine at hand.

A child who received vaccination against DPT at the age of 4 months, had suffered encephalopathy, i.e. impairment of brain function after vaccination. The parents of the child claimed compensation against the State through Secretary of Health and Human Services. The United States Supreme Court,[16] denied the claim of compensation to the parents of the child on the ground that the child had been microcephalic before vaccination which was evidence of encephalopathy, though the child had suffered seizures within three days of the vaccination.

(vi) *Neonatal screening* Neonatal screening for some diseases are very important as omission of their diagnosis in many cases cause mental retardation. Early diagnosis of hypothyroid state and its therapy before 2 months of age is mandatory for normal physical and mental development. Screening is done by estimation of T_4 levels but definitive diagnosis of congenital hypothyridim is based on elevated TSH level. Its worldwide prevalence is in the range of one per 4000 infants. Recently it has been shown that over 4 per cent of infants born to mothers belonging to endemic iodine deficient belt in India having biochemical evidences of

16 *Donna E. Shalala* v *Margaret Whitecotton* [1995]131 L Ed 2d 374; 115 S Ct 1477.

neonatal hypothyroidism. These babies should receive replacement hormone therapy as early as possible to avoid mental retardation.

Deficiency of enzyme phenylalanine hydroxylase causes accumulation of phenylalanine in body fluids in a condition termed phenylketonuria—a disorder of autosomal recessive inheritance. Brain cells are deprived of amino acid which are essential nutrients for their maturation and myelination during the period of rapid neurological development in infancy and early childhood. In newbron periodical diagnosis is made by routine screening of all neonates specially in siblings of known patients by Guthrie's test. If the dietary treatment is initiated within a few weeks of birth mental retardation can be prevented.

Galactosemia is another autosomal recessive disorder manifesting within a few days after birth after ingestion of milk. Prolonged physiologial jaundice is found in newborn. Liver is enlarged and cataract appears within a few weeks. Children become mentally retarded. Vomiting or diarrhoea, failure to thrive are common manifestations. Galactose free diet started early leads to rapid clinical improvement.

The view expressed by the Supreme Court on the basis of expert opinion is that all infants with birth weight of less than 1500 grams or gestational age of less than 32 weeks are required to be screened for Retinopathy of Prematurity (in short ROP) during 2 to 4 weeks of age to avoid permanent blindness.[17]

(vii) *Surgical conditions*

(A) CHOANAL ATRASIA. Choanal atrasia is a condition where posterior nasal air passage is blocked by a bony or membranous septum so baby suffers from severe respiratory difficulties since birth. The inability to pass a catheter through the nose confirms diagnosis.

(B) CONGENITAL DIAPHRAGMATIC HERNIA. The persistence of pleuroperitoneal canal results in herniation of abdominal contents into thorax resulting in mediastinum shifting and

17 *V. Krishnakumar* v *State of Tamil Nadu* (2015)9 SCC 388.

compression of lung, with difficult resuscitation. Alertness and prompt action is vital for saving these babies. Breathing with bag and mask should never be attempted as it causes gaseous distension of bowel and respiratory difficulty worsens.

(C) CONGENITAL DISLOCATION OF HIP JOINTS. It is found in 10-20 per 1000 live born infants. Condition is more common among first born, post term or large infants and female babies delivered following breech presentation. Routine examination of hips of all infants by Ortolani Barlow manoeuvre is essential for early diagnosis and early management is essential for optimal functional recovery.

(viii) *Infection* Infection may present in a number of insiduous ways throughout infancy. Meningitis may be considered as possible diagnosis when there is no obvious focus for the child's illness. Once meningitis is suspected, investigations like blood for bacterial culture and lumbar puncture for cerebro-spinal fluid examination, need to be undertaken promptly. Widal test in the second week of the disease and the blood culture in first seven days are mandatory to confirm the diagnosis of enteric fever. Oral rehydration solution (ORS) should be used in the treatment of gastroenteritis without delay because electrolyte imbalance is rapid in children. The ORS prevents the fatal outcome. The chest x-ray is mandatory for confirmatory diagnosis of pneumonia. Failure to diagnose septicaemia in early stage is fatal to the child. Similarly, failure to estimate serum-bilirubin at regular interval for diagnosis of congenital hyper-bilirubinemia and its fatal outcome as Kernicterus is negligence on the part of a paediatrician.

8 Surgery

(i) *Common errors of surgeons*[1]

(A) DISCLOSURE OF INFORMATION. The dissatisfaction of the patients following surgery stems from inadequate communication between patient and surgeon during pre-

1 *General Surgery*, Professor Michael Hobsley, PhD, FRCS; Mr. John Scurr, BSc, MB, FRCS referred to *Medical Negligence* by Michael J. Powers and Nigel H. Harris, Chapter 28, Edition 1990; Dr. Sudip C. Chakraborty, MS, MNAMS, MCh.

operative stage. The expected chances of success and failure, the risk and benefit of the procedure, the hazards and complications of the particular surgery and the procedure of anesthesia should be explained to the patient and his relatives in the language understood by them before obtaining written consent for the operation. The surgeon should not hesitate to explain and inform the patient and his relatives about the actual procedure of surgery with associated risks and complications, so that failure of the surgery or the adverse consequences may not be construed by the patient and his relatives as negligence of the surgeon. To avoid future allegation of negligence the surgeon may record in the case history the points of discussion as far as practicable.

For example, the surgeon is duty bound to inform the patient of the risk of alteration of voice following any operation to remove thyroid gland. The patient undergoing parotid surgery or complicated mastoid operation has right to know about occasional unavoidable complications of injury to facial nerve and the risk of facial nerve injury.

The duty of the plastic surgeon[2] is to explain that the surgeon cannot remove the scars, but can place the scar where it is not seen. The patient must be warned of the risk of losing nipple sensation in surgery of breast augmentation or reduction. The patient undergoing gastric surgery must know the recognised complications like alteration in digestion which leads to dumping syndrome. It is mandatory to warn the patients undergoing prostatectomy that retrograde ejaculation and sexual impotency may occur. The patients undergoing vasectomy operation must know that sterility is not achieved immediately after the operation and that normal contraception should continue until a few consecutive semen analysis proves the absence of spermatozoa. The leakage of bile or jaundice due to inadvertent injury to the bile duct is complication of gall bladder surgery. Moreover, the risk or failure of vasectomy operation should be disclosed to the patient pre-operatively.

2 *Medical Negligence in Plastic Surgery*, Mr. John R. Cobbett, MB, FRCS referred to *Medical Negligence* by Michael J. Powers and Nigel H. Harris, Chapter 33, Edition 1990.

Any patient having wax syringed from the external auditory meatus should be warned of the complications like vasovagal attack, rupture of old healed perforation, and damage to the external auditory meatus from unexpected movements of the patient. The swelling of the face, numbness in face, and minor haemorrhage are common complications of operation on maxillary antrum. The surgeon must discuss pre-operatively about dislocation of teeth and reactionary secondary haemorrhage in the surgery of removal of tonsils and adenoids. The advantage and disadvantage of stapedectomy must be explained to the patient because hearing aid is an effective alternative method of treatment.[3]

It is not always possible to make a diagnosis other than by surgical means i.e. exploratory operation or biopsy. In case of acute abdomen, sometimes it is not possible to diagnose clinically and laparotomy is indicated for diagnosis. The negative outcome does not necessarily amount to negligence, provided pre-operative discussion with the patient is done.

(B) TREATMENT BEFORE SURGERY. It is the duty of the surgeon to make some routine investigations before every surgery. (*a*) Haemoglobin, TC, DC, ESR; (*b*) bleeding time, clotting time; (*c*) blood urea, creatinine, blood sugar (fasting and PP); (*d*) X-ray chest, ECG and cardiology check up should be done before undertaking operation. Tetanus toxoid injection (of two doses) should be given as prophylaxis against tetanus before any open elective surgery. That apart, special investigations should be done as per requirement in individual cases of super speciality. For example, in cholecystectomy, the surgeon should advise for oral cholecystography to confirm the existence and location of stone in gall bladder, apart from ultrasonography. The blood sugar of a known diabetic should be controlled pre-operatively, so that the patient becomes euglycaemic before surgery. Similarly, effort should be made to control the hypertension as far as possible pre-operatively with proper medication under the guidance of a cardiologist.

3 *Otorhinolaryngology*, Sir Donald Harrison, MD, PhD, FRCS referred to *Medical Negligence* by Michael J. Powers and Nigel H. Harris, Chapter 35, Edition 1990.

The duty of the surgeon is to review the history of the patient, make clinical examination of his own, and persue the result of investigations before undertaking surgery. Failure to obtain the history of the patient may result in omission to make proper clinical examination leading to inappropriate therapy resulting tragic end of the patient. For example, patient presenting back pain is not asked to show the site of pain. Without examining the location of pain, the orthopaedic surgeon orders a lumbar spine x-ray which is negative. The review of history of the patient detected that the pain was lower dorsal spreading to the lumbar region. Taking careful history and proper clinical examination could have indicated that there was lower dorsal spine pathology and an appropriate x-ray could have revealed the tuberculous vertebra.

As an abundant precaution before any operation to remove thyroid tissue, the vocal cords should be examined to check whether they move normally, in default the paralysis of vocal cords may be ascribed to damage to the nerve during the operation. Similarly, any one presenting with a lump in the breast should be carefully examined and depending on findings of examination, appropriate investigations should be advised. Patients with history of excessive bleeding require pre-operative investigation like full blood count, platelet count, and prothrombin time. Bleeding diathesis like haemophilia, Christmas disease may be detected pre-operatively by specific history taking including family history and detailed coagulation profile study. To embark upon a surgical procedure unaware of the coagulation problem, in spite of a definite history and consequently without adequate blood readily available for replacing losses may constitute negligence. For patients with AB Negative and O Negative blood group, adequate blood of that particular group should be arranged after grouping and cross-matching pre-operatively, if the situation so demands. It is also considered negligent to operate on a patient with pre-existing chest infection without taking steps to reduce the risks to the patients in the pre-operative stage. Patients with already established infections should be treated pre-operatively with specific drug as per culture sensitivity report whenever possible e.g. urine culture, pus culture, blood culture and CSF culture.

It is important to enquire about the drug history of the patient before surgery because many commonly used drugs have serious complications if continued during the operation. Specific drug history and specially history of allergy to any drug will help the surgeon to avoid complications and to facilitate post operative management of the patient. Skin test for allergic manifestation should be done in certain injectable drugs which are known to cause severe sometimes fatal drug reaction like anaphylactic shock e.g. penicillin group, I.V. Iodine contrast. The patient should be warned of the side effect of the drug before surgery. The surgeon must consider whether his skill and resources available will have any impact on the risk and result of the surgery. The error of operation on wrong limb must be avoided by following clear written medical record and correctly labelled x-ray by the surgeon immediately before the operation. Before removal of vital organs like eye, kidney etc. the surgeon must be absolutely certain about the side of affected disease. It is mandatory to ascertain the normal function of the unaffected kidney before removal of the contralateral kidney with even malignancy or non-functioning kidney.

(c) **Delay in surgery.** The delay in surgical treatment is considered negligence where the correct diagnosis indicates urgent surgery. For example, a child presents with two days' history of increasing pain in the hip, limb and high fever, which is diagnosed as septic arthritis with or without acute osteomyelitis. Failure to improve significantly after 24 hours of administering antibiotics is an indication for urgent surgical drainage of the abscess.

The strangulated inguinal hernia is diagnosed by clinical examination. The undue delay for adequate resuscitation without taking the patient to the operation theatre may constitute negligence. Similarly, delay in operation of acute appendicitis, may develop ruptured appendix and pelvic sepsis causing death or fertility problem in young girls. It is advisable that the actual critical condition of the patient should be documented at the time of first presentation to and examination by the surgeon. The surgeon attached to general hospital, Ernakulam confirmed the diagnosis of acute appendicitis, but did not perform surgery on the patient who died due to perforated appendix. The surgeon was held negligent by Kerala High Court.[4]

(D) DAMAGE DURING SURGERY. Bleeding is inevitable in surgery. The bloodless operation requires application of tourniquet which very often causes damage to normal nerves. The surgeon must apply reasonable care not only in application and removal of the tourniquet, but also the duration and pressure of application of the same. Failure to remove the tourniquet at the end of the operation is actionable negligence. Retention of instrument or foreign body within the abdominal cavity excites reaction which invariably involves additional adhesion formation and may be associated with some local sepsis. The surgeons were held negligent for leaving artery forceps,[5] a metallic tip of suction tube,[6] sponge,[7] and mop,[8] inside abdomen of the patient during surgery. It is the duty of the surgeon to ascertain the cause of complications during surgery and to take effective remedial measures as far as practicable.

The surgeon often asks the anaesthetist to administer drugs that lowers blood pressure during operation involving territory with abundant blood supply, e.g. face, neck etc. In such cases, it is the duty of the surgeon to ask the anaesthetist to raise the blood pressure back to normal before closing the

4 *Dr. T.T. Thomas* v *Elisa* AIR 1987 Ker 52; 1987(1) ACC 461; 1987(1) ACJ 192; (1987)2 TAC 50; 1986 Ker LT 1026.

5 *Ms Sau Madhuri* v *Dr. Rajendra* 1996(3) CPR 174 (NC); III(1996) CPJ 75 (NC); (1997)5 CTJ 43 (CP) (NCDRC); 1997 CCJ 1499 (NC).

6 *Smt. Rohini Pritam Kabadi* v *Dr. R.T. Kulkarni* 1998(1) CPR 142 (Bangalore); III(1996) CPJ 441 (Bangalore); (1997)5 CTJ 83 (CP) (SCDRC); 1998 CCJ 910 (Kant).

7 *Aleyamma Varghese* v *Dewan Bahadur Dr. V. Varghese* 1996 CTJ 911; 1997(1) CPR 310 (Ker); III(1997) CPJ 165 (Ker); 1998 CCJ 1310 (Ker).

8 *Achutrao Haribhau Khodwa* v *State of Maharashtra* (1996)2 SCC 634; (1996)4 CTJ 950 (SC) (CP); 1996 ACJ 505.

wound. The absence of this precaution may precipitate bleeding imperfectly sealed blood vessels which is indicative of negligence on the part of the surgeon. Omission to recognise the injury resulting in post-operative bleeding may also amount to negligence on the part of the surgeon.

The nerve damaged directly in the field of operation is usually by cutting or by traction or pressure on a nerve beyond the field of the operation. Damage may be the result of ischaemia from blockage of a main vessel such as femoral or brachial arteries. The excessive pressure or traction on the nerve may result in partial paralysis. It is very difficult to decide on the precise nature of nerve injury. To avoid the allegation of negligence the proper course of action is to explore the nerve as soon as convenient and to undertake the appropriate repair.[9]

It is clear from medical literature that in case of cholecystectomy it is the duty of the surgeon to have put the tube for draining out the bile liquid, because failure to drain out bile liquid may lead to biliary peritonitis resulting in death of the patient.[10] The young surgeons are cautioned against adopting the method of laproscopic surgery without gaining sufficient experience of performing abdominal operations i.e. general surgery and in particular removal of gall bladder in open surgery. Cutting of common bile duct in the process of removal of gall bladder by way of laparoscopic surgery may amount to negligence.[11]

(E) **Postoperative monitoring.** The commonest allegation against one surgeon is failure to attend promptly the patient during postoperative period and in times of crisis after the operation. The duty of the surgeon is to observe the patient during postoperative stage in order to check abnormalities

9 *Neuro Surgery*, Prof. John Hankinson, MBBS, FRCS, referred to *Medical Negligence* by Michael J. Powers and Nigel H. Harris, Chapter 34, Edition 1990.

10 *Altaf Hussain Farooqui* v *Dr. Ashok Mathure* 1998(1) CPR 427 (Bom).

11 *Smt. Gurmit Mahal* v *Chauhan Nursing Home* 1998(3) CPR 405 (Chandigarh); 1999 CTJ 55 (CP) (SCDRC); *N.K. Kohli* v *Bajaj Nursing Home through Dr. Nilam Bajaj* 1999(2) CPR 79 (Bhopal); II(2000) CPJ 308.

in pulse rate, blood pressure, respiration, urine out put, temperature and level of consciousness. Failure to carry out necessary monitoring at a frequency required by the patient's condition or to respond appropriately to the situation as evidenced by monitoring may constitute negligence.

Patients undergoing surgical procedure often suffer considerable disturbances in their fluid balance. Too little fluid leads to fluid depletion and the patient becomes dehydrated and the urine output falls. Similarly, excessive fluid replacement overloads the patient producing symptoms of cardiac failure. It is important to monitor the fluid balance of the patient during postoperative period. Omission to monitor the fluid balance of the patient by preparing the chart of intake and output of fluid and by deciding the nature and volume of the fluid may amount to negligence.

The development of hematoma or wound infection is very common after any surgery. The formation of hematoma cannot be considered negligence on the part of surgeon where adequate steps have been taken to prevent it, but failure to diagnose and treat hematoma appropriately may constitute negligence. Infection is a natural hazard of all surgical procedure. Superficial infection known as stitch abscess does not form the subject-matter of negligence, but failure to recognise deep infection in appropriate time and delay of treatment may constitute negligence.

It is the duty of the surgeon conducting quadruple vessel coronary artery bypass surgery to diagnose postoperative sternal infection early and give prompt treatment by prescribing proper antibiotics after making prompt pus culture.[12] The vascular injury for multiple fractures of arm and leg must be referred to the vascular surgeon within 6 to 8 hours, in default vascular injury may lead to formation of gangrene and delay in referring the patient may amount to negligence.[13]

12 *John Andrade* v *P.D. Hinduja National Hospital & Medical Research Centre* 1998(1) CPR 579 (Bom).

13 *Lekh Raj* v *Bharaj Nursing Home* 1998(2) CPR 450 (Chandigarh); II(1998) CPJ 335 (Chandigarh); 1999 CCJ 1537 (Punj).

(ii) ***Common errors of orthopaedics***[14] The non-union of fractures may be due to various factors like impaired blood supply at the fracture site or osteotomy site, inadequate immobilisation of the fracture, and poor apposition of the bone ends. The surgeon is negligent if non-union of fractures is the result of poor standard of primary treatment viz, failure to achieve an acceptable position of the bone fragments, so that a gap exists at the fracture site causing inappropriate internal fixation. The reduction of the fracture by using traction with the help of attendants without taking elementary caution of giving anaesthetic agent to the patient was considered negligence by Indian Supreme Court.[15]

Owing to swelling the initially satisfactory plaster cast may become tight causing severe pain, numbness in digits, impaired circulation leaving necrosis of soft tissues and neurological deficit resulting loss of limb or functionally useless limb. The duty of the surgeon is to anticipate swelling, to make sure that the cast is adequately padded, and to monitor the patient carefully, so that urgent action may be taken if the impaired circulation is exhibited through pain, impaired sensation, pale skin, loss of arterial pulsation and failure to extend the digits fully.

It is difficult to diagnose fractures and dislocation of the cervical spines. It is suggested that where clinical and radiological examinations do not reveal anything in a patient responsive to neck pain, tenderness or neurological deficit in the face of normal plain radiographs, a hard cervical collar must be prescribed till the patient undergoes further investigations such as repetition of plain x-rays or C.T. Scan to avoid iatrogenic spinal insult.[16]

When the patient was operated upon for an ulcer of the heel of left foot, the surgeon was held negligent for not passing

14 *Trauma and Orthopaedics*, Mr. Nigel Harris, FRCS referred to *Medical Negligence* by Michael J. Powers and Nigel H. Harris, Chapter 30, Edition 1990.

15 *Dr. Laxman Balkrishna Joshi* v *Dr. Trimbak Bapu Godbole* AIR 1969 SC 128; 1968 ACJ 183 (SC); 1968 SCD 866; (1968)2 SCWR 73; 1968 Mah LJ 599.

16 JIMA, vol. 90, p. 181.

on information regarding limited debridement under general anaesthesia and regarding gangrene in the mid and second toes, and for not attending the patient for three days, particularly when the condition of patient was deteriorating day by day.[17] The surgeon must take precaution for open reduction of fracture of tibia at the junction of lower and middle of shaft; otherwise it may lead to infection.[18] It is the duty of the surgeon to take all precautionary measures for ensuring asepsis, during any orthopaedic surgery, specially during open reduction or internal fixation of any fracture.

(iii) ***Common errors of ophthalmologists***[19] The allegation of dimmed vision due to delay in diagnosis of squint is common against the ophthalmologist. Omission to advise x-ray examination is considered negligent if there is suggestive history of perforating wounds with no signs of foreign body. It is the duty of the doctor to advise for x-ray or ultrasound scan when foreign body could not be detected in the eye of a patient treated for receiving injury when a small iron particle hit the eye.[20] Failure to examine the visual fields may lead to form incorrect opinion that the declining vision is due to cataract and thereby cause delay in diagnosing glaucoma, which is considered as negligence. Similarly, omission to dilate the pupil for examination leads to error in diagnosing retinal detachment. It may be difficult to resist a claim for compensation when the patient has to undergo a major operation instead of simple prophylactic treatment due to delayed diagnosis of retinal detachment. The duty of the surgeon is to monitor the patient treated with steroid continually and to warn the patient about the dangerous side-effects of steroids. The use of steroid must be avoided by

17 *V. Vassanda Coumary* v *Dr. T. Ramachandrudu* 1998(3) CPR 227 (Pondicherry).

18 *P.P. Ismail* v *Mrs. K.K. Radha* 1997(2) CPR 171 (NC); I(1998) CPJ 16 (NC); (1997)5 CTJ 685 (CP) (NCDRC); 1999 CCJ 99 (NC).

19 *Ophthalmology*, Mr. Patrick J. Holmes Sellors, FRCS referred to *Medical Negligence* by Michael J. Powers and Nigel H. Harris, Chapter 36, Edition 1990.

20 *Dr. Jyothi Vivek* v *Vijayashree Eye Hospital* 1997(3) CPR 220 (Ker); *Dr. Jyothi Vivek* v *Pradeep* I(1998) CPJ 191 (Ker); 1999 CCJ 720 (Ker).

the ophthalmologist for undiagnosed irritable red eyes, because steroid aggravates herpetic disease of the cornea.

Retinopathy of Prematurity (RoP) is one of the major emerging causes of childhood blindness. The retina of a pre-term baby remains immature at the time of birth. The post-natal developments of retinal vessels may lead to RoP. All infants with birth weight of less than 1500 grams or gestational age of less than 32 weeks, are required to be mandatorily screened for RoP, which usually takes about 4 to 5 weeks to be diagnosed. The routine screening for RoP should be done between 2 to 4 weeks.[1]

Opacification of crystalline lens is called cataract which is mostly an age-related disease. Cataract is one of the few diseases which have an excellent and easy cure. Extra-capsular extraction of lens (ECEL) with posterior chamber intra-ocular lens implantation (PCIOL) can very easily place the person back to the general stream. One ECEL requires about 45 minutes during which period three cases of ICEL can be performed. The surgeon is duty-bound to explain the merits and demerits of traditional cataract operation in comparison with IOL implantation.[2]

The doctor must make the vision test and note down the same in prescription before cataract operation. The cataract operation is not advisable if vision is 6/12 or even 6/18. Moreover, IOP (Intra-Ocular Pressure) of the patient must be checked when pre-operative investigations are carried out for intra-ocular operations, such as cataract and glaucoma.[3] The vitreous haemorrhage after serious operation for retinal detachment must invite serious attention of the surgeon for effective treatment, because absence of proper post-operative follow up may result in complete loss of vision of the patient.[4]

1 *Maharaja Agrasen Hospital* v *Master Rishabh Sharma* 2019 SCC Online SC 1658.

2 JIMA, vol. 91, p. 74.

3 *K.N. Lal* v *R.K. Akhaury* III(1997) CPJ 112 (Pat); 1998 CCJ 1223 (Bihar).

4 *Shri Ram Babu* v *Dr. Anjani Kishore Prasad* 1998(2) CPR 223 (Pat); II(1998) CPJ 684 (Pat); 1998 CTJ 606 (CP) (SCDRC); 2000 CCJ 314.

(iv) *Common errors of otorhinolaryngologists*[5] Haemorrhage is the common side effect of all nasal surgery even after pre-operative instillation of vasoconstrictor drops. The most common operation within the nasal passage is removal of nasal polyp which is benign swelling of the nasal mucosa arising primarily from the region of the middle meatus and ethmoidal cells. Removal of nasal polypi or extensive intranasal surgery may lead to anosmia i.e. severe impairment of smell. Pre-operative counselling with the patient may save the surgeon from the allegation of causing damage to cribriform plate due to lack of visibility, previous surgery, or anatomical variations. The patient must be warned of the possibility of facial nerve injury and its consequence following any surgery in the parotid gland. The possibility of producing noticeable neurological deficit should form the essence of every pre-operative discussion with patients undergoing thyroid surgery.

5 *Otorhinolaryngology*, Sir Donald Harrison, PhD, FRCS referred to *Medical Negligence* by Michael J. Powers and Nigel H. Harris, Chapter 35, Edition 1990.

CHAPTER

7

Judicial Pronouncement—What May or May Not be Negligence

(A) MISCELLANEOUS ACTS AMOUNTING TO NEGLIGENCE

Anaesthetist

(i) *Death due to administration of wrong mode and dose of anaesthesia* The patient was admitted to the hospital for second delivery. She had undergone caesarean section under general anaesthesia, though she was given spinal anaesthesia during previous caesarean operation. The condition of the patient became critical for administering wrong mode and dose of anaesthesia and there was no reversal from anaesthesia after surgery. Ultimately the patient was shifted to another hospital where she expired.

The National Commission[1] held the anaesthetist and the hospital negligent for not giving proper dose of anaesthesia and for not monitoring the patient during surgery and for not managing reversal from anaesthesia post surgery, particularly when there was no evidence of foetal distress for urgent caesarean section.

(ii) *Death due to cardiorespiratory arrest during operation* The patient had undergone operation for insertion of plate and

1 *Rajiv Sharma* v *Helvita Clinic Pvt. Ltd.* II(2010) CPJ 68.

screws in his right forearm. The patient developed pain and deformity at the operation site. The x-rays were taken and the patient was referred to the cardiologist for examination and opinion whether he can go for surgery. The cardiologist noted the blood pressure of the patient as 150/100mm and STT changes in anterolateral leads in ECG, but did not recognise the condition as hypertension. So, the operation was started under general anaesthesia. The patient developed cardiorespiratory arrest in the midst of the operation and collapsed.

The State Commission, Gujarat,[2] held the anaesthetist negligent for not assessing the patient's condition for anaesthesia by ignoring blood pressure of 150/100mm and STT changes in ECG; and for not ensuring whether defibrillator was provided in the operation theatre before starting anaesthesia; and also for not maintaining proper oxygenation, particularly when lack of oxygen as probable cause of cardiac arrest could not be ruled out. The order of the State Commission was affirmed by the National Commission.[3]

(iii) *Permanent brain damage after tonsillectomy* The patient underwent tonsillectomy operation in a Government hospital. The consistent expert evidence is that tonsillectomy is an elective operation. On the commencement of operation the respiratory arrest occurred on account of the anaesthetist removing the tube from the mouth of the patient without giving fresh breaths of oxygen and there was delay on the part of the anaesthetist in noticing the respiratory arrest and inserting the tube for the second time, and in the meanwhile the respiratory arrest led to cardiac arrest which made the anaesthetist give massage and chest compression to assist circulation of blood. The faulty method of induction of anaesthetic led to cerebral anoxia and thus permanently damaged the brain.

2 *Arunaben D. Kothari* v *Navdeep Clinic* 1996(3) CPR 20 (Guj); III(1996) CPJ 605 (Guj); (1997)5 CTJ 533 (CP) (SCDRC); 1998 CCJ 972 (Guj).

3 *Rashmi Vora* v *Arunaben D. Kothari* 2006(1) CPC 66; IV(2005) CPJ 164.

It is held by Andhra Pradesh High Court[4] that the anaesthetist was negligent by removing endotracheal tube from the mouth of the patient and for failure to begin respiratory resuscitation by oxygenating the patient with a mask and bag or by mouth to mouth ventilation before attempting to pass endotracheal tube for the second time. The surgeon was held negligent, because he commenced the operation and completed the same and thereby served to precipitate damage to the patient, although he was aware that the patient had respiratory arrest and that the anaesthetist did massage and external compression of the chest to revive respiration of the patient who had almost reached the point of death before commencement of operation.

(iv) *Permanent brain damage after Fallopian Tube Test* The patient had undergone Fallopian Tube Test (FTT) under general anaesthesia. She developed breathing trouble due to inadequacy of the dose of general anaesthesia and thereby hypoxia occurred which led to brain damage. The patient started living in vegetative state on account of brain damage suffered due to hypoxia.

The National Commission[5] held that there was serious deficiency in service on the part of the doctors in providing treatment to the patient.

(v) *Paralysis of lower limbs after caesarean section* The patient was admitted to the hospital for delivery of the child. The anaesthesia is administered in spinal cord for caesarean delivery. The child was born, but the lower limbs of the patient were paralysed. No postoperative care was taken by referring the patient to the neurosurgeon for surgical decompression of cord, though MRI was done. The National Commission[6] found the anaesthetist negligent in discharge of duty.

4 *Dr. P. Narasimha Rao* v *Gundavarapu Jaya Prakash* 1990(1) ACJ 350; AIR 1990 AP 207; (1990)1 ACC 468; (1989)3 Andh LT 564; (1989)2 APLJ (HC) 491.

5 *Sanjay Mutha* v *Dr. Jayashree Desai* I(2013) CPJ 727.

6 *Sutapa Dasgupta (Dr.)* v *Tapan Kar* II(2017) CPJ 649; 2017(3) CLT 265; 2017(4) CPR 334 (NC).

2 Cardiologist

(i) *Death due to cardiorespiratory arrest during operation* The patient had undergone operation for insertion of plate and screws in his right forearm. The patient developed pain and deformity at the operation site. The x-rays were taken and the patient was referred to the cardiologist for examination and opinion whether he can go for surgery. The cardiologist noted the blood pressure of the patient as 150/100mm and STT changes in anterolateral leads in ECG, but did not recognise the condition as hypertension. The operation started under general anaesthesia. The patient developed cardiorespiratory arrest in the midst of the operation and collapsed.

The State Commission, Gujarat,[7] held the cardiologist negligent for declaring the patient fit for operation without making adequate diagnosis of condition of heart and cardiovascular system by advising proper investigation and treatment of the patient, which was affirmed by the National Commission.[8]

(ii) *Death after coronary angiography test* The patient had undergone Tread Mill Test (TMT) and reported positive for Reversible Myocardial Infarction (RMI) and Ischemia. Without recommending non-invasive investigations like blood test for lipid profile, KFT, LFT, allergy test for contrast media, echocardiography and Holter Meter Test for ascertaining contradictions, the doctor hurriedly proceeded for coronary angiography test (CART) even when there was no emergency. The patient suffered prolonged severe hypoglycaemia leading to death.

The National Commission[9] held the doctor negligent in giving treatment to the patient.

7 *Arunaben D. Kothari* v *Navdeep Clinic* 1996(3) CPR 20 (Guj); III(1996) CPJ 605 (Guj); (1997)5 CTJ 533 (CP) (SCDRC); 1998 CCJ 972 (Guj).

8 *Rashmi Vora* v *Arunaben D. Kothari* 2006(1) CPC 66; IV(2005) CPJ 164.

9 *Manjeet Chawla* v *Escorts Heart Institute and Research Centre* 2015(1) Andh LD 5; 2014(3) CPR 452; IV(2014) CPJ 81 (NCDRC).

3 Dermatologist

Failure to distinguish between Measles and Toxic Epidermal Necrolysis (TEN) The patient suffering from TEN was wrongly diagnosed as measles and thereby his improper treatment led to the death of the patient. The expert opinion is against the doctor who treated the patient.

The National Commission[10] held the dermatologist negligent and awarded compensation.

4 Dentist

(i) ***Failure to warn of alteration in sensation*** The patient suffered permanent damage to the lingual nerve during surgery to remove three wisdom teeth. This resulted in pain and loss of taste. It was alleged that the surgeon was negligent in conducting surgery and in not explaining the possibility of alteration in sensation due to surgery.

It is held by the Queen's Bench in U.K.[11] that damage to the nerve was not caused by unavoidable manipulation of the retractor, but by lack of due care and skill on the part of the surgeon who allowed the drill to cut into the lingual nerve. However, the negligence on the part of the surgeon in not issuing the warning was not established, because a responsible body of professional opinion was in favour of not issuing warning of the risk of the symptoms involving partial loss of taste and unpleasant sensation in the mouth.

(ii) ***Sufferings due to slipping of needle into stomach during extraction of molar teeth*** The patient approached the hospital with complaint of pain in right molar teeth. The doctor extracted the right molar teeth of lower jaw and the patient started bleeding from the mouth. The doctor wanted to irrigate the mouth to clean the socket by inserting syringe into the mouth of the patient. The needle got detached from the syringe and slipped into throat of the patient, which ultimately slipped into stomach. The operation was conducted to remove the needle from the intestine of the patient.

10 *Billroth Hospitals Ltd.* v *R. Vijayalakshmi* 2017(2) CPR 321; III(2017) CPJ 367 (NCDRC).

11 *Heath* v *Berkshire Health Authority* (1991)8 BMLR 98.

The State Commission, Karnataka,[12] held the doctor negligent for not exercising due care and skill at the time of irrigating the mouth of the patient by applying the principle of *res ipsa loquitur*, as the doctor could not explain as to why the needle was detached from the syringe while irrigating the mouth of the patient.

(iii) ***Sufferings for defective dentures*** The complainant got prepared dentures for himself and his wife from a doctor. Both the sets of dentures did not fit properly to the respective recipients who suffered from pain and injury in the mouth.

The National Commission reversed the order of State Commission and upheld the order of District Forum which held the doctor negligent and awarded compensation of ₹1000 against the doctor.[13]

5 Doctors other than allopathic

(i) ***Damage caused to the baby by Ayurvedic doctor*** A baby aged about six months was suffering from convulsions during high fever and was under treatment of the neurologist. The father of the patient was attracted by advertisement of the respondent Ayurvedic doctor who gave allopathic medicine in the garb of Ayurvedic medicine for treatment of fits during high fever.

By upholding the decision of the National Commission it is held by the Supreme Court[14] that the respondent Ayurvedic doctor is guilty of unfair trade practice and negligent for passing off allopathic medicine as Ayurvedic medicine and thereby causing damage to the baby.

(ii) ***Death due to inadequate treatment without diagnosis*** The patient approached the registered homeopathic practitioner for treatment of fever. The doctor administered strong antibiotics for eight days initially for treatment of viral fever and subsequently for typhoid without confirming the

12 *Amblappa* v *Sriman D. Veerendra Heggade* 1999(3) CPR 72 (Bangalore).
13 *Ishwar Das* v *Vinay Kumar Gupta* II(1992) CPJ 118 (NC).
14 *Bhanwar Kanwar* v *R.K. Gupta* (2013)4 SCC 252.

diagnosis by any pathological test. The doctor also prescribed intra-muscular injections of Sodium compound to relieve the patient of pain without ascertaining the cause for the pain. The patient was shifted to a nursing home where he was treated for six days. As the condition of the patient deteriorated, he was shifted to another hospital where he expired.

The Supreme Court of India[15] held the doctor guilty of negligence in giving allopathic medicines to the patient without being qualified in that system of medicine and without being registered under the Medical Council Act 1956 or State Medical Council Act. The Supreme Court also directed the Medical Council of India to consider the feasibility of initiating prosecution against the doctor under s. 15(3) of the Indian Medical Council Act 1956.

(iii) ***Death due to administration of injection by Ayurvedic doctor*** The patient suffering from breathlessness was treated in OPD without advising for hospitalisation. The Ayurvedic practitioner gave injection to the patient, which led to infection, septicemia and gangrene and ultimate death.

The Ayurvedic doctor being not qualified to administer allopathic medicine was found guilty of negligence in discharge of duty by the National Commission.[16]

(iv) ***Death due to unskilled termination of pregnancy*** The patient was admitted to the nursing home for termination of pregnancy. She expired due to cardiorespiratory failure after the operation. The doctors registered under Mysore Ayurvedic and Unani Practitioner Registration and Medical Practitioner Miscellaneous Provisions Act 1961, and having no recognised qualification defined in s. 2(*h*) of Indian Medical Council Act 1956, conducted MTP, though they were not entitled to practise modern scientific medicines beyond the territory of State of Karnataka.

15 *Poonam Verma* v *Aswin Patel* AIR 1996 SC 2111; (1996)4 SCC 332; 1996(3) CPR 205 (SC); II (1996) CPJ 1 (SC); (1996)4 CTJ 465 (SC) (CP).

16 *Harishbhai Shamjibhai* v *Dr. D.C. Gohil* I(2015) CPJ 231; 2015(1) CLT 342; 2015(1) CPR 345 (NCDRC).

It is held by the State Commission, Kerala,[17] that the doctors were not qualified for conducting MTP, and that the nursing home was not recognised Institute for conducting MTP, and as such the doctors have violated the provisions of ss. 3 and 4 of Medical Termination of Pregnancy Act 1971. The doctors were held guilty of negligence by the State Commission on three scores: first, they were not qualified to practise medicine in Kerala, secondly, they have violated the provisions of Medical Termination of Pregnancy Act 1971, and thirdly, they did not show the reasonable care expected of a doctor in conducting MTP of the patient.

(v) *Loss of eyesight due to adverse reaction of drugs* The patient aged 10 years was treated by the doctor for fever. The doctor who is a licensed homeopathic practitioner, prescribed Septran tablets and other tablets for two days for treatment of fever. The patient developed adverse reaction (patches on the whole body) after taking medicines. He was shifted to better equipped clinic where his condition improved, but he lost his eyesight even after two operations.

The State Commission, Karnataka,[18] held the doctor negligent for prescribing allopathic medicines, when he is qualified to practise homeopathic medicines only.

(vi) *Permanent disability due to administration of injection* (*a*) The patient was treated by the doctor for severe pain in the stomach. The doctor administered an injection of optineuron resulting in paralysis of right leg of the patient. Ultimately the patient suffered permanent disability to the extent of 20 percent.

The State Commission[19] held the doctor guilty of negligence in administering injection causing permanent disability of the patient, as the Commission disbelieved the version of the doctor who being merely R.M.P. prescribed the

17 *Dr. K. Mahabala Bhat* v *K. Krishna* 2000(1) CPR 369 (Ker).

18 *Dr. A.M. Mulla* v *Maghaksab Ismailsab Nonawada* 1999(2) CPR 353 (Bangalore); 1999 CTJ 504 (CP) (SCDRC).

19 *Rajender Lal* v *Dr. Rudra Singh* 1996(2) CPR 364 (Chandigarh); (1996)4 CTJ 649 (CP) (SCDRC).

injection to the patient, but denied to have administered it by himself.

(*b*) The patient approached the doctor for treatment of abdominal pain. The doctor administered injection containing four medicines, *viz,* fortwin, calmpose, anafortan and morphen. The patient developed infection resulting in gangrene and amputation of fingers. It is alleged that the patient suffered 50% disability, physical pain, mental agony and financial loss due to administration of injection in the artery instead of vein of the patient by the doctor.

The State Commission, Punjab,[20] held the doctor negligent, as it was established from expert evidence that three fingers of the patient were amputated on account of development of gangrene which was the result of administration of injection in the artery of the patient.

(vii) *Sufferings due to complications after unskilled endoscopy*
The patient was advised to undergo Upper Gastro Intestinal Endoscopy (UGIE) in the Army hospital. The damage caused to esophagus during UGIE resulted in formation of thick yellow pass in both lungs. The patient survived after prolonged treatment in another hospital for almost three months.

The National Commission[1] held the gastroenterologist and the hospital negligent in conducting UGIE undergone by the patient resulting in prolonged illness and sufferings.

6 Gynaecologist and obstetrician

(i) *Artery forceps left inside abdomen during caesarean operation*
The patient was operated for delivery of caesarean child under general anaesthesia. She complained of pain and nausea continuously for two weeks after the operation. She was shifted to another hospital where the doctor took an x-ray of her abdomen and found a pair of scissors, medically known

20 *Kharaitilal* v *Kewal Krishan* I(1998) CPJ 181 (Chandigarh); 1999 CCJ 725 (Punj).

1 *Sudha Garg* v *Union of India* 2009(156) DLT 498; 2009 CTJ 382 (CP); I(2009) CPJ 297.

as "artery forceps" inside the abdomen. She was operated on and the scissors were removed from the abdomen. The patient claimed compensation against the doctors. The State Commission, Maharashtra, held the doctor negligent and awarded compensation towards expenditure incurred for medical treatment.

On appeal, the National Commission,[2] enhanced the amount of compensation in addition to costs and expenses for medical treatment.

(ii) ***Brain damage after attempted ventouse extraction and subsequent forceps delivery*** The plaintiff born with severe brain damage claimed compensation through his father on the ground that the obstetrician of the defendant health authority first attempted to deliver him using a ventouse extractor and after failure of this attempt, forceps delivery was carried out, and thereby he suffered brain damage. It is established from evidence that the brain damage of the plaintiff was the result of intermittent hypoxia caused by inappropriate amount of force which the obstetrician had used to deliver him.

The Queen's Bench Division of U.K.[3] held the obsterician negligent for using untoward force to deliver the baby, as no competent obstetrician would have used that amount of force in the circumstances.

(iii) ***Damage due to improper D&E operation*** The patient had undergone D&E operation for termination of pregnancy. She developed pain in abdomen and suffered from fever, nausea and vomiting during postoperative period. As the condition of the patient deteriorated, she was shifted to better equipped hospital where the doctor had gone through the report of investigations and opined that there were perforations in the uterus and intestine and that pus had collected in the abdomen. The patient was operated and after improving the

2 *Ms Sau Madhuri* v *Rajendra* 1996(3) CPR 174 (NC); III(1996) CPJ 75 (NC); (1997)5 CTJ 43 (CP) (NCDRC); 1997 CCJ 1499 (NC).

3 *Townsend* v *Worcester and District Health Authority* (1994)23 BMLR 31 (QBD).

condition of the patient another operation for "faecal fistula" was performed on the patient.

It is held by the State Commission, Gujarat,[4] that the patient suffered physical pain and mental agony due to negligence on the part of the doctor in performing D&E operation.

(iv) *Damage to small intestine during post partum sterilization*
The patient gave birth to a male child and had undergone post partum sterilization. The doctor conducted the operation without administering even local anaesthesia. The patient was brought back to the hospital on the next date of discharge with complaints of pus and faecal matter oozing through the surgical slit. The laparotomy findings of another hospital shows that the abdominal cavity of the patient was filled with faecal matter and thick foul smelling pus. When surgeon opened abdomen the terminal 10" of the ileum was found to be perforated in many places with massive peritonitis with pockets of pus. The patient was again operated, but her condition deteriorated and she ultimately expired. The expert evidence and the post-mortem report indicate that the small intestine of the deceased was cut and left unsutured, instead of cutting of knuckle of the fallopian tube.

The Kerala High Court[5] held the doctor negligent in performing post partum sterilization, because, first the doctor had cut the small intestine and left it unsutured, instead of cutting the knuckle of the fallopian tube of the deceased; secondly, the expert evidence established that if the patient undergoing surgical operation happened to sustain a cut injury to the intestine and the injury remained unsutured for a period of 7 to 8 days, the patient would suffer from peritonitis leading to the fatal stage; and thirdly, the post-mortem report indicated that the cause of death was peritonitis which developed as a complication of the injury sustained to the intestine during port partum sterilization.

4 *Vinubhai Parsottamdas Patel* v *Dr. Vijay Kumar Ajmera* 1997(1) CPR 348 (Guj).

5 *Joseph* alias *Pappachan* v *Dr. George Moonjely* 1995(1) ACJ 253.

(v) *Death after giving birth of dead baby by normal delivery* The patient was pregnant after a gap of 12 years after the birth of her second child. The doctor categorised the patient as high risk having regard to severe toxemia of pregnancy, 37 years of age, and gap of 12 years between the present delivery and past one. There is no explanation as to why the foetal death occurred and why the doctor failed to detect the dead foetus in time. There was profuse uncontrolled bleeding leading to death of the patient. It is established from expert evidence that the doctor failed to take proper care for removal of dead foetus in time on emergency basis by undertaking caesarean section. It is alleged that the patient died due to failure on the part of the doctor to make surgical intervention to stop profuse bleeding by requisitioning the services of the anaesthetist and by making prior arrangement for supply of blood.

The National Commission,[6] held the doctor negligent for inadequate treatment and improper management of the deceased patient.

(vi) *Death after caesarean section due to lack of laboratory test* The patient was suffering from pregnancy induced hypertension (PIH) and Pre-eclampsia. Without conducting any investigations like blood test, urine test, renal and liver function tests and tests for foetal well-being, the patient was asked to undergo caesarean section, which resulted in her death.

On consideration of the lapses on the part of the doctor, the National Commission[7] held the doctor negligent in providing reasonable care to the patient.

(vii) *Death after hysterectomy operation* The patient had multiple fibroids of varying sizes in uterus. She had severe bleeding and was advised for hysterectomy by the respondent gynaecologist. The BP of the patient was 180/100 and her hemoglobin level in the blood was 7 mg. The patient died

6 *Vijay H. Mankar* v *Dr. (Mrs.) Mangla Bansad* 2000 CTJ 101 (CP) (NCDRC); I(2000) CPJ 37 (NC); 2000 CCJ 610.

7 *K.K. Kakkar (Dr.)* v *Neetu Singh* III(2014) CPJ 642 (NCDRC).

after the operation. Two fold allegations were made against the gynaecologist: first, the doctor should have performed surgery after controlling blood pressure and hemoglobin, and secondly, the doctor should not have performed surgery of a critical patient in a nursing home without having facility of ICU.

The Supreme Court[8] held that the gynaecologist was justified in performing surgery for controlling bleeding, but he was held guilty of negligence for performing operation in a nursing home without having ICU, particularly when the patient was suffering from high blood pressure and low hemoglobin.

(viii) ***Death after total abdominal hysterectomy*** The doctor came to the decision that the patient was suffering from fibroid uterus and conducted total abdominal hysterectomy (TAH). She suffered postoperative pancreatitis with sepsis resulting in cardiorespiratory arrest and death. The USG of abdomen revealed that the patient was suffering from menorrhagia fibroid uterus and ovarian cyst, which could not be detected by the operating doctor.

The National Commission[9] held the doctor negligent for failure to diagnose the patient properly.

(ix) ***Death due to complications after delivery of child*** The patient was admitted to the nursing home for delivery of the child under the care of the gynaecologist who treated her from 32 weeks of pregnancy. The haemoglobin level of the patient was 10.7 gm during 18 weeks of pregnancy and BP was below normal at the time of admission to the nursing home. The baby was born after inducing labour with medicine, but died due to birth asphyxia with APGAR score of $^1/_{10}$. The postpartum haemorrhage (PPH) took place after delivery and the patient died on the way to another hospital.

8 *Bijay Sinha Roy (D) represented by LR* v *Biswanath Das* 2017 SCC Online SC 1101.

9 *Madan Lal* v *R.K. Chaudhary (Dr.)* 2016(2) CPR 657; IV(2016) CPJ 370 (NCDRC).

The National Commission[10] held on the basis of expert evidence that there was deficiency in service on the part of the gynaecologist for failure to insist on hematological investigations and cardiological consultation to ascertain whether the patient was anaemic and hypotensive during last trimester.

(x) ***Death due to leaving of mop during hysterectomy*** The patient was admitted to the nursing home for removal of fibroid from uterus by way of hysterectomy. She complained about abdominal pain, loss of appetite, nausea, vomiting, vaginal discharge and loss of weight during periodical check up after discharge from the nursing home. After almost two and half months of operation she was advised by another doctor for ultrasound and swab test. Two mops were detected in abdominal cavity. The second surgery was performed for removal of mops, but her intestine was ruptured and she suffered from septicemia. Ultimately the patient died after prolonged suffering.

The UT Commission, Chandigarh[11] held the gynaecologist and nursing home liable for deficiency in service during operation and during post operative period resulting in death of the patient, which was affirmed by the National Commission.

(xi) ***Death due to postpartum haemorrhage (PPH) after delivery of child*** The doctor did not attend the patient at the time of delivery and when the complications developed. It is not established from record that any attempt was made to operate the patient by calling an anaesthetist when her condition was deteriorating for excessive haemorrhage.

Under the above circumstances the doctor was found to be negligent in providing treatment to the patient by the National Commission.[12]

10 *Deep Nursing Home Through Dr. Gurdeep Singh Kochhar* v *Manmeet Singh Mattewal* 2012(2) CPR 569; III(2012) CPJ 154.

11 *Jaswinder Singh* v *Santokh Nursing Home* 2006(1) CLT 442; I(2006) CPJ 85 being affirmed in *Santokh Nursing Home* v *Jaswinder Singh* 2009(3) CPR 46; I(2010) CPJ 204.

12 *Sabita (Dr.), Kallianpurkar Nursing Home* v *Shreepad* IV(2015) CPJ 230 (NCDRC).

(xii) ***Death due to wrong treatment of cancer*** The patient was admitted to the hospital with complaints of stomach pain and menstrual discharge during pregnancy. The investigations confirmed ectopic pregnancy and abdominal mass of about 4" diameter above the uterus. The laparotomy was conducted to end ectopic pregnancy and the pathological test of the specimens suggested carcinoma, but the same needed to be co-related with other tests before reaching to the clear and conclusive finding. Without conducting any biopsy of the abdominal mass, the doctor administered 5 cycles of chemotherapy. The second pathological report indicated that the patient had no malignancy. Ultimately she died at a very young age.

The National Commission[13] held the doctor and the hospital negligent for giving wrong treatment resulting in death of the patient.

(xiii) ***Death due to unskilled dilatation and curettage (D&C)*** The patient had undergone dilatation and curettage (D&C) for termination of pregnancy. She suffered abdominal pain, excessive bleeding and vomitting during postoperative period and her condition was deteriorating. She was shifted to higher speciality centre where exploratory laparotomy revealed multiple perforations of ileum, which were resected and uterine wall repaired, but she ultimately died.

The National Commission[14] held the doctor negligent for causing uterine perforation and intra abdominal damage during D&C operation of the patient.

(xiv) ***Death during operation of uterine fibromyometosis*** The patient approached the gynaecologist for excess bleeding and white discharge during her monthly period. She was subjected to various tests including X-ray, ECG, Blood test etc. and thereafter she was operated for "uterine fibromyometosis". The patient collapsed on the operation table.

13 *Dr. Kurien Joseph* v *Govindarajan* 2013(2) CPR 230.

14 *R.P. Unniyal* v *S.V. Nursing Home* 2015(2) Andh LD 18; IV(2014) CPJ 435 (NCDRC).

The National Commission,[15] upheld the order of State Commission, Bombay in awarding compensation against the doctors, but the anaesthetist was excluded from the liability to pay compensation as negligence was not established against him. It is also held by the National Commission that the act of carrying out the operation of a patient with rare blood group and morbid obesity for "uterine fibromyometosis" without making arrangement for blood, artificial respirator, by prolonging the duration of operation upto 7 hours and by shifting the patient from well-equipped hospital to ill-equipped hospital for monetary gain, amounts to deficiency in service on the part of the doctors.

(xv) ***Diagnosis of pregnancy without investigation*** The patient was suffering from abnormal absence of menstruation over two months. She did not wish to have a child, but she apprehended pregnancy. She was referred to a consultant gynaecologist. She was examined by the consultant who on clinical examination found her not to be pregnant and advised her to continue contraceptive pill. The consultant told her that she was not pregnant without recommending any test to determine pregnancy. Six months later, the patient found that she was pregnant.

It is held by the Queen's Bench of U.K. that the consultant gynaecologist was negligent in rejecting the possibility of pregnancy without recommending blood test or urine test for pregnancy.[16]

(xvi) ***Disability of child for failure to give warning*** A child was born with congenital rubella syndrome. The parents of the child alleged that the health authority was negligent for the failure to diagnose and warn the mother that the child she was carrying might be affected by rubella syndrome with the result that she was unable to have the pregnancy terminated.

15 *Dr. (Mrs.) Rashmi B. Fadnavis* v *Mumbai Grahak Panchayat* III(1998) CPJ 21 (NC); 1998(3) CPR 34 (NC); 1998 CTJ 742 (CP) (NCDRC); 1999 CCJ 391 (NC).

16 *Gardinar* v *Mounfield* (1989)5 BMLR 1 (QBD).

The health authority admitted liability before the Court of Appeal in U.K. for its negligent failure to diagnose and warn the mother that the child in the womb might be infected with rubella.[17]

(xvii) ***Permanant disability of child due to failure to terminate pregnancy*** The doctor performed an abortion to terminate the pregnancy of the patient. The specialist miscalculated the date of conception and used a curette of the wrong size, with the result that the pregnancy was not terminated. Two months later it was detected that the patient was still pregnant. It was then too late for a legal therapeutic abortion. Subsequently the baby delivered by caesarean section, was found suffering from severe and permanent disabilities. It was alleged that the doctor was negligent for failure to diagnose the continuing pregnancy during postoperative care.

The British Columbia Supreme Court[18] found the doctor negligent in determining the age of the foetus, with the result that he used a curette of wrong size to perform the abortion. The doctor was held negligent in respect of his postoperative attendance on the patient, when he examined her and concluded that the abortion procedure had been successful. The doctor was also negligent in carrying out unsuccessful abortion procedure whereby injuries were caused to the foetus.

(xviii) ***Sufferings for leaving metallic tip of suction tube in abdomen during caesarean operation*** The patient had undergone caesarean operation for delivery of a baby. She suffered from urine trouble and severe pain in abdomen after the operation. The symptoms were diagnosed as urine infection, but the medicines prescribed by the doctor did not work. The patient was taken to the consultant gynaecologist, who advised ultrasonography of uterus. The report of ultrasonography showed a mass adherent to the bladder. The patient had to undergo operation for removal of the

17 *Salith* v *Enfield Health Authority* (1991)7 BMLR 1 (CA).

18 *Cherry et al* v *Borsman* (1992)94 DLR (4th) 487 (British Columbia Court of Appeal); (1991)75 DLR (4th) 668 (British Columbia Supreme Court).

mass which was opened and a foreign body *i.e.* metallic tip of the suction tube was found in the cavity of the mass.

The State Commission, Bangalore,[19] held the doctor negligent in performing the caesarean operation, because the patient suffered from physical pain and mental distress for leaving a metallic tip of suction tube in the abdomen of the patient during caesarean operation.

(xix) ***Sufferings for leaving sponge in abdomen after caesarean section and tubectomy*** The patient had undergone caesarean operation followed by tubectomy. She complained of pain in abdomen after discharge from the hospital, but the gynaecologist did advise for investigations for ascertaining the cause of pain. The report of x-ray, scanning of abdomen and needle test conducted on the advice of another surgeon revealed that there was foreign body (mass) and thick pass at the left side of abdomen just above umbilicus level. The second surgeon removed the sponge from peritoneal cavity.

The State Commission, Punjab[20] held the gynaecologist negligent in performing operation and by not advising proper investigation to ascertain the cause of pain in abdomen during postoperative period.

(xx) ***Sufferings due to removal of reproductive organs without consent*** The patient suffering from prolonged menstrual bleeding was admitted to the hospital and gave consent for diagnostic operative laparoscopy. The doctor performed hysterectomy and salpingo-oopherectomy for removal of uterus, ovaries and fallopian tubes after obtaining consent from the mother of the patient in the midst of the operation on the ground that the patient was suffering from endometriosis.

By reversing the decision of the National Commission, the Supreme Court held the doctor negligent for conducting hysterectomy and salpingo-oopherectomy for removal of

19 *Smt. Rohini Pritam Kabadi* v *Dr. R.T. Kulkarni* 1998(1) CPR 142 (Bangalore); III(1996) CPJ 441 (Bangalore); (1997)5 CTJ 83 (CP) (SCDRC); 1998 CCJ 910 (Kant).

20 *Harvinder Kaur* v *Dr. (Mrs.) Sushma Chawla* III(2001) CPJ 143.

reproductive organs of an unmarried woman without consent, when there was no emergency and the matter was still at the stage of investigation.[1]

(xxi) ***Sufferings due to removal of ovaries and one kidney without consent.*** The patient was suffering from irregular bleeding which was diagnosed as dysfunctional uterine bleeding. She was admitted to the hospital for hysterectomy. Her consent was obtained for removal of uterus through abdominal route. The gynaecologist performed hysterectomy through vaginal route and removed ovaries without consent. The subsequent surgery was required during postoperative period as one of the kidneys was removed, large intestine was exposed and small intestine was infected with adhesions at various places and for repair and closure of fistula.

The National Commission[2] held the gynaecologist and the hospital negligent for removal of ovaries and one kidney without consent.

(xxii) ***Sufferings due to unskilled hysterectomy*** The bladder injury of the patient detected after 10 days of hysterectomy was diagnosed as vesico vaginal fistula (VVF). She had to undergo two major operations for repair of VVF in second hospital and third operation in the third hospital. She was not treated with medicines like injection Lupride or Danzole for endometriosis before hysterectomy. Having noted multiple fibroids and dense adhesions between anterior uterine wall and bladder, the doctor should have taken more care while separating and dissection of the bladder and should have sought assistance of an urologist.

The doctor was found to be negligent in conducting hysterectomy by the National Commission.[3]

1 *Samira Kohli* v *Dr. Prabha Manchanda* (2008)2 SCC 1; 2008 ACJ 747; AIR 2008 SC 1385; JT 2008(1) SC 399; (2008)1 Scale 442.

2 *Smt. Saroj Chandhoke* v *Sir Ganga Ram Hospital* 2007(3) CPR 209; III(2007) CPJ 189.

3 *Stepheena (Dr.)* v *Lilly Joseph* I(2015) CPJ 203; 2015(1) CLT 509; 2015(1) CPR 347 (NCDRC).

(xxiii) ***Sufferings for leaving abdominal pad in the abdomen during hysterectomy*** The patient was admitted to the hospital for removal of ovarian cyst. The gynaecologist removed the uterus after obtaining oral consent of the husband in the midst of the operation. She developed pain, dysentery, nausea, vomiting followed by intestinal obstruction during postoperative period. The x-ray report revealed foreign material covered with intestine and pus. The abdominal pad measuring about 12"x12" was found in the junction of small and large intestine during second surgery conducted by another doctor.

The Division Bench of Madras High Court[4] held the gynaecologist and the hospital negligent for keeping abdominal pad inside the body during surgery for removal of uterus and thereby causing pain, mental agony and unnecessary medical expenditure.

(xxiv) ***Survival of pregnancy after dilatation and curettage*** The patient underwent an operation for dilatation and curettage (D&C) and sterilization at a hospital managed by the health authority. After three months of operation the patient discovered that her pregnancy had survived the operation.

It is held by the Queen's Bench in England[5] that the doctor was negligent in discharging his duty towards the patient who is entitled to get damages, *inter alia*, for the financial loss incurred in the upkeep of the unplanned child.

(xxv) ***Unwanted child after sterilization and D&C operation*** The plaintiff, mother of three children, suffering from an ectopic pregnancy, had undergone laparoscopic sterilization and dilatation and curettage under care of the consultant gynaecologist. The plaintiff disclosed that her menstruation period was late before the operation. Moreover, the plaintiff understood that D&C operation would remove any fertilized egg from the uterus, and not a partial operation for diagnostic

4 *Soni Hospital* v *Arun Balakrishnan Iyer* AIR 2011 Mad 208; 2011(3) CTC 699.

5 *Allen* v *Bloomsbury Health Authority* 13 BMLR 47 (QB).

purposes. The plaintiff refused to undergo termination of pregnancy of about 15 weeks gestation.

The consultant gynaecologist was held negligent by the Queen's Bench Division[6] for not communicating adequately with the patient before undertaking the operation, particularly when the plaintiff disclosed about her late menstruation period during pre-operative consultation.

(xxvi) ***Unwanted child after sterilization operation*** (*a*) The patient, mother of three normal children, got terminated the fourth pregnancy and sterilization was also performed by the doctors employed by the health authority. Subsequently she became pregnant and gave birth to a congenitally abnormal child.

The Court of Appeal in England[7] held the doctor negligent in performing sterilization and awarded damages for pain, suffering and loss of amenities including extra-care which will have to be given to the congenitally abnormal child over the years.

(*b*) The plaintiff aged 40 years, was the mother of three children—all delivered by caesarean section. The plaintiff had undergone sterilization, but she became pregnant after 15 months of the operation. It is alleged that the health authority failed to warn her of the risk that the sterilization operation might fail.

The Court of Appeal in U.K.[8] held the health authority negligent for not giving proper warning to the plaintiff about the risk of failure of sterilization. It is further held that the plaintiff would have used contraception in addition to sterilization in order to avoid fourth caesarean section, had appropriate warning been given to the plaintiff about the risk of failure of the operation.

6 *Cronchman* v *Burke* 40 BMLR 163 (QBD).

7 *Emeh* v *Kensington and Chelsea and Westminster Area Health Authority* [1985]11 ACC (BJ) 1; [1985] QB 1012; [1985]2 WLR 233; [1984]3 All ER 1044; 128 Sol Jo 705 (CA).

8 *Lybert* v *Warrington Health Authority* 25 BMLR 91 (CA); [1996]7 Med LR 71.

(*c*) A poor lady had undergone sterilization at the Government Hospital after giving birth to seven children. She conceived and ultimately gave birth to a female child due to negligent performance of sterilization by the doctor who operated upon the right fallopian tube without touching the left fallopian tube.

The civil court awarded compensation with interest @ 12% per annum and the same was affirmed by the High Court and the Supreme Court of India.[9]

7 Hospital

(i) ***Admission of patient without proper infrastructure*** A patient was admitted to the nursing home and shifted to Medical College Hospital under the circumstances which were not explained.

The State Commission, Orissa, held that there was deficiency in service on the part of the nursing home by admitting and continuing the treatment of a patient whose sufferings required sophisticated treatment of Medical College Hospital. This decision of the State Commission was set aside by the National Commission[10] on appeal, but the National Commission did not direct the complainant to refund ₹50,000 to the Nursing Home, which was paid by the Nursing Home as out of court settlement.

(ii) ***Brain damage due to delay in delivery of the child*** The plaintiff's mother was admitted to the hospital of the health authority for delivery of child. She delivered the first twin spontaneously at 7.27p.m. and brisk vaginal bleeding was noted between 7.45 and 7.55p.m. Attempts made to call the Registrar was unsuccessful and the consultant obstetrician delivered the second twin at 8.35p.m. It is alleged that the second twin suffered brain damage due to birth asphyxia resulting from delay of 68 minutes in delivery of the child.

9 *State of Haryana* v *Santra (Smt.)* (2000)3 Scale 417; I(2000) CPJ 53; AIR 2000 SC 1888; 2000 ACJ 1188; JT 2000(5) SC 34.

10 *Anurekha Sahoo* v *Orissa Nursing Home* II(1992) CPJ 803 (Ori); 1993(1) CPR 51 (Ori) reversed by NC; 1995(1) CPR 494 (NC); (1994)2 CTJ 885 (CP) (NCDRC).

It is held by the Court of Appeal in U.K.[11] that the brain damage resulted from birth asphyxia and that failure to summon the Registrar or Consultant obstetrician promptly for delivery of the second twin was attributed to the negligence of the health authority.

(iii) *Cerebral palsy due to delay in conducting caesarean operation* The plaintiff aged 10 years was diagnosed as suffering from Multicystic Leuco Encephalo Malacia (MCLE). She had severe spastic quadriplegic cerebral palsy with developmental retardation. The mother of the plaintiff was admitted to the hospital of the health authority at 37 weeks gestation with complaint of reduction in foetal movements. She had undergone a series of cardiotocograph (CTG) traces. There was delay of six hours in conducting caesarean section. The plaintiff was born with Apgar score of 4 and displayed asphyxia. It is alleged that the catastrophic injuries of the plaintiff were caused, pre-birth was attributed to lack of care in conducting CTG traces and in failing to respond appropriately to the results of those traces by performing caesarean section earlier.

The health authority was held negligent by the Court of Appeal in U.K.[12] for delay in conducting the caesarean section, which materially contributed to the damage suffered by the plaintiff.

(iv) *Death after coronary artery bypass graft (CABG)* The patient was not connected to pulse oximeter in ICU after coronary artery bypass graft in order to monitor the condition of BP, heart rate and arterial blood oxygen saturation. The condition of the patient was checked on hourly basis. The patient suffered irreversible damage in ICU, which could not be checked and monitored and thereby the patient died.

The National Commission[13] held that there was negligence on the part of the hospital during postoperative period in ICU.

11 *Bull* v *Devon Area Health Authority* 22 BMLR 79 (CA); [1993]4 Med LR 117.

12 *Re, R* (a minor) (No. 2) 33 BMLR 178 (CA).

13 *Consumer Education and Research Society* v *Madras Medical Mission* 2016(4) CPR 97; 2016(4) CLT 227 (NCDRC).

(v) ***Death after falling on bathroom*** The patient was admitted to the hospital, as he was suffering from acute myeloid leukemia. While the patient was suffering from high fever, he fell down in the bathroom. No doctor assessed the effect of falling down in the bathroom by prescribing CT scan or other investigations. The doctor prescribed medicine over phone and the patient died.

The National Commission[14] held both the hospital and the doctor negligent for the lapses in the treatment after fall of the patient in the bathroom.

(vi) ***Death due to infection of burn injury*** The patient suffering from burn injury was admitted to the hospital. The patient was shifted to another bed in order to accommodate another critically burnt patient who expired. The patient was again shifted to the previous bed without disinfecting the bed and without changing the bed sheet and thereby the infection was aggravated and the patient died.

The National Commission[15] was of the view that there was deficiency of service on the part of the hospital staff.

(vii) ***Death due to transfusion of wrong group of blood*** The patient suffered burn injury accidently from a stove. She was shifted to PGI, Chandigarh for treatment of 50% burn. The blood group of the patient was A+. The patient was transfused B+ group of blood on two different dates and she expired. It is alleged that the patient died due to transfusion of wrong group of blood in the hospital.

It is held by the State Commission, Chandigarh,[16] that there was negligence on the part of the attending doctors and staff of PGI for transfusing wrong group of blood to the patient resulting in her death. The decision of the State

14 *Smt. N. Shree Mani* v *Nizam Institute of Medical Sciences* 2011(4) CPR 196; IV(2011) CPJ 513.

15 *Gita Rani Kakkar* v *Chandigarh Administration* II(2017) CPJ 188; 2017(1) CPR 548 (NCDRC).

16 *Jaspal Singh* v *Post Graduate Institute of Medical Education and Research (PGI), Chandigarh* 2000(2) CPR 300 (Chandigarh); II(2000) CPJ 439 (Chandigarh).

Commission was affirmed by the National Commission and the Supreme Court of India.[17]

(viii) ***Death of patient during delivery*** The patient was admitted to the nursing home for second delivery. Owing to carelessness of the doctor the baby was delivered in asphyxiated condition and the mother died.

The National Commission awarded compensation against the nursing home and declared the doctor negligent for not using reasonable care and skill that a doctor should have taken at the time of delivery of high risk pregnancy.[18]

(ix) ***Death of patient for treatment by Unani specialist in emergency.*** The patient was admitted to the hospital for repeated attack of epistaxis (nasal bleeding). One Unani specialist attended the patient and administered allopathic drug and intravenous drip. The patient died of chocking consequent to aspiration of blood in the air passage, though the ENT surgeon was called at the last moment, who blocked the airpassages after repeated nasal bleeding for about ten hours.

The National Commission[19] held the hospital negligent for engaging Unani specialist for providing treatment in an emergency, particularly when the patient was suffering from repeated attack of epistaxis.

(x) ***Death for prescribing overdose of steroid and for not providing supportive therapy*** The patient was admitted to the hospital with fever and skin rash. The physician prescribed "depomedrol" injection at dose of 40 mg three times per day for first 3 days. The dose of "depomedrol" was repeated by the physician without diagnosing the nature of

17 *Post-Graduate Institute of Medical Education and Research, Chandigarh* v *Jaspal Singh* (2009)7 SCC 330; JT 2009(7) SC 527; 2009 ACJ 2672.

18 *Dr. Sr. Louie* v *Smt. Kannolil Pathumma* 1993(1) CPR 422 (NC); I(1993) CPJ 30 (NC); 1993 CTJ. 32 (NCDRC) affirmed by S.C. in *Indian Medical Association* v *V.P. Shantha* AIR 1996 SC 550; (1995)6 SCC 651; III(1995) CPJ 1 (SC); 1995(3) CPR 412 (SC); 1995 CTJ 969 (SC) (CP); 1996 CCJ 1 (SC).

19 *Prof. P.N. Thakur* v *Hans Charitable Hospital* 2008 CTJ 380 (CP); 2007(3) CPR 157; III(2007) CPJ 340.

the disease which was subsequently diagnosed as Toxic Epidermal Nercolysis, i.e. TEN. The physician prescribed long acting steroid in high dose without prescribing quick acting steroid required for the disease and without foreseeing its implications.

There was no record to show that the hospital examined the vital parameters of the patient viz, body temperature, respiration rate, pulse, blood pressure and urine input and output. The hospital also failed to provide supportive therapy including IV fluids/electrolyte replacement, dressing of skin wounds and close monitoring of infection, which is mandatory for proper treatment of TEN patients. The patient ultimately died of infections in another hospital.

By setting aside the judgment of the National Commission, the Supreme Court of India,[20] held the hospital negligent in performance of duty for not providing supportive therapy to the patient suffering from TEN and for not recording the vital parameters of the patient.

(xi) ***Disability after angiography without consent*** The patient had to undergo laparoscopy in the hospital. He had to undergo angiography when the doctors suspected vascular tumour. He was administered local anaesthesia and a catheter was inserted through the Trass femoral route into the aorta and test dose of dye was injected to the patient. The catheter was removed when the patient started convulsions. Ultimately the patient suffered from paraphasia.

By setting aside the order of the State Commission, the National Commission[1] held the hospital liable in negligence for not referring the patient to the neurologist for removal of elevated cerebrospinal fluid by immediate lumber puncture.

(xii) ***Disability for lack of care by the hospital*** The patient aged about 31 years was admitted to the hospital with

20 *Malay Kumar Ganguly* v *Dr. Sukumar Mukherjee* 2009(7) SCJ 124; (2009)9 SCC 221; AIR 2010 SC 1162; (2009)10 Scale 675; III(2009) CPJ 17; 2009(3) CCR 558; 2010 AIR SCW 769.

1 *K.N. Koteshwara Bhatta* v *Kastuba Hospital* 2007(1) CPR 21; I(2007) CPJ 258.

complaint of acute fever. He was shifted to CCU located in the 3rd floor of the hospital. He fell down from the 3rd floor of the hospital and sustained injuries resulting in disability.

The State Commission, Kerala[2] held the hospital negligent for failure to take care of the patient resulting in disability and further medical treatment.

(xiii) ***Permanent brain damage due to administration of lariago injection by unqualified nurse*** The minor patient was treated for seven days for typhoid in Spring Meadows Hospital. The consultant doctor prescribed "Chloramphenicol" injection, but the unqualified nurse misread it as "Chloroquine" and indented for purchase of injection "lariago" (i.e. chloroquine). The nurse injected chloroquine 5 mg. i.v. which is at least $3\frac{1}{2}$ times of the normal pediatric dose, resulting in cardiac arrest. The delay in resuscitation of the child after cardiac arrest contributed to irreversible brain damage of the child. The patient suffered irreparable brain damage and was compelled to live in vegetative state after treatment of 21 days in All India Institute of Medical Sciences, New Delhi.

The National Commission held the nurse negligent in indenting for a wrong injection and in administering the injection intravenously by herself. The National Commission also came to the conclusion that the attending doctor was negligent, as he allowed the unqualified nurse to give intravenous injection, defying the advice of the consultant doctor. As a result, the hospital was held liable to pay compensation for the negligence of its employees. On appeal, the Supreme Court of India[3] confirmed the award of compensation passed by the National Commission.

2 *Kannan* V.*R. Vithayathil House* v *Sree Sudheendra Medical Mission Hospital* 2002(2) CPC 376.

3 *Harjot Ahluwalia (minor) through parents* v *Spring Meadows Hospital* 1997(3) CPR 1 (NC); II(1997) CPJ 98 (NC); (1997)5 CTJ 734 (CP) (NCDRC); 1998 CCJ 405 (NC) confirmed by Supreme Court of India in *Spring Meadows Hospital* v *Harjot Ahluwalia through K.S. Ahluwalia* AIR 1998 SC 1801; (1998)4 SCC 39; 1998(1) CPR 1 (SC); I(1998) CPJ 1 (SC); 1998 CTJ 81 (SC) (CP); 1998 CCJ 521 (SC); JT 1998(2) SC 620; III(1998) SLT 684.

(xiv) ***Permanent disability after surgery for excision biopsy through thoracotomy*** The patient was admitted to the hospital for treatment of benign tumour in left thorax. The patient complained of weight loss and fever for last one year and x-ray revealed erosion of 2nd, 3rd and 4th ribs of left side. Since benign lesions are very unlikely to be present with fever for one year and since rapidly growing benign lesions can also erode ribs, a biopsy of the mass for confirmation of diagnosis was recommended. When four attempts of FNAC (Fine Needle Aspiration Cytology) could not yield any conclusive pathological diagnosis, the patient had to undergo excision biopsy by thoracotomy. After undergoing surgery for excision biopsy the patient became paraplegic, confined to wheel chair, developed spasticity and flexor spasms and diffuse pain in the lower limbs.

The National Commission,[4] held the doctors and the hospital negligent on the following counts:

(A) PRE-OPERATIVE STAGE. The C.T. Surgeon and physician not only failed to utilise the available pre-operative clinical information about vertebral erosion and infection of vertebrae, but also failed to conduct necessary pre-operative diagnostic tests like MRI and myelogram which would have provided information pre-operatively on the extension of mass into intervertebral foramen and would have brought the neuro-surgeon into action from the very beginning. So the patient was deprived of the service of neuro-surgeon from the very beginning.

(B) OPERATIVE STAGE. The object of surgery was to know about the pathology of tumour, but the entire tumour was excised before knowing its pathology as a benign schwannoma. The doctor could not explain why removal of benign tumour in chest wall resulted in spinal cord injury and paraplegia.

(C) POSTOPERATIVE STAGE. The operating surgeon did not inform the anxious parents of the removal of tumour and rib and

4 *Prasanth S. Dhananka* v *Nizam's Institute of Medical Sciences* 1999 CTJ 163 (CP) (NCDRC); I(1999) CPJ 43 (NC); 1999(1) CPR 42 (NC); 1999 CCJ 1099 (NC).

the nature of the tumour after surgery. The hospital did not exchange opinion with sister institutions for postoperative management of the patient.

The order of the National Commission was affirmed by the Supreme Court which enhanced the amount of compensation.[5]

(xv) ***Respiratory arrest for delay in providing ambulance service*** The patient suffering from asthma was attended by a doctor who telephoned the defendant ambulance service to send an ambulance to take the patient to the hospital. The ambulance did not arrive for 40 minutes, although the records were manipulated to show that it had arrived after 22 minutes. The patient suffered respiratory arrest.

The trial judge held the defendant ambulance service liable for the respiratory arrest of the patient, which would have been averted had the ambulance service been provided within reasonable time. By confirming the decision of the trial judge on appeal, it is held by the Court of Appeal in U.K.[6] that the defendant ambulance service was negligent for providing service, which was part of the health service provided by the hospital.

(xvi) ***Sufferings due to wrong treatment suspecting pulmonary embolism*** The patient suffering from high blood sugar was admitted to the hospital for breathlessness and severe pain. The doctor suspected pulmonary embolism and advised investigations for D-Dimer test, repeat Echo test and spinal CT chest scan. The hospital ignored to carry out the investigations. When the condition of the patient deteriorated injection TPA (Actilyse) was administered along with other medicines, but it had negative effect. The patient had to be shifted from one hospital to another hospital for proper treatment.

5 *Nizam's Institute of Medical Sciences* v *Prasanth S. Dhananka* (2009)6 SCC 1; JT 2009(2) SC 385; 2009 AIR SCW 3563; 2010 ACJ 38; (2009)4 Supreme 165.

6 *Kent* v *Griffiths* [2000]2 All ER 474 (CA); [2000]2 WLR 1158.

The National Commission[7] found deficiency of service on the part of the hospital for not following the standard protocol of treatment.

(xvii) *Suffering from hepatitis after transfusion of blood without screening* The patient was admitted to the hospital with high malarial fever. Her platelet count was 59,000. Her liver was found to be normal from ultrasound test and HCV (Hepatitis) anti-bodies and HB antigens were found to be negative. The hospital transferred platelet from five donors without proper testing of blood when platelet count of the patient was 35,000, whereas it is established from medical literature that platelet transfusion is necessary only when platelet count is between 15,000 and 20,000.

The National Commission[8] held the hospital negligent in providing treatment to the patient resulting in development of acute attack of hepatitis C.

8 Hospital and others

(i) *Death due to adverse reaction of anaesthesia* The patient aged about $2^1/_2$ years suffered injury on the forehead for which three stitches were given. The father of the baby took him to the clinic of the doctor apprehending visible scar on the forehead of the baby. The baby was taken to the operation theatre for giving micro stitches under local anaesthesia, but the child did not regain senses. The child was shifted to Ganga Ram Hospital where he died after three days.

The Delhi State Commission[9] held the hospital and the anaesthetist negligent for not taking care to decide the quantity of anaesthetic drug (Ketamine) on consideration of age, weight and metabolic capacity of the child who died due to adverse reaction of anaesthetic drug.

(ii) *Death due to complications after surgery for removal of implant* The patient was admitted to the hospital for removal

7 *Inscol Hospital* v *Inderjit Arora* 2017(2) CLT 108; 2017(2) CPR 34; II(2017) CPJ 402 (NCDRC).

8 *Ms. Shefali Bhargava* v *Indra Prastha Apollo Hospital* 2003(3) CPR 58; I(2003) CPJ 216 (NC); 2003(3) CLT 402.

9 *Madhu Sudan* v *Dr. Suresh Gupta* II(2006) CPJ 348.

of fibular implant by surgery. The surgeon overlooked the back history of undergoing surgery of right ankle of the patient and failed to prescribe proper investigations to confirm or rule out Deep Vein Thrombosis (DVT) before undertaking planned surgery. The surgeon was careless in continuing surgery after development of cardiac complications of the patient under general anaesthesia. The anaesthetist administered general anaesthesia in preference to spinal anaesthesia and did not record the cause of cardiac arrest, though he claimed that it happened due to pre-existing DVT followed by pulmonary embolism (PE). The hospital did not call any cardiologist in proper time and did not provide any bed to the patient after complicated surgery for about six hours during postoperative period.

The National Commission[10] held the hospital, surgeon and anaesthetist negligent in discharge of professional duty and thereby the patient died of cardiac arrest.

(iii) ***Death due to delay in treatment of cancer for non-supply of biopsy report*** The patient approached the surgeon for feeling of hardness in the tongue. The whole of the nodule was removed by surgery and biopsy was done, but the surgeon or the hospital did not disclose the biopsy report to the patient. After lapse of about five months the patient again developed hardness in the tongue and malignancy was detected by CT scan. The patient died in spite of treatment in Tata Memorial Hospital, Bombay and in cancer department of AIIMS.

The National Commission[11] held the hospital and the surgeon negligent for delaying the treatment of the deceased by not disclosing the biopsy report to the patient or his relatives and thereby expediting the death by 5 to 7 years.

(iv) ***Death due to transfusion of blood of wrong group.*** The pregnant lady was transfused B+ve blood after her first delivery, whereas her blood group was B-ve-Rh sensitisation,

10 *M.C. Katare* v *Bombay Hospital and Medical Research Centre* 2010(1) CPR 269; II(2010) CPJ 128.

11 *Mrs. Sushma* v *Dr. G.D. Goel* IV(2010) CPJ 410.

i.e. development of anti Rh antibodies in blood causing destruction of foetus in subsequent pregnancies. The compatibility test (cross-matching) should be done in such cases to evade major mishap. The blood bank issued blood without compatibility test in careless manner and thereby mishap took place.

The National Commission[12] held the hospital and the doctor who gave the wrong report, liable for negligence.

(v) ***Death for overdose of medicine without monitoring adverse effect.*** The patient was diagnosed to be a case of RTI, but the report of blood test revealed malaria parasite called plasmodium vivax. When the patient did not respond to the treatment of administering Falcigo injection in overdose, he was taken to another doctor who treated the patient for plasmodium vivax without conducting second blood test. The condition of the patient deteriorated and ultimately he died.

The National Commission[13] held the hospital and the doctors negligent in providing overdose of falcigo without taking precaution to assess the adverse effect of overdose of medicine.

(vi) ***Permanent disability due to birth asphyxia*** The pregnant lady was admitted to the hospital due to absence of labour pain on expected date of delivery. The administration of pitocin drip failed to induce labour pain for almost two days. The baby was born after inducing the method called Artificial Rupture Membrane (ARM). The baby was not sucking and found to be suffering from birth asphyxia.

The National Commission[14] held the hospital and the doctor negligent for not taking into account the warning signals of foetal distress and for not taking step to conduct caesarean delivery to avert asphyxia.

12 *Anil Kumar Mittal (Dr.)* v *Neelam Gupta* IV(2015) CPJ 597; 2016(1) Andh LD 33 (NCDRC).

13 *Ashok Kumar Upadhaya* v *Dr. D.N. Misra* I(2011) CPJ 194.

14 *Baby Geetha* v *Cosmopolitan Hospitals (P) Ltd.* 2006(2) CPC 398; III(2006) CPJ 89.

(vii) *Permanent disability due to complications after surgery* The patient had undergone surgical procedure called "chemical sympathectomy"— a procedure used for destruction of the periarterial sympathetic nerves as in Doppler's operation by a corrosive such as phenol. The procedure was conducted under local anaesthesia on Sunday in the ward instead of operation theatre. No senior doctor was present during the procedure, which was abandoned when the patient complained of numbness in his leg. A test dose of mild solution of ethanol was not used to test its susceptibility and reaction of the therapeutic chemical, i.e. phenol. Ultimately the patient suffered from lower limb paresis and urine retention and bowel movements could be re-habilitated by digital evacuation.

The National Commission[15] found the hospital and the operating surgeon negligent for causing permanent disability of the patient.

(viii) *Refusal to admit patient in the hospital for treatment* The patient was taken to the ESI hospital for treatment of acute pain in abdomen. She is a card-holder of ESI hospital and is entitled to medical assistance from the ESI hospital. The attending doctor examined the patient after five hours of attendance, but refused to admit her in the hospital for non-availability of bed. The admission of the patient was refused in other hospitals and ultimately she was admitted in a nursing home where she expired.

The State Commission, West Bengal,[16] held the hospital and the attending doctor negligent on the grounds of not giving timely medical treatment to the patient and refusal to admit the patient in the hospital for treatment of acute pain in abdomen.

(ix) *Sufferings due to unskilled laparoscopic surgery* The surgeon punctured small intestine during surgery. He failed to correct the leak by resuturing by performing laparotomy

15 *Om Parkash Lokre* v *Christian Medical College & Hospital* 2009(2) CPR 116; 2009 CTJ 849 (CP); II(2009) CPJ 178.

16 *Ranjit Kumar Das* v *Medical Officer, ESI Hospital, Manicktola, Calcutta* 1998(1) CPR 165 (Cal); III(1997) CPJ 336 (Cal); 1999 CCJ 70 (WB).

and discharged the patient for admission in another hospital where another surgeon made eleven unsuccessful attempts before referring the patient to another higher speciality centre. Both the surgeons were found to be negligent and deficient in service and the hospitals were also held vicariously liable for the sufferings of the patient by the National Commission.[17]

(x) ***Sufferings due to unskilled lumber puncture.*** The baby of 45 days old was admitted to the hospital for abdominal distention and one episode of general convulsion. The lumber puncture done on the child resulted in blood stained cerebro spinal fluid (CSF). The child developed paraplegia accompanied by paralysis of bladder and rectum. The child suffered due to lumber puncture which resulted in hematoma in the spine within next few days.

The National Commission[18] held the hospital and the doctor negligent for undertaking two episodes of lumber puncture resulting in hematoma in the spine of the child.

9 Nephrologist/Urologist

(i) ***Death after renal transplantation*** The patient diagnosed as Hepatitis C virus (HCV) with End Stage Renal Disease (ESRD) was admitted for chronic renal failure. A known diabetic for more than a decade, the patient was on regular dialysis. He had undergone Kidney transplant and discharged after treatment of high blood sugar. He was re-admitted for vomitting, nausea and other complications in ICU and kept on ventilator. The four fingers of left hand of the patient had to be amputated due to thermal burn during Kidney transplant. Ultimately he died of septicaemia and multi-organ failure.

The National Commission[19] did not hold the doctor negligent for Kidney transplant, but negligence was

17 *Vijay Health Centre* v *Chandra Das* 2015(2) CLT 494; II(2015) CPJ 578 (NCDRC).

18 *Subhash Chand* v *M.D. Jaipur Golden Hospital* IV(2011) CPJ 536.

19 *Rashmi Taryon* v *Noida Medicare Centre Ltd.* 2015(4) CPR 548; I(2016) CPJ 228 (NCDRC).

attributed to the doctor and the hospital for additional trauma of thermal injury to the patient's fingers during Kidney transplant.

(ii) ***Sufferings due to improper treatment of Kidney stone*** The patient was admitted to the hospital a number of times and various procedures were performed on him for Kidney stone, but his condition was deteriorating. Ultimately the right Kidney of the patient had to be removed by surgery in another hospital as the same was damaged due to repeated ultrasound scan.

The National Commission[20] held the doctor and the hospital negligent in providing treatment to the patient.

10 Nurse

(i) ***Damage due to unskilled treatment of high risk pregnancy*** One midwife-cum-nurse was running a hospital in the name of "Jeevan Hospital" on Tanjore Road near Tiruchirapalli in Tamil Nadu. The complainant bearing a child of 35 weeks old with normal activities was admitted to the hospital. The pregnancy had ensued within one year of the previous caesarean operation and the patient was of a rare blood-group R-H Negative. The midwife took the complainant to the delivery ward and started giving treatment by administering two injections followed by four more injections on hands and hips. The complainant had started heavy bleeding from her uterus. Then she was shifted to City Hospital where she underwent operation and a dead male child was delivered. The uterus was removed as the same was ruptured.

The State Commission, Tamil Nadu,[1] held the midwife guilty of negligence for taking up treatment of complicated case of pregnancy when she was only a nurse-cum-midwife. The Commission also held her fully responsible for the harm caused to the complainant and her child.

20 *A.J. Mohammad Shah alias A.J. Shanavas* v *Kerala Institute of Medical Science (KIMS)* III(2015) CPJ 155; 2015(5) Andh LD 16 (NCDRC).

1 *M. Jeeva* v *R. Lalitha* 1994(2) CPR 517 (NC); II(1994) CPJ 73 (NC); (1994)2 CTJ 498 (CP) (NCDRC).

(ii) ***Sufferings for leaving surgical sponge in abdominal cavity after caesarean operation*** The complainant was admitted to the hospital at an advanced stage of pregnancy. An attempt was made to induce labour pain and ultimately a caesarean operation was performed on the complainant. The complainant complained of recurring pain in abdomen. The complainant was shifted to a better equipped hospital where CT Scan report revealed that surgical sponge was left in abdominal cavity. The complainant got relief after removal of sponge by way of emergency operation.

It is held by the State Commission, Kerala,[2] that the post operational complications developed for leaving surgical sponge in the abdominal cavity of the complainant during caesarean operation. The surgeon was not held negligent, as it is the duty of the nursing staff to count the sponges during operation. The State Commission held the nurse responsible for not counting the sponges leading to postoperative complications of the complainant and made the hospital vicariously liable to pay compensation as employer of the negligent nurse.

11 Oncologist

(i) ***Death after hysterectomy for cervical cancer*** The patient had undergone radical hysterectomy for cancer, but the disease reappeared after 10 months and she developed metastasis resulting in death. It is established from evidence that the doctor did not make clear diagnosis post surgery resulting in failure to commence requisite treatment.

The doctor was found to be negligent by the National Commission.[3]

(ii) ***Death after surgery for cervical cancer*** The doctor removed uterus, ovaries, fallopian tubes and ureters of the patient and made holes in abdomen for draining out urine. The doctor

2 *Aleyamma Varghese* v *Dewan Bahadur Dr. Varghese* 1996 CTJ 911 (CP) (SCDRC); 1997(1) CPR 310 (Ker); III(1997) CPJ 165 (Ker); 1998 CCJ 1310 (Ker).

3 *Rajiv Gandhi Cancer Institute and Research Centre* v *Lt. Col. (Retd.) Zile Singh Dahiya* 2014(2) CPR 475; II(2014) CPJ 464 (NCDRC).

of another hospital reconstructed urinary tract and joined it to urinary bladder. It is alleged that the life span of the patient would have been prolonged, had proper treatment been planned by conducting biopsy for ascertaining the stage of cancer.

The National Commission[4] held the doctor negligent for performing surgery without the help of anaesthetist and without conducting biopsy to ascertain the stage of cancer.

(iii) Sufferings due to wrong surgery The patient was suffering from cancer. She was admitted to the hospital due to vaginal bleeding. With consent of the patient the assistant to the senior oncologist opened the abdomen and closed it without performing surgery. She was declared to be inoperable case of cancer in USA. She suffered during prolonged period for conducting unnecessary surgery by advice of the senior oncologist.

The Bombay High Court[5] held the hospital and the senior oncologist negligent in advising surgery against the advice of the doctor in USA and thereby causing unnecessary medical expenditure, mental agony, pain and suffering of the patient.

12 Ophthalmologist

(i) *Damage for failure to warn of risk before surgery* The patient had been almost blind in her right eye since a penetrating injury to it at the age of nine. Despite this early misfortune, she had continued to lead a substantially normal life. She decided to have an eye-examination at the age of forty. The ophthalmologist advised her that an operation on the right eye would not only improve its appearance by removing scar tissue, but would probably restore significant sight to that eye. The surgical procedure was carried out. After the operation there was no improvement in the right eye. On the other hand, she developed inflammation in the left eye as an element of sympathetic ophthalmia. Ultimately the patient lost the sight in the left eye and thus became blind. It is

4 *R.M. Gautam (Dr.)* v *Master Nav Kshitij* III(2015) CPJ 351; 2015(3) CPR 496 (NCDRC).

5 *Padam Chandra Singhi* v *Dr. P.B. Desai* 2011(113) BLR 3409; 2012(1) All MR 510.

alleged that the ophthalmic surgeon was negligent for failure to warn of the risk of sympathetic ophthalmia.

The High Court of Australia held the Ophthalmic Surgeon negligent for failure to warn of the risk of damage to left eye as a result of operation on the right eye, because sympathetic ophthalmia was the only danger whereby both the eyes might be rendered sightless.[6]

(ii) *Injury to cornea and left eye-ball due to defective operation*

The complainant aged 6 years was born with physical deformity in the size of two eyes. The disease was diagnosed as ptosis *i.e.* drooping of left eyelid. The patient had undergone operation under the care of the surgeon in P.G.I., Chandigarh. There was further drooping of eyelid instead of lifting of the same after the operation. The patient suffered a serious damage to the tear gland resulting in non-formation of tears requiring use of medicines every three hourly and insertion of costly plug in the left eye. It is alleged that the surgeon caused injury to the left eye-ball and cornea of the patient by negligent performance of the operation, resulting in double vision and permanent disability.

It is held by the State Commission, Chandigarh,[7] that the surgeon was negligent in performing the operation, resulting in double vision and further drooping of left eyelid of the patient.

(iii) *Loss of vision for cataract operation without waiting for B Scan report.* The patient had undergone surgery for removal of cataract from his right eye. The doctor advised the patient to undergo B Scan EKO X-ray, but conducted operation without waiting for B Scan report of the patient. The B Scan report was required to ascertain the retinal problem of the patient. The patient lost his vision in the right eye after the operation.

The State Commission, W.B.[8] held the doctor negligent in conducting cataract operation without waiting for B Scan report of the patient's eye.

6 *Rogers* v *Whitaker* 109 ALR 625 (H.C. of Australia); 16 BMLR 148.
7 *Jaswinder Singh* v *Dr. J.S. Saini* II(2000) CPJ 262 (Chandigarh).
8 *Sourindra Mohon Ghosh* v *Dr. V. Pahwa* 2000 CTJ 475 (CP) (SCDRC).

(iv) ***Loss of vision for not screening of RoP of premature baby.*** The female baby weighing 1250 grams was born with gestational age of 29 weeks in the Government hospital and remained under the care of the neonatologists till 13 weeks of age. The neonatologists did not advise for screening the baby for Retinopathy of Prematurity (in short RoP) till 13 weeks of age and thereby the baby became blind due to detachment of retina which turned into funnel shaped.

The Supreme Court[9] held the neonatologists and the state liable in negligence for causing loss of vision of the baby girl by not advising for screening of RoP of the premature baby within 2 to 4 weeks after birth.

(v) ***Loss of vision of child for not screening him for RoP*** The baby weighing 1.49 kg and 32 weeks gestation was born in the hospital. The baby was under the care of the paediatrician and opthalmologist during his stay in the hospital. He was not screened for RoP either during his stay in the hospital for 4 weeks or during his review and routine check up in OPD of the hospital on two dates after his discharge from the hospital. Ultimately, it was established that the child became blind for total detachment of retina.

The Supreme Court[10] held the hospital, paediatrician and opthalmologist guilty of medical negligence for their failure to carry out mandatory check up of RoP on a pre-term baby, which ultimately led to his blindness.

(vi) ***Loss of vision after cataract surgery*** The complainant had undergone cataract surgery, but lost vision in the right eye. The surgeon did not instil 5% povidone iodine solution in the affected area before surgery. The surgeon also did not administer antibiotic in any form after surgery. The surgeon started steroid very late and in haphazard manner without prescribing intravitreal injection throughout the stay of the complainant in the hospital.

9 *V. Krishna Kumar* v *State of Tamil Nadu* (2015)9 SCC 388.
10 *Maharaja Agrasen Hospital* v *Master Rishabh Sharma* 2019 SCC Online SC 1658.

The National Commission[11] held the opthalmologist and the hospital negligent in providing medical treatment to the complainant.

(vii) ***Loss of vision after unskilled surgery*** The complainant suffered congenital disorder in his left eye, which looked a little smaller than the right one. The vision in both the eyes of the complainant was 6/9. Without disclosing the possibility of residual imperfections and potential complications, the doctor performed the surgery causing injury to the cornea and eye ball of the complainant, resulting in diminishing vision in the eye and double vision.

By setting aside the order of the State Commission, Chandigarh on appeal, the National Commission held the doctor negligent for loss of vision of the complainant.[12]

13 Orthopaedician

(i) ***Amputation of leg after operation to cure ulcer of the heel*** The patient was suffering from diabetes mellitus and hypertension. She had undergone operation for an ulcer of the heel of her left foot. She developed gangrene and was not attended by the surgeon for three days. Ultimately her left leg was amputated.

The State Commission, Pondicherry,[13] held the surgeon negligent on two counts: first, the surgeon did not pass on information regarding debridement under general anaesthesia and regarding gangrene in the mid and second toes of the patient; secondly, the surgeon left the patient for three days without giving any instruction for treatment, particularly when the condition of the patient was deteriorating day by day.

(ii) ***Death due to complications after surgery for displacement of left forearm*** The patient sustained simple fracture with

11 *Director, Jawaharlal Institute for Post Graduate Medical Education & Research (JIPMER), Puducherry* v *S. Varrery Srinivas* 2012(3) CPR 256; III(2012) CPJ 467.

12 *Jaswinder Singh* v *Dr. Neeraj Sud* 2011(3) CPR 406.

13 *V. Vassanda Coumary* v *Dr. T. Ramachandrudu* 1998(3) CPR 227 (Pondicherry).

displacement in radius of left forearm. The orthopaedic surgeon conducted operation in spite of pre-anaesthetic drug reaction, which led to acute respiratory depression of the patient. While both the kidneys were damaged, the patient was referred to the gastroenterologist for loose motion and vomiting, whose prescribed drugs further damaged the kidneys leading to the death of the patient.

The State Commission, Andhra Pradesh[14] held the surgeon negligent for performing surgery without taking care of drug reaction and acute respiratory depression. The hospital was held negligent for discharging the patient when he developed hyperthermia during postoperative period.

(iii) ***Death due to delay in conducting surgery of fractured leg*** The patient suffered crush injury in an accident, but no urgent surgery of the fractured leg was done. She developed gangrene and septicemia and the leg had to be amputated. Ultimately the condition of the patient deteriorated leading to death.

The National Commission[15] held the doctor negligent on the ground that he did not conduct surgery for two days and thereby the gangrene and septicemia developed leading to amputation of leg and ultimate death of the young girl of 16 years of age.

(iv) ***Death due to mismatched blood transfusion*** The patient sustained fracture in the neck of the femur and was admitted in the nursing home of the orthopaedic surgeon. The operation was done and blood was transfused. The orthopaedician signed on the requisition slip sent to the blood bank by enclosing with it wrong specimen of B+ group of blood, whereas the patient had A+ group of blood. Ultimately, the patient died of mismatched blood transfusion.

14 *Dr. M.A. Gafoor* v *Medwin Hospital* I(2009) CPJ 167.

15 *Post Graduate Institute of Medical Education and Research* v *Amit Sarkar* 2015(3) RCR (Civil) 410 (NCDRC); *Amit Sarkar* v *PGIMER* III(2015) CPJ 357 (NCDRC).

The National Commission[16] held the orthopaedician negligent by observing that wrong blood transfusion is an error which no doctor or hospital exercising ordinary skill would have made.

(v) ***Death due to repair of femur of leg without anaesthesia*** Owing to accident the patient was suffering from fracture of the femur of his left leg. On screening it was found that he had an overlapping fracture of the femur which required pin-traction. A morphia injection was given to the patient. The doctor used manual traction with the help of three male attendants at the time of putting the fractured leg in plaster. This kind of rough manipulation was calculated to cause conditions favourable for embolism or shock and proved fatal to the patient. The doctor described the cause of death as fat embolism.

The Supreme Court of India held that the doctor was guilty of negligence and carelessness, because he did not make thorough preliminary examination before injecting morphia and he reduced the fracture without taking elementary caution of giving anaesthetic to the patient.[17]

(vi) ***Death due to unskilled surgery for disc prolapse*** A young lady of 23 years of age had undergone surgery due to lumbar disc prolapse. It is alleged that the surgeon committed grave mistake by not setting right the flesh in the operated area, which resulted in grave complications leading to cardiac arrest and death. No explanation is forthcoming why a young lady will have so many grave complications leading to cardiac arrest after surgery.

By invoking the doctrine of *res ipsa loquitur*, the National Commission,[18] held the surgeon negligent in performing the surgery.

16 *Dr. Sunil Thakur* v *Gorachand Goswami* 2013(1) CPR 340; I(2013) CPJ 646; 2013(3) ALD (Cons) 20.

17 *Dr. Laxman Balkrishna Joshi* v *Dr. Trimbak Bapu Godbole* 1968 ACJ 183 (SC); AIR 1969 SC 128; 1968 Mah LJ 599; (1968)2 SCWR 73; 1968 SCD 866.

18 *Thayira Begum* v *Padmini Nursing Home* IV(2017) CPJ 106; 2018(1) CLT 31; 2017(3) CPR 603 (NCDRC).

(vii) *Death during operation due to cardiorespiratory arrest* The patient had sustained injury to his right arm and undergone operation for insertion of plate and screws in his right forearm. The patient developed pain and deformity at the operation site. The orthopaedician conducted the operation after obtaining opinion of the cardiologist and after getting x-rays done. The patient developed cardio-respiratory arrest in the midst of the operation and collapsed.

The State Commission, Gujarat,[19] held the orthopaedician, cardiologist and anaesthetist negligent for the death of patient in the midst of the operation, which was affirmed by the National Commission.[20]

(viii) *Deformity due to defective treatment of hairline fracture in neck of femur* The patient was admitted to the hospital for treatment of hairline fracture in neck of femur. The surgeon performed hemi-orthoplasty without having trained staff in the hospital. Ultimately the patient had to undergo total hip replacement surgery within $3^1/_2$ years and thereafter to lead his life with crutches.

The National Commission[1] held the orthopaedic surgeon negligent in providing treatment to the patient on the following grounds:

(*i*) by not following the procedure of internal fixation;

(*ii*) the defective performance of hemi-orthoplasty;

(*iii*) the adoption of procedure of hemi-orthoplasty not justified at the age of 42 as per medical literature;

(*iv*) the lack of infrastructure including trained staff for carrying out surgery in the hospital.

(ix) *Disability due to defective treatment of fracture of lower part of left leg* The patient was admitted to the hospital consequent on a fracture sustained on the lower part of her

19 *Arunaben D. Kothari* v *Navdeep Clinic* 1996(3) CPR 20 (Guj); III(1996) CPJ 605 (Guj); (1997)5 CTJ 533 (CP) (SCDRC); 1998 CCJ 972 (Guj).

20 *Rashmi Vora* v *Arunaben D. Kothari* 2006(1) CPC 66; IV(2005) CPJ 164.

1 *S. Ramanujam* v *Dr. C.P. Sree Kumar* 2007(1) CLT 155; IV(2006) CPJ 365.

left leg above the ankle. The left leg was put in plaster cast by the doctor and the patient was discharged. An abscess was noticed at the operation site when plaster was removed.

On examination of x-ray photo, it was seen that there were foreign substances left inside the leg. The patient was thereafter treated by another doctor who conducted operation to remove the foreign bodies found inside the leg in order to prevent further damage. The patient was discharged with plaster cast after three weeks and the same was reviewed after one month and thereafter the plaster was recast and she was advised to come after six weeks for follow up action. The patient was advised to walk with the help of crutch. It was alleged that the patient suffered not only severe pain and discomfiture, but also became permanently disabled on account of the negligent, defective and inadequate treatment given to her by the doctor of the first hospital.

It is held by the State Commission, Kerala,[2] that the doctor of the first hospital was negligent in the treatment of the patient because, first, the doctor got compression plate purchased by the patient, but the same was not used for the treatment without any cogent explanation; secondly, the doctor used wires and screws instead of compression plate which was complete deviation from the standard treatment of fracture of Tibia; and thirdly, the broken drill bits were found inside the leg, which caused the complications leading to disability of the patient. On appeal, the National Commission,[3] confirmed the decision of the State Commission.

(x) ***Permanent disability due to improper treatment*** The patient suffering from swelling and pain in his right foot had undergone operation, but the problems went on increasing. The sample taken during excision was not sent for biopsy test. The biopsy done in another hospital revealed cancerous lesion and highly malignant tumour, and the foot was amputated. The patient suffered permanent disability.

2 *Mrs. K.K. Radha* v *Dr. G.U. Sekhar* III(1994) CPJ 376 (Ker); (1994)2 CTJ 790 (CP) (SCDRC).

3 *P.P. Ismail* v *Mrs. K.K. Radha* 1997(2) CPR 171 (NC); I(1998) CPJ 16 (NC); (1997)5 CTJ 685 (CP) (NCDRC); 1999 CCJ 99 (NC).

The National Commission[4] found deficiency in service for not making proper diagnosis and treatment by sending the sample taken during excision for biopsy test.

(xi) *Disability due to unskilled surgery* The complainant was allured by the advertisement for increasing the height of the body by way of surgery. The surgery performed by the orthopaedician comprised corticotomy on both the legs (middle tibia) and putting of fixators on both the legs. While fixator of 120 mm was put on the left leg, fixator of 150 mm was put on the right leg. The bone was increased by 3 cm in length, but the complainant suffered from pain and swelling. The ring fixator was removed due to infection and the leg was put on plaster cast, but the complainant was unable to do normal duties due to pain.

It is held by the National Commission[5] that the deformity and sinus discharge from the left leg resulting in abnormal mobility and bone infection were the result of negligent surgery of the orthopaedician.

(xii) *Permanent disability due to failure to diagnose compound fracture* The x-rays clearly revealed that the patient suffered fracture of femur shaft and fracture of femur neck. The doctor missed to diagnose both the fractures and treated only for fracture of the shaft of femur. The x-rays taken later in another hospital revealed that the fracture of neck of femur remained untreated. The patient was advised to undergo total hip replacement (THR) for non-union of old fracture of neck of femur, but he refused further surgery due to poor financial condition. As a result, the patient suffered 58% permanent disability including shortening of the leg.

The National Commission[6] held the surgeon negligent and awarded compensation of ₹10 lakh.

4 *Post Graduate Institute of Medical Education & Research* v *Mamta Rani alias Babli* II(2017) CPJ 177 (NCDRC).

5 *Managing Director, Fathima Hospital Kozhikode* v *K.K. Jose, Kottakkakath House Kodanchal* 2011(3) CPR 293; III(2011) CPJ 206.

6 *Manu* v *Dr. Akhilesh Kumar* III(2015) CPJ 462; 2015(3) CLT 1; 2015(3) CPR 443 (NCDRC).

(xiii) ***Permanent disability due to unskilled treatment of fractured arm*** The complainant suffered fracture in the humerus bone of the left arm. The doctor got the x-ray done and the arm was put in plaster by the doctor. The doctor removed the plaster after a few days as the plaster became loose due to reduction in swelling. The doctor took about 25 x-rays within two years, but the complainant recovered after surgical treatment by another doctor. It is alleged that the complainant suffered permanent disability, as the doctors did not advise for any surgical treatment when he came to know from x-ray reports that there was no callous formation and there was no possibility of union of broken ends of bone.

It is held by the State Commission, U.P.[7] that the doctor was negligent by not advising or adopting for surgical treatment in spite of the fact that there was no union of broken ends of the bone.

14 Otorhinolaryngologist

(i) ***Death after stapedotomy surgery*** The patient died after stapedotomy operation. The post mortem report indicated subdural haemorrhage all across the brain due to injury inside the skull during surgery. The cause of death was pulmonary oedema and cerebral oedema which according to expert opinion, must have been the result of internal injury during operation or due to delayed effect of anaesthesia administered by the surgeon himself. The contention of the surgeon that the death was due to SUDEP (sudden unexpected death in epilepsy) was not accepted in the absence of any history of epilepsy of the patient.

The National Commission[8] held the surgeon negligent in conducting the surgery.

(ii) ***Permanent disability due to unskilled surgery of nasal septum.*** The patient approached ENT surgeon for correction of nasal septum with enlargement of inferior concha. The

7 *Mohd. Ubaid Siddiqui* v *Dr. Ramesh Kumar Upadhaya* 2000 CTJ 284 (CP) (SCDRC); 2000(1) CPR 77 (Lucknow).

8 *G.V.S. Rao (Dr.)* v *K. Chinna Reddy* 2016(4) CPR 193 (NCDRC).

surgeon advised septoplasty. While the patient was under general anaesthesia, the surgeon injected inside the nostrils 2% xylocaine with adrenaline using a syringe without consulting anaesthetist and thereby the patient suffered temporary cardiac arrest resulting vegetative life.

The National Commission held the surgeon and the hospital liable in negligence for causing permanent disability of the patient.[9]

(iii) *Sufferings after cataract operation* The IOL of the patient was detached or dislocated after cataract surgery. Nothing is on record to indicate what advice or mode of treatment was prescribed by the doctor during postoperative period. The second surgery was done in another hospital for correction of implantation of IOL and thereby the patient suffered financial loss and harassment.

The National Commission[10] held the surgeon negligent for performance of cataract surgery and in discharge of duty during postoperative period.

15 Paediatrician

(i) *Permanent disability due to wrong diagnosis and treatment* The patient aged 12 years was treated by one doctor for fever for about three days. As the fever did not subside and the patient developed swelling on lips, followed by lesions both inside and outside the mouth, he was referred to the paediatrician who gave treatment for measles for about five days. When rash had spread all over the body, the patient was referred to ENT surgeon and dermatologist who diagnosed the case as Stevens Johnson Syndrome; which was reaction of sulphur drug. As the disease was in the last stage, the patient's vision was permanently impaired even after giving treatment by an ophthalmologist. It is alleged that the patient lost eyesight and became permanently disabled due to wrong diagnosis and treatment given by the paediatrician.

9 *St. Gregorious Mission Hospital* v *Roji George* 2008(1) CPR 7; I(2008) CPJ 68.

10 *Saint Francis Hospital Bawar Road* v *Kamla* I(2016) CPJ 302 (NCDRC).

It is held by the State Commission, Gujarat,[11] that the paediatrician was guilty of negligence in not diagnosing Stevens Johnson Syndrome, but he could not be held liable for loss of vision of the patient resulting in permanent disability for the whole life.

(ii) *Permanent vegetative state after circumcision operation* The patient aged about $2^1/_2$ years had undergone circumcision operation under general anaesthesia, but did not regain consciousness. It is established from evidence that the patient suffered respiratory distress during operation for failure of the surgeon and the anaesthetist in taking adequate precautionary measures and thereby the patient will have to remain in vegetative state for the rest of his life.

The Supreme Court of India[12] held the doctor negligent in performance of duty towards the patient by affirming the decision of the National Commission.

16 Pathologist

(i) *Death expedited for submission of wrong report* The patient aged about 25 years had undergone surgery and tissues were removed for biopsy. The pathologist who conducted biopsy gave the report indicating the disease as tuberculosis. When the condition of the patient deteriorated, she was shifted to the hospital where the illness was diagnosed as synovial sarcoma (a form of cancer) after pathological test. The patient died as the disease had affected the vital organs of the body by the time the disease was diagnosed as cancer in the hospital.

The Kerala High Court[13] held that the pathologist who conducted the first biopsy, failed to exercise due care and thereby committed medical negligence.

11 *Jayendra Maganlal Padiya* v *Dr. Lalit P. Trivedi* I(1997) CPJ 11 (Ahmedabad); 1998 CCJ 496 (Guj).

12 *Shilaben Aswin Kumar Rana* v *Dr. Bhavin Kumar Shah* 2014(2) CPR 816; II(2014) CPJ 707 (NCDRC) affirmed by Supreme Court of India in 2019(2) RCR (Civil) 184; JT 2019(2) SC 289.

13 *Dr. U. Ummer* v *K.M. Hameed* ILR (2013)2 Ker 535; 2013(2) KLJ 568.

(ii) ***Sufferings due to delay in diagnosing cancer by detecting abnormal cells in cervical smear test*** The plaintiff had undergone a routine cervical smear test at the age of 24, but no abnormality was detected. She married and gave birth to a female baby. She complained of heavy and frequent vaginal bleeding and got temporary relief after undergoing D&C operation. When plaintiff became pregnant for the second time, her cervical cancer was detected, which required immediate termination of her pregnancy followed by a wertheim's hysterectomy and radiotherapy.

The Queen's Bench Division[14] held the doctor negligent for failure to diagnose cervical cancer earlier and the defendant health authority admitted liability for not detecting abnormal cells in the cervical smear three years back.

(iii) ***Sufferings due to wrong report of VDRL test*** The patient was referred to the doctor for ante-natal laboratory examination when she was seven months' pregnant. The report given by the doctor indicated VDRL (Venereal Disease Research Laboratory) test as "positive" for "Titre 1.8", which meant that either of the spouses was suffering from venereal disease. There was no indication that the report should be treated as preliminary result, subject to confirmatory tests. The patient was subjected to another test in other laboratory where the report of VDRL test was found to be negative. It is alleged that the patient suffered mental agony and humiliation due to wrong report of VDRL test given by the doctor.

The State Commission, Maharashtra,[15] held the doctor negligent in giving the report of VDRL test as positive for titre 1.8 without mentioning the same as preliminary result, subject to confirmatory tests.

(iv) ***Sufferings due to wrong report of FNAC Test.*** The patient was treated in the hospital for her lump in her right breast.

14 *Thurman* v *Wiltshire and Bath Health Authority* (1997)36 BMLR 63 (QBD).

15 *Chandrasagar D. Rajput* v *Dr. Dinesh J. Shah* II(1999) CPJ 165 (Mumbai).

The pathologist of the hospital repeated Fine Needle Aspiration Cytology (FNAC) Test and the report was positive indicating "Aspirates from right breast lump had shown well differentiated carcinoma." Based on that report surgery was performed on right breast and tumour was sent for histopathological test. The report indicated that the tumour was benign and there was no carcinoma. The second opinion on the slides in UK also confirmed that there was no cancer.

The National Commission[16] held the pathologist and the hospital negligent for causing mental agony, trauma and emotional suffering due to submission of wrong report of FNAC Test.

17 Physician

(i) ***Blood transfusion without consent*** The patient was severely injured in an automobile accident and was taken to the hospital. The doctor advised for blood transfusion, but a nurse discovered a card in patient's purse identifying her as a Jehovah's witness. The physician of the hospital personally administered transfusion to the patient to preserve her life and health disregarding the religious convictions of the patient. The patient recovered and brought an action against the physician and the hospital authority.

The Ontario Court of Appeal in Canada[17] held that the physician and the hospital authority were liable for administering transfusion to the patient who had the right to refuse life-preserving medical treatment.

(ii) ***Death after penicillin injection without test dose*** A female patient had an ulcer on her right ankle. The doctor prescribed an injection of procaine penicillin without making appropriate enquiry about the history of the patient. She was allergic to penicillin. The injection proved fatal. It was alleged that the doctor had failed in his duty in not making appropriate enquiry before prescribing the injection.

16 *All India Institute of Medical Sciences through its Director* v *Mrs. Ayesha Begum* IV(2010) CPJ 112.

17 *Malette* v *Shulman et al* (1990)67 DLR (4th) 321.

It is held by the Privy Council that the doctor failed in his duty to make appropriate enquiry before causing the penicillin injection to be given, which was the admitted cause of death of the patient and as such the doctor was negligent.[18]

(iii) *Death due to complications after administering dextrose saline drip* The patient was suffering from fever, headache and pain. The doctor gave her paracetamol injection and amoxicillin and advised her to bring to the hospital on the next day. On the next day the doctor administered dextrose saline drip through untrained nurse and left the hospital. The patient started shivering within a few minutes of administration of drip, but the doctor prescribed only a few tablets over phone. The patient lost the vision, became unconscious and ultimately died after shifting to another hospital.

The National Commission[19] upheld the order of the State Commission, Tamil Nadu, which held the doctor negligent for failure to take reasonable care when the condition of the patient deteriorated after administration of dextrose saline drip.

(iv) *Death due to failure to refer the patient to the hospital for better treatment* A nine-year-old boy suffered from vomiting for about 30 hour period. The vomit was dark coloured and his appearance became sallow and sunken eyed and his foot become inverted and he was unable to walk unaided. The medicines prescribed by the general physician did not work. The physician referred the patient to the hospital after giving treatment for 12 hours and the patient collapsed before arriving at the hospital. It is alleged that the general physician was negligent for not referring the patient to the hospital promptly after recognising the risk of dehydration in the child and need for constant monitoring the condition of the child.

The court of UK,[20] held the general physician negligent in failing to refer the child to the hospital promptly by

18 *Chin Keow* v *Government of Malaysia* 1967 ACJ 379; [1967]1 WLR 813; 111 Sol Jo 333 (PC).

19 *Dr. A. Jeyaseelan* v *Anandan* 2007(1) CPR 469; II(2007) CPJ 101.

20 *Fisher* v *McKenzie* (1994)26 BMLR 98 CS (OH).

recognising the risk of dehydration and need for constant monitoring of the child.

(v) ***Death due to improper treatment of dengue*** The patient suffering from high fever with feeling of nausea and vomiting was treated by the doctor without making any diagnosis and without prescribing any blood test. It was not possible to review the medication and rule out dengue infection for not disclosing symptoms of the disease suffered by the patient in the treatment sheet. Under the above circumstances the National Commission[21] found deficiency in service on the part of the doctor who treated the patient.

(vi) ***Death due to lack of monitoring during dengue fever*** The patient, aged 56 years, with cardiac complications, was diagnosed as dengue fever and required hospitalisation. The patient died due to deficiency in timely monitoring the condition of the patient when suffering from abdominal discomfort.

According to the Supreme Court of India[22] the doctor failed to meet the standard of reasonable care expected from medical service by the critical patient.

(vii) ***Death due to overdose of steroid and lack of supportive treatment*** The patient was admitted to the hospital with fever and skin rash. The physician prescribed "depomedrol" injection at dose of 40 mg three times per day for first 3 days. The dose of "depomedrol" was repeated by the physician without diagnosing the nature of the disease which was subsequently diagnosed as Toxic Epidermal Nercolysis. The physician prescribed long acting steroid in high dose without prescribing quick acting steroid required for the disease and without foreseeing its implications. The supportive treatment including IV fluid/electrolyte replacement, dressing of skin wounds and close monitoring of infection was not given to the patient. The effect of immunosuppression caused due to

21 *Hardwari Lal* v *A.K. Agarwal (Dr.)* 2017(3) CLT 295; IV(2017) CPJ 218; 2017(4) CPR 295 (NCDRC).

22 *Arun Kumar Manglik* v *Chirayu Health and Medicare Pvt. Ltd.* (2019)3 Scale 333; 2019(2) CPR 27; JT 2019(5) SC 379; III(2019) CPJ 1 (SC).

the use of steroid in overdose affected the immunity of the patient who ultimately died of infection in another hospital.

By setting aside the judgment of the National Commission,[23] the Supreme Court of India, held the physician negligent in performance of duty for prescribing high dose of long acting steroid in violation of the dose prescribed by the experts for the patients suffering from TEN *i.e.* Toxic Epidermal Nercolysis.[1]

(viii) ***Death due to wrong treatment of typhoid instead of malaria*** The patient was admitted to the hospital with complaint of intermittent fever and chill. The doctor gave the treatment of typhoid, but the patient was not responding to the treatment. The patient was shifted to another hospital in critical condition, where the smear for malaria parasite was found to be positive and the widal test was found to be negative. The patient died in the said hospital due to cardio respiratory arrest and malaria.

By setting aside the decision of the State Commission and National Commission and by restoring the order of the District Forum, the Supreme Court of India held the doctor negligent for giving wrong treatment to the patient even without the aid of expert evidence.[2]

(ix) ***Loss of eye-sight for administering drug having severe allergic reaction.*** The doctor prescribed tablet "amalar" for treatment of malaria of the patient aged about 32 years without ascertaining her allergic reaction to sulphur drug, when this drug is used in case of resistance to chloroquine and is prone to reaction like "dry eye syndrome". The doctor again prescribed drug like cibexinio and glycerine for alleviation of allergic condition of the patient without clinical

23 *Dr. Kunal Saha* v *Dr. Sukumar Mukherjee* 2006(2) CLT 609; 2006(2) CPR 14; III(2006) CPJ 142.

1 *Malay Kumar Ganguly* v *Dr. Sukumar Mukherjee* 2009(7) SCJ 124; (2009)9 SCC 221; AIR 2010 SC 1162; (2009)10 Scale 675; III(2009) CPJ 17; 2009(3) CCR 558; 2010 AIR SCW 769.

2 *V. Kishan Rao* v *Nikhil Super Speciality Hospital* (2010)5 SCC 513; 2010(4) SCJ 690; 2010 AIR SCW 4252; III(2010) CPJ 1; 2010(5) SLT 349; CDJ 2010 SC 428.

examination of the patient. She lost her eye-sight without having any chance of repair of her ratina.

The State Commission, Andhra Pradesh[3] held the doctor guilty of negligence for prescribing drug without monitoring the dangerous side effect of the drug, which resulted in loss of eye-sight of the patient.

18 Radiologist

(i) *Abnormality of foetus not detected by ultrasound scanning*

The patient obtained three reports at different periods of her pregnancy from the scan centre. All the reports revealed that there were no obvious anomalies in the unborn child and that limbs were visualised. When the child was born she was shocked that the left hand of the child was deformed with only a stump just below the elbow.

The State Commission, Tamil Nadu,[4] held the doctor and the scan centre negligent in taking ultrasound scan, and did not accept the contention to the effect that the scan findings would not be 100% accurate and there would be possibility of unobserved anomalies. It is held that the scan findings may not be 100% accurate in case of small anomalies, but in the present case the anomaly was so large (viz, no forearm except a small stump below the elbow) that such an anomaly cannot escape notice in the scan.

(ii) *Life expectancy reduced due to failure to diagnose PPH*

The plaintiff had undergone medical examination including chest x-ray. The radiologist had failed to report the presence of a significant abnormality, which if reported, would have been diagnosed as primary pulmonary hypertension (PPH), whereby life-expectancy is reduced if the sufferer becomes pregnant. The plaintiff became pregnant and thereafter PPH was diagnosed. She gave birth to a daughter and thereafter she had to undergo hysterectomy and cardiac catheterisation. It is alleged that failure to diagnose PPH in time caused

3 *Devi Rani* v *N. Prakash Rao* III(2002) CPJ 123.
4 *Mrs. Shanthi Sridharan* v *Senthil Scan Centre* 1998 CTJ 759 (CP) (SCDRC).

pregnancy and subsequent sufferings including reduced life expectancy of the plaintiff.

The Court of Appeal in UK,[5] held the health authority liable for failure to diagnose PPH at initial stage by the radiologist and awarded general damages for pain and suffering resulting from complications of pregnancy attributable to PPH, heart catheterisation and complications of hysterectomy.

(iii) *Sufferings due to complications after laparoscopic sterilization operation* The laparoscopic sterilization operation was performed on the patient in a local camp along with hundreds of other patients. The patient had to undergo several operations during postoperative period and the patient also suffered from infection due to lack of hygiene and infrastructure in the camp of the operation.

The Karnataka High Court[6] held the State vicariously liable for negligence of the doctors resulting in pain, suffering and medical expenditure of the patient.

(iv) *Sufferings due to unnecessary operation on the basis of wrong MRI report* The complainant developed a suspected tumour in her back. The first MRI scan report revealed meningioma or neurofibroma at D10-10 level on the left side. The surgeon performed laminectomy, but no tumour was found, and a small operation of spinal cord was planned for histopathology. The second MRI scan showed laminectomy defects at D 8-9-10 levels, along with slight swelling of spinal cord. Thereafter second operation was carried out for removal of tumour. It is alleged that the complainant suffered due to wrong report of first MRI, which resulted in unnecessary first operation.

The State Commission, Maharashtra,[7] held the hospital vicariously liable for negligence of the radiologist in supplying

5 *R.* v *Croydon Health Authority* 40 BMLR 40 (CA); [1998] Lloyd's Rep Med 44.

6 *Sou Shevanta* v *State of Karnataka* CDJ 2005 Kar HC 343; 2006 ACJ 2677.

7 *Sharifabi I. Sayed* v *Bombay Hospital and Medical Research Centre* 1998 CCJ 1106 (Mah).

wrong report of MRI, which resulted in unnecessary first operation.

(v) *Unwanted operation for wrong report of ultrasound test* The patient had undergone ultrasound test of her abdomen under the care of the doctor. The report revealed multiple shadows of stones in gall bladder. The patient was operated, but no stone was found in gall bladder. The expert evidence indicates that there could be 2% to 3% cases of error in the report.

The State Commission, Chandigarh,[8] held the doctor negligent for supplying wrong report to the patient.

19 State

(i) *Damage for leaving mop inside abdomen during caesarean operation* The patient had undergone caesarean operation in a Government hospital. The patient developed severe pain and other complications after the operation. Ultimately the scan report revealed that foreign body (mop) was left in paraspinal region during caesarean operation. By subsequent operation the foreign body was removed and the pus was sucked out, but for complete recovery of the patient another operation was required.

The High Court of Andhra Pradesh,[9] invoked its jurisdiction under Art. 226 of the Constitution of India and held the State of Andhra Pradesh liable for negligent treatment of the patient by the doctors in a Government hospital.

(ii) *Death caused by insertion of pneumoperitoneal needle during laparoscopic tubectomy* The patient had undergone laparoscopic tubectomy at primary health centre of the State of Rajasthan. The patient died during the operation. It was established from the report of enquiry that the death of the patient was caused by neurogenic shock resulting in cardiac arrest, caused by insertion of pneumoperitoneal needle.

8 *Darshan Kaur* v *Dr. J.S. Sodhi* I(1999) CPJ 557 (Chandigarh); 1999(1) CPR 522 (Chandigarh); 1999 CTJ 337 (CP) (SCDRC).

9 *Mrs. Shanta* v *State of Andhra Pradesh* III(1997) CPJ 481 (HC of AP).

The High Court[10] held the State of Rajasthan vicariously liable for the death of the patient whose operation was done by the doctor in Government hospital without having adequate resuscitative facilities and cardiac monitoring equipments and assistance of trained anaesthetist.

(iii) *Death for leaving mop inside peritoneal cavity during sterilization operation* The patient had undergone sterilization operation in a Government hospital. The patient developed high fever, abnormal pain and her condition deteriorated, but no step was taken to ascertain the cause of her ailment. When the condition of the patient became serious, the doctors reopened the abdomen and a mop (towel) left inside the peritoneal cavity during previous operation was removed and the abdomen was closed after draining out the collected pus. The patient ultimately expired.

The trial court held the doctors of the Government hospital negligent in conducting the sterilization operation. On appeal the High Court reversed the decision of the trial court. On further appeal, the Supreme Court[11] had set aside the order of the High Court and restored the order passed by the trial court and held that once death by negligence in Government hospital is established, the State would be liable to pay compensation.

(iv) *Unwanted child after sterilization operation* The mother of seven children had undergone sterilization operation at the Government hospital, as she wanted to take advantage of the scheme of sterilization launched by the Government of Haryana. The hospital issued a certificate that her operation was successful. She conceived and ultimately gave birth to a female child. It is established from evidence that only her right fallopian tube was operated upon and the left fallopian tube remained untouched.

10 *Rajmal* v *State of Rajasthan* 1996 ACJ 1166.

11 *Achutrao Haribhau Khodwa* v *State of Maharashtra* (1996)2 SCC 634; 1996 ACJ 505; (1996)4 CTJ 950 (SC) (CP).

It is held by the Supreme Court[12] that the doctor who performed the operation acted in the most negligent manner. It is also held that the State is vicariously liable for negligence of the doctor in Government hospital in performance of sterilization operation resulting in birth of unwanted child.

20 Surgeon

(i) *Damage for failure to diagnose breast cancer at initial stage* The plaintiff aged 38 years complained of a lump in her left breast and the general practitioner referred her to a consultant surgeon of the health authority. The surgeon could not detect discreet lump, but found two areas of benign modularity and the same was diagnosed as fibroadenoma which did not need further attention. The plaintiff developed discomfort and was admitted to the hospital for excision of the lump under care of the consultant surgeon. The lump was found to be cancerous after one year of initial consultation of the surgeon. It is alleged that the plaintiff suffered substantial reduction in expectation of life for failure of the consultant surgeon to discover lump during initial consultation and to arrange excision and biopsy of the lump and for discharging her without further action.

It is held by the Queen's Bench Division in UK,[13] that the consultant surgeon was negligent for not detecting the lump in left breast of the plaintiff during initial consultation, particularly when the plaintiff asserted that there was a lump and the letter of referral from the general practitioner also indicated lump in left breast of the plaintiff.

(ii) *Death after surgery for removal of stone of kidney* The patient was admitted to the hospital with diagnosis of bilateral kidney stones with hydronephrosis. The right kidney was damaged for development of stone with grade IV hydronephrosis and left kidney developed stone with grade II hydronephrosis. She had undergone surgery

12 *State of Haryana* v *Smt. Santra* 2000 CTJ 481 (SC) (CP); I(2000) CPJ 53 (SC).

13 *Judge* v *Huntingdon Health Authority* 27 BMLR 107 (QBD); [1995]6 Med LR 223.

for removal of stone of left kidney. When the patient was recovering after lapse of seven days of first surgery, she was again operated for removal of stone of right kidney with consent of the husband of the patient. The surgeon had knowledge about poor tolerance of anaesthesia during first surgery. The condition of the patient deteriorated after administration of anaesthesia during second surgery and died of cardiac arrest.

The National Commission[14] found the surgeon and the anaesthetist negligent for conducting surgery on the right kidney within a span of seven days of conducting surgery on left kidney, particularly when the patient had poor tolerance of anaesthesia during first surgery.

(iii) *Death for surgery despite critical platelet count* The patient was operated for removal of round worms from stomach. There was no evidence of critical condition of the patient, though he was admitted with pain in abdomen, fever and haemorrhage in both eyes. The patient died.

The Supreme Court of India,[15] held that the surgeon was negligent in taking decision to operate upon the patient in spite of critical platelet count, particularly when there was no immediate necessity to conduct the surgery.

(iv) *Death after complicated surgery without informed consent* The patient had undergone surgical repair of aneurysm, as he was suffering from pain in leg and had difficulty in walking due to tightening sensation in the leg. The surgeon found ischaemic change in both lower limbs and impending gangrene after seeing the result of Digital Sub-Traction Angiography (DSA). Without disclosing the merits and demerits of the surgery to the relatives of the patient, the surgeon conducted operation and the patient became unconscious and put on ventilator. The second surgery was conducted after considerable delay and edema developed in both the legs. The senior surgeon went abroad to attend the

14 *Shri Joginder Singh* v *Dr. Rajeev Kumar Majumdar* IV(2009) CPJ 9.
15 *Nand Kishore Prasad* v *Mohib Hamidi (Dr.)* AIR 2019 SC 2385; JT 2019(5) SC 398; II(2019) CPJ 124; 2019(2) CPR 635 (SC).

conference and the orthopaedician ultimately amputated both the legs, but the patient died of septicemia.

The National Commission[16] held the surgeon and the hospital negligent in performing complicated surgery without disclosing the risks and benefits of the surgery and for not taking prompt corrective measures during post operative period and for not referring the patient to the orthopaedician in proper time.

(v) *Death due to appendicitis operation without proper diagnosis* The female patient was suffering from abdominal pain. The doctor diagnosed the case as one of acute appendicitis requiring immediate operation. The doctor proceeded to undertake the operation in a hospital lacking basic facilities. The operation was performed without the help of any trained anaesthetist. The total blood count and urine test were not done. Finding appendix to be normal he proceeded to remove the gall bladder without further investigation and without caring for the ill-effects of keeping the patient under chloroform for two hours especially when her kidney was affected. No preventive steps were taken to counteract the toxic effects of chloroform on the kidney and liver by giving glucose and vitamins. As a result, chloroform anaesthesia damaged the kidneys and the liver, resulting in hepato-renal failure leading to the death of the patient. The question was whether the surgeon was liable for damages.

It was held by Jabalpur Bench of Madhya Pradesh High Court that the surgeon failed in his duty of care in undertaking the operation without taking necessary precautions and was liable to pay damages.[17]

(vi) *Death due to complications after laparoscopic cholecystectomy* The patient was diagnosed with stones in gall bladder. She had undergone laparoscopic cholecystectomy.

16 *Dinesh Jaiswal (deceased) through LRs* v *Bombay Hospital and Medical Research Centre* I(2010) CPJ 176.

17 *Ram Bihari Lal* v *Dr. J.N. Shrivastava* 1982 ACJ (Supp) 142 (MP) reversed by 1985 ACJ 424; AIR 1985 MP 150; 1985 Jab LJ 259; (1985)1 Cur CC 987; 1985 MPLJ 288; 1985 Cur Civ LJ 149.

The patient had to consult the surgeon after discharge from the hospital for stomach ache, constipation and vomiting. The surgeon did not prescribe diagnostic tests till visible signs of jaundice. By conducting second laparotomy a tube was inserted to drain out bile stained fluid from peritoneal cavity of the patient. Ultimately, Endoscopic Retrograde Cholangio Pancreatograply (ERCP) conducted on the patient at PGI, Chandigarh detected leak in the area of cystic duct and narrowing of central bile duct, and surgery was done, but the patient died of sepsis.

The National Commission[18] held the surgeon and the nursing home negligent for not prescribing diagnostic tests till visible signs of jaundice and for failure to detect the cause of bile leakage by referring the patient for ERCP and thereby aggravating the sufferings of the patient who ultimately died.

(vii) ***Death due to delay in appendicitis operation*** The patient was admitted to the Hospital with complaint of severe abdominal pain. It was diagnosed as a case of acute appendicitis, but no surgery was performed on the patient on the day of his admission in the hospital. On the next date he died of perforated appendix.

It is held by Kerala High Court[19] that the doctor was negligent in not performing the operation on the patient when he was in a condition to undergo the operation.

(viii) ***Death due to delay in conducting surgery of acute appendicitis*** The patient was diagnosed as acute appendicitis requiring emergency surgery. There was inordinate delay of 17 hours in conducting surgery, despite clinical signs of acute emergency. Ultimately the patient died due to cardiovascular arrest resulting from acute necrotizing perforating appendicitis with peritonitis.

18 *Rajinder Singh Dogra* v *Dr. P.N. Gupta, P.N. Urology and Surgical Centre* I(2013) CPJ 2[illegible]6.

19 *Dr. T.T. Thomas* v *Elisa* 1987(1) ACJ 192; (1987)1 ACC 461; AIR 1987 Ker 52; 1986 Ker LT 1026; (1987)2 TAC 50.

The National Commission,[20] awarded ₹40 lakh as compensation after holding the surgeon negligent for inordinate delay in conducting surgery in emergency.

(ix) ***Death due to negligence in conducting cholecystectomy*** The patient was diagnosed as having stones in the gall bladder. She had undergone laparoscopic cholecystectomy under the care of the surgeon for removal of stones. The patient died of cardiac arrest in the operation theatre. It is established from evidence that the surgeon had undertaken the task of performing major surgery on a patient without any assistance from the qualified anaesthetist and without arranging for blood before conducting surgery.

By reversing the decision of the State Commission, HP, the surgeon was held negligent by the National Commission[1] in providing treatment to the patient in utter disregard of the prevalent practice and procedure and settled protocol in that behalf.

(x) ***Death due to surgery without proper precaution*** The patient was advised for surgery after attaining two years of age due to persistent complaint of pneumonia resulting from cleft palate since birth. The surgeon operated in spite of existence of respiratory problem without any pre-operative test and pre-anaesthetic test and thereby the patient went into coma before surgery and remained in vegetative state.

The National Commission[2] held the surgeon and the hospital negligent on three counts: first, for not conducting pre-operative test and pre-anaesthetic test, secondly, for performing operation of the patient with respiratory tract infection in spite of having no emergency, and thirdly, for not taking due care in administering anaesthesia and giving drug Thiopentone having risk for patients with respiratory problems.

20 *Manika Roy* v *B.L. Chitlangra* 2016(1) CLT 374; 2016(1) CPR 380; II(2016) CPJ 348 (NCDRC).

1 *Suresh Nanda* v *Dr. Anoop Kumar* II(2012) CPJ 228.

2 *Karamveer Singh* v *Garg Nursing Home* 2012(3) CPR 490; III(2012) CPJ 630.

(xi) ***Severe burn injury during hernia operation*** The patient is a baby of 65 days old. He was born with inguinal hernia. The patient had undergone operation in the hospital. The patient suffered severe burn injury on both the legs for keeping an extremely hot water bag under the child's leg while the child was under anaesthesia during the operation.

It is held by the State Commission, Karnataka,[3] that the paediatric surgeon and anaesthetist did not exercise reasonable care in discharge of their duties during the operation. It is further held that the need to bring up the temperature of the body of the patient by keeping hot water bag arose, because fall of the temperature upto 2.9 degree was due to negligence in checking and monitoring the temperature of the operation theatre and for lack of modern equipment like radiant heater in the operation theatre.

(xii) ***Sufferings due to unskilled laparoscopic cholecystectomy*** The surgeon conducted laparoscopic cholecystectomy without proper and clinical investigations. The surgeon observed that gall bladder and surroundings strictures had dense adhesions, but failed to diagnose any anatomical changes, in spite of CT scan. The surgeon had to convert laparoscopic surgery to open surgery, as severe haemorrhage took place for cutting of hepatic vein during laparoscopic surgery. The patient was shifted to higher speciality centre for development of post-cholecystectomy biliary fistula and strictures.

Under the above circumstances the National Commission[4] found the surgeon guilty of negligence in conducting surgery.

(xiii) ***Sufferings for leaving mop in abdomen during exploratory laparotomy*** The girl child aged about 13 years was diagnosed as immature teratoma—Right ovary with secondary Norris Grade I for which exploratory laparotomy was done. The patient was discharged from the hospital after seven days

3 *Master P.M. Aswin* v *Manipal Hospital, Bangalore* 1997(1) CPR 393 (Bangalore); I(1997) CPJ 238 (Bangalore); 1998 CCJ 1079 (Kant).

4 *S.P. Gupta (Dr.)* v *Sukhdeb Raj Kaushal* 2016(3) CPR 494; 2016(3) CLT 579 (NCDRC).

of the operation. The patient was brought back to the hospital after seven days when pass started oozing out from the sutures. It was detected during second surgery that mop was left in abdomen when first surgery was done.

The National Commission[5] held the doctor negligent in carrying out exploratory laparotomy.

(xiv) *Sufferings for leaving needle holder in abdomen during surgery* The patient had undergone surgery for removal of ovarian cyst and repair of umbilical hernia. She complained for persistent pain in her pelvic and abdominal region during postoperative period, but the surgeon never advised for x-ray or ultrasound to detect the cause of pain. Ultimately she had to undergo another surgery in the second hospital, where surgical needle holder was recovered from her abdomen after about 4 to 5 months of the first surgery.

By invoking the doctrine of *res ipsa loquitur* the surgeon was held negligent by the National Commission.[6]

(B) MISCELLANEOUS ACTS NOT AMOUNTING TO NEGLIGENCE

1 Anaesthetist

(i) *Damage due to procedure adopted by anaesthetist during surgery* The plaintiff had undergone surgery for removal of gall bladder under general anaesthesia. It is alleged that the plaintiff suffered damage to the brachial plexus, which was caused during administration of an intravenous drip by hyper abduction of the arm causing excessive strain upon a nerve.

The Court of Appeal in UK,[7] did not hold the anaesthetist negligent, as the anaesthetist adopted universally accepted practice and the arm of the plaintiff was never placed even, accidentally, in any position during surgery, which could have caused injury to the plaintiff.

5 *K. Ravindra Nath (Dr.)* v *Vitta Veera Surya Prakasam* IV(2006) CPJ 105; 2006(2) CPC 652; 2007(1) CLT 31.

6 *Leela G. Nair* v *Prof. (Dr.) K.P. Haridas* 2015(2) CLT 244; 2015(2) CPR 340; II(2015) CPJ 763 (NCDRC).

7 *Delaney* v *Southmead Health Authority* 26 BMLR 111 (CA); [1995]6 Med LR 355.

(ii) ***Death due to cardiac arrest during surgery for cure of disc prolapse*** The patient aged 21 years was admitted to the hospital for surgery due to prolapsed disc at L_4 and L_5 level. It was decided to conduct surgery in the prone position on a frame known as scoliosis frame or relton-hall frame. It is alleged that the patient was turned from supine position to prone position under anaesthesia and the patient developed bradycardia followed by hypertension, which were not reversed with drugs. It is further alleged that the patient suffered cardiac arrest when endotracheal tube affixed to the mouth became loose and moved out of its position during emergency manoeuvre.

The National Commission[8] did not hold the doctors negligent in handling the patient in OT causing slip of endotracheal tube from the mouth causing cardiac arrest in the absence of expert evidence.

(iii) ***Death due to overdose of anaesthetic*** The patient was admitted for removal of stones from gall bladder. The patient expired. The post mortem report revealed that the death was caused due to excessive dose of Thiopental by the anaesthetist. However, the expert opined that administration of Thiopental of 14.3 mg was within normal limit and the same cannot be the cause of death of the patient.

The anaesthetist was not held negligent by the National Commission.[9]

(iv) ***Paralysis of lower limbs after hernia operation*** The patient had undergone hernia operation in the hospital under the care of the surgeon. The anaesthetist administered spinal anaesthesia to the patient at the time of the operation. The patient lost senses of his body below the waist after the operation. The patient suffered paraplegic condition and was treated by an orthopaedician who opined that there was blood clot in the spinal cord and therefore conducted two operations unsuccessfully. It is alleged that the patient had

8 *Shrinath Chaturvedi* v *Dr. G.S. Ambedkar* III(2009) CPJ 203.

9 *Vijaya Nirmala (Dr.)* v *Udhiya alias Udhiyakumari* IV(2017) CPJ 528; 2018(1) CPR 317 (NCDRC).

suffered paraplegic condition due to gross negligence of the doctors.

The State Commission, Karnataka,[10] did not hold the surgeon and anaesthetist negligent, as there was no expert evidence to establish the fact that paraplegia suffered by the patient was the result of administration of spinal anaesthesia or the result of negligence in conducting hernia operation.

2 Cardiologist

(i) ***Death after double valve replacement*** The patient was advised for surgery of aortic valve replacement (AVR) on the basis of report of angiography. The doctor performed the combined procedure of double valve replacement (DVR), i.e. both AVR and MVR (mitral valve replacement) as TTE (transesophageal echocardiography) report confirmed the status of valves thickened, calcified, deformed, severe aortic stenosis (AS) and moderate mitral stenosis (MS).

The patient suffered massive intracranial haemorrhage leading to death. The allegation that the doctor performed DVR without informed consent was not substantiated from the evidence on record.

The National Commission[11] did not hold the doctor guilty of negligence.

(ii) ***Death due to delay in conducting heart surgery*** The patient suffering from unstable angina was admitted to the hospital. It is alleged that procedure of CABG should have been done promptly to save the life of the patient, but it is established from evidence that CABG operation depended on health condition and as such the doctors had to wait. However, the operation was done when the condition of the patient deteriorated in spite of best efforts of the treating doctors and ultimately the patient died.

10 *S. Rama Rao* v *Bantwal Sulochana Madhava Shenoy Trust (Regd.)* I(1997) CPJ 301 (Bangalore).

11 *Amarnath Kakkar* v *Escorts Heart Institute and Research Centre Ltd.* 2015(4) CPR 174; II(2016) CPJ 570 (NCDRC).

The deficiency in service on the part of the doctors was not established as held by the National Commission.[12]

(iii) *Death after giving streptokinase injection* The patient suffering from diabetes mellitus and hypertension with myocardial infarction with CCF was admitted to the hospital. It is alleged that the patient died due to administration of streptokinase injection by an MBBS doctor when the BP of the patient was high, whereas the same injection should have been given by a specialist doctor if the BP of the patient is low. The expert opinion is that all MBBS doctors and trained paramedics can give streptokinase injection.

The National Commission[13] did not hold the doctor negligent in providing treatment to the patient.

(iv) *Suffering due to aortic dissection during angiography procedure* The patient suffering from hypertension had undergone angiography procedure by one competent coronary expert. The emergency open heart surgery is required in case of acute aortic dissection, but treatment of patient with medicine is sufficient in case of sub-acute aortic dissection. The patient suffered abdominal pain, as the passage of the catheter through aortic space was not smooth due to some associated causes.

The Supreme Court of India[14] is of the view that the allegation of negligence against the doctor is not established.

(v) *Sufferings due to defective angiography* The patient aged about 55 years suffered acute chest pain. The cardiologist conducted angiography for confirmation of blockage. With the consent of the son of the patient the cardiologist performed angioplasty for removal of 95% blockage, but gave up the procedure in the midway after 15-20 minutes. The patient was shifted to another hospital where CT scan and

12 *Susmita Roy Chowdhury* v *B.M. Birla Heart Research Centre* 2017(2) CLT 507; 2017(2) CPR 466; III(2017) CPJ 658 (NCDRC).

13 *Parwati Devi* v *Dr. Raman* 2014(2) CPR 415; II(2014) CPJ 559 (NCDRC).

14 *Kanta* v *Tagore Heart Care and Research Centre Pvt. Ltd.* (2014)8 Scale 475; (2014)12 SCC 206; 2015 ACJ 1141; AIR 2014 SC 3355; JT 2014(9) SC 41; III(2014) CPJ 3 (SC).

MRI revealed that the patient suffered aorta dissection. The second cardiologist conducted angiography and the procedure of angioplasty and the patient recovered gradually.

The Supreme Court[15] did not hold the defendant cardiologist negligent, as the patient could not establish by adducing cogent evidence whether he suffered from aorta dissection during angiography or after angiography due to high blood pressure.

(vi) *Sufferings due to lack of postoperative care* The complainant was admitted to the Hospital with chest pain as indoor patient. He was operated for coronary artery bypass graft surgery. The complainant paid for postoperative care, but the surgeon did not take care of the complainant after operation.

The State Commission, Bombay awarded compensation against the doctor whose indifferent attitude to the patient during post-operational complicacies caused serious mental and physical distress to the patient. On appeal the National Commission[16] reversed the decision of State Commission, Bombay and held that the private doctor who is performing the operation for a fee in the hospital, cannot be expected to undertake and provide postoperative treatment and care and that the deficiency of service on the part of the doctor was not established.

3 Dermatologist

Death for improper treatment of Toxic Epidermal Nercolysis (TEN) The patient suffered from severe drug allergy caused by wrong medication, viz Proton Pump Inhibitor. The patient approached the dermatologist after initial treatment from another doctor who was not made party in the proceeding. The dermatologist got the opportunity to treat the

15 *Kanta* v *Tagore Heart Care and Research Centre Private Limited* (2014)12 SCC 206.

16 *B. Sekhar Hegde* v *Dr. Sudhanshu Bhattacharya* II(1992) CPJ 449 (Bom); (1993)1 CTJ 523 (SCDRC) reversed by III(1993) CPJ 388 (NC); 1993(3) CPR 414 (NC); (1994)2 CTJ 10 (CP) (NCDRC).

complication developed after giving drug by the first doctor. It is also established from medical literature that Stevens-Johnson-Syndrome (SJS)/TEN are caused by antibiotics or anti-inflammatory medicines rather than by PPI group of medicines.

Under the above circumstances the dermatologist was not held negligent by the National Commission.[17]

4 Dentist

(i) *Damage due to non-disclosure of risk of hepatitis in administering blood product* The patient suffered delayed bleeding due to extraction of molar tooth and was found to be suffering from mild hemophilia. The doctor administered a blood product called "Cryoprecipitate" which was replaced with another blood product called "Hemofil" which was packaged with the express warning of the risk that it might transmit hepatitis. The risk of hepatitis was not disclosed to the patient who developed post-transfusion non-A and non-B hepatitis.

The dentist was held not negligent by the Court of Appeal in New Brunswick,[18] because even if the risk of contracting hepatitis from an infusion of blood products particularly Hemofil would have been disclosed, a reasonable man in the patient's position would still have consented to the treatment to stop bleeding in his mouth.

(ii) *Headache and heavy bleeding after extraction of tooth* The doctor removed one tooth of the patient without taking the history of the patient. On the next day the patient complained to the doctor for heavy bleeding, but only a few pain killers were prescribed by the doctor. The patient also suffered from severe headache. Subsequently the condition of the patient improved after proper treatment and management of high blood pressure in the nursing home. The patient claimed compensation against the doctor.

17 *Prem Lata* v *Arun Kumar Sinha (Dr.)* 2016(4) CPR 294 (NCDRC).
18 *Kitchen* v *McMullen* (1989)5 BMLR 59 (CA).

The State Commission dismissed the complaint. On appeal, the National Commission[19] upheld the order of the State Commission on the ground that the complainant did not adduce evidence to establish the link between headache and extraction of tooth and to prove his approach to the doctor for heavy bleeding after extraction of tooth.

5 Doctors other than allopathic

(i) ***Sufferings by homoeopathic medicines*** The complainant had undergone medical treatment under homoeopathic doctor for acidity, nasal problem and mental irritation. It is alleged that the prolonged homoeopathic treatment resulted in suffering of the complainant from anxiety, lack of concentration, acidity, mental disturbances and depression.

The State Commission, Maharashtra, awarded compensation against the doctor. On appeal the National Commission[20] had set aside the order of the State Commission on the ground that the complainant did not lead any evidence to prove that he had suffered from the alleged ailments after taking medicines prescribed by the doctor or that the homoeopathic medicines prescribed by the doctor might have resulted in suffering of the ailments narrated by the complainant.

(ii) ***Sufferings due to complications after MTP*** The doctor conducted medical termination of pregnancy of the patient and discharged her within a couple of hours with prescription for subsequent treatment at home. The patient developed pain and profuse bleeding and had to undergo MTP for the second time for recovery. It is alleged that the patient suffered due to negligence of the doctor in conducting medical termination of pregnancy.

The State Commission, Punjab,[1] did not hold the doctor negligent as he was qualified to conduct MTP and as no

19 *S.B. Tiwari* v *Dr. G. Pranavadhyani* I(1996) CPJ 301 (NC); (1996)4 CTJ 406 (CP) (NCDRC).

20 *Mrs. Suvarna Baljekar* v *Rohit Bhatt* 1996(2) CPR 13 (NC); II(1996) CPJ 75 (NC); (1996)4 CTJ 677 (CP) (NCDRC).

1 *Smt. Neelam* v *Dr. Rajib Kaur* 2000 CTJ 472 (CP) (SCDRC).

expert evidence was adduced to prove negligence of the doctor in conducting MTP.

6 Gynaecologist and obstetrician

(i) ***Brain damage of the child by forceps delivery*** It was alleged that in course of carrying out a trial of forceps delivery the doctor pulled too long and too strongly on the baby's head—thereby causing the brain damage. The decision of the trial court to award compensation was reversed by majority of the Court of Appeal. The House of Lords[2] affirmed the decision of the Court of Appeal by holding that the expert medical evidence together with the evidence of the complainant was not sufficient to lead to a finding of professional negligence.

(ii) ***Damage due to D&C operation*** The patient had undergone dilation and curettage under the care of a gynaecologist for treatment of pain in abdomen. As the pain did not subside she had undergone dilation and curettage for the second time under the care of another doctor. The patient did not get any relief. Ultimately it was detected that there were perforations in intestine due to earlier operations and the patient got relief after three successive operations. It is alleged that the patient had to undergo three successive operations due to negligence of the doctors in conducting D&C operations.

The State Commission, Gujarat,[3] did not hold the doctors negligent, as there was no evidence to establish that two D&C operations were conducted on the patient and that there was nexus between the sufferings of the patient and the treatment given by the doctors.

(iii) ***Death after caesarean operation*** The patient was admitted to the clinic of the doctor for delivery of the child. She delivered a child by caesarean operation, but she died. It is

2 *Whitehouse* v *Jordan* 1982 ACJ 107; [1980]1 All ER 650 (CA) affirmed [1981]1 All ER 267; 125 Sol Jo 167 (HL); [1981]1 WLR 246.

3 *Dakshaben Ramniklal* v *Dr. K.D. Lakhani* 1996(1) CPR 539 (Ahmedabad).

alleged that the doctor was negligent in conducting caesarean operation without assistance of an anaesthetist and that the doctor was not qualified to conduct the operation.

The State Commission, Punjab,[4] did not hold the doctor negligent, because, first, no expert evidence was adduced to establish that the treatment given by the doctor was below the prescribed standard, and secondly, the doctor was qualified to conduct caesarean operation. The question whether conducting caesarean operation without the assistance of an anaesthetist was negligent, was not decided by the Commission.

(iv) *Death due to complications after caesarean operation*

(1) The patient was admitted to the nursing home for delivery of the child. She delivered a female baby by caesarean section under general anaesthesia. She developed acute pain in the abdomen and bled profusely and her condition deteriorated. The wound was twice operated and stitched up by the doctor, but the soaking of blood could not be arrested. The renowned surgeons and gynaecologists were called and according to their advice, three bottles of fresh blood were transfused. Thereafter the patient was shifted to better equipped hospital at Calcutta, where she expired. It is alleged that the doctor is guilty of negligence in giving treatment to the patient, which resulted in her death.

The doctor was not held negligent by the State Commission, W.B.,[5] because no expert evidence was adduced to establish that there was negligence on the part of the doctor in giving treatment to the patient.

(2) The patient developed complications after caesarean delivery during postoperative period. It is alleged that the patient died, as the operation was done in undue baste, nurses were not qualified and record was not maintained properly, which constituted negligence. On the other hand, the expert

4 *Surinder Kumar (Laddi)* v *Dr. Santosh Menon* 2000(1) CPR 23 (Chandigarh).

5 *Prasanta Kumar Chakraborty* v *Dr. Jahar Debnath* III(2000) CPJ 91 (Cal).

opinion of qualified gynaecologist was that the complications developed during postoperative period were known complications of surgery.

Accordingly, the deficiency in service was not established against the doctor in the opinion of the National Commission.[6]

(v) ***Death due to complications after hysterectomy*** The patient was admitted to the nursing home with complaint of bleeding per vagina. The doctor conducted hysterectomy operation for removal of uterus and ovaries. The patient developed pain, cough and abdominal distension. The doctor found disruption after removal of two sutures and conducted emergency operation for closure of abdomen under general anaesthesia. The patient died of cardiac arrest during the operation.

It is held by the State Commission, Orissa that the patient developed infection and wound did not heal up due to contributory negligence of the patient who did not follow the advice of the doctor during postoperative period. So the doctor was not held negligent in giving treatment to the patient. On appeal, the order of the State Commission was confirmed by the National Commission.[7]

(vi) ***Death of child due to improper delivery*** The patient was admitted to the hospital with complaint of abdominal pain for delivery of child. The patient gave birth to a child who expired. It is alleged that the doctor could not monitor the condition of the patient properly, as she was profusely bleeding and thereby the baby expired.

The State Commission dismissed the complaint on the ground that there was no negligence on the part of the doctor and hospital. On appeal the National Commission,[8] upheld the order of the State Commission, because the allegation of negligence was belied by the fact of requisitioning the service of a paediatrician even before delivery of the child.

6 *Ajay Khandel* v *Prakash Nursing Home* 2017(4) CPR 552 (NCDRC).

7 *Md. Aslam* v *Ideal Nursing Home* 1994(1) CPR 619 (Ori) confirmed by 1997(2) CPR 109 (NC); III(1997) CPJ 81 (NC); (1997)5 CTJ 824 (CP) (NCDRC); 1998 CCJ 1244 (NC).

8 *Yasmin Sultana* v *Dr. Rupaben D. Patel* 1998(2) CPR 20 (NC); II(1998) CPJ 40 (NC); 1998 CTJ 737 (CP) (NCDRC); 1999 CCJ 28 (NC).

(vii) *Failure to re-canalise blocked fallopian tubes* The patient had undergone sterilization operation after having a female child. The patient desired of getting another child after 12 years of operation. On assurance of the doctor the patient had undergone re-canalisation operation. It is alleged that during follow up after three months of the operation, the x-ray report revealed that left side fallopian tube was completely blocked in violation of the assurance given by the doctor.

The State Commission, Delhi,[9] did not hold the doctor negligent in conducting the operation, particularly when it is established from evidence that both sides of the tube were found to be re-canalised at the time of passing dye through catheter after the operation. It is held that the examinations carried out by other clinics also found the right side tube to be fully re-canalised and that conception can take place if one of the two tubes is re-canalised. Moreover, the Commission did not believe that the doctor guaranteed 100% chances of pregnancy in case of re-canalisation.

(viii) *Hysterectomy causing vesico vaginal fistula* The patient had undergone operation for removal of uterus and entrometriosis in urinary bladder. The patient developed problem of incontinence and the ailment was diagnosed as VVF (Vesico Vaginal Fistula). The patient had to undergo another operation for recovery in another hospital. It is alleged that the patient developed VVF due to removal of in dwelling catheter by the doctor only after ten days of the operation.

The State Commission, Bihar,[10] did not hold the doctor negligent, as it is established from medical literature that VVF (Vesico Vaginal Fistula) is a known complication of hysterectomy, which may result from injury to the bladder during hysterectomy. It is also held that no expert evidence is adduced to substantiate the allegation that complication

9 *Dr. (Mrs.) Madhu Rana* v *Smt. Bimla Gupta* III(1999) CPJ 224 (Del).

10 *Dr. Rameshwar Prasad Agarwal* v *Md. Abas Ansari* 1999(2) CPR 386 (Pat); 1999 CTJ 664 (CP) (SCDRC); I(2000) CPJ 433 (Pat).

of VVF occurred due to removal of in dwelling catheter within ten days of the operation.

(ix) ***Removal of uterus without consent*** The complainant was advised to terminate her pregnancy for protection of health. The doctor took the complainant to labour room but subsequently the doctor informed the husband of the complainant that she was bleeding and needed immediate operation. Subsequently the doctor informed the husband of the complainant that it was a case of cervical pregnancy and her uterus has been removed. The complainant alleged that the doctor was negligent in conducting the operation and removal of the uterus.

The National Commission[11] came to the conclusion that the doctor acted with due care, circumspection, skill and competence and that the doctor saved the life of the patient by administering prompt and efficient surgical treatment to the patient on discovery of her cervical pregnancy.

(x) ***Rupture of uterus due to delay in conducting caesarean operation*** The patient was admitted to the hospital for delivery of second child. The doctor induced labour with oxytocin gel/ pitocin in low doses (1/2 unit) under observation. As there was no satisfactory progress of labour, the medicine was stopped and the patient was prepared for caesarean operation. However, the uterus of the patient was ruptured, and subsequently repaired. The patient could conceive subsequently and deliver another child.

It is held by the State Commission, Chandigarh,[12] that there is no negligence on the part of the doctor, as the trial of labour is justified for having less risk than caesarean operation.

(xi) ***Sufferings after intrauterine foetal death*** The doctor did not perform caesarean section for removal of baby after intrauterine foetal death, as spontaneous expulsion occurs within two weeks of death in 80% cases, failing which

11 *Vinitha Ashok* v *Lakshmi Hospital* II(1992) CPJ 372 (NC).
12 *Kiranjeet* v *Dr. Nirlep Kaur* III(1999) CPJ 208 (Chandigarh).

intervention by surgery is required. The allegation that timely caesarean section would have saved the life of the baby is not substantiated from the facts and circumstances of the case.

Accordingly, the doctor was not found to be negligent by the National Commission.[13]

(xii) ***Sufferings for leaving gauze in abdomen during caesarean operation*** The patient was admitted to the hospital for delivery and gave birth to a male child by caesarean operation. The patient developed pain in abdomen after about four months of the operation. The report of ultrasound and x-ray revealed "inflammatory mass foreign body inside the abdomen". The doctor operated upon the patient for the second time, but she was not relieved of pain. Ultimately the patient recovered after removal of segment of gauze piece from the abdomen of the patient by way of operation in PGI, Chandigarh.

The State Commission, Chandigarh,[14] did not hold the doctor negligent, as there was no evidence to connect the doctor with the deficiency in giving treatment to the patient. Moreover, the segment of gauze piece taken out by way of operation had quite fresh and smooth margins which indicated possibility of receiving medical treatment in some other places by the patient.

(xiii) ***Sufferings due to adverse effect of oral contraceptive*** The plaintiff aged 22 years was advised to take oral contraceptive by the doctor, though her blood pressure was 150/100. After taking the medicines the plaintiff suffered a serious brain stem stroke as a result of thrombosis in the basilar artery, and was rendered almost completely disabled. It is alleged that the doctor was negligent in prescribing oral contraceptive to the plaintiff, as the plaintiff was suffering from hypertension and migraine.

13 *Ashok Kumar Rai (Dr.)* v *Seema Singh* II(2015) CPJ 600 (NCDRC).
14 *Rajni Bansal* v *Dr. D.C. Mittal* III(1997) CPJ 511 (Chandigarh).

It is held by the Court of Appeal in UK,[15] that the defendant doctor was not negligent in prescribing oral contraceptive, as it is established from evidence that the plaintiff was not suffering from hypertension or migraines at the time of prescribing the medicine and that a single recording of high blood pressure is insufficient to establish hypertension.

(xiv) *Sufferings due to failure of sterilization operation* The patient became pregnant after sterilization operation and carried the pregnancy upto 35 weeks. The child born after sterilization operation for not carrying out medical termination of pregnancy cannot claim compensation for being brought up as unwanted child.

The National Commission,[16] did not hold the doctor negligent for failure of sterilization operation.

(xv) *Sufferings for failure of medical termination of pregnancy* The patient had undergone MTP (Medical Termination of Pregnancy) under the care of the doctor. The patient had to undergo second MTP for evacuation of the product which was not taken out by the doctor. It is alleged that the patient suffered mental agony and financial loss for undergoing second MTP due to negligence of the doctor.

The State Commission, Kerala,[17] did not hold the doctor negligent, as it is established from expert evidence that there is possibility of missing the product when MTP is performed before six weeks of pregnancy, particularly when the doctor adopted the approved method for conducting MTP of the patient.

(xvi) *Sufferings for failure to diagnose ectopic pregnancy during D&C operation* The patient was admitted to the private hospital for termination of pregnancy. She started bleeding

15 *Vadera* v *Shaw* 45 BMLR 162 (CA).

16 *Mithlesh* v *Primary Health Centre, Dhowlana, Hapur* I(2015) CPJ 15 (NCDRC).

17 *Dr. P.N. Bhaskaran* v *Mrs. Molly Robinson* 1999(3) CPR 442 (Ker); I(2000) CPJ 81 (Ker). [This is not good authority because the issue whether risk of failure of MTP was disclosed to the patient before undertaking treatment was neither urged, nor decided by the Commission].

after insertion of laminaria tent and her uterus was removed by conducting an emergency operation as she had cervical pregnancy. She claimed compensation for negligence in carrying out dilation and curettage procedure resulting in removal of uterus at a very young age.

The Supreme Court[18] and the National Commission did not hold the doctor negligent because, first, the procedure adopted for dilation and curettage by the doctors for medical termination of pregnancy is commonly in practice in Kerala, though there may be difference of opinion amongst the experts; secondly, the ultrasonogram not recommended by the doctors before D&C would not have established ectopic pregnancy in the cervical canal; thirdly, the treatment of hysterectomy was the only solution on account of profuse bleeding of the patient.

(xvii) ***Unwanted child after sterilization operation*** (*a*) The plaintiff had undergone vasectomy operation after proper counselling by the doctor of the health authority. The literature provided by the health authority to the plaintiff, explained the procedure to be carried out and the need for two consecutive negative sperm samples before unprotected intercourse. The plaintiff provided two clear negative sperm tests after the operation and thereafter the couple ceased to use oral contraception. The wife of the plaintiff became pregnant. It is alleged that the counsellor of the health authority did not inform the plaintiff of the risk of failure of the operation.

The Queen's Bench Division of U.K.,[19] did not hold the health authority liable in negligence, as the court believed that the counsellor of the health authority must have explained about the small risk of failure of vasectomy operation.

(*b*) The wife of the complainant had undergone sterilization operation after having one son and two daughters from the

18 *Vinitha Ashok (Smt.)* v *Lakshmi Hospital* (2001)8 SCC 731; AIR 2001 SC 3914; JT 2001(8) SC 142; (2001)6 Scale 476.

19 *Stobie* v *Central Birmingham Health Authority* (1994)22 BMLR 135 (QBD).

wedlock. She became pregnant and gave birth to a female child after undergoing tubectomy operation under the care of a lady doctor in the Government hospital. The complainant claimed compensation against the State and the lady doctor.

The Supreme Court[20] did not hold the lady doctor negligent for failure of tubectomy operation resulting in birth of unwanted female child as it is established from medical literature that failure rate of sterilization operation is from 0.3% to 7% depending on the techniques chosen for performing the operation.

(xviii) ***Unwanted child after termination of pregnancy and sterilization*** The patient had undergone medical termination of pregnancy and sterilization operation in the hospital. Subsequently the patient became pregnant. It is alleged that the patient became pregnant after sterilization operation due to negligence of the doctor in conducting the operation.

The State Commission, Delhi,[1] did not hold the doctor negligent for failure of sterilization operation, as the risk of failure is inherent in all methods of female sterilization including tubal ligation.

7 Hospital

(i) ***Cerebral palsy due to delay in conducting caesarean section*** The doctor of the health authority attempted to deliver the baby with a keillends forceps, using the long wandering techniques. One blade of the forceps became entangled with the baby's arm and the doctor attempted to remove it and to deliver the baby using the blade of a second pair of forceps. This attempt failed and the baby was delivered by emergency caesarean section. The baby suffered a short period of severe hypoxic distress for about 50 minutes and found to be suffering from cerebral palsy.

20 *State of Punjab* v *Shiv Ram* (2005)7 SCC 1.

1 *Smt. Jaiwati* v *Parivan Seva Sanstha* III(1999) CPJ 167 (Del); 1999 CTJ 601 (CP) (SCDRC); 2000(1) CPR 538 (Del). [This is not good law, because omission to warn of the risk of failure of sterilization operation, which amounts to negligence, was neither urged, nor decided by the Commission].

The Queen's Bench Division of U.K.,[2] did not hold the health authority liable in negligence, as there were conflicting expert opinions about the procedure adopted by the doctor and it is impossible to hold the opinion of the (health authority) as untenable.

(ii) ***Damage due to transfusion of wrong group of blood*** It is alleged that the patient suffered harassment and mental agony for transfusing wrong group of blood by the hospital.

The State Commission, West Bengal held the hospital negligent and awarded compensation. By setting aside the order of the State Commission on appeal, it is held by the National Commission,[3] that there is no evidence to link the blood transfusion with the resultant complications of the patient and that the certificate issued by the expert in support of the allegation made out by the patient is neither haematologist nor pathologist.

(iii) ***Death due to complications following kidney transplantation*** The patient was suffering from non-olyguric renal failure. She had undergone fistula operation for preparation to dialysis. Thereafter she had undergone kidney transplant operation for avoiding inconvenience of regular dialysis as per advice of the doctor. The dopler test after the operation indicated that there was no supply of blood in the newly transplanted kidney of the patient. The second operation was conducted, but the output of urine was reduced and the urea and creatinine level in the blood gradually increased. The team of doctors who conducted the operation left for Bangladesh to attend conference leaving the patient in critical condition under care of other doctors of the hospital.

The National Commission[4] did not hold the hospital and the team of doctors negligent, as deficiency of service was not established in high risk operation of kidney transplantation.

2 *Nash* v *Kingston and Richmond Health Authority* 36 BMLR 123 (QBD).
3 *Calcutta Medical Research Institute* v *Bimalesh Chatterjee* I(1999) CPJ 13 (NC); 1999(1) CPR 3 (NC); 1999 CCJ 499 (NC).
4 *P.B. Rao* v *Dr. S. Sundar* II(2006) CPJ 223; 2006(2) CLT 354.

(iv) ***Death due to delay in conducting surgery*** The patient was admitted to the hospital with history of long standing hypertension for 18 years coupled with an attack of myocardial infraction about 15 years back, renal failure for last one year, and also recurrent episodes of pulmonary oedema. The necessary investigations revealed that the patient was suffering from heart and kidney problem and needed surgery. It is alleged that the patient expired for not conducting surgery within two weeks from the date of admission and that the dead body was not released by the hospital authority before settling the bills.

The State Commission, Tamil Nadu,[5] did not hold the hospital negligent for asking the patient party to settle the bills before releasing the dead body from the hospital. It is also held that the hospital was not liable for negligence for not conducting the surgery, as the general condition of the patient did not permit such surgery, though attempts were made on two different occasions for surgery.

(v) ***Death due to improper treatment*** The patient was admitted to private hospital in serious condition. The disease was diagnosed as pancreatitis by the consulting surgeon. The patient was kept in an ordinary room instead of intensive care unit where the facilities for close monitoring of the patient by the doctor and nurses are available. The patient was required to be operated in order to save his life, but the operation was not performed and the patient was left to the care of nurses and junior doctors—resulting in death.

The State Commission, Delhi held the hospital authority negligent for not providing the required I.C.U. facilities to the patient, but on appeal the National Commission[6] reversed the decision of the State Commission and held that the surgeon and the hospital authority were not negligent.

5 *Mrs. Usha Mehrotra* v *Appollo Hospitals Enterprises Ltd.* 1999(2) CPR 453 (Chennai).

6 *D.P. Bhandari* v *Sri Ganga Ram Hospital* II(1991) CPJ 409 (Del) reversed by *Sri Ganga Ram Hospital* v *D.P. Bhandari* II(1992) CPJ 397 (NC); 1992(1) CPR 796 (NC).

(vi) *Death due to wrong diagnosis and treatment* The patient was admitted to the hospital with complaint of persistent vomiting. He was diagnosed as chronic duodenal ulcer with obstruction after considering the reports of several investigations. He had to undergo surgery, but he was not relieved of pain and vomiting. He was referred to a hematologist. The patient was ultimately taken to a Government hospital where the doctor after perusing the discharge summary of the previous hospital opined that the patient should have consulted nephrologist, and that the previous hospital wrongly diagnosed the disease as auto immune hemolytic anaemia. The patient ultimately died in the said hospital. It is alleged that the first hospital was negligent for not diagnosing the renal problem of the deceased, for undertaking operation in spite of very low blood haemoglobin, and for not reflecting blood pressure and other details of blood test in the discharge certificate.

The State Commission, Tamil Nadu,[7] did not hold the hospital negligent on the grounds: (*a*) that the cause of action of the deceased was not established by evidence, (*b*) that emergency operation required for gastric outlet obstruction due to duodenal ulcer was performed after raising hemoglobin level upto 9.8 mg. by blood transfusion, and (*c*) that the details of blood test like blood urea etc. and blood pressure could not be supplied in the discharge certificate due to some limitations of the computer service.

(vii) *Infection of HIV after blood transfusion* The wife of the complainant had undergone hysterectomy in the hospital. Two units of blood were transfused to the patient during postoperative care in the hospital. The patient got infected with HIV and ultimately died of AIDS due to blood transfusion.

The State Commission, Tamil Nadu,[8] dismissed the complaint, as there was no reliable evidence to prove that the blood transfused to the patient contained HIV and that

7 *Mrs. Saraswati* v *M/s. Vimala Hospital* I(2000) CPJ 115 (Chennai).
8 *M. Chinnaiyan* v *Shri Gokulam Hospital* I(1999) CPJ 587 (Chennai).

the patient was free from HIV before blood transfusion in the hospital.

(viii) ***Permanent brain damage due to delay in shifting the patient to intensive therapy unit*** The patient aged eight months, was suffering from pneumonia and acute myocarditis. There was delay in calling Senior Registrar in order to transfer the patient to intensive therapy unit. On the way to intensive therapy unit the patient suffered cardiac arrest, which resulted in permanent brain damage.

The Court of Appeal in U.K.[9] did not hold the health authority negligent, as it is established from evidence that the patient would not have been transferred to intensive therapy unit earlier had Senior Registrar been called in time, and that the patient would have suffered cardiac arrest had he been transferred to intensive therapy unit earlier.

(ix) ***Permanent disability after spine surgery*** The patient was suffering from advanced degenerative changes in the lumber spine with large posterocentral subligamentus extrusion $L^4/_5$ disc causing thecal sac and cauda equina nerve root compression. She was operated by orthopaedic surgeon, though the hospital took consent for surgery by neurosurgeon. She lost sensation in the lower part of the body after operation and became totally bed-ridden.

It is held by the National Commission[10] on the basis of expert opinion that the hospital is not liable for deficiency in service for performance of surgery by orthopaedic surgeon, as the instant surgery could have been performed either by orthopaedic surgeon or by neurosurgeon.

(x) ***Permanent disability due to inadequate treatment*** The complainant was admitted to the hospital with complaint of high fever, brancho pneumonia and measles. She was treated for five days with medicines and injections. She was shifted to another hospital where she was treated for ten days. She developed gangrene and her left arm was amputated.

9 *Sherlock* v *North Birmingham Health Authority* 40 BMLR 103 (CA).
10 *Shri Virendra Singh* v *National Institute of Medical Sciences, Sobha Nagar* III(2011) CPJ 27.

The State Commission, Chandigarh,[11] did not hold the doctor negligent, because there was no evidence to substantiate the allegation of negligence, particularly when the patient did not respond to the conventional treatment prescribed by texts and followed by the specialists.

(xi) *Unwanted child after sterilization operation* The husband of the plaintiff had undergone vasectomy operation arranged by the pregnancy advisory service. The plaintiff came to learn that the operation had been successful and that she needed no contraception in future. The plaintiff commenced sexual relationship with her husband on reliance of the statement that he had undergone vasectomy. She did not use any form of contraception during sexual intercourse nor did her husband use any contraceptive device. As a result, the plaintiff became pregnant and later gave birth to a daughter. She claimed damages for child birth, loss of income and cost of bringing up the child.

The County Court Judge dismissed the suit on the ground that it disclosed no reasonable cause of action. On appeal it is held by the Court of Appeal,[12] in UK that the plaintiff had no reasonable cause of action. It is also held that the plaintiff had no special relationship with the pregnancy advisory service, so as to give rise to a duty of care. Moreover, the plaintiff had received advice from her family physician that she might be pregnant by her husband despite the vasectomy and as such the plaintiff could not claim to have had sexual intercourse with her husband without using any contraceptive solely by relying on advice of the pregnancy advisory service.

8 Hospital and others

(i) *Death due to complications after angiography* The patient was admitted to the hospital for angiography. He was advised for repeat surgery for replacement of mitral valve which

11 *Miss Maya Devi* v *Escorts Medical Centre* I(1999) CPJ 449 (Chandigarh); 2000 CCJ 1078 (Haryana).

12 *Goodwill* v *British Pregnancy Advisory Service* [1996]2 All ER 161 (CA); [1996]1 WLR 1397 (CA); 31 BMLR 83 (CA); [1996] Fam Law 471; [1996] NLJR 173; 140 Sol Jo LB 37 (CA).

was damaged as per report of angiography. He was taken to operation theatre without pre-operative check up. The patient extubated himself in ICCU and the physician attempted endotracheal intubation, but failed. The patient expired by the time the outside anaesthetist was called to the hospital.

The National Commission[13] did not hold the hospital, surgeon and anaesthetist negligent in performance of duty only because intubation could not be carried out immediately after extubation by the patient, in spite of making all attempts by the attending doctors and nurses of the hospital.

(ii) *Death due to delay in attending the patient* The patient was admitted to the hospital with complaint of Diabetes Mellitus, Hypertension and Broncho pneumonia. The investigations were done and treatment was given, but the patient collapsed due to heart failure. It is alleged that there was delay in attending the patient by the senior doctor and that proper diagnosis and treatment were not given to the patient, resulting in her death.

The State Commission, Punjab,[14] did not hold the doctor and the hospital negligent as there was no evidence to establish that the diagnosis made and treatment given by the attending doctor was not proper, and that there was delay on the part of the senior doctor to attend the patient.

(iii) *Death due to inadequate treatment* (*a*) The patient was admitted to the hospital with burning sensation in stomach, vomiting and diarrhoea. She was also suffering from chronic renal failure. The laparoscopy was performed for confirmation of diagnosis of tuberculosis of lower abdomen. She developed intestinal fistula leading to serious infection *i.e.* septicaemia and ultimately expired.

The Supreme Court of India affirmed the decision of the National Commission which did not hold the doctor and the

13 *Mrs. Shantaben Muljibhai Patel* v *Breach Candy Hospital & Research Centre* 2005(1) CLT 515; 2005(1) CPC 183; I(2005) CPJ 10.

14 *N.S. Sahota* v *New Ruby Hospital* II(2000) CPJ 345 (Chandigarh).

hospital negligent due to want of the opinion of experts in support of the allegations of medical negligence.[15]

(*b*) The baby was admitted to the hospital for cardiac catheterization and angiography, as she was suffering from cyanotic congenital heart disease. The surgery was not performed as she was suffering from upper respiratory tract infection. She was discharged from the hospital by prescribing xitamia e drops and iron drops. The baby died of severe cyanotic heart disease with broncho pneumonia. The allegation of the father of the baby was that the doctors did not prescribe any medicine for pneumonia at the time of discharge from the hospital, though surgery was postponed due to URTI.

The National Commission[16] did not hold the hospital and the doctor negligent, as there was no evidence to prove that the baby was suffering from pneumonia at the time of discharge from the hospital.

(iv) *Death due to jaundice during pregnancy* The patient developed jaundice during eight months of her pregnancy. She was admitted to the nursing home with complaint of vomiting and fever. The patient gave birth to a dead baby and ultimately she died. It is established from expert evidence that there is no specific treatment of jaundice, even when the serum bilirubin of the patient was 8.60 mg. The baby died due to hypoxia during uterine contraction and placental dysfunction. The question of removing the baby by caesarean section was ruled out due to severity of jaundice.

The National Commission[17] did not hold the doctor and the nursing home negligent for the death of the patient after delivery of the dead baby.

(v) *Sufferings due to wrong diagnosis and treatment* The first child of the complainant was suffering from Thalassaemia

15 *Ins Malhotra (Ms.)* v *Dr. A Kriplani* (2009)4 SCC 705.

16 *Ruben Banerjee* v *Ehirc Heart Institute and Research Centre* 2008(1) CPR 207; 2008 CTJ 604 (CP); I(2008) CPJ 239.

17 *K. Muniasamy* v *Harley Ram Nursing Home* 2007(3) CPR 112; I(2008) CPJ 293.

Major. She contacted the doctor of AIIMS when she became pregnant for the second time. She had undergone chronic villus biopsy for pre-natal diagnosis for Thalassaemia Major as per advice of the doctor, who advised the complainant to go ahead with the pregnancy. However, after the birth the child was diagnosed as Thalassaemia Major.

The view of the National Commission[18] is that there was no deficiency in service provided by the hospital or the doctor, as it is established from evidence that there is possibility of 1% to 2% error in the result of all pre-natal tests based on DNA technology.

(vi) ***Sufferings for improper treatment of back pain*** The patient developed pain in the buttock after prostate operation in a private hospital at Chandigarh. The patient was admitted to P.G.I. where the doctors conducted open surgery suspecting epidural abscess in the spine. The patient developed unbearable pain stretching towards lower extremities of the body. The condition of the patient improved after second operation in Apollo Hospital for setting the failed back syndrome with spondylitis L_4S_1.

The State Commission, Chandigarh,[19] did not hold the hospital and the Surgeon negligent, as the patient had not brought on record the details of surgical treatment received at the private hospital before admission to P.G.I and as the patient was admitted to P.G.I. with large number of problems such as severe back pain, inability to get up, fever, and weakness in the legs.

(vii) ***Sufferings due to improper treatment by overdose of medicine*** The patient was suffering from renal failure and severe urinary tract infection. The doctor prescribed amikacin injection of 500 mg twice a day, as methenamine mandelate could not be used for renal failure of the patient. The patient

18 *Sailesh Manjul* v *All India Institute of Medical Sciences* 2004(3) CPR 27; 2004(3) CLT 269; 2004(2) CPC 514; III(2004) CPJ 93.

19 *Dr. S.L. Dhawan* v *Post Graduate Medical Institute & Research Centre* 1998(2) CPR 425 (Chandigarh); III(1998) CPJ 128 (Chandigarh); 1998 CTJ 627 (CP) (SCDRC).

got himself discharged from the hospital and continued taking amikacin against medical advice. The kidney transplantation of the patient was done in another hospital. The patient suffered from impairment of hearing due to overdose of amikacin injection.

The Supreme Court[20] did not hold the doctor negligent in prescribing amikacin injection as a life saving measure, in spite of side effect of impairment of hearing of the patient.

9 Nephrologist/Urologist

(i) *Death due to delay in kidney transplantation* The patient suffering from diabetes, nephropathy and acute pulmonary edema Grade-I was admitted to the hospital for kidney transplant due to renal failure. The blood group of the patient was identified as A+ from the report produced by the patient, but later the blood group was found to be AB-universal. It is alleged that there was delay on the part of the doctor to carry out emergent kidney transplant and as such the patient had to be shifted to another hospital where kidney transplant was done, but the patient expired.

Under the above circumstances the National Commission[1] did not hold the doctor and the first hospital negligent in providing treatment to the patient.

(ii) *Death after renal failure* The patient aged about 78 years, suffering from multiple health problems, was admitted to the hospital for renal damage. The doctor resorted to hemodialysis as per standard treatment protocol, as the patient was a known case of diabetes and hypertension for last 15 years. However, the patient died of uremia leading to renal failure.

The National Commission[2] is of the view that the negligence has not been established against the doctor.

20 *Martin F. D'Souza* v *Mohd Ishfaq* (2009)3 SCC 1; 2009 ACJ 1695; AIR 2009 SC 2049; JT 2009(2) SC 486; (2009)2 Scale 620.

1 *Naveena Bharathi* v *K.C. Gurudev* III(2017) CPJ 231 (NCDRC).

2 *Charan Kamal Chopra* v *R.K. Gupta (Dr.)* II(2019) CPJ 414 (NCDRC).

(iii) *Sufferings due to incomplete surgery* The patient suffering from urinary incontinence (i.e. continuous flow of urine) was advised surgery for bladder augmentation with appendicular vesicostomy. The urologist performed surgery only for bladder augmentation. He did not perform the second part of the surgery, i.e. appendicular vesicostomy as the anatomical and physiological condition of the patient did not permit for carrying out the said surgery.

Since carrying out appendicular vesicostomy surgery is always subject to anatomical and physiological condition of the patient, the doctor was not found to be negligent by the National Commission.[3]

10 Nurse

Death after administration of injection by duty nurse The husband of the complainant had undergone hydrocele operation under the care of the doctor. It is alleged that during postoperative period the duty nurse gave an injection to the patient without having any test dose and without checking up the condition of the patient and thereby the patient collapsed.

The State Commission, Tamil Nadu,[4] did not hold the duty nurse negligent, as the allegation of administration of injection by duty nurse without test dose, has not been substantiated by cogent evidence on behalf of the complainant.

11 Oncologist

(i) *Death for cancer in liver* The patient visited the hospital with abdominal pain, which was diagnosed as appendicitis. The surgery was performed, but the pain continued. After one month cancer in liver was detected by way of investigation in another hospital. Ultimately the patient died. It is alleged

3 *Raghavendra Rao* v *Dr. Santosh J. Karmakar* 2014(4) CPR 383; IV(2014) CPJ 478 (NCDRC).

4 *Smt. Packia Retnam* alias *A.P. Ratna Singh* v *Dr. N.C. Thanu* I(1999) CPJ 314 (Chennai); 1998(1) CPR 222 (Chennai).

that the doctor failed to diagnose the disease and conducted surgery wrongly for appendicitis.

The Consumer Forum[5] held that it was a case of error of judgment, which cannot be construed as negligence. It is also held that the chance of survival of the patient was bleak even if the cancer in liver (HCC) would have been detected at the initial stage of acute abdominal pain, and as such causative link was not established to prove negligence.

(ii) ***Sufferings due to wrong diagnosis of breast cancer*** It is alleged that the left breast lump of the patient was wrongly diagnosed and treated for cancer. However, the medical record, i.e. HPE and FNAC report proved that the patient was suffering from malignancy of breast and treatment was found to be correct.

There was no deficiency of service on the part of the doctor as held by National Commission.[6]

12 Ophthalmologist

(i) ***Damage to retina due to administration of excess oxygen*** The infant patient was born prematurely and suffering from various illnesses including oxygen deficiency. A catheter was twice inserted into the vein of the patient rather than an artery and on both occasions the patient was given excess oxygen. The patient was later discovered to be suffering from an incurable condition of the retina resulting in near blindness. It is alleged that the doctors administered excess oxygen in patient's bloodstream which caused or materially contributed to the patient's retinal condition.

The House of Lords[7] did not hold the doctors negligent, because it was not established that the patient's retinal

5 *Nallan Chandra Sekhar Reddy* v *Desai Thippa Reddy (Dr.)* 2017(1) CPR 588; 2017(2) CLT 30; II(2017) CPJ 481.

6 *Bimla Devi (deceased)* v *Ajay Aggarwal (Dr.)* 2018(1) CPR 541; II(2018) CPJ 545 (NCDRC).

7 *Wilsher* v *Essex Area Health Authority* [1987] QB 730; [1986]3 All ER 801; [1987]2 WLR 425; 130 Sol Jo 749 (CA) reversed by [1988]1 All ER 871; [1988]2 WLR 557; 132 Sol Jo 418; 3 BMLR 37 (HL).

condition could have been caused only by failure to prevent excess oxygen being given to him.

(ii) ***Loss of eyesight after cataract operation*** (*a*) The patient was operated in one of his eyes for cataract and intraocular lens was implanted by the doctor. It is alleged that the patient lost vision in the operated eye due to negligence of the doctor in conducting the operation.

The State Commission dismissed the complaint as there was no iota of evidence to substantiate the contention that loss of vision was due to improper implantation of I.O.L. or negligence of the doctor to conduct the operation. The order of the State Commission was confirmed by National Commission,[8] on appeal.

(*b*) The complainant had undergone cataract operation in his right eye under the care of the doctor. The complainant developed irritation in eye and unbearable headache and the medicines prescribed did not work. The doctor conducted the second operation, but the patient lost his eyesight. It is alleged that the complainant lost his eyesight due to negligence of the doctor in conducting the operation.

The State Commission, Punjab,[9] did not hold the doctor negligent, as the injury in the operated eye was noticed during prolonged postoperative period due to absence of proper care by the complainant. It is also held that every operation has its risk which includes post operational hazards for which the doctor cannot be held responsible.

(*c*) The patient had undergone cataract operation in his left eye. It is alleged that the operation was done by the trainee doctors by ignoring the fact that the patient was suffering from thyroid and diabetes. The patient lost complete vision in the left eye after the operation.

8 *Kailash Kumar Sharma* v *Dr. Hari Charan Mathur* 1997(2) CPR 126 (NC); III(1997) CPJ 41 (NC); 1998 CTJ 245 (CP) (NCDRC); 1998 CCJ 955 (NC).

9 *Charan Singh* v *Khosla Hospital* II(1999) CPJ 633 (Chandigarh); 2000 CTJ 123 (CP) (SCDRC).

The Delhi High Court[10] did not hold the surgeon and the hospital negligent, as it was established from evidence that the Senior Resident Surgeon conducted the surgery and that there was no evidence of negligence on the part of the surgeon and the hospital.

(iii) ***Loss of eyesight after glaucoma operation*** The patient was operated for glaucoma in left eye, but her eyesight did not revive. She was examined by the surgeon on five occasions after her discharge from the hospital and she was operated upon thrice on her left eye,·but these were of no avail.

The State Commission, Chandigarh,[11] did not hold the surgeon negligent, as the complainant failed to adduce evidence to prove negligence on the part of the surgeon. It is further held that the doctor refunded the expenses incurred by the complainant by issuing cheque, but the same does not establish deficiency in service on the part of the doctor.

(iv) ***Loss of vision after cataract surgery*** The patient had undergone cataract surgery and made no complaint of loss of vision during three routine check up within 21 days after surgery. Subsequently the patient got treatment from two other hospitals where retinal detachment was detected and thereby the patient suffered loss of vision.

Since retinal detachment is uncommon complication of cataract surgery and since there was no complaint of loss of vision even when spectacle was given to the patient after cataract surgery, the National Commission[12] did not hold the doctor negligent in conducting cataract surgery.

(v) ***Loss of vision after surgery for injury caused by wooden splinter.*** The patient sustained injury to the left eye caused by wooden splinter. Two opthalmologists conducted surgery and administered steroids, but the patient suffered from fungal endophthalmitis. However, the left eye was found to be full of

10 *Government of NCT of Delhi* v *Maharaj Kishan* CDJ 2013 DHC 1508.

11 *Mrs. Asha Rani* v *Dr. Rohit Grover* 1997(1) CPR 55 (Chandigarh); III(1996) CPJ 259 (Chandigarh); 1998 CCJ 100 (Chandigarh).

12 *Dilip C. Shah (Dr.)* v *Subhash Chandra Thro* 2015(1) CLT 490 (NCDRC).

pass and fungal endophthalmitis and another opthalmologist conducted corneal grafting, but the patient lost vision in the left eye.

The National Commission[13] did not hold two opthalmologists, who conducted surgery at the initial stage, negligent on the allegation of conducting surgery without maintaining proper hygiene and without using proper sterilized instruments.

(vi) ***Loss of vision for improper treatment*** The patient received injury when a small iron particle hit in his left eye. He was examined by two eye-surgeons who could not detect the iron foreign body in the left eye of the patient. Nor did they advice for x-ray or ultrasound scan. Subsequently on advice of the third eye-surgeon the patient got x-ray and ultrasound scan done and the iron foreign body was removed by way of surgery.

The District Forum held two eye-surgeons and the hospital guilty of negligence and awarded compensation. On appeal, the State Commission, Kerala,[14] reversed the decision of the District Forum and dismissed the complaint on the ground that nothing substantial was brought out in the evidence of the expert to establish that there was deficiency in service on the part of the two eye-surgeons and the hospital.

(vii) ***Permanent damage to left eye after operation*** The complaint was filed by the mother of the minor patient whose left eye was operated by the doctor without proper care and thereby the operation resulted in the permanent damage to the left eye of the patient.

The complaint was dismissed by the State Commission, Delhi, on the grounds that the allegation of use of improper and dangerous medicines was not substantiated by evidence, and that the service rendered by the defendant doctor was

13 *Master Aayush Dhar* v *K.C. Garg* II(2010) CPJ 55.

14 *Dr. Jyothi Vivek* v *Vijayasree Eye Hospital* 1997(3) CPR 220 (Ker); *Dr. Jyothi Vivek* v *Pradeep* I(1998) CPJ 191 (Ker); 1999 CCJ 720 (Ker).

not found to be deficient. The order of dismissal was affirmed by the National Commission.[15]

(viii) ***Removal of right eye by way of operation for treatment of injury to the eye*** The complainant, a minor boy, received severe injury in his right eye while bursting fire crackers at the school ground. The surgeon who treated the complainant, removed the whole eye by operation known as evisceration with the consent of the school authority. It is alleged that the complainant lost his right eye for negligence in conducting the operation by the surgeon without the consent of the parents.

It is held by the State Commission, Tamil Nadu,[16] that the surgeon was not negligent for removing the damaged right eye of the complainant, as evisceration was the only remedy available for preventing damage to the other eye and brain of the complainant. The surgeon was also held not negligent for conducting emergency operation with the consent of the school authority as the parents of the minor complainant were residing at a distance of 140 km. from the school.

13 Orthopaedician

(i) ***Amputation of leg due to defective plaster cast*** A minor girl sustained injuries due to fall from a moving bus. She was rushed to the hospital run by Kerala State Electricity Board. She was diagnosed to have sustained fracture on the left tibia. Her injured leg was immobilised by a plaster cast extending from mid-thigh to the ankle. She was given penicillin injection and glucose saline diet and on complain of severe pain in the leg, she was given sedatives. Since pain did not subside, the patient was removed to another hospital where the doctor found that the toes were swollen blue, immobile and anaesthetic. On removal of plaster it

15 *Miss Gurpreet Kaur (minor)* v *Dr. R.K. Bhutrni* I(1992) CPJ 257 (Del) affirmed by National Commission 1993(3) CPR 659 (NC); III(1993) CPJ 355 (NC); (1993)1 CTJ 1028 (NCDRC).

16 *Tamarino Marcel D'cruz* v *Management of St. Joseph's Boys Higher Secondary School* 1999 CCJ 1043 (Chennai).

was found that there was no pulsation or any other evidence of blood supply to the foot and leg. The patient was removed to C.M.C. Hospital at Vellore where her left leg was amputated to prevent gangrene and to save the life of the patient. The patient brought an action for damages on the ground of shortened expectation of life, pain and suffering, cost of treatment and expenses for providing an artificial leg.

The Ernakulam Bench of the Kerala High Court[17] did not hold the doctor of S.E.B. Hospital negligent, because first, he gave adequate treatment to the patient in the hospital, and secondly, the plaster would become tight if there was swelling after the plaster cast.

(ii) ***Disability after operation to cure injury on left knee*** A girl aged nine years received injury on left knee. She was taken to the hospital where doctor prescribed some medicines and gave first aid. The patient developed pain and swelling. The doctor got the x-ray done and gave plaster cast and thereafter the patient developed pain and swelling. The patient was shifted to another hospital where the doctor operated her for faciotomy under anaesthesia, but she suffered permanent disability. It is alleged that the girl suffered disability, physical pain and mental agony for negligence of the doctor.

The State Commission, Kerala,[18] did not hold the doctor negligent, because sufficient evidence was not adduced to warrant the conclusion that the complications of the child developed due to deficiency in service on the part of the doctor, particularly when the possibility of arising the complications on account of faciotomy operation cannot be ruled out.

(iii) ***Disability due to defective operation of fractured wrist*** The complainant had undergone operation for fracture of the wrist. The doctor removed the plaster after almost six weeks. The wrist of the complainant was disfigured and the pain

17 *Usha* v *Dr. G.P. Namboodiri* 1986(1) ACJ 141.

18 *P.R. Sumangi* v *Kairali Medical Centre* 1997(3) CPR 418 (Ker); I(1998) CPJ 203 (Ker); 1999 CCJ 1050 (Ker).

continued. It is alleged that the pain was subsisting and wrist was disfigured due to negligence of the doctor in conducting the operation.

It is held by the State Commission, Punjab,[19] that the doctor was not negligent in performing the operation, because the deformities of the wrist were due to anatomical feature of the bone which being spongy was compressed on account of severity of the fracture.

(iv) *Disability for defective operation of fractured elbow* The complainant, a child aged 8 years, was treated by orthopaedic surgeon for fractured elbow of the left hand. The X-ray of the left hand elbow was taken, the fracture was reduced and set by the doctor under general anaesthesia. Thereafter x-ray revealing well-set of the fracture was taken and the plaster cast was given. As the elbow pain continued unabated, the complainant was treated by another orthopaedic surgeon. It is alleged that the complainant was not cured completely due to negligence and lack of care of the first orthopaedic surgeon.

The complaint was dismissed by the State Commission, Karnataka,[20] on the grounds that the complainant failed to establish deficiency of service on the part of the first orthopaedic surgeon, and that the deformity of the complainant was due to contributory negligence of the complainant in tampering with plaster and giving movement to the fractured elbow without waiting for the full period for removal of the plaster.

(v) *Permanent disability after treatment of fracture of right femur* The complainant, aged 43 years sustained hairline fracture at neck of right femur. The doctor gave plaster of paris bandage for about one foot length from the bottom of right foot and advised for six weeks bed rest. The complainant had to undergo surgery known as hemiarthroplasty for not

19 *Suresh Kumar Sharma* v *Dr. Hardas Singh Sandhu* 1998 CCJ 1143 (Punj).

20 *Master Ashok Kumar* v *M/s. Agadi Nursing Home* III(1995) CPJ 142 (Bangalore); 1995(1) CPR 517 (Bangalore).

following the advice of the doctor. It is alleged that the complainant suffered permanent disability due to negligence of the doctor in conducting surgery.

The State Commission, Tamil Nadu,[1] did not hold the doctor negligent for selecting the particular method of surgery after assessing the type of fracture as garden Type III fracture and for known complications of hemiarthroplasty, such as infection, loosening of prosthesis, and erosion of bone, which caused disability of the patient.

(vi) ***Permanent disability after treatment of multiple injury in left leg*** The complainant sustained multiple injury in his left leg in an accident. The doctor plastered the left leg and prescribed some medicines. The patient developed severe pain, but the doctor did not pay any attention. The complainant was taken to another specialist doctor who advised for physical exercise under guidance of a physiotherapist. It is alleged that the complainant suffered permanent disability to the extent of 43.50% due to negligent treatment of the doctor.

The State Commission, Bihar,[2] did not hold the doctor negligent, as there was no iota of evidence to establish that the treatment given by the doctor was negligent or deficient resulting in permanent disability of the complainant.

(vii) ***Sufferings after repair of fracture of right leg*** The doctor put plaster cast on fractured right leg after examination of x-ray. After removal of plaster, the patient suffered from foot drop, which was confirmed by osteotomy. It is alleged that the patient became physically handicapped due to cutting of peroneal nerve by the doctor during the procedure.

The National Commission[3] did not hold the doctor negligent as the expert opinion revealed that the patient got proper treatment of malunited fracture and there was no evidence of peroneal nerve cut.

1 *Mr. S. Ramanujam* v *Dr. C.P. Sree Kumar* I(1999) CPJ 666 (Chennai).
2 *Ashok Kumar Singh* v *Dr. Mohan Thakur* II(2000) CPJ 220 (Pat).
3 *Bhushan Kumar Batra* v *S.P. Mandal (Dr.)* IV(2017) CPJ 304; 2017(4) CPR 638 (NCDRC).

(viii) ***Sufferings due to defective operation*** The complainant met with a motor accident and was treated in the hospital. The injury was bandaged and the leg was kept on a stand without any movement. Fortwin injection was given. On the next day the complainant was operated under anaesthesia with consent of the patient. He was taken away from the hospital against medical advice. He was shifted to another hospital where the doctor opened the plaster and found the formation of haematoma and infection. The doctors of the later hospital removed the fixtures and fixed new fixtures. It is alleged that the complainant suffered pain and damage due to deficiency of medical service rendered in first the hospital.

The State Commission, Tamil Nadu did not hold the surgeon of the first hospital guilty of negligence in performing surgery, because no evidence was adduced to show that the method adopted by the doctor was not accepted professional practice and that the damage suffered by the complainant was due to first surgery performed in the first hospital. The National Commission[4] also upheld the decision of the State Commission.

(ix) ***Sufferings due to inadequate treatment of fracture of leg*** The patient aged 42 years suffered hairline fracture of the neck of right femur of his leg. The conservative treatment of putting the fractured leg in a plaster of paris bandage did not yield result. The doctor adopted the procedure of hemiarthoplasty i.e. partial hip joint replacement operation instead of internal fixation method for treatment. The patient suffered complications and had to undergo total hip replacement surgery for negligence of the orthopaedician.

The National Commission held the doctor guilty of negligence, but the Supreme Court reversed the decision and refused to grant any compensation to the patient in view of divergence of opinion as to the choice of

4 *R. Gopinathan* v *Eskeycee Medical Foundation* 1994(2) CPR 488 (NC); I(1994) CPJ 147 (NC); (1994)2 CTJ 97 (CP) (NCDRC) affirming decision of State Commission 1993(1) CPR 456 (Mad).

procedure of treatment between internal fixation and hemiarthoplasty.[5]

(x) ***Sufferings due to unskilled surgery of fracture of elbow.*** The patient suffering from olecranon osteotomy had undergone treatment for fracture of elbow. It is alleged after two years of surgery that the patient suffered numbness in little finger due to damage to ulnar nerve during surgery for use of inferior and substandard implants.

The National Commission[6] did not hold the doctor negligent for lack of proof of causative relationship between injury like damage to ulnar nerve and surgery undertaken by the doctor.

(xi) ***Sufferings for unskilled surgery of fracture of hands*** The patient had undergone surgery for plating of fractures, fracture of zygoma right elevated and bone grafting. Subsequent x-rays revealed loosening of implants in both fore-arms. The further surgery for stabilization of fracture and bone grafts applied to right fore-arm cast, but the right fore-arm bones remained ununited, while the left fore-arm was cured. The patient refused to undergo further surgery for removal of implant, though subsequently steel plates were removed by surgery in another hospital.

Under the above circumstances the National Commission[7] did not hold the doctor negligent for sustaining disability by the patient.

14 Otorhinolaryngologist

(i) ***Death after nasal surgery*** The patient had undergone nasal surgery, but died of cardiac arrest during surgery. The patient was normal during pre-anaesthetic check up and the anaesthetist started endotracheal intubation in the OT

5 *C.P. Sreekumar (Dr.)* v *S. Ramanujam* 2009 ACJ 2305; JT 2009(6) SC 221; (2009)7 SCC 130; 2009 AIR SCW 3878; (2009)6 Scale 613.

6 *Tarun Garg* v *Dr. R.K. Gupta* II(2014) CPJ 700; 2014(4) Andh LD 24 (NCDRC).

7 *Manik Maliba Tarade* v *Sushrut Medical Care & Research Societies, Hardikar Hospital* 2015(3) Andh LD 30; IV(2014) CPJ 428 (NCDRC).

after 45 minutes. The allegation that Butram 2 mg. IV was given to the patient who developed laryngospasm and respiratory arrest within five minutes of administration of injection, is not proved from the case-sheet of the patient.

The National Commission[8] did not hold the surgeon negligent in performance of duty.

(ii) ***Death due to complications after removal of foreign body from throat*** The patient approached the doctor when a piece of meat got struck in throat. The patient had undergone oesophaguscopy for removal of foreign body under general anaesthesia. As the piece of meat was too large to be negotiated it was dislodged to the stomach. The patient developed discomfort after discharge from the hospital and ultimately she passed away after ten days. It is alleged that the doctor was negligent in conducting oesophaguscopy under general anaesthesia and in managing post operational complications resulting in death of the patient.

The State Commission, Kerala,[9] did not hold the doctor negligent, because, first, no fault in the treatment of the doctor was established from evidence and secondly, there was no vital signs of perforations of oesophagus during four days of treatment of the patient after operation in the hospital.

(iii) ***Death during operation of sinusitis*** The patient was admitted to the nursing home for operation of sinusitis. The patient developed convulsion and lost her B.P. and pulse before commencement of operation and ultimately died of massive heart attack in the operation theatre.

The State Commission did not hold the doctor negligent on two grounds: first, nothing was on record to disbelieve the operation notes which refuted the allegation of not giving proper treatment to the patient; secondly, no expert evidence was adduced by the complainant to dispute the affidavits given by four doctors on behalf of the operating surgeon,

8 *Archana Sharma* v *North Star Hospital & Joint Replacement Centre* I(2016) CPJ 269; 2015(4) CPR 893 (NCDRC).

9 *M.J. Joseph* v *Dr. P.J. John* 2000(2) CPR 5 (Ker).

which proved that the surgeon exercised proper skill in giving treatment to the patient. The order of dismissal of the complaint passed by State Commission, was upheld by the National Commission.[10]

(iv) *Death during surgery to plug the hole in ear drum* The patient had occasional slight discharge of watery liquid from his left ear. The doctor advised for surgery to plug the small hole in the ear drum. The doctor conducted the operation, but the patient entered into coma after administration of local anaesthesia and ultimately expired. It is alleged that the doctor is not qualified to give local anaesthesia and that he was negligent in administering anaesthesia without giving any test dose.

The State Commission, Tamil Nadu,[11] did not hold the doctor negligent, as there was no expert evidence to prove that the ENT Surgeon was not qualified to give local anaesthesia, or that only general anaesthesia should have been administered in the particular case, or that the test dose of anaesthesia was not given before administering anaesthesia.

15 Paediatrician

(i) *Death after treatment of diarrhoea* A male child, aged two months fell ill and was admitted to the hospital for treatment of diarrhoea. The child expired. It is alleged that the death of the child was due to wrong medicine prescribed by the paediatrician.

The National Commission,[12] dismissed the complaint on the grounds that there was no evidence to establish the causal connection between the death of the male child and the medical treatment given by the paediatrician, and that the cause of death was not diarrhoea, but cyanotic CHD with

10 *Sethuraman Subramaniam Iyer* v *Triveni Nursing Home* 1997(2) CPR 144 (NC); I(1998) CPJ 10 (NC); 1998 CTJ 7 (CP) (NCDRC); 1998 CCJ 1532 (NC).

11 *A. Sambi Reddy* v *K.K.R. ENT Hospital and Research Institute* 1997(3) CPR 316 (Chennai); I(1999) CPJ 165 (Chennai).

12 *Ramjilal* v *M/s. Sarvodaya Medical* II(1995) CPJ 234 (NC); 1995(1) CPR 833 (NC); (1995)3 CTJ 890 (CP) (NCDRC).

CHF (cyanotic Congenital Heart disease with congestive heart failure).

(ii) ***Death due to excessive dosage of phenergan*** The infant suffering from pneumonia was given 6 tea-spoon full of phenergan. The infant died. It is alleged that the infant died due to excessive dosage of phenergan prescribed by the doctor. However, it is established from evidence that the doctor prescribed half tea-spoon of phenergan for three times a day for two days only.

The National Commission[13] did not hold the doctor negligent for causing death of the patient by prescribing excessive dosage of phenergan.

(iii) ***Sufferings due to administration of wrong medicines in heavy dose*** The complainant approached the doctor for treatment of his son at the age of three years. The doctor prescribed ciprofloxacin 250 mg. to the child for two weeks for treatment of typhoid. The child was treated with the same drug for the same disease at the age of $1^1/_2$ years. It is alleged that the physical condition of the child is deteriorated after treatment due to adverse effect of the drug and the dose in which it was administered.

The State Commission, U.P.,[14] did not hold the doctor negligent on the grounds: (*a*) that there was difference of opinion about the use of the drug ciprofloxacin on the children below 12 years of age, and (*b*) that there was no evidence of any damage caused to the child by use of the drug in the dose prescribed by the doctor.

16 Pathologist

(i) ***Sufferings due to error in blood grouping*** The patient was admitted to the hospital with complaint of profuse bleeding with her actual blood group as 'B' positive. The blood group test of the patient carried out by the doctor thrice indicated her blood group as 'B' negative. It is alleged that the patient

13 *Kadar Khan* v *G.L. Gupta (Dr.)* 2015(3) WBLR 358; IV(2014) CPJ 150 (NCDRC).

14 *Dr. Rakesh Nath Mehrotra* v *Atul Pradhan* 2000(1) CPR 405 (Lucknow).

suffered restlessness and swelling in her body for transfusion of 'B' negative blood due to wrong report of her blood group in the laboratory of the doctor.

It is held by the State Commission, Punjab,[15] that negligence cannot be attributed to the doctor for the following reasons: first, there is no expert evidence to prove that the causes of restlessness and swelling in the body of the patient were due to transfusion of wrong blood group; secondly, transfusion of 'B' negative blood to the patient with 'B' positive blood has been recognised as accepted professional practice.

(ii) *Sufferings due to wrong report of pregnancy test* There was delay of five days in menstruation period of the complainant. The doctor after conducting urine test confirmed the pregnancy of the complainant. Subsequently another doctor found no pregnancy after conducting the urine test.

The State Commission, Chandigarh,[16] did not hold the doctor negligent, as the standard medical literature indicates that the result of pregnancy test may not be accurate beyond 98%. However, the Commission upheld the order of warning to the doctor passed by the District Forum.

17 Physician

(i) *Advice to minor girl on contraception without parent's consent* A doctor who in the exercise of his clinical judgment gave contraceptive advice and treatment to a minor girl without her parent's consent was not found guilty by the House of Lords,[17] because the *bona fide* exercise of the clinical judgment by the doctor negated the *mens rea* and as such advice to minor girl on contraception without parent's consent was not considered unlawful interference with parental rights.

(ii) *Damage to heart muscle for wrong treatment* The complainant, was admitted to the hospital, where he was

15 *Mrs. Meenakshi* v *Dr. Surkha Sachar* II(1999) CPJ 60 (Chandigarh).

16 *Mrs. Manpreet Kaur* v *Dr. (Mrs.) A.K. Sawhney* I(1999) CPJ 149 (Chandigarh).

17 *Gillick* v *West Norfolk and Wisbech Area Health Authority* (1985)2 BMLR 11; [1986] AC 112; [1985]3 All ER 402; [1985]3 WLR 830; 129 Sol Jo 738 (HL).

treated as an inpatient for seven days. The complainant allegedly complained of severe pain in chest and hands. It is further alleged that the complainant was treated by a consultant Gastroenterologist for abdominal pain. The complainant claimed compensation against the doctor on the allegation that the complainant suffered severe damage to his heart muscles resulting in impairment of his earning capacity for negligence and deficiency in service on the part of the doctor.

The National Commission[18] on consideration of evidence came to the conclusion that the complainant was admitted into the hospital with severe upper abdominal infection which was brought under control by prompt treatment of consultant gastroenterologist. The National Commission dismissed the complaint as frivolous and vexatious with cost to be paid to the doctor and the hospital, because, first, the records maintained in the hospital did not indicate that the complainant had ever complained of any pain in the chest, and secondly, there was no iota of evidence to prove negligence, lack of reasonable skill, care and competence or deficiency in service on the part of the doctor.

(iii) ***Damage to nerve affecting vocal cord by an exploratory operation to confirm diagnosis*** The patient was suffering from chest complaint. The consultants diagnosed that she was suffering from tuberculosis but also considered the possibility of her suffering from Hodgkin's disease. Before conducting the tests to confirm whether she was suffering from tuberculosis, the consultants performed an exploratory operation to determine whether she was suffering from Hodgkin's disease. The result of the operation showed her in fact to be suffering from tuberculosis and not Hodgkin's disease. As a result of the operation the patient suffered damage to a nerve affecting her vocal cords which caused her speech to be impaired. It is alleged that the consultants were negligent in deciding to carry out the operation before obtaining the result of the tuberculosis test.

18 *Brij Mohan Kher* v *Dr. N.B. Banka* 1994(3) CPR 197 (NC); III(1994) CPJ 140 (NC); I(1995) CPJ 99 (NC); (1994)2 CTJ 862 (CP) (NCDRC).

The House of Lords[19] did not hold the consultants guilty of an error of judgment amounting to breach of their duty of care to their patients; because, first, there existed conflicting medical opinion as to the necessity of operation, and secondly, there was no basis for preferring one body of expert opinion to the other.

(iv) ***Death due to administration of wrong dose of medicine*** The patient was treated by the doctor for renal disease with stone in kidney. As the patient complained of pain in right side of abdomen, the doctor gave morphine intravenous injection. As the pain did not subside even after waiting for half an hour, the doctor gave another dose of morphine with calmpose intravenous injection. The patient did not regain consciousness and ultimately expired. It is alleged that the patient died due to administration of wrong dose of medicine.

The expert opinion on behalf of the patient party is that if dose of morphine and calmpose is combined and given intravenous with interval of half an hour, it could prove to be fatal, whereas the expert evidence on behalf of the doctor is that there would not be any effect of the two medicines referred to above after six hours of administration. It is held that there is divergence of opinions as to whether dose of morphine and calmpose could be repeated with interval of half an hour.

The State Commission, Punjab,[1] did not hold the doctor negligent, as the patient died after about 8-9 hours of administration of the drugs, and as the administration of drugs with interval of half an hour was not proved to be fatal.

(v) ***Death due to allergy caused by antibiotics*** The patient was treated by the doctor for fever. The doctor prescribed

19 *Maynard* v *West Midlands Regional Health Authority* (1983)1 BMLR 122; [1985]1 All ER 635; [1984]1 WLR 634; 128 Sol Jo 317 (HL).

1 *Nita Singla* v *Dr. Karnail Singh* III(1998) CPJ 39 (Chandigarh); 1998 CTJ 538 (CP) (SCDRC); 2000 CCJ 335. [This is not good authority as the question whether treatment given was as per accepted professional practice, was neither urged nor decided by the State Commission].

ampicillin tablets and Cosavil tablets, but she developed eye trouble. She was treated by another doctor who continued the same medicines. The patient developed rashes on her face and swelling on her eye lids. She was admitted to the hospital for treatment of "Stevens Johnson Syndrome" in which the patient's skin gets peeled off. She was shifted to another hospital where she expired due to "septicaemia" caused by 75% skin loss due to drug reaction. It is alleged that the patient died of "Stevens Johson Syndrome" due to administration of antibiotics by the doctors without giving a test dose.

The doctors were held not negligent by the State Commission, Maharashtra,[2] because it was established from evidence that the treatment given to the patient under the given circumstances was proper, and the patient was never found to be allergic to antibiotics during last several years of treatment by the doctor.

(vi) ***Death due to treatment without diagnosis*** The patient, an employee of Philips India Ltd., fell ill suddenly and the Medical Officer of the company treated him without making proper diagnosis of disease. The patient died of smallpox. The question was whether the doctor was guilty of negligence.

It is held by Bombay High Court[3] that the doctor was not negligent because the duty cast on the company's doctor in respect of company's employee is not higher or lower than the duty of an average doctor towards his patient.

(vii) ***Permanent brain damage due to improper treatment*** The five-year-old patient severely injured herself. A cut in one of her elbows substantially severed her muscles and nerves and the humeral artery, causing an extensive haemorrhage and blood loss. The doctor administered emergency treatment in a small general hospital and arranged for the transfer of the child to a pediatrics teaching hospital for skilled

2 *Kashiram Bhimrao Kamble* v *Dr. Udaya A. Patil* III(1998) CPJ 614 (Bom).

3 *Phillips India Ltd.* v *Kanju Punnu* 1975 ACJ 311; AIR 1975 Bom 306; 77 Bom LR 337; 1975 Mah LJ 792.

treatment. The condition of the patient began to deteriorate in the second hospital where the child suffered cardio-respiratory arrest causing permanent brain damage.

The Supreme Court of Canada[4] held that the doctor had not been negligent in the discharge of his duty towards his patient, and that a physician was not liable for a mere error of judgment that did not amount to professional fault.

(viii) *Permanent brain damage for delay in giving treatment* A two-year-old boy was treated for breathing difficulties in a hospital managed by the health authority. Owing to failure of the doctor to attend the patient in response to urgent summons of the ward sister, the patient suffered a respiratory and cardiac arrest. He was resuscitated, but sustained severe brain damage. The question before the Court of Appeal in U.K. was whether the patient's brain damage was caused by the negligence of the doctor.

The doctor of the health authority was held not negligent by the Court of Appeal in U.K.[5] because it was not established that the doctor would have probably intubated the patient had he attended the patient in time, and that failure to intubate was contrary to accepted medical practice.

(ix) *Permanent disability due to improper diagnosis and treatment without investigation* The patient was suffering from swelling of his feet and had difficulty in passing urine. He approached the doctor who got various tests conducted, but did not advise for ultrasound to rule out the possibility of stone in kidney. It is alleged that the doctor started giving steroid suspecting "Nephrotic Syndrome" of the patient without recommending any confirmatory tests for proper diagnosis and thereby the patient became completely disabled.

The State Commission, Chandigarh,[6] did not hold the doctor negligent, as it was established from evidence that

4 *Lapointe et al* v *Chevrette* (1992)90 DLR (4th) 7.

5 *Bolitho* v *City and Hackney Health Authority* 13 BMLR 111 (CA) affirmed by House of Lords [1997]4 All ER 771; [1998] AC 232.

6 *Hans Raj* v *Dr. K.S. Chugh* 2000 CTJ 577 (CP) (SCDRC); 2000(1) CPR 310 (Chandigarh).

the patient was taking extra doses of steroids without contracting the doctor for three months and thereby contributed to the disability suffered by him.

(x) ***Sufferings due to inadequate treatment of acute bronchial problem*** The patient was treated by the doctors for acute bronchial problems. The doctors refused to follow the advice of the senior consultants of their field in giving treatment to the patient. It is alleged that the patient suffered due to wrong treatment given by the doctors for long period.

The State Commissioner, W.B. held the doctors negligent and directed them to pay compensation to the patient. By setting aside the order of the State Commission on appeal, it is held by the National Commission,[7] that the doctors cannot be held negligent in the absence of expert evidence to prove that the treatment given to the patient was wrong or not adequate and thereby the patient suffered.

(xi) ***Sufferings due to infection of Hepatitis-B after blood transfusion*** The complainant got himself admitted to a nursing home for treatment of his prostate gland. The doctor performed surgery upon the complainant. The blood transfusion was also started simultaneously with the commencement of surgery. He was discharged after five days of operation. After four months it was diagnosed that he was suffering from Hepatitis-B infection.

The National Commission[8] did not hold the doctor or the nursing home or the blood bank negligent, because the allegations that the cause of the disease of the complainant was supply of infected blood by blood bank and that the blood transfused to the complainant was contaminated with Hepatitis-B virus, were not substantiated from evidence.

(xii) ***Sufferings due to delay in making proper diagnosis*** The lump under the left arm of the patient could not be detected by the general practitioner and thereby there was delay of

7 *Subhashish Dhar (Dhir)* v *Smt. Sanjukta Sengupta* III(1999) CPJ 29 (NC); 1999(3) CPR 13 (NC); 1999 CTJ 573 (CP) (NCDRC).

8 *A. Narain Rao* v *Dr. G. Ramakrishna Reddy* 1994((1) CPR 687 (NC); I(1993) CPJ 110 (NC); I(1994) CPJ 54 (NC); (1993)1 CTJ 387 (NCDRC).

nine months in making diagnosis of non-Hodgkin's lymphoma. The patient claimed damages for reduction of life-span due to negligence of the doctors in making proper diagnosis.

It is held by the House of Lords[9] that the delay of nine months in making diagnosis due to negligence of the doctor was not the cause of reduction of life span of the patient, as the patient would have lived for ten years had the diagnosis been made without delay, and thereby the doctor cannot be held liable for payment of compensation.

(xiii) ***Sufferings due to wrong diagnosis leading to kidney transplantation*** The patient was admitted to the nursing home with complaint of vomiting. The bone marrow sample of the patient was sent to the pathologist whose report revealed deposit of Hodgkin's Lymphoma, and the doctor without referring the patient to any specialist started administering Endoxan injections. Subsequently, the bone marrow sample was analysed by an Oncologist whose report indicated that the patient had myelopatic anaemia in the marrow and the clinical features did not fit with Hodgkin's disease. It is alleged that the patient suffered renal failure and underwent surgical transplantation of kidney due to administration of Endoxan injection on the basis of wrong diagnosis of Hodgkin's Lymphoma.

The doctors were not held negligent by the State Commission, as there was no expert evidence to prove that renal failure was due to administration of Endoxan injections and as the old slides were not re-examined by any other pathologist for second opinion. The order of dismissal of the complaint by State Commission, was confirmed by the National Commission.[10]

(xiv) ***Sufferings for failure to inform diagnosis of cancer*** The physician diagnosed cancer and removed a lump from the breast of the patient, but failed to inform her that the lump.

9 *Gregg* v *Scott* [2005]2 WLR 268; [2005] UKHL 2.

10 *Consumer Protection Counsel* v *Dr. M. Sundaram* 1997(2) CPR 164 (NC); II(1998) CPJ 3 (NC); (1997)5 CTJ 582 (CP) (NCDRC); 1999 CCJ 199 (NC).

was cancerous. The patient was informed of the diagnosis after four years when further symptoms developed. It is alleged that the doctor was neligent by not informing the patient of the diagnosis.

The Supreme Court of Canada[11] did not hold the physician liable for depriving the patient of an opportunity of obtaining proper treatment on the ground that the patient's chances of survival would not have been greater if she had been informed of the diagnosis, because the medical opinion was divided in 1971 on the proper method of treating breast cancer.

18 Psychiatrist

Permanent disability due to administration of electro-convulsive therapy (*a*) The patient was advised by a specialist to undergo electro-convulsive therapy for recovery from mental illness. He was not warned of the risks of fractures involved in the treatment. The risk of fracture was in the order of one in ten thousand. To exclude the risk of fracture, no relaxant drug or manual control was used. There were two bodies of opinion among the professionals—one body preferred the use of relaxant drugs and manual control and the other body preferred to avoid use of drugs because of mortality risks. There was no uniformity of opinion on the use of manual control. As a result of not using relaxant drugs the patient sustained severe physical injuries consisting in dislocation of both hip joints with fractures of the pelvis.

The doctor was not held negligent by the Queen's Bench of U.K.,[12] because, first, he acted in accordance with a practice accepted as proper by a responsible body of medical men skilled in that particular art; secondly the doctors did not disclose the risk to the patient believing the dangers involved in the treatment to be minimal; and thirdly, it was not established that the patient would not have consented to the treatment had he been warned of the risks.

11 *Lawson* v *Laferriere* (1991)78 DLR (4th) 609.

12 *Bolam* v *Friern Hospital Management Committee* [1957]2 All ER 118; [1957]1 WLR 582; 101 Sol Jo 357; 1 BMLR 1 (QBD).

(*b*) The patient was treated by the doctor for some psychiatric problems. He was administered five ECTs (electro convulsive therapy) as outdoor patient and four more ECTs as indoor patient under general anaesthesia and in O.T. The patient, aged 60 years, received injury on cervical spine, as he had fallen from the bed. It is alleged that the patient suffered permanent disability due to negligence of the doctor and hospital in giving treatment.

The State Commission, Delhi,[13] did not hold the doctor negligent for two reasons, first, there was expert evidence to prove that the drugs prescribed and ECTs given to the patient were in accordance with well-established professional practice and secondly, there was no expert evidence to prove that the fracture in apophyseal area and injury in cervical spine received by the patient by falling from bed, resulted in his permanent disability.

19 Radiologist

(i) *Death due to allergic reaction in diagnostic medical test* A patient died in consequence of an allergic reaction to a dye used in a diagnostic medical test (IVP). Severe reaction was known to occur in about one in 2,000 cases and death in between one in 40,000 and one in 1,00,000. The defendant radiologist did not warn the patient of these risks. He acted in accordance with the advice of the Canadian Association of Radiologists.

It is held by the Ontario Court of Appeal in Canada[14] that the radiologist ought to have informed the patient of the risk, because there was no exception to the principle by way of therapeutic privilege. However, the radiologist was held not negligent for failure to disclose the risk to the patient on the ground that a fully informed reasonable person in patient's position would have chosen to consent to the diagnostic test.

(ii) *Death due to improper treatment based on wrong report of C.T. Scan* The patient had a medical history of cancer and was operated for removal of uterine tumour in Tata Memorial

13 *Ganga Singh* v *Dr. I.C. Sethi* 1999 CTJ 302 (CP) (SCDRC).
14 *Meyer et al* v *Rogers et al* (1991)78 DLR (4th) 307 (O.C. of Appeal).

Hospital at Bombay and the biopsy report at that time indicated that the tumour was malignant. She was also administered chemotherapy and the doctors found everything under control. After three months the C.T. Scan of abdomen and pelvis of the patient was done by the radiologist who ruled out any trace of cancer of the patient. Accordingly no treatment of cancer was administered for stomach pain and allied trouble of the patient. After five months of the first treatment a lesion in right low Hepatic lobe was found by the doctors of Tata Memorial Hospital on examination of the same C.T. Scan plate of the patient who ultimately expired. It is alleged that the radiologist was negligent in reading the C.T. Scan report which aggravated the pain and sufferings and expedited the death of the patient.

The National Commission[15] did not hold the radiologist negligent, because the physician of Tata Memorial Hospital before prescribing the line of treatment should have carefully examined the reasons for lesion in right low hepatic lobe in a patient with history of cancer.

(iii) ***Sufferings due to wrong report of ultrasound scan*** The patient suffering from severe abdominal pain and jaundice had undergone ultrasound scan. The USG report of the radiologist revealed existence of stone in CBD. The surgeon operated the patient, but no stone was found in CBD. However, the surgeon detected a tumour in the head of the pancreas. The patient was shifted to the higher speciality centre where bulky head of pancreas was found to be normal by ERCP and other investigations.

The National Commission[16] did not hold the radiologist negligent, as the expert opined that the stone in CBD could have passed out naturally in the intervening period between the date of USG and the date of surgery, particularly when it was not possible to detect any shadow or lesion in the pancreas due to previous cholecystectomy with all tough adhesions.

15 *Rahul Sinha* v *Dr. Ashok Mitra* II(1995) CPJ 227 (NC); 1995(1) CPR 835 (NC); (1995)3 CTJ 618 (CP) (NCDRC).

16 *Kiran Sinha* v *Dr. A.K. Vishwakarma* 2015(4) CPR 348; II(2016) CPJ 204 (NCDRC).

(iv) ***Sufferings for failure to detect abnormality in foetus by ultrasound scan*** The patient was about 26 weeks pregnant. She had an ultrasound scan at a hospital administered by the health authority. The radiographer taking the scan doubted possible abnormality in the foetus. The consultant radiologist decided that no further action should be taken because there was no firm evidence of abnormality. After three months the baby was born and was found to be suffering from *spina bifida.* It is alleged that the radiologist was negligent in not ascertaining whether foetus was abnormal and thereby deprived the patient of the possibility of having the pregnancy terminated.

The Queen's Bench of U.K.[17] did not hold the consultant radiologist negligent in failing to direct a rescan when the radiographer raised his suspicions of abnormality, since by then it was 27 weeks of pregnancy, which was too late to carry out a lawful termination.

20 State

Brain damage after vaccination (*a*) The complainant, an infant who was administered the triple antigen injection as well as anti-polio drops for immunization against contracting diptheria, tetanus, whooping cough and poliomyelitis, developed severe reaction resulting in damage to his brain causing muscular deformity and deficiency as in the case of poliomyelitis.

The State Commission dismissed the complaint on the ground that no negligence is made out against the State Government doctors, because other children immunized from the same vaccine did not suffer and the complainant was not consumer inasmuch as the services of the doctors were not hired for consideration. The order of dismissal of the complaint was upheld by the National Commission.[18]

(*b*) A child, aged about 4 months, received vaccination against diphtheria, pertussis and tetanus (DPT). The parents of the child claimed compensation against the Secretary of

17 *Rance* v *Mid-Downs Health Authority* (1990)5 BMLR 75 (QBD).

18 *Tapan Kumar Nayak* v *State of Orissa* 1997(2) CPR 104 (NC); II(1997) CPJ 14 (NC); (1997)5 CTJ 410 (CP) (NCDRC); 1998 CCJ 193 (NC).

Health and Human Services under the National Childhood Vaccine Injury Act, on the ground that the child had suffered encephalopathy i.e. impairment of brain function after the vaccination.

The United States Court of Federal Claims denied compensation to the claimants on the ground that the child had been microcephalic before vaccination which was evidence of encephalopathy, though the child had suffered seizures within three days of the vaccination. On appeal, the United States Court of Appeals for Federal Circuit reversed the decision and held that the Secretary of Health and Human Services had not rebutted the *prima facie* case made out by the parents of the child by proving the symptoms of encephalopathy during 3-day period after vaccination. Ultimately, the United States Supreme Court,[19] reversed the decision on the ground that the child experienced symptoms of injury after receiving vaccination, but the claimants failed to establish that the child had no symptoms of that injury before the vaccination.

21 Surgeon

(i) *Continuous flow of urine after prostate operation* The patient had undergone prostate operation. The patient developed acute pain in thigh muscles and backbone. The continuous and regular flow of urine which had started immediately after the operation continued. It is alleged that the patient was suffering from incontinence due to damage caused to the sphincter muscle during the operation performed by the doctor.

The National Commission,[1] did not hold the doctor negligent on the following grounds: first, there was no expert evidence to prove that damage of sphincter muscle would result in incontinence of the patient; secondly, the doctor who prescribed injection for treatment of sphincter damage, was not examined as witness; and thirdly, the fact that the patient was suffering from incontinence, was not reported to

19 *Donna E. Shalala* v *Margaret Whitecotton* [1995]131 L Ed 2d 374; 115 S Ct 1477.

1 *Tarachand Jain* v *Ganga Ram Hospital* III(1999) CPJ 53 (NC); 1999(3) CPR 38 (NC); 1999 CTJ 734 (CP) (NCDRC); 2000 CCJ 457.

the hospital authority during the period of two months after his discharge from the hospital.

(ii) *Damage to spinal cord for non-disclosure of risk of surgery* The patient suffering from persistent pain in her neck and shoulders was advised by the specialist to undergo an operation on her spinal column to relieve the pain. The patient was warned of the possibility of disturbing nerve root, but was not informed of the possibility of damage to the spinal cord. The risk of damage to the spinal cord was less than 1%, but if the risk materialised the resulting injury could range from mild to very severe. The patient suffered injury to her spinal cord which resulted in her being severely disabled.

The surgeon was held not negligent by the House of Lords, because non-disclosure of the risk of damage to the patient's spinal cord accorded with a practice accepted as proper by a responsible body of neuro-surgeon.[2]

(iii) *Death expedited due to wrong diagnosis and treatment* The patient approached the doctor for treatment of swelling on the abdomen over and above the hip portion. The doctor diagnosed the disease as lymphoma and conducted two operations for removal of the lump. The excision biopsy was done when the doctor suspected neurofibroma. As the report of biopsy revealed cancer, the patient was referred to better equipped hospital for treatment by radiotherapy and chemotherapy. The patient ultimately expired. It is alleged that the doctor conducted two operations hurriedly without proper investigations and thereby helped to spread the disease quickly resulting in death of the patient.

The State Commission, Tamil Nadu,[3] did not hold the doctor negligent as the treatment given by the doctor was the standard surgical practice prevalent throughout the world.

(iv) *Disability for non-disclosure of risk of surgery* The patient underwent hernia operation. Following the operation she suffered chronic and intractable pain in the area surrouding

2 *Sidaway* v *Bethlem Royal Hospital Governors* [1985] AC 871; [1985]1 All ER 643; [1985]2 WLR 480; 129 Sol Jo 154; (1985)1 BMLR 132 (HL).

3 *T.M.T. Chandra* v *Dr. Mahesh* I(2000) CPJ 361 (Chennai); 2000(2) CPR 129 (Chennai).

the operation scar. She was referred to the specialist who operated on her by injecting a solution near the spinal cord with the object of destroying pain conducting nerves which served the scar area. It is alleged that the patient was not warned that the treatment involved the risk of numbness and possible loss of muscle power. As a result of treatment undertaken by the specialist, the patient found her right leg completely numb, which considerably impaired her mobility.

The Queen's Bench of U.K.[4] did not hold the surgeon negligent because, first, he carried out his duty to inform the patient of the implications of the operation in broad terms, secondly, he had no duty to warn the patient of the possibility of numbness in her leg which was not a foreseeable risk of the operation and thirdly, it is not established that the patient would have refused to undergo the operation had she been properly informed of the risks.

(v) *Gauze towel left in the splenic bed of the patient during surgery* The patient had to undergo emergency operation after road accident. Thereafter the patient suffered physical agony for about three weeks. Ultimately after second operation in the Hospital at Bombay the doctors found gauze towel of 6"x6" in the splenic bed of the patient.

The State Commission, Goa found the allegation of deficiency of service as proved and awarded compensation. On appeal, the National Commission[5] had set aside the order of the State Commission on the ground that the State Commission did not give permission to cross-examine the surgeon who performed the operation in Jaslok Hospital, Bombay, though he was available for giving evidence.

(vi) *Permanent brain damage during heart transplant surgery* The plaintiff, aged 15 months, had undergone heart transplant surgery. His heart stopped immediately after administration of anaesthetic. When attempts to restart the heart by use of drugs and external massage failed, the chest

4 *Chatterton* v *Gerson* (1980)1 BMLR 80; [1981]1 All ER 257; [1981] QB 432; [1981]3 WLR 1003.

5 *Salgaokar Medical Research Centre* v *R.B. Raikar* 1996(2) CPR 50 (NC); II(1996) CPJ 209 (NC); (1996)4 CTJ 576 (CP) (NCDRC).

was opened and the heart started working after giving internal massage. The plaintiff suffered irreversible brain damage as oxygen was not supplied to the brain during the period when the heart was stopped. It is alleged that the parents of the plaintiff would have refused consent to the surgery had they been informed of the risk of brain damage.

It is held by the Queen's Bench Division,[6] that failure to warn of less than 1% risk does not amount to negligence, because the parents of the plaintiff would have given consent to the transplant surgery even if information of small risk of serious brain damage had been disclosed.

(vii) ***Permanent disability after hernia operation*** The patient was admitted to the hospital with complaint of recurrent direct hernia. He had undergone operation. The patient developed pain in pubic region and he was unable to move or walk. The patient was treated by other doctor who diagnosed the ailment as "osteitis pubic" caused by infection of bone due to hernia operation. The patient suffered from permanent disability on the leg even after three operations at the pubic area of the patient.

It is held by the State Commission, Kerala,[7] that expert evidence and observation made in the standard text books indicate that the cause of osteitis pubic was not known. The Commission did not hold the doctor negligent, as it was not established from evidence that the permanent disability on the left leg of the patient was consequent upon osteitis pubic which resulted from hernia operation.

(viii) ***Sufferings due to unskilled cholecystectomy*** The patient was suffering from obstructive jaundice due to wrong surgery of cholecystectomy. The patient was called for corrective surgery, but she went to another hospital. It is established from evidence that the known complication of cholecystectomy is obstruction to the bile flow and subsequent development of obstructive jaundice for which corrective surgery is required during postoperative period.

6 *Poynter* v *Hillington Health Authority* 37 BMLR 192 (QBD).

7 *K.K. Ummer* v *Jubilee Mission Hospital, Trichur* III(1997) CPJ 432 (Ker).

The National Commission[8] did not hold the surgeon negligent, as the injuries suffered by the patient are inherent risks of the surgery.

(ix) *Sufferings due to wrong diagnosis and unwanted surgery*
The patient aged 14 years was admitted to the hospital with complaint of pain in upper abdomen, vomiting and fever. The patient was operated for acute appendicitis. As the pain, vomiting and fever did not subside, the patient had to undergo second operation within 55 hours of the first operation. As the symptoms continued even after the second operation, the patient was shifted to better equipped hospital where his condition became stable after prolonged treatment. It is alleged that the patient suffered mental agony and physical pain during prolonged postoperative complications due to wrong diagnosis and unwanted surgery.

The National Commission,[9] did not hold the surgeons negligent, as the differential diagnosis of acute appendicitis is essentially the diagnosis of "acute abdomen" which may produce same alterations of functions as acute appendicitis. The surgeon was duty bound to conduct the first operation as the patient's clinical condition pointed to acute appendicitis. It is also held that the second operation was required as the surgeon suspected perforative intestines and advised laparotomy.

(x) *Sufferings for non-removal of stones from kidney by operation*
The patient approached the doctor for treatment of acute retention of urine and supra pubic pain. He was operated upon for removal of stones from urinary bladder. It is alleged that the patient suffered from pain due to non-removal of stone from left kidney while operating upon urinary bladder for removal of stones.

The State Commission, Punjab,[10] did not hold the doctor negligent for conducting the operation, as it is established

8 *Sanjay Gadekar (Dr.)* v *Sangamitra* alias *Sandhya Khobragade* 2016(3) CLT 14; 2016(3) CPR 270 (NCDRC).

9 *Kanhaiya Kumar Singh* v *Park Medicare and Research Centre* III(1999) CPJ 9 (NC); 1999 CTJ 644 (CP) (NCDRC); 2000 CCJ 249.

10 *Sewa Ram* v *Dr. Vitul K. Gupta, K.R. Mission Hospital and Maternity Home* 1999(2) CPR 68 (Chandigarh).

from expert evidence that the stones cannot be removed from the kidney while performing operation for removal of stones from urinary bladder.

(xi) *Sufferings for open surgery after obtaining consent for laparoscopic surgery* The patient gave consent for laparoscopic surgery for removal of gall stone. The surgeon noticed swelling, inflammation and adhesion on gall bladder and proceeded to remove gall bladder by conventional procedure of surgery after obtaining consent from the husband of the patient. It is alleged that she suffered various ailments for open surgery and removal of gall bladder for which consent was not obtained by the surgeon.

The Supreme Court of India[11] did not hold the surgeon guilty of negligence for converting laparoscopic surgery to open surgery and for removal of gall bladder even if the same is done without consent on the ground that the additional procedure though unauthorised may be performed by the surgeon under the original consent to save the life of the patient.

(xii) *Death due to pyogenic meningitis after surgery for removal of abdominal tumour* The patient had undergone surgery for removal of abdominal tumour. The tumour was found to be malignant. It is alleged that the body of pancreas was damaged during surgery and a channel was fixed to drain out the fluids. The patient had to undergo second surgery and two bags were fitted to drain out the fluids. The patient was treated in other hospitals for pancreatic fistula and chronic fistula, but ultimately died.

The National Commission did not hold the surgeons and the hospital negligent in performance of duty on the basis of the medical literature and the evidence of the experts in the field. On appeal, the Supreme Court of India[12] affirmed the decision of the National Commission.

11 *S.K. Jhunjhunwala (Dr.)* v *Dhanwanti Kumar* JT 2018(9) SC 435; AIR 2018 SC 4625; 2018(4) CPR 738; (2019)2 SCC 282.

12 *Kusum Sharma* v *Batra Hospital and Medical Research Centre* 2010(2) CTC 461; 2010(3) SCJ 349; (2010)3 SCC 480; AIR 2010 SC 1050; 2010 AIR SCW 1315; 2010(1) Supreme 519; (2010)2 Scale 267; JT 2010(2) SC 7; 2010(2) SLT 73.

Part B

COMPENSATION

CHAPTER

8

Eligibility and Liability

1 Compensation under general law—entitlement An action for personal injury including medical negligence is a claim for compensation (*i*) by the person who has sustained injury or damage; or (*ii*) where death of the person is caused, by the executor, administrator or representative of the person deceased.[1] If the plaintiff establishes that the doctor was negligent, but fails to prove that any loss or injury was caused thereby, then he will not be entitled to claim any compensation.[2]

Any adult person of sound mind is entitled to claim for compensation provided he suffers damage due to medical negligence. This claim for personal injury may be made by any minor or person of unsound mind through next friend by invoking the provisions of Or. 32 of the Code of Civil Procedure. So, the persons who are incapable of protecting their own interest due to immaturity of mind or mental infirmity are entitled to claim for compensation through their next friend.[3]

1 Section 1A of the Fatal Accidents Act 1855.

2 *Sidhraj Dhadda* v *State of Rajasthan* AIR 1994 Raj 68; 1993(1) Raj LW 532.

3 Order 32 of the Code of Civil Procedure 1908.

The personal injury action cannot be commenced by the executor, administrator or representative of the deceased under the provisions of the Legal Representatives' Suits Act 1855 because the said Act is intended to protect suits for wrongs done to the property of the deceased. However, the executor, administrator or representative of the deceased person is entitled to claim for compensation for the benefit of the wife, husband, parent and child under s. 1A of the Fatal Accidents Act 1855. Woodroffe, J[4] held that the term "legal representative" is not limited to administrators, executors, and heirs, and that it must be held to include any person who in law represents the estate of the deceased. It would be relevant to point out that the view expressed by Woodroffe, J has been embodied by s. 2(11) of the Code of Civil Procedure 1908, which is as follows:

"Legal representative" means a person who in law represents the estate of a deceased person, and includes any person who intermeddles with the estate of the deceased and where a party sues or is sued in a representative character the person on whom the estate devolves on the death of the party so suing or sued. Gajendragadkar, J[5] held that the clause—a person who in law represents the estate of a deceased person—must include different legatees under the will.

Every action for personal injury under s. 1A of the Fatal Accidents Act 1855 shall be brought by and in the name of executor, administrator or representative of the deceased for the benefit of the spouse, parent, and child of the deceased, irrespective of whether they are "legal representatives" within the meaning of s. 2(11) of the Code of Civil Procedure 1908, because the word "parent" includes father, mother, grandfather, and grandmother, and the word "child" includes son, daughter, grandson, granddaughter, step-son, and step-daughter.[6]

4 *Dinomoni Chaudhurani* v *Elahadut Khan* 8 CWN 843.
5 *Andhra Bank Ltd.* v *Srinivasan* AIR 1962 SC 232.
6 Section 4 of the Fatal Accidents Act 1855.

The Madras High Court[7] has held that the word "representative" used in the Fatal Accidents Act 1855 means and includes all or any of the persons for whose benefit a suit under the Act can be maintained, and that the persons are the representatives in the sense that they are the persons taking the place of the deceased in obtaining reparation for the wrong done. The view of Madras High Court is adopted by Calcutta High Court,[8] which laid down that the word "representative" in the Fatal Accidents Act 1855 means not the legal representatives of the deceased, but the wife, husband, parent and children of the deceased, and that any one of them can bring the suit for the benefit of others. The consistent view of the Punjab,[9] Mysore,[10] Madras,[11] and Rajasthan[12] High Courts is that the father also can bring an action for personal injury as a representative of the deceased. It, therefore, follows that under the Fatal Accidents Act 1855, compensation is available to all those members of the family of the deceased, who suffer monetary loss as a result of death of the said person caused by wrongful act, neglect or default. The maxim *actio personalis moritur cum persona* is modified by s. 306 of the Indian Succession Act 1925, which provides that all rights to prosecute or defend any action for or against a person at the time of his death, survive to or against his executor or administrator, excepting causes of action for defamation, assault or other personal injuries not causing death.[13]

In a complaint for compensation on the ground of medical negligence, the right to sue would survive in the legal heirs who would be entitled to compensation.[14]

7 *Johnson* v *The Madras Railway Company* ILR (1905)28 Mad 479.
8 *Jeet Kumari* v *Chittagong E & E Supply Co*. AIR 1947 Cal 195.
9 *Himachal Government Transport* v *Joginder Singh* 1970 ACJ 57 (Punj).
10 *M. Vasavalingaiah* v *T.P. Papanna* AIR 1972 Mys 63; 1971 ACJ 404; (1971) Mys LJ 351.
11 *Palani Ammal* v *Safe Service Ltd*. 1966 ACJ 19 (Mad).
12 *State of Rajasthan* v *Parwati Devi* AIR 1966 Raj 210.
13 *Maharani Dey* v *Debabrata Bardhan* 1984 ACJ 95; AIR 1983 Gau 84.
14 *Mukesh Kumari (minor & dead) by LRs* v *M. Lal Oswal Cancer Treatment and Research Foundation* (2004)13 SCC 69.

2 Compensation under consumer law

(i) ***Ambit of jurisdiction*** A consumer can claim compensation before District Commission[15] for amount not exceeding rupees one crore, before State Commission[16] for amount exceeding rupees one crore, but not exceeding rupees ten crore, and before National Commission[17] for amount exceeding rupees ten crore by filing complaint for deficiency of service availed of on payment of consideration.

The amicable settlement of a dispute between the doctor and the patient over a number of complications after lipolysis before the State Commission, was reopened by the order of the National Commission, when multiple abdominal hernias due to careless handling of lipolysis operation, were detected after one month of amicable settlement of the dispute before State Commission.[18]

However, it would not be proper to direct the consumers to approach the civil court in all cases involving evidence of experts. In view of the procedure open to the Commission under the enabling provisions of the Consumer Protection Act for examination of experts by putting written questions to be replied on affidavits or through video-conference by appointing a Commissioner, there is no scope for delay in examination of experts involving medical negligence. According to the Supreme Court, it would be totally wrong assumption that justice cannot be done by following the procedure of summary trial adopted by the Consumer Courts, where complicated questions of facts involving medical negligence are required to

15 Section 11 of the Consumer Protection Act 1986 prescribing pecuniary jurisdiction of District Forum not exceeding rupees twenty lakh, is replaced by s. 34 of the Consumer Protection Act 2019 w.e.f. 9th August 2019.

16 Section 17 of the Consumer Protection Act 1986 prescribing pecuniary jurisdiction of State Commission exceeding rupees twenty lakh, but not exceeding rupees one crore, is replaced by s. 47 of the Consumer Protection Act 2019 w.e.f. 9th August 2019.

17 Section 21 of the Consumer Protection Act 1986 prescribing pecuniary jurisdiction of National Commission exceeding rupees twenty crore, is replaced by s. 58 of the Consumer Protection Act 2019 w.e.f. 9th August 2019.

18 *Dr. (Miss) Jasmine Patel* v *Dr. R.J. Manekshah* (1997)5 CTJ 766 (CP) (NCDRC); 1997(2) CPR 223 (NC); III(1997) CPJ 14 (NC); 2000(1) CPR 421 (Bom).

be dealt with.[19] Even the Division Bench of Kerala High Court held that the dispute with regard to medical negligence can be decided by Permanent Lok Adalat.[20]

The National Commission dismissed the complaint filed against the hospital for negligent performance of operation for removal of stone from urethra, resulting in paralysis on the right side of the body and necessitating second operation for removal of left kidney. By reversing the decision of the National Commission, it is held by the Supreme Court[1] that the complaint should have been taken to its logical conclusion by asking the parties to adduce evidence and rendered its findings on merit.

It is held by the Supreme Court,[2] that in complaints involving complicated issues requiring recording of evidence of experts, the complainant can be asked to approach the civil court for necessary relief. The view of the National Commission[3] is that the pendency of the civil suit cannot bar the proceedings before Consumer Forum when the complaint is filed against the doctor for deficiency in service. However, the issue with regard to concurrent jurisdiction of the Consumer Forum and other Forums to decide any dispute is resolved by the Supreme Court by holding that the jurisdiction of the Consumer Forum would not be barred and the power of the Consumer Forum to adjudicate upon the dispute could not be negated, if two different forums have jurisdiction to entertain the dispute in respect of the same subject-matter.[4] The enquiry contemplated under Consumer Protection Act 1986 would not permit cross-examination of large number of witnesses and production of documentary

19 *J.J. Merchant (Dr.)* v *Shrinath Chaturvedi* II(2002) CPJ 8; JT 2002(6) SC 1; (2002)6 SCC 635; AIR 2002 SC 2931; (2002)5 Scale 545.

20 *Dr. Ambika Kumary* v *State of Kerala* 2011(2) KLT 673; AIR 2012 Ker 16.

1 *Charan Singh* v *Healing Touch Hospital* (2000)7 SCC 668; AIR 2000 SC 3138; 2000(3) CPR 1; JT 2000 (Supp) 1 SC 26; (2000)6 Scale 431.

2 *Indian Medical Association* v *V.P. Shantha* AIR 1996 SC 550; (1995)6 SCC 651; III(1995) CPJ 1 (SC); 1995(3) CPR 412 (SC); (1995)3 CTJ 969 (SC) (CP); 1996 CCJ 1 (SC).

3 *Dr. (Mrs.) K. Sankari* v *Shailesh More* CDJ 2004 (Cons) Case No. 013.

4 *Kishore Lal* v *Chairman, Employees State Insurance Corporation* AIR 2007 SC 1819; (2007)4 SCC 579; II(2007) CPJ 25; JT 2007(6) SC 541; (2007)4 Supreme 775.

evidence by both parties.[5] The contrary view expressed by the State Commission, Chandigarh[6] is that instead of relegating the complainant to the remedy of the civil court, the Consumer Forum should decide the disputed questions on the basis of materials produced by the parties. The plea raised by the Nizam's Institute of Medical Sciences before the Supreme Court that the complicated questions of facts involving medical negligence cannot be decided by the National Commission was turned down, as the hospital and the attending doctors contested the complaint throughout without challenging the propriety of adjudication of the said dispute by the Commission.[7] The view of the National Commission[8] is that the consumer forum cannot come to the conclusion whether the hospital and the operating surgeon were negligent without the evidence of the experts as well as extracts of medical literature and without cross-examination of the experts giving evidence on affidavit.

The Consumer Courts cannot decide the dispute whether the professional fee charged by a doctor is reasonable or exorbitant, because the amount of professional fee charged by a doctor depends on number of factors *viz.*, qualification, experience, nature and quality of service rendered by him.[9] Similarly, the Consumer Court cannot entertain the complaint that the rates charged in a hospital were in excess of those mentioned in the brochure, because the price charged for rendering service is not a consumer dispute under s. 2(1)(*c*)* of the Consumer Protection Act 1986.[10] The law

5 *N.C. Sarin* v *Moolchand Kharaitiram Hospital* 1996(3) CPR 350 (Del); II(1996) CPJ 418 (Del).

6 *Pradeep Seth* v *Dr. Ashok Sarwal* I(1998) CPJ 612 (Chandigarh); 1998 CTJ 687 (CP) (SCDRC).

7 *Nizam's Institute of Medical Sciences* v *Prasanth S. Dhananka* (2009)6 SCC 1; JT 2009(2) SC 385; 2009 AIR SCW 3563; 2010 ACJ 38; (2009)4 Supreme 165.

8 *Baburao Satappa Irrannanavar* v *Kle Society's Hospital & Research Centre* 2006(3) CPR 92; 2006(2) CPC 623; IV(2006) CPJ 71.

9 *Dr. K.B. Kapoor* v *Phool Dev Parshad* III(1996) CPJ 477 (Chandigarh); *Bakshish Singh* v *Post Graduate Institute, Chandigarh* I(1999) CPJ 431 (Chandigarh); 1999 CCJ 483 (Chandigarh).

* Replaced by s. 2(6) of the Consumer Protection Act 2019 w.e.f. 9.8.2019.

10 *Bakshish Singh* v *Post Graduate Institute, Chandigarh* 1999 CCJ 483 (Chandigarh); I(1999) CPJ 431.

laid down by the National Commission[11] is that demand and acceptance of an exorbitant fee by a doctor cannot be deemed to be deficiency in service and as such the same is beyond the scope of scrutiny of the Consumer Courts in India.

The complainant had undergone bypass surgery in Calcutta, but he started feeling chest pain after coming back to his residence at Patna. It is held that the cause of action had arisen partly in Patna and therefore, the State Commission, Patna has jurisdiction to entertain the complaint.[12] The contrary view expressed by State Commission, Maharashtra,[13] is that the District Forum, Nasik had no jurisdiction to entertain the complaint when the doctor was in Bombay and treated the patient in Bombay.

(ii) ***Consumer—criteria for determination*** A consumer[14] means any person who hires or avails of any service for consideration which has been paid or promised or partly paid and partly promised, or under any system of deferred payment, and includes any beneficiary of such services other than the person who hires or avails of them, when such services are availed of with the approval of the person who paid or promised the consideration. The term "hire" used in s. 2(1)(*d*)(*ii*) of the Consumer Protection Act 1986 means "employ person for wages"[15] or "to procure the temporary use of services for stipulated payment".[16] Accordingly, a nursing home or a private hospital[17] hiring the service of a medical practitioner for consideration may be a consumer. However, it is held by the

11 *B.S. Hegde* v *Dr. Sudhansu Bhattacharya* (1994)2 CTJ 10 (CP) (NCDRC); 1993(3) CPR 414 (NC); III(1993) CPJ 388 (NC) reversing II(1992) CPJ 449 (Bom); (1993)1 CTJ 523 (SCDRC).

12 *Sarju Prasad* v *B.N. Birla Heart Research Centre* (1995)3 CTJ 183 (CP) (SCDRC).

13 *Deepak Behl* v *Dr. Narendra M. Rege* II(1999) CPJ 601 (Mumbai); 1999 CTJ 840 (CP) (SCDRC).

14 Section 2(1)(*d*)(*ii*) of the Consumer Protection Act 1986 since replaced by s. 2(7)(*ii*) of the Consumer Protection Act 2019 w.e.f. 9.8.2019.

15 *Concise Oxford Dictionary* by Judy Pearsall, 10th Ed. 1999.

16 *Shorter Oxford English Dictionary,* vol. I, 3rd Ed. 1944, reprinted with corrections and revised addenda 1959.

17 Section 2(1)(*d*) of the Consumer Protection Act 1986 since replaced by s. 2(6) of the Consumer Protection Act 2019 w.e.f. 9.8.2019.

Apex Court[18] that the service rendered by a medical officer to his employer under the contract of employment would be outside the purview of "Service" as defined in s. 2(1)(*o*) of the Consumer Protection Act 1986.*

The activity of providing medical assistance for payment carried on by hospitals and members of the medical profession falls within the scope of the expression "service" as defined in s. 2(1)(*o*)* of the Consumer Protection Act 1986, and in the event of any deficiency in the performance of such service the aggrieved party can invoke the remedies by filing a complaint before the Consumer Forum having jurisdiction.[19] A person claiming himself as consumer must satisfy three conditions *viz.* (*a*) service should be rendered to him; (*b*) service should be hired by him, and (*c*) for hiring service he should have paid consideration in the manner envisaged by s. 2(1)(*d*)(*ii*)** of the Consumer Protection Act 1986.[20] The law is now well-settled by the National Commission[1] that a patient availing of the professional service of medical practitioner on payment of fees is a consumer within the meaning of s. 2(1)(*d*)(*ii*)** of the Consumer Protection Act. The view of the National Commission is upheld by the Apex Court,[2] but the concept of professional service rendered on payment is made wider. According to the Apex Court, there are medical practitioners, Government hospitals, non-government hospitals,

18 *Indian Medical Association* v *V.P. Shantha* AIR 1996 SC 550; (1995)6 SCC 651; III(1995) CPJ 1 (SC); 1995(3) CPR 412 (SC); (1995)3 CTJ 969 (SC) (CP); 1996 CCJ 1 (SC).

* Replaced by s. 2(42) of the Consumer Protection Act 2019 w.e.f: 9.8.2019.

19 *Smt. Vasantha P. Nair* v *Messrs Cosmopolitan Hospital* 1991(2) CPR 155 (Ker); II(1991) CPJ 444 (Ker) affirmed by National Commission 1992(1)CPR 820 (NC); I(1992) CPJ 302 (NC).

** Replaced by s. 2(7)(*ii*) of the Consumer Protection Act 2019 w.e.f. 9.8.2019.

20 *Consumer Unity and Trust Society, Jaipur* v *State of Rajasthan* 1991(1) CPR 30 (Raj); II(1991) CPJ 56 (Raj).

1 *Dr. Sr. Louie* v *Smt. Kannolil Pathumma* I(1993) CPJ 30 (NC); 1993(1) CPR 422 (NC); (1993)1 CTJ 32 (NCDRC); *Consumer Education and Research Society* v *Dr. Ratilal B. Patel* III(1992) CPJ 25 (NC); (1993)1 CTJ 89 (NCDRC); *Cosmopolitan Hospital* v *Smt. Vasantha P. Nair* 1992(1) CPR 820 (NC); I(1992) CPJ 302 (NC).

2 *Indian Medical Association* v *V.P. Shantha* AIR 1996 SC 550; (1995)6 SCC 651; III(1995) CPJ 1 (SC); 1995(3) CPR 412 (SC); (1995)3 CTJ 969 (SC) (CP); 1996 CCJ 1 (SC).

nursing homes and dispensaries where free professional service is rendered to the patients belonging to the poor class but the bulk of the service is rendered to the patients on payment basis. The expenses incurred for providing free service are met out of the income from the service rendered to the paying patients. All persons who avail of the services by such doctors and hospitals are required to be treated on the same footing irrespective of the fact that some of them pay for the service and others avail of the same free of charge. The doctors and hospitals falling under this category are amenable to the provisions of the Consumer Protection Act along with the management of the hospital jointly and severally because the recipients of such free services are consumers. Where medical services rendered by the hospital are not free of charge for all patients, and the hospital collected fees for various items from the patient, he becomes consumer for any deficiency-in-service rendered by the doctor of the hospital.[3]

The scope of the Consumer Protection Act 1986 is not limited to the person who has the privity of contract with the person hiring the services, but also subsequent beneficiaries thereof, even though the latter may not be a party to the original contract. To be precise, the Consumer Protection Act has not confined itself to the original hirer alone, but equally extended it to subsequent beneficiaries of the services as well.[4] The law laid down by the Supreme Court[5] is that under s. 2(1)(*d*)(*ii*)* of the Consumer Protection Act 1986, a consumer would mean a person who hires or avails of any services and includes any beneficiary of such services other than the person who hires or avails of the services. When a young child is taken to a hospital by his parents and the child is treated by the doctor, the parents would come within the definition of "consumer" having hired the services and the young child would also become a consumer under the inclusive definition being a beneficiary of such services.

3 *Amblappa* v *Sriman D. Veerendra Heggade* 1999(3) CPR 72 (Bangalore).

4 *Dr. B.S. Sidhu* v *Secretary, Central Govt.* II(1991) CPJ 90 (Haryana).

5 *Spring Meadows Hospital* v *Harjot Ahluwalia through K.S. Ahluwalia* AIR 1998 SC 1801; (1998)4 SCC 39; 1998(1) CPR 1 (SC); I(1998) CPJ 1 (SC); 1998 CTJ 81 (SC) (CP); 1998 CCJ 521 (SC); JT 1998(2) SC 620; III(1998) SLT 684.

* Replaced by s. 2(7)(*ii*) of the Consumer Protection Act 2019 w.e.f. 9.8.2019.

According to the National Commission,[6] the parents of a young man having hired the services of the hospital, are consumers. When parents are maintaining the upkeep of the married daughter who is in a vegetative state, and parents are required to spend for the medical treatment of the married daughter, the claim of compensation of the parents cannot be refused on the ground that the husband of the married woman did not file the complaint.[7] The issue whether legal heirs of deceased consumer can invoke the jurisdiction of consumer courts is decided by the National Commission[8] by holding that the expression "consumer" defined in s. 2(1)(*d*)* of the Consumer Protection Act 1986, includes legal representatives of the deceased consumer. The contrary view expressed by the State Commission, Tamil Nadu,[9] is no longer good law. The contrary view that the legal representative of the deceased complainant has no right to sue for personal injury suffered by the deceased complainant cannot be the good law.[10]

The consistent view of the State Commission, Rajasthan,[11] Delhi,[12] Madras,[13] Punjab,[14] Karnataka,[15]

6 *Prasanth S. Dhananka* v *Nizam's Institute of Medical Sciences* 1999 CTJ 163 (CP) (NCDRC); I(1999) CPJ 43 (NC); 1999(1) CPR 42 (NC); 1999 CCJ 1099 (NC).

7 *Rajaram S. Parab* v *Dr. Kalpana Desai* 1998(3) CPR 398 (Mumbai); *Nirmala R. Parab* v *Dr. Kalpana Desai* III(1998) CPJ 66, 527, 692 (Mumbai); 1998 CTJ 807 (CP) (SCDRC); 1999 CCJ 1296 (Mah).

8 *Dr. Sr. Louie* v *Smt. Kannolil Pathumma* I(1993) CPJ 30 (NC); 1993(1) CPR 422 (NC); (1993)1 CTJ 32 (NCDRC); *Cosmopolitan Hospital* v *Smt. Vasantha P. Nair* 1992(1) CPR 820 (NC); I(1992) CPJ 302 (NC).

* Replaced by s. 2(7) of the Consumer Protection Act 2019 w.e.f. 9.8.2019.

9 *Mrs. Hemalatha Saptharishi* v *The Indian Oil Corporation Ltd.* III(1998) CPJ 533 (Chennai); *S. Tharani* v *Southern Railway Headquarters Hospital* II(1999) CPJ 485 (Chennai); 1999(3) CPR 336 (Chennai); *Aparna Doraisamy* v *Dr. Anandan* 1999(2) CPR 5 (Chennai).

10 *Malnad Hospital and Institute of Oncology Super Speciality Surgical Centre* v *H.C. Eranna* III(2012) CPJ 253.

11 *Hanuman Prasad Darban* v *Dr. C.S. Sharma* 1991(1) CPR 63 (Raj).

12 *Smt. Ram Kali* v *Delhi Administration* I(1991) CPJ 309 (Del).

13 *Kadarkarai Nadar* v *Rakkappan* 1994(1) CPR 359 (Mad).

14 *Pavitar Singh* v *State of Punjab* I(1994) CPJ 397 (Punj); 1994(1) CPR 367 (Punj); (1994)2 CTJ 88 (SCDRC); *Paramjit Kaur* v *State of Punjab* 1998 CCJ 1384.

15 *Sowbhagya Prasad* v *State of Karnataka* I(1994) CPJ 402 (Bangalore); (1994)2 CTJ 93 (CP) (SCDRC).

Maharashtra[16] and Madhya Pradesh,[17] is that a patient enjoying professional service of the doctor free of cost from Government hospitals cannot be considered as a consumer within the meaning of s. 2(1)(*d*)* of the Consumer Protection Act 1986. The patient who avails of medical treatment from a doctor free of charge as family friend, is not a consumer for the purpose of the Consumer Protection Act 1986.[1] A gratuitous patient is not a consumer for availing of medical services free of cost.[2] The donation collected from the patient cannot be treated as consideration for the professional service rendered by the doctor.[3] Mere charging of room rent from affluent patients for the wards in private charitable hospital, would not bring the patients within the ambit of a consumer.[4] Similarly, the complaint filed against Central Government Health Scheme for deficiency of service is dismissed because the professional service under CGHS is rendered free of charge.[5] The professional service rendered to the railway employees by railway hospital, on payment of nominal charges is beyond the scope of scrutiny of the Consumer Courts in India.[6] The payment of a token amount for registration or a token compulsory contribution for medical treatment cannot be classified as "consideration" for availing the "service" under s. 2(1)(*o*)** of the Consumer Protection Act 1986.[7] However,

16 *Laxman Thamappa Kotgiri* v *Union of India* 1998 CCJ 1093 (Bom); 1998(1) CPR 665 (Bom).

17 *Smt. Rajbai* v *Madhya Pradesh Shasan Sachiv Lok Swasthya Avam Pariwar Kalyan Nibhag* I(1999) CPJ 578 (Bhopal); 2000 CTJ 379 (CP) (SCDRC); *Pushpa Bai* v *Dr. S. Joseph* II(2000) CPJ 566 (Bhopal).

* Replaced by s. 2(7) of the Consumer Protection Act 2019 w.e.f. 9.8.2019.

1 *Mappooyan* v *Dr. Premavathy Elango* 1991(2) CPR 460 (Mad).

2 *Harbhajan Singh* v *Dayanand Medical College* 1994(1) CPR 518 (Punj); (1994)2 CTJ 258 (CP) (SCDRC); III(1996) CPJ 263; 1997 CCJ 952 (Punj).

3 *C.V. Madhusudhana* v *Director, Jayadeva Institute of Cardiology* II(1992) CPJ 519 (Bangalore).

4 *Dr. Ravinder Gupta* v *Ganga Devi* 1993(3) CPR 255 (Haryana).

5 *Prem Chand Sharma* v *Director, Central Government Health Scheme* 1992(2) CPR 51 (Del).

6 *Laxman Thamappa Kotgiri* v *Union of India* 1998(1) CPR 665 (Bom); 1998 CCJ 1093 (Mah); *S. Tharani* v *Southern Railway Headquarters Hospital* II(1999) CPJ 485 (Chennai); 1999(3) CPR 336 (Chennai).

** Replaced by s. 2(42) of the Consumer Protection Act 2019 w.e.f. 9.8.2019.

7 *Anthony Dass A* v *Ex Engineer, Earth Movers Division, BEML* III(1997) CPJ 224 (Bangalore); 1998 CCJ 1301 (Kant).

the view of the National Commission[8] is that an employee of Visakhapatnam Port Trust and members of his family, who are entitled to receive free medical treatment as per conditions of service, can be considered as consumers under the Consumer Protection Act 1986.

The principle of law enunciated by the National Commission[9] is that persons who avail themselves of the facility of medical treatment in Government hospitals are not consumers and the said facility offered in Government hospitals cannot be regarded as service "hired" for "consideration" for the purpose of the Consumer Protection Act 1986. The Supreme Court[10] has augmented and amplified the rights of the patients who are availing medical services free of charge, so that some recipients of the free services can invoke the remedies provided under the Consumer Protection Act 1986. Accordingly service rendered by doctor or hospitals or nursing homes to some patients on payment of charges and to other patients free of charge, would fall within the ambit of "service" as defined in s. 2(1)(*o*)* of the Consumer Protection Act 1986 and the recipients of such free professional service would be "consumers" under s. 2(1)(*d*)** of the Consumer Protection Act 1986.

It is held by the National Commission[11] that the complainant who, being a close relation of colleague doctor, availed of free medical treatment from the doctor, is a consumer, because all other patients pay for the service of the doctor. Accordingly, service rendered gratuitously by the doctor to the relation of colleague doctor in nursing home where patients are treated on payment of charges will fall within the ambit of "service" under s. 2(1)(*o*)* of the Consumer

8 *G. Kondala Rao* v *The Board of Trustees* III(2006) CPJ 97.

9 *Consumer Unity and Trust Society, Jaipur* v *State of Rajasthan* 1991(1) CPR 241 (NC); 1(1992) CPJ 259 (NC); (1993)1 CTJ 89 (NCDRC); *Mrs. Mable Roosevelt* v *State of Kerala* 1991(1) CPR 330 (NC).

10 *Indian Medical Association* v *V.P. Shantha* AIR 1996 SC 550; (1995)6 SCC 651; III(1995) CPJ 1 (SC); 1995(3) CPR 412 (SC); (1995)3 CTJ 969 (SC) (CP); 1996 CCJ 1 (SC).

* Replaced by s. 2(42) of the Consumer Protection Act 2019 w.e.f. 9.8.2019.

** Replaced by s. 2(7) of the Consumer Protection Act 2019 w.e.f. 9.8.2019.

11 *Vijay H. Mankar* v *Dr. (Mrs.) Mangla Bansod* 2000 CTJ 101 (CP) (NC DRC); I(2000) CPJ 37 (NC); 2000 CCJ 610.

Protection Act 1986. It is held by the State Commission, West Bengal,[12] that a patient being an employee of the employer registered under the ESI Scheme is consumer for availing of medical service from the ESI hospitals.

3 Liability under general law

(i) ***Individual liability*** Under the general principles of tortious liability the medical practitioner who caused injury or damage by negligence is bound to pay compensation. The medical man is bound to compensate to the family of the deceased patient whose death is caused by his wrongful act, neglect or default.[13] Even the executors, administrators, heirs or representatives of any deceased medical practitioner are liable to pay compensation for any wrong committed by the deceased in his lifetime and for which he would have been subjected to an action.[14] The maxim *actio personalis moritur cum persona* is modified in India by s. 306 of the Indian Succession Act 1925, which lays down that all rights to prosecute or defend any action for or against a person at the time of his death, survive to or against his executor or administrator, excepting causes of action for defamation, assault or other personal injuries not causing death.[15] In *Sidaway*[16] the House of Lords did not object to action brought by Mrs. Sidaway against the executors of the estate of the deceased neurosurgeon, Mr. Murray A. Falconer, though the allegation of negligence was not established in this case. Where the complainant hired the service of the hospital and there was no privity of contract between the doctor and the complainant, the doctor would not be liable to pay compensation, but the hospital would be liable to pay compensation awarded to the complainant.[17] The National Commission[18] has clarified that

12 *Ranjit Kumar Das* v *Medical Officer, ESI Hospital, Manicktola* 1998(1) CPR 165 (Cal); III(1997) CPJ 336 (Cal); 1999 CCJ 70 (WB).

13 Section 1A of the Fatal Accidents Act 1855.

14 Section 1 of the Legal Representatives' Suits Act 1855.

15 *Maharani Dey* v *Debabrata Bardhan* 1984 ACJ 95; AIR 1983 Gau 84.

16 *Sidaway* v *Bethlem Royal Hospital Governors* [1985] AC 871; [1985]1 All ER 643; [1985]2 WLR 480; 129 Sol Jo 154; (1985)1 BMLR 132 (HL).

17 *Shibu* v *St. Joseph Hospital* 1995(3) CPR 177 (Ker).

18 *Balbir Singh Makol* v *Chairman, Sir Ganga Ram Hospital* 2001(1) CLT 495.

the liability of a doctor sued for causing personal injury due to negligence extinguishes on his death and his legal representatives cannot be brought on record. However, if the award is passed against the doctor on completion of the proceeding, the amount of compensation can be recovered from the estate of the deceased doctor by bringing his legal representatives on record.

(ii) *Vicarious liability* "Vicarious" means one "that takes or supplies the place of another".[19] The vicarious liability means a taking of liability of one person by another person.[20] The liability of the hospital authorities extends to the fault of doctors and other employees whether their employment is permanent or temporary or casual, paid or honorary, whole-time or part-time as in the case of visiting physicians or surgeons.[21] The hospital authority is vicariously liable for the negligence of its Radiographers,[1] House-surgeons,[2] whole-time Assistant Medical Officers[3] and Anaesthetists.[4] The private hospital or nursing home will be liable to pay compensation for negligence of its staff including medical practitioner, if there is an implied contract of treatment between the patient and the said hospital or nursing home. To paraphrase Lord Denning:[5]

> "The authorities who run a hospital, be they local authorities, Government boards, or any other corporation,

19 *The Shorter Oxford English Dictionary*, vol. II, (3rd Ed. 1944, Reprinted with corrections and revised addenda 1959).

20 Lord Denning, MR. in *Launchbury* v *Morgans* [1971]2 QB 245 reversed by *Morgans* v *Launchbury* [1973] AC 127; [1972]2 WLR 1217; 116 Sol Jo 396; [1972]2 All ER 606; [1972]1 Lloyd's Rep 483.

21 Ramaswamy Ayer's *Law of Torts*, 8th Ed., p. 521.

1 *Gold* v *Essex County Council* [1942]2 KB 293; [1942]2 All ER 237; 112 LJKB 1; 167 LT 166; 86 Sol Jo 295 (CA).

2 *Collins* v *Hertfordshire County Council* [1947] KB 598; [1947]1 All ER 633; *Cassidy* v *Ministry of Health* [1951]2 KB 343; [1951]1 All ER 574; 95 Sol Jo 253 (CA).

3 *Cassidy* v *Ministry of Health* [1951]2 KB 343; [1951]1 All ER 574; 95 Sol Jo 253 (CA).

4 *Roe* v *Minister of Health* [1954]2 QB 66; [1954]2 All ER 131; [1954]2 WLR 915; 98 Sol Jo 319 (CA).

5 *Cassidy* v *Ministry of Health* [1951]2 KB 343; [1951]1 All ER 574; 95 Sol Jo 253 (CA).

are in law under the self-same duty as the humblest doctor; whenever they accept a patient for treatment, they must use reasonable care and skill to cure him of his ailment. .... They must do it by the staff which they employ; and if their staff are negligent in giving the treatment, they are just as liable for that negligence as is anyone else who employs others to do his duties for him."

A young footballer aged 17 years suffered a cardiac arrest resulting in catastrophic brain damage while he was playing for the club after signing contract with the club. He had an abnormal report of ECG suggesting cardiac disease. The cardiologist recommended for clinical review even when scan did not indicate any sign of hypertrophic cardiomyopathy. The club doctor did not carry out clinical review and formed opinion that the young footballer is not at risk and may continue to play football. The club was held vicariously liable for the negligence of the club doctor who ignored the advice of the cardiologist for clinical review.[6]

The Supreme Court of India,[7] held the hospital liable to pay compensation for the negligence of its attending doctor and unqualified nurse, as the doctor allowed the nurse to give intravenous injection to the patient against advice of the consultant doctor and thereby contributed to the irreparable brain damage of the minor patient. The State Commission, West Bengal,[8] directed the ESI Hospital to pay compensation for not giving timely medical treatment to the patient and for refusal to admit the patient for treatment of acute pain in abdomen due to non-availability of bed. The hospital was directed to pay compensation to the father of the minor patient suffering from partial disability of the left leg on account of negligence of the unqualified nurse of the hospital in administering paracetamol injection on the left

6 *Hamed* v *Mills* [2015] EWHC 298 (QB).

7 *Spring Meadows Hospital* v *Harjot Ahluwalia through K.S. Ahluwalia* AIR 1998 SC 1801; (1998)4 SCC 39; 1998(1) CPR 1 (SC); I(1998) CPJ 1 (SC); 1998 CTJ 81 (SC) (CP); 1998 CCJ 521 (SC); JT 1998(2) SC 620; III(1998) SLT 684.

8 *Ranjit Kumar Das* v *Medical Officer, ESI Hospital, Manicktola* 1998(1) CPR 165 (Cal); III(1997) CPJ 336 (Cal); 1999 CCJ 70 (WB).

buttock.[9] The hospital was held vicariously liable to pay compensation for slipping of needle into the stomach of the patient after getting detached from the syringe when the doctor of the said hospital was irrigating the mouth after extraction of right molar teeth of the patient.[10] The hospital was held vicariously liable for negligence of the doctors on the panel of the hospital and the visiting doctors of the hospital, who treated the patient with overdose of steroid contrary to the established treatment protocol and thereby the patient died.[11]

The Supreme Court of India[12] held the hospital vicariously liable for the acts of negligence of the paediatrician and ophthalmologist who did not screen the pre-term baby for Retinopathy of Prematurity (RoP) during four weeks of stay in the hospital and even during review and routine check up on two dates in the OPD of the hospital after his discharge and thereby the child became blind.

The State is vicariously liable for the tortious acts of its servants or agents which are not committed in the exercise of its sovereign functions or in the exercise of sovereign powers delegated to such public servants.[13] The work of medical relief undertaken by Government through Primary Health Centre is not a sovereign function of the State and as such the defence of sovereign immunity must fail.[14] Running a hospital for treatment of the general public is a welfare activity undertaken by the Government and it cannot be in exercise of sovereign power of the State.[15] Accordingly, the

9 *A.M. Mathew* v *Director, Karuna Hospital* 1998(1) CPR 39 (Ker); I(1998) CPJ 476 (Ker); 1999 CCJ 960 (Ker).

10 *Amblappa* v *Sriman D. Veerendra Heggade* 1999(3) CPR 72 (Bangalore).

11 *Balaram Prasad* v *Kunal Saha* (2014)1 SCC 384.

12 *Maharaja Agrasen Hospital* v *Master Rishabh Sharma* 2019 SCC Online SC 1658.

13 *State of Rajasthan* v *Vidyawati* AIR 1962 SC 933; 1958-68 ACJ 296 (SC); (1963)1 SCJ 307.

14 *The "Ad Hoc" Committee, the Indian Insurance Company Association Pool, Bombay* v *Smt. Radhabai* AIR 1976 MP 164.

15 *State of Haryana* v *Smt. Santra* 2000 CTJ 481 (SC) (CP); I(2000) CPJ 53 (SC).

State would be vicariously liable for damages payable on account of negligence of its doctors and other employees.[16] The Supreme Court[17] held the State of Haryana vicariously liable for negligence of the doctor in a Government Hospital in performance of sterilization operation resulting in birth of an unwanted child. The Union Territory of Chandigarh and the hospital authority were also held vicariously liable for deficiency-in-service on the part of the doctors of the Government Hospital in rendering postoperative care of the patient resulting in her permanent disability by way of amputation of leg.[18]

The view of the UK Supreme Court[19] is that the vicarious liability can apply to any relationship where damage is caused wrongfully by an individual carrying on activities as an integral part of the employer and for the benefit of the employer. The Union of India and States are liable for damages occasioned by the negligence of employees in the service of the Government if the negligence is such as would render an ordinary employer liable.[20] The Government is required to be impleaded as a party to the suit instituted against a Medical Officer of Government Hospital for damages in respect of any act alleged to have been done by him in his official capacity.[1] Like a private employer, the State is liable to pay compensation for negligence of its medical practitioner who have committed the wrong in course of their employment as public servant. However, the State is not vicariously liable for negligence committed by medical practitioners of Government hospitals in course of their private practice or beyond the course of their employment as public officers.

16 *Achutrao Haribhau Khodwa* v *State of Maharashtra* (1996)2 SCC 634; (1996)4 CTJ 950 (SC) (CP); 1996 ACJ 505.

17 *State of Haryana* v *Smt. Santra* 2000 CTJ 481 (SC) (CP); I(2000) CPJ 53 (SC).

18 *Sukhwarsha Rani* v *General Hospital, through its Medical Superintendent* 2000(1) CPR 337 (Chandigarh).

19 *Cox* v *Ministry of Justice* [2016] UKS 10; [2016] AC 660.

20 *Kasturi Lal* v *State of Uttar Pradesh* AIR 1965 SC 1039; (1965)1 SCR 375.

1 Order 27, r. 5A of the Code of Civil Procedure 1908.

The Supreme Court has observed that non-joinder of the treating doctor and nursing staff cannot result in dismissal of the claim petition filed against the hospital or the nursing home on the ground of medical negligence. The hospital or the clinic is vicariously responsible for the acts of their permanent staff as well as staff whose services are temporarily requisitioned for the treatment of the patients. When the hospital fails to discharge its duties through its doctors employed on permanent basis or contract basis, the hospital will be vicariously liable and the complaint filed against the hospital cannot be dismissed for not impleading a particular doctor employed on contract basis.[2]

The State was exempted from paying compensation to the victim of medical negligence, where the claim was made against the surgeon as the person primarily liable for damages and against the State of Kerala as vicariously liable for non-performance of an emergency operation by the surgeon of the Government Hospital.[3] However, the Government could not escape vicarious liability for negligence of the surgeon and anaesthetist attached to Government hospital.[4] The complainant suffered damage due to deficiency of service rendered by the doctor of the hospital. As the discharge certificate issued by the hospital was signed by the said doctor and as the bill of the hospital included the professional fees of the said doctor, the hospital was held vicariously liable in respect of the claim for compensation.[5] The National Commission[6] held the hospital vicariously liable for negligence of the staff of ICCU, who did not keep vigil when

2 *Savita Garg (Smt.)* v *Director, National Heart Institute* (2004)8 SCC 56.

3 *Dr. T.T. Thomas* v *Elisa* AIR 1987 Ker 52; 1987(1) ACJ 192; (1987)1 ACC 461; (1987)2 TAC 50; 1986 Ker LT 1026.

4 *Dr. P. Narasimha Rao* v *Gundavarapu Jaya Prakash* AIR 1990 AP 207; (1990)1 ACC 468; 1990(1) ACJ 350; (1989)3 Andh LT 564; (1989)2 APLJ (HC) 491.

5 *Mrs. K.K. Radha* v *Dr. G.U. Sekhar* III(1994) CPJ 376 (Ker); (1994)2 CTJ 790 (CP) (SCDRC) confirmed by N.C. in *P.P. Ismail* v *Mrs. K.K. Radha* 1997(2) CPR 171 (NC); I(1998) CPJ 16 (NC); (1997)5 CTJ 685 (CP) (NCDRC); 1999 CCJ 99 (NC).

6 *Bhajanlal Gupta* v *Mool Chand Kharaiti Ram Hospital* I(2001) CPJ 31 (NC).

the oxygen tube was pulled out by the patient resulting in acute breathlessness.

The nurse gave injection "Tracurium" in the postoperative ward and thereby the patient died, whereas the injection should have been given in the operation theatre only by or under the supervision of an anaesthetist. The National Commission[7] held the hospital vicariously liable for negligent act of the nurse and enhanced the amount of compensation awarded by the State Commission from ₹5 lakh to ₹20 lakh.

The doctor conducted the operation as an employee of the nursing home owned by the wife of the doctor. It is held by Kerala High Court that the doctor is primarily liable for his negligent act and the owner of the nursing home is vicariously liable for the negligent conduct of its employee doctor.[8] The orthopaedician, cardiologist and anaesthetist were held jointly and severally liable for the death of the patient in the midst of the operation, though the liability was apportioned as 30%, 60% and 10% respectively.[9] The Supreme Court[10] directed the State of Maharashtra to pay compensation to the legal representatives of a deceased patient who died due to negligence of the Government doctors in conducting sterilization operation in Government hospital. The State of Rajasthan was held vicariously liable for death of a patient during laparoscopic tubectomy operation in a Government hospital without having adequate resuscitative facilities *e.g.* endotracheal anaesthesia, defibrillator and cardiac monitoring equipments.[11] The State of Karnataka was held vicariously liable for pain, suffering and medical expenditure of a lady who had undergone laparoscopic sterilization operation in a local camp along with hundreds of other ladies under the care of the doctors working under State of Karnataka.[12]

7 *B.T. Sridhar* v *Vokkaligara Sangha* IV(2015) CPJ 215 (NCDRC).
8 *Joseph* alias *Pappachan* v *Dr. George Moonjely* 1995(1) ACJ 253.
9 *Arunaben D. Kothari* v *Navdeep Clinic* 1996(3) CPR 20 (Guj); III(1996) CPJ 605 (Guj); (1997)5 CTJ 533 (CP) (SCDRC); 1998 CCJ 972 (Guj).
10 *Achutrao Haribhau Khodwa* v *State of Maharashtra* (1996)2 SCC 634; (1996)4 CTJ 950 (SC) (CP); 1996 ACJ 505.
11 *Rajmal* v *State of Rajasthan* 1996 ACJ 1166.
12 *Sou Shevanta* v *State of Karnataka* CDJ 2005 Kar HC 343; 2006 ACJ 2677.

4 Liability under consumer law

(i) ***Professional service under consumer law*** The "service" defined in s. 2(1)(*o*)* of the Consumer Protection Act 1986 brings within its sweep service of any description available to potential users. It is true that the professional services of doctors, engineers, lawyers are not specifically mentioned in s. 2(1)(*o*)* of the Consumer Protection Act 1986. The facilities of some services mentioned in s. 2(1)(*o*)* of the Consumer Protection Act 1986 are merely illustrative of the definition of service, which is wide, but not exhaustive. Naturally, the professional services of doctors, lawyers, engineers, architects and technical services of mechanics, contractors, builders, fall within the ambit of s. 2(1)(*o*)* of the Consumer Protection Act 1986 because these services are available to potential users on payment of consideration.

The professional service rendered by a medical practitioner for consideration is service within the ambit of the Consumer Protection Act 1986.[13] The National Commission[14] has settled the law by holding that the professional service rendered by a medical practitioner in his consulting room or clinic or hospital on payment of consideration amounts to hiring of service for consideration, which is amenable to the jurisdiction of the Consumer Courts established under Consumer Protection Act 1986. The view of the National Commission is upheld by the Supreme Court[15] by arriving at the conclusion that service rendered to a patient by a medical practitioner (except where the doctor renders service free of charge to every patient or under a contract of personal service), by way of consultation, diagnosis and treatment, both medicinal and surgical, would fall within the ambit of

* Replaced by s. 2(42) of the Consumer Protection Act 2019 w.e.f. 9.8.2019.

13 Section 2(1)(*o*) and s. 1(4) of the Consumer Protection Act 1986 now replaced by s. 2(42) and s. 1(4) of the Consumer Protection Act 2019 respectively w.e.f. 9.8.2019.

14 *Cosmopolitan Hospital* v *Smt. Vasantha P. Nair* 1992(1) CPR 820 (NC); I(1992) CPJ 302 (NC); *Dr. Sr. Louie* v *Smt. Kannolil Pathumma* I(1993) CPJ 30 (NC); 1993(1) CPR 422 (NC); (1993)1 CTJ 32 (NCDRC); *Consumer Education and Research Society* v *Dr. Ratilal B. Patel* III(1992) CPJ 25 (NC); (1993)1 CTJ 89 (NCDRC).

15 *Indian Medical Association* v *V.P. Shantha* AIR 1996 SC 550; (1995)6 SCC 651; III(1995) CPJ 1 (SC); 1995(3) CPR 412 (SC); (1995)3 CTJ 969 (SC) (CP); 1996 CCJ 1 (SC).

"service" as defined in s. 2(1)(*o*)* of the Consumer Protection Act. The fact that medical practitioners belong to the medical profession and are subject to the disciplinary control of the Medical Council of India or State Medical Councils constituted under the provisions of the Indian Medical Council Act would not exclude the services rendered by them from the ambit of the Consumer Protection Act.

The hospital is liable to take reasonable care about the treatment of the patient, if the services of the hospital are hired by the patient. When a patient is admitted to the hospital on payment and put in charge of a doctor, what really takes place is hiring of the service of the doctor by the patient. If the hospital provides other services, the patient is really hiring these services also.[16] A pensioner who avails of the facility of free supply of medicines under the Rajasthan State Pensioners' Medical Concessions Scheme by making monthly contributions at the rate prescribed, while in service, has hired the services in exchange for the contribution, and is, therefore, a consumer within the meaning of s. 2(1)(*d*)** of the Consumer Protection Act 1986.[17] An employee of the employer registered under ESI Scheme is consumer for availing of medical service from the ESI hospitals.[18]

Relying on *"V.P. Shantha"*[19] wherein the Apex Court expounded the proposition that where medical service is rendered as part of terms and conditions of service, the same would not amount to free service and would constitute "service" for the purpose of Consumer Protection Act, the National Commission[20] held that the doctors who provide medical treatment under the Central Government Health Scheme in a Government hospital free of charge, would be covered under the Consumer Protection Act.

* Replaced by s. 2(42) of the Consumer Protection Act 2019 w.e.f. 9.8.2019.

16 *Muralidhar Eknath Masane* v *Sushrusha Citizen Co-op. Hospital* 1995(1) CPR 606 (Bom).

** Replaced by s. 2(7) of the Consumer Protection Act 2019 w.e.f. 9.8.2019.

17 *Treasury Officer and Member Secretary, Pensioner Medical Fund* v *G.K. Joshi* I(1996) CPJ 22 (Raj).

18 *Ranjit Kumar Das* v *Medical Officer, ESI Hospital, Manicktola* 1998(1) CPR 165 (Cal); III(1997) CPJ 336 (Cal); 1999 CCJ 70 (WB).

19 *Indian Medical Association* v *V.P. Shantha* (supra footnote 15).

20 *Arvind Pandey* v *Dr. (Mrs.) Sulekha Saran* 2012(3) CPR 142; III(2012) CPJ 357.

The two categories of services are exempted from the purview of the Consumer Protection Act 1986. Section 2(1)(*o*)* of the Consumer Protection Act excludes service rendered free of charge and contract of personal service.

(ii) *Professional service free of cost* It is well-settled by the National Commission[1] that the facility of medical treatment offered in the Government hospital free of charge does not constitute service within the meaning of s. 2(1)(*o*)* of the Consumer Protection Act. This view of the National Commission is upheld by the Apex Court in the case of *Indian Medical Association* v *V.P. Shantha*[2] wherein it is laid down that the service rendered by a medical practitioner or hospital or nursing home free of charges, falls outside the expression "service" defined in s. 2(1)(*o*)* of the Consumer Protection Act.

Professional service rendered gratuitously by the doctor is beyond the scope of scrutiny of the Consumer Courts.[3] The question whether the patients of "paying ward" in Government hospital are availing of medical service for consideration was the subject-matter of scrutiny before the National Commission[4] which has held that with regard to "paying wards" the payments are specifically related to special rooms or beds, and the medical facilities available in a Government hospital are common to all patients inclusive of those in the pay wards, without any discrimination.

The question whether contribution to Central Government Health Scheme is consideration for medical service availed of in appropriate Government hospital is settled by the National Commission[5] which lays down that the contribution

* Replaced by s. 2(42) of the Consumer Protection Act 2019 w.e.f. 9.8.2019.

1 *Consumer Unity and Trust Society, Jaipur* v *State of Rajasthan* 1991(1) CPR 241 (NC); I(1992) CPJ 259 (NC); (1993)1 CTJ 89 (NCDRC); *Mrs. Mable Roosevelt* v *State of Kerala* 1991(1) CPR 330 (NC).

2 AIR 1996 SC 550; (1995)6 SCC 651; III(1995) CPJ 1 (SC); 1995(3) CPR 412 (SC); (1995)3 CTJ 969 (SC) (CP); 1996 CCJ 1 (SC).

3 *Harbhajan Singh* v *Dayanand Medical College* 1994(1) CPR 518 (Punj); (1994)2 CTJ 258 (CP) (SCDRC); III(1996) CPJ 263; 1997 CCJ 952 (Punj); *Mapooyan* v *Dr. Premavathy Elango* 1991(2) CPR 460 (Mad).

4 *Consumer Unity and Trust Society, Jaipur* v *State of Rajasthan* 1991(1) CPR 241 (NC); I(1992) CPJ 259 (NC); (1993)1 CTJ 89 (NCDRC).

5 *Consumer Unity and Trust Society, Jaipur* v *State of Rajasthan* 1991(1) CPR 241 (NC); I(1992) CPJ 259 (NC); (1993)1 CTJ 89 (NCDRC).

to CGHS should be taken to be in lieu of free treatment in the diverse dispensaries as well as the free provision of medicines from those dispensaries. The principle enunciated by the National Commission[6] is that a Government servant under the Central Government Health Scheme is not a "consumer" within the meaning of s. 2(1)(*d*)* of the Consumer Protection Act 1986, and the services rendered to him under CGHS, do not constitute "service" as defined under s. 2(1)(o)** of the said Act. The complaint filed against Central Government Health Scheme for deficiency of service was dismissed because the professional service under CGHS is rendered free of charge.[7] Accordingly, the professional service rendered by the doctors free of cost in Government hospital is beyond the scope of scrutiny of the Consumer Courts in India. The service rendered by the railway hospitals for railway employees on payment of nominal charges, cannot be said to be service for consideration and as such remedy for deficiency in service is not available under the Consumer Protection Act 1986.[8]

The law well-settled by the Supreme Court[9] is that the service rendered by a medical practitioner attached to Government hospital, non-government hospital or nursing home or health centre or dispensary where such services are rendered free of charge to everybody, would not be service under s. 2(1)(*o*)** of the Consumer Protection Act 1986. The payment of a token amount for registration purpose only at the hospital or nursing home would not alter the position. It is also made clear by the Supreme Court that service rendered at a Government hospital or non-government hospital or nursing home where services are rendered on payment of charges to

6 *Additional Director, CGHS, Pune* v *Dr. R.L. Butani* 1996(1) CPR 136 (NC); I(1996) CPJ 255 (NC); 1996 CCJ 1017 (NC).

* Replaced by s. 2(7) of the Consumer Protection Act 2019 w.e.f. 9.8.2019.

** Replaced by s. 2(42) of the Consumer Protection Act 2019 w.e.f. 9.8.2019.

7 *Prem Chand Sharma* v *Director, Central Government Health Scheme* 1992(2) CPR 51 (Del).

8 *Laxman Thamappa Kotgiri* v *Union of India* 1998(1) CPR 665 (Bom); 1998 CCJ 1093 (Mah).

9 *Indian Medical Association* v *V.P. Shantha* AIR 1996 SC 550; (1995)6 SCC 651; III(1995) CPJ 1 (SC); 1995(3) CPR 412 (SC); (1995)3 CTJ 969 (SC) (CP); 1996 CCJ 1 (SC).

some persons and rendered free of charge to other persons availing of such services, would fall within the ambit of expression "service" defined in s. 2(1)(*o*)* of the Consumer Protection Act, irrespective of the fact that the service is rendered free of charge to persons who are not in a position to pay for such services. Accordingly free service rendered by a medical practitioner may be service under s. 2(1)(*o*)* of the Consumer Protection Act, and the recipient a "consumer" under the said Act. By following the decision of the Supreme Court it is held by the National Commission[10] that "service" rendered gratuitously by the doctor to the relation of colleague doctor in the nursing home where patients are treated on payment of charges, fall within the ambit of "service" under s. 2(1)(*o*)* of the Consumer Protection Act 1986.

According to the dictum of the Apex Court,[11] service rendered by a medical practitioner or hospital or nursing home cannot be regarded as service rendered free of charge, if the person availing of the service has taken an insurance policy for medical care whereunder the charges will be reimbursed by the insurance company. Similarly, where, as a part of the condition of service, the employer bears the expenses of medical treatment of an employee and his dependants, the medical service rendered to such an employee and his dependants would not be considered free of charge.

(iii) *Contract of personal service* The "contract of personal service" refers, *inter alia*, to the relationship of master and servant where the latter has entered into an agreement with the former for employment.[12] There is distinction between "contract of personal service" and "contract for professional service". Hilbery, J[13] has pointed out that in contract for service master can order what is to be done, but in contract of service master cannot only order what is to be done, but

* Replaced by s. 2(42) of the Consumer Protection Act 2019 w.e.f. 9.8.2019.

10 *Vijay H. Mankar* v *Dr. (Mrs.) Mangla Bansod* 2000 CTJ 101 (CP) (NCDRC); I(2000) CPJ 37 (NC); 2000 CCJ 610.

11 *Indian Medical Association* v *V.P. Shantha,* (supra footnote 9).

12 *Life Insurance Corporation of India* v *Sheela Devi* 1992(1) CPR 318 (Haryana).

13 *Collins* v *Hertfordshire County Council* [1947] KB 598; [1947]1 All ER 633.

also how it is to be done. The contract for professional service is distinguished from contract of personal service by Fletcher Moulton, LJ[14] in following ways:

> "The greater the amount of direct control exercised over the person rendering the services by the person contracting for them the stronger the grounds for holding it to be a contract of (personal) service, and similarly, the greater the degree of independence of such control the greater the probability that the services rendered are of the nature of professional services."

The National Commission[15] has categorically laid down that a contract of personal service involves a master-servant relationship which is wholly different from a doctor-patient relationship and it will be totally wrong to call the professional service rendered by a medical man to his patients as "personal service" coming within the exempted category mentioned in s. 2(1)(*o*)* of the Consumer Protection Act 1986.

The conflict of judicial opinion among the State Commissions as to whether the relationship between medical practitioner and his patient is contract of personal service and thereby excluded from the term "service" in s. 2(1)(*o*)* of the Consumer Protection Act, has been set at rest by the National Commission[16] which has laid down that the professional service rendered by the doctor on receiving consideration paid by the patient cannot be a contract of personal service and therefore such medical services fall within the ambit of s. 2(1)(*o*)* of the Consumer Protection Act 1986.

A "contract of personal service" has to be distinguished from "contract for personal services". It is laid down by our

14 *Simmons* v *Health Laundry Co.* [1910]1 KB 543; 79 LJKB 395; 102 LJ 210; 54 Sol Jo 392 (CA).

15 *Cosmopolitan Hospital* v *Smt. Vasantha P. Nair* 1992(1) CPR 820 (NC); I(1992) CPJ 302 (NC).

* Replaced by s. 2(42) of the Consumer Protection Act 2019 w.e.f. 9.8.2019.

16 *Cosmopolitan Hospital* v *Smt. Vasantha P. Nair* 1992(1) CPR 820 (NC); I(1992) CPJ 302 (NC); *Consumer Education and Research Society* v *Dr. Ratilal B. Patel* III(1992) CPJ 25 (NC); (1993)1 CTJ 89 (NCDRC); *Dr. Sr. Louie* v *Smt. Kannolil Pathumma* 1993(1) CPR 422 (NC); I(1993) CPJ 30 (NC); (1993)1 CTJ 32 (NCDRC).

Apex Court[17] that since there is no relationship of master and servant between the doctor and the patient, the contract between the medical practitioner and his patient cannot be treated as a contract of personal service, but is a contract for services and the service rendered by the medical practitioner to his patient under such a contract is not covered by the exclusionary part of the definition of "service" contained in s. 2(1)(*o*)* of the Consumer Protection Act. Accordingly, the service rendered by a Medical Officer to his employer under the contract of employment would be outside the purview of "service" as defined in s. 2(1)(*o*)* of the Consumer Protection Act.

The State Commission, Bombay,[18] did not award any compensation against an anaesthetist, because there was no "privity of contract" between the patient and the anaesthetist whose service was hired by the surgeon for the patient. On appeal, it is held by the National Commission that the anaesthetist who participated in the process of delivery of medical services to the beneficiary is as much liable as the main surgeon if negligence is established, and that privity of contract need not be established for a claim to be made under Consumer Protection Act, so long as there is hiring or availing of services for consideration.

(iv) *Deficiency in service—criteria for* "Deficiency" which has been defined in s. 2(1)(*g*)** of the Consumer Protection Act, means, "imperfection, shortcoming, or inadequacy in the quality, nature and manner of performance which is required to be maintained under any law for the time being in force or has been undertaken to be performed by a person in pursuance of a contract or otherwise in relation to any

17 *Indian Medical Association* v *V.P. Shantha* AIR 1996 SC 550; (1995)5 SCC 651; III(1995) CPJ 1 (SC); 1995(3) CPR 412 (SC); (1995)3 CTJ 969 (SC) (CP); 1996 CCJ 1 (SC).

* Replaced by s. 2(42) of the Consumer Protection Act 2019 w.e.f. 9.8.2019.

18 *Mumbai Grahak Panchayat* v *Dr. (Mrs.) Rashmi B. Fadnavis* 1996(1) CPR 137 (NC); (1996)4 CTJ 286 (CP) (NCDRC); 1998 CCJ 766 (NC) confirmed by NC in *Dr. (Mrs.) Rashmi B. Fadnavis* v *Mumbai Grahak Panchayat* III(1998) CPJ 21 (NC); 1998(3) CPR 34 (NC); 1998 CTJ 742 (CP) (NCDRC); 1999 CCJ 391 (NC).

** Replaced by s. 2(11) of the Consumer Protection Act 2019 w.e.f. 9.8.2019.

service".[19] The deficiency of service under consumer jurisdiction undoubtedly includes what is negligence in the law of torts but is somewhat wider.[20] The doctor may be personally liable or the hospital may be vicariously liable for the deficiency of professional service rendered on payment. It is held by the Supreme Court[1] that a determination about deficiency of service for the purpose of s. 2(1)(*g*)* of the Consumer Protection Act has to be made by applying the same test as is applied in an action for damages for negligence.

The National Commission[2] is of the view that the private doctor who performed the operation for a fee in the hospital, could not be expected to undertake and provide postoperative care and treatment to the hospital's patient and as such the award of compensation by State Commission was set aside. Where the operation is performed in a hospital, i.e. an institution, it is the duty of the institution to render postoperative care and treatment and the surgeon was not held negligent. The National Commission[3] affirmed the decision of Kerala State Commission which held the hospital liable for deficiency in service. The decision of National Commission was also upheld by the Supreme Court.[4] The National Commission[5] also affirmed the decision of the Madras State Commission

19 *Yasmin Sultana* v *Dr. Rupaben D Patel* 1994(1) CPR 407 (Guj).

20 *Dr. Ravinder Gupta* v *Ganga Devi* 1993(3) CPR 255 (Haryana); (1993)1 CTJ 1004 (SCDRC).

1 *Indian Medical Association* v *V.P. Shantha* AIR 1996 SC 550; (1995)6 SCC 651; III(1995) CPJ 1 (SC); 1995(3) CPR 412 (SC); (1995)3 CTJ 969 (SC) (CP); 1996 CCJ 1 (SC).

* Replaced by s. 2(11) of the Consumer Protection Act 2019 w.e.f. 9.8.2019.

2 *B.S. Hegde* v *Dr. Sudhanshu Bhattacharya* II(1992) CPJ 449 (Bom); (1993)1 CTJ 523 (SCDRC) reversed by National Commission 1993(3) CPR 414 (NC); III(1993) CPJ 388 (NC); (1994)2 CTJ 10 (CP) (NCDRC).

3 *Cosmopolitan Hospital* v *Smt. Vasantha P. Nair* 1991(2) CPR 155 (Ker); II(1991) CPJ 444 (Ker) affirmed by 1992(1) CPR 820 (NC); I(1992) CPJ 302 (NC).

4 *Indian Medical Association* v *V.P. Shantha* AIR 1996 SC 550; (1995)6 SCC 651; III(1995) CPJ 1 (SC); 1995(3) CPR 412 (SC); (1995)3 CTJ 969 (SC) (CP); 1996 CCJ 1 (SC).

5 *R. Gopinathan* v *Eskeycee Medical Foundation* 1993(1) CPR 456 (Mad) affirmed by I(1994) CPJ 147 (NC); 1994(2) CPR 488 (NC); (1994)2 CTJ 97 (CP) (NCDRC).

which laid down that the hospital authorities could be made liable to the patient for injury caused to him by the negligence or other fault of the doctors, surgeons, nurses, anaesthetists and other members of the hospital in course of their work.

The National Commission[6] has held that the act of carrying out the operation of a patient with rare blood group and morbid obesity for "uterine fibromyometosis" without making arrangement for blood and artificial respirator, by prolonging the duration of operation upto seven hours, and by shifting the patient from well-equipped hospital to ill-equipped hospital for monetary gain, amounts to deficiency in service on the part of the attending doctor. Similarly, the fact of leaving critically ill patient under the care of unqualified compounder, particularly when the situation demands constant monitoring of the patient, amounts to deficiency in service on the part of the doctor.[7] Whenever sample is taken for any laboratory test and charges for test are collected, it is implied that delivery of test report will be completion of "service" hired for charges paid. When samples were collected by the hospital staff two times for corean biopsy and the samples got spoiled for the delay in sending the same to the laboratory, deficiency in service was attributed to the hospital.[8]

The hospital was found to be vicariously liable for negligence of the doctor whose deficiency of service caused the death of the mother and baby in a case of high risk pregnancy.[9] The Supreme Court[10] upheld this decision of

6 *Dr. (Mrs.) Rashmi B. Fadnavis* v *Mumbai Grahak Panchayat* III(1998) CPJ 21 (NC); 1998(3) CPR 34 (NC); 1998 CTJ 742 (CP) (NCDRC); 1999 CCJ 391 (NC).

7 *Pravinbhai Khubchandbhai Soni* v *Dr. Rajendra R. Shah* 1997(3) CPR 224 (Guj); II(1998) CPJ 627 (Guj); 1998 CTJ 797 (CP) (SCDRC); 1999 CCJ 1323 (Guj).

8 *Mayo Hospital* v *Sunil Tiwari* 1997(3) CPR 574 (Bhopal); III(1997) CPJ 387 (Bhopal); 1998 CTJ 156 (CP) (SCDRC); 1999 CCJ 51 (MP).

9 *Dr. Sr. Louie* v *Smt. Kannolil Pathumma* 1993(1) CPR 422 (NC); I(1993) CPJ 30 (NC); (1993)1 CTJ 32 (NCDRC).

10 *Indian Medical Association* v *V.P. Shantha* AIR 1996 SC 550; (1995)6 SCC 651; III(1995) CPJ 1 (SC); 1995(3) CPR 412 (SC); (1995)3 CTJ 969 (SC) (CP); 1996 CCJ 1 (SC).

National Commission. The Supreme Court is of the view that the performance of hysterectomy and salpingo-oopherectomy for removal of uterus, ovaries and fallopian tubes of an unmarried women of 44 years of age without consent during diagnostic operative laparoscopy is undoubtedly an unauthorised invasion and interference with the body of the patient, which amounts to a tortious act of assault and battery and therefore a "deficiency in service".[11]

The National Commission[12] has observed that failure on the part of the hospital to accede to the request of the complainant to furnish all the papers relating to his operation and treatment, cannot amount to "deficiency in service" within the meaning of the expression used in the Consumer Protection Act 1986. The hospital is not found to be liable for deficiency in service for asking the patient party to settle the bills before releasing the dead body from the hospital.[13]

5 Liability of State under constitutional law

The right to health and health care is protected under Art. 21 of the Constitution of India as a right to life. When doctors performed their duties towards the patient negligently in a Government hospital, the servants of the State violated the fundamental right of the patient guaranteed under Art. 21 of the Constitution. By following the principle of law enunciated by the Supreme Court in *Nilabati Behera's* case,[14] the Andhra Pradesh High Court[15] exercised its jurisdiction under Art. 226 of the Constitution of India to award compensation to a patient whose treatment was done negligently by the doctors in a Government hospital. The High Court directed the State of Andhra Pradesh to pay compensation to the patient for negligent treatment by the

11 *Samira Kohli* v *Dr. Prabha Manchanda* (2008)2 SCC 1; 2008 ACJ 747; AIR 2008 SC 1385; JT 2008(1) SC 399; (2008)1 Scale 442.

12 *Poona Medical Foundation Ruby Hall Clinic* v *Marutirao L. Titkare* I(1995) CPJ 232 (NC); 1995(1) CPR 661 (NC).

13 *Mrs. Usha Mehrotra* v *Apollo Hospitals Enterprises Ltd.* 1999(2) CPR 453 (Chennai).

14 *Nilabati Behera* v *State of Orissa* AIR 1993 SC 1960.

15 *Mrs. Shanta* v *State of AP* III(1997) CPJ 481 (HC of AP).

doctors in a Government hospital. Similarly, the High Court of Rajasthan,[16] directed the State Government to pay compensation for the death of the patient whose laparoscopic tubectomy was done by the doctor of the State Government in Primary Health Centre without adequate resuscitative facilities and cardiac monitoring equipment. The High Court of Madhya Pradesh[17] awarded compensation against the state for giving birth of two children after failure of vasectomy operation of the husband on the ground that public policy in India is in favour of control of the population and thereby unwanted child due to failure of sterilization operation is not a matter of delight and pleasure to the family. The Madurai Bench of Madras High Court[18] directed the state to pay compensation for the death of the mother and baby under the care of staff nurse and mid-wife of Government hospital due to absence of the doctor on duty. The Madurai Bench of Madras High Court[19] directed the State of Tamil Nadu to pay compensation for the death of a young lady of 22 years in Primary Health Centre, as no doctor attended the patient in spite of profuse bleeding after delivery of the child.

16 *Rajmal* v *State of Rajasthan* 1996 ACJ 1166.
17 *Jyoti Kewat* v *State of MP* CDJ 2002 MPHC 388; 2003(1) MPHT 482.
18 *V. Raman* v *Director of Medical and Rural Health Services, Chennai* 2010(1) MLJ 1409; 2010(1) CWC 303.
19 *Thangapandi* v *Director of Primary Health Services* 2011(1) MLJ 1329.

CHAPTER

9

Pleading and Proof

1 Particulars of pleadings It is trite law that the decision of a case cannot be based on grounds outside the pleadings of the parties.[1] To paraphrase Lord Dunedin,[2] "No amount of evidence can be looked into upon a plea which was never put forward". The statement of material facts on which the party relies for his claim or defence must be pleaded concisely.[3] The negligence, special damage and other particulars required to be proved must be pleaded with specificity, particularity and precision.[4] The particulars of contributory negligence, set off, counter-claim and other grounds of defence must be specifically pleaded by the defendant.[5] In the absence of any averment in the pleading, the Consumer Court[6] did not consider the evidence of the complainant that he paid ₹500 to the doctor for medical treatment.

Lord Diplock[7] has enunciated with force and clarity the principle that one can recover special damage which has been pleaded and, proved. If a plaintiff has suffered damage

1 *Trojan & Co.* v *Nagappa* AIR 1953 SC 235.
2 *Siddik Md.* v *Saran* 43 IA 27; AIR 1930 PC 57.
3 Order 6, r. 2 of the Code of Civil Procedure 1908.
4 Order 6, r. 4 of the Code of Civil Procedure 1908.
5 Order 8, rr. 2 to 6 of the Code of Civil Procedure 1908.
6 *Kadakarai Nadar* v *Rakkapan* 1994(2) CPR 417 (Mad).
7 *Ilkiw* v *Samuels* [1963]2 All ER 879; [1963]1 WLR 991; 107 Sol Jo 680 (CA).

of a kind which is not the necessary and immediate consequence of the wrongful act, he must warn the defendant in the pleadings that the compensation claimed will extend to this damage. This principle gives rise to the plaintiff's undoubted obligation to plead and particularise any item of damage which represents out-of-pocket expenses, or loss of earnings, incurred prior to the trial, and which is capable of substantially exact calculation.[8]

The concept of liability without negligence is opposed to the basic principles of law. The proof of negligence remains the lynch pin to recover compensation.[9] To succeed in an action for damage and compensation, the claimant has to establish some negligence or breach of duty by the defendant towards him and its causal connection with the injuries sustained by the claimant.[10] In order to succeed in an action for negligence against a doctor the plaintiff must prove (1) that the doctor was under a duty to take reasonable care towards the plaintiff to avoid the damage complained of or not to cause damage to the plaintiff by failure to take reasonable care; (2) that there was a breach of that duty on the part of the doctor; and (3) that breach of duty was the real cause of damage complained of and such damage was reasonably foreseeable.[11] The master becomes liable for the conduct of the servant, when the servant is proved to have acted negligently in course of his employment.

2 Construction of pleadings The general rule is that the relief should be founded on pleadings made by the parties. Pleadings are loosely drafted in the courts, and as such, the courts should not scrutinise the pleadings with such meticulous care, so as to result in genuine claims being

8 *Perestrello* v *United Paint Co. Ltd.* [1969]3 All ER 479; [1969]1 WLR 570; 113 Sol Jo 36 (CA).

9 *Minu B. Mehta* v *Balkrishna Ramchandra Nayan* AIR 1977 SC 1248; 1977 ACJ 118; (1977)2 SCC 441; 1977 TAC 320; (1977)2 SCR 886; (1977)2 APLJ (SC) 1.

10 *Calcutta State Transport Corporation* v *Kamal Prakash De* AIR 1976 Cal 2; 1976 ACJ 58; 1976 TAC 182.

11 *Philips India Ltd.* v *Kanju Punnu* AIR 1975 Bom 306; 1975 ACJ 311; 77 Bom LR 337; 1975 Mah LJ 792.

defeated on trivial grounds.[12] The function of the pleadings is only to state the material facts and it is for the court to determine the legal result of those facts and to mould the relief in accordance with that result.[13]

In the absence of clear plea of negligence the Supreme Court[14] held the driver of a vehicle negligent on the ground that the pleadings have to be interpreted not with formalistic rigour, but with latitude or awareness of low legal literacy of poor people. If a plea is not specifically made and yet it is covered by an issue by implication and the parties knew that the said plea was involved in the trial, then the mere fact that the plea was not expressly taken in the pleadings would not disentitle a party from relying upon it, if it is satisfactorily proved by evidence.[15] There is no dispute as regards the proposition that the plea of inevitable accident can be raised as defence even though it is not specifically pleaded, if it is so made out from the materials on record.[16]

By modifying the decision of the National Commission it is held by the Supreme Court of India[17] that without making amendment to the claim petition, the claimant is entitled to make additional claim or enhanced amount of claim and that it is the duty of the Consumer Forum to consider such claim for the purpose of awarding just and reasonable compensation.

3 **Burden of proof** The general rule is that the burden of proving negligence as cause of the accident lies on the party who alleges it. The elementary principle is that it is for the

12 *Madan Gopal Kanodia* v *Mamraj Maniram* AIR 1976 SC 461.

13 *Moolji Jaitha and Co.* v *Khandesh Spinning and Weaving Mills Co. Ltd.* AIR 1950 FC 83; 1950 SCJ 51; 1949 FCR 849.

14 *Manjushri Raha* v *B.L. Gupta* AIR 1977 SC 1158; 1977 ACJ 134; (1977)2 SCC 174; 1977 TAC 297; (1977)2 SCR 944.

15 *Bhagwati Prasad* v *Chandramaul* AIR 1966 SC 735; (1966)2 SCR 286; 1966 All LJ 799; 1966 SCD 888.

16 *Krishan Dayal* alias *Keshavdayal* v *Vishnu Prasad* 1985 ACJ 450; *Bhagwati Prasad* v *Chandramaul* AIR 1966 SC 735; 1966 SCD 888; 1966 All LJ 799; (1966)2 SCR 286.

17 *Dr. Balaram Prasad* v *Dr. Kunal Saha* (Civil Appeal No. 2867 of 2012, 692 of 2012, 2866 of 2012, 731 of 2012 and 858 of 2012), CDJ 2013 SC 937; 2013(7) MLJ 781; (2014)1 SCC 384.

plaintiff to prove that damage under any particular head has resulted from the wrongful act of the defendant.[18] So, the burden of proving negligence of the doctor is on the plaintiff. The plaintiff has to stand on his own feet and not to take benefit of any lacunae in the evidence of the doctor.[19] However, the party can take advantage of presumptions which may be available to him, to lighten the burden. Presumptions are of three types: (*i*) permissive presumption or presumption of fact, (*ii*) compelling presumption or rebuttable presumption of law, (*iii*) conclusive proof or irrebuttable presumption of law.[20] It is held by Chagla, ACJ and Bhagwati, J that actions for negligence in India are to be determined according to the principles of English Common Law.[1] The law laid down by the House of Lords[2] is that where a breach of duty of care is proved or admitted, the burden still lies on the plaintiff to prove that such breach caused the injury suffered. In cases where breach of duty consists of an omission to do an act which ought to be done (e.g. failure of a doctor to attend the patient), that factual inquiry is in the realms of hypothesis. Accordingly the burden of proving negligence and resultant damage is on the plaintiff or complainant.[3] The complainant has to succeed on the strength of his own case and in case of medical negligence the complainant has to allege the specific acts of negligence and prove the same by establishing the facts constituting negligence.[4]

18 *Carslogie SS Co.* v *Royal Norwegian Government* [1952] AC 292; [1952]1 All ER 20; [1951]2 TLR 1099; 95 Sol Jo 801; [1951]2 Lloyd's Rep 441 (HL).

19 *Harbhajan Singh* v *Dayanand Medical College & Hospital* III(1996) CPJ 263 (Chandigarh); 1994(1) CPR 518 (Punj); (1994)2 CTJ 88 (CP) (SCDRC); 1997 CCJ 952 (Punj).

20 *Syad Akbar* v *State of Karnataka* AIR 1979 SC 1848; (1980)1 SCC 30; 1980 SCC (Cri) 59; 1980 ACJ 88; 1979 Cr App R (SC) 273.

1 *Amelia Flounders* v *Dr. Clement Perreira* (1947) OCJ Appeal No. 27 of 1947 (unreported).

2 *Bolitho (Administratrix of the estate of Bolitho)* v *City and Hackney Health Authority* [1997]4 All ER 771 (HL); [1998] AC 232 (HL); [1997]3 WLR 1151 (HL); 39 BMLR 1 (HL); 141 Sol Jo LB 238 (HL).

3 *Calcutta Medical Research Institute* v *Bimalesh Chatterjee* I(1999) CPJ 13 (NC); 1999(1) CPR 3 (NC); 1999 CCJ 499 (NC).

4 *Kumari Mahua Daripa* v *Dr. Aniruddha Ghorai* III(2015) CPJ 671 (NCDRC).

Where a claimant suffered injury due to negligence of two or more persons, but claimed compensation against one person only, that person would be liable only to the extent that he had contributed towards the injury. In such circumstances the onus of proving causation remained on the claimant and the defendant might not plead that others were responsible in part. The court would decide on consideration of the evidence whether the claimant had proved that the defendant was responsible for the whole or a quantifiable part of the injury.[5]

A surgeon who failed to perform an emergency operation must prove with satisfactory evidence that the patient refused to undergo the operation, not only at the initial stage, but even after the patient was informed about the dangerous consequences of not undergoing the operation. When a surgeon or medical man advances a plea that the patient did not give his consent for the surgery or the course of treatment advised by him, the burden is on him to prove that non-performance of the surgery or non-administration of the treatment was on account of the refusal of the patient to give consent thereto.[6]

Viscount Simon[7] lays down the principle that a man cannot call upon the other party to compensate him in full, when he is a part-author of his own injury. When contributory negligence is set up as defence, its existence does not depend on any duty owed by the injured party to the party sued, and all that is necessary to establish such a defence is to prove that the injured party did not in his own interest take reasonable care of himself and contributed by his want of care to his own injury.[8] The burden of proving contributory negligence is solely on the defendant; the onus is not on the plaintiff to disprove contributory negligence.

5 *Holtby* v *Brigham & Cowan (Hill) Ltd.* [2000]3 All ER 421 (CA).

6 *Dr. T.T. Thomas* v *Elisa* AIR 1987 Ker 52; 1986 Ker LT 1026; (1987)2 TAC 50; 1987(1) ACJ 192; (1987)1 ACC 461.

7 *Nance* v *British Columbia Ele Rly. Co. Ltd.* [1951] AC 601; [1951]2 All ER 448; 95 Sol Jo 543.

8 *Nance* v *British Columbia Ele Rly. Co. Ltd.* (supra).

Peter Pan, J[9] has laid down the criteria for onus of proof as follows:

> "Although in an action in negligence the onus of proof normally rested on the plaintiff, in a case where a general duty of care arose and there was a failure to take a recognised precaution and that failure was followed by the very damage which that precaution was designed to prevent, the burden of proof lay on the defendant to show, first, that he was not in breach of any duty and, second, if he failed to prove that he had not been in breach of duty, that the damage suffered by the plaintiff did not result from the breach."

It is difficult to discover any causal connection between the defendant's wrongful act and the damage suffered by the plaintiff, particularly in situations where damage has resulted from the act of another person who is independent of the defendant himself.[10] The court can refuse the claim for compensation in these situations by applying the maxim "*novus actus interveniens*", which means an independent supervening act. The surgeon was not held negligent for unwanted pregnancy of the plaintiff due to failure of sterilization operation, as the plaintiff's decision to have unprotected sexual intercourse with the knowledge that she was not sterile, was a *novus actus interveniens*, breaking the chain of causation.[11]

The maxim "*actio personalis moritur cum persona*" has application when the action is one for damages for a personal wrong. The meaning of the maxim is that a personal action dies with the person and the effect is that the death extinguishes the liability in tort. The death of the doctor extinguishes his liability for damages.[12] It is held by the Supreme Court,[13] that the maxim operates in a limited class

9 *Clark* v *Maclennan* [1983]1 All ER 416.

10 Charlesworth & Percy on *Negligence*, 9th Ed., p. 402 (5·39).

11 *Sabri-Tabrizi* v *Lothian Health Board* 43 BMLR 190 CS (OH).

12 *G. Jayaprakash* v *State of Andhra Pradesh* AIR 1977 AP 20; 1976 Andh LT 393; (1976)2 APLJ (HC) 300; 1976 ACJ 492; 1977 TAC 146.

13 *Girijanandini* v *Bijendra Narain* AIR 1967 SC 1124.

of actions, such as actions for damages for defamation, assault, or other personal injuries not causing the death of the party. Where in a case of medical negligence the complaint relates to an action for personal injuries not causing death of the party, the cause of action will not survive, as the action is for personal injuries not causing death of the party.[14] By applying this maxim, the claim for compensation against legal representatives of the deceased doctor on the allegation of negligence in performance of operation on the complainant was dismissed by the State Commission.[15] However, if the complainant dies during the pendency of the proceeding against the doctor on the allegation of medical negligence, the legal representatives of the deceased complainant will be substituted, as the claim based on breach of legal duty survives to the legal representatives.[16]

The doctrine of "*res ipsa loquitur*" is a rule of evidence affecting onus of proof. The maxim "*res ipsa loquitur*" may apply, if the cause of the accident is unknown and no reasonable explanation as to the cause is coming forth from the defendant. In such cases (*a*) the event or accident must be of a kind which does not happen in the ordinary course of things if those who have the management and control use due care and (*b*) it has to be further satisfied that the event which caused the accident was within the management and control of the defendant.[17] There are some cases in which the accident speaks for itself so that it is sufficient for the plaintiff to prove the accident and nothing more. It will then be for the defendant to establish that the accident happened due to some other causes than his own negligence.[18] The

14 *Sujith K.P.* v *The National Hospital* 1997(1) CPR 231 (Ker).

15 *G. Bharat* v *Dr. G. Sarangapani (dead) by LRs.* 1997(1) CPR 466 (Hyderabad); *Dr. (Smt.) Mandakini Vasant Lal* v *Sarangdhar Shivaji Ingle* (1994)2 CTJ 261 (CP) (SCDRC).

16 *N.K. Joshi (deceased) through LRs* v *Dr. Neelam Kaul* 2000 CCJ 196 (Del).

17 *Syad Akbar* v *State of Karnataka* AIR 1979 SC 1848; (1980)1 SCC 30; 1980 SCC (Cri) 59; 1980 ACJ 88; 1979 CrLJ 1374; 1979 Cr LR (SC) 527; 1979 Cr App R (SC) 273.

18 *Pushpabai Parshottam Udeshi* v *Ranjit Ginning & Pressing Co. Pvt. Ltd.* AIR 1977 SC 1735; (1977)2 SCC 745; 1977 ACJ 343; 1977 TAC 387; (1977)3 SCR 372.

burden of proving inevitable accident is upon the defendant who takes the plea of inevitable accident.[19] Similarly, to establish the plea of "latent defect", it must be shown by the defendant that he had taken all reasonable care and that despite this, the defect remained hidden.[20]

The State Commission, Gujarat,[1] has summed up the principles of burden of proof as follows: "Ordinarily it is for the complainant to prove that the doctor whose treatment he had taken was negligent in giving his treatment. It is true that the doctor cannot be held negligent, simply because something happens to go wrong. However, the details of the operation and findings in the course of operation are within the special knowledge of the doctor performing the operation and his team. It is, therefore, for the doctor to explain satisfactorily as to what he had done in the course of the operation and if the operation was not successful or if it results in complications, it is for him to explain as to how it so happened". So the onus lies on the doctors in the operation theatre to explain events and the ultimate outcome i.e. the death of the patient.[2] When keratotomy operation was performed on left eye of a teenager in violation of accepted professional practice, resulting in loss of his eyesight, the burden of proof is on the doctor to establish that he was not in breach of any duty in giving treatment to the minor patient.[3] The onus of proof shifts upon the attending doctors to prove that there was no negligence in performance of operation when the patient died within 10 hours of admission in the operation theatre in mysterious circumstances.[4] Where the complainant is not aware of what took place inside the

19 *C. Chinnaswami* v *M. Vijay* 1966 ACJ 317 (Mad); *Parmeswari Das* v *Soman Devi* 1958-65 ACJ 63 (Punj); *Krishan Dayal* alias *Keshavdayal* v *Vishnu Prasad* 1985 ACJ 450; *Bhagwati* v *Chandramaul* AIR 1966 SC 735; 1966 SCD 888; 1966 All LJ 799; 1966 All WR (HC) 609; (1966)2 SCR 286.

20 *Henderson* v *Henry E. Jenkins and Sons* 1970 ACJ 198 (HL).

1 *Aphraim Jayanand Rathod* v *Dr. Shailesh Shah* 1996(1) CPR 547 (Guj); I(1996) CPJ 243 (Guj); 1997 CCJ 1573 (Guj).

2 *Arunaben D. Kothari* v *Navdeep Clinic* 1996(3) CPR 20 (Guj); III(1996) CPJ 605 (Guj); (1997)5 CTJ 533 (CP) (SCDRC); 1998 CCJ 972 (Guj).

3 *Smt. Adarsh Bararia* v *Dr. P.S. Hardia* 2000(2) CPR 188 (Bhopal).

4 *Smt. Bhanupal* v *Dr. Prakash Padode* II(2000) CPJ 384 (Bhopal).

operation theatre, the onus of proof lies on the doctor to establish that there was no negligence on his part resulting in permanent disability of the patient.[5]

4 Expert evidence

(i) ***Value of expert evidence*** The role of the expert medical witness is to assist the judge in order to guide him to come to the correct conclusion. It must be for the judge to guess the weight and usefulness of such assistance as he is given and to reach his own conclusion accordingly.[6] The expert evidence must be adduced to prove the allegation of negligence by the doctor.[7] In the absence of expert evidence on behalf of the complainant the National Commission,[8] declined to hold that the treatment given by the doctor was not proper or was given in a slipshod manner or that there was over transfusion of blood resulting in cardiac decompensation.

The Consumer Forum has the discretion to decide the necessity of expert evidence in a case of medical negligence but the Consumer Forum must keep in mind that an expert witness discharges two functions: first, the duty of the expert is to explain the technical issues as clearly as possible so that it can be understood by a common man, and secondly, the function of the expert is to assist the forum in deciding whether the acts or omissions of the medical practitioner or the hospital constitute negligence.[9]

The order of dismissal of the complaint was confirmed on appeal by the State Commission, Chandigarh,[10] on the ground

5 *S.A. Qureshi* v *Padode Memorial Hospital and Research Centre* II(2000) CPJ 463 (Bhopal).

6 *Vernon* v *Bosley* [1997]1 All ER 577 (CA).

7 *Dr. C.V. Mathew* v *P. Babu* I(2000) CPJ 134 (Ker); 1999(3) CPR 461 (Ker).

8 *Dr. T.N. Subrahmanyam* v *Dr. B. Krishna Rao* 1996(2) CPR 247 (NC); II(1996) CPJ 233 (NC); (1996)4 CTJ 785 (CP) (NCDRC); 1997 CCJ 1138 (NC).

9 *V. Kishan Rao* v *Nikhil Super Speciality Hospital* (2010)5 SCC 513; (2010)4 SCJ 690; 2010 AIR SCW 4252; III(2010) CPJ 1; 2010(5) SLT 349; CDJ 2010 SC 428.

10 *Mrs. Satwant Kaur* v *Dr. Kanwaljit Kaur* 1998(2) CPR 458 (Chandigarh); I(1998) CPJ 298 (Chandigarh); 1998 CTJ 557 (CP) (SCDRC); 1999 CCJ 781 (Punj).

that the complainant could not adduce any expert evidence to prove that either in the process of caesarean operation or tubectomy the cotton sponge could have been left in the colon of the patient. The National Commission,[11] confirmed the order of dismissal of the complaint by the State Commission, which, in the absence of expert evidence on behalf of the complainant, relied upon affidavits filed by four doctors on behalf of the doctor in order to refute the allegation of want of skill in giving medical treatment. The proposition of law laid down by the National Commission[12] is that the medical man cannot be held negligent unless there is expert evidence to substantiate the allegation of negligence. The Supreme Court affirmed the order of dismissal of the compliant by the National Commission for not producing expert evidence in support of the allegation of medical negligence.[13]

The two judge Bench of the Supreme Court of India[14] is of the view that whenever a complaint is received against a doctor or hospital by the Consumer Forum or by the Criminal Court, then before issuing notice to the doctor or hospital against whom the complaint was made, the Consumer Forum or the Criminal Court should first refer the matter to a competent doctor or committee of doctors specialised in the field relating to which the medical negligence is attributed and only if the doctor or committee of doctors gives expert opinion that there is a *prima facie* case of medical negligence and notice should be issued to the doctor or the hospital concerned.

It is declared by the Supreme Court[15] that the judgment rendered in *Martin F. D'Souza* (supra) is *per incuriam*. The Supreme Court reiterates that the ratio of the judgment in *Jacob Mathew* v *State of Punjab*[16] is confined to the question

11 *Sethuraman Subramaniam Iyer* v *Triveni Nursing Home* 1997(2) CPR 144 (NC); I(1998) CPJ 10 (NC); 1998 CTJ 7 (CP) (NCDRC); 1998 CCJ 1532 (NC).

12 *Darshani Devi* v *Rajashri* I(1998) CPJ 358 (NC).

13 *Ins Malhatra (Ms.)* v *Dr. A Kriplani* (2009)4 SCC 705.

14 *Martin F. D'Souza* v *Mohd. Ishfaq* (2009)3 SCC 1; 2009 ACJ 1695; AIR 2009 SC 2049; JT 2009(2) SC 486; (2009)2 Scale 620.

15 *V. Kishan Rao* v *Nikhil Super Speciality Hospital* (2010)5 SCC 513.

16 (2005)6 SCC 1; 2005 SCC (Cri) 1369.

of medical negligence leading to criminal prosecution either on the basis of a criminal complaint or on the basis of an FIR. The ratio of *Jacob Mathew* (supra) is, thus, limited to prosecution of doctors for the offence under s. 304A of the Indian Penal Code. The expert opinion of the doctor cannot be pre-condition of filing a complaint before consumer court or a plaint before the civil court for compensation on the ground of medical negligence. The view of the Supreme Court that the judgment rendered in *V. Kishan Rao* (supra) by declaring the judgment of *Martin F. D'Souza* (supra) as *per incuriam*, is followed as correct position of law.[17]

The decision of the Apex Court in "D'souza" is also held to be "*per incuriam*" by the subsequent three Judge-Bench of the Apex Court,[18] because the directions of "D'souza" are not only contrary to the earlier larger Bench decision in *Jacob Mathew*[19] which distinguishes civil liability of medical negligence from criminal liability but also contrary to the larger Bench in "*Dr. J.J. Merchant*"[20] wherein it is laid down that only in appropriate cases examination of expert may be necessary and the same is left to the discretion of the Commission.

It is held by the Supreme Court of India[1] that the duty of an expert witness is to furnish the judge with the necessary scientific criteria for testing the accuracy of the conclusions so as to enable the judge to form his independent judgment by the application of these criteria to the facts proved by the evidence of the case. The credibility of such a witness depends

17 *A. Srimannarayana* v *Dasari Santakumari* (2013)9 SCC 496.

18 *V. Kishan Rao* v *Nikhil Super Speciality Hospital* (2010)5 SCC 513; (2010)4 SCJ 690; 2010 AIR SCW 4252; III(2010) CPJ 1; 2010(5) SLT 349.

19 *Jacob Mathew* v *State of Punjab* (2005)6 SCC 1; 2005 ACJ 1840; AIR 2005 SC 3180; III(2005) CPJ 9; 2005(3) CPR 70; 2005 CrLJ 3710; JT 2005(6) SC 584.

20 *Dr. J.J. Merchant* v *Shrinath Chaturvedi* II(2002) CPJ 8; JT 2002(6) SC 1; (2002)6 SCC 635; AIR 2002 SC 2931; (2002)5 Scale 545.

1 *Malay Kumar Ganguly* v *Dr. Sukumar Mukherjee* (2009)9 SCC 221; AIR 2010 SC 1162; (2009)10 Scale 675; III(2009) CPJ 17; 2009(3) CCR 558; (2009)7 SCJ 124; 2010 AIR SCW 769; *Ramesh Chandra Agrawal* v *Regency Hospital Ltd.* 2009(4) KLT 81 (SC); (2009)9 SCC 709; (2009)7 SCJ 748; 2009 AIR SCW 7308; AIR 2010 SC 806.

on the reasons stated in support of his conclusions and the data and materials furnished which form the basis of his conclusions.

(ii) *Authority to summon expert witness* The District Forum (now District Commission) refused to summon two doctors along with case records of the patient to prove the allegation of medical negligence by expert evidence on the ground that the pleading does not disclose that the complainant failed to secure the affidavits of the doctors. By setting aside the order of the District Forum, it is held by the State Commission, Chandigarh,[2] that in case of medical negligence the Consumer Forum can be requested to summon expert witnesses under s. 13(4)(*i*)* of the Consumer Protection Act 1986 in order to prove the allegation of medical negligence.

The court can also issue commission to record the evidence by way of video-conferencing, where the attendance of a witness cannot be procured without an amount of delay, expense or inconvenience.[3]

The National Commission asked the expert to give opinion, but the expert could not form the complete opinion due to non-availability of original record of treatment and X-ray films. The National Commission refused to direct the expert to reconsider his opinion after making all the records of treatment available to him, though the records were not available to the expert due to negligence of the staff of the Commission. The Supreme Court of India[4] reversed the decision of the National Commission and directed for the expert opinion after making all the records of the treatment available to the expert, because a fair opportunity should be given to the complainant to prove his claim based on the report of the expert.

2 *Darshan Singh Basra* v *Dr. Jasbir Singh* 1998(1) CPR 304 (Chandigarh); I(1998) CPJ 45 (Chandigarh); 1998 CTJ 202 (CP) (SCDRC).

* Replaced by s. 38(9)(*a*) of the Consumer Protection Act 2019 w.e.f. 9.8.2019.

3 *State of Maharastra* v *Dr. Praful B Desai* (2003)4 SCC 601; AIR 2003 SC 2053; JT 2003(3) SC 382.

4 *Ramesh Chandra Agrawal* v *Regency Hospital Ltd* (2009)9 SCC 709; (2009)7 SCJ 748; 2009 AIR SCW 7308; AIR 2010 SC 806.

(iii) *Cross-examination of expert under Consumer Forum* It is true that reception of evidence on affidavit is permissible before Consumer Forum, but when a party insists that he wants to cross-examine the deponent of the affidavit to prove that the affidavit cannot be relied upon, natural justice demands that permission to cross-examine that witness should be given.[5]

(iv) *Criteria for accepting expert evidence* A doctor charged with negligence can clear himself if he shows that he acted in accordance with the prevailing professional practice. The judge accepted the expert evidence in favour of surgery undertaken by the doctor to alleviate suspected nerve root compression of the patient even in the absence of radicular, although normal medical opinion would not have countenance surgery in that situation, because the decision of the doctor to operate was one which a responsible body of surgeons practising in the doctor's specialisation would not have considered it unreasonable. The judge has the discretion to decide whether a body of doctors would constitute a responsible body for acceptance of expert opinion, because a small number may constitute the necessary defence.[6]

(v) *Criteria for condemning expert evidence* The principle of law enunciated by the House of Lords[7] is that a doctor could be liable for negligence in respect of diagnosis and treatment despite a body of professional opinion sanctioning his conduct where it had not been demonstrated to the judge's satisfaction that the body of opinion relied on was reasonable or responsible. In the vast majority of cases the fact that distinguished experts in the field were of a particular opinion would demonstrate the reasonableness of that opinion. However, in a rare case, if it could be demonstrated that the

5 *Salgaokar Medical Research Centre* v *R.B. Raikar* 1996(2) CPR 50 (NC); II(1996) CPJ 209 (NC); (1996)4 CTJ 576 (CP) (NCDRC).

6 *De Freitas* v *O'Brien* 25 BMLR 51 (CA); [1993]4 Med LR 281, affirmed [1995]6 Med LR 108.

7 *Bolitho (Administratrix of the estate of Bolitho)* v *City and Hackney Health Authority* [1997]4 All ER 771 (HL); [1998] AC 232 (HL); [1997]3 WLR 1151 (HL); 39 BMLR 1 (HL); 141 Sol Jo LB 238 (HL).

professional opinion was not capable of withstanding logical analysis, the judge would be entitled to hold that the body of opinion was not reasonable or responsible. The judge has the right to come to the conclusion that the views genuinely held by a competent medical expert are unreasonable when he is satisfied that the body of expert opinion cannot be logically supported at all and that such opinion will not provide the bench mark by reference to which the doctor's conduct falls to be assessed.

The judge is permitted to take the view that the expert is simply wrong, because he has not considered all the factors, or that he does not speak for a responsible body but for himself. In other words, the judge can reject the evidence of expert as unreliable or partisan on consideration of the cross-examination of the expert witness.[8] Moreover, the judge may take the view that, whatever the experts say about what they would have done under the situation, they are wrong, i.e. faced with the actual situation they would not have acted as the doctor did. This principle is illustrated in the dissenting judgment of Simon Brown, LJ in "Bolitho".[9] It is held by the Queen's Bench that Coroner cannot return a verdict of lack of care resulting in death during surgery under anaesthetic.[10] The National Commission,[11] did not consider the certificate issued by an eminent physician to substantiate the allegation of transfusing wrong group of blood to the patient, as the physician was neither a hematologist nor pathologist. The Supreme Court of India is of the view that the consumer courts are at liberty to reject the evidence of medical expert on scrutinising and evaluating the relevant evidence and

8 *Bowers* v *Harrow Health Authority* [1995]6 Med LR 16; *Murphy* v *Wirral Health Authority* [1996]7 Med LR 232; *Wisziewski* v *Central Manchester Health Authority* [1996]7 Med LR 248; *Le Page* v *Kingston and Richmond Health Authority* [1997]8 Med LR 229.

9 *Bolitho (Administratrix of the estate of Bolitho)* v *City and Hackney Health Authority* [1997]4 All ER 771 (HL); [1998] AC 232 (HL); [1997]3 WLR 1151 (HL); 39 BMLR 1 (HL); 141 Sol Jo LB 238 (HL).

10 *Regina* v *Surrey Coroner, Ex parte Wright* [1997] QB 786.

11 *Calcutta Medical Research Institute* v *Bimalesh Chatterjee* I(1999) CPJ 13 (NC); 1999(1) CPR 3 (NC); 1999 CCJ 499 (NC).

other circumstances in order to adjudicate the appropriate standard of care required in cases of medical negligence.[12]

(vi) *Conflicting expert evidence—duty of court* A child suffered cardiac arrest and brain damage, as the doctor had not attended and intubated the child in response to the call made by the night sister. The plaintiff's expert said that it would have been mandatory to intubate; the defendants' expert said that he would not have intubated, had he attended the patient in the night. There were clearly two schools of thought about the need to intubate and there was no material which entitled the court to say that on the balance of probabilities the child would have been intubated, had the doctor responded to the call of the night sister; nor could it be shown that the decision not to intubate would have been negligent. The House of Lords,[13] accepted the expert opinion of the defendants on the ground that the plaintiff could not show that the doctor would have intubated, nor that it would have been mandatory to intubate. Similarly, in *Joyce* case[14] the court preferred the defendant's expert opinion, as the plaintiff could not establish that a vascular surgeon would have operated within the crucial 48 hour period, nor that it would have been mandatory for him to have done so. The judge should give reasons for preference of one body of expert opinion. Stuart-Smith, LJ[15] has observed:

> "What the judge has to decide is which of two explanations (of the experts) is to be preferred. That is a question of fact which the judge has to determine on the ordinary basis on a balance of probability. It is a question for the judge to weigh up the evidence on both

12 *Sathy M. Pillay* v *S. Sharma* 2017(4) RCR (Civil) 324; 2018(1) AICLR 698; 2018 All SCR 443; 2018(2) ICC 141 (SC).

13 *Bolitho (Administratrix of the estate of Bolitho)* v *City and Hackney Health Authority* [1997]4 All ER 771 (HL); [1998] AC 232 (HL); [1997]3 WLR 1151 (HL); 39 BMLR 1 (HL); 141 Sol Jo LB 238 (HL) affirming [1993]4 Med LR 381 (CA); 13 BMLR 111 (CA).

14 *Joyce* v *Merton, Sutton and Wandsworth Health Authority* [1996]7 Med LR 1.

15 *Fallows* v *Randle* [1997]8 Med LR 160 (CA).

sides, and he is entitled in a situation to prefer the evidence of one expert witness to that of the other."

The Court of Appeal in UK[16] was critical of a Deputy High Court Judge for accepting the evidence of expert witness for the defendant on the ground that the witness was highly reputed and for not giving any suggestion that he did not represent the view of responsible body of surgeons. Wall, LJ agreeing with Leveson and Sir Mark Patter P observed as follows:

"Where there is a clear conflict of medical opinion, the court's duty is not merely to say which view it prefers, but to explain why it prefers one to the other."

Two conflicting expert opinions were available with regard to hospitalisation of a patient aged about 55 years who was suffering from eye infection, fever, difficulty in breathing and pain in abdomen. The opinion of first expert was in favour of hospitalisation, while the opinion of the second expert was against hospitalisation of the patient. The National Commission relied on the opinion of the second expert on the ground that the same was well reasoned and justified in the facts and circumstances of the case.[17]

5 Res ipsa loquitur

(i) *Object and purport* *"Res ipsa loquitur"* is no more than a convenient label to describe situations where, notwithstanding the plaintiff's inability to establish the exact cause of the accident, the fact of the accident by itself is sufficient, in the absence of an explanation, to justify the conclusion that most probably the defendant was negligent and that his negligence caused the injury.[18] The general purport of the words *"res ipsa loquitur"* is that the accident speaks for itself or tells its own story. The normal rule is that it is for the plaintiff to prove negligence, but in some

16 *Smith* v *Southampton University Hospitals NHS Trust* [2007] EWCA Civ 387; (2007)96 BMLR 79.

17 *Post Graduate Institute of Medical Education and Research* v *Jasmine* 2018(2) All MR 93; III(2018) CPJ 72 (NCDRC).

18 John G. Fleming, *Law of Torts,* 5th Ed., p. 302.

cases considerable hardship is caused to the plaintiff as the true cause of the accident is not known to him, but is solely within the knowledge of the defendant who caused it, the plaintiff can prove the accident but cannot prove how it happened to establish negligence on the part of the defendant. This hardship is sought to be avoided by invoking the principle of *res ipsa loquitur*.[19] Where the thing is shown to be under the management of the defendant or his servants, and the accident is such as in the ordinary course of things does not happen if those who have the management use proper care, it affords reasonable evidence, in the absence of explanation by the defendant, that the accident arose for want of care.[20]

The Supreme Court of India is of the view that in a case where negligence on the part of the doctor or the hospital is evident, the principle of *res ipsa loquitur* operates and the complainant does not have to prove anything as the thing proves itself and in such a case it is for the doctor or the hospital to prove that he has taken care and done his duty to repel the charge of negligence.[1]

(ii) *Criteria for application* The maxim comes into operation: (*a*) on proof of the happening of an unexplained occurrence; (*b*) when the occurrence is one, which would not have happened in the ordinary course of things without negligence on the part of somebody other than the plaintiff; and (*c*) the circumstances point to the negligence in question being that of the defendant, rather than that of any other person.[2] The Bombay High Court has observed[3] that the following three

19 *Pushpabai Parshottam Udeshi* v *Ranjit Ginning & Pressing Co. Pvt. Ltd.* AIR 1977 SC 1735; (1977)2 SCC 745; 1977 ACJ 343; 1977 TAC 387; (1977)3 SCR 372.

20 *Scott* v *London & Katherine Docks* (1865)3 H & C 596 quoted in "*Shyam Sunder* v *State of Rajasthan*" AIR 1974 SC 890; 1974 Lab IC 598; (1974)1 SCC 690; 1974 ACJ 296; 76 Punj LR 550; (1974)2 SCJ 317.

1 *V. Kishan Rao* v *Nikhil Super Speciality Hospital* (2010)5 SCC 513; (2010)4 SCJ 690; 2010 AIR SCW 4252; III(2010) CPJ 1; 2010(5) SLT 349; CDJ 2010 SC 428.

2 Charlesworth & Percy on *Negligence*, 9th Ed., p. 425 (5·88).

3 *Ashish Kumar Majumdar* v *Aishi Ram Batra Charitable Trust* CDJ 2009 DHC 1059.

conditions are required to be satisfied for invoking the doctrine of *res ipsa loquitur*: first, the happening should be unexplained, secondly, the happening would not have remained unexplained in ordinary course without negligence on the part of somebody, and thirdly, circumstances are a pointer to negligence of the defendant rather than any other person.

It is well-settled that where in an action for negligence the thing causing fatal injury to the deceased and consequent pecuniary loss to the plaintiff is shown to be under the management of the defendant or his servants and the accident is such as in the ordinary course of events does not happen, if those who have the management use proper care, that affords reasonable evidence, in the absence of explanation by the defendant, that the accident arose from want of care.[4] The normal rule is that it is for the plaintiff to prove negligence and not for the defendant to disprove it. An exception to this rule applies where the circumstances surrounding the thing which causes the damage are at the material time exclusively under the control or management of the defendant or his servant and the happening is such, which cannot occur in the ordinary course of things without negligence on the part of the defendant.[5]

To invoke the maxim of *res ipsa loquitur* the following two-steps process need to be established: first, whether the accident is the kind that would usually be caused by negligence; and secondly, whether or not the opposite party had exclusive control over the instrumentality that caused the accident.[6]

It is important to note that when complications and death of patient occurred within four walls of operation theatre

4 *The Krishna Bus Service Ltd.* v *Smt. Mangli* AIR 1976 SC 700; (1976)1 SCC 793; 1976 ACJ 183; 1976 TAC 260; (1976)3 SCR 178; (1976)1 APLJ (SC) 52.

5 *Municipal Corporation of Delhi* v *Subhagwanti* AIR 1966 SC 1750; (1966)2 SCA 96; 1966 Cur LJ 820; (1966)68 Punj LR 307; (1966)2 SCWR 533.

6 *Monica Singla (Dr.)* v *Tej Bhan* 2015(4) CPR 540; I(2016) CPJ 588 (NCDRC).

where patient's relatives had no access, the onus lies on the doctors in the operation theatre to explain events and the ultimate outcome, i.e. the death of the patient.[7] By invoking the maxim of *res ipsa loquitur*. The National Commission[8] held the surgeon guilty of medical negligence for leaving surgical needle holder in the abdomen of the patient during surgery for removal of ovarian cyst and repair of umbilical hernia and for not taking any corrective measures like taking of x-ray or ultrasound, despite repeated complaint of the patient for a period of about 4-5 months after the surgery. By applying the doctrine of *res ipsa loquitur*, the National Commission[9] held the doctor negligent for development of gangrene in right palm of the infant, who was given IV infusion in right hand and tight bandage cast, as he was suffering from septicaemia.

The Supreme Court[10] applied the doctrine of *res ipsa loquitur* where the patient had to undergo second operation in critical condition for removal of a mop (towel) left inside the peritoneal cavity of the patient during sterilization operation in a Government hospital. The High Court of Rajasthan,[11] invoked the doctrine of *res ipsa loquitur* to hold the State Government liable for the death of a patient during laparoscopic tubectomy operation in a Government hospital. The State Commission, Karnataka[12] held the dental surgeon liable in negligence for slipping of needle into the stomach of the patient at the time of irrigating the mouth after extraction of right molar teeth of the patient by applying the principle of *res ipsa loquitur*, as the surgeon could not explain as to why the needle was detached from the syringe while irrigating the mouth of the patient. By

7 *Arunaben D. Kothari* v *Navdeep Clinic* 1996(3) CPR 20 (Guj); III(1996) CPJ 605 (Guj); (1997)5 CTJ 533 (CP) (SCDRC); 1998 CCJ 972 (Guj).

8 *Leela G. Nair* v *Prof. Dr. K.P. Haridas* 2015(2) CLT 244; 2015(2) CPR 340; II(2015) CPJ 763 (NCDRC).

9 *Doon Valley Hospital* v *Master Shivabshu* IV(2016) CPJ 43 (NCDRC).

10 *Achutrao Haribhau Khodwa* v *State of Maharashtra* (1996)2 SCC 634; (1996)4 CTJ 950 (SC) (CP); 1996 ACJ 505.

11 *Rajmal* v *State of Rajasthan* 1996 ACJ 1166.

12 *Amblappa* v *Sriman D. Veerendra Heggade* 1999(3) CPR 72 (Bangalore).

applying the doctrine of *res ipsa loquitur* the National Commission[13] held the doctors and the hospital negligent when a healthy lady of 38 years was admitted to the hospital for hysterectomy, but died in the operation theatre before commencement of surgery.

The Supreme Court of India[14] applied the principle of *res ipsa loquitur* when the doctor gave the wrong treatment of typhoid to the patient suffering from malaria and ultimately the patient was shifted to another hospital in critical condition where she died. The plaintiff lodged in a room on the third floor of the hospital, was suffering from high fever and was in delirious state. He fell down on the ground at night and suffered multiple fracture of lumber vertebrae and became a paraplegic below waist. The Supreme Court[15] observed that the trial court rightly invoked the principle of *res ipsa loquitur* to the facts of the present case for shifting the burden of proof on the hospital that there was no negligence in taking due care of the patient who was an indoor patient in the said hospital.

When there was allegation of brain damage of the child due to birth asphyxia resulted by delay of 68 minutes in delivery of the child, the court shifted the evidentiary burden on the health authority to justify the delay in securing the attendance of the consultant obstetrician for delivery of the child. By invoking the principle of *res ipsa loquitur,* the Court of Appeal in UK[16] held the health authority liable in negligence for failure to secure the attendance of Registrar or consultant obstetrician promptly for delivery of the child suffering from brain damage. The doctor caused damage to

13 *Baburao Vithal Lohakpure* v *Suniti Devi Singhania Hospital and Medical Research Centre* 2008(3) CPR 264; II(2008) CPJ 31.

14 *V. Kishan Rao* v *Nikhil Super Speciality Hospital* (2010)5 SCC 513; 2010(4) SCJ 690; 2010 AIR SCW 4252; III(2010) CPJ 1; 2010(5) SLT 349; CDJ 2010 SC 428.

15 *Ashish Kumar Majumdar* v *Aishi Ram Batra Charitable Hospital Trust* (2014)9 SCC 256; AIR 2014 SC 2061; 2014 ACJ 1393; (2014)5 Scale 340.

16 *Bull* v *Devon Area Health Authority* 22 BMLR 79 (CA); [1993]4 Med LR 117.

the common bile duct in course of operation to remove the gall bladder of the patient. The Court of Appeal[17] held the doctor negligent for causing injury in an area beyond the area of operation by applying the principle of *res ipsa loquitur*.

(iii) *Criteria for rejection* There are conflicting judicial opinions regarding applicability of the maxim when an object or an operation is under the control of two persons who are not in law responsible for the acts of each other. Lord Denning, J[18] favours application of the maxim on the ground that the plaintiff can call on each of the persons responsible for an explanation.

In an action in torts if the defendant gives no rebutting evidence but a reasonable explanation, equally consistent with the presence as well as with the absence of negligence, the presumption or inference based on *res ipsa loquitur* can no longer be sustained. The burden of proving the affirmative that the defendant was negligent and the accident occurred by his negligence still remains with the plaintiff, and in such a situation it will be for the court to determine at the time of judgment whether the proven or undisputed facts, as a whole, disclose negligence.[19]

However, simply because a patient has not favourably responded to a treatment given by a doctor or a surgery has failed, the doctor cannot be held straight way liable for medical negligence by applying the doctrine of *res ipsa loquitur*.[20]

The doctor sued for professional negligence by invoking the maxim of *res ipsa loquitur*, can rebut the allegation by adducing expert evidence that the accepted method of treatment undertaken by him had unavoidable risk.[1]

17 *Thomas* v *Curley* [2013] Med LR 141; (2013)131 BMLR 111.

18 *Roe* v *Minister of Health* [1954]2 QB 66; [1954]2 All ER 131; [1954]2 WLR 915; 98 Sol Jo 319 (CA).

19 *Syad Akbar* v *State of Karnataka* AIR 1979 SC 1848; (1980)1 SCC 30; 1980 SCC (Cri) 59; 1980 ACJ 88; 1979 CrLJ 1374; 1979 Cr LR (SC) 527; 1979 Cr App R (SC) 273.

20 *Martin F. D'Souza* v *Mohd Ishfaq* (2009)3 SCC 1; 2009 ACJ 1695; AIR 2009 SC 2049; JT 2009(2) SC 486; (2009)2 Scale 620.

1 *Direndra Rao Jachak* v *Usha Mullapudi Cardiac Centre* IV(2014) CPJ 745 (NCDRC).

The State Commission, Maharashtra,[2] refused to invoke the doctrine of *res ipsa loquitur* to prove negligence of the doctor in conducting tubectomy operation when the hospital notes did not indicate negligence on the part of the doctor and the post-mortem report indicated post operational shock as the cause of death of the patient. Similarly, the State Commission, Kerala[3] refused to apply the principle of *res ipsa loquitur* to establish negligence in conducting oesophaguscopy under general anaesthesia and in managing postoperative complications resulting in death of the patient. The State Commission, Andhra Pradesh,[4] also refused to apply the principles of *res ipsa loquitur* where the patient developed infection in his right eye with a typical coliform bacteria resulting in loss of eyesight after cataract operation. The Court of Appeal in UK,[5] refused to apply the maxim *res ipsa loquitur* to fix liability of an anaesthetist, as the practice adopted by the anaesthetist was universally acceptable. Similarly, the Court of Appeal in UK,[6] refused to invoke the principle of *res ipsa loquitur* to fix the liability of a surgeon for giving spinal anaesthetic for post operation pain relief of a patient and thereby causing total loss of sensation in legs and penile numbness leading to ejaculatory problems, as the causes of neurological defects were in doubt.

Even in civil jurisdiction, the rule of *res ipsa loquitur* is not of universal application and has to be applied with extra care and caution to the cases of professional negligence and in particular that of the doctor.[7]

2 *Laxman Thamappa Kotgiri* v *Union of India* 1998 CCJ 1093 (Bom); 1998(1) CPR 665 (Bom).

3 *M.J. Joseph* v *Dr. P.J. John* 2000(2) CPR 5 (Ker).

4 *Air Commodore Satyanarayana* v *L.V. Prasad Eye Institute* I(1998) CPJ 110 (Hyderabad); 1998 CTJ 548 (CP) (SCDRC); 1999 CCJ 550 (AP).

5 *Delancy* v *Southmead Health Authority* 26 BMLR 111 (CA); [1995]6 Med LR 355.

6 *Ratcliffe* v *Plymouth and Torbay Health Authority* 42 BMLR 64 (CA).

7 *Jacob Mathew* v *State of Punjab* (2005)6 SCC 1; 2005 ACJ 1840; AIR 2005 SC 3180; III(2005) CPJ 9; 2005(3) CPR 70; 2005 CrLJ 3710; JT 2005(6) SC 584.

6 Contributory negligence

(i) ***Ambit and purport*** The term 'contributory negligence' squarely and solely applies to the conduct of the claimant alone. If the claimant is guilty of an act or omission, which has materially contributed to the accident and the resultant injury and damages, the matter comes within the ambit of contributory negligence and the courts are enjoined to apportion the loss between the parties as the facts and circumstances may justify.[8] Lord Denning[9] points out that a person is guilty of contributory negligence if he ought reasonably to have foreseen that, if he did not act as a reasonably prudent man, he might hurt himself; and in his reckonings he must take into account the possibility of others being careless.

It is held by the Supreme Court of India[10] that even if there was interference by the patient party during the treatment, it will in no way diminish the primary responsibility and default in duty on the part of the doctors and the hospital.

(ii) ***Criteria for application*** The general rule of law with respect to negligence is that although there may have been negligence on the part of the plaintiff, yet unless he could by exercise of ordinary care have avoided the consequences of defendant's negligence, he is entitled to recover damages.[11]

To establish the defence of contributory negligence the defendant must prove first, that the plaintiff failed to take ordinary care of himself, and secondly, that his failure to take care was a contributory cause of the accident.[12] When

8 *Andhra Marine Exports (P) Ltd.* v *P. Radhakrishnan* AIR 1984 Mad 358; (1984)97 Mad LW 144; (1984)2 Mad LJ 12; 1984 ACJ 355; (1984)2 TAC 114.

9 *Jones* v *Livox Quarries Ltd.* [1952]2 QB 608; [1952]1 TLR 1377; 96 Sol Jo 344.

10 *Malay Kumar Ganguly* v *Dr. Sukumar Mukherjee* (2009)7 SCJ 124; (2009)9 SCC 221; AIR 2010 SC 1162; (2009)10 Scale 675; III(2009) CPJ 17; 2009(3) CCR 558; 2010 AIR SCW 769.

11 *Sindhu Mohanty* v *Gourkrishna Mohanty* AIR 1976 Ori 213; (1976)1 Cut WR 119; 1976 ACJ 114; 1976 TAC 554.

12 *Lewis* v *Denye* [1939]1 KB 540 affirmed [1940] AC 921; 109 LJKB 817; 163 LT 249.

contributory negligence is set up as defence, its existence does not depend on any duty owed by the injured party to the party sued, and all that is necessary to establish such a defence is to prove that the injured party did not in his own interest take reasonable care of himself and contributed by his want of care to his own injury.[13]

The patient had undergone hysterectomy operation for removal of uterus and ovary. The patient developed infection and the wound did not heal up for not following the advice of the doctor. The patient had to undergo emergency operation for closure of abdomen under general anaesthesia and the patient died of cardiac arrest during the operation. Owing to contributory negligence of the patient, the doctors were not held negligent.[14] The doctor was not held negligent as it was established from evidence that the patient was taking extra dose of steroid without contacting the doctor for three months and thereby contributed to the disability suffered by him.[15] The State Commission, Uttar Pradesh,[16] turned down the allegation of negligence of the doctor in performance of operation of broken bones on the ground of contributory negligence of the patient in breaking of the entire plaster by careless conduct. Similarly, the State Commission, Kerala[17] held the patient liable for contributory negligence for making delay of about two months in getting admitted into the hospital for surgery for reconstruction of right ureter, even after specific advice for admission and management at the earliest, and thereby reduced the total compensation by 50%.

13 *Nance* v *British Columbia Ele Rly. Co. Ltd.* [1951] AC 601; [1951]2 All ER 448; 95 Sol Jo 543.

14 *Md. Aslam* v *Ideal Nursing Home* 1997(2) CPR 109 (NC); III(1997) CPJ 81 (NC); (1997)5 CTJ 824 (CP) (NCDRC); 1998 CCJ 1244 (NC) affirming 1994(1) CPR 619 (Ori).

15 *Hans Raj* v *Dr. K.S. Chugh* 2000 CTJ 577 (CP) (SCDRC); 2000(1) CPR 310 (Chandigarh).

16 *Suraj Singh* v *Dr. Manoj Kankaney* II(2000) CPJ 293 (Lucknow).

17 *A.J. Mohammad Shah* alias *A.J. Shanavas* v *Kerala Institute of Medical Sciences* CDJ 2009 Ker SC DRC 061.

(iii) ***Criteria for rejection*** When a person is injured without any negligence on his part, but as a result of negligence on the part of the other person or as a result of the combined negligence of two other persons it is not a case of contributory negligence.[18] The contributory negligence is the fault on the part of claimant in the very occurrence of the accident. The conduct of claimant subsequent to the accident cannot be termed as contributory negligence for mitigating the amount of compensation.[19]

(iv) ***Theory of last opportunity*** When an accident happens through the combined negligence of two persons he alone is liable to the other who had the last opportunity of avoiding the accident by reasonable care, and who then knew or ought to have known of the danger caused by the other's negligence.[20] The rule of last opportunity is clearly illogical if it means that in every case the person whose negligence came last in time is solely responsible for the damage, irrespective of whether it is based upon remoteness of damage.[1]

7 Composite negligence When the accident occurs and the resultant injuries and damages flow without any negligence on the part of the claimant, but as a result of the negligence on the part of two or more persons, it is a case normally styled in legal parlance as "composite negligence". The principles of composite negligence are that the person wronged has a choice of proceeding against all or anyone or more than one of the wrong doers where more than one person are responsible in the commission of the wrong.[2] The

18 *Andhra Marine Exports (P) Ltd.* v *P. Radhakrishnan* AIR 1984 Mad 358; (1984) 97 Mad LW 144; (1984)2 Mad LJ 12; 1984 ACJ 355; (1984)2 TAC 114.

19 *Fuljibhai Motibhai Govabhai Dela* v *Fakirmohmad Saiyadali Saiyed* AIR 1982 Guj 241; 1984 Guj LH 578.

20 *Davies* v *Mann* (1842)12 LJ Ex 10 quoted in *Sindhu Mohanty* v *Gourkrishna Mohanty* AIR 1976 Ori 213; (1976)1 Cut WR 119; 1976 ACJ 114; 1976 TAC 554.

1 Winfield and Jolowicz on *Tort*, 15th Ed., p. 233.

2 *Andhra Marine Exports (P) Ltd.* v *P. Radhakrishnan* AIR 1984 Mad 358; (1984)97 Mad LW 144; (1984)2 Mad LJ 12; 1984 ACJ 355; (1984)2 TAC 114.

Gujarat State Commission,[3] apportioned the liability of orthopaedician, çardiologist, and anaesthetist as 30%, 60% and 10% respectively though they were held jointly and severally liable for the death of the patient in the midst of an operation.

8 Volenti non fit injuria A person, who makes an agreement, whether expressly or by implication, with another to run the risk of harm, which has been created by that other person, cannot recover in respect of the damage so suffered by him in consequence of any of the risks that he had agreed to run. The effect of such consent or assent is expressed by the maxim "*volenti non fit injuria*".[4] The injuries received in the course of lawful surgical operation are examples of '*volenti non fit injuria*'. The doctrine embodies voluntary assumption of risk, that is, assent or consent to the risk of harm. The risk must be construed to be what any reasonable man would expect in the circumstances and no more. The doctrine is not to be construed to mean that a person always assents to a risk, merely because he has knowledge of it.[5] The defence of '*volenti non fit injuria*' involves the answers to two queries, viz. whether (*a*) the plaintiff had agreed to the breach of a duty of care, which was owed to him by the defendant; and (*b*) the plaintiff had consented to waive his right of action against the defendant in respect of that breach.[6]

The surgeon was not held negligent for unwanted pregnancy of the plaintiff due to failure of sterilization operation as the plaintiff took the decision to have unprotected sexual intercourse after having knowledge that she was not sterile. The court did apply the maxim *volenti non fit injuria*, as the plaintiff accepted the risk of the defendant's negligence in the performance of his legal duty, absolving the defendant from the consequences of that negligence.[7]

3 *Arunaben D. Kothari* v *Navdeep Clinic* 1996(3) CPR 20 (Guj); III(1996) CPJ 605 (Guj); (1997)5 CTJ 533 (CP) (SCDRC); 1998 CCJ 972 (Guj).
4 Charlesworth & Percy on *Negligence*, 9th Ed., p. 225 (para 3·68).
5 *Om Parkash Sekhri* v *Pritam Singh* 1984 ACJ 435 (P&H).
6 Charlesworth & Percy on *Negligence*, 9th Ed., p. 225 (para 3.68).
7 *Sabri Tabrizi* v *Lothian Health Board* 43 BMLR 190 CS (OH).

9 Inevitable accident The defence of 'inevitable accident', 'act of God', or 'latent defect' in fact mean the same thing.[8] Sir Frederick Pollock[9] defined 'inevitable accident' as an accident not avoidable by any such precautions as a reasonable man, doing such an act then and there, could be expected to take. The expression 'inevitable accident' has assumed a special meaning in legal parlance and is understood for a long time to connote only those accidents which cannot be foreseen and consequently cannot be averted with care and skill.[10] There can be no 'inevitable accident' unless the defendant can prove that something happened over which he had no control and the effect of which could not have been avoided by the exercise of care and skill.[11] The burden of proof rests on the party who takes the plea of 'inevitable accident'.[12]

An act of God will be an extraordinary occurrence due to natural causes which is not the result of any human intervention and which could not be avoided by any amount of foresight and care.[13] In order to succeed in a defence that the accident was due to latent defect, it must be established that the defect was latent and not discoverable by use of reasonable care.[14] To establish the plea of latent defect, it must be proved that the defect remained hidden in spite of taking all reasonable care.[15]

8 *Bimala Devi* v *Pepsu Road Transport Corporation* 1984 ACJ 473 (P&H).

9 Pollock on *Torts*, 15th Ed., p. 97.

10 *State of M.P.* v *Pehlajrai Dwarkadas* AIR 1976 MP 208; 1976 ACJ 222; 1976 MPLJ 311.

11 Charlesworth & Percy on *Negligence*, 7th Ed., p. 197.

12 *C. Chinnaswami* v *M. Vijay* 1966 ACJ 317 (Mad); *Bhagwati* v *Chandramaul* AIR 1966 SC 735; *Krishan Dayal* alias *Keshavdayal* v *Vishnu Prasad* 1985 ACJ 450.

13 *P.K. Kalasami Nadar* v *K. Ponnuswami Mudaliar* AIR 1962 Mad 44; 74 Mad LW 495; ILR (1961) Mad 1091.

14 *Minu B. Mehta* v *Balkrishna Ramchandra Nayan* AIR 1977 SC 1248; 1977 ACJ 118; (1977)2 SCC 441; 1977 TAC 320; (1977)2 SCR 886; (1977)2 APLJ (SC) 1.

15 *Henderson* v *Henry E Jenkins and Sons* [1969]2 QB 188 reversed [1970] AC 282; [1969]3 WLR 732; 113 Sol Jo 856; [1969]3 All ER 756; 1970 ACJ 198 (HL).

10 Evaluation of evidence The provisions of the Indian Evidence Act are not applicable to the proceedings before the consumer court. The National Commission is merely to comply with principles of natural justice.[16] The hospital was held guilty of deficiency in service in giving treatment to the patient, as the case papers and treatment sheets of the patient were not produced to refute the allegation of lack of standard care and treatment to the patient.[17] The State Commission[18] disbelieved the evidence of the surgeon for producing two sets of photocopy of case papers in order to substantiate his evidence without any cogent explanation about non-availability of the original. The State Commission, Mumbai,[19] disbelieved the evidence of the complainant on the ground that the post-mortem report, inquest report and expert evidence did not support the allegation of massive bleeding from the operation site, and that the risk of pulmonary embolism is a known, but unforeseeable complication in case of fracture of long bone, which perhaps was the cause of death.

The duty nurse gave an injection to the patient during post-operative period without any test dose and immediately thereafter the patient emitted froth and collapsed. The State Commission, Tamil Nadu,[20] disbelieved the evidence of the complainant on the ground that the complainant could not disclose the name of the injection administered by the nurse to the patient. The leg of the patient was amputated as a result of development of gangrene. The allegation of deficiency in service attributed to the doctor for not promptly referring the patient to better equipped hospital even after detecting vascular injury with fractures, was negated by the State

16 *Malay Kumar Ganguly* v *Dr. Sukumar Mukherjee* (2009)9 SCC 221; (2009)7 SCJ 124; AIR 2010 SC 1162; (2009)10 Scale 675; III(2009) CPJ 17; 2009(3) CCR 558; 2010 AIR SCW 769.

17 *Kanaiyalal Ramanlal Trivedi* v *Dr. Satyanarayan Vishwakarma* 1996(3) CPR 24 (Guj); I(1997) CPJ 332 (Guj); 1998 CCJ 690 (Guj).

18 *Devendra Kantilal Nayak* v *Dr. Kalyaniben Dhruv Shah* 1996(3) CPR 56; I(1997) CPJ 103; 1998 CCJ 544 (Guj).

19 *Smt. Archana* v *Chudhari Trust Hospital* 1998(1) CPR 556 (Mumbai).

20 *Smt. Packia Retnam* alias *A.P. Ratna Singh* v *Dr. N.C. Thanu* 1998(1) CPR 222 (Chennai); I(1999) CPJ 314 (Chennai).

Commission, Chandigarh[1] on the basis of expert evidence to the effect that the treatment given by the doctor to stabilise the condition of the patient before referring the patient to the hospital was proper. The patient was admitted to PGI, Chandigarh with large number of problems such as severe pain in the back, inability to get up, shivering and fever, and weakness in the legs etc. The allegation of negligence on the part of the doctors of PGI was ruled out by the State Commission[2] on the ground that the patient had not brought on record the details of surgical treatment received at the private hospital before admission to PGI, Chandigarh.

The patient suffered permanent loss of voice due to paralysis of vocal cord following PDA (surgery of congenital heart disease), but the surgeon was not held negligent on the grounds that 4% vocal cord paralysis following PDA was established from standard medical literature, and that there was no categorical proof of injury to laryngeal nerve during surgery. Moreover, the allegation that the patient was not informed of the chances of impairment of vocal cord due to surgery, was negated from the detailed written consent of the patient.[3]

The State Commission, Karnataka,[4] did not hold the doctor negligent for giving wrong treatment of typhoid, as the patient got discharged from the hospital without complying with the instruction of the doctor for bone marrow aspiration test. The wife of the complainant died of massive heart attack during operation of sinusitis. In the absence of expert evidence on behalf of the complainant, the State Commission rightly relied on the affidavits filed by the four doctors to refute the

1 *Lekh Raj* v *Bharaj Nursing Home* 1998(2) CPR 450 (Chandigarh); II(1998) CPJ 335 (Chandigarh); 1999 CCJ 1537 (Punj).

2 *Dr. S.L. Dhewan* v *Post Graduate Medical Institute & Research Centre* 1998(2) CPR 425 (Chandigarh); III(1998) CPJ 128 (Chandigarh); 1998 CTJ 627 (CP) (SCDRC).

3 *C. Anjani Kumar* v *Madras Medical Mission* 1998(2) CPR 308 (Chennai); I(1998) CPJ 533 (Chennai); 1998 CTJ 504 (CP) (SCDRC); 1999 CCJ 915 (TN).

4 *P.N. Sudhakar Gupta* v *Shri Anugraha Vittala Nursing Home* 1997(2) CPR 169 (Bangalore); I(1997) CPJ 266 (Bangalore).

allegation that the surgeon did not possess professional skill or that life saving drugs were not given for treatment of anaphylactic shock which risk was inherent in administration of xylocaine anaesthesia. Moreover, the State Commission[5] relied upon the operation notes, as nothing was brought on record to show that the operation notes were fabricated and were prepared after the death of the patient.

The patient had undergone abdominal hysterectomy and one bottle of blood was given after surgery. The patient developed fever and the blood test revealed malaria and hepatitis virus B infection. The State Commission, Tamil Nadu,[6] refused to hold the hospital and doctor negligent because the patient did not prove that she was negative for hepatitis-B virus infection before surgery and blood transfusion. The State Commission, Chandigarh,[7] did not hold the doctor negligent as it was established from evidence that the patient was taking extra doses of steroids without contacting the doctor for three months and thereby contributed to the disability suffered by him.

The hospital was held vicariously liable for negligence of the doctor on the basis of two documents: first, bill of the hospital included the professional fees of the doctor; secondly, discharge certificate was issued by the hospital under its letter head and under the signature of the doctor.[8] When it was established from evidence that there were perforations in uterus and intestine and complications of "faecal fistula" after D&E operation for termination of pregnancy, and no explanation was forthcoming as to why the patient was kept in the hospital for three days after D&E operation and non-disclosure of treatment given to the patient during

5 *Sethuraman Subramaniam Iyer* v *Triveni Nursing Home* 1997(2) CPR 144 (NC); I(1998) CPJ 10 (NC); 1998 CTJ 7 (CP) (NCDRC); 1998 CCJ 1532 (NC).

6 *V. Chitralekha* v *Director and Superintendent, IOG* I(1998) CPJ 124 (Chennai).

7 *Hans Raj* v *Dr. K.S. Chugh* 2000 CTJ 577 (CP) (SCDRC); 2000(1) CPR 310 (Chandigarh).

8 *P.P. Ismail* v *Mrs. K.K. Radha* 1997(2) CPR 171 (NC); I(1998) CPJ 16 (NC); (1997)5 CTJ 685 (CP) (NCDRC); 1999 CCJ 99 (NC).

postoperative complications, the operating surgeon was held negligent by the State Commission, Gujarat.[9]

The doctor has failed to produce the case-history with operating notes on the pretext of destroying the same as per prevalent practice in various nursing homes of the State of Madhya Pradesh. The complaint was filed after one year and eight months of the operation and the doctor gave reply within seven months of filing complaint. The State Commission, M.P. held that it was the duty of the doctor to preserve the case-history of the patient after submitting reply in court. The plea of destroying the case-history appeared to the court as an attempt to suppress certain facts likely to be revealed from history-sheet. On the basis of medical literature it is held by the State Commission, M.P.[10] that the doctor was negligent in performing operation resulting in permanent disability of the patient.

11 Principles of res judicata The parents of a baby boy approached the State Commission for compensation against the doctor and the hospital on the allegation that the baby died due to medical negligence of the hospital and the doctor. The claim of medical negligence was dismissed by the State Commission. The appeal preferred against the decision of the State Commission was withdrawn and a civil suit was filed on the same set of facts alleging medical negligence. The Bombay High Court,[11] held that the suit is barred by the principles of *res judicata*, as the issues involved in the suit have already been decided finally by the State Commission.

9 *Vinubhai Parsottamdas Patel* v *Dr. Vijay Kumar Ajmera* 1997(1) CPR 348 (Guj).

10 *S.A. Qureshi* v *Padode Memorial Hospital and Research Centre* II(2000) CPJ 463 (Bhopal).

11 *Miraj Medical Centre* v *Sunil Tukaram Danane* (Writ Petition No. 10897 of 2014 decided on 15.10.2019).

CHAPTER

10

Amount and Assessment

1 Object of compensation The compensation paid for personal injuries is neither punishment nor reward. The principle on which damages for negligence are assessed is that they are to be regarded as compensation for an injury sustained and not as punishment for a wrong inflicted. The sole basis of awarding compensation to the dependants of the deceased is that on account of culpable negligence or default of the offender, a valuable life who was the source of livelihood to the claimants is cut short. The abrupt termination of life results in loss to the dependants or to the estate. The determination of the amount of compensation is basically a net balance of the loss and gain to the survivors or the dependants. It is held by the Court of Appeal in UK[1] that the purpose of an award of damages in tort is to make good to the injured plaintiff, so far as money could do, the loss that he had suffered as a result of the wrong done to him. Relying on the principle *restitutio in integrum* it is held by the Supreme Court of India[2] that the aggrieved person should get that sum of money as compensation, which would put him in the same position if he had not sustained the wrong. It must result in compensating not only the financial

1 *Wells* v *Wells* [1999]1 AC 345.
2 *V. Krishnakumar* v *State of Tamil Nadu* AIR 2015 SC 2836; (2015)9 SCC 388; 2015 ACJ 2028; (2015)7 Scale 275; III(2015) CPJ 15 (SC).

loss suffered due to the injuries, but also pain and suffering undergone by the aggrieved person.

The basic figure of annual dependency has to be determined after excluding the amount which the deceased was spending on himself or which he was investing in some capital investment or formation of the estate. In order to do justice between the parties the method of multiplying the annual dependency by the number of years by which the life has been cut short without any further reduction is unreasonable and unrealistic. The principle of working out the suitable multiplier with which annual dependency be multiplied and capital amount arrived at appears to be the only just and reasonable method, because the same takes into consideration not only the age of the victim but also the ages of the dependants and all uncertainties of life—both in the realm of enhancement in the income as well as factors justifying reduction in the amount of compensation.[3]

2 Damage—reasonable foreseeability It is held by the Privy Council that if a defendant is guilty of negligence he is liable only for those consequences of his act which were reasonably foreseeable.[4] The law does not require that the precise nature of the injury must be reasonably foreseeable before liability is attributed. It is sufficient if the type, kind, degree or order of harm could have been foreseen in a general way.[5] Where the plaintiff suffers no damage to his person or property, but has sustained only economic loss the law does not usually permit him to recover that loss because it is too remote to be a head of damage.[6] Mere economic loss unaccompanied by damage to the plaintiff's person or property is irrecoverable in an action for negligence. The test of foreseeability

3 *Lachhman Singh* v *Gurmit Kaur* AIR 1979 P&H 50 (FB); (1979)81 Punj LR 1; ILR (1979)1 P&H 186; 1979 ACJ 170; 1979 TAC 221.

4 *Overseas Tankship (U.K.) Ltd.* v *Morts Dock and Engineering Co. Ltd. (The Wagon Mound)* [1961] AC 388; [1961]1 All ER 404; [1961]2 WLR 126; 105 Sol Jo 85; [1961]1 Lloyd's Rep 1.

5 *Bradford* v *Robinsons Rentals Ltd.* [1967]1 All ER 267; [1967]1 WLR 337; 111 Sol Jo 33.

6 *SCM (UK) Ltd.* v *W.J. Whittall & Son Ltd.* [1971]1 QB 337; [1970]3 All ER 245; [1970]3 WLR 694; 114 Sol Jo 706 (CA).

determines liability in damages for the result of wrongful act. The questions of remoteness of damages and breaking of chain of causation by intervening action should be taken into consideration before ascertaining the damages.

3 Mode of assessment Much thought is devoted by the Judiciary on the question of the appropriate test to be applied to the quantification of damages.[7] The Supreme Court of India[8] adopted multiplier system for assessing damages on the basis of the principle enunciated by the House of Lords. Lord Wright[9] has laid down the general rule of assessing damages in the following ways: The damages are to be based on the reasonable expectation of pecuniary benefit or benefit reducible to money value. In assessing the damages which may be legitimately pleaded in diminution of the damages must be considered. The actual pecuniary loss of each individual entitled to sue can only be ascertained by balancing, on the one hand, the loss to him of the future pecuniary benefit, and, on the other hand, any pecuniary advantage which from whatever source comes to him by reason of the death.

Viscount Simon[10] formulated the following tests for ascertaining damages: first, the expectation of life of the deceased has to be estimated having regard to his age, bodily health and the possibility of premature determination of his life by later accidents; secondly, the amount required for future provision of his wife shall be estimated having regard to the amount he used to spend on her during his lifetime and other circumstances; thirdly, the estimated annual sum is multiplied by the number of years of the estimated span of life of the deceased, and the said amount must be

7 *Municipal Corporation of Delhi* v *Subhagwanti* AIR 1966 SC 1750; (1966)2 SCA 96; 1966 SCWR 533; 1966 ACJ 57 (SC).

8 *Sheikhupura Transport Co. Ltd.* v *Northern India Transporters Insurance Co. Ltd.* AIR 1971 SC 1624; 1971 ACJ 206; 1971 SCD 535; 73 Punj LR 722; (1971)1 Civ Ap J 166 (SC).

9 *Davies* v *Powell Duffryn Associated Collieries Ltd.* [1942] AC 601; [1942]1 All ER 657; 167 LT 74; 111 LJKB 418; 86 Sol Jo 294 (HL).

10 *Nance* v *British Columbia Electric Rly. Co. Ltd.* [1951] AC 601; [1951]2 All ER 448; 95 Sol Jo 543 (PC).

discounted so as to arrive at the equivalent in the form of a lump sum payable on his death; fourthly, further deductions must be made for the benefit accruing to the widow from the acceleration of her interest in his estate; and fifthly, further amount has to be deducted for the possibility of the wife dying earlier if the husband had lived the full span of life, and it should also be taken into account that there is the possibility of the widow remarrying much to the improvement of her financial position.

Lord Wright[11] pointed out the manner of assessment of damages by certain years' purchase in the following way: The starting point is the amount of damages which the deceased was earning, the ascertainment of which to some extent may depend upon the regularity of his employment. Then there is an estimate of how much was required or expended for his own personal and living expenses. The balance will give data or basic figures which will generally be turned into a lump sum by taking a certain number of years' purchase. That sum, however, has to be taxed down by having due regard to uncertainties, for instance, that the widow might have again married and thus ceased to be dependant, and other like matters of speculation and doubt.

Lord Diplock[12] enunciated the following principles for the purpose of working out annual dependency: To assess the damages it is necessary to form a view on three matters—each of which is in greater or lesser degree one of speculation: (*i*) the value of the material benefits for his dependants which the deceased would have provided out of his earnings for each year in the future during which he would have provided them had he not been killed, (*ii*) the value of any material benefits which the dependants would have obtained in each such year from sources (other than insurance) which would not have been available to them had the deceased lived, but which will become available to them as a result of his death,

11 *Davies* v *Powell Duffryn Associated Collieries Ltd.* [1942] AC 601; [1942]1 All ER 657; 167 LT 74; 111 LJKB 418; 86 Sol Jo 294 (HL).

12 *Mallet* v *Mc Monagle* [1970] AC 166; [1969]2 All ER 178; [1969]2 WLR 767; 113 Sol Jo 207 (HL).

(*iii*) the amount of the capital sum which with prudent management will produce annual amount equal to the difference between (*i*) and (*ii*) (i.e. the dependency) for each of the years during which the deceased would have provided material benefits for the dependants had he not been killed.

To determine the quantum of damages in case of fatal accidents, a basic figure indicative of the annual loss to the dependants from the premature death has to be arrived at. This basic figure has to be converted into a lump sum by applying a suitable multiplier. For the purpose of determining the multiplier to be applied to the annual dependency the factors like prospects of increase in wages, recession in trade, spells of unemployment, possibilities of the children beginning to earn when grown up, remarriage of the widow as well as the presence of the children diminishing the chances of remarriage have to be taken into consideration.[13]

The majority of the Privy Council[14] held that exemplary damages can be awarded in exceptional and rare cases of negligent conduct of the defendant, which was so outrageous as to call for condemnation and punishment, though the defendant might not have intended to cause harm or been subjectively reckless to the risks involved.

4 Assessment by application of multiplier The multiplier method of assessing damages is to calculate the net pecuniary loss upon an annual basis and to arrive at the total award by multiplying the figure assessed as the amount of the annual dependency by a number of years' purchase, i.e. the number of years the benefit was expected to last by taking into consideration the imponderable factors in fixing either the multiplier or the multiplicand.[15]

When a person is on the threshold of his career, his income is less, but he has a longer period to serve and as such a

13 *Lachhman Singh* v *Gurmit Kaur* AIR 1979 P&H 50 (FB); (1979)81 Punj LR 1; ILR (1979)1 P&H 186; 1979 ACJ 170; 1979 TAC 221.

14 *A.* v *Bottrill* [2002]3 WLR 1406; [2002] UKPC 44.

15 *Madhya Pradesh State Road Transport Corporation* v *Sudhakar* AIR 1977 SC 1189; 1977 Cur LJ (Civ) 283; (1977)3 SCC 64; 1977 TAC 503; (1977)3 SCR 627.

higher "multiplier" is called for. A lower "multiplier" is justified as the person grows old, and his income and contribution to the family increases. The multiplier of 16 is commonly invoked by our High Courts and the Supreme Court where the deceased is in his twenties. Similarly, the multiplier of 15 has been used where the deceased is over the age of thirty.[16]

The deceased was 30 years old at the time of the accident. The multiplier of 15 years was used by the Supreme Court in calculating the amount of compensation.[17] The deceased lady was aged about 23 years. She had 35 years of service before her when she died. The claimant's loss was reasonably worked out by keeping in mind all the relevant facts and contingencies and taking 20 as the suitable multiplier by the Supreme Court.[18]

The deceased was aged 60 years. The annual income of the deceased was ₹5,00,000 as per Income Tax Return. By deducting one-third amount towards personal expenditure of the deceased, the annual loss of dependency comes to ₹29,70,000. By applying the multiplier of 9 and by taking into consideration the fact of pendency of the litigation for about 20 years, a sum of ₹40,00,000 was awarded as compensation in addition to ₹10,00,000 towards mental agony, loss of consortium and loss of love and affection.[19] The Delhi High Court[20] and the Full Bench of Punjab and Haryana High Court[1] applied 16 as multiplier when the deceased was aged 24 years and 23 years respectively.

16 *Smt. Krishna Kumari Gupta* v *Gurbux Sheesh Singh* 1985 ACJ 457; AIR 1985 All 85; (1985)1 ACC 68; 1985 All CJ 23; (1985)11 All LR 121.

17 *Municipal Corporation of Delhi* v *Subhagwanti* AIR 1966 SC 1750; (1966)2 SCA 96; 1966 SCWR 533; 1966 ACJ 57 (SC).

18 *Madhya Pradesh State Road Transport Corporation* v *Sudhakar* AIR 1977 SC 1189; 1977 Cur LJ (Civ) 283; (1977)3 SCC 64; 1977 TAC 503; (1977)3 SCR 627.

19 *Sheela Hirba Naik Gaunekar* v *Apollo Hospitals Ltd.* 2016(4) RCR (Civil) 879; (2016)10 Scale 18 (SC).

20 *Chameli Wati* v *Delhi Municipal Corporation* 1984 ACJ 134 (Del).

1 *Lachhman Singh* v *Gurmit Kaur* AIR 1979 P&H 50 (FB); (1979)81 Punj LR 1; ILR (1979)1 P&H 186; 1979 ACJ 170; 1979 TAC 221.

Without selecting the multiplier on the basis of the guidelines given in the second schedule annexed to s. 163A of the Motor Vehicles Act 1988, the Supreme Court of India[2] applied the multiplier of 30 instead of 15 for assessing the loss of dependency of the claimant when the deceased was aged about 45 years. An Advocate aged 45 years had no proof of income at the time of death. His annual income was taken as ₹50,000 which was not taxable in the relevant financial year 2000-01. By taking his active legal practice for another 25 years and by deducting 1/3rd amount towards his personal expenses and by considering rate of inflation, the National Commission[3] assessed loss of dependency to the tune of ₹11,50,000 and awarded total compensation of ₹13.8 lakh including ₹2 lakh for distress and mental agony and ₹25,000 as litigation cost. A lady who died of medical negligence was aged about 56 years. She was housewife and not employed. The Supreme Court of India[4] assessed her contribution to the family in terms of money by taking into consideration her educational qualification status of bringing up and income of the husband and enhanced the amount of compensation from ₹5 lakh to ₹15 lakh towards her husband.

The Supreme Court warned against the straight jacket approach of using multiplier method for calculation of damages in cases of medical negligence. By taking into consideration various aspects of awarding damages the Supreme Court granted huge amount of compensation in *Balaram Prasad* v *Kunal Saha,*[5] *Nizam's Institute of Medical Sciences* v *Prasanth S. Dhanuka*[6] and *V. Krishnakumar* v *State of Tamil Nadu.*[7]

2 *Dr. Balaram Prasad* v *Dr. Kunal Saha* (Civil Appeal No. 2867 of 2012, 692 of 2012, 2866 of 2012, 731 of 2012 and 858 of 2012), CDJ 2013 SC 937; 2013(7) MLJ 781.

3 *Pushpa Bhatnagar* v *Varun Hospital* 2016(3) CLT 71; 2016(3) CPR 123; IV(2016) CPJ 140 (NCDRC).

4 *Arun Kumar Manglik* v *Chirayu Health and Medicare Pvt. Ltd.* (2019)3 Scale 333; 2019(2) CPR 27; JT 2019(5) SC 379.

5 (2014)1 SCC 384.

6 (2009)6 SCC 1.

7 (2015)9 SCC 388.

5 Assessment by interest theory The interest theory laid down by the Full Bench comprising three Judges of Punjab and Haryana High Court,[8] was discarded by the five Judges' Full Bench of the same High Court[9] on the ground that in present day India when our economy is not so highly developed as in western countries and the banking system has not taken deep roots especially in the villages, it is too unrealistic to adopt interest theory for determining the damages. The unanimous opinion of the Full Bench comprising five Judges of the Punjab and Haryana High Court[10] is that the interest theory is impracticable and unrealistic and will not be a proper yardstick for determining the correct amount of compensation.

6 Assessment—benefits deducted In view of the well-recognised principle that damages are compensatory and not punitive, the Court of Appeal in England[11] held that where the plaintiff received unemployment benefit to which the defendant was a contributing party, such sums must be deducted from his award of damages. Like unemployment benefit, the family income supplement is not only deductive from the special damages for loss of earnings, but also from the general damages in respect of future loss of earnings where the likely receipts are capable of being calculated with a degree of certainty.[12]

The Supreme Court refused to grant any compensation for the medical expenses incurred by the patient, which have already been defrayed by the employer of the father of the patient.[13] The National Commission also held that the

8 *Joki Ram* v *Smt. Naresh Kanta* (1977)79 Punj LR 328; TLR (1977)2 Punj 208; AIR 1977 P&H 214 (FB).

9 *Lachhman Singh* v *Gurmit Kaur* AIR 1979 P&H 50 (FB); (1979)81 Punj LR 1; ILR (1979)1 P&H 186; 1979 ACJ 170; 1979 TAC 221.

10 *Lachhman Singh* v *Gurmit Kaur* (supra).

11 *Parsons* v *B.N.M. Laboratories Ltd.* [1964]1 QB 95; [1963]2 WLR 1273; 107 Sol Jo 294; [1963]2 All ER 658; *Nabi* v *British Leyland (U.K.) Ltd.* [1980]1 WLR 529; 124 Sol Jo 83; [1980]1 All ER 667.

12 *Gas Kill* v *Preston* [1981]3 All ER 427.

13 *Nizam's Institute of Medical Sciences* v *Prasanth S. Dhananka* (2009)6 SCC 1; JT 2009(2) SC 385; 2009 AIR SCW 3563; 2010 ACJ 38; (2009)4 Supreme 165.

amount received by the patient towards his treatment from the employer will be deducted from the total amount of compensation awarded by the consumer court.[14]

7 Assessment—benefits not deducted The general rule is that the injured party should give credit for all sums which he received in diminution of his loss, save for exceptional cases such as insurance benefits.[15] To paraphrase Lord Bridge,[16] "The classic heads of exception to the basic rule are: Money accruing to the injured plaintiff under policies of insurance for which he had paid the premium". The disablement pension does not operate to reduce the damages because there is no reason in setting off what the plaintiff was entitled to under a contract with third person.[17] Where a plaintiff becomes entitled to receive a pension, not by reason of the accident, but by reason of the contributions he had made, during his service with his employer, a wrong doer should not be allowed to appropriate the said benefit, and as such the pension should be disregarded in assessing damages, whether or not the contribution to the superannuation fund was compulsory.[18] The plaintiff—a member of police service made compulsory contribution to a police pension fund out of his pay which entitled him as of right to a pension on his being discharged from police force for disablement. The House of Lords[19] held that the invalid pension was not deductible in assessing damages for loss of earnings on the ground that the pension was delayed remuneration for current work through insurance.

Money received by the plaintiff from the bounty or benevolence of third parties motivated by sympathy for his

14 *S.P. Gupta (Dr.)* v *Sukhdeb Raj Kaushal* 2016(3) CPR 494; 2016(3) CLT 579 (NCDRC).

15 *Parry* v *Cleaver* [1970] AC 1; [1969]1 All ER 555; [1969]2 WLR 821; 113 Sol Jo 147; [1969]1 Lloyd's Rep 83 (HL).

16 *Hodgson* v *Trapp* [1988]3 WLR 1281; [1988]3 All ER 870 (HL).

17 *Payne* v *Railway Executive* [1952]1 KB 26; [1951]2 All ER 910; [1951]2 TLR 929; 95 Sol Jo 710 (CA).

18 *Judd* v *Hammersmith West London and St. Mark's Hospitals (Board of Governors)* [1960]1 WLR 328; [1960]1 All ER 607; 104 Sol Jo 270.

19 *Parry* v *Cleaver* [1970] AC 1; [1969]1 All ER 555; [1969]2 WLR 821; 113 Sol Jo 147; [1969]1 Lloyd's Rep 83 (HL).

misfortune cannot be deducted in computing the amount of compensation.[20] Similarly, the *ex gratia* payment from employer is not deductible in assessment of damages for loss of earnings.[1] It is decided by the Supreme Court[2] that the amount of ₹13,500 as death-cum-retirement gratuity which the dependants of the deceased would have got, must be added to the amount of compensation awarded on the basis of salary. The High Court fell in error in deducting ₹10,000 on account of pensionary benefit of the dependants of the deceased.[3] The Supreme Court of India[4] deducted dearness allowance from income of the deceased. With all humility it is submitted that the proposition of deducting dearness allowance from income of the deceased is not sound proposition of law.

The deceased was 37 years of age at the time of his death. He was drawing a salary of ₹620 per month at the time of his death. The certificate from the Accountant General's office showed that the deceased would have drawn ₹1,88,000 till the time of superannuation. Even if half of this amount be spent by the deceased to cover day-to-day domestic expenses, payment of income-tax and other charges, the actual income lost to the family including the value of the estate and the loss to the dependants would be ₹94,000. The Supreme Court[5] held that the High Court was wrong in not taking into account the salary of the deceased at the time of his retirement.

20 *Redpath* v *Belfast and County Down Railway* [1947] NI 167; *Peacock* v *Amusement Equipment Co. Ltd.* [1954]2 QB 347; [1954]2 All ER 689; [1954]3 WLR 288; 98 Sol Jo 533 (CA).

1 *Cunningham* v *Harrison* [1973] QB 942; [1973]3 All ER 463; [1973]3 WLR 97; 117 Sol Jo 547 (CA).

2 *Smt. Manjushri Raha* v *B.L. Gupta* AIR 1977 SC 1158; 1977 ACJ 134; 1977 UJ (SC) 212; (1977)2 SCC 174; 1977 TAC 297; (1977)2 SCR 944.

3 *N. Sivammal* v *Managing Director, Pandian Roadways Corporation* 1985 ACJ 75 (SC); AIR 1985 SC 106; (1985)1 TAC 302.

4 *Pushpabai Parshottam Udeshi* v *M/s. Ranjit Ginning & Pressing Co. Pvt Ltd.* AIR 1977 SC 1735; (1977)2 SCC 745; 1977 ACJ 343; 1977 TAC 387; (1977)3 SCR 372; (1977)2 SCWR 174.

5 *Smt. Manjushri Raha* v *B.L. Gupta* AIR 1977 SC 1158; 1977 ACJ 134; 1977 UJ (SC) 212; (1977)2 SCC 174; 1977 TAC 297; (1977)2 SCR 944.

8 Compensation to severely handicapped person—principle of computation The court has to strike a balance between the inflated and unreasonable demand of the victim and the equally untenable claim of the opposite party urging for no compensation. The court must not be charry of awarding compensation to ensure steady and reasonable income to a severely handicapped person for a time, when he is unable to earn for himself. The complainant developed acute paraplegia with complete loss of control over the lower limbs and other related complications immediately after surgery for excision biopsy. The compensation was computed keeping in mind the fact that the complainant suffered from complete paralysis of lower limbs requiring continuous physiotherapy and nursing on account of infection of the urinary tract, that his brilliant career has been cut short at the early age of 20 years and that there is no possibility of improvement of his condition in future. The multiplier method was not adopted by the Supreme Court for calculation of compensation on consideration of the nature of damage suffered by the complainant, the expenditure for medical treatment incurred and likely to be incurred by him in future, and the restriction of his rising in the professional career due to his physical condition. The Supreme Court[6] awarded compensation of Rupees one crore to the severely handicapped young man.

9 Compensation under Fatal Accidents Act The injured person is entitled to get damages against the offender under the Law of Torts. The specific provision for getting damages by the dependants of the deceased was enacted for the first time in 1855 when the Fatal Accidents Act came into force. In an action under the Fatal Accidents Act 1855 it is not sufficient for the plaintiff to prove that he lost by the death of the deceased a mere speculative possibility of pecuniary benefit. In order to succeed it is necessary for him to establish that he has lost a reasonable probability of pecuniary advantage. Compulsory damages under s. 1A of the Fatal

6 *Nizam's Institute of Medical Sciences* v *Prasanth S. Dhananka* (2009)6 SCC 1; JT 2009(2) SC 385; 2009 AIR SCW 3563; 2010 ACJ 38; (2009)4 Supreme 165.

Accidents Act 1855 for wrongful death must be limited to the pecuniary loss to the beneficiaries. Since the elements which go to make up the value of the life of the deceased to the designated beneficiaries are necessarily personal to each case, in the very nature of things, there can be no exact or uniform rule for measuring the value of human life.[7] The general principle is that the pecuniary loss can be ascertained only by balancing on the one hand, the loss to the claimants of the future pecuniary benefit and, on the otherhand, any pecuniary advantage which from whatever source comes to them by reason of the death, that is, the balance of loss and gain to a dependant by the death must be ascertained.[8]

The compensation for pecuniary loss sustained by the dependants is payable under s. 1 of the Fatal Accidents Act 1855 and damages for mental agony, suffering and loss of expectation of life are payable under s. 2 of the said Act of 1855. As the claims under two sections of the Act are based upon different causes of action, the claimants—whether the same or different, would be entitled to recover compensation separately under both the heads. If a person taking benefit under both the sections is the same, he cannot be permitted to recover twice for the same loss. In awarding damages under both the heads, there shall not be duplication of the same claim, that is, if any part of the compensation representing the loss to the estate goes into calculation of the personal loss under s. 1, that portion shall be excluded in giving compensation under s. 2 and *vice versa*. There is no duplication in awarding damages under both the heads when the court gave compensation for pecuniary loss under s. 1 and awarded damages for loss to the estate, which represented the damages for mental agony, suffering and loss of expectation of life under s. 2 of the Fatal Accidents Act 1855.[9]

7 *C.K. Subramonia Iyer* v *T. Kunhikuttan Nair* AIR 1970 SC 376; 1969 SCWR 779.

8 *Gobald Motor Service Ltd.* v *R.M.K. Veluswami* AIR 1962 SC 1; (1962)1 SCR 929; 1962 Mad LJ (Cri) 120; (1962)1 SCJ 206; (1962)1 Mad LJ (SC) 105.

9 *Gobald Motor Service Ltd.* v *R.M.K. Veluswami* AIR 1962 SC 1; (1962)1 SCR 929; 1962 Mad LJ (Cri) 120; (1962)1 SCJ 206; (1962)1 Mad LJ (SC) 105.

10 Compensation under Constitutional law Right to health and health care is protected as fundamental right under Art. 21 of the Constitution of India. Where the doctors treated a patient in a Government hospital negligently, the State violated the fundamental right of the patient guaranteed under Art. 21 of the Constitution of India. The High Court of Andhra Pradesh,[10] invoked its jurisdiction under Art. 226 of the Constitution of India in order to award compensation to a patient who was the victim of medical negligence of the doctors in a Government hospital.

11 Heads of damage The award of damages in personal injury claims is an award of one figure only, a composite figure, made up of several parts. Some of the parts may be capable of being estimated in terms of money, such as loss of future earnings. Others cannot truly be estimated in terms of money at all, but must proceed on a conventional basis, such as compensation for pain and suffering and loss of amenities. At the end all the parts must be brought together to give fair compensation for the injuries.[11] Damages are awarded for pecuniary loss and non-pecuniary loss. Damages awarded under the head "pecuniary loss" are called "special damages". Loss of earnings, expenses incurred for treatment as a result of the accident, and future pecuniary loss fall under the head "special damages". Damages awarded under the head non-pecuniary loss are called "general damages". Non-pecuniary loss is of three kinds: (*a*) pain and suffering, (*b*) loss of amenities of life, and (*c*) shortened expectation of life.[12]

The Supreme Court of India[13] awarded compensation for medical negligence under the following heads: (*i*) loss of income of the deceased; (*ii*) cost of medical treatment; (*iii*) travel

10 *Mrs. Shanta* v *State of A.P.* III(1997) CPJ 481 (HC of AP).

11 Lord Denning, MR. in *Watson* v *Powles* [1968]1 QB 596; [1967]3 All ER 721; [1967]3 WLR 1364; 111 Sol Jo 562 (CA).

12 *Dr. P. Narasimha Rao* v *Gundavarapu Jaya Prakash* 1990(1) ACJ 350; (1990)1 ACC 468; AIR 1990 AP 207; (1989)3 Andh LT 564; (1989)2 APLJ (HC) 491.

13 *Dr. Balaram Prasad* v *Dr. Kunal Saha* (Civil Appeal No. 2867 of 2012, 692 of 2012, 2866 of 2012, 731 of 2012 and 858 of 2012), CDJ 2013 SC 937; 2013(7) MLJ 781.

and hotel expenses; (*iv*) loss of consortium; (*v*) pain and suffering and (*vi*) cost of litigation.

(i) ***General damage*** It is difficult to frame any formula by which general damages can be assessed for pain and suffering, loss of amenities of life and loss of expectation of life. The principles governing assessment of damages are that the damages must be fair and reasonable, that a just proportion must be observed between damages for less serious and those for more serious injuries, and that attempt must be made to award a sum in accordance with the general run of assessments made over the years in comparable cases. There must be a rational nexus between the assessment of damage and the award of damage. The Judge has no obligation to follow the award of comparable cases, but he is duty bound to consider the awards of comparable cases. It is pertinent to summarise the mode of assessment in the words of Lord Salmon,[14] "the damages awarded should be such that the ordinary sensible man would not instinctively regard them as either mean or extravagant, but would consider them to be sensible and fair in all the circumstances". The general damages awarded for failure to diagnose cervical cancer by detecting abnormal cells in cervical smear test, included compensation for surgery and radiotherapy, for abortion of much wanted foetus, for loss of reproductive abilities, for abnormal scarring, a deformed and shortened vagina with impairment of the enjoyment of sexual intercourse and fear, anxiety and psychological damage.[15]

(A) PAIN AND SUFFERING. Damages for pain and suffering are not capable of exact estimation and their assessment is a matter of degree, based on the facts of each case. The medical care and treatment are included within the actual and prospective suffering. The court must consider what is a fair amount to be awarded as compensation for pain and bodily suffering. The unconsciousness of the plaintiff eliminates the

14 *Fletcher* v *Autocar and Transporters Ltd.* [1968]2 QB 322; [1968]1 All ER 726; [1968]2 WLR 743; 112 Sol Jo 96 (CA).

15 *Thurman* v *Wiltshire and Bath Health Authority* (1997)36 BMLR 63 (QBD).

damage for pain and suffering which exist by being felt, thought, or experienced, irrespective of the serious nature of the injuries.[16] Where it is impossible to quantify in terms of money this head of claim, it is assessed by the Judges on a conventional basis.[17] Where the plaintiff realises the extent and severity of injuries by which his activities are reduced permanently to a lower level, he must be compensated for the mental anguish suffered from such injuries.[18]

It is now well-recognised that an action will lie for injury by shock sustained through the medium of the eye or the ear without direct contact.[19] The Court of Appeal in U.K. has described the shock as a state of mind between nervous shock resulting in psychiatric illness, on the one hand, and sorrow and grief on the other hand.[20] No damage will be awarded if the distress of mind is not accompanied by physical injury.[1]

(B) LOSS OF AMENITIES OF LIFE. The loss of amenities and enjoyment of life can be evaluated subjectively where the loss depends entirely upon mental suffering. The loss of enjoyment of life can be determined objectively where the loss is of a personal asset, something both in the nature of property and deprivation of a limb. The objective test is invoked when the loss is independent of mental suffering and victim's sense of loss experienced in the mind. It is authoritatively settled by the House of Lords[2] that it is in respect of objective loss of amenities that the damages will be determined, together with an additional sum for mental suffering, if the same is proved. In *H. West's* case[3] the plaintiff

16 *Wise* v *Kaye* [1962]1 QB 638; 106 Sol Jo 14; [1962]1 All ER 257; [1962]2 WLR 96 (CA); *Andrews* v *Freeborough* [1967]1 QB 1; [1966]2 All ER 721; [1966]3 WLR 342; 110 Sol Jo 407 (CA).

17 *Croke* v *Wiseman* [1982]1 WLR 71; [1981]3 All ER 852.

18 *Birkett* v *Hayes* [1982]1 WLR 816; [1982]2 All ER 710; 126 Sol Jo 399 (CA).

19 *Bourhill* v *Young* [1943] AC 92; 167 LT 261; [1942]2 All ER 396.

20 *Hinz* v *Berry* [1970]2 QB 40; [1970]1 All ER 1074; [1970]2 WLR 684; 114 Sol Jo 111 (CA).

1 *Schneider* v *Eisovitch* [1960]2 QB 430; [1960]1 All ER 169; [1960]2 WLR 169; 104 Sol Jo 89.

2 *H. West & Son Ltd.* v *Shephard* [1964] AC 326; [1963]2 All ER 625 (HL).

3 *H. West & Son Ltd.* v *Shephard* (supra).

was unable to do anything for herself due to severe head injury resulting in cerebral atrophy and paralysis of all the limbs and accordingly huge amount was awarded for loss of amenities and for loss of expectation of life.

The loss of enjoyment of life must be assessed on proper consideration of the effect of injuries on the health and spirit of the injured in carrying out the normal social and personal life. In an action for personal injuries it is irrelevant to consider whether the victim is unable to enjoy personally the award of damage. The loss of mother's care suffered by a child was valued on the basis of employing a "nanny" keeping in mind that the extent of such care decreases as the child grows up.[4]

The court awarded substantial damages for loss of amenities to a 16-year-old athletic, intelligent schoolboy who turned into a spastic, remained paralysed, mute, and in a state of coma due to a road-accident.[5] Damages were also awarded in representative actions arising out of large number of children born pitifully deformed after their mother had taken the drug thalidomide, as a tranquilliser, during their pregnancy.[6] The following facts are to be taken into account in assessment of damages for loss of enjoyment of life: the dependence of the injured on the help of others in his daily life,[7] the inability to look after, care for and render services to the dependant by the injured,[8] the sexual impotency,[9] the premature onset of menopause,[10] the loss of prospect of marriage,[11] and the inability to lead the life which the

4 *Spittle* v *Bunney* [1988]3 All ER 1031; [1988]1 WLR 847 (CA).

5 *Maxwell* v *Maxwell Scientific International (Distribution Services), The Times*, 23rd June 1963.

6 *S.* v *Distillers Co. (Biochemicals) Ltd.* [1970]1 WLR 114; [1969]3 All ER 1412; 113 Sol Jo 672.

7 *Heaps* v *Perrite Ltd.* [1937]2 All ER 60; 81 Sol Jo 236.

8 *Rourke* v *Bouton*, *The Times*, 23rd June 1982.

9 *Cook* v *J.L. Kier & Co. Ltd.* [1970]1 WLR 774; [1970]2 All ER 513; 114 Sol Jo 207.

10 *Sutton* v *Population Services Family Planning Programme Ltd.*, *The Times*, 7th November 1981.

11 *Harris* v *Harris* [1973]1 Lloyd's Rep 445.

injured used to lead or which he might have led or wanted to lead.[12]

(c) Loss of expectation of life. Each person has a right to his own life.[13] The prospect of an enjoyable, vigorous and happy life may be shortened or reduced by the injuries sustained by the injured person. The reduction of the prospect of happy and enjoyable life by injury to health must be taken into consideration in assessment of damages under this head. It is decided by the House of Lords[14] that the damage for loss of expectation of life is available on behalf of a deceased person's estate. The claim for loss of expectation of life can be advanced even when the deceased had been killed.[15] The moderate approach is followed by the courts of England in assessment of damages of alive plaintiffs with shortened expectation of life. It is decided by the House of Lords[16] that if a man is cut off in the prime of life, then no matter how bright his prospects only a conventional sum can be awarded in respect of lost years.

(ii) *Special damage* Special damage denotes pecuniary loss. The general principle is that the pecuniary loss can be ascertained only by balancing on the one hand, the loss to the claimants of the future pecuniary benefit, and on the otherhand, any pecuniary advantage which from whatever sources come to them by reason of the death, that is, the balance of loss and gain to a dependant by the death must be ascertained. The pecuniary loss to the aggrieved party would depend upon data which cannot be ascertained accurately, but must necessarily be an estimate or even partly

12 *Owen* v *Sykes* [1936]1 KB 192; 80 Sol Jo 15; 105 LJKB 32; 154 LT 82; *Keating* v *Elvan Reinforced Concrete Co. Ltd.* [1967]3 All ER 611 affirmed [1968]2 All ER 139; [1968]1 WLR 722; 112 Sol Jo 193.

13 Article 21 of the Constitution of India; Article 1 of International Covenant on Economic, Social and Cultural Rights 1966.

14 *Rose* v *Ford* [1936]1 KB 90 reversed [1937] AC 826; 106 LJKB 576; 157 LT 174; 81 Sol Jo 683; [1937]3 All ER 359.

15 *Morgan* v *Scoulding* [1938]1 KB 786; 158 LT 230; 81 Sol Jo 1041; [1938]1 All ER 28.

16 *H. West & Son Ltd.* v *Shephard* [1964] AC 326; [1963]2 All ER 625 (HL).

a conjecture.[17] The basic figure of annual dependency has to be determined after excluding the amount which the deceased was spending on himself or which he was investing in some capital investment or formation of the estate. In order to do justice between the parties the method of multiplying the annual dependency by the number of years by which the life has been cut short without any further reduction is unrealistic and unreasonable. The principle of working out the suitable multiplier with which annual dependency is to be multiplied and capital amount arrived at appears to be the only just and reasonable method because the same takes into consideration not only the age of the victim, but also the age of the dependents and all uncertainties of life, both in the realm of enhancement of the income as well as factors justifying reduction in the amount of compensation.[18]

Loss of earnings, expenses incurred for treatment as a result of the accident, and future pecuniary loss fall under the head—"special damage".[19]

(A) LOSS OF EARNINGS. Loss of earnings should be assessed as special damage between the date of accident and the trial. An injured plaintiff is entitled to recover damages in respect of any resultant loss of wages, salaries and fees. The plaintiff's real claim for special damage is the amount of his net loss and the particulars are necessary in order to enable this special damage to be calculated.[20] When special damages are being calculated there should be deduction of the amount of any national insurance contributions the plaintiff would have had to make if he had remained in work.[1] Other

17 *Sheikhupura Transport Co. Ltd.* v *Northern India Transporters Insurance Co. Ltd.* AIR 1971 SC 1624; 1971 ACJ 206; 1971 SCD 535; 73 Punj LR 722; (1971)1 Civ Ap J 166 (SC).

18 *Lachhman Singh* v *Gurmit Kaur* AIR 1979 P&H 50 (FB); ILR (1979)1 P&H 186; 1979 ACJ 170; 1979 TAC 221.

19 *Dr. P. Narasimha Rao* v *Gundavarapu Jaya Prakash* AIR 1990 AP 207; 1990(1) ACJ 350; (1990)1 ACC 468; (1989)3 Andh LT 564; (1989)2 AP LJ (HC) 491.

20 *Phipps* v *Orthodox Unit Trusts Ltd.* [1958]1 QB 314; [1957]3 WLR 856; 101 Sol Jo 884; [1957]3 All ER 305.

1 *Cooper* v *Firth Brown Ltd.* [1963]1 WLR 418; 107 Sol Jo 295; [1963]2 All ER 31.

deductions to be made are the income tax which the plaintiff would have paid, any compulsory deductions that would have been made, e.g. the contributions paid for national insurance, trade union and similar obligatory payments and superannuation or other pension contributions.[2] The basic principle for assessment of loss of earnings is that the injured person should be placed in the same financial position, as far as it can be done by an award of money, as he would have been, had the accident not happened.[3] The assessment can be made on broad lines and it is not necessary to do it with mathematical accuracy.[4]

(B) EXPENSES FOR MEDICAL TREATMENT. It is axiomatic to state that the expenses incurred by the injured plaintiff on medical treatment must be reimbursed by the defendent whose negligence has caused the injuries. The plaintiff is entitled to the cost of medical treatment—even if it is subsequently discovered that the treatment was incorrect. The cost of medical treatment includes the cost of nursing, fees of the consultants, cost of medicine and other ancillary charges. The injured plaintiff is not obliged to avail himself of free hospital treatment. The claimant can elect to be treated as a private patient but the court may be reluctant to award damages on what would be a speculative basis.[5]

(C) LOSS OF FUTURE EARNINGS. There is difference between an award for loss of earnings and for loss of earning capacity. Compensation for loss of future earnings is awarded for real assessable loss proved by evidence. On the other hand, compensation for diminution of earning capacity is awarded as part of general damages for pain and suffering as well as loss of amenities. The damages for future earning capacity is quantified separately in England after pronouncement of

2 *Colledge* v *Bass Mitchells & Butlers Ltd.* [1988]1 All ER 536; [1988] ICR 125 (CA).

3 *Hodgson* v *Trapp* [1988]3 All ER 870; [1988]3 WLR 1281 (HL).

4 *British Transport Commission* v *Gourley* [1956] AC 185; [1956]2 WLR 41; 100 Sol Jo 12; [1955]3 All ER 796; [1955]2 Lloyd's Rep 475.

5 *Lim Poh Choo* v *Camden and Islington Area Health Authority* [1980] AC 174; [1979]2 All ER 910; [1979]3 WLR 44; 123 Sol Jo 457 (HL).

judgment.[6] The problem of assessing quantum of damages for loss of future earning capacity arises where the plaintiff is in employment after the accident. To arrive at a decision the court must consider the factors like the risk of losing the present job and being thrown into the competitive market for another job. The fact of impairment of a person's capacity to do work, even if it is gratuitous, can result in a loss and become part of future earning capacity. For example, the proper measure of damages for the future partial loss of housekeeping capacity of an injured housewife is the estimated cost of employing labour in order to provide housekeeping services, which she would need in future, even if the award may not be used by her for that purpose at all.[7]

The determination of the amount of compensation under this head is basically a net balance of the loss and gain to the survivors or the dependants. In this calculation it is not possible to visualise or measure in exact terms all the uncertainties, hazards and the windfalls of life. There is bound to be some sort of general estimate, but mere speculations or wild guesswork has to be avoided.

12 Interest on award The court should distinguish between damages in respect of loss already incurred, for which interest may be awarded, and damages for future loss. In the latter case, far from the plaintiff being kept out of his money, the damages represent an accelerated receipt and interest in respect of future pecuniary loss should therefore not in principle be awarded.

General damages in respect of pain, suffering and loss of amenities should attract interest calculated at the appropriate rate, normally from the date of service of the writ to the date of trial. Damages in respect of loss of future earnings should attract no interest. Special damages, which usually relate to loss of earnings, medical expenses and the like which would have been incurred at various times, should be dealt with on

6 *Jefford* v *Gee* [1970]2 QB 130; [1970]2 WLR 702; [1970]1 All ER 1202; 114 Sol Jo 206 (CA).

7 *Daly* v *General Steam Navigation Co. Ltd*. [1981]1 WLR 120; [1980]3 All ER 696; 125 Sol Jo 100; [1980]2 Lloyd's Rep 415 (CA).

broad lines by awarding interest, at one-half of the appropriate rate allowed on other damages, from the date of accident to the date of trial, thus averaging the loss and expenditure over this period. In exceptional cases such as when one party or the other has been guilty of gross delay the court may depart from the above guidelines by diminishing or increasing the award of interest or altering the period for which it is allowed.[8]

There are plethora of precedents in which interest is awarded from the date of application for compensation.[9] The object of payment of interest during the period between the date of making application and the date of payment is to compel the person concerned to make payment of compensation without delay.[10] The Supreme Court awarded interest at the rate of 6% per annum on the compensation awarded.[11] The dictum of the Supreme Court[12] is that the amount of compensation will carry interest at the rate of 12% per annum from the date of the order, if the compensation amount is not deposited within four weeks. However, in another case[13] the Supreme Court awarded interest at the rate of 12% from the date of the accident till payment.

13 Forum for assessment The damages are awarded either by the Civil Court or by the Consumer Forum. Every suit shall be instituted in the court of the lowest grade competent to try it.[14] A suit for compensation may be instituted at the option of the plaintiff either in the court within the local limits of whose jurisdiction the wrong is done and the cause of action arises or in the court within the local limits of whose jurisdiction the defendant resides, or carries on business, or personally works for gain.[15] Similarly, a complaint for compensation not exceeding

8 Halsbury's *Laws of England*, 4th Ed., vol. 12, p. 490.

9 *K.G. Bhaskaran* v *K.A. Thankamma* 1973 ACJ 539 (Ker); *Hanuman Dass* v *Usha Rani* 1978 ACJ 310; *Suman Bai* v *State of M.P.* AIR 1982 MP 62; *Dayabhai Patel* v *Smt. Sundarbai* AIR 1987 MP 45.

10 *Ramesh Chandra* v *Randhir Singh* AIR 1977 All 330.

11 *Bishan Devi* v *Sirbaksh Singh* AIR 1979 SC 1862; 1979 UJ (SC) 736; 1979 ACJ 496; (1980)1 SCC 272; 1980 Cur LJ (Civ) 40.

12 *Pushpa Thakur* v *Union of India* 1984 ACJ 559.

13 *Narcinva V. Kamat* v *Alfredo Antonio Doe Martins* 1985 ACJ 397.

14 Section 15 of the Code of Civil Procedure 1908.

15 Sections 19 & 20 of the Code of Civil Procedure 1908.

₹20 lakh* before enforcement of the Consumer Protection Act 2019 may be instituted at the option of the complainant either (*i*) in the District Forum** within whose territorial jurisdiction the cause of action arises wholly or in part, or (*ii*) in the District Forum** within whose territorial jurisdiction the opposite party resides or carries on business or personally works for gain, or (*iii*) in the District Forum** within whose territorial jurisdiction any of the opposite parties resides or carries on business or personally works for gain, provided the permission of the District Forum** or the consent of the opposite parties beyond the territorial jurisdiction of the Forum is obtained.[16] The amount of compensation from rupees twenty lakh to rupees one crore can be awarded by the State Commission.[17] The National Commission can entertain complaint for compensation exceeding rupees one crore.[18] When the complainant's assessment of loss has patently been inflated in order to bring the matter within the pecuniary jurisdiction of the State Commission, the complaint is to be returned for presentation to the competent District Forum.[19]

The huge amount of court fees is required to be paid in any suit for compensation on the allegation of medical negligence. The quicker and cheaper remedy is available to the consumers of medical service under different Consumer Disputes Redressal Agencies established by the Consumer Protection Act 1986.

14 Amount assessed by civil court—case laws

(1) ***Death after operation of appendicitis*** The patient, mother of seven minor children, was treated by the doctor who

* Now 'not exceeding one crore rupees' under s. 34 of the Consumer Protection Act 2019.

** According to the Consumer Protection Act 2019 the 'District Forum' is now District Commission.

16 Section 11 of the Consumer Protection Act 1986 replacing by s. 34 of the Consumer Protection Act 2019 w.e.f. 9.8.2019.

17 Section 17 of the Consumer Protection Act 1986. According to s. 47 of the Consumer Protection Act 2019 the amount of compensation from ₹1 crore to ₹10 crore may be awarded by the State Commission.

18 Section 21 of the Consumer Protection Act 1986. According to s. 58 of the Consumer Protection Act 2019 the National Commission can entertain a complaint for compensation exceeding ₹10 crore.

19 *Jagannath* v *Jindal Dental and Orthopaedic Clinic of Koithal* II(1994) CPJ 119 (Haryana).

diagnosed the case as one of acute appendicitis. The doctor did not take the preliminary precautions like total blood count, urine test before proceeding with the operation. The help of trained anaesthetist was not obtained. No preventive step was taken to counter-act the toxic effects of chloroform on the kidney and liver by giving glucose and vitamins. On making grid iron incision the doctor found the appendix to be normal, but he proceeded to remove the gall bladder without further investigation, without preparing the patient for the second operation and without the consent of the patient party. The negligence and rashness of the surgeon in conducting the operation using chloroform anaesthesia damaged the kidneys and liver, resulting in hepato-renal failure leading to the death of the patient.

As the plaintiff claimed only symbolical damages, the court awarded ₹3,000 to the plaintiff for loss of service of his deceased wife at the rate of ₹25 per month for 10 years. The court also held that the award of ₹1,000 for mental agony and physical suffering was too low.[20]

(2) *Death due to delay in performing appendicitis operation*

The plaintiff's husband was admitted to the General Hospital, Ernakulam for complaints of severe abdominal pain which was diagnosed as a case of acute appendicitis, but no surgery was performed on the patient for two days. The patient breathed his last due to perforated appendix.

The High Court affirmed the decision of the trial court which granted a decree against the doctor for a total sum of ₹37,000.[1]

(3) *Death due to cardiorespiratory failure as reaction of anaesthesia*

The patient had undergone tubectomy under the care of the gynaecologist. There was nothing in the bed-head ticket to indicate whether sensitivity test was conducted before

20 *Ram Bihari Lal* v *Dr. J.N. Srivastava* 1985 ACJ 424; AIR 1985 MP 150; 1985 Jab LJ 259; (1985)1 Cur CC 987; 1985 MPLJ 288; 1985 Cur Civ LJ 149 reversing single Bench decision 1982 ACJ (Supp) 142 (MP).

1 *Dr. T.T. Thomas* v *Elisa* AIR 1987 Ker 52; (1987)1 ACC 461; 1987(1) ACJ 192; 1986 Ker LT 1026; (1987)2 TAC 50.

administering xylocaine 2% as local anaesthesia and what was the dose of administering anaesthesia to the patient. The doctors were held negligent for death of the patient due to cardiorespiratory failure as a reaction of anaesthesia.

The patient aged about 28 years was housewife and mother of four children. By assessing the loss of dependency at the rate of ₹36,000 per annum and by applying the multiplier of 20, the High Court of Himachal Pradesh[2] assessed the total amount of compensation as ₹3,50,000 to be paid by the defendants jointly and severally to the legal heirs of the deceased patient.

(4) ***Death due to unskilled treatment of fractured leg*** The patient aged about 20 years, son of the plaintiff, met with an accident resulting in the fracture of the femur of his left leg. The doctor was negligent in putting the fractured leg in plaster by using manual traction and excessive force with the help of three attendants and by giving single morphine injection and without caring to give anaesthetic to the patient, which caused conditions favourable for embolism or shock and proved fatal to the patient.

The trial court awarded the plaintiff general damages for a sum of ₹3,000 which was upheld by the Apex Court.[3]

(5) ***Death during laparoscopic tubectomy in Government hospital*** The patient had undergone laparoscopic tubectomy in Government hospital. The patient died due to neurogenic shock resulting in cardiac arrest, caused by insertion of pneumoperitoneal needle during the operation. The State of Rajasthan was held vicariously liable for the death of the patient whose operation was done by the doctor in Government hospital without having adequate resuscitative facilities and cardiac monitoring equipments.

The patient used to earn ₹500 per month from tailoring business. She was aged about 30 years only. The High Court

2 *Jagdish Ram* v *State of HP* 2008 ACJ 433.

3 *Dr. Laxman Balkrishna Joshi* v *Dr. Trimbak Bapu Godbole* 1968 ACJ 183 (SC); AIR 1969 SC 128; 1968 SCD 866; 1968 Mah LJ 599; (1968)2 SCWR 73.

directed the State Government to pay ₹1,00,000 to the husband of the deceased patient as compensation along with interest @12% per annum from the date of the order till realisation.[4]

(6) ***Death during tubectomy operation in Government hospital*** The patient had undergone tubectomy operation in Government hospital. She was aged 30 years and used to earn ₹280 per month as auxiliary nurse-cum-midwife. She had suffered cardiac arrest and sustained irreparable damage to the brain and did not regain consciousness. The state was held vicariously liable for negligence of the doctors of the hospital.

The High Court of Kerala[5] directed the state and the doctor to pay compensation of ₹3,80,944 jointly and severally.

(7) ***Death of a housewife after sterilization operation*** The deceased was only 24 years of age at the time of death. She was admitted to the Medical Centre, for post partum sterilization operation after her third delivery. She died on account of negligence of the doctor in performing the P.P.S. operation in the Medical Centre. The deceased was a housewife. She also used to derive income from her poultry business. She was survived by her husband and three young children including a baby of two months old.

The Kerala High Court[6] awarded compensation of ₹1,60,000 to the legal heirs of the deceased together with interest at the rate of 12% per annum from the date of institution of the suit till realisation of the amount. A sum of ₹1,00,000 was considered reasonable compensation under different heads like loss of consortium, pecuniary loss, loss of amenities of life and shortened expectation of life.

(8) ***Death of a teacher after sterilization operation*** The patient had undergone sterilization operation in a Government hospital in the State of Maharashtra. The patient developed high fever and abnormal pain and her condition deteriorated,

4 *Rajmal* v *State of Rajasthan* 1996 ACJ 1166.
5 *Dr. M.K. Gourikutty* v *M.K. Raghavan* CDJ 2001 Ker HC 296; AIR 2001 Ker 398.
6 *Joseph* alias *Pappachan* v *Dr. George Moonjely* 1995(1) ACJ 253.

but nothing was done to ascertain the cause of her ailment. When the condition of the patient became serious, abdomen was reopened and a mop (towel) left inside the peritoneal cavity during previous operation, was removed, and the pus drained out. The patient ultimately expired.

The patient was a teacher in a Government school. She died due to negligence of the doctors of Government hospital in conducting sterilization operation. The trial court awarded compensation of ₹36,000 only. The High Court had set aside the order of the trial court and held that negligence of the doctors was not proved. By setting aside the judgment of the High Court, the Supreme Court[7] restored the order of compensation passed by the trial court, and directed the State of Maharashtra to pay compensation of ₹36,000.

(9) ***Permanent brain damage after tonsillectomy*** The plaintiff, normal healthy youth of 17 years of age, had extraordinary brilliant academic career. He had a bright future of being a promising Engineer with decent job. He underwent tonsillectomy in the Government hospital. The anaesthetist and the surgeon were held negligent for causing permanent brain damage to the plaintiff.

Considering the brilliant academic career of the plaintiff which ended in permanent brain damage, the court assessed ₹2,00,000 as reasonable compensation under the head "future pecuniary loss". Damage for pain and suffering, loss of amenities of life was assessed at ₹2,00,000. Since the plaintiff cannot get a decree for more than what he has asked, the court passed a decree in favour of the plaintiff for a sum of ₹50,000 with interest at the rate of 12% from the date of filing the suit.[8]

(10) ***Permanent disability due to carelessness of the hospital*** The patient lodged in a room on the third floor of the hospital, was suffering from high fever and was in delirious state. He

7 *Achutrao Haribhau Khodwa* v *State of Maharashtra* (1996)2 SCC 634; (1996)4 CTJ 950 (SC) (CP); 1996 ACJ 505.

8 *Dr. P. Narasimha Rao* v *Gundavarapu Jaya Prakash* (1990)1 ACC 468; 1990(1) ACJ 350; AIR 1990 AP 207; (1989)3 Andh LT 564; (1989)2 APLJ (HC) 491.

fell down on the ground at night and suffered multiple fracture of lumber vertebrae and became a paraplegic below waist.

The Supreme Court[9] affirmed the award of total compensation of ₹11,00,000 under three broad heads: (*i*) loss of future prospect of employment ₹4,00,000; (*ii*) cost of engagement of attendant ₹4,00,000; and (*iii*) non-pecuniary loss including pain and suffering, loss of limb etc. ₹3,00,000.

(11) ***Sufferings for leaving foreign body in abdomen during caesarean operation*** The patient had undergone caesarean operation in a Government hospital. She developed pain and other complications after the operation. Ultimately the scan report revealed that a foreign body (mop) was left in paraspinal region during caesarean operation. By subsequent operation the foreign body was removed and pus sucked out, but another operation was required for complete recovery of the patient.

The High Court of Andhra Pradesh[10] invoked its jurisdiction under Art. 226 of the Constitution and directed the State of Andhra Pradesh to pay compensation of ₹3,00,000 to the patient for negligent treatment given to her by the doctors in a Government hospital.

(12) ***Sufferings for leaving abdominal pad inside the body during hysterectomy*** The complainant was admitted to the hospital for removal of ovarian cyst, but her uterus was removed after obtaining consent of her husband in the midst of the operation. She developed pain, dysentery, nausea, vomiting followed by intestinal obstruction during postoperative period. The x-ray report revealed foreign material covered with intestine and pus. The second surgeon removed abdominal pad measuring 12"x12" from the junction of small and large intestine during second surgery.

The Division Bench of Madras High Court[11] directed the gynaecologist and the hospital to pay compensation of

9 *Ashish Kumar Majumdar* v *Aishi Ram Batra Charitable Hospital Trust* (2014)9 SCC 256.

10 *Shanta* v *State of A.P.* III(1997) CPJ 481 (HC of AP).

11 *Soni Hospital* v *Arun Balakrishnan Iyer* AIR 2011 Mad 208; 2011(3) CTC 699.

₹2,00,000 for pain and suffering, ₹1,00,000 for mental agony and ₹35,000 for expenditure incurred for medical treatment.

(13) ***Unwanted child of a poor lady after sterilization operation*** The complainant, a poor lady having seven children, had undergone sterilization operation in a Government hospital. She conceived and gave birth to a female child due to negligence of the doctor in performing sterilization operation.

The Supreme Court[12] directed the State of Haryana to pay compensation of ₹54,000 to the complainant along with interest at the rate of 12% per annum from the date of institution of the suit till the date of payment of the decretal amount.

15 Amount assessed by consumer court—case laws

(1) ***Amputation of right hand for intra-arterial injection*** A two year old baby girl suffering from pneumonia was given intravenous fluids by inserting needle into artery instead of vein resulting in blockage of blood supply to the right forearm. The patient had to undergo amputation of right hand for development of gangrene due to inadvertent intra-arterial injection in the radial artery.

The Supreme Court[13] enhanced the amount of compensation against the hospital from ₹10,00,000 to ₹20,00,000 with interest @ 9% p.a. from the date of order of the court.

(2) ***Amputation of right arm above elbow*** The patient admitted to the hospital for Dilation and Curettage (D&C), was administered intravenous injection of phenergan and fortwin by the doctor. The excruciating pain suffered by the patient did not abate and she was shifted to another hospital. She was diagnosed with acute arterial occlusion with ischemia of limb caused by intra arterial injection. Ultimately her right arm above the elbow had to be amputated.

12 *State of Haryana* v *Smt. Santra* 2000 CTJ 481 (SC) (CP); I(2000) CPJ 53 (SC).

13 *Alfred Benedict* v *Manipal Hospital, Bangalore* (2015)11 SCC 423; 2014 SCC Online SC 1089.

The Supreme Court[14] enhanced the amount of compensation from ₹4,93,526 to ₹10,00,000 in an appeal preferred against the decision of the National Commission.

(3) ***Amputation of leg due to unskilled treatment of fracture of femur*** The complainant suffered fracture of her right femur. The right leg of the complainant upto the joint of the knee was amputated due to negligence of the doctor and the hospital in giving medical treatment and rendering postoperative care to the complainant.

The complainant suffered permanent disability. The hospital authority and Union Territory of Chandigarh were directed to pay a sum of ₹1,50,000 to the complainant as compensation.[15]

(4) ***Cerebral palsy due to delay in caesarean section*** The mother suffered long hours of labour pain causing pressure on umbilical cord and placenta due to delay in conducting caesarean section. The child suffered birth asphyxia leading to cerebral palsy and survived for 12 years with multiple health problems due to negligence of the doctor in causing delay in caesarean section.

The National Commission[16] awarded compensation of rupees one crore out of which `80 lakh to be paid by the hospital and `20 lakh to be paid by the doctor.

(5) ***Damage caused to the baby by Ayurvedic doctor*** A baby aged about six months was suffering from convulsions during high fever and was under treatment of the neurologist. The father of the patient was attracted by advertisement of the Ayurvedic doctor who gave allopathic medicine in the garb of Ayurvedic medicine for treatment of fits during high fever.

The baby suffered damage due to the treatment of the Ayurvedic doctor. The compensation of ₹5,00,000 awarded by the National Commission was enhanced to ₹15,00,000 by

14 *Shoda Devi* v *D.D.U. / Ripon Hospital, Shimla* (Civil Appeal No. 2557 of 2019 arising out of SLP (Civil) No. 26789 of 2018 decided on 07.03.2019).

15 *Sukhwarsha Rani* v *General Hospital through its Medical Superintendent* 2000(1) CPR 337 (Chandigarh).

16 *Indu Sharma (Dr.)* v *Indraprastha Apollo Hospital* III(2015) CPJ 248; 2015(2) CLT 454 (NCDRC).

the Supreme Court which directed the Ayurvedic doctor to pay ₹15,00,000 to the father of the baby within three months.[1]

(6) ***Damage due to deficiency in postoperative care*** The patient had undergone quadruple vessel coronary artery bypass surgery. The patient developed postoperative sternal infection and started purulent discharge from the site of the operation. The hospital was negligent in removing the sternal wires in two different stages and the doctor was negligent in his casual approach of prescribing antibiotics and for failure to make early diagnosis and prompt treatment of postoperative sternal infection.

The State Commission, Maharashtra,[2] directed the hospital and the cardiologist to pay jointly and severally ₹2,00,000 to the patient—the break up being ₹50,000 for delay in prescribing antibiotics, ₹50,000 for third operation, ₹80,000 for postoperative treatment, and ₹20,000 as costs.

(7) ***Damage during D&E operation*** The patient had undergone D&E operation for termination of pregnancy. She developed pain in abdomen and suffered from fever, nausea and vomiting during postoperative period. The patient was shifted to another hospital where report of investigations revealed that there were perforations in the uterus and intestine and that pus had collected in the abdomen. The patient suffered physical pain and mental agony due to want of skill on the part of the doctor in performing D&E operation.

The State Commission, Gujarat,[3] awarded compensation of ₹50,000 for physical pain and mental agony of the patient and ₹1,50,000 for the expenditure incurred for medical treatment of the patient. So, the total amount of compensation was ₹2,00,000 in addition to cost of ₹2,000.

(8) ***Damage during delivery of child*** The complainant was admitted to the nursing home with labour pain for delivery of her normal child. The pregnancy had ensued within one

1 *Bhanwar Kanwar* v *R.K. Gupta* (2013)4 SCC 252.
2 *John Andrade* v *P.D. Hinduja National Hospital & Medical Research Centre* 1998(1) CPR 579 (Bom).
3 *Vinubhai Parsottamdas Patel* v *Dr. Vijay Kumar Ajmera* 1997(1) CPR 348 (Guj).

year of the previous caesarean operation and the complainant was of a rare blood group R-H negative. The child of the complainant died and the uterus of the complainant was ruptured and removed by subsequent operation only because of want of skill and competence on the part of the nurse who took up the treatment of complicated case of pregnancy.

The State Commission, Tamil Nadu awarded compensation of ₹2,50,000 which was reduced to ₹2,00,000 by National Commission on appeal, because the amount of ₹1,00,000 towards pain and suffering was considered to be on higher side.[4]

(9) *Damage for leaving artery forceps during caesarean operation*
The patient complained of pain and nausea after caesarean operation continuously for two weeks. Subsequently on x-ray of abdomen a pair of scissors, medically known as "artery forceps" were detected inside the abdomen. The artery forceps were removed by operation.

The State Commission, Maharashtra, awarded compensation of ₹31,175. On appeal, the National Commission,[5] enhanced the amount from ₹31,175 to ₹39,175 in addition to costs of ₹2,000.

(10) *Damage for leaving foreign body during caesarean operation*
The patient suffered from urine trouble and severe pain in abdomen after caesarean operation. The report of ultrasonograph showed a mass adherent to the bladder. The patient had to undergo second operation for removal of the mass which was opened and a foreign body, *i.e.* metallic tip of the suction tube was found in the cavity of the mass.

The State Commission, Karnataka[6] directed the doctor to pay compensation of ₹2 lakh to the patient for performing

4 *M. Jeeva* v *R. Lalitha* II(1994) CPJ 73 (NC); 1994(2) CPR 517 (NC); (1994)2 CTJ 498 (CP) (NCDRC).

5 *Ms Sau Madhuri* v *Dr. Rajendra* 1996(3) CPR 174 (NC); III(1996) CPJ 75 (NC); (1997)5 CTJ 43 (CP) (NCDRC); 1997 CCJ 1499 (NC).

6 *Smt. Rohini Pritam Kabadi* v *Dr. R.T. Kulkarni* 1998(1) CPR 142 (Bangalore); 1998 CCJ 910; III(1996) CPJ 441 (Bangalore); (1997)5 CTJ 83 (CP) (SCDRC).

caesarean operation negligently leaving a metallic tip of suction tube in the abdomen of the patient.

(11) *Damage for slipping of needle into stomach during extraction of molar teeth* The doctor inserted syringe into the mouth of the complainant in order to irrigate the mouth and to clean the socket to stop bleeding after extraction of molar teeth. The needle got detached and slipped into stomach. The doctor is held guilty of negligence for not exercising due care at the time of irrigating the mouth of the complainant.

The complainant is a clerk in a company. The hospital is held vicariously liable for negligence of its doctor. The State Commission, Karnataka,[7] directed the hospital to pay to the complainant compensation of ₹1,00,000 by way of general damages and ₹200 for actual expenditure on treatment and ₹3,000 as cost of the proceeding.

(12) *Damage to cornea and left eyeball due to defective operation* The complainant, aged six years, had undergone an operation for removal of deformity of left eye. Owing to negligence in performance of operation the complainant suffered from further drooping of eyelid instead of lifting of the same, and serious damage to cornea resulting in double vision, and damage to the tear gland resulting in non-formation of tears requiring use of medicines at an interval of three hours.

The State Commission, Chandigarh,[8] directed the hospital to pay compensation of ₹2,00,000 to the guardian of the minor complainant along with cost of ₹5,000.

(13) *Damage to eyes due to wrong diagnosis and treatment* The son of the complainant, aged 8 years was treated for measles, though he was ultimately found to have been suffering from SJS (drug induced immunological, mucocutaneous disorder) resulting in damage to the eyes. The expert evidence established that the disability from which the patient suffered can be largely, but not entirely attributed to the treatment provided by the doctor and the hospital.

7 *Amblappa* v *Sriman D. Veerendra Heggde* 1999(3) CPR 72 (Bangalore).
8 *Jaswinder Singh* v *Dr. J.S. Saini* II(2000) CPJ 262 (Chandigarh).

The National Commission[9] awarded compensation of ₹9,00,000 against the hospital and the doctors by apportioning the amount of compensation to be paid by each doctor.

(14) *Death after coronary artery bypass graft (CABG)* The patient was not connected to pulse oximeter in ICU after coronary artery bypass graft in order to monitor the condition of BP, heart rate and arterial blood oxygen saturation. The patient suffered irreversible damage leading to death during postoperative period.

The National Commission[10] found deficiency in service during postoperative period and awarded compensation of ₹10 lakh along with litigation cost of ₹25,000.

(15) *Death after insertion of stent due to renal failure* The patient aged about 36 years was working with HSBC bank and drawing salary of ₹20,000 per month. She died of renal failure after insertion of stent in the hospital. The husband lost companionship and the children lost love and affection of the mother. By taking life expectancy to be 65 years, the lump sum amount of compensation of ₹20 lakh was awarded by the National Commission.[11]

(16) *Death after delivery of baby by caesarean section* The patient had undergone caesarean operation and delivered a baby girl. The patient was bleeding profusely and remained unconscious after the operation. She was shifted to another hospital where she collapsed.

The patient was housewife aged 35 years. Her service to the family is assessed at ₹1,500 per month or ₹18,000 per annum. After excluding 1/3 of the value for personal expenses of the deceased, and by using 15 as proper multiplier, the amount of compensation is calculated at ₹1,80,000. In addition

9 *Jayendra Maganlal Padia* v *Dr. Lalit P. Trivedi* 2011(3) CPR 326; III(2011) CPJ 249.

10 *Consumer Education and Research Society* v *Madras Medical Mission* 2016(4) CPR 97; IV(2016) CPJ 227 (NCDRC).

11 *Sri Kanth Sri Kande* v *Sun Shine Hospitals* 2019(1) CPR 780 (NCDRC).

the legal representatives of the deceased are awarded ₹20,000 for loss of expectancy of life, ₹10,000 for pain, shock and suffering and ₹25,000 for medical treatment of the deceased. So, the State Commission,[12] awarded total compensation of ₹2,35,000.

(17) ***Death after giving birth of dead baby by normal delivery*** The patient aged 37 years became pregnant after a gap of 12 years after the birth of her second child. The patient died after giving birth to a dead baby due to carelessness and negligence of the doctor in giving treatment to the patient.

The National Commission,[13] directed the doctor to pay compensation of ₹2.50 lakh to the complainant on account of mental agony and suffering caused to the family of the deceased and irreparable loss of mother of two children at their very young age.

(18) ***Death after hernia operation*** The patient started bleeding through anus and developed loose motion and vomiting after hernia operation. The patient was shifted to better equipped hospital where he was treated for 28 days. The patient died of septicaemia with acute renal failure. The hospital did not carry out necessary treatment with regard to blood culture, pus culture and other bacteriological tests, which could have saved the life of the patient by giving early treatment for septicaemia.

The State Commission, Maharashtra,[14] held the hospital guilty of negligence and awarded compensation of ₹3,74,000 in addition to cost of ₹10,000. The patient was 50 years old. He had monthly income of ₹3,000 only. The loss of contribution of ₹1,500 per month for 15 years would come to about ₹2,70,000. The Commission also awarded ₹35,000 for loss of consortium and loss of expectation of life and ₹69,000 for the expenditure incurred for medical treatment of the deceased.

12 *Devendra Kantilal Nayak* v *Dr. Kalyaniben Dhruv Shah* 1996(3) CPR 56; I(1997) CPJ 103; 1998 CCJ 544 (Guj).

13 *Vijay H. Mankar* v *Dr. (Mrs.) Mangla Bansod* 2000 CTJ 101 (CP) (NCDRC); I(2000) CPJ 37 (NC); 2000 CCJ 610.

14 *Fakruddin Abbas Bharmal* v *Dr. B. Dasgupta* 1998(3) CPR 365 (Mumbai); III(1998) CPJ 677 (Mumbai); 1998 CTJ 857 (CP) (SCDRC).

(19) *Death after hysterectomy operation* The patient was admitted to the nursing home without ICU facility for hysterectomy due to heavy bleeding. The gynaecologist conducted the operation in spite of high blood pressure and low hemoglobin of the patient. The patient died after the operation. The gynaecologist was held guilty of negligence for performing operation in a nursing home without having ICU, particularly when the patient was suffering from high blood pressure and low hemoglobin.

The Supreme Court[15] directed the gynaecologist to pay ₹5,00,000 to the legal heirs of the deceased as compensation within three months, failing which the amount will carry interest @ 12% per annum.

(20) *Death after D&C operation* The patient was admitted to the hospital for termination of pregnancy of 4½ months. The doctor had undertaken D&C operation after ten days of administration of glucose injection. She had to be re-admitted for high fever and abdominal pain after two days of discharge from the hospital. The condition of the patient did not improve after the second operation. Ultimately she died in another hospital due to septicaemia arising from peritonitis as a result of uterine perforation.

The National Commission[16] affirmed the order of the State Commission, Punjab which directed the doctor and the hospital to pay compensation of ₹4,50,000 to the husband of the deceased patient.

(21) *Death after operation of left hip* The patient was admitted to the hospital for operation of his left hip. Owing to continuous bleeding from the operational wounds and absence of adequate medical care by the hospital authority the patient died.

The Bombay State Commission[17] awarded compensation of ₹7,00,000 to the legal heirs of the deceased patient together

15 *Bijay Sinha Roy (D) represented by LR* v *Biswanath Das* 2017 SCC Online SC 1101.

16 *Dr. Ramesh Jain* v *Jagroop Singh* 2008(1) CPR 221; 2008 CTJ 480 (CP); I(2008) CPJ 233.

17 *Arvind Kumar Himmatlal Shah represented by LRs.* v *Bombay Hospital Trust* 1992(2) CPR 154 (Bom).

with interest at the rate of 12% per annum from the date of filing the complaint till realisation.

(22) *Death after surgery for removal of stone of kidney* The patient was admitted to the hospital with diagnosis of bilateral kidney stones with hydronephrosis. The right kidney was damaged for development of stone with grade IV hydronephrosis and left kidney developed stone with grade II hydronephrosis. She had undergone surgery for removal of stone of left kidney. When the patient was recovering after lapse of seven days of first surgery, she was again operated for removal of stone of right kidney with consent of the husband of the patient. The surgeon had knowledge about poor tolerance of anaesthesia during first surgery. The condition of the patient deteriorated after administration of anaesthesia during second surgery and died of cardiac arrest. The surgeon and the anaesthetist were held negligent for conducting second elective surgery when the patient had poor tolerance of anaesthesia.

The National Commission[18] awarded compensation of ₹17,00,000 along with interest @ 9% to the husband and two minor children of the deceased patient with the following break up: (*i*) ₹50,000 for medical expenditure; (*ii*) ₹10,000 for funeral expenses; (*iii*) ₹15,000 for conveyance charge; (*iv*) ₹10,00,000 for loss of love and affection; (*v*) ₹1,00,000 for loss of consortium; (*vi*) ₹25,000 for miscellaneous expenditure and (*vii*) ₹5,00,000 loss of income as claimed, in default the loss of income would have been ₹9,00,000.

(23) *Death after complicated surgery without informed consent* The deceased aged about 42 years was admitted to the hospital due to pain in the leg and difficulty in walking. The surgeon found ischaemic change in both lower limbs and impending gangrene after seeing the result of Digital Subtraction Angiography (DSA). The surgeon conducted the operation without disclosing the risks and benefits of the surgery. The patient became unconscious and developed edema in both the legs. The orthopaedician was called in the

18 *Shri Joginder Singh* v *Dr. Rajeev Kumar Majumdar* IV(2009) CPJ 9

last moment for amputation of the legs, but the patient died of septicaemia. The surgeon and the hospital were held negligent for conducting complicated surgery without informed consent, for not taking prompt corrective measures during postoperative period and for not referring the patient to the orthopaedician in proper time.

The National Commission[19] directed the surgeon and the hospital to pay compensation of ₹8,64,000 towards loss of income, ₹4,08,800 towards cost of medical expenditure for treatment of the deceased and ₹1,00,000 towards pain and suffering of the deceased.

(24) ***Death after coronary angiography test*** The patient had undergone Tread Mill Test (TMT) and reported positive for Reversible Myocardial Infarction and Ischemia. Without recommending non-invasive investigations like blood test for lipid profile, KFT, LFT, echocardiography and Halter Meter Test, the doctor hurriedly proceeded for coronary angiography test, even when there was no emergency. The patient suffered prolonged severe hypoglycemia leading to death.

The National Commission[20] held the doctor negligent and awarded compensation of ₹25 lakh apart from litigation cost of ₹2 lakh.

(25) ***Death due to administration of heavy dose of anaesthesia without precaution*** The patient aged 34 years died during operation of hernia due to negligence of the anaesthetist in administering heavy dose of anaesthesia without proper precaution. The surgeon was also negligent for performing operation on a patient who was not properly prepared for anaesthesia. The hospital was also liable for delay of two hours in supplying blood to the patient and for not possessing life saving drugs to treat the patient.

The patient was earning about ₹4,000 to ₹5,000 per month. The dependency of the wife and son is assessed at ₹1,000 per month and ₹12,000 yearly. By applying multiplier of 14, the

19 *Dinesh Jaiswal (deceased) through LRs* v *Bombay Hospital and Medical Research Centre* I(2010) CPJ 176.

20 *Manjeet Chawla* v *Escorts Heart Institute and Research Centre* 2014(3) CPR 452; IV(2014) CPJ 81 (NCDRC).

amount would be worked out to ₹1,68,000. A sum of ₹7,000 was added for loss of consortium to his wife and love and affection to the child. Accordingly, the State Commission, M.P.,[1] awarded a total sum of ₹1,75,000 as compensation with 12% interest for a period of five years along with cost of ₹2,000.

(26) ***Death due to complications after angioplasty*** The patient had undergone angioplasty in the hospital. The patient died of heart failure after four days of surgery due to negligence of the hospital and the doctor during postoperative period. The deceased aged about 60 years had annual income of ₹5,00,000. The loss of dependency was assessed at ₹29,70,000 after deduction of $^1/_3$rd amount towards personal expenditure of the deceased and by applying multiplier of 9. The non-pecuniary damages towards pain and suffering, mental agony, loss of consortium and loss of love and affection were assessed at ₹10,00,000.

The Supreme Court[2] assessed the total amount of compensation at ₹50,00,000 out which the hospital was directed to pay ₹40,00,000 with 9% interest p.a. and the doctor who was negligent in taking postoperative care, was directed to pay ₹10,00,000 with 9% interest p.a.

(27) ***Death due to administration of overdose of steroid*** A 36 years old US based child psychologist suffering from Toxic Epidermal Necrolysis (TEN) was admitted to AMRI Hospital at Kolkata. She was treated with overdose of steroid by the specialist in medicine and the specialist in dermatology. The hospital also did not provide proper care and treatment to the patient. Ultimately the patient died after shifting to Breach Candy Hospital at Mumbai. The AMRI hospital and three doctors who treated the patient were held liable in negligence in providing treatment contrary to established medical protocol.

The Supreme Court[3] assessed the loss of income of the deceased by fixing annual income of $40,000. The future loss

1 *Smt. Bhanupal* v *Dr. Prakash Padode* II(2000) CPJ 384 (Bhopal).
2 *Sheela Hirba Naik Gaunekar* v *Apollo Hospitals Limited* (2018)12 SCC 699; 2016 SCC Online SC 1394.
3 *Balaram Prasad* v *Kunal Saha* (2014)1 SCC 384.

of income was determined by adding 30% to the annual income of the deceased. By taking life expectancy of the deceased at 70 years and by deducting 1/3rd of the income towards personal expenditure and by applying the multiplier of 30, the compensation for loss of income was assessed at ₹5,72,00,550. A sum of ₹10,00,000 was awarded for pain and suffering of the deceased and a sum of ₹1,00,000 was awarded for loss of consortium. The Supreme Court awarded compensation of ₹10,00,000 towards travel expenses of the husband, ₹5,00,000 towards travel expenses for shifting the patient from Kolkata to Mumbai, ₹7,00,000 towards medical expenses of the deceased and ₹1,50,000 towards cost of litigation. Ultimately, the Supreme Court directed AMRI hospital to pay compensation of ₹5,83,00,550 along with interest and the specialist doctor in medicine, the specialist in dermatology and another doctor were directed to pay ₹10,00,000, ₹10,00,000 and ₹5,00,000 respectively.

(28) ***Death due to shock following spinal anaesthesia*** A young lady aged about 25 years was admitted to the hospital for encirclement of the cervix by making sutures at the mouth of uterus to retain the pregnancy and prevent miscarriage. The patient died of shock following spinal anaesthesia within 24 hours of surgery. The hospital and the gynaecologist were held negligent for performance of duty, as there was no noting of the doctor about what type of anaesthesia was used and whether consent of the patient was obtained.

The National Commission[4] enhanced the amount of compensation from ₹3,00,000 to ₹6,00,000.

(29) ***Death due to administration of wrong blood after delivery*** The patient was admitted to the nursing home for second delivery. The gynaecologist who conducted the first delivery by caesarean section gave syntocinon with 20 drops per minute without making any preparation for caesarean section in case of emergency. The syntocinon drip led to rupture of uterus resulting in profuse bleeding. The blood group of the patient was A negative, but A positive blood was given due to non-availability of A negative blood. The patient went into

4 *Dr. Sathy M. Pillai* v *S. Sharma* 2007(3) CPR 176; IV(2007) CPJ 131.

shock from which she never recovered. The gynaecologist and the hospital were held liable for deficiency in service for not making advance preparation for caesarean section by collecting A negative blood. The State Commission, Andhra Pradesh[5] awarded compensation of ₹3,00,000 against the hospital and the gynaecologist for their deficiency in service.

(30) ***Death due to administration of wrong mode and dose of anaesthesia*** The wife of the complainant aged about 39 years was admitted to the hospital for second delivery. She had undergone caesarean section under general anaesthesia, though she was given spinal anaesthesia during previous caesarean operation. The condition of the patient became critical for administering wrong mode and dose of anaesthesia and there was no reversal from anaesthesia after surgery. Ultimately the patient died due to negligence of the anaesthetist and the hospital for not giving proper dose of anaesthesia and for not monitoring the patient during surgery and for not managing reversal from anaesthesia after surgery.

The National Commission[6] directed the anaesthetist and the hospital to pay ₹10,00,000 to the minor children of the deceased, ₹1,00,000 to the husband of the deceased for loss of consortium and ₹1,15,754 as medical expenditure incurred by the husband for the treatment of the wife.

(31) ***Death due to complications after laparoscopic cholecystectomy*** The wife of the complainant, aged about 46 years had undergone laparoscopic cholecystectomy for stones in gall bladder. The patient had to consult the surgeon after discharge from the hospital due to stomach ache, constipation and vomiting. The surgeon failed to prescribe diagnostic tests till visible signs of jaundice. The second laparotomy was done for insertion of tube to drain out bile stained fluid from peritoneal cavity of the patient. Ultimately, Endoscopic Retrograde Cholangio Pancreatography (ERCP) conducted on the patient at PGI, Chandigarh, detected leak in the area of cystic duct and narrowing of central bile duct, and surgery was done, but the patient died of sepsis.

5 *Katra Satyanarayana* v *Lakshmi Nursing Home* II(2003) CPJ 262.
6 *Rajiv Sharma* v *Helvita Clinic Pvt. Ltd.* II(2010) CPJ 68.

The National Commission[7] directed the surgeon and the nursing home to pay compensation of ₹7,00,000 for loss of income by taking into consideration the income of the patient as house wife @ ₹10,000 per month and by deducting $^1/_3$rd amount for personal expenses and by invoking multiplier of 10 only.

(32) ***Death due to complications after cholecystectomy*** The wife of the complainant was operated for cholelithias (removal of stone from gall bladder) by the doctor, who had not put the tube for draining out the bile liquid after cholecystectomy. The patient developed about 8000cc of bile liquid which was infected leading to biliary peritonitis. The patient ultimately died of septicaemia.

The patient was aged 26 years. By quantifying her services as ₹500 p.m. and by applying the multiplier of 20, the State Commission, Maharashtra,[8] awarded compensation of ₹2,50,000 in addition to costs of ₹5,000. The break up of ₹2,50,000 is as follows: ₹1,20,000 for compensation, ₹30,000 for loss of consortium to the complainant, ₹1,00,000 for expenditure incurred on medical treatment of the patient.

(33) ***Death due to complications after surgery for removal of implant*** A young lady aged about 30 years and mother of two children was admitted to the hospital for removal of fibular implant by surgery. The surgeon overlooked the back-history of undergoing surgery of right ankle of the patient and failed to prescribe proper investigations to confirm or rule out Deep Vein Thrombosis (DVT) before undertaking planned surgery. The surgeon was careless in continuing surgery after development of cardiac complications of the patient under general anaesthesia. The anaesthetist also administered general anaesthesia in preference to spinal anaesthesia and did not record the cause of cardiac arrest, though it happened due to pre-existing DVT followed by pulmonary embolism (PE). The hospital was liable for not

7 *Rajinder Singh Dogra* v *Dr. P.N. Gupta, P.N. Urology and Surgical Centre* I(2013) CPJ 286.

8 *Altaf Hussain Farooqui* v *Dr. Ashok Mathure* 1998(1) CPR 427 (Bom).

calling cardiologist in proper time and for not providing bed to the patient for about six hours after complicated surgery.

The National Commission[9] directed the surgeon to pay ₹3,00,000 and both the anaesthetist and the hospital to pay ₹1,00,000 each within six weeks from the date of the order, failing which the award will carry interest @ 9% per annum.

(34) ***Death due to complications after surgery for cure of displacement of left forearm*** The son of the complainant, aged 29 years and a software Engineer, sustained simple fracture with displacement in radius of left forearm. The orthopaedic surgeon conducted operation, in spite of pre-anaesthetic drug reaction, which led to acute respiratory depression of the patient. While both the kidneys were damaged, the patient was referred to the gastro-enterologist for loose motion and vomiting, where prescribed drugs further damaged the kidneys leading to the death of the patient. The surgeon was held negligent for performing surgery without taking care of drug reaction and acute respiratory depression, while the hospital was found to be negligent for discharging the patient without referring him to the nephrologist when he developed hyperthermia during postoperative period.

The State Commission, Andhra Pradesh[10] awarded compensation of ₹15,20,000 including ₹20,000 for loss of estate. The hospital was directed to pay ₹13,00,000 and the orthopaedic surgeon was directed to pay the balance amount of ₹2,20,000 with interest @ 9% per annum.

(35) ***Death due to complications after delivery of child*** The wife of the complainant was admitted to the nursing home for delivery of the child under the care of the gynaecologist. The baby was born after inducing labour with medicine, but died due to birth asphyxia with APGAR score of $^1/_{10}$. The Post Partum Haemorrhage (PPH) took place after delivery and the patient died on the way to another hospital. The

9 *M.C. Katare* v *Bombay Hospital and Medical Research Centre* 2010(1) CPR 269; II(2010) CPJ 128.

10 *Dr. M.A. Gafoor* v *Medwin Hospital* CDJ APSC DRC 022; I(2009) CPJ 167.

gynaecologist was found to be negligent for failure to insist on hematological investigations and cardiological consultation to ascertain whether the patient was anaemic and hypotensive during last trimester on consideration of haemoglobin level and blood pressure of the patient.

The National Commission[11] directed the gynaecologist and nursing home to pay compensation of ₹20,26,000 to the complainant.

(36) ***Death due to deficiency in giving treatment of kidney trouble*** The patient aged 18 years, was admitted to the hospital for treatment of chronic kidney trouble. The date of operation for replacement of kidney was fixed. In the meantime one needle was pricked in the groin and the same was kept in his body with adhesive tape until the injury was infected resulting in pus formation leading to gangrene of the leg. Ultimately the patient died due to negligence of the doctors of the hospital.

The State Commission, Maharashtra[12] directed the hospital to pay ₹2 lakh towards compensation and ₹1,000 towards cost along with interest at the rate of 18% per annum from the date of order till realisation of compensation.

(37) ***Death due to deficiency in administration of anaesthesia before surgery*** A healthy lady of 38 years was admitted to the hospital for hysterectomy, but died in the operation theatre before commencement of surgery. The anaesthetist did not conduct proper pre-anaesthetic check up before surgery. By applying the doctrine of *res ipsa loquitur* the doctors and the hospital were held negligent in providing treatment.

The National Commission[13] awarded compensation of ₹10,00,000 out of which the anaesthetist was directed to pay ₹6,00,000 and the gynaecologist and the hospital were directed to pay ₹2,00,000 each.

11 *Deep Nursing Home through Dr. Gurdeep Singh Kochhar* v *Manmeet Singh Mattewal* 2012(2) CPR 569; III(2012) CPJ 154.

12 *Shivaji Gendeo Chavan* v *Chief Director, Wanless Hospital* III(1995) CPJ 43 (Bom).

13 *Baburao Vithal Lohakpure* v *Suniti Devi Singhania Hospital and Medical Research Centre* 2008(3) CPR 264; II(2008) CPJ 31.

(38) ***Death due to deficiency in giving treatment of neurological problem*** The patient, aged 13 years, was treated by a neuro-physician, as he fell down three to four times while playing. The adverse reaction of the medicines prescribed by the doctor was duly reported to the doctor who advised the patient to be admitted into the hospital where injections were given to the patient without consulting the doctor. The neuro-physician did not attend the patient in the hospital even when his condition was critical on the plea that those days were Saturday and Sunday. Even after admission of the patient to the hospital as per advice of the neuro-physician, he did not give any instruction to the hospital staff for treatment of the patient and visited the hospital at an interval of 24 hours knowing fully well the critical condition of the patient who ultimately expired.

The State Commission at Maharashtra[14] held the neuro-physician guilty of negligence and directed him to pay ₹50,000 to the legal heirs of the deceased. The hospital did not take reasonable care for treatment of the deceased and as such the hospital was directed to pay ₹3 lakh as compensation.

(39) ***Death due to deficiency in service of hospital staff.*** The patient suffering from burn injury was shifted from the bed in order to accommodate another critically burnt patient who expired. Thereafter the patient was again shifted to the previous bed without disinfecting the same and without changing the bed sheet and thereby the infection of the patient was aggravated leading to death.

The National Commission[15] upheld the award of compensation of ₹8,00,000.

(40) ***Death due to delay in conducting caesarean operation*** The patient was admitted to the hospital with complaint of acute labour pain. The doctor conducted the operation after waiting

14 *Muralidhar Eknath Masane* v *Sushrusha Citizen Co-operative Hospital* 1995(1) CPR 606 (Bom).

15 *Gita Rani Kakkar* v *Chandigarh Administration* II(2017) CPJ 188; 2017(1) CPR 548 (NCDRC).

for four hours for a particular anaesthetist, when the patient could have been shifted to better equipped hospital within two hours. The result of delay in conducting the operation was the death of the patient as well as the child.

The patient was aged 34 years. She died leaving behind husband and a child of $3^1/_2$ years of age. The State Commission, Tamil Nadu,[16] directed the doctor to pay compensation of ₹5,00,000 to the legal representatives of the deceased patient along with 18% interest and cost of ₹2,000.

(41) ***Death due to delay in giving treatment*** The wife of the complainant was taken to the hospital for treatment of acute pain in her abdomen. The attending doctor refused to admit her to the hospital for non-availability of bed. The other hospitals also refused the admission of the patient who was ultimately admitted to a nursing home where she expired on the next day.

The patient was 34 years old. She used to earn ₹700 per month. The State Commission, West Bengal,[17] awarded compensation of ₹2 lakh against the hospital. The State Commission also directed the attending doctor of the hospital to pay compensation of ₹5,000 to the complainant.

(42) ***Death due to delay in treatment of cancer for non-supply of biopsy report*** The patient was treated by the surgeon for feeling of hardness in the tongue. The whole of the nodule was removed by surgery and biopsy was done, but the surgeon or the hospital did not disclose the biopsy report to the patient. The patient again developed hardness in the tongue after lapse of about five months and malignancy was detected by CT scan. The patient died in spite of treatment in Tata Memorial Hospital, Bombay and in cancer department of AIIMS. Both the hospital and the surgeon were held negligent for delaying the treatment of the deceased by not disclosing the biopsy report to the patient or his relatives.

16 *K. Murugesan* v *Dr. S. Sarala Devi* I(1999) CPJ 542 (Chennai).
17 *Ranjit Kumar Das* v *Medical Officer, E.S.I. Hospital, Manicktola* 1998(1) CPR 165 (Cal); III(1997) CPJ 336 (Cal); 1999 CCJ 70 (WB).

The National Commission[18] awarded compensation of ₹4,20,000 towards loss of income of the deceased by taking into consideration ₹5,000 as income per month and by applying multiplier of 7 and ₹2,50,000 towards non-pecuniary damages for loss of company and mental agony and ₹1,00,000 towards expenditure for medical treatment of the deceased.

(43) ***Death due to improper care after normal delivery*** The patient was bleeding profusely after giving birth of a baby by normal delivery. The doctor called the anaesthetist to carry out surgery when conservative treatment of packing failed to check profuse bleeding after five hours of normal delivery. The patient died due to negligence of the doctor in making attempt to carry out surgical intervention after delay of five hours of commencement of profuse bleeding.

The deceased was a housewife aged 25 years. As she was not contributing financially, the normal earning of the deceased was taken as ₹15,000 per year and half of the said amount was deducted for her personal expenses. The contribution of the deceased to the family was taken as ₹7,500 per year and by applying the multiplier 15, the amount was worked out at ₹1,12,500. An amount of ₹5,000 was awarded for loss of love and affection to the daughter and ₹2,000 for funeral expenses. Accordingly, total amount of ₹1,19,500 was awarded as compensation with interest at the rate of 12% per annum for a period of five years by the State Commission, M.P.[19]

(44) ***Death due to mismatched blood transfusion*** The father of the complainant sustained fracture in the neck of the femur and was admitted in the nursing home of the orthopaedic surgeon. The operation was done and blood was transfused, but the patient died of mismatched blood transfusion. The orthopaedician was held negligent for signing on the requisition slip sent to the blood bank by enclosing with it wrong specimen of B+ group of blood, whereas the patient had A+ group of blood.

18 *Mrs. Sushma* v *Dr. G.D. Goel* IV(2010) CPJ 410.

19 *Hemant Bahadur Singh Parihar* v *Dr. (Mrs.) Maya Pathak* 2000(1) CPR 191 (Bhopal).

The National Commission[20] awarded compensation of ₹5,38,000 in favour of the son of the deceased patient.

(45) *Death due to overdose of steroid and lack of supportive treatment* The patient aged about 45 years, a citizen of USA was admitted to the hospital in Calcutta for fever and skin rash. The condition of the patient deteriorated for administration of overdose of long acting steroid without diagnosing the nature of the disease and without foreseeing the adverse effect of such steroid. The supportive treatment including IV fluid/electrolyte replacement, dressing of skin wounds and close monitoring of infection was not given to the patient. The effect of immunosuppression caused due to use of steroid in overdose affected the immunity of the patient who ultimately died of infection in another hospital in Mumbai.

By modifying the order of the National Commission, the Supreme Court of India,[1] enhanced the amount of compensation from ₹1,34,66,000 to ₹6,08,00,550 with 6% interest per annum from the date of complaint till the date of payment. The Apex Court directed two physicians to make payment of ₹10,00,000 each as compensation and directed one junior doctor to pay ₹5,00,000 as compensation. The Apex Court also directed the hospital to make payment of ₹6,08,00,550 to the claimant as compensation as per the following break up: (*i*) loss of income including future prospect of the deceased ₹5,72,00,550; (*ii*) cost of medical treatment of the deceased at Calcutta and Mumbai ₹7,00,000; (*iii*) travel and hotel expenses at Mumbai ₹6,50,000; (*iv*) loss of consortium ₹1,00,000; (*v*) pain and suffering ₹10,00,000; (*vi*) cost of litigation ₹11,50,000.

(46) *Death due to transfusion of wrong group of blood* The blood group of the patient was A+. The patient was transfused B+ group of blood on two different dates, resulting in her death. The attending doctors, staff and the hospital authority

20 *Dr. Sunil Thakur* v *Gorachand Goswami* 2013(1) CPR 340; I(2013) CPJ 646; 2013(3) ALD (Cons) 20.

1 *Dr. Balaram Prasad* v *Dr. Kunal Saha* (Civil Appeal No. 2867 of 2012, 692 of 2012, 2866 of 2012, 731 of 2012 and 858 of 2012), CDJ 2013 SC 937; 2013(7) MLJ 781.

were held liable for transfusing wrong group of blood to the patient resulting in her death.

The State Commission, Chandigarh,[2] directed the hospital to pay compensation of ₹2 lakh to the legal heirs of the deceased patient along with cost of ₹5,000.

The decision of the State Commission was affirmed by the National Commission and the Supreme Court of India.[3]

(47) ***Death due to surgery without proper precaution*** The child patient was suffering from persistent pneumonia due to cleft palate since birth. The doctor advised for surgery after attaining two years of age. The surgeon operated in spite of existence of respiratory problem without pre-operative test and pre-anaesthetic check up and thereby the child went into coma before surgery and remained in vegetative state. The surgeon and the hospital were found negligent for operating the patient with respiratory tract infection in spite of having no emergency and without conducting pre-operative test and pre-anaesthetic check up and for not taking due care in administering anaesthesia.

The National Commission[4] increased the amount of compensation against the surgeon and the nursing home from ₹3,00,000 to ₹7,00,000 with interest @ 9% per annum from the date of the order till the date of payment.

(48) ***Death due to unskilled treatment for delivery of child*** The wife of the complainant was taken to the doctor for delivery of dead foetus. The doctor undertook the treatment of the patient in critical condition and made surgical intervention in a complicated case of delivery of dead foetus without being qualified to do so. The doctor was held negligent for causing death of the patient by giving unskilled treatment.

2 *Jaspal Singh* v *Post Graduate Institute of Medical Education and Research (PGI), Chandigarh* II(2000) CPJ 439 (Chandigarh); 2000(2) CPR 300 (Chandigarh).

3 *Post Graduate Institute of Medical Education and Research, Chandigarh* v *Jaspal Singh* (2009)7 SCC 330; JT 2009(7) SC 527; 2009 ACJ 2672.

4 *Karamveer Singh* v *Garn Nursing Home* 2012(3) CPR 490; III(2012) CPJ 630.

The State Commission, Punjab,[5] directed the doctor to pay compensation of ₹2 lakh to the complainant along with costs of ₹10,000.

(49) *Death due to unskilled termination of pregnancy* The doctors being not qualified to conduct Medical Termination of Pregnancy, conducted termination of pregnancy of the patient resulting in her death. The doctors were held liable in negligence for causing death of the patient.

The deceased was aged 35 years and a concrete worker earning ₹100 per day. The District Forum assessed her contribution to the family as ₹500 per month. By assuming that she would have lived for another 25 years, the District Forum awarded total compensation of ₹2,01,000 including ₹15,000 for pain and suffering, and ₹18,000 for pecuniary loss. On appeal, the State Commission, Kerala,[6] upheld the order of the District Forum.

(50) *Death due to wrong treatment of typhoid instead of malaria* The patient aged about 45 years was admitted to the hospital with complaint of intermittent fever and chill. The patient was not responding to the treatment of typhoid given by the doctor. The patient was shifted to another hospital in critical condition where the smear for malaria parasite was found to be positive and the widal test was found to be negative. The patient died in the said hospital due to cardio respiratory arrest and malaria.

The District Forum held the doctor negligent for giving wrong treatment and awarded compensation of ₹2 lakh. The State Commission and National Commission reversed the decision of the District Forum (now District Commission) on the ground that the doctor cannot be held negligent without expert evidence. By setting aside the decision of the National Commission, the Supreme Court of India held the doctor negligent for making wrong diagnosis and treatment without

5 *Dilbagh Hussain* v *Harjinder Kaur* III(2000) CPJ 17 (Chandigarh).
6 *Dr. K. Mahabala Bhat* v *K. Krishna* 2000(1) CPR 369 (Ker).

evidence of expert and affirmed the award of compensation of ₹2 lakh given by the District Forum.[7]

(51) *Death due to unskilled treatment of Unani Specialist in Emergency* A young man of 23 years of age having post graduate degree was admitted to the hospital for repeated attack of epistaxis (nasal bleeding). One Unani Specialist administered allopathic drugs and intravenous drip. The patient died of chocking consequent to aspiration of blood in the air passage, though ENT surgeon was called at the last moment, who blocked the air passages after repeated nasal bleeding for about 10 hours. The hospital was held liable in negligence for engaging unani specialist for providing treatment in emergency.

The National Commission[8] awarded compensation of ₹7,50,000 against the hospital only.

(52) *Death due to wrong treatment by homoeopathic doctor* The patient was treated with strong antibiotics for eight days by a registered homoeopathic practitioner without confirming the diagnosis by any pathological test. As the condition of the patient deteriorated, he was shifted to nursing home where he was treated for six days. The condition of the patient did not improve and he was shifted to another hospital where he expired.

The National Commission dismissed the complaint filed by the legal representatives of the deceased patient. On appeal, the Supreme Court,[9] reversed the decision of the National Commission and directed the doctor to pay compensation of ₹3,00,000 in addition to cost of ₹30,000 on consideration of the fact that the deceased patient was 35 years old and was earning ₹5,700 per month as salary.

7 *V. Kishan Rao* v *Nikhil Super Speciality Hospital* (2010)5 SCC 513; 2010(4) SCJ 690; 2010 AIR SCW 4252; III(2010) CPJ 1; 2010(5) SLT 349; CDJ 2010 SC 428.

8 *Prof. P.N. Thakur* v *Hans Charitable Hospital* 2008 CTJ 380 (CP); 2007(3) CPR 157; III(2007) CPJ 340.

9 *Poonam Verma* v *Aswin Patel* AIR 1996 SC 2111; (1996)4 SCC 332; 1996(3) CPR 205 (SC); II(1996) CPJ 1 (SC); (1996)4 CTJ 465 (SC) (CP).

(53) ***Death due to wrong treatment of cancer*** The patient was suffering from stomach pain and menstrual discharge during pregnancy. She was admitted to the hospital and investigations confirmed ectopic pregnancy and abdominal mass of about 4" diameter above the uterus. The laparotomy was conducted to end ectopic pregnancy and the pathological test of the specimens suggested carcinoma, but the same needed to be co-related with other tests before reaching to the clear and conclusive finding. Without conducting any biopsy of the abdominal mass, the doctor administered 5 cycles of chemotherapy. However, the second pathological report indicated that the patient had no malignancy. Ultimately she died at a very young age. The doctor and the hospital were held negligent for providing wrong treatment to the patient.

The National Commission[10] awarded compensation of ₹5,00,000 with interest @ 9% per annum, if the amount of compensation is not paid within a period of 8 weeks.

(54) ***Death during operation of right forearm*** The patient was operated for insertion of plate and screws in right forearm. The patient developed pain and deformity at operation site. The patient was operated after obtaining opinion of the cardiologist and reports of other investigations. The patient developed cardiorespiratory arrest in the midst of the operation and was declared dead. The orthopaedician, cardiologist and the anaesthetist were held negligent for the death of the patient.

The income of the patient was ₹3,000 per month. After deducting 1/3rd for personal expenditure and by using 15 as multiplier, the compensation is calculated at ₹24,000 x 15 i.e. ₹3,60,000. The State Commission, Gujarat,[11] awarded total compensation of ₹4,15,000 including ₹40,000 for loss of estate and ₹15,000 for medical and other expenses and cost of ₹5,000, which was affirmed by the National Commission.[12]

10 *Dr. Kurien Joseph* v *Govindarajan* 2013(2) CPR 230.

11 *Arunaben D. Kothari* v *Navdeep Clinic* 1996(3) CPR 20 (Guj); III(1996) CPJ 605 (Guj); (1997)5 CTJ 533 (CP)(SCDRC); 1998 CCJ 972 (Guj).

12 *Rashmi Vora* v *Arunaben D. Kothari* 2006(1) CPC 66; IV(2005) CPJ 164.

(55) ***Death during sterilization operation*** The wife of the complainant had undergone sterilization. The operation was conducted under local anaesthesia without calling any anaesthetist to the operation theatre. The patient died during operation conducted by the doctor.

The complainant lost his wife at the age of 35 years. She had two children of 5 years and 8 months of age respectively. The State Commission, Tamil Nadu,[13] directed the doctor to pay compensation of ₹2,50,000 for loss of consortium and ₹1,50,000 for mental agony and hardship, along with 18% interest per annum till realisation.

(56) ***Death during Tread Mill Test*** The patient aged 47 years, mother of two children went to the hospital for check up of the whole body due to irregular long cycles, four abortions and menopause. She was subjected to Tread Mill Test (TMT) in the absence of any doctor and she collapsed. The hospital was held negligent in providing service to the deceased.

The National Commission[14] awarded compensation of ₹7,00,000 to the husband of the deceased, ₹5,00,000 to the two children of the deceased for loss of companion, love and affection respectively. The additional compensation of ₹5,00,000 was awarded for trauma and mental agony of the legal heirs of the deceased due to sad, sudden and pre-mature death.

(57) ***Death during laparoscopic cholecystectomy*** The wife of the complainant aged about 55 years was diagnosed as having stones in the gall bladder. She had undergone laparoscopic cholecystectomy under the care of the surgeon. The patient died of cardiac arrest in the operation theatre. It is established from evidence that the surgeon had undertaken the task of performing major surgery without any assistance from the qualified anaesthetist. The surgeon was held negligent in providing medical treatment in utter disregard of the prevalent protocol and practice.

13 *A. Ravi* v *Dr. (Mrs.) Usha Rani* I(1999) CPJ 581 (Chennai).

14 *S.N. Verma* v *Indraprastha Appollo Hospital through its Director Medical Superintendent* CDJ 2010 (Cons) Case No. 071.

The National Commission[15] awarded compensation of ₹4,20,000 towards loss of income of the deceased and ₹1,00,000 towards loss of consortium and mental agony.

(58) ***Death expedited for not conducting routine investigations***
The patient had undergone decortication surgery for removal of thickened pleura covering the lung. The doctor did not send the specimen removed by surgery for histopathology test. The patient had to undergo another operation for histopathology test and the report indicated malignant mesothelioma of the pleura. The patient expired. The doctor was held negligent for not conducting routine investigations to assess or confirm the diagnosis.

The deceased patient was aged 42 years. The State Commission, Maharashtra,[16] directed the doctor to pay compensation of ₹2,25,000 including ₹10,000 as cost, ₹50,000 for travel expense and ₹1,65,000 for medical treatment of the deceased.

(59) ***Death following complications of administration of injection***
The doctor being not qualified to practise allopathic medicine, administered injection on gluteal region and prescribed steroid tablets to the patient. The patient developed pain and tumour at the site of the injection. The subsequent treatment in two different hospitals failed to improve the condition of the patient who ultimately expired.

The patient was housewife aged 35 years. The value of her service is assessed at ₹1,500 per month or ₹18,000 per annum After deducting $^1/_3$ for her personal expenses and by using 15 as proper multiplier, the amount of compensation is calculated at ₹1,80,000. To this ₹20,000 is added for loss of estate. The State Commission, Gujarat,[17] directed the doctors and the hospital to pay ₹2,00,000 jointly and severally to the legal representatives of the patient, in addition to cost of ₹5,000.

15 *Suresh Nanda* v *Dr. Anoop Kumar* II(2012) CPJ 228.

16 *S.V. Panchori* v *Dr. Kaushal Pandey* II(1999) CPJ 332 (Bom); 1999 CTJ 296 (CP) (SCDRC).

17 *Kanaiyalal Ramanlal Trivedi* v *Dr. Satyanarayan Vishwakarma* 1996(3) CPR 24 (Guj); I(1997) CPJ 332 (Guj); 1998 CCJ 690 (Guj).

(60) *Death for leaving mops in abdomen during hysterectomy* The patient was admitted to the nursing home for removal of fibroid from uterus by way of hysterectomy. She was discharged from the nursing home after four days of operation. She complained about abdominal pain, loss of appetite, nausea, vomiting and vaginal discharge and loss of weight during periodical check up after discharge from the nursing home. After about two and half months two mops were detected in abdominal cavity by way of ultrasound on the advice of another doctor. The second surgery was performed for removal of mops, but her intestine was ruptured. Ultimately she died of septicemia after prolonged suffering. The gynaecologist and the nursing home were held liable for deficiency in service.

The National Commission[1] awarded compensation of ₹8,00,000 out of which the nursing home was directed to pay ₹5,00,000 being indemnified by the Insurance Company and the surgeon was directed to pay ₹3,00,000.

(61) *Death for overdose of medicine without monitoring adverse effect* The son of the complainant, aged 16 years, was diagnosed to be a case of RTI, but the report of blood test revealed malaria parasite called plasmodium vivax. When the patient did not respond to the treatment of administering falcigo injection in overdose, he was taken to another doctor who treated the patient for plasmodium vivax without conducting second blood test. The patient ultimately died of adverse effect of overdose of falcigo administered without monitoring the patient to assess the adverse effect of the medicine.

The National Commission[2] directed the hospital and the doctors to pay compensation of ₹1,00,000 for reimbursement of medical expenditure, ₹6,00,000 for lump sum economic loss and ₹4,00,000 for mental trauma and agony of the parents of the deceased.

1 *Santokh Nursing Home* v *Jaswinder Singh* 2009(3) CPR 46; I(2010) CPJ 204.
2 *Ashok Kumar Upadhaya* v *Dr. D.N. Misra* I(2011) CPJ 194.

(62) ***Death immediately after operation to stop excess bleeding and discharge*** The patient was operated for excess bleeding and white discharge during monthly period. The patient died immediately after the operation. The State Commission, Bombay directed both doctors to pay jointly and severally ₹2,55,355 in addition to cost of ₹5,000. This order was upheld on appeal by the National Commission.[3]

(63) ***Deformity due to unskilled surgery for improvement of height*** A girl aged about 15 years underwent cosmetic surgery with ring fixation for improving height, but her left leg became shorter by 1.5 inches than right leg and the deformity could not be removed after several operations. The hospital was found to be negligent in providing treatment resulting in deformity of the patient.

The State Commission, Kerala[4] directed the hospital to pay compensation of ₹5,00,000 to the complainant.

(64) ***Disability due to falling from 3rd floor of the hospital*** The patient aged about 31 years was admitted to the hospital with complaint of acute fever. He was shifted to CCU located in the 3rd floor of the hospital. He fell down from the 3rd floor of the hospital and sustained injuries resulting in disability. The hospital was held negligent for failure to take care of the patient resulting in disability and further medical treatment.

The State Commission, Kerala[5] directed the hospital to pay compensation of ₹2,00,000 for mental agony, physical disability and for expenditure incurred for medical treatment.

(65) ***Irreversible brain damage after administration of injection*** The minor patient was treated for seven days in Spring

3 *Mumbai Grahak Panchayat* v *Dr. (Mrs.) Rashmi B. Fadnavis* 1996(1) CPR 137 (NC); (1996)4 CTJ 284 (CP) (NCDRC); 1998 CCJ 766 (NC) affirmed by NC in *Dr. (Mrs.) Rashmi B. Fadnavis* v *Mumbai Grahak Panchayat* III(1998) CPJ 21 (NC); 1998(3) CPR 34 (NC); 1998 CTJ 742 (CP)(NCDRC); 1999 CCJ 391 (NC).

4 *Nadiya* v *Proprietor, Fatima Hospital* III(2001) CPJ 572.

5 *Kannan V.R. Vithayathil House* v *Sree Sudheendra Medical Mission Hospital* 2002(2) CPC 376.

Meadows Hospital for typhoid. The consultant doctor prescribed "chloramphenicol" injection and the unqualified nurse misread it as "chloroquine" and indented for purchase of injection "lariago" (i.e. chloroquine). The nurse injected chloroquine 5mg iv which was at least $3\frac{1}{2}$ times of the normal paediatric dose, resulting in cardiac arrest. The patient suffered irreversible brain damage and was compelled to live in vegetative state after treatment of 21 days in All India Institute of Medical Sciences, New Delhi.

The National Commission came to the conclusion that the attending doctor was negligent, as he allowed the unqualified nurse to give intravenous injection, while the consultant doctor advised that the injection must be given by the attending doctor himself. The hospital is liable to pay compensation for negligence of its staff. The Supreme Court of India,[6] confirmed the order of the National Commission to award compensation of ₹12.5 lakh to the minor patient. A sum of ₹10 lakh towards compensation to the minor and ₹2.5 lakh for purchase of equipments required by the minor. The Supreme Court also confirmed the order of the National Commission to award compensation to the tune of ₹5 lakh to the parents for acute mental agony for reducing their only son to the vegetative state of life. The hospital and the nurse are jointly and severally liable to pay the amount of compensation, though Insurance Company is liable to indemnify the amount of ₹12,37,500 in terms of the policy on account of the liability of the hospital.

(66) *Loss of eyesight after cataract operation* The complainant had undergone cataract surgery. He lost vision in the right eye due to deficiency in providing service by the surgeon and the hospital.

6 *Harjot Ahluwalia (minor) through parents* v *Spring Meadows Hospital* 1997(3) CPR 1 (NC); II(1997) CPJ 98 (NC); (1997)5 CTJ 734 (CP) (NCDRC); 1998 CCJ 405 (NC) confirmed by Supreme Court of India in *Spring Meadows Hospital* v *Harjot Ahluwalia through K.S. Ahluwalia* AIR 1998 SC 1801; (1998)4 SCC 39; 1998(1) CPR 1 (SC); I(1998) CPJ 1 (SC); 1998 CTJ 81 (SC) (CP); 1998 CCJ 521 (SC); JT 1998(2) SC 620; III(1998) SLT 684.

The National Commission[7] awarded compensation of ₹5,00,000 against the surgeon and the hospital.

(67) ***Loss of eyesight of lawyer after cataract operation*** The patient had undergone cataract operation in his right eye. The patient lost his eyesight in the right eye even after prolonged treatment in different hospitals. It is established from evidence that the patient lost his eyesight due to negligence of the doctor in conducting the operation.

The patient was a practising lawyer. The patient lost ten years of active life due to disability to the extent of 30% by loss of eyesight. The State Commission, Bihar[8] awarded total compensation of ₹5,55,000 against the doctor. The break up of the amount of compensation is as follows: (*i*) ₹25,000 for mental agony; (*ii*) ₹50,000 for medical treatment after operation; (*iii*) ₹1,80,000 for loss of earning; (*iv*) ₹2,00,000 for disability to the extent of 30% for loss of eyesight; and (*v*) ₹1,00,000 for cost of maintaining a driver to drive the car of the patient.

(68) ***Loss of eyesight after operation for retinal detachment*** The patient was operated for retinal detachment of the right eye. The patient lost eyesight of the right eye beyond repair after the operation. The surgeon was held negligent in carrying out the operation and during post operation follow up.

In the absence of any evidence to assess the quantum of compensation, the State Commission, Bihar,[9] assumed the patient as unskilled labourer who might have saved only ₹25 per day, which works out to ₹9,000 per annum. By taking into consideration the age of the patient as 40 years and by taking into consideration about 20 years of active service, the patient was awarded compensation of ₹1,80,000 in

7 *Director, Jawaharlal Institute for Postgraduate Medical Education & Research (JIPMER), Puducherry* v *S. Varrery Srinivas* 2012(3) CPR 256; III(2012) CPJ 467.

8 *K.N. Lal* v *R.K. Akhaury* III(1997) CPJ 112 (Pat); 1998 CCJ 1223 (Bihar).

9 *Shri Ram Babu* v *Dr. Anjani Kishore Prasad* 1998(2) CPR 223 (Pat); II(1998) CPJ 684 (Pat); 1998 CTJ 606 (CP) (SCDRC); 2000 CCJ 314.

addition to ₹10,000 on account of travel, lodging, consultation fees and purchase of medicines.

(69) *Loss of vision for not screening of RoP of premature baby* The female baby weighing 1250 grams was born with gestational age of 29 weeks in the Government hospital and remained under the care of the neonatologists till 13 weeks of age. The neonatologists did not advise for screening the baby for Retinopathy of Prematurity (in short RoP) till 13 weeks of age and thereby baby became blind due to detachment of retina which turned into funnel shaped. The neonatologists, the hospital and the state were held liable for loss of vision of the baby girl.

The Supreme Court[10] directed the doctors, hospital and the state to pay compensation of ₹42,87,921 along with interest under the heading "Past Medical Expenses" and ₹82,95,048 under the heading "Future Medical Expenses" by taking into consideration life expectancy of the baby at 70 years and the said amount is increased to ₹1,38,00,000 on the basis of rate of inflation as per guidelines of RBI. The amount of compensation is apportioned as follows: (*i*) ₹1,30,00,000 and ₹40,00,000 along with interest to be paid jointly and severally by state and the hospital; and (*ii*) ₹8,00,000 and ₹2,87,921 along with interest to be paid by two doctors in charge of Neo-Natology unit of the hospital in equal half share.

(70) *Loss of vision of pre-term baby for not screening of RoP.* The paediatrician and ophthalmologist did not screen the pre-term baby weighing 1.49 kg. and 32 weeks gestation for Retinopathy of Prematurity (RoP) during his stay in the hospital for four weeks and even during review and routine check on two different dates in the OPD of the hospital after his discharge and thereby the child became blind due to complete detachment of the retina.

The compensation of ₹64,00,000 awarded by the National Commission was enhanced to ₹76,00,000 by the Supreme

10 *V. Krishna Kumar* v *State of Tamil Nadu* (2015)9 SCC 388.

Court of India[11] which was to be paid jointly and severally by the hospital and the doctors within specific period of time.

(71) ***Loss of vision in one eye after surgery for not maintaining hygiene by hospital*** The complainant suffered loss of vision in one eye after surgery, which was caused due to infection for not maintaining hygiene by the hospital. The complainant was a Government employee drawing salary of ₹6,400 per month, but he was forced to take voluntary retirement nine years before the date of superannuation for permanent disability of loss of vision in one eye. The complainant was forced to take pension of ₹2,500 per month and thereby suffered financial loss of ₹3,900 per month.

The State Commission awarded compensation of ₹40,000 which was enhanced to ₹1,00,000 by the National Commission. On appeal, the Supreme Court of India[12] enhanced the amount of compensation from ₹1,00,000 to ₹4,32,000 in addition to litigation cost of ₹50,000 and cost of treatment to the tune of ₹13,000.

(72) ***Paraplegia after surgery for excision biopsy through thoracotomy*** The complainant had undergone excision biopsy by thoracotomy to confirm the diagnosis about the nature of the tumour in left thorax, when four attempts of FNAC (Fine Needle Aspiration Cytology) could not yield any conclusive pathological diagnosis. After undergoing surgery for excision biopsy the complainant became paraplegic, confined to wheel chair, developed spasticity and flexor spasms and diffuse pain in lower limbs. The hospital and its surgeons and physician were held liable for paraplegic condition of the complainant.

The complainant is only 20 years old and a student of engineering. By increasing the amount of compensation from ₹15.5 lakh to ₹1 crore with interest @ 6% per annum from the date of award of the National Commission till the date

11 *Maharaja Agrasen Hospital* v *Master Rishabh Sharma* 2019 SCC Online SC 1658.

12 *A.U. Sukumaran* v *N.S.D. Raju* (Civil Appeal No. 64 of 2009 arising out of SLP (C) No. 3146 of 2007 decided on 9th January 2009) CDJ 2009 SC 180.

of payment, it is held by the Supreme Court[13] that multiplier method would not be applicable for computation of compensation in this case. The break up of the amount of compensation is as follows: (*i*) ₹7.2 lakh for driver-cum-attendant for a period of 30 years @ ₹2,000 per month; (*ii*) ₹14.40 lakh towards cost of nursing for 30 years @ ₹4,000 per month; (*iii*) ₹10.80 lakh for physiotherapy for 30 years @ ₹3,000 per month; (*iv*) ₹25 lakh towards continuous medical expenses involving costly medicine; (*v*) ₹25 lakh for loss of future earning; and (*vi*) ₹10 lakh for pain and suffering.

(73) ***Paraplegia after angiography without consent*** The complainant had to undergo mini laparoscopy in the hospital. He had to undergo angiography when the doctors suspected vascular tumour. He was administered local anaesthesia and a catheter was inserted through the Tran femoral route into the aorta and test dose of dye was injected to the patient. The catheter was removed due to convulsion, but the patient suffered from paraplegia. The hospital was held negligent for not referring the patient to the neurologist for removal of elevated cerebrospinal fluid by immediate lumber puncture.

By setting aside the order of the State Commission, the National Commission[14] directed the hospital to pay compensation of ₹6,30,000 to the complainant.

(74) ***Permanent brain damage after circumcision operation*** A child of $2^1/_2$ years of age had undergone circumcision operation under general anaesthesia. He did not regain consciousness and remained in vegetative state due to negligence of the anaesthetist

By taking into consideration the condition of the child and sufferings of the parents for the entire life of the child, the National Commission[15] enhanced the amount of

13 *Nizam's Institute of Medical Sciences* v *Prasanth S. Dhananka* (2009)6 SCC 1; JT 2009(2) SC 385; 2009 AIR SCW 3563; 2010 ACJ 38; (2009)4 Supreme 165.

14 *K.N. Koteshwara Bhatta* v *Kastenba Hospital* 2007(1) CPR 21; I(2007) CPJ 258.

15 *Shilaben Ashwin Kumar Rana* v *Dr. Bhavin Kumar Shah* 2014(2) CPR 816; II(2014) CPJ 707 (NCDRC).

compensation from ₹5 lakh awarded by State Commission to ₹10 lakh in addition to litigation cost of ₹30,000.

(75) ***Permanent brain damage after caesarean operation*** The patient had undergone caesarean operation under spinal anaesthesia. The patient suffered permanent brain damage for not providing oxygen to her in emergency during suturing the lower segment and later during the transit of the patient to other hospital. The anaesthetist was held liable for causing permanent brain damage of the patient.

The patient, aged 30 years, was the mother of four children. The husband of the patient will have to engage a female attendant for household duties and for looking after his children, whose remuneration is calculated at ₹1,000 per month. This expenditure comes to ₹12,000 per annum and by applying the multiplier of 25, the amount comes to ₹3,00,000. Moreover, ₹50,000 is awarded for loss of marital pleasure of the husband, ₹50,000 for loss of mother's love and affection by the children and ₹50,000 is awarded for cost of medicines and ₹10,000 as cost. The anaesthetist was directed to pay ₹4,60,000 as compensation within one month, failing which 15% interest would carry on the amount of compensation.[16]

(76) ***Permanent brain damage after septoplasty*** The patient approached ENT surgeon for correction of nasal septum with enlargement of inferior concha. The surgeon advised septoplasty. While the patient was under general anaesthesia, the surgeon injected inside the nostrils 2% xylocaine with adrenaline using a syringe without consulting the anaesthetist and thereby the patient suffered temporary cardiac arrest resulting vegetative life due to negligence of the surgeon.

The State Commission directed the surgeon and the hospital to pay ₹6,00,000 as compensation which was increased to ₹7,50,000 by the National Commission.[17]

16 *Mr. Sakil Mohammed Vakil Khan* v *Dr. Miss Perin Irani* 1999(2) CPR 515 (Bom); 1999 CTJ 679 (CP) (SCDRC).

17 *St. Gregorious Mission Hospital* v *Roji George* 2008(1) CPR 7; I(2008) CPJ 68.

(77) *Permanent brain damage after Fallopian Tube Test* The complainant had undergone Fallopian Tube Test (FTT) under general anaesthesia. She developed breathing trouble due to inadequacy of the dose of general anaesthesia and thereby hypoxia developed, which led to brain damage. The complainant started living in vegetative state on account of brain damage suffered due to hypoxia.

The National Commission[18] awarded compensation of ₹38,40,000 with the following break up: (*i*) ₹6,00,000 towards expenses incurred for Medical treatment, (*ii*) ₹14,40,000 towards expenses to be incurred for future maintenance in vegetative state, and (*iii*) ₹18,00,000 towards physical and mental suffering.

(78) *Permanent disability of a student after administration of injection* The doctor administered injection in right hip of the patient, resulting in severe pain and amputation of right leg from hip joint after fifteen days of giving injection.

The patient was aged 16 years. He was studying in class XI. He suffered 90% disability due to negligence of the doctor in administering injection. The father of the patient had to spend ₹70,000 for treatment of the patient. So, the State Commission, Punjab,[19] directed the doctor to pay a sum of ₹1,25,000 to the patient within one month, in default to pay interest @18% per annum from the date of the order till realisation.

(79) *Permanent disability due to amputation of fingers of right hand* The patient aged about 22 years was doing fitter course in ITI. All fingers of his right hand had to be amputated due to negligence of the doctor. His family consisted of 10 members including old parents.

By taking into consideration the age, income, impairment of future earning capacity, number of dependants, and

18 *Sanjay Mutha* v *Dr. Jayashree Desai* I(2013) CPJ 727.
19 *Gursewak Singh* v *Dr. Jaskaran Singh* III(1996) CPJ 300 (Chandigarh); (1997)5 CTJ 68 (CP) (SCDRC); 1998 CCJ 942 (Chandigarh).

inflation, the Bombay High Court[20] awarded compensation of ₹10 lakh in addition to ₹1 lakh as litigation cost.

(80) ***Permanent disability due to amputation of right hand of an infant*** The child lost right hand due to negligence of the doctor, which requires artificial prostheses periodically as per the age.

The National Commission[1] enhanced the amount of compensation from ₹6,17,320 awarded by State Commission to ₹15 lakh.

(81) ***Permanent disability due to birth asphyxia*** The patient was admitted to the hospital for child birth, as labour pain was not started on the expected date of delivery. The administration of pitocin drip failed to induce labour pain for almost two days. The baby was born after inducing the method called Artificial Rupture Membrane (ARM). The baby was not sucking and found to be suffering from birth asphyxia. The hospital and the doctor were held negligent for not taking into account the warning signals of foetal distress and for not taking steps for caesarian delivery to avert asphyxia.

The National Commission[2] awarded compensation of ₹4,50,000 against the hospital and the doctor by way of calculation of expenditure for the baby @ ₹3,500 p.m. for employment of servant, ₹2,000 p.m. for anti-convulsion drug and ₹2,250 for physiotherapy.

(82) ***Permanent disability due to complications after surgery*** The complainant had undergone surgical procedure called "chemical sympathectomy" a procedure used for destruction of the periarterial sympathetic nerves as in Doppler's operation by a corrosive such as "phenol". The procedure

20 *Umakant Kisan Mane* v *Dean, Rajawadi Municipal Hospital* 2016(2) BCR 55; 2016(2) Mah LJ 266 (Bom) (DB).

1 *Doon Valley Hospital* v *Master Shivabshu* IV(2016) CPJ 43 (NCDRC).

2 *Baby Geetha* v *Cosmopolitan Hospitals (P) Ltd.* 2006(2) CPC 398; III(2006) CPJ 89.

was conducted under local anaesthesia in the ward instead of operation theatre and in the absence of any senior doctor. The procedure was abandoned when the patient complained of numbness in his leg. A test dose of mild solution of ethanol was not used to test its susceptibility and reaction of the therapeutic chemical, i.e. phenol. Ultimately the patient suffered from permanent disability due to deficiency in service on the part of the hospital and the surgeon.

The National Commission[3] directed the hospital and the surgeon to pay total compensation of ₹10,00,000 jointly and severally with the following break up: (*i*) ₹5,00,000 towards permanent disability; (*ii*) ₹2,00,000 towards past and future medical expenditure; (*iii*) ₹3,00,000 towards mental agony, physical trauma and life-long sufferings.

(83) ***Permanent disability due to deficiency in treatment of fractured leg*** The complainant had to undergo five operations in the hospital and to pay huge amount for medical treatment and transport charges. Owing to negligence of the doctor and hospital the complainant suffered severe physical pain, mental agony and permanent disabilities. There was evidence of restriction of movement of ankle joint and decimal shortening of the leg. She could walk with crutch.

The State Commission, Kerala, awarded a total sum of ₹2,00,000 as compensation against the hospital by holding it vicariously liable for negligence of the doctor. The Commission fixed ₹1 lakh as just and reasonable compensation for mental pain, agony and disability suffered by the complainant. Taking into consideration the huge amount spent on purchase of medicine, medical expenses for surgery and other incidental expenses, an amount of ₹75,000 was fixed as reasonable compensation. An award of ₹25,000 was fixed as compensation for making several trips from Payyannur to Mangalore by taxi and other vehicles.

3 *Om Prakash Lokre* v *Christian Medical College and Hospital* 2009(2) CPR 116; 2009 CTJ 849 (CP); II(2009) CPJ 178.

On appeal, the order of the State Commission was upheld by the National Commission[4] which directed the hospital authority to pay ₹2,00,000 to the complainant.

(84) *Permanent disability due to unskilled treatment of fractured arm* The complainant sustained fracture in the humerus bone of the left arm. There was no union of broken ends of the bone due to defective treatment of the doctor. The doctor was held guilty of negligence for not advising or adopting for surgical intervention when there was no possibility of union of the bone. The complainant suffered from permanent disability due to negligent treatment of the doctor.

The State Commission, U.P.[5] directed the doctor to pay compensation of ₹1,63,000 and cost of ₹5,000 to the complainant. The complainant was awarded ₹1,00,000 for mental tension, agony, harassment and permanent disability and ₹63,000 for medical expenses incurred by him.

(85) *Permanent disability of penis after operation* The patient had undergone circumcision operation. The nerve had been cut during the operation resulting in complete impotency as the penis had to be completely amputated except the small stump. The patient suffered permanent damage to the penis and permanent disability to pass urine due to negligence in conducting circumcision operation.

The patient is aged 23 years only. He cannot lead a married life and enjoy sex for the rest of the life. The State Commission, Tamil Nadu,[6] awarded compensation of ₹8,00,000 against the doctor along with interest @ 15% per annum from the date of order till realisation and cost of ₹2,000.

4 *Mrs. K.K. Radha* v *Dr. G.U. Sekhar* III(1994) CPJ 376 (Ker); (1994)2 CTJ 790 (CP) (SCDRC) confirmed by NC in *P.P. Ismail* v *Mrs. K.K. Radha* 1997(2) CPR 171 (NC); I(1998) CPJ 16 (NC); (1997)5 CTJ 685 (CP)(NCDRC); 1999 CCJ 99 (NC).

5 *Mohd. Ubaid Siddiqui* v *Dr. Ramesh Kumar Upadhaya* 2000 CTJ 284 (CP) (SCDRC); 2000(1) CPR 77 (Lucknow).

6 *C. Sivakumar* v *Dr. John Arthur* III(1998) CPJ 436 (Chennai); 2000 CCJ 673.

(86) *Permanent vegetative state of the child after circumcision operation* A child of $2^1/_2$ years old had undergone circumcision operation under general anaesthesia, but did not regain consciousness. It is established from evidence that the child will remain in vegetative state for negligence of the doctor in conducting surgery under general anaesthesia.

The amount of compensation of ₹5 lakh awarded by the State Commission was enhanced to ₹10 lakh by the National Commission, which was further enhanced by ₹7 lakh by the Supreme Court of India.[7]

(87) *Severe burn injury to a baby during inguinal hernia operation* A baby born with inguinal hernia had undergone operation when he was only 65 days old. The baby suffered severe burn injury on both the legs for keeping an extremely hot water bag under his legs while he was under anaesthesia during the operation.

The State Commission, Karnataka,[8] directed the hospital, paediatric surgeon and anaesthetist to pay jointly and severally ₹5,00,000 along with 18% interest, in addition to cost of ₹3,500.

(88) *Sufferings due to birth of deformed child* The complainant obtained three reports at different periods of her pregnancy from the opposite party scan centre. All the reports revealed that there was no obvious anomalies in the unborn child and that limbs were visualised. The complainant was shocked to find that the left hand of the child was deformed with only a stump just below the elbow. It is held by the State Commission, Tamil Nadu that the scan findings may not be 100% accurate in the case of small anomalies but in the present case the anomaly was so glaring that it cannot escape notice in the scan.

7 *Shilaben Ashwin Kumar Rana* v *Dr. Bhavin Kumar Shah* 2014(2) CPR 816; II(2014) CPJ 707 (NCDRC) affirmed by Supreme Court of India JT 2019(2) SC 289; 2019(2) ALT 12; 2019(1) Law Herald (SC) 552.

8 *Master P.M. Aswin* v *Manipal Hospital, Bangalore* 1997(1) CPR 393 (Bangalore); I(1997) CPJ 238 (Bangalore); 1998 CCJ 1079 (Kant).

The State Commission, Tamil Nadu,[9] awarded compensation of ₹5,00,000 against the scan centre along with interest @15% per annum till payment in addition to cost of ₹3,000. However, the doctor was exempted from making any payment on account of compensation, as there was no privity of contract between the complainant and the doctor who signed the scan reports.

(89) *Sufferings due to complications after unskilled endoscopy* The complainant was admitted to the Army Hospital for treatment of gastritis and heart burn. She was advised to undergo upper Gastro Intestinal Endoscopy (UGIE) in the hospital. The damage caused to esophagus during UGIE resulted in formation of thick yellow pass in both lungs. She survived after prolonged treatment for about three months in another hospital. Both the hospital and gastroenterologist were held to be negligent in conducting UGIE undergone by the patient.

The National Commission[10] directed Union of India and the doctor to pay compensation of ₹10,47,488 towards expenditure incurred for medical treatment. The compensation of ₹2,00,000 was also awarded towards non-pecuniary damage like pain and suffering.

(90) *Sufferings due to wrong report of MRI* The patient suffered for unnecessary operation conducted by the doctor on the basis of MRI report in which site of tumour was wrongly shown. This avoidable operation compelled the patient to be confined to the hospital for 3-4 weeks. The patient aged 67 years suffered from physical pain and mental agony due to negligence of the doctor and the hospital.

The State Commission, Maharashtra,[11] directed the hospital to pay compensation of ₹1,30,000 plus cost of ₹5,000

9 *Mrs. Shanthi Sridharan* v *Santhil Scan Centre* 1998 CTJ 759 (CP) (SCDRC).

10 *Sudha Garg* v *Union of India* 2009(156) DLT 498; 2009 CTJ 382 (CP); I(2009) CPJ 297.

11 *Sharifabi I. Sayed* v *Bombay Hospital & Medical Research Centre* 1998 CCJ 1106 (Mah).

to the patient. The break up of the amount is ₹70,000 towards hospital charges for unnecessary operation, ₹50,000 for physical pain and mental agony, and ₹10,000 for ancillary expenses. The amount of compensation will carry interest of 18% from the date of complaint till actual payment, if compensation is not paid within four months from the date of the order.

(91) ***Sufferings for lack of care after operation of inguinal hernia*** The complainant aged about 65 years had undergone operation of left inguinal hernia. He had to undergo 10 (ten) major and minor operations during postoperative period of 145 days, as he suffered from peritonitis and septicemia during post operative period. The surgeon was held liable in deficiency of service for the sufferings of the complainant.

The State Commission, Maharashtra[12] awarded compensation of ₹6,00,000 towards expenditure incurred by the complainant for medical treatment and ₹1,00,000 towards pain and mental agony of the complainant.

(92) ***Sufferings due to wrong report of FNAC Test*** The complainant was treated in the hospital for lump in her right breast. The pathologist of the hospital repeated Fine Needle Aspiration Cytology (FNAC) Test and the report was found to be positive indicating "Aspirates from right breast lump had shown well differential carcinoma". Based on that report surgery was performed on right breast and the tumour was sent for histopathological test. The report indicated that the tumour was benign and there was no carcinoma. The second opinion on the slides in UK also confirmed that there was no cancer. The pathologist and the hospital were held negligent for submission of wrong report of FNAC Test.

12 *Abdul Kader Suleman Allana* v *Saptarshi Medical and Research Centre Pvt. Ltd.* III(2000) CPJ 258.

The National Commission[13] awarded compensation of ₹5,00,000 for mental agony, trauma, emotional suffering and disfigurement of the body of the complainant.

(93) ***Sufferings due to unskilled lumber puncture*** The baby of 45 days old was admitted to the hospital for abdominal distention and one episode of general convulsion. The lumber puncture was done and blood stained cerebro spinal fluid (CSF) came out. The child developed paraplegia accompanied by paralysis of bladder and rectum.

The National Commission[14] directed the hospital and the doctor to pay compensation of ₹3,00,000 for traumatic lumber puncture, ₹5,00,000 for pain, suffering and mental agony of the child and the parents and ₹2,00,000 towards expenditure incurred for the medical treatment of the child.

(94) ***Sufferings due to unskilled LSCS surgery*** The lady admitted in the hospital with complaint of labour pain, had undergone LSCS surgery under the care of the doctor. The complications developed, as the patient sustained Iatragenic Cecal Perforation during surgery due to negligence of the doctor. She had to undergo second and third surgery in another hospital for recovery from the injuries sustained during LSCS surgery.

The Madras High Court[15] awarded compensation of ₹7,90,350 under different heads like pain and sufferings, mental agony and medical expenses etc.

(95) ***Sufferings due to wrong surgery by oncologist*** The patient was suffering from cervical cancer. She was admitted to the hospital for vaginal bleeding. With the consent of the patient the Assistant to the senior oncologist opened the abdomen and closed it without performing surgery. She was declared to be inoperable case of cancer in USA. The hospital and the

13 *All India Institute of Medical Sciences through its Director* v *Mrs. Ayesha Begum* IV(2010) CPJ 112.

14 *Subhash Chand* v *M.D. Jaipur Golden Hospital* IV(2011) CPJ 536.

15 *K. Latha* v *Madharasi* A.S. No. 610 of 2019, CMP Nos. 18541, 25841 and 25842 of 2019 decided on 23.01.2020.

senior oncologist were held negligent for unnecessary medical expenditure, pain and suffering, distress and mental agony of the patient.

The Bombay High Court[16] directed the hospital and the senior oncologist to pay compensation of ₹42,375 towards medical expenditure, ₹38,880 towards nursing expenditure and ₹15,00,000 towards distress, mental agony, pain and suffering of the patient.

(96) *Sufferings for removal of reproductive organs without consent* The patient, an unmarried women of 44 years, gave consent for diagnostic operative laparascopy for prolonged menstrual bleeding. The doctor was held negligent for performing hysterectomy and salpingo-oophorectomy for removal of uterus, ovaries and fallopian tubes without consent of the patient.

The Supreme Court[17] directed the doctor to pay ₹25,000 to the patient as compensation for unauthorised AH-BSO surgery along with interest @ 10% per annum from the date of order of the National Commission till the date of payment on consideration of mitigating circumstances like age of the patient and good faith of the doctor in carrying out surgery for treatment of endometriosis. The Supreme Court also directed the doctor to return the professional fees to the patient.

(97) *Sufferings due to removal of ovaries and one kidney without consent* The patient aged about 43 years was admitted to the hospital for hysterectomy due to dysfunctional uterine bleeding. Her consent was obtained for removal of uterus through abdominal route. The gynaecologist performed hysterectomy and removed ovaries without consent. The subsequent surgery was required during postoperative period as one of the kidneys was removed, large intestine was

16 *Padam Chandra Singhi* v *Dr. P.B. Desai* 2011(113) BLR 3409; 2012(1) All MR 510.

17 *Samira Kohli* v *Dr. Prabha Manchanda* (2008)2 SCC 1; 2008 ACJ 747; AIR 2008 SC 1385; JT 2008(1) SC 399; (2008)1 Scale 442.

exposed and small intestine was infected with adhesions at various places and for repair and closure of fistula. The gynaecologist and the hospital were held negligent for removal of ovaries and one kidney without consent.

The National Commission[18] awarded compensation of ₹5,00,000 against the gynaecologist and the hospital who were made jointly and severally liable for making payment of compensation.

(98) ***Sufferings for leaving mop in abdomen during exploratory laparotomy*** The girl child aged about 13 years was diagnosed as immature teratoma-Right ovary with secondary Norris Grade I for which exploratory laparotomy was done. She was discharged from the hospital after seven days of the operation. She was brought back to the hospital after seven days when pass started oozing out from the sutures. It was detected from second surgery that mop was left in abdomen when first surgery was done. The doctor was held negligent in carrying out exploratory laparotomy.

The National Commission[19] affirmed the order of the State Commission, which awarded compensation of ₹3,50,000 towards medical expenditure, mental agony, and trauma faced by the applicant.

(99) ***Sufferings for transfusion of blood without screening*** The complainant was admitted to the hospital with high fever and platelet count of 59,000. Her liver was found to be normal from ultrasound test and HCV (Hepatitis) anti bodies and HB antigens were found to be negative. The hospital transfused platelet from five donors without proper testing of blood, when platelet count of the patient was 35,000 whereas it is established from medical literature that platelet transfusion is necessary only when platelet count varies between 15,000 and 20,000. The hospital was found to be

18 *Smt. Saroj Chandhoke* v *Sir Ganga Ram Hospital* 2007(3) CPR 209; III(2007) CPJ 189.

19 *K. Ravindra Nath (Dr.)* v *Vitta Veera Surya Prakasam* IV(2006) CPJ 105; 2006(2) CPC 652; 2007(1) CLT 31.

negligent in providing treatment to the patient resulting in development of acute attack of hepatitis C.

The National Commission[20] awarded compensation of ₹10,00,000 towards cost of medical treatment already incurred and ₹8,00,000 towards future medical treatment and for mental agony and suffering.

20 *Ms Shefali Bhargava* v *Indra Prastha Appollo Hospital* 2003(3) CPR 58; I(2003) CPJ 216 (NC); 2003(3) CLT 402.

Part C

APPENDICES

APPENDIX

1

The Indian Medical Council (Professional Conduct, Etiquette and Ethics) Regulations, 2002*

MEDICAL COUNCIL OF INDIA

NOTIFICATION

New Delhi, dated 11th March, 2002

No. MCI-211(2)/2001/Registration. In exercise of the powers conferred under section 20A read with section 33(m) of the Indian Medical Council Act, 1956 (102 of 1956), the Medical Council of India, with the previous approval of the Central Government, hereby makes the following regulations relating to the Professional Conduct, Etiquette and Ethics for registered medical practitioners, namely:

Short Title and Commencement (1) These Regulations may be called the Indian Medical Council (Professional Conduct, Etiquette and Ethics) Regulations, 2002. (2) They shall come into force on the date of their publication in the Official Gazette.

CHAPTER 1

1 Code of medical ethics

A. DECLARATION. Each applicant, at the time of making an application for registration under the provisions of the Act, shall be provided a

* Published in Part III, s. 4 of the Gazette of India, dated 6th April, 2002.

copy of the declaration and shall submit a duly signed Declaration as provided in Appendix 1. The applicant shall also certify that he/she had read and agreed to abide by the same.

B. DUTIES AND RESPONSIBILITIES OF THE PHYSICIAN IN GENERAL.

1.1 *Character of Physician* (Doctors with qualification of MBBS or MBBS with post graduate degree/ diploma or with equivalent qualification in any medical discipline):

1.1.1 A physician shall uphold the dignity and honour of his profession.

1.1.2 The prime object of the medical profession is to render service to humanity; reward or financial gain is a subordinate consideration. Who- so-ever chooses his profession, assumes the obligation to conduct himself in accordance with its ideals. A physician should be an upright man, instructed in the art of healings. He shall keep himself pure in character and be diligent in caring for the sick; he should be modest, sober, patient, prompt in discharging his duty without anxiety; conducting himself with propriety in his profession and in all the actions of his life.

1.1.3 No person other than a doctor having qualification recognised by Medical Council of India and registered with Medical Council of India/State Medical Council (s) is allowed to practice Modern system of Medicine or Surgery. A person obtaining qualification in any other system of Medicine is not allowed to practice Modern system of Medicine in any form.

1.2 *Maintaining good medical practice*

1.2.1 The Principal objective of the medical profession is to render service to humanity with full respect for the dignity of profession and man. Physicians should merit the confidence of patients entrusted to their care, rendering to each a full measure of service and devotion. Physicians should try continuously to improve medical knowledge and skills and should make available to their patients and colleagues the benefits of their professional attainments. The physician should practice methods of healing founded on scientific basis and should not associate professionally with anyone who violates this principle. The honoured ideals of the medical profession imply that the responsibilities of the physician extend not only to individuals but also to society.

1.2.2 Membership in Medical Society: For the advancement of his profession, a physician should affiliate with associations and societies of allopathic medical professions and involve actively in the functioning of such bodies.

1.2.3 A Physician should participate in professional meetings as part of Continuing Medical Education programmes, for at least 30 hours every five years, organized by reputed professional academic bodies or any other authorized organisations. The compliance of this requirement shall be informed regularly to Medical Council of India or the State Medical Councils as the case may be.

1.3 *Maintenance of medical records*

1.3.1 Every physician shall maintain the medical records pertaining to his/her indoor patients for a period of 3 years from the date of commencement of the treatment in a standard proforma laid down by the Medical Council of India and attached as Appendix 3.

1.3.2. If any request is made for medical records either by the patients/authorised attendant or legal authorities involved, the same may be duly acknowledged and documents shall be issued within the period of 72 hours.

1.3.3 A Registered medical practitioner shall maintain a Register of Medical Certificates giving full details of certificates issued. When issuing a medical certificate he / she shall always enter the identification marks of the patient and keep a copy of the certificate. He / She shall not omit to record the signature and/or thumb mark, address and at least one identification mark of the patient on the medical certificates or report. The medical certificate shall be prepared as in Appendix 2.

1.3.4 Efforts shall be made to computerize medical records for quick retrieval.

1.4 *Display of registration numbers*

1.4.1 Every physician shall display the registration number accorded to him by the State Medical Council / Medical Council of India in his clinic and in all his prescriptions, certificates, money receipts given to his patients.

1.4.2 Physicians shall display as suffix to their names only recognized medical degrees or such certificates/diplomas and memberships/ honours which confer professional knowledge or recognizes any exemplary qualification/achievements.

1.5 *Use of Generic names of drugs.* *[Every physician should prescribe drugs with generic names legibly and preferably in capital letters and

---

* *Substituted* vide MCI Notification No. MCI-211(2)2016(Ethics)/131118 dated 8.10.2016.

he/she shall ensure that there is a rational prescription and use of drugs.]

1.6 *Highest Quality Assurance in patient care.* Every physician should aid in safeguarding the profession against admission to it of those who are deficient in moral character or education. Physician shall not employ in connection with his professional practice any attendant who is neither registered nor enlisted under the Medical Acts in force and shall not permit such persons to attend, treat or perform operations upon patients wherever professional discretion or skill is required.

1.7 *Exposure of Unethical Conduct.* A Physician should expose, without fear or favour, incompetent or corrupt, dishonest or unethical conduct on the part of members of the profession.

1.8 *Payment of Professional Services.* The physician, engaged in the practice of medicine shall give priority to the interests of patients. The personal financial interests of a physician should not conflict with the medical interests of patients. A physician should announce his fees before rendering service and not after the operation or treatment is under way. Remuneration received for such services should be in the form and amount specifically announced to the patient at the time the service is rendered. It is unethical to enter into a contract of "no cure no payment". Physician rendering service on behalf of the state shall refrain from anticipating or accepting any consideration.

1.9 *Evasion of Legal Restrictions.* The physician shall observe the laws of the country in regulating the practice of medicine and shall also not assist others to evade such laws. He should be cooperative in observance and enforcement of sanitary laws and regulations in the interest of public health. A physician should observe the provisions of the State Acts like Drugs and Cosmetics Act, 1940; Pharmacy Act, 1948; Narcotic Drugs and Psychotropic Substances Act, 1985; Medical Termination of Pregnancy Act, 1971; Transplantation of Human Organ Act, 1994; Mental Health Act, 1987; Environmental Protection Act, 1986; Pre–natal Sex Determination Test Act, 1994; Drugs and Magic Remedies (Objectionable Advertisement) Act, 1954; Persons with Disabilities (Equal Opportunities and Full Participation) Act, 1995 and Bio-Medical Waste (Management and Handling) Rules, 1998 and such other Acts, Rules, Regulations made by the Central/State Governments or local Administrative Bodies or any other relevant Act relating to the protection and promotion of public health.

CHAPTER 2

2 Duties of physicians to their patients

2.1 *Obligations to the Sick*

2.1.1 Though a physician is not bound to treat each and every person asking his services, he should not only be ever ready to respond to the calls of the sick and the injured, but should be mindful of the high character of his mission and the responsibility he discharges in the course of his professional duties. In his treatment, he should never forget that the health and the lives of those entrusted to his care depend on his skill and attention. A physician should endeavour to add to the comfort of the sick by making his visits at the hour indicated to the patients. A physician advising a patient to seek service of another physician is acceptable, however, in case of emergency a physician must treat the patient. No physician shall arbitrarily refuse treatment to a patient. However for good reason, when a patient is suffering from an ailment which is not within the range of experience of the treating physician, the physician may refuse treatment and refer the patient to another physician.

2.1.2 Medical practitioner having any incapacity detrimental to the patient or which can affect his performance vis-à-vis the patient is not permitted to practice his profession.

2.2 *Patience, Delicacy and Secrecy.* Patience and delicacy should characterize the physician. Confidences concerning individual or domestic life entrusted by patients to a physician and defects in the disposition or character of patients observed during medical attendance should never be revealed unless their revelation is required by the laws of the State. Sometimes, however, a physician must determine whether his duty to society requires him to employ knowledge, obtained through confidence as a physician, to protect a healthy person against a communicable disease to which he is about to be exposed. In such instance, the physician should act as he would wish another to act toward one of his own family in like circumstances.

2.3 *Prognosis.* The physician should neither exaggerate nor minimize the gravity of a patient's condition. He should ensure himself that the patient, his relatives or his responsible friends have such knowledge of the patient's condition as will serve the best interests of the patient and the family.

2.4 *The Patient must not be neglected.* A physician is free to choose whom he will serve. He should, however, respond to any request for his assistance in an emergency. Once having undertaken a case, the physician should not neglect the patient, nor should he withdraw from the case without giving adequate notice to the patient and his family. Provisionally or fully registered medical practitioner shall not willfully commit an act of negligence that may deprive his patient or patients from necessary medical care.

2.5 *Engagement for an Obstetric case.* When a physician who has been engaged to attend an obstetric case is absent and another is sent for and delivery accomplished, the acting physician is entitled to his professional fees, but should secure the patient's consent to resign on the arrival of the physician engaged.

CHAPTER 3

3 Duties of physician in consultation

3.1 *Unnecessary consultations should be avoided*

3.1.1 However in case of serious illness and in doubtful or difficult conditions, the physician should request consultation, but under any circumstances such consultation should be justifiable and in the interest of the patient only and not for any other consideration.

3.1.2 Consulting pathologists /radiologists or asking for any other diagnostic Lab investigation should be done judiciously and not in a routine manner.

3.2 *Consultation for Patient's Benefit.* In every consultation, the benefit to the patient is of foremost importance. All physicians engaged in the case should be frank with the patient and his attendants.

3.3 *Punctuality in Consultation.* Utmost punctuality should be observed by a physician in making themselves available for consultations.

3.4 *Statement to Patient after Consultation*

3.4.1 All statements to the patient or his representatives should take place in the presence of the consulting physicians, except as otherwise agreed. The disclosure of the opinion to the patient or his relatives or friends shall rest with the medical attendant.

3.4.2 Differences of opinion should not be divulged unnecessarily but when there is irreconcilable difference of opinion the circumstances should be frankly and impartially explained to the patient or his relatives or friends. It would be opened to them to seek further advice as they so desire.

3.5 *Treatment after Consultation.* No decision should restrain the attending physician from making such subsequent variations in the treatment if any unexpected change occurs, but at the next consultation, reasons for the variations should be discussed/ explained. The same privilege, with its obligations, belongs to the consultant when sent for in an emergency during the absence of attending physician. The attending physician may prescribe medicine at any time for the patient, whereas the consultant may prescribe only in case of emergency or as an expert when called for.

3.6 *Patients Referred to Specialists.* When a patient is referred to a specialist by the attending physician, a case summary of the patient should be given to the specialist, who should communicate his opinion in writing to the attending physician.

3.7 *Fees and other charges*

3.7.1 A physician shall clearly display his fees and other charges on the board of his chamber and/or the hospitals he is visiting. Prescription should also make clear if the Physician himself dispensed any medicine.

3.7.2 A physician shall write his name and designation in full along with registration particulars in his prescription letter head.

NOTE: In Government hospital where the patient–load is heavy, the name of the prescribing doctor must be written below his/her signature.

*[3.8 *Consultation by Telemedicine*

3.8.1 Consultation through Telemedicine by the Registered Medical Practitioner under the Indian Medical Council Act, 1956 shall be permissible in accordance with the Telemedicine Practice Guidelines contained in Appendix 5.

3.8.2 Telemedicine Practice Guidelines are designed to serve as an aid and tool to enable Registered Medical Practitioners to effectively leverage telemedicine to enhance health services and access to all in India.

3.8.3 Telemedicine Practice Guidelines are not applicable to the use of digital technology to conduct surgical or invasive procedure remotely.

3.8.4 Any of the drugs lists contained in Telemedicine Practice Guidelines can be modified by the Board of Governors in super-session of the Medical Council of India/Medical Council of India from time to time, as required.

* *Inserted* vide MCI Notification No. MCI-211(2)/2019(Ethics)/100659 dated 12.05.2020.

3.8.5 The Board of Governors in super-session of the Medical Council of India may issue necessary directions or advisories or clarifications in regard to these Guidelines, as required.

3.8.6 The Telemedicine Practice Guidelines can be amended from time to time in larger public interest with the prior approval of Central Government [Ministry of Health and Family Welfare, Government of India].

CHAPTER 4

4. Responsibilities of physicians to each other

4.1 *Dependence of Physicians on each other.* A physician should consider it as a pleasure and privilege to render gratuitous service to all physicians and their immediate family dependants.

4.2 *Conduct in consultation.* In consultations, no insincerity, rivalry or envy should be indulged in. All due respect should be observed towards the physician in-charge of the case and no statement or remark be made, which would impair the confidence reposed in him. For this purpose no discussion should be carried on in the presence of the patient or his representatives.

4.3 *Consultant not to take charge of the case.* When a physician has been called for consultation, the Consultant should normally not take charge of the case, especially on the solicitation of the patient or friends. The Consultant shall not criticize the referring physician. He / she shall discuss the diagnosis treatment plan with the referring physician.

4.4 *Appointment of substitute.* Whenever a physician requests another physician to attend his patients during his temporary absence from his practice, professional courtesy requires the acceptance of such appointment only when he has the capacity to discharge the additional responsibility along with his / her other duties. The physician acting under such an appointment should give the utmost consideration to the interests and reputation of the absent physician and all such patients should be restored to the care of the latter upon his/her return.

4.5 *Visiting another Physician's case.* When it becomes the duty of a physician occupying an official position to see and report upon an illness or injury, he should communicate to the physician in attendance so as to give him an option of being present. The medical officer / physician occupying an official position should avoid remarks upon the diagnosis or the treatment that has been adopted.

CHAPTER 5

5 Duties of physician to the public and to the paramedical profession

5.1 *Physicians as Citizens.* Physicians, as good citizens, possessed of special training should disseminate advice on public health issues. They should play their part in enforcing the laws of the community and in sustaining the institutions that advance the interests of humanity. They should particularly co-operate with the authorities in the administration of sanitary/public health laws and regulations.

5.2 *Public and Community Health.* Physicians, especially those engaged in public health work, should enlighten the public concerning quarantine regulations and measures for the prevention of epidemic and communicable diseases. At all times the physician should notify the constituted public health authorities of every case of communicable disease under his care, in accordance with the laws, rules and regulations of the health authorities. When an epidemic occurs a physician should not abandon his duty for fear of contracting the disease himself.

5.3 *Pharmacists / Nurses.* Physicians should recognize and promote the practice of different paramedical services such as, pharmacy and nursing as professions and should seek their cooperation wherever required.

CHAPTER 6

6 Unethical acts A physician shall not aid or abet or commit any of the following acts which shall be construed as unethical—

6.1 *Advertising*

6.1.1 Soliciting of patients directly or indirectly, by a physician, by a group of physicians or by institutions or organisations is unethical. A physician shall not make use of him / her (or his / her name) as subject of any form or manner of advertising or publicity through any mode either alone or in conjunction with others which is of such a character as to invite attention to him or to his professional position, skill, qualification, achievements, attainments, specialities, appointments, associations, affiliations or honours and/or of such character as would ordinarily result in his self aggrandizement. A physician shall not give to any person, whether for compensation or otherwise, any approval, recommendation, endorsement, certificate, report or statement with respect of any drug, medicine, nostrum remedy, surgical, or therapeutic article, apparatus or appliance or any commercial product or article with respect of any property, quality or use thereof or any test, demonstration or trial thereof, for use in connection with his name, signature, or photograph in any form or manner of advertising through any mode nor shall he boast of cases, operations, cures or remedies or permit the publication of report thereof through any mode. A medical practitioner is however permitted to make a formal announcement in press regarding the following:

(1) On starting practice.

(2) On change of type of practice.

(3) On changing address.

(4) On temporary absence from duty.

(5) On resumption of another practice.

(6) On succeeding to another practice.

(7) Public declaration of charges.

6.1.2 Printing of self photograph, or any such material of publicity in the letter head or on sign board of the consulting room or any such clinical establishment shall be regarded as acts of self advertisement and unethical conduct on the part of the physician. However, printing of sketches, diagrams, picture of human system shall not be treated as unethical.

6.2 *Patent and copy rights.* A physician may patent surgical instruments, appliances and medicine or Copyright applications, methods and procedures. However, it shall be unethical if the benefits of such patents or copyrights are not made available in situations where the interest of large population is involved.

6.3 *Running an open shop (Dispensing of Drugs and Appliances by Physicians).* A physician should not run an open shop for sale of medicine for dispensing prescriptions prescribed by doctors other than himself or for sale of medical or surgical appliances. It is not unethical for a physician to prescribe or supply drugs, remedies or appliances as long as there is no exploitation of the patient. Drugs prescribed by a physician or brought from the market for a patient should explicitly state the proprietary formulae as well as generic name of the drug.

6.4 *Rebates and commission*

6.4.1 A physician shall not give, solicit, or receive nor shall he offer to give solicit or receive, any gift, gratuity, commission or bonus in consideration of or return for the referring, recommending or procuring of any patient for medical, surgical or other treatment. A physician shall not directly or indirectly, participate in or be a party to act of division, transference, assignment, subordination, rebating, splitting or refunding of any fee for medical, surgical or other treatment.

6.4.2 Provisions of para 6.4.1 shall apply with equal force to the referring, recommending or procuring by a physician or any person, specimen or material for diagnostic purposes or other study / work. Nothing in this section, however, shall prohibit payment of salaries by a qualified physician to other duly qualified person rendering medical care under his supervision.

6.5 *Secret Remedies.* The prescribing or dispensing by a physician of secret remedial agents of which he does not know the composition, or the manufacture or promotion of their use is unethical and as such prohibited. All the drugs prescribed by a physician should always carry a proprietary formula and clear name.

6.6 *Human Rights.* The physician shall not aid or abet torture nor shall he be a party to either infliction of mental or physical trauma or concealment of torture inflicted by some other person or agency in clear violation of human rights.

6.7 *Euthanasia.* Practicing euthanasia shall constitute unethical conduct. However on specific occasion, the question of withdrawing supporting devices to sustain cardio-pulmonary function even after brain death, shall be decided only by a team of doctors and not merely by the treating physician alone. A team of doctors shall declare withdrawal of support system. Such team shall consist of the doctor in charge of the patient, Chief Medical Officer / Medical Officer in charge of the hospital and a doctor nominated by the in-charge of the hospital from the hospital staff or in accordance with the provisions of the Transplantation of Human Organ Act, 1994.

The Clause No. 6.8, as under, is included in terms of Notification published on 14.12.2009 in Gazette of India & the same is also enclosed as Annexure - I.

"6.8 Code of conduct for doctors *[.....] in their relationship with pharmaceutical and allied health sector industry.

The section 6.8.1 (*b*) shall be substituted in terms of Notification published on 01.02.2016 in Gazette of India, as under: (*b*) Travel Facilities: A medical practitioner shall not accept any travel Facility inside the country or outside, including rail, road, air,

* *Deleted* vide Notification published dated 1.2.2016.

ship, cruise tickets, paid vacation, etc. from any pharmaceutical or allied healthcare industry or their representatives for self and family members for vacation or for attending conferences, seminars, workshops, CME Programme, etc. as a delegate.

(iii) Action to be taken by the Council for violation of section 6.8, as *amended* vide notification dated 10/12/2009, shall be prescribed by further amending the section 6.8.1 as under:

6.8.1 In dealing with Pharmaceutical and allied health sector industry, a medical practitioner shall follow and adhere to the stipulations given below:—

(A) GIFTS: A medical practitioner shall not receive any gift from any pharmaceutical or allied health care industry and their sales people or representatives.

(B) TRAVEL FACILITIES: A medical practitioner shall not accept any travel facility inside the country or outside, including rail, road, air, ship, cruise tickets, paid vacations etc. from any pharmaceutical or allied healthcare industry or their representatives for self and family members for vacation or for attending conferences, seminars, workshops, CME programme etc. as a delegate.

(c) HOSPITALITY: A medical practitioner shall not accept individually any hospitality like hotel accommodation for self and family members under any pretext.

(d) CASH OR MONETARY GRANTS: A medical practitioner shall not receive any cash or monetary grants from any pharmaceutical and allied healthcare industry for individual purpose in individual capacity under any pretext. Funding for medical research, study etc. can only be received through approved institutions by modalities laid down by law / rules / guidelines adopted by such approved institutions, in a transparent manner. It shall always be fully disclosed.

(e) MEDICAL RESEARCH: A medical practitioner may carry out, participate in, work in research projects funded by pharmaceutical and allied healthcare industries. A medical practitioner is obliged to know that the fulfillment of the following items (i) to (vii) will be an imperative for undertaking any research assignment/project funded by industry – for being proper and ethical. Thus, in accepting such a position a medical practitioner shall:

(i) Ensure that the particular research proposal(s) has the due permission from the competent concerned authorities.

(ii) Ensure that such a research project(s) has the clearance of national/state/institutional ethics committees/bodies.

(iii) Ensure that it fulfils all the legal requirements prescribed for medical research.

(iv) Ensure that the source and amount of funding is publicly disclosed at the beginning itself.

(v) Ensure that proper care and facilities are provided to human volunteers, if they are necessary for the research project(s).

(vi) Ensure that undue animal experimentations are not done and when these are necessary they are done in a scientific and a humane way.

(vii) Ensure that while accepting such an assignment a medical practitioner shall have the freedom to publish the results of the research in the greater interest of the society by inserting such a clause in the MoU or any other documents/agreement for any such assignment.

(f) **MAINTAINING PROFESSIONAL AUTONOMY**: In dealing with pharmaceutical and allied healthcare industry a medical practitioner shall always ensure that there shall never be any compromise either with his/her own professional autonomy and/or with the autonomy and freedom of the medical institution.

(g) **Affiliation**: A medical practitioner may work for pharmaceutical and allied healthcare industries in advisory capacities, as consultants, as researchers, as treating doctors or in any other professional capacity. In doing so, a medical practitioner shall always:

(i) Ensure that his professional integrity and freedom are maintained.

(ii) Ensure that patients interest are not compromised in any way.

(iii) Ensure that such affiliations are within the law.

(iv) Ensure that such affiliations/employments are fully transparent and disclosed.

(h) **Endorsement**: A medical practitioner shall not endorse any drug or product of the industry publically. Any study conducted on the efficacy or otherwise of such products shall be presented to and/or through appropriate scientific bodies or published in appropriate scientific journals in a proper way.

CHAPTER 7

7 Misconduct The following acts of commission or omission on the part of a physician shall constitute professional misconduct rendering him/her liable for disciplinary action

7.1 *Violation of the Regulations.* If he/she commits any violation of these Regulations.

7.2 If he/she does not maintain the medical records of his/her indoor patients for a period of three years as per regulation 1.3 and refuses to provide the same within 72 hours when the patient or his/her authorised representative makes a request for it as per the regulation 1.3.2.

7.3 If he/she does not display the registration number accorded to him/her by the State Medical Council or the Medical Council of India in his clinic, prescriptions and certificates etc. issued by him or violates the provisions of regulation 1.4.2.

7.4 *Adultery or Improper Conduct.* Abuse of professional position by committing adultery or improper conduct with a patient or by maintaining an improper association with a patient will render a Physician liable for disciplinary action as provided under the Indian Medical Council Act, 1956 or the concerned State Medical Council Act.

7.5 *Conviction by Court of Law.* Conviction by a Court of Law for offences involving moral turpitude / Criminal acts.

7.6 *Sex Determination Tests.* On no account sex determination test shall be undertaken with the intent to terminate the life of a female foetus developing in her mother's womb, unless there are other absolute indications for termination of pregnancy as specified in the Medical Termination of Pregnancy Act, 1971. Any act of termination of pregnancy of normal female foetus amounting to female foeticide shall be regarded as professional misconduct on the part of the physician leading to penal erasure besides rendering him liable to criminal proceedings as per the provisions of this Act.

7.7 *Signing Professional Certificates, Reports and other Documents.* Registered medical practitioners are in certain cases bound by law to give, or may from time to time be called upon or requested to give certificates, notification, reports and other documents of similar character signed by them in their professional capacity for subsequent use in the courts or for administrative purposes etc. Such documents, among others, include the ones given at Appendix –4. Any registered practitioner who is shown to have signed or given under his name and authority any such certificate, notification, report or document of a similar character which is untrue, misleading or improper, is liable to have his name deleted from the Register.

7.8 A registered medical practitioner shall not contravene the provisions of the Drugs and Cosmetics Act and regulations made there under. Accordingly,

(*a*) Prescribing steroids/ psychotropic drugs when there is no absolute medical indication;

(*b*) Selling Schedule 'H' & 'L' drugs and poisons to the public except to his patient;

in contravention of the above provisions shall constitute gross professional misconduct on the part of the physician.

7.9 Performing or enabling unqualified person to perform an abortion or any illegal operation for which there is no medical, surgical or psychological indication.

7.10 A registered medical practitioner shall not issue certificates of efficiency in modern medicine to unqualified or non-medical person.

(Note: The foregoing does not restrict the proper training and instruction of bonafide students, midwives, dispensers, surgical attendants, or skilled mechanical and technical assistants and therapy assistants under the personal supervision of physicians.)

7.11 A physician should not contribute to the lay press articles and give interviews regarding diseases and treatments which may have the effect of advertising himself or soliciting practices; but is open to write to the lay press under his own name on matters of public health, hygienic living or to deliver public lectures, give talks on the radio/TV/ internet chat for the same purpose and send announcement of the same to lay press.

7.12 An institution run by a physician for a particular purpose such as a maternity home, nursing home, private hospital, rehabilitation centre or any type of training institution etc. may be advertised in the lay press, but such advertisements should not contain anything more than the name of the institution, type of patients admitted, type of training and other facilities offered and the fees.

7.13 It is improper for a physician to use an unusually large sign board and write on it anything other than his name, qualifications obtained from a University or a statutory body, titles and name of his speciality, registration number including the name of the State Medical Council under which registered. The same should be the contents of his prescription papers. It is improper to affix a sign-board on a chemist's shop or in places where he does not reside or work.

7.14 The registered medical practitioner shall not disclose the secrets of a patient that have been learnt in the exercise of his / her profession except–

(*i*) in a court of law under orders of the Presiding Judge;
(*ii*) in circumstances where there is a serious and identified risk to a specific person and / or community; and
(*iii*) notifiable diseases.

In case of communicable / notifiable diseases, concerned public health authorities should be informed immediately.

7.15 The registered medical practitioner shall not refuse on religious grounds alone to give assistance in or conduct of sterility, birth control, circumcision and medical termination of Pregnancy when there is medical indication, unless the medical practitioner feels himself/herself incompetent to do so.

7.16 Before performing an operation the physician should obtain in writing the consent from the husband or wife, parent or guardian in the case of minor, or the patient himself as the case may be. In an operation which may result in sterility the consent of both husband and wife is needed.

7.17 A registered medical practitioner shall not publish photographs or case reports of his / her patients without their permission, in any medical or other journal in a manner by which their identity could be made out. If the identity is not to be disclosed, the consent is not needed.

7.18 In the case of running of a nursing home by a physician and employing assistants to help him / her, the ultimate responsibility rests on the physician.

7.19 A Physician shall not use touts or agents for procuring patients.

7.20 A Physician shall not claim to be specialist unless he has a special qualification in that branch.

7.21 No act of invitro fertilization or artificial insemination shall be undertaken without the informed consent of the female patient and her spouse as well as the donor. Such consent shall be obtained in writing only after the patient is provided, at her own level of comprehension, with sufficient information about the purpose, methods, risks, inconveniences, disappointments of the procedure and possible risks and hazards.

7.22 Research: Clinical drug trials or other research involving patients or volunteers as per the guidelines of ICMR can be undertaken, provided ethical considerations are borne in mind. Violation of existing ICMR guidelines in this regard shall constitute misconduct. Consent taken from the patient for trial of drug or therapy which is not as per the guidelines shall also be construed as misconduct.

The following Clause No. 7.23 & 7.24 are deleted in terms of Notification published on 22.02.2003 in Gazette of India & the same is also enclosed as Annexure - II.

7.23 If a physician posted in rural area is found absent on more than two occasions during inspection by the Head of the District Health Authority or the Chairman, Zila Parishad, the same shall be construed as a misconduct if it is recommended to the Medical Council of India/ State Medical Council by the State Government for action under these Regulations.

7.24 If a physician posted in a medical college/institution both as teaching faculty or otherwise shall remain in hospital/college during the assigned duty hours. If they are found absent on more than two occasions during this period, the same shall be construed as a misconduct if it is certified by the Principal/Medical Superintendent and forwarded through the State Government to Medical Council of India/State Medical Council for action under these Regulations.

CHAPTER 8

8. Punishment and disciplinary action

8.1 It must be clearly understood that the instances of offences and of Professional misconduct which are given above do not constitute and are not intended to constitute a complete list of the infamous acts which calls for disciplinary action, and that by issuing this notice the Medical Council of India and or State Medical Councils are in no way precluded from considering and dealing with any other form of professional misconduct on the part of a registered practitioner. Circumstances may and do arise from time to time in relation to which there may occur questions of professional misconduct which do not come within any of these categories. Every care should be taken that the code is not violated in letter or spirit. In such instances as in all others, the Medical Council of India and/or State Medical Councils have to consider and decide upon the facts brought before the Medical Council of India and/or State Medical Councils.

8.2 It is made clear that any complaint with regard to professional misconduct can be brought before the appropriate Medical Council for Disciplinary action. Upon receipt of any complaint of professional misconduct, the appropriate Medical Council would hold an enquiry and give opportunity to the registered medical practitioner to be heard in person or by pleader. If the medical practitioner is found to be guilty of committing professional misconduct, the appropriate Medical Council may award such punishment as deemed necessary or may direct the removal altogether or for a specified period, from the register of the name of the delinquent registered practitioner. Deletion from the Register shall be widely publicized in local press as well as in the publications of different Medical Associations/ Societies/Bodies.

8.3 In case the punishment of removal from the register is for a limited period, the appropriate Council may also direct that the name so removed shall be restored in the register after the expiry of the period for which the name was ordered to be removed.

8.4 Decision on complaint against delinquent physician shall be taken within a time limit of 6 months.

8.5 During the pendency of the complaint the appropriate Council may restrain the physician from performing the procedure or practice which is under scrutiny.

8.6 Professional incompetence shall be judged by peer group as per guidelines prescribed by Medical Council of India.

The following Clause No. 8.7 & 8.8 are included in terms of Notification published on 27.05.2004 in Gazette of India & the same is also enclosed as Annexure - III.

"8.7 Where either on a request or otherwise the Medical Council of India is informed that any complaint against a delinquent physician has not been decided by a State Medical Council within a period of six months from the date of receipt of complaint by it and further the MCI has reason to believe that there is no justified reason for not deciding the complaint within the said prescribed period, the Medical Council of India may—

(*i*) Impress upon the concerned State Medical Council to conclude and decide the complaint within a time bound schedule;

(*ii*) May decide to withdraw the said complaint pending with the concerned State Medical Council straightaway or after the expiry of the period which had been stipulated by the MCI in accordance with para (*i*) above, to itself and refer the same to the Ethical Committee of the Council for its expeditious disposal in a period of not more than six months from the receipt of the complaint in the office of the Medical Council of India."

"8.8 Any person aggrieved by the decision of the State Medical Council on any complaint against a delinquent physician, shall have the right to file an appeal to the MCI within a period of 60 days from the date of receipt of the order passed by the said Medical Council:

Provided that the MCI may, if it is satisfied that the appellant was prevented by sufficient cause from presenting the appeal within the aforesaid period of 60 days, allow it to be presented within a further period of 60 days.

APPENDIX 1

A. Declaration

At the time of registration, each applicant shall be given a copy of the following declaration by the Registrar concerned and the applicant shall read and agree to abide by the same:

1) I solemnly pledge myself to consecrate my life to service of humanity.
2) Even under threat, I will not use my medical knowledge contrary to the laws of Humanity.
3) I will maintain the utmost respect for human life from the time of conception.
4) I will not permit considerations of religion, nationality, race, party politics or social standing to intervene between my duty and my patient.
5) I will practice my profession with conscience and dignity.
6) The health of my patient will be my first consideration.
7) I will respect the secrets which are confined in me.
8) I will give to my teachers the respect and gratitude which is their due.
9) I will maintain by all means in my power, the honour and noble traditions of medical profession.
10) I will treat my colleagues with all respect and dignity.
11) I shall abide by the code of medical ethics as enunciated in the Indian Medical Council (Professional Conduct, Etiquette and Ethics) Regulations, 2002.

I make these promises solemnly, freely and upon my honour.

Signature ....

Name ....

Place ....

Address..

....

Date ....

APPENDIX 2

1. Form of certificate recommended for leave or extension or communication of leave and for fitness

Signature of patient
or thumb impression ________________________

To be filled in by the applicant in the presence of the Government Medical Attendant, or Medical Practitioner.

Identification marks:—

1. ____________________
2. ____________________

I, Dr. ____________________ after careful examination of the case certify hereby that __________ whose signature is given above is suffering from ____________ and I consider that a period of absence from duty of ______________ with effect from ______________ is absolutely necessary for the restoration of his health.

I, Dr. ____________________ after careful examination of the case certify hereby that ______________ on restoration of health is now fit to join service.

Place ________________ Signature of Medical attendant.

Date ______________ Registration No. ____________
(Medical Council of India / State Medical Council of .... State)

NOTE: The nature and probable duration of the illness should also be specified . This certificate must be accompanied by a brief resume of the case giving the nature of the illness, its symptoms, causes and duration.

APPENDIX 3

Format for medical record

(see regulation 3.1)

Name of the patient :

Age :

Sex :

Address :

Occupation :

Date of 1st visit :

Clinical note (summary) of the case :

Prov. : Diagnosis :

Investigations advised with reports :

Diagnosis after investigation :

Advice :

Follow up :

Date:

Observations:

Signature in full ....

Name of Treating Physician

APPENDIX 4

List of certificates, reports, notifications etc. Issued by doctors for the purposes of various acts / administrative requirements

a) Under the acts relating to birth, death or disposal of the dead.

b) Under the Acts relating to Lunacy and Mental Deficiency and under the Mental illness Act and the rules made thereunder.

c) Under the Vaccination Acts and the regulations made thereunder.

d) Under the Factory Acts and the regulations made thereunder.

e) Under the Education Acts.

f) Under the Public Health Acts and the orders made thereunder.

g) Under the Workmen's Compensation Act and Persons with Disability Act.

h) Under the Acts and orders relating to the notification of infectious diseases.

i) Under the Employee's State Insurance Act.

j) In connection with sick benefit insurance and friendly societies.

k) Under the Merchant Shipping Act.

l) For procuring / issuing of passports.

m) For excusing attendance in courts of Justice, in public services, in public offices or in ordinary employment.

n) In connection with Civil and Military matters.

o) In connection with matters under the control of Department of Pensions.

p) In connection with quarantine rules.

q) For procuring driving licence.

FOOT NOTE: The Principal Regulations namely, "Indian Medical Council (Professional Conduct, Etiquette and Ethics) Regulations, 2002" were published in Part – III, section (4) of the Gazette of India on the 6th April, 2002, and amended vide MCI notifications dated 22/02/2003, 26/05/2004 & 14.12.2009.

APPENDIX

2

The Consumer Protection Act, 2019

No. 35 of 2019

[9th August, 2019

An Act to provide for protection of the interests of consumers and for the said purpose, to establish authorities for timely and effective administration and settlement of consumers' disputes and for matters connected therewith or incidental thereto.

Be it enacted by Parliament in the Seventieth Year of the Republic of India as follows:—

Chapter I

Preliminary

1. Short title, extent, commencement and application. (1) This Act may be called the Consumer Protection Act, 2019.

(2) It extends to the whole of India except the State of Jammu and Kashmir.

(3) It shall come into force on such date as the Central Government may, by notification, appoint and different dates may be appointed for different States and for different provisions of this Act and any reference in any such provision to the commencement of this Act shall be construed as a reference to the coming into force of that provision.

(4) Save as otherwise expressly provided by the Central Government, by notification, this Act shall apply to all goods and services.

2. Definitions. In this Act, unless the context otherwise requires,—

(1) "advertisement" means any audio or visual publicity, representation, endorsement or pronouncement made by means of light, sound, smoke, gas, print, electronic media, internet or website and includes any notice, circular, label, wrapper, invoice or such other documents;

(2) "appropriate laboratory" means a laboratory or an organisation—

(*i*) recognised by the Central Government; or

(*ii*) recognised by a State Government, subject to such guidelines as may be issued by the Central Government in this behalf; or

(*iii*) established by or under any law for the time being in force, which is maintained, financed or aided by the Central Government or a State Government for carrying out analysis or test of any goods with a view to determining whether such goods suffer from any defect;

(3) "branch office" means—

(*i*) any office or place of work described as a branch by the establishment; or

(*ii*) any establishment carrying on either the same or substantially the same activity carried on by the head office of the establishment;

(4) "Central Authority" means the Central Consumer Protection Authority established under section 10;

(5) "complainant" means—

(*i*) a consumer; or

(*ii*) any voluntary consumer association registered under any law for the time being in force; or

(*iii*) the Central Government or any State Government; or

(*iv*) the Central Authority; or

(*v*) one or more consumers, where there are numerous consumers having the same interest; or

(*vi*) in case of death of a consumer, his legal heir or legal representative; or (*vii*) in case of a consumer being a minor, his parent or legal guardian;

(6) "complaint" means any allegation in writing, made by a complainant for obtaining any relief provided by or under this Act, that—

(*i*) an unfair contract or unfair trade practice or a restrictive trade practice has been adopted by any trader or service provider;

(*ii*) the goods bought by him or agreed to be bought by him suffer from one or more defects;

(*iii*) the services hired or availed of or agreed to be hired or availed of by him suffer from any deficiency;

(*iv*) a trader or a service provider, as the case may be, has charged for the goods or for the services mentioned in the complaint, a price in excess of the price—

(*a*) fixed by or under any law for the time being in force; or

(*b*) displayed on the goods or any package containing such goods; or

(*c*) displayed on the price list exhibited by him by or under any law for the time being in force; or

(*d*) agreed between the parties;

(*v*) the goods, which are hazardous to life and safety when used, are being offered for sale to the public—

(*a*) in contravention of standards relating to safety of such goods as required to be complied with, by or under any law for the time being in force;

(*b*) where the trader knows that the goods so offered are unsafe to the public;

(*vi*) the services which are hazardous or likely to be hazardous to life and safety of the public when used, are being offered by a person who provides any service and who knows it to be injurious to life and safety;

(*vii*) a claim for product liability action lies against the product manufacturer, product seller or product service provider, as the case may be;

(7) "consumer" means any person who—

(*i*) buys any goods for a consideration which has been paid or promised or partly paid and partly promised, or under any system of deferred payment and includes any user of such goods other than the person who buys such goods for consideration paid or promised or partly paid or partly promised, or under any system of deferred payment, when such use is made with the approval of such person, but does not include a person who obtains such goods for resale or for any commercial purpose; or

(*ii*) hires or avails of any service for a consideration which has been paid or promised or partly paid and partly promised, or under any system of deferred payment and includes any beneficiary of such service other than the person who hires or avails of the services for consideration paid or promised, or partly paid and partly promised, or under any system of deferred payment, when such services are availed of with the approval of the first mentioned person, but does not include a person who avails of such service for any commercial purpose.

Explanation.—For the purposes of this clause,—

(*a*) the expression "commercial purpose" does not include use by a person of goods bought and used by him exclusively for the purpose of earning his livelihood, by means of self-employment;

(*b*) the expressions "buys any goods" and "hires or avails any services" includes offline or online transactions through electronic means or by teleshopping or direct selling or multi-level marketing;

(8) "consumer dispute" means a dispute where the person against whom a complaint has been made, denies or disputes the allegations contained in the complaint;

(9) "consumer rights" includes,—

(*i*) the right to be protected against the marketing of goods, products or services which are hazardous to life and property;

(*ii*) the right to be informed about the quality, quantity, potency, purity, standard and price of goods, products or services, as the case may be, so as to protect the consumer against unfair trade practices;

(*iii*) the right to be assured, wherever possible, access to a variety of goods, products or services at competitive prices;

(*iv*) the right to be heard and to be assured that consumer's interests will receive due consideration at appropriate fora;

(*v*) the right to seek redressal against unfair trade practice or restrictive trade practices or unscrupulous exploitation of consumers; and

(*vi*) the right to consumer awareness;

(10) "defect" means any fault, imperfection or shortcoming in the quality, quantity, potency, purity or standard which is required to be maintained by or under any law for the time being in force or under any contract, express or implied or as is claimed by the trader in any manner whatsoever in relation to any goods or product and the expression "defective" shall be construed accordingly;

(11) "deficiency" means any fault, imperfection, shortcoming or inadequacy in the quality, nature and manner of performance which is required to be maintained by or under any law for the time being in force or has been undertaken to be performed by a person in pursuance of a contract or otherwise in relation to any service and includes—

(*i*) any act of negligence or omission or commission by such person which causes loss or injury to the consumer; and

(*ii*) deliberate withholding of relevant information by such person to the consumer;

(12) "design", in relation to a product, means the intended or known physical and material characteristics of such product and includes any intended or known formulation or content of such product and the usual result of the intended manufacturing or other process used to produce such product;

(13) "direct selling" means marketing, distribution and sale of goods or provision of services through a network of sellers, other than through a permanent retail location;

(14) "Director-General" means the Director-General appointed under sub-section (2) of section 15;

(15) "District Commission" means a District Consumer Disputes Redressal Commission established under sub-section (1) of section 28;

(16) "e-commerce" means buying or selling of goods or services including digital products over digital or electronic network;

(17) "electronic service provider" means a person who provides technologies or processes to enable a product seller to engage in advertising or selling goods or services to a consumer and includes any online market place or online auction sites;

(18) "endorsement", in relation to an advertisement, means—

(*i*) any message, verbal statement, demonstration; or

(*ii*) depiction of the name, signature, likeness or other identifiable personal characteristics of an individual; or

(*iii*) depiction of the name or seal of any institution or organisation,

which makes the consumer to believe that it reflects the opinion, finding or experience of the person making such endorsement;

(19) "establishment" includes an advertising agency, commission agent, manufacturing, trading or any other commercial agency which carries on any business, trade or profession or any work in connection with or incidental or ancillary to any commercial activity, trade or profession, or such other class or classes of persons including public utility entities in the manner as may be prescribed;

(20) "express warranty" means any material statement, affirmation of fact, promise or description relating to a product or service warranting that it conforms to such material statement, affirmation, promise or description and includes any sample or model of a product warranting that the whole of such product conforms to such sample or model;

(21) "goods" means every kind of movable property and includes "food" as defined in clause (*j*) of sub-section (1) of section 3 of the Food Safety and Standards Act, 2006 (34 of 2006);

(22) "harm", in relation to a product liability, includes—

(*i*) damage to any property, other than the product itself;

(*ii*) personal injury, illness or death;

(*iii*) mental agony or emotional distress attendant to personal injury or illness or damage to property; or

(*iv*) any loss of consortium or services or other loss resulting from a harm referred to in sub-clause (*i*) or sub-clause (*ii*) or sub-clause (*iii*),

but shall not include any harm caused to a product itself or any damage to the property on account of breach of warranty conditions or any commercial or economic loss, including any direct, incidental or consequential loss relating thereto;

(23) "injury" means any harm whatever illegally caused to any person, in body, mind or property;

(24) "manufacturer" means a person who—

(*i*) makes any goods or parts thereof; or

(*ii*) assembles any goods or parts thereof made by others; or

(*iii*) puts or causes to be put his own mark on any goods made by any other person;

(25) "mediation" means the process by which a mediator mediates the consumer disputes;

(26) "mediator" means a mediator referred to in section 75;

(27) "member" includes the President and a member of the National Commission or a State Commission or a District Commission, as the case may be;

(28) "misleading advertisement" in relation to any product or service, means an advertisement, which—

(*i*) falsely describes such product or service; or

(*ii*) gives a false guarantee to, or is likely to mislead the consumers as to the nature, substance, quantity or quality of such product or service; or

(*iii*) conveys an express or implied representation which, if made by the manufacturer or seller or service provider thereof, would constitute an unfair trade practice; or

(*iv*) deliberately conceals important information;

(29) "National Commission" means the National Consumer Disputes Redressal Commission established under sub-section (1) of section 53;

(30) "notification" means a notification published in the Official Gazette and the term "notify" shall be construed accordingly;

(31) "person" includes—

(*i*) an individual;

(*ii*) a firm whether registered or not;

(*iii*) a Hindu undivided family;

(*iv*) a co-operative society;

(*v*) an association of persons whether registered under the Societies Registration Act, 1860 or not;

(*vi*) any corporation, company or a body of individuals whether incorporated or not;

(*vii*) any artificial juridical person, not falling within any of the preceding sub-clauses;

(32) "prescribed" means prescribed by rules made by the Central Government, or, as the case may be, the State Government;

(33) "product" means any article or goods or substance or raw material or any extended cycle of such product, which may be in gaseous, liquid, or solid state possessing intrinsic value which is capable of delivery either as wholly assembled or as a component part and is produced for introduction to trade or commerce, but does not include human tissues, blood, blood products and organs;

(34) "product liability" means the responsibility of a product manufacturer or product seller, of any product or service, to compensate for any harm caused to a consumer by such defective product manufactured or sold or by deficiency in services relating thereto;

(35) "product liability action" means a complaint filed by a person before a District Commission or State Commission or National Commission, as the case may be, for claiming compensation for the harm caused to him;

(36) "product manufacturer" means a person who—

(*i*) makes any product or parts thereof; or

(*ii*) assembles parts thereof made by others; or

(*iii*) puts or causes to be put his own mark on any products made by any other person; or (*iv*) makes a product and sells, distributes, leases, installs, prepares, packages, labels, markets, repairs, maintains such product or is otherwise involved in placing such product for commercial purpose; or

(*v*) designs, produces, fabricates, constructs or re-manufactures any product before its sale; or

(*vi*) being a product seller of a product, is also a manufacturer of such product;

(37) "product seller", in relation to a product, means a person who, in the course of business, imports, sells, distributes, leases, installs, prepares, packages, labels, markets, repairs, maintains, or otherwise is involved in placing such product for commercial purpose and includes—

(*i*) a manufacturer who is also a product seller; or

(*ii*) a service provider,

but does not include—

(*a*) a seller of immovable property, unless such person is engaged in the sale of constructed house or in the construction of homes or flats;

(*b*) a provider of professional services in any transaction in which, the sale or use of a product is only incidental thereto, but furnishing of opinion, skill or services being the essence of such transaction;

(*c*) a person who—

(I) acts only in a financial capacity with respect to the sale of the product;

(II) is not a manufacturer, wholesaler, distributor, retailer, direct seller or an electronic service provider;

(III) leases a product, without having a reasonable opportunity to inspect and discover defects in the product, under a lease arrangement in which the selection, possession, maintenance, and operation of the product are controlled by a person other than the lessor;

(38) "product service provider", in relation to a product, means a person who provides any service in respect of such product;

(39) "regulations" means the regulations made by the National Commission, or as the case may be, the Central Authority;

(40) "Regulator" means a body or any authority established under any other law for the time being in force;

(41) "restrictive trade practice" means a trade practice which tends to bring about manipulation of price or its conditions of delivery or to affect flow of supplies in the market relating to goods or services in such a manner as to impose on the consumers unjustified costs or restrictions and shall include—

(*i*) delay beyond the period agreed to by a trader in supply of such goods or in providing the services which has led or is likely to lead to rise in the price;

(*ii*) any trade practice which requires a consumer to buy, hire or avail of any goods or, as the case may be, services as condition precedent for buying, hiring or availing of other goods or services;

(42) "service" means service of any description which is made available to potential users and includes, but not limited to, the provision of facilities in connection with banking, financing, insurance, transport, processing, supply of electrical or other energy, telecom, boarding or lodging or both, housing construction, entertainment, amusement or the purveying of news or other information, but does not include the rendering of any service free of charge or under a contract of personal service;

(43) "spurious goods" means such goods which are falsely claimed to be genuine;

(44) "State Commission" means a State Consumer Disputes Redressal Commission established under sub-section (1) of section 42;

(45) "trader", in relation to any goods, means a person who sells or distributes any goods for sale and includes the manufacturer thereof, and where such goods are sold or distributed in package form, includes the packer thereof;

(46) "unfair contract" means a contract between a manufacturer or trader or service provider on one hand, and a consumer on the other, having such terms which cause significant change in the rights of such consumer, including the following, namely:—

(*i*) requiring manifestly excessive security deposits to be given by a consumer for the performance of contractual obligations; or (*ii*) imposing any penalty on the consumer, for the breach of contract thereof which is wholly disproportionate to the loss occurred due to such breach to the other party to the contract; or

(*iii*) refusing to accept early repayment of debts on payment of applicable penalty; or

(*iv*) entitling a party to the contract to terminate such contract unilaterally, without reasonable cause; or

(*v*) permitting or has the effect of permitting one party to assign the contract to the detriment of the other party who is a consumer, without his consent; or

(*vi*) imposing on the consumer any unreasonable charge, obligation or condition which puts such consumer to disadvantage;

(47) "unfair trade practice" means a trade practice which, for the purpose of promoting the sale, use or supply of any goods or for the provision of any service, adopts any unfair method or unfair or deceptive practice including any of the following practices, namely:—

(*i*) making any statement, whether orally or in writing or by visible representation including by means of electronic record, which—

(*a*) falsely represents that the goods are of a particular standard, quality, quantity, grade, composition, style or model;

(*b*) falsely represents that the services are of a particular standard, quality or grade;

(*c*) falsely represents any re-built, second-hand, renovated, reconditioned or old goods as new goods;

(*d*) represents that the goods or services have sponsorship, approval, performance, characteristics, accessories, uses or benefits which such goods or services do not have;

(*e*) represents that the seller or the supplier has a sponsorship or approval or affiliation which such seller or supplier does not have;

(*f*) makes a false or misleading representation concerning the need for, or the usefulness of, any goods or services;

(*g*) gives to the public any warranty or guarantee of the performance, efficacy or length of life of a product or of any goods that is not based on an adequate or proper test thereof:

Provided that where a defence is raised to the effect that such warranty or guarantee is based on adequate or proper test, the burden of proof of such defence shall lie on the person raising such defence;

(*h*) makes to the public a representation in a form that purports to be—

(A) a warranty or guarantee of a product or of any goods or services; or

(B) a promise to replace, maintain or repair an article or any part thereof or to repeat or continue a service until it has achieved a specified result,

if such purported warranty or guarantee or promise is materially misleading or if there is no reasonable prospect that such warranty, guarantee or promise will be carried out;

(*i*) materially misleads the public concerning the price at which a product or like products or goods or services, have been or are, ordinarily sold or provided, and, for this purpose, a representation as to price shall be deemed to refer to the price at which the product or goods or services has or have been sold by sellers or provided by suppliers generally in the relevant market unless it is clearly specified to be the price at which the product has been sold or services have been provided by the person by whom or on whose behalf the representation is made;

(*j*) gives false or misleading facts disparaging the goods, services or trade of another person.

Explanation.—For the purposes of this sub-clause, a statement that is,—

(A) expressed on an article offered or displayed for sale, or on its wrapper or container; or

(B) expressed on anything attached to, inserted in, or accompanying, an article offered or displayed for sale, or on anything on which the article is mounted for display or sale; or

(C) contained in or on anything that is sold, sent, delivered, transmitted or in any other manner whatsoever made available to a member of the public,

shall be deemed to be a statement made to the public by, and only by, the person who had caused the statement to be so expressed, made or contained;

(*ii*) permitting the publication of any advertisement, whether in any newspaper or otherwise, including by way of electronic record, for the sale or supply at a bargain price of goods or services that are not intended to be offered for sale or supply at the bargain price, or for a period that is, and in quantities that are, reasonable, having regard to the nature of the market in which the business is carried on, the nature and size of business, and the nature of the advertisement.

Explanation.—For the purpose of this sub-clause, "bargain price" means,—

(A) a price that is stated in any advertisement to be a bargain price, by reference to an ordinary price or otherwise; or

(B) a price that a person who reads, hears or sees the advertisement, would reasonably understand to be a bargain price having regard to the prices at which the product advertised or like products are ordinarily sold;

(*iii*) permitting—

(*a*) the offering of gifts, prizes or other items with the intention of not providing them as offered or creating impression that something is being given or offered free of charge when it is fully or partly covered by the amount charged, in the transaction as a whole;

(*b*) the conduct of any contest, lottery, game of chance or skill, for the purpose of promoting, directly or indirectly, the sale, use or supply of any product or any business interest, except such contest, lottery, game of chance or skill as may be prescribed;

(*c*) withholding from the participants of any scheme offering gifts, prizes or other items free of charge on its closure, the information about final results of the scheme.

Explanation.—For the purpose of this sub-clause, the participants of a scheme shall be deemed to have been informed of the final results of the scheme where such results are within a reasonable time published, prominently in the same newspaper in which the scheme was originally advertised;

(*iv*) permitting the sale or supply of goods intended to be used, or are of a kind likely to be used by consumers, knowing or having reason to believe that the goods do not comply with the standards prescribed by the competent authority relating to performance, composition, contents, design, constructions, finishing or packaging as are necessary to prevent or reduce the risk of injury to the person using the goods;

(*v*) permitting the hoarding or destruction of goods, or refusal to sell the goods or to make them available for sale or to provide any service, if such hoarding or destruction or refusal raises or tends to raise or is intended to raise, the cost of those or other similar goods or services;

(*vi*) manufacturing of spurious goods or offering such goods for sale or adopting deceptive practices in the provision of services;

(*vii*) not issuing bill or cash memo or receipt for the goods sold or services rendered in such manner as may be prescribed;

(*viii*) refusing, after selling goods or rendering services, to take back or withdraw defective goods or to withdraw or discontinue deficient services and to refund the consideration thereof, if paid, within the period stipulated in the bill or cash memo or receipt or in the absence of such stipulation, within a period of thirty days;

(*ix*) disclosing to other person any personal information given in confidence by the consumer unless such disclosure is made in accordance with the provisions of any law for the time being in force.

Chapter II

CONSUMER PROTECTION COUNCILS

3. Central Consumer Protection Council. (1) The Central Government shall, by notification, establish with effect from such date as it may specify in that notification, the Central Consumer Protection Council to be known as the Central Council.

(2) The Central Council shall be an advisory council and consist of the following members, namely:—

(*a*) the Minister-in-charge of the Department of Consumer Affairs in the Central Government, who shall be the Chairperson; and

(*b*) such number of other official or non-official members representing such interests as may be prescribed.

4. Procedure for meetings of Central Council. (1) The Central Council shall meet as and when necessary, but at least one meeting of the Council shall be held every year.

(2) The Central Council shall meet at such time and place as the Chairperson may think fit and shall observe such procedure in regard to the transaction of its business as may be prescribed.

5. Objects of Central Council. The objects of the Central Council shall be to render advice on promotion and protection of the consumers' rights under this Act.

6. State Consumer Protection Councils. (1) Every State Government shall, by notification, establish with effect from such date as it may specify in such notification, a State Consumer Protection Council for such State to be known as the State Council.

(2) The State Council shall be an advisory council and consist of the following members, namely:—

(*a*) the Minister-in-charge of Consumer Affairs in the State Government who shall be the Chairperson;

(*b*) such number of other official or non-official members representing such interests as may be prescribed;

(*c*) such number of other official or non-official members, not exceeding ten, as may be nominated by the Central Government.

(3) The State Council shall meet as and when necessary but not less than two meetings shall be held every year.

(4) The State Council shall meet at such time and place as the Chairperson may think fit and shall observe such procedure in regard to the transaction of its business, as may be prescribed.

7. Objects of State Council. The objects of every State Council shall be to render advice on promotion and protection of consumer rights under this Act within the State.

8. District Consumer Protection Council. (1) The State Government shall, by notification, establish for every District with effect from such date as it may specify in such notification, a District Consumer Protection Council to be known as the District Council.

(*2*) The District Council shall be an advisory council and consist of the following members, namely:—

(*a*) the Collector of the district (by whatever name called), who shall be the Chairperson; and

(*b*) such number of other official and non-official members representing such interests as may be prescribed.

(3) The District Council shall meet as and when necessary but not less than two meetings shall be held every year.

(4) The District Council shall meet at such time and place within the district as the Chairperson may think fit and shall observe such procedure in regard to the transaction of its business as may be prescribed.

9. Objects of District Council. The objects of every District Council shall be to render advice on promotion and protection of consumer rights under this Act within the district.

Chapter III

CENTRAL CONSUMER PROTECTION AUTHORITY

10. Establishment of Central Consumer Protection Authority. (1) The Central Government shall, by notification, establish with effect from such date as it may specify in that notification, a Central Consumer Protection Authority to be known as the Central Authority to regulate matters relating to violation of rights of consumers, unfair trade practices and false or misleading advertisements which are prejudicial to the interests of public and consumers and to promote, protect and enforce the rights of consumers as a class.

(*2*) The Central Authority shall consist of a Chief Commissioner and such number of other Commissioners as may be prescribed, to be appointed by the Central Government to exercise the powers and discharge the functions under this Act.

(3) The headquarters of the Central Authority shall be at such place in the National Capital Region of Delhi, and it shall have regional and other offices in any other place in India as the Central Government may decide.

11. Qualifications, method of recruitment, etc., of Chief Commissioner and Commissioners. The Central Government may, by notification, make rules to provide for the qualifications for appointment, method of recruitment, procedure for appointment, term of office, salaries and allowances, resignation, removal and other terms and conditions of the service of the Chief Commissioner and Commissioners of the Central Authority.

12. Vacancy, etc., not to invalidate proceedings of Central Authority. No act or proceeding of the Central Authority shall be invalid merely by reason of—

(*a*) any vacancy in, or any defect in the constitution of, the Central Authority; or

(*b*) any defect in the appointment of a person acting as the Chief Commissioner or as a Commissioner; or

(*c*) any irregularity in the procedure of the Central Authority not affecting the merits of the case.

13. Appointment of officers, experts, professionals and other employees of Central Authority. (1) The Central Government shall provide the Central Authority such number of officers and other employees as it considers necessary for the efficient performance of its functions under this Act.

(2) The salaries and allowances payable to, and the other terms and conditions of service of, the officers and other employees of the Central Authority appointed under this Act shall be such as may be prescribed.

(3) The Central Authority may engage, in accordance with the procedure specified by regulations, such number of experts and professionals of integrity and ability, who have special knowledge and experience in the areas of consumer rights and welfare, consumer policy, law, medicine, food safety, health, engineering, product safety, commerce, economics, public affairs or administration, as it deems necessary to assist it in the discharge of its functions under this Act.

14. Procedure of Central Authority. (1) The Central Authority shall regulate the procedure for transaction of its business and allocation of its business amongst the Chief Commissioner and Commissioners as may be specified by regulations.

(2) The Chief Commissioner shall have the powers of general superintendence, direction and control in respect of all administrative matters of the Central Authority:

Provided that the Chief Commissioner may delegate such of his powers relating to administrative matters of the Central Authority, as he may think fit, to any Commissioner (including Commissioner of a regional office) or any other officer of the Central Authority.

15. Investigation Wing. (1) The Central Authority shall have an Investigation Wing headed by a Director-General for the purpose of conducting inquiry or investigation under this Act as may be directed by the Central Authority.

(2) The Central Government may appoint a Director-General and such number of Additional Director-General, Director, Joint Director, Deputy Director and Assistant Director, from amongst persons who have experience in investigation and possess such qualifications, in such manner, as may be prescribed.

(3) Every Additional Director-General, Director, Joint Director, Deputy Director and Assistant Director shall exercise his powers, and discharge his functions, subject to the general control, supervision and direction of the Director-General.

(4) The Director-General may delegate all or any of his powers to the Additional Director-General or Director, Joint Director or Deputy Director or Assistant Director, as the case may be, while conducting inquiries or investigations under this Act.

(5) The inquiries or the investigations made by the Director-General shall be submitted to the Central Authority in such form, in such manner and within such time, as may be specified by regulations.

16. Power of District Collector. The District Collector (by whatever name called) may, on a complaint or on a reference made to him by the Central Authority or the Commissioner of a regional office, inquire into or investigate complaints regarding violation of rights of consumers as a class, on matters relating to violations of consumer rights, unfair trade practices and false or misleading advertisements, within his jurisdiction and submit his report to the Central Authority or to the Commissioner of a regional office, as the case may be.

17. Complaints to authorities. A complaint relating to violation of consumer rights or unfair trade practices or false or misleading advertisements which are prejudicial to the interests of consumers as a class, may be forwarded either in writing or in electronic mode, to any one of the authorities, namely, the District Collector or the Commissioner of regional office or the Central Authority.

18. Powers and functions of Central Authority. (1) The Central Authority shall—

(*a*) protect, promote and enforce the rights of consumers as a class, and prevent violation of consumers rights under this Act;

(*b*) prevent unfair trade practices and ensure that no person engages himself in unfair trade practices;

(*c*) ensure that no false or misleading advertisement is made of any goods or services which contravenes the provisions of this Act or the rules or regulations made thereunder;

(*d*) ensure that no person takes part in the publication of any advertisement which is false or misleading.

(2) Without prejudice to the generality of the provisions contained in sub-section (1), the Central Authority may, for any of the purposes aforesaid,—

(*a*) inquire or cause an inquiry or investigation to be made into violations of consumer rights or unfair trade practices, either *suo motu* or on a complaint received or on the directions from the Central Government;

(*b*) file complaints before the District Commission, the State Commission or the National Commission, as the case may be, under this Act;

(*c*) intervene in any proceedings before the District Commission or the State Commission or the National Commission, as the case may be, in respect of any allegation of violation of consumer rights or unfair trade practices;

(*d*) review the matters relating to, and the factors inhibiting enjoyment of, consumer rights, including safeguards provided for the protection of consumers under any other law for the time being in force and recommend appropriate remedial measures for their effective implementation;

(*e*) recommend adoption of international covenants and best international practices on consumer rights to ensure effective enforcement of consumer rights;

(*f*) undertake and promote research in the field of consumer rights;

(g) spread and promote awareness on consumer rights;

(*h*) encourage non-Governmental organisations and other institutions working in the field of consumer rights to co-operate and work with consumer protection agencies;

(*i*) mandate the use of unique and universal goods identifiers in such goods, as may be necessary, to prevent unfair trade practices and to protect consumers' interest;

(*j*) issue safety notices to alert consumers against dangerous or hazardous or unsafe goods or services;

(*k*) advise the Ministries and Departments of the Central and State Governments on consumer welfare measures;

(*l*) issue necessary guidelines to prevent unfair trade practices and protect consumers' interest.

19. Power of Central Authority to refer matter for investigation or to other Regulator. (1) The Central Authority may, after receiving any information or complaint or directions from the Central Government or of its own motion, conduct or cause to be conducted a preliminary inquiry as to whether there exists a *prima facie* case of violation of consumer rights or any unfair trade practice or any false or misleading advertisement, by any person, which is prejudicial to the public interest or to the interests of consumers and if it is satisfied that there exists a *prima facie* case, it shall cause investigation to be made by the Director-General or by the District Collector.

(2) Where, after preliminary inquiry, the Central Authority is of the opinion that the matter is to be dealt with by a Regulator established under any other law for the time being in force, it may refer such matter to the concerned Regulator along with its report.

(3) For the purposes of investigation under sub-section (1), the Central Authority, the Director-General or the District Collector may call upon a person referred to in sub-section (1) and also direct him to produce any document or record in his possession.

20. Power of Central Authority to recall goods, etc. Where the Central Authority is satisfied on the basis of investigation that there is sufficient evidence to show violation of consumer rights or unfair trade practice by a person, it may pass such order as may be necessary, including—

(*a*) recalling of goods or withdrawal of services which are dangerous, hazardous or unsafe;

(*b*) reimbursement of the prices of goods or services so recalled to purchasers of such goods or services; and

(*c*) discontinuation of practices which are unfair and prejudicial to consumers' interest:

Provided that the Central Authority shall give the person an opportunity of being heard before passing an order under this section.

21. Power of Central Authority to issue directions and penalties against false or misleading advertisements. (1) Where the Central Authority is satisfied after investigation that any advertisement is false or misleading and is prejudicial to the interest of any consumer or is in contravention of consumer rights, it may, by order, issue directions to the concerned trader or manufacturer or endorser or advertiser or publisher, as the case may be, to discontinue such advertisement or to modify the same in such manner and within such time as may be specified in that order.

(2) Notwithstanding the order passed under sub-section (1), if the Central Authority is of the opinion that it is necessary to impose a penalty in respect of such false or misleading advertisement, by a manufacturer or an endorser, it may, by order, impose on manufacturer or endorser a penalty which may extend to ten lakh rupees:

Provided that the Central Authority may, for every subsequent contravention by a manufacturer or endorser, impose a penalty, which may extend to fifty lakh rupees.

(3) Notwithstanding any order under sub-sections (1) and (2), where the Central Authority deems it necessary, it may, by order, prohibit the endorser of a false or misleading advertisement from making endorsement of any product or service for a period which may extend to one year:

Provided that the Central Authority may, for every subsequent contravention, prohibit such endorser from making endorsement in respect of any product or service for a period which may extend to three years.

(4) Where the Central Authority is satisfied after investigation that any person is found to publish, or is a party to the publication of, a misleading advertisement, it may impose on such person a penalty which may extend to ten lakh rupees.

(5) No endorser shall be liable to a penalty under sub-sections (2) and (3) if he has exercised due diligence to verify the veracity of the claims made in the advertisement regarding the product or service being endorsed by him.

(6) No person shall be liable to such penalty if he proves that he had published or arranged for the publication of such advertisement in the ordinary course of his business:

Provided that no such defence shall be available to such person if he had previous knowledge of the order passed by the Central Authority for withdrawal or modification of such advertisement.

(7) While determining the penalty under this section, regard shall be had to the following, namely:—

(*a*) the population and the area impacted or affected by such offence;

(*b*) the frequency and duration of such offence;

(*c*) the vulnerability of the class of persons likely to be adversely affected by such offence; and

(*d*) the gross revenue from the sales effected by virtue of such offence.

(8) The Central Authority shall give the person an opportunity of being heard before an order under this section is passed.

22. Search and seizure. (1) For the purpose of conducting an investigation after preliminary inquiry under sub-section (1) of section 19, the Director-General or any other officer authorised by him in this behalf, or the District Collector, as the case may be, may, if he has any reason to believe that any person has violated any consumer rights or committed unfair trade practice or causes any false or misleading advertisement to be made, shall,—

(*a*) enter at any reasonable time into any such premises and search for any document or record or article or any other form of evidence and seize such document, record, article or such evidence;

(*b*) make a note or an inventory of such record or article; or

(*c*) require any person to produce any record, register or other document or article.

(2) The provisions of the Code of Criminal Procedure, 1973 (2 of 1974), relating to search and seizure shall apply, as far as may be, for search and seizure under this Act.

(3) Every document, record or article seized under clause (*a*) of sub-section (1) or produced under clause (*c*) of that sub-section shall be returned to the person, from whom they were seized or who produced the same, within a period of twenty days of the date of such seizure or production, as the case may be, after copies thereof or extracts therefrom certified by that person, in such manner as may be prescribed, have been taken.

(4) Where any article seized under sub-section (1) are subject to speedy or natural decay, the Director-General or such other officer may dispose of the article in such manner as may be prescribed.

(5) In the case of articles other than the articles referred to in sub-section (4), provisions contained in clause (*c*) of sub-section (2) of section 38 shall *mutatis mutandis* apply in relation to analysis or tests.

23. Designation of any statutory authority or body to function as Central Authority. The Central Government may, if it considers necessary, by notification, designate any statutory authority or body to exercise the powers and perform the functions of the Central Authority referred to in section 10.

24. Appeal. A person aggrieved by any order passed by the Central Authority under sections 20 and 21 may file an appeal to the National Commission within a period of thirty days from the date of receipt of such order.

25. Grants by Central Government. The Central Government may, after due appropriation made by Parliament by law in this behalf, make to the Central Authority grants of such sums of money as that

Government may think fit for being utilised for the purposes of this Act.

26. Accounts and audit. (1) The Central Authority shall maintain proper accounts and other relevant records and prepare an annual statement of accounts in such form and manner as may be prescribed in consultation with the Comptroller and Auditor-General of India.

(2) The accounts of the Central Authority shall be audited by the Comptroller and Auditor-General of India at such intervals as may be specified by him and any expenditure incurred in connection with such audit shall be payable by the Central Authority to the Comptroller and Auditor-General of India.

(3) The Comptroller and Auditor-General of India or any other person appointed by him in connection with the audit of the accounts of the Central Authority shall have the same rights, privileges and authority in connection with such audit as the Comptroller and Auditor-General of India generally has, in connection with the audit of the Government accounts and, in particular, shall have the right to demand the production of books, accounts, connected vouchers and other documents and papers and to inspect any of the offices of the Central Authority.

(4) The accounts of the Central Authority as certified by the Comptroller and Auditor-General of India or any other person appointed by him in this behalf together with the audit report thereon shall be forwarded annually to the Central Government which shall cause the same to be laid before each House of Parliament.

27. Furnishing of annual reports, etc. (1) The Central Authority shall prepare once in every year, in such form, manner and at such time as may be prescribed, an annual report giving full account of its activities during the previous year and such other reports and returns, as may be directed, and copies of such report and returns shall be forwarded to the Central Government.

(2) A copy of the annual report received under sub-section (1) shall be laid, as soon as may be after it is received, before each House of Parliament.

Chapter IV

CONSUMER DISPUTES REDRESSAL COMMISSION

28. Establishment of District Consumer Disputes Redressal Commission. (1) The State Government shall, by notification, establish a District Consumer Disputes Redressal Commission, to be known as the District Commission, in each district of the State:

Provided that the State Government may, if it deems fit, establish more than one District Commission in a district.

(2) Each District Commission shall consist of—

(a) a President; and

(b) not less than two and not more than such number of members as may be prescribed, in consultation with the Central Government.

29. Qualifications, etc. of President and members of District Commission. The Central Government may, by notification, make rules to provide for the qualifications, method of recruitment, procedure for appointment, term of office, resignation and removal of the President and members of the District Commission.

30. Salaries, allowances and other terms and conditions of service of President and members of District Commission. The State Government may, by notification, make rules to provide for salaries and allowances and other terms and conditions of service of the President, and members of the District Commission.

31. Transitional provision. Any person appointed as President or, as the case may be, a member of the District Commission immediately before the commencement of this Act shall hold office as such as President or, as the case may be, as member till the completion of his term for which he has been appointed.

32. Vacancy in office of member of District Commission. If, at any time, there is a vacancy in the office of the President or member of a District Commission, the State Government may, by notification, direct—

(a) any other District Commission specified in that notification to exercise the jurisdiction in respect of that district also; or

(b) the President or a member of any other District Commission specified in that notification to exercise the powers and discharge the functions of the President or member of that District Commission also.

33. Officers and other employees of District Commission. (1) The State Government shall provide the District Commission with such officers and other employees as may be required to assist the District Commission in the discharge of its functions.

(2) The officers and other employees of the District Commission shall discharge their functions under the general superintendence of the President of the District Commission.

(3) The salaries and allowances payable to, and the other terms and conditions of service of, the officers and other employees of the District Commission shall be such as may be prescribed.

34. Jurisdiction of District Commission. (1) Subject to the other provisions of this Act, the District Commission shall have jurisdiction to entertain complaints where the value of the goods or services paid as consideration does not exceed one crore rupees:

Provided that where the Central Government deems it necessary so to do, it may prescribe such other value, as it deems fit.

(2) A complaint shall be instituted in a District Commission within the local limits of whose jurisdiction,—

(*a*) the opposite party or each of the opposite parties, where there are more than one, at the time of the institution of the complaint, ordinarily resides or carries on business or has a branch office or personally works for gain; or

(*b*) any of the opposite parties, where there are more than one, at the time of the institution of the complaint, actually and voluntarily resides, or carries on business or has a branch office, or personally works for gain, provided that in such case the permission of the District Commission is given; or

(*c*) the cause of action, wholly or in part, arises; or

(*d*) the complainant resides or personally works for gain.

(3) The District Commission shall ordinarily function in the district headquarters and may perform its functions at such other place in the district, as the State Government may, in consultation with the State Commission, notify in the Official Gazette from time to time.

35. Manner in which complaint shall be made. (1) A complaint, in relation to any goods sold or delivered or agreed to be sold or delivered or any service provided or agreed to be provided, may be filed with a District Commission by—

(*a*) the consumer,—

(*i*) to whom such goods are sold or delivered or agreed to be sold or delivered or such service is provided or agreed to be provided; or (*ii*) who alleges unfair trade practice in respect of such goods or service;

(*b*) any recognised consumer association, whether the consumer to whom such goods are sold or delivered or agreed to be sold or delivered or such service is provided or agreed to be provided, or who alleges unfair trade practice in respect of such goods or service, is a member of such association or not;

(*c*) one or more consumers, where there are numerous consumers having the same interest, with the permission of the District Commission, on behalf of, or for the benefit of, all consumers so interested; or

(*d*) the Central Government, the Central Authority or the State Government, as the case may be:

Provided that the complaint under this sub-section may be filed electronically in such manner as may be prescribed.

Explanation.—For the purposes of this sub-section, "recognised consumer association" means any voluntary consumer association registered under any law for the time being in force.

(2) Every complaint filed under sub-section (1) shall be accompanied with such fee and payable in such manner, including electronic form, as may be prescribed.

36. Proceedings before District Commission. (1) Every proceeding before the District Commission shall be conducted by the President of that Commission and atleast one member thereof, sitting together:

Provided that where a member, for any reason, is unable to conduct a proceeding till it is completed, the President and the other member shall continue the proceeding from the stage at which it was last heard by the previous member.

(2) On receipt of a complaint made under section 35, the District Commission may, by order, admit the complaint for being proceeded with or reject the same:

Provided that a complaint shall not be rejected under this section unless an opportunity of being heard has been given to the complainant:

Provided further that the admissibility of the complaint shall ordinarily be decided within twenty-one days from the date on which the complaint was filed.

(3) Where the District Commission does not decide the issue of admissibility of the complaint within the period so specified, it shall be deemed to have been admitted.

37. Reference to mediation. (1) At the first hearing of the complaint after its admission, or at any later stage, if it appears to the District Commission that there exists elements of a settlement which may be acceptable to the parties, except in such cases as may be prescribed, it may direct the parties to give in writing, within five days, consent to have their dispute settled by mediation in accordance with the provisions of Chapter V.

(2) Where the parties agree for settlement by mediation and give their consent in writing, the District Commission shall, within five days of receipt of such consent, refer the matter for mediation, and in such case, the provisions of Chapter V, relating to mediation, shall apply.

38. Procedure on admission of complaint. (1) The District Commission shall, on admission of a complaint, or in respect of cases referred for mediation on failure of settlement by mediation, proceed with such complaint.

(2) Where the complaint relates to any goods, the District Commission shall,—

(*a*) refer a copy of the admitted complaint, within twenty-one days from the date of its admission to the opposite party mentioned in the complaint directing him to give his version of the case within a period of thirty days or such extended period not exceeding fifteen days as may be granted by it;

(*b*) if the opposite party on receipt of a complaint referred to him under clause (*a*) denies or disputes the allegations contained in the complaint, or omits or fails to take any action to represent his case within the time given by the District Commission, proceed to settle the consumer dispute in the manner specified in clauses (*c*) to (*g*);

(*c*) if the complaint alleges a defect in the goods which cannot be determined without proper analysis or test of the goods, obtain a sample of the goods from the complainant, seal it and authenticate it in the manner as may be prescribed and refer the sample so sealed to the appropriate laboratory along with a direction that such laboratory to make an analysis or test, whichever may be necessary, with a view to finding out whether such goods suffer from any defect alleged in the complaint or from any other defect and to report its findings thereon to the District Commission within a period of forty-five days of the receipt of the reference or within such extended period as may be granted by it;

(*d*) before any sample of the goods is referred to any appropriate laboratory under clause (*c*), require the complainant to deposit to the credit of the Commission such fees as may be specified, for payment to the appropriate laboratory for carrying out the necessary analysis or test in relation to the goods in question;

(*e*) remit the amount deposited to its credit under clause (*d*) to the appropriate laboratory to enable it to carry out the analysis or test mentioned in clause (*c*) and on receipt of the report from the appropriate laboratory, it shall forward a copy of the report along with such remarks as it may feel appropriate to the opposite party;

(*f*) if any of the parties disputes the correctness of the findings of the appropriate laboratory, or disputes the correctness of the methods of analysis or test adopted by the appropriate laboratory, require the opposite party or the complainant to submit in writing his objections with regard to the report made by the appropriate laboratory;

(*g*) give a reasonable opportunity to the complainant as well as the opposite party of being heard as to the correctness or otherwise of the report made by the appropriate laboratory and also as to the objection made in relation thereto under clause (*f*) and issue an appropriate order under section 39.

(3) The District Commission shall, if the complaint admitted by it under sub-section (2) of section 36 relates to goods in respect of which the procedure specified in sub-section (2) cannot be followed, or if the complaint relates to any services,—

(*a*) refer a copy of such complaint to the opposite party directing him to give his version of the case within a period of thirty days or such extended period not exceeding fifteen days as may be granted by the District Commission;

(*b*) if the opposite party, on receipt of a copy of the complaint, referred to him under clause (*a*) denies or disputes the allegations contained in the complaint, or omits or fails to take any action to represent his case within the time given by the District Commission, it shall proceed to settle the consumer dispute—

(*i*) on the basis of evidence brought to its notice by the complainant and the opposite party, if the opposite party denies or disputes the allegations contained in the complaint, or

(*ii*) *ex parte* on the basis of evidence brought to its notice by the complainant, where the opposite party omits or fails to take any action to represent his case within the time given by the Commission;

(*c*) decide the complaint on merits if the complainant fails to appear on the date of hearing.

(4) For the purposes of sub-sections (2) and (3), the District Commission may, by order, require an electronic service provider to provide such information, documents or records, as may be specified in that order.

(5) No proceedings complying with the procedure laid down in sub-sections (1) and (2) shall be called in question in any court on the ground that the principles of natural justice have not been complied with.

(6) Every complaint shall be heard by the District Commission on the basis of affidavit and documentary evidence placed on record:

Provided that where an application is made for hearing or for examination of parties in person or through video conferencing, the District Commission may, on sufficient cause being shown, and after recording its reasons in writing, allow the same.

(7) Every complaint shall be disposed of as expeditiously as possible and endeavour shall be made to decide the complaint within a period of three months from the date of receipt of notice by opposite party where the complaint does not require analysis or testing of commodities and within five months if it requires analysis or testing of commodities:

Provided that no adjournment shall ordinarily be granted by the District Commission unless sufficient cause is shown and the reasons for grant of adjournment have been recorded in writing by the Commission:

Provided further that the District Commission shall make such orders as to the costs occasioned by the adjournment as may be specified by regulations:

Provided also that in the event of a complaint being disposed of after the period so specified, the District Commission shall record in writing, the reasons for the same at the time of disposing of the said complaint.

(8) Where during the pendency of any proceeding before the District Commission, if it appears necessary, it may pass such interim order as is just and proper in the facts and circumstances of the case.

(9) For the purposes of this section, the District Commission shall have the same powers as are vested in a civil court under the Code of Civil Procedure, 1908 (5 of 1908) while trying a suit in respect of the following matters, namely:—

(*a*) the summoning and enforcing the attendance of any defendant or witness and examining the witness on oath;

(*b*) requiring the discovery and production of any document or other material object as evidence;

(*c*) receiving of evidence on affidavits;

(*d*) the requisitioning of the report of the concerned analysis or test from the appropriate laboratory or from any other relevant source;

(*e*) issuing of commissions for the examination of any witness, or document; and

(*f*) any other matter which may be prescribed by the Central Government.

(10) Every proceeding before the District Commission shall be deemed to be a judicial proceeding within the meaning of sections 193 and 228 of the Indian Penal Code (48 of 1860), and the District Commission shall be deemed to be a criminal court for the purposes of section 195 and Chapter XXVI of the Code of Criminal Procedure, 1973.

(11) Where the complainant is a consumer referred to in sub-clause (*v*) of clause (5) of section 2, the provisions of Order I, Rule 8

of the First Schedule to the Code of Civil Procedure, 1908 (5 of 1908) shall apply subject to the modification that every reference therein to a suit or decree shall be construed as a reference to a complaint or the order of the District Commission thereon.

(12) In the event of death of a complainant who is a consumer or of the opposite party against whom the complaint has been filed, the provisions of Order XXII of the First Schedule to the Code of Civil Procedure, 1908 (5 of 1908) shall apply subject to the modification that every reference therein to the plaintiff and the defendant shall be construed as reference to a complainant or the opposite party, as the case may be Commission.

39. Findings of District Commission. (1) Where the District Commission is satisfied that the goods complained against suffer from any of the defects specified in the complaint or that any of the allegations contained in the complaint about the services or any unfair trade practices, or claims for compensation under product liability are proved, it shall issue an order to the opposite party directing him to do one or more of the following, namely:—

(*a*) to remove the defect pointed out by the appropriate laboratory from the goods in question;

(*b*) to replace the goods with new goods of similar description which shall be free from any defect;

(*c*) to return to the complainant the price, or, as the case may be, the charges paid by the complainant along with such interest on such price or charges as may be decided;

(*d*) to pay such amount as may be awarded by it as compensation to the consumer for any loss or injury suffered by the consumer due to the negligence of the opposite party:

Provided that the District Commission shall have the power to grant punitive damages in such circumstances as it deems fit;

(*e*) to pay such amount as may be awarded by it as compensation in a product liability action under Chapter VI;

(*f*) to remove the defects in goods or deficiencies in the services in question;

(*g*) to discontinue the unfair trade practice or restrictive trade practice and not to repeat them;

(*h*) not to offer the hazardous or unsafe goods for sale;

(*i*) to withdraw the hazardous goods from being offered for sale;

(*j*) to cease manufacture of hazardous goods and to desist from offering services which are hazardous in nature;

(*k*) to pay such sum as may be determined by it, if it is of the opinion that loss or injury has been suffered by a large number of consumers who are not identifiable conveniently:

Provided that the minimum amount of sum so payable shall not be less than twenty-five per cent. of the value of such defective goods sold or service provided, as the case may be, to such consumers;

(*l*) to issue corrective advertisement to neutralise the effect of misleading advertisement at the cost of the opposite party responsible for issuing such misleading advertisement;

(*m*) to provide for adequate costs to parties; and

(*n*) to cease and desist from issuing any misleading advertisement.

(2) Any amount obtained under sub-section (1) shall be credited to such fund and utilised in such manner as may be prescribed.

(3) In any proceeding conducted by the President and a member and if they differ on any point or points, they shall state the point or points on which they differ and refer the same to another member for hearing on such point or points and the opinion of the majority shall be the order of the District Commission:

Provided that the other member shall give his opinion on such point or points referred to him within a period of one month from the date of such reference.

(4) Every order made by the District Commission under sub-section (1) shall be signed by the President and the member who conducted the proceeding:

Provided that where the order is made as per majority opinion under sub-section (3), such order shall also be signed by the other member.

40. Review by District Commission in certain cases. The District Commission shall have the power to review any of the order passed by it if there is an error apparent on the face of the record, either of its own motion or on an application made by any of the parties within thirty days of such order.

41. Appeal against order of District Commission. Any person aggrieved by an order made by the District Commission may prefer an appeal against such order to the State Commission on the grounds of facts or law within a period of forty-five days from the date of the order, in such form and manner, as may be prescribed:

Provided that the State Commission may entertain an appeal after the expiry of the said period of forty-five days, if it is satisfied that there was sufficient cause for not filing it within that period:

Provided further that no appeal by a person, who is required to pay any amount in terms of an order of the District Commission, shall be entertained by the State Commission unless the appellant has deposited fifty per cent. of that amount in the manner as may be prescribed:

Provided also that no appeal shall lie from any order passed under sub-section (1) of section 81 by the District Commission pursuant to a settlement by mediation under section 80.

42. Establishment of State Consumer Disputes Redressal Commission. (1) The State Government shall, by notification, establish a State Consumer Disputes Redressal Commission, to be known as the State Commission, in the State.

(2) The State Commission shall ordinarily function at the State capital and perform its functions at such other places as the State Government may in consultation with the State Commission notify in the Official Gazette:

Provided that the State Government may, by notification, establish regional benches of the State Commission, at such places, as it deems fit.

(3) Each State Commission shall consist of—

(*a*) a President; and

(*b*) not less than four or not more than such number of members as may be prescribed in consultation with the Central Government.

43. Qualifications etc., of President and members of State Commission. The Central Government may, by notification, make rules to provide for the qualification for appointment, method of recruitment, procedure of appointment, term of office, resignation and removal of the President and members of the State Commission.

44. Salaries, allowances and other terms and conditions of service of President and members of State Commission. The State Government may, by notification, make rules to provide for salaries and allowances and other terms and conditions of service of the President and members of the State Commission.

45. Transitional provision. Any person appointed as President or, as the case may be, a member of the State Commission immediately before the commencement of this Act shall hold office as such, as President or member, as the case may be, till the completion of his term.

46. Officers and employees of State Commission. (1) The State Government shall determine the nature and categories of the officers and other employees required to assist the State Commission in the discharge of its functions and provide the Commission with such officers and other employees as it may think fit.

(2) The officers and other employees of the State Commission shall discharge their functions under the general superintendence of the President.

(3) The salaries and allowances payable to and the other terms and conditions of service of, the officers and other employees of the State Commission shall be such as may be prescribed.

47. Jurisdiction of State Commission. (1) Subject to the other provisions of this Act, the State Commission shall have jurisdiction—

(*a*) to entertain—

(*i*) complaints where the value of the goods or services paid as consideration, exceeds rupees one crore, but does not exceed rupees ten crore:

Provided that where the Central Government deems it necessary so to do, it may prescribe such other value, as it deems fit;

(*ii*) complaints against unfair contracts, where the value of goods or services paid as consideration does not exceed ten crore rupees;

(*iii*) appeals against the orders of any District Commission within the State; and (*b*) to call for the records and pass appropriate orders in any consumer dispute which is pending before or has been decided by any District Commission within the State, where it appears to the State Commission that such District Commission has exercised a jurisdiction not vested in it by law, or has failed to exercise a jurisdiction so vested or has acted in exercise of its jurisdiction illegally or with material irregularity.

(*2*) The jurisdiction, powers and authority of the State Commission may be exercised by Benches thereof, and a Bench may be constituted by the President with one or more members as the President may deem fit:

Provided that the senior-most member shall preside over the Bench.

(3) Where the members of a Bench differ in opinion on any point, the points shall be decided according to the opinion of the majority, if there is a majority, but if the members are equally divided, they shall state the point or points on which they differ, and make a reference to the President who shall either hear the point or points himself or refer the case for hearing on such point or points by one or more of the other members and such point or points shall be decided according to the opinion of the majority of the members who have heard the case, including those who first heard it:

Provided that the President or the other members, as the case may be, shall give opinion on the point or points so referred within a period of one month from the date of such reference.

(4) A complaint shall be instituted in a State Commission within the limits of whose jurisdiction,—

(*a*) the opposite party or each of the opposite parties, where there are more than one, at the time of the institution of the complaint, ordinarily resides or carries on business or has a branch office or personally works for gain; or

(*b*) any of the opposite parties, where there are more than one, at the time of the institution of the complaint, actually and voluntarily resides, or carries on business or has a branch office or personally works for gain, provided in such case, the permission of the State Commission is given; or

(c) the cause of action, wholly or in part, arises; or

(d) the complainant resides or personally works for gain.

48. Transfer of cases. On the application of the complainant or of its own motion, the State Commission may, at any stage of the proceeding, transfer any complaint pending before a District Commission to another District Commission within the State if the interest of justice so requires.

49. Procedure applicable to State Commission. (1) The provisions relating to complaints under sections 35, 36, 37, 38 and 39 shall, with such modifications as may be necessary, be applicable to the disposal of complaints by the State Commission.

(2) Without prejudice to the provisions of sub-section (1), the State Commission may also declare any terms of contract, which is unfair to any consumer, to be null and void.

50. Review by State Commission in certain cases. The State Commission shall have the power to review any of the order passed by it if there is an error apparent on the face of the record, either of its own motion or on an application made by any of the parties within thirty days of such order.

51. Appeal to National Commission. (1) Any person aggrieved by an order made by the State Commission in exercise of its powers conferred by sub-clause (*i*) or (*ii*) of clause (*a*) of sub-section (1) of section 47 may prefer an appeal against such order to the National Commission within a period of thirty days from the date of the order in such form and manner as may be prescribed:

Provided that the National Commission shall not entertain the appeal after the expiry of the said period of thirty days unless it is satisfied that there was sufficient cause for not filing it within that period:

Provided further that no appeal by a person, who is required to pay any amount in terms of an order of the State Commission, shall be entertained by the National Commission unless the appellant has deposited fifty per cent. of that amount in the manner as may be prescribed.

(2) Save as otherwise expressly provided under this Act or by any other law for the time being in force, an appeal shall lie to the National Commission from any order passed in appeal by any State Commission, if the National Commission is satisfied that the case involves a substantial question of law.

(3) In an appeal involving a question of law, the memorandum of appeal shall precisely state the substantial question of law involved in the appeal.

(4) Where the National Commission is satisfied that a substantial question of law is involved in any case, it shall formulate that question and hear the appeal on that question:

Provided that nothing in this sub-section shall be deemed to take away or abridge the power of the National Commission to hear, for reasons to be recorded in writing, the appeal on any other substantial question of law, if it is satisfied that the case involves such question of law.

(5) An appeal may lie to the National Commission under this section from an order passed *ex parte* by the State Commission.

52. Hearing of appeal. An appeal filed before the State Commission or the National Commission, as the case may be, shall be heard as expeditiously as possible and every endeavour shall be made to dispose of the appeal within a period of ninety days from the date of its admission:

Provided that no adjournment shall ordinarily be granted by the State Commission or the National Commission, as the case may be, unless sufficient cause is shown and the reasons for grant of adjournment have been recorded in writing by such Commission:

Provided further that the State Commission or the National Commission, as the case may be, shall make such orders as to the costs occasioned by the adjournment, as may be specified by regulations:

Provided also that in the event of an appeal being disposed of after the period so specified, the State Commission or the National Commission, as the case may be, shall record in writing the reasons for the same at the time of disposing of the said appeal.

53. Establishment of National Consumer Disputes Redressal Commission. (1) The Central Government shall, by notification, establish a National Consumer Disputes Redressal Commission, to be known as the National Commission.

(2) The National Commission shall ordinarily function at the National Capital Region and perform its functions at such other places as the Central Government may in consultation with the National Commission notify in the Official Gazette:

Provided that the Central Government may, by notification, establish regional Benches of the National Commission, at such places, as it deems fit.

54. Composition of National Commission. The National Commission shall consist of—

(*a*) a President; and

(*b*) not less than four and not more than such number of members as may be prescribed.

55. Qualifications etc., of President and members of National Commission. (1) The Central Government may, by notification, make rules to provide for qualifications, appointment, term of office, salaries and allowances, resignation, removal and other terms and conditions of service of the President and members of the National Commission:

Provided that the President and members of the National Commission shall hold office for such term as specified in the rules made by the Central Government but not exceeding five years from the date on which he enters upon his office and shall be eligible for re-appointment:

Provided further that no President or members shall hold office as such after he has attained such age as specified in the rules made by the Central Government which shall not exceed,—

(*a*) in the case of the President, the age of seventy years;

(*b*) in the case of any other member, the age of sixty-seven years.

(2) Neither the salary and allowances nor the other terms and conditions of service of President and members of the National Commission shall be varied to his disadvantage after his appointment.

56. Transitional provision. The President and every other member appointed immediately before the commencement of section 177 of the Finance Act, 2017 (7 of 2017) shall continue to be governed by the Provisions of the Consumer Protection Act, 1986 (68 of 1986) and the rules made thereunder as if this Act had not come into force.

57. Other officers and employees of National Commission. (1) The Central Government shall provide, in consultation with the President of the National Commission, such number of officers and other employees to assist the National Commission in the discharge of its functions as it may think fit.

(2) The officers and other employees of the National Commission shall discharge their functions under the general superintendence of the President of the National Commission.

(3) The salaries and allowances payable to, and the other terms and conditions of service of, the officers and other employees of the National Commission shall be such as may be prescribed.

58. Jurisdiction of National Commission. (1) Subject to the other provisions of this Act, the National Commission shall have jurisdiction—

(*a*) to entertain—

(*i*) complaints where the value of the goods or services paid as consideration exceeds rupees ten crore:

Provided that where the Central Government deems it necessary so to do, it may prescribe such other value, as it deems fit;

(*ii*) complaints against unfair contracts, where the value of goods or services paid as consideration exceeds ten crore rupees;

(*iii*) appeals against the orders of any State Commission;

(*iv*) appeals against the orders of the Central Authority; and

(*b*) to call for the records and pass appropriate orders in any consumer dispute which is pending before or has been decided by any State Commission where it appears to the National Commission that such State Commission has exercised a jurisdiction not vested in it by law, or has failed to exercise a jurisdiction so vested, or has acted in the exercise of its jurisdiction illegally or with material irregularity.

(2) The jurisdiction, powers and authority of the National Commission may be exercised by Benches thereof and a Bench may be constituted by the President with one or more members as he may deem fit:

Provided that the senior-most member of the Bench shall preside over the Bench.

(3) Where the members of a Bench differ in opinion on any point, the points shall be decided according to the opinion of the majority,

if there is a majority, but if the members are equally divided, they shall state the point or points on which they differ, and make a reference to the President who shall either hear the point or points himself or refer the case for hearing on such point or points by one or more of the other members and such point or points shall be decided according to the opinion of the majority of the members who have heard the case, including those who first heard it:

Provided that the President or the other member, as the case may be, shall give opinion on the point or points so referred within a period of two months from the date of such reference.

59. Procedure applicable to National Commission. (1) The provisions relating to complaints under sections 35, 36, 37, 38 and 39 shall, with such modifications as may be considered necessary, be applicable to the disposal of complaints by the National Commission.

(2) Without prejudice to sub-section (1), the National Commission may also declare any terms of contract, which is unfair to any consumer to be null and void.

60. Review by National Commission in certain cases. The National Commission shall have the power to review any of the order passed by it if there is an error apparent on the face of the record, either of its own motion or on an application made by any of the parties within thirty days of such order.

61. Power to set aside ex parte orders. Where an order is passed by the National Commission *ex parte*, the aggrieved party may make an application to the Commission for setting aside such order.

62. Transfer of cases. On the application of the complainant or of its own motion, the National Commission may, at any stage of the proceeding, in the interest of justice, transfer any complaint pending before the District Commission of one State to a District Commission of another State or before one State Commission to another State Commission.

63. Vacancy in office of President of National Commission. When the office of President of the National Commission is vacant or a person occupying such office is, by reason of absence or otherwise, unable to perform the duties of his office, these shall be performed by the senior-most member of the National Commission:

Provided that where a retired Judge of a High Court or a person who has been a Judicial Member is a member of the National Commission, such member or where the number of such members is more than one, the senior-most person amongst such members, shall preside over the National Commission in the absence of President of that Commission.

64. Vacancies or defects in appointment not to invalidate orders. No act or proceeding of the District Commission, the State Commission or the National Commission shall be invalid by reason only of the existence of any vacancy amongst its members or any defect in the constitution thereof.

65. Service of notice, etc. (1) All notices, required by this Act to be served, shall be served by delivering or transmitting a copy thereof by registered post acknowledgment due addressed to opposite party against whom complaint is made or to the complainant by speed post or by such courier service, approved by the District Commission, the State Commission or the National Commission, as the case may be, or by any other mode of transmission of documents including electronic means.

(2) Without prejudice to the provisions contained in sub-section (1), the notice required by this Act may be served on an electronic service provider at the address provided by it on the electronic platform from where it provides its services as such and for this purpose, the electronic service provider shall designate a nodal officer to accept and process such notices.

(3) When an acknowledgment or any other receipt purporting to be signed by the opposite party or his agent or, as the case may be, by the complainant is received by the District Commission, the State Commission or the National Commission, as the case may be, or postal article containing the notice is received back by such District Commission, State Commission or the National Commission, with an endorsement purporting to have been made by a postal employee or by any person authorised by the courier service to the effect that the opposite party or his agent or complainant had refused to take delivery of the postal article containing the notice or had refused to accept the notice by any other means specified in sub-section (1) when tendered or transmitted to him, the District Commission or the State Commission or the National Commission, as the case may be, shall declare that the notice has been duly served on the opposite party or to the complainant, as the case may be:

Provided that where the notice was properly addressed, pre-paid and duly sent by registered post acknowledgment due, a declaration referred to in this sub-section shall be made notwithstanding the fact that the acknowledgment has been lost or misplaced, or for any other reason, has not been received by the District Commission, the State

Commission or the National Commission, as the case may be, within thirty days from the date of issue of notice.

(4) All notices required to be served on an opposite party or to complainant, as the case may be, shall be deemed to be sufficiently served, if addressed in the case of the opposite party, to the place where business or profession is carried on, and in case of the complainant, the place where such person actually and voluntarily resides.

66. Experts to assist National Commission or State Commission. Where the National Commission or the State Commission, as the case may be, on an application by a complainant or otherwise, is of the opinion that it involves the larger interest of consumers, it may direct any individual or organisation or expert to assist the National Commission or the State Commission, as the case may be.

67. Appeal against order of National Commission. Any person, aggrieved by an order made by the National Commission in exercise of its powers conferred by sub-clause (*i*) or (*ii*) of clause (*a*) of sub-section (1) of section 58, may prefer an appeal against such order to the Supreme Court within a period of thirty days from the date of the order:

Provided that the Supreme Court may entertain an appeal after the expiry of the said period of thirty days if it is satisfied that there was sufficient cause for not filing it within that period:

Provided further that no appeal by a person who is required to pay any amount in terms of an order of the National Commission shall be entertained by the Supreme Court unless that person has deposited fifty per cent. of that amount in the manner as may be prescribed.

68. Finality of orders. Every order of a District Commission or the State Commission or the National Commission, as the case may be, shall, if no appeal has been preferred against such order under the provisions of this Act, be final.

69. Limitation period. (1) The District Commission, the State Commission or the National Commission shall not admit a complaint unless it is filed within two years from the date on which the cause of action has arisen.

(2) Notwithstanding anything contained in sub-section (1), a complaint may be entertained after the period specified in sub-section (1), if the complainant satisfies the District Commission, the State Commission or the National Commission, as the case may be, that he had sufficient cause for not filing the complaint within such period:

Provided that no such complaint shall be entertained unless the District Commission or the State Commission or the National Commission, as the case may be, records its reasons for condoning such delay.

70. Administrative control. (1) The National Commission shall have the authority to lay down such adequate standards in consultation with the Central Government from time to time, for better protection of the interests of consumers and for that purpose, shall have administrative control over all the State Commissions in the following matters, namely:—

(*a*) monitoring performance of the State Commissions in terms of their disposal by calling for periodical returns regarding the institution, disposal and pendency of cases;

(*b*) investigating into any allegations against the President and members of a State Commission and submitting inquiry report to the State Government concerned along with copy endorsed to the Central Government for necessary action;

(*c*) issuance of instructions regarding adoption of uniform procedure in the hearing of matters, prior service of copies of documents produced by one party to the opposite parties, furnishing of english translation of judgments written in any language, speedy grant of copies of documents;

(*d*) overseeing the functioning of the State Commission or the District Commission either by way of inspection or by any other means, as the National Commission may like to order from time to time, to ensure that the objects and purposes of the Act are best served and the standards set by the National Commission are implemented without interfering with their quasi-judicial freedom.

(2) There shall be a monitoring cell to be constituted by the President of the National Commission to oversee the functioning of the State Commissions from the administrative point of view.

(3) The State Commission shall have administrative control over all the District Commissions within its jurisdiction in all matters referred to in sub-section (1).

(4) The National Commission and the State Commissions shall furnish to the Central Government periodically or as and when required, any information including the pendency of cases in such form and manner as may be prescribed.

(5) The State Commission shall furnish, periodically or as and when required to the State Government any information including pendency of cases in such form and manner as may be prescribed.

71. Enforcement of orders of District Commissions, State Commission and National Commission. Every order made by a District Commission, State Commission or the National Commission shall be enforced by it in the same manner as if it were a decree made by a Court in a suit before it and the provisions of Order XXI of the First Schedule to the Code of Civil Procedure, 1908 (5 of 1908) shall, as far as may be, applicable, subject to the modification that every reference therein to the decree shall be construed as reference to the order made under this Act.

72. Penalty for non-compliance of order. (1) Whoever fails to comply with any order made by the District Commission or the State Commission or the National Commission, as the case may be, shall be punishable with imprisonment for a term which shall not be less than one month, but which may extend to three years, or with fine, which shall not be less than twenty-five thousand rupees, but which may extend to one lakh rupees, or with both.

(2) Notwithstanding anything contained in the Code of Criminal Procedure, 1973 (2 of 1974), the District Commission, the State Commission or the National Commission, as the case may be, shall have the power of a Judicial Magistrate of first class for the trial of offences under sub-section (1), and on conferment of such powers, the District Commission or the State Commission or the National Commission, as the case may be, shall be deemed to be a Judicial Magistrate of first class for the purposes of the Code of Criminal Procedure, 1973.

(3) Save as otherwise provided, the offences under sub-section (1) shall be tried summarily by the District Commission or the State Commission or the National Commission, as the case may be.

73. Appeal against order passed under section 72. (1) Notwithstanding anything contained in the Code of Criminal Procedure, 1973, where an order is passed under sub-section (1) of section 72, an appeal shall lie, both on facts and on law from—

(*a*) the order made by the District Commission to the State Commission;

(*b*) the order made by the State Commission to the National Commission; and

(*c*) the order made by the National Commission to the Supreme Court.

(2) Except as provided in sub-section (1), no appeal shall lie before any court, from any order of a District Commission or a State Commission or the National Commission, as the case may be.

(3) Every appeal under this section shall be preferred within a period of thirty days from the date of order of a District Commission or a State Commission or the National Commission, as the case may be:

Provided that the State Commission or the National Commission or the Supreme Court, as the case may be, may entertain an appeal after the expiry of the said period of thirty days, if it is satisfied that the appellant had sufficient cause for not preferring the appeal within the said period of thirty days.

Chapter V

MEDIATION

74. Establishment of consumer mediation cell. (1) The State Government shall establish, by notification, a consumer mediation cell to be attached to each of the District Commissions and the State Commissions of that State.

(2) The Central Government shall establish, by notification, a consumer mediation cell to be attached to the National Commission and each of the regional Benches.

(3) A consumer mediation cell shall consist of such persons as may be prescribed.

(4) Every consumer mediation cell shall maintain—

(*a*) a list of empanelled mediators;

(*b*) a list of cases handled by the cell;

(*c*) record of proceeding; and

(*d*) any other information as may be specified by regulations.

(5) Every consumer mediation cell shall submit a quarterly report to the District Commission, State Commission or the National Commission to which it is attached, in the manner specified by regulations.

75. Empanelment of mediators. (1) For the purpose of mediation, the National Commission or the State Commission or the District Commission, as the case may be, shall prepare a panel of the mediators to be maintained by the consumer mediation cell attached to it, on the recommendation of a selection committee consisting of the President and a member of that Commission.

(2) The qualifications and experience required for empanelment as mediator, the procedure for empanelment, the manner of training empanelled mediators, the fee payable to empanelled mediator, the terms and conditions for empanelment, the code of conduct for empanelled mediators, the grounds on which, and the manner in which, empanelled mediators shall be removed or empanelment shall be cancelled and other matters relating thereto, shall be such as may be specified by regulations.

(3) The panel of mediators prepared under sub-section (1) shall be valid for a period of five years, and the empanelled mediators shall be eligible to be considered for re-empanelment for another term, subject to such conditions as may be specified by regulations.

76. Nomination of mediators from panel. The District Commission, the State Commission or the National Commission shall, while nominating any person from the panel of mediators referred to in section 75, consider his suitability for resolving the consumer dispute involved.

77. Duty of mediator to disclose certain facts. It shall be the duty of the mediator to disclose—

(*a*) any personal, professional or financial interest in the outcome of the consumer dispute;

(*b*) the circumstances which may give rise to a justifiable doubt as to his independence or impartiality; and

(*c*) such other facts as may be specified by regulations.

78. Replacement of mediator in certain cases. Where the District Commission or the State Commission or the National Commission, as the case may be, is satisfied, on the information furnished by the mediator or on the information received from any other person including parties to the complaint and after hearing the mediator, it shall replace such mediator by another mediator.

79. Procedure for mediation. (1) The mediation shall be held in the consumer mediation cell attached to the District Commission, the State Commission or the National Commission, as the case may be.

(2) Where a consumer dispute is referred for mediation by the District Commission or the State Commission or the National Commission, as the case may be, the mediator nominated by such Commission shall have regard to the rights and obligations of the parties, the usages of trade, if any, the circumstances giving rise to the consumer dispute and such other relevant factors, as he may deem necessary and shall be guided by the principles of natural justice while carrying out mediation.

(3) The mediator so nominated shall conduct mediation within such time and in such manner as may be specified by regulations.

80. Settlement through mediation. (1) Pursuant to mediation, if an agreement is reached between the parties with respect to all of the issues involved in the consumer dispute or with respect to only some of the issues, the terms of such agreement shall be reduced to writing accordingly, and signed by the parties to such dispute or their authorised representatives.

(2) The mediator shall prepare a settlement report of the settlement and forward the signed agreement along with such report to the concerned Commission.

(3) Where no agreement is reached between the parties within the specified time or the mediator is of the opinion that settlement is not possible, he shall prepare his report accordingly and submit the same to the concerned Commission.

81. Recording settlement and passing of order. (1) The District Commission or the State Commission or the National Commission, as the case may be, shall, within seven days of the receipt of the settlement report, pass suitable order recording such settlement of consumer dispute and dispose of the matter accordingly.

(2) Where the consumer dispute is settled only in part, the District Commission or the State Commission or the National Commission, as the case may be, shall record settlement of the issues which have been so settled and continue to hear other issues involved in such consumer dispute.

(3) Where the consumer dispute could not be settled by mediation, the District Commission or the State Commission or the National Commission, as the case may be, shall continue to hear all the issues involved in such consumer dispute.

Chapter VI

Product liability

82. Application of Chapter. This Chapter shall apply to every claim for compensation under a product liability action by a complainant for any harm caused by a defective product manufactured by a product manufacturer or serviced by a product service provider or sold by a product seller.

83. Product liability action. A product liability action may be brought by a complainant against a product manufacturer or a product service provider or a product seller, as the case may be, for any harm caused to him on account of a defective product.

84. Liability of product manufacturer. (1) A product manufacturer shall be liable in a product liability action, if—

(*a*) the product contains a manufacturing defect; or

(*b*) the product is defective in design; or

(*c*) there is a deviation from manufacturing specifications; or

(*d*) the product does not conform to the express warranty; or

(*e*) the product fails to contain adequate instructions of correct usage to prevent any harm or any warning regarding improper or incorrect usage.

(2) A product manufacturer shall be liable in a product liability action even if he proves that he was not negligent or fraudulent in making the express warranty of a product.

85. Liability of product service provider. A product service provider shall be liable in a product liability action, if—

(*a*) the service provided by him was faulty or imperfect or deficient or inadequate in quality, nature or manner of performance which is required to be provided by or under any law for the time being in force, or pursuant to any contract or otherwise; or (*b*) there was an act of omission or commission or negligence or conscious withholding any information which caused harm; or

(*c*) the service provider did not issue adequate instructions or warnings to prevent any harm; or

(*d*) the service did not conform to express warranty or the terms and conditions of the contract.

86. Liability of product seller. A product seller who is not a product manufacturer shall be liable in a product liability action, if—

(*a*) he has exercised substantial control over the designing, testing, manufacturing, packaging or labelling of a product that caused harm; or

(*b*) he has altered or modified the product and such alteration or modification was the substantial factor in causing the harm; or

(*c*) he has made an express warranty of a product independent of any express warranty made by a manufacturer and such product failed to conform to the express warranty made by the product seller which caused the harm; or

(*d*) the product has been sold by him and the identity of product manufacturer of such product is not known, or if known, the service of notice or process or warrant cannot be effected on him or he is not subject to the law which is in force in India or the order, if any, passed or to be passed cannot be enforced against him; or

(*e*) he failed to exercise reasonable care in assembling, inspecting or maintaining such product or he did not pass on the warnings or instructions of the product manufacturer regarding the dangers involved or proper usage of the product while selling such product and such failure was the proximate cause of the harm.

87. Exceptions to product liability action. (1) A product liability action cannot be brought against the product seller if, at the time of harm, the product was misused, altered, or modified.

(2) In any product liability action based on the failure to provide adequate warnings or instructions, the product manufacturer shall not be liable, if—

(*a*) the product was purchased by an employer for use at the workplace and the product manufacturer had provided warnings or instructions to such employer;

(*b*) the product was sold as a component or material to be used in another product and necessary warnings or instructions were given by the product manufacturer to the purchaser of such component or material, but the harm was caused to the complainant by use of the end product in which such component or material was used;

(*c*) the product was one which was legally meant to be used or dispensed only by or under the supervision of an expert or a class of experts and the product manufacturer had employed reasonable means to give the warnings or instructions for usage of such product to such expert or class of experts; or

(*d*) the complainant, while using such product, was under the influence of alcohol or any prescription drug which had not been prescribed by a medical practitioner.

(3) A product manufacturer shall not be liable for failure to instruct or warn about a danger which is obvious or commonly known to the user or consumer of such product or which, such user or consumer, ought to have known, taking into account the characteristics of such product.

Chapter VII

OFFENCES AND PENALTIES

88. Penalty for non-compliance of direction of Central Authority. Whoever, fails to comply with any direction of the Central Authority under sections 20 and 21, shall be punished with imprisonment for a term which may extend to six months or with fine which may extend to twenty lakh rupees, or with both.

89. Punishment for false or misleading advertisement. Any manufacturer or service provider who causes a false or misleading advertisement to be made which is prejudicial to the interest of consumers shall be punished with imprisonment for a term which may extend to two years and with fine which may extend to ten lakh rupees; and for every subsequent offence, be punished with imprisonment for a term which may extend to five years and with fine which may extend to fifty lakh rupees.

90. Punishment for manufacturing for sale or storing, selling or distributing or importing products containing adulterant. (1) Whoever, by himself or by any other person on his behalf, manufactures for sale or stores or sells or distributes or imports any product containing an adulterant shall be punished, if such act—

(*a*) does not result in any injury to the consumer, with imprisonment for a term which may extend to six months and with fine which may extend to one lakh rupees;

(*b*) causing injury not amounting to grievous hurt to the consumer, with imprisonment for a term which may extend to one year and with fine which may extend to three lakh rupees;

(*c*) causing injury resulting in grievous hurt to the consumer, with imprisonment for a term which may extend to seven years and with fine which may extend to five lakh rupees; and

(*d*) results in the death of a consumer, with imprisonment for a term which shall not be less than seven years, but which may extend to imprisonment for life and with fine which shall not be less than ten lakh rupees.

(2) The offences under clauses (*c*) and (*d*) of sub-section (1) shall be cognizable and non-bailable.

(3) Notwithstanding the punishment under sub-section (1), the court may, in case of first conviction, suspend any licence issued to the person referred to in that sub-section, under any law for the time being in force, for a period up to two years, and in case of second or subsequent conviction, cancel the licence.

Explanation.—For the purposes of this section,—

(*a*) "adulterant" means any material including extraneous matter which is employed or used for making a product unsafe;

(*b*) "grievous hurt" shall have the same meaning as assigned to it in section 320 of the Indian Penal Code.

91. Punishment for manufacturing for sale or for storing or selling or distributing or importing spurious goods. (1) Whoever, by himself or by any other person on his behalf, manufactures for sale or stores or sells or distributes or imports any spurious goods shall be punished, if such act—

(*a*) causing injury not amounting to grievous hurt to the consumer, with imprisonment for a term which may extend to one year and with fine which may extend to three lakh rupees;

(*b*) causing injury resulting in grievous hurt to the consumer, with imprisonment for a term which may extend to seven years and with fine which may extend to five lakh rupees;

(*c*) results in the death of a consumer, with imprisonment for a term which shall not be less than seven years, but may extend to imprisonment for life and with fine which shall not be less than ten lakh rupees.

(2) The offences under clauses (*b*) and (*c*) of sub-section (1) shall be cognizable and non-bailable.

(3) Notwithstanding the punishment under sub-section (1), the court may, in case of first conviction, suspend any licence issued to the person referred to in that sub-section, under any law for the time being in force, for a period up to two years, and in case of second or subsequent conviction, cancel the licence.

92. Cognizance of offence by court. No cognizance shall be taken by a competent court of any offence under sections 88 and 89 except on a complaint filed by the Central Authority or any officer authorised by it in this behalf.

93. Vexatious search. The Director General or any other officer, exercising powers under section 22, who knows that there are no reasonable grounds for so doing, and yet—

(*a*) searches, or causes to be searched any premises; or

(*b*) seizes any record, register or other document or article, shall, for every such offence, be punished with imprisonment for a term which may extend to one year, or with fine which may extend to ten thousand rupees or with both.

Chapter VIII

MISCELLANEOUS

94. Measures to prevent unfair trade practices in e-commerce, direct selling, etc. For the purposes of preventing unfair trade practices in e-commerce, direct selling and also to protect the interest and rights of consumers, the Central Government may take such measures in the manner as may be prescribed.

95. Presidents, members, Chief Commissioner, Commissioner and certain officers to be public servants. The Presidents and members of the District Commission, the State Commission and the National Commission, and officers and other employees thereof, the Chief Commissioner and the Commissioner of the Central Authority, the Director General, the Additional Director General, the Director, the Joint Director, the Deputy Director and the Assistant Director and all other officers and employees of the Central Authority and other persons performing any duty under this Act, while acting or purporting to act in pursuance of any of the provisions of this Act, shall be deemed to be public servants within the meaning of section 21 of the Indian Penal Code.

96. Compounding of offences. (1) Any offence punishable under sections 88 and 89, may, either before or after the institution of the prosecution, be compounded, on payment of such amount as may be prescribed:

Provided that no compounding of such offence shall be made without the leave of the court before which a complaint has been filed under section 92:

Provided further that such sum shall not, in any case, exceed the maximum amount of the fine, which may be imposed under this Act for the offence so compounded.

(2) The Central Authority or any officer as may be specially authorised by him in this behalf, may compound offences under sub-section (1).

(3) Nothing in sub-section (1) shall apply to person who commits the same or similar offence, within a period of three years

from the date on which the first offence, committed by him, was compounded.

Explanation.—For the purposes of this sub-section, any second or subsequent offence committed after the expiry of a period of three years from the date on which the offence was previously compounded, shall be deemed to be a first offence.

(4) Where an offence has been compounded under sub-section (1), no proceeding or further proceeding, as the case may be, shall be taken against the offender in respect of the offence so compounded.

(5) The acceptance of the sum of money for compounding an offence in accordance with sub-section (1) by the Central Authority or an officer of the Central Authority empowered in this behalf shall be deemed to amount to an acquittal within the meaning of the Code of Criminal Procedure, 1973.

97. Manner of crediting penalty. The penalty collected under section 21 and the amount collected under section 96 shall be credited to such fund as may be prescribed.

98. Protection of action taken in good faith. No suit, prosecution or other legal proceeding shall lie against the Presidents and members of the District Commission, the State Commission and the National Commission, the Chief Commissioner, the Commissioner, any officer or employee and other person performing any duty under this Act, for any act which is in good faith done or intended to be done in pursuance of this Act or under any rule or order made thereunder.

99. Power to give directions by Central Government. (1) Without prejudice to the foregoing provisions of this Act, the Central Authority, shall, in exercise of its powers or the performance of its functions under this Act, be bound by such directions on questions of policy, as the Central Government may give in writing to it from time to time:

Provided that the Central Authority shall, as far as practicable, be given an opportunity to express its views before any direction is given under this sub-section.

(2) The decision of the Central Government whether a question is one of policy or not shall be final.

100. Act not in derogation of any other law. The provisions of this Act shall be in addition to and not in derogation of the provisions of any other law for the time being in force.

101. Power of Central Government to make rules. (1) The Central Government may, by notification, make rules for carrying out any of the provisions contained in this Act.

(2) Without prejudice to the generality of the foregoing power, such rules may provide for, —

(*a*) the other class or classes of persons including public utility entities under clause (19) of section 2;

(*b*) the contest, lottery, game of chance or skill which are to be exempted under item (*b*) of sub-clause (*iii*) of clause (47) of section 2;

(*c*) the manner of issuing bill or cash memo or receipt for goods sold or services rendered under sub-clause (*vii*) of clause (47) of section 2;

(*d*) the number of other official or non-official members of the Central Council under clause (*b*) of sub-section (2) of section 3;

(*e*) the time and place of meeting of Central Council and the procedure for the transaction of its business under sub-section (2) of section 4;

(*f*) the number of Commissioners in the Central Authority under sub-section (2) of section 10;

(*g*) the qualifications for appointment, method of recruitment, procedure of appointment, term of office, salaries and allowances, resignation, removal and other terms and conditions of service of the Chief Commissioner and other Commissioners of the Central Authority under section 11;

(*h*) the salaries and allowances payable to, and the other terms and conditions of service of, the officers and other employees of the Central Authority under sub-section (2) of section 13;

(*i*) the qualifications for appointment of Director General, Additional Director General, Director, Joint Director, Deputy Director and Assistant Director and the manner of appointment under sub-section (2) of section 15;

(*j*) the manner of taking copies or extracts of document, record or article seized or produced before returning to the person under sub-section (3) of section 22;

(*k*) the officer and the manner of disposing of articles which are subject to speedy or natural decay under sub-section (4) of section 22;

(*l*) the form and manner for preparing annual statement of accounts by the Central Authority in consultation with the Comptroller and Auditor-General of India under sub-section (1) of section 26;

(*m*) the form in which, and the time within which, an annual report, other reports and returns may be prepared by the Central Authority under sub-section (1) of section 27;

(*n*) the qualifications for appointment, method of recruitment, procedure for appointment, term of office, resignation and removal of President and members of the District Commission under section 29;

(*o*) the other value of goods and services in respect of which the District Commission shall have jurisdiction to entertain complaints under proviso to sub-section (1) of section 34;

(*p*) the manner of electronically filing complaint under the proviso to sub-section (1) of section 35;

(*q*) the fee, electronic form and the manner of payment of fee for filing complaint under sub-section (2) of section 35;

(*r*) the cases which may not be referred for settlement by mediation under sub-section (1) of section 37;

(*s*) the manner of authentication of goods sampled in case of the National Commission under clause (*c*) of sub-section (2) of section 38;

(*t*) any other matter which may be prescribed under clause (*f*) of sub-section (9) of section 38;

(*u*) the fund where the amount obtained may be credited and the manner of utilisation of such amount under sub-section (2) of section 39;

(*v*) the form and the manner in which appeal may be preferred to the State Commission under section 41;

(*w*) the qualifications for appointment, method of recruitment, procedure for appointment, term of office, resignation and removal of the President and members of the State Commission under section 43;

(*x*) the other value of goods and services in respect of which the State Commission shall have jurisdiction under the proviso to sub-clause (*i*) of clause (*a*) of sub-section (1) of section 47;

(*y*) the form and manner of filing appeal to the National Commission, and the manner of depositing fifty per cent. of the amount before filing appeal, under sub-section (1) of section 51;

(*z*) the number of members of the National Commission under clause (*b*) of section 54;

(*za*) the qualifications, appointment, term of office, salaries and allowances, resignation, removal and other terms and conditions of service of the President and members of the National Commission under sub-section (1) of section 55;

(*zb*) the salaries and allowances payable to, and other terms and conditions of service of, the officers and other employees of the National Commission under sub-section (3) of section 57;

(*zc*) the other value of goods and services in respect of which the National Commission shall have jurisdiction under the proviso to sub-clause (*i*) of clause (*a*) of sub-section (1) of section 58;

(*zd*) the manner of depositing fifty per cent. of the amount under the second proviso to section 67;

(*ze*) the form in which the National Commission and the State Commission shall furnish information to the Central Government under sub-section (4) of section 70;

(*zf*) the persons in the consumer mediation cell under sub-section (3) of section 74;

(*zg*) the measures to be taken by the Central Government to prevent unfair trade practices in e-commerce, direct selling under section 94;

(*zh*) the amount for compounding offences under sub-section (1) of section 96;

(*zi*) the fund to which the penalty and amount collected shall be credited under section 97; and

(*zj*) any other matter which is to be, or may be, prescribed, or in respect of which provisions are to be, or may be, made by rules.

102. Power of State Government to make rules. (1) The State Governments may, by notification, make rules for carrying out the provisions of this Act:

Provided that the Central Government may, frame model rules in respect of all or any of the matters with respect to which the State Government may make rules under this section, and where any such model rules have been framed in respect of any such matter, they shall apply to the State until the rules in respect of that matter is made by the State Government and while making any such rules, so far as is practicable, they shall conform to such model rules.

(2) In particular, and without prejudice to the generality of the foregoing power, such rules may provide for all or any of the following matters, namely:—

(*a*) the other class or classes of persons including public utility entities under clause (19) of section 2;

(*b*) the contest, lottery, game of chance or skill which are to be exempted under item (*b*) of sub-clause (*iii*) of clause (47) of section 2;

(*c*) the number of other official or non-official members of the State Council under clause (*b*) of sub-section (2) of section 6;

(*d*) the time and place of meeting of the State Council and the procedure for the transaction of its business under sub-section (4) of section 6;

(*e*) the number of other official and non-official members of District Council under clause (*b*) of sub-section (2) of section 8;

(*f*) the time and place of meeting of the District Council and procedure for the transaction of its business under sub-section (4) of section 8;

(*g*) the number of members of the District Commission under clause (*b*) of sub-section (2) of section 28;

(*h*) the salaries and allowances payable to, and other terms and conditions of service of, the President and members of the District Commission under section 30;

(*i*) the salaries and allowances payable to, and other terms and conditions of service of, the officers and other employees of the District Commission under sub-section (3) of section 33;

(*j*) the manner of authentication of goods sampled by the State Commission and the District Commission under clause (*c*) of sub-section (2) of section 38;

(*k*) the manner of depositing fifty per cent. of the amount before filing appeal under second proviso to section 41;

(*l*) the number of members of the State Commission under sub-section (3) of section 42;

(*m*) the salaries and allowances payable to, and other terms and conditions of service of, the President and members of the State Commission under section 44;

(*n*) the salaries and allowances payable to, and other terms and conditions of service of, the officers and other employees of the State Commission under sub-section (3) of section 46;

(*o*) the form in which the State Commission shall furnish information to the State Government under sub-section (5) of section 70;

(*p*) the persons in the consumer mediation cell under sub-section (3) of section 74;

(*q*) any other matter which is to be, or may be prescribed, or in respect of which provisions are to be, or may be made by rules.

103. Power of National Commission to make regulations. (1) The National Commission may, with the previous approval of the Central Government, by notification, make regulations not inconsistent with this Act to provide for all matters for which provision is necessary or expedient for the purpose of giving effect to the provisions of this Act.

(2) In particular, and without prejudice to the generality of the foregoing power, such regulations may make provisions for—

(*a*) the costs for adjournment to be imposed by the District Commission under the second proviso to sub-section (7) of section 38;

(*b*) the costs for adjournment to be imposed by the State Commission or the National Commission, as the case may be, under the second proviso to section 52;

(*c*) the maintenance of any other information by the consumer mediation cell under sub-section (4) of section 74;

(*d*) the manner of submission of quarterly report by consumer mediation cell to the District Commission, the State Commission or the National Commission under sub-section (5) of section 74;

(*e*) the qualifications and experience required for empanelment as mediator, the procedure for empanelment, the manner of training empanelled mediators, the fee payable to empanelled mediator, the terms and conditions for empanelment, the code of conduct for empanelled mediators, the grounds on which, and the manner in which, empanelled mediators shall be removed or empanelment shall be cancelled and the other matters relating thereto under sub-section (2) of section 75;

(*f*) the conditions for re-empanelment of mediators for another term under sub-section (3) of section 75;

(*g*) the other facts to be disclosed by mediators under clause (*c*) of section 77;

(*h*) the time within which, and the manner in which, mediation may be conducted under sub-section (3) of section 79; and (*i*) such other matter for which provision is to be, or may be, made by regulation.

104. Power of Central Authority to make regulations. (1) The Central Authority may, with the previous approval of the Central Government, by notification, make regulations not inconsistent with this Act, for the purpose of giving effect to the provisions of this Act.

(2) In particular, and without prejudice to the generality of the foregoing power, such regulations may provide for all or any of the following matters, namely:—

(*a*) the procedure for engaging experts and professionals and the number of such experts and professionals under sub-section (3) of section 13;

(*b*) the procedure for transaction of business and the allocation of business of the Chief Commissioner and Commissioner under sub-section (1) of section 14;

(*c*) the form, manner and time within which, inquiries or investigation made by the Director-General shall be submitted to the Central Authority under sub-section (5) of section 15; and

(*d*) such other matter for which provision is to be, or may be, made by regulation.

105. Rules and regulations to be laid before each House of Parliament. (1) Every rule and every regulation made under this Act shall be laid, as soon as may be after it is made, before each House of Parliament, while it is in session, for a total period of thirty days which may be comprised in one session or in two or more successive sessions, and if, before the expiry of the session immediately following the session or the successive sessions aforesaid, both Houses agree in making any modification in the rule or regulation or both Houses agree that the rule or regulation shall thereafter have effect only in such modified form or be of no effect, as the case may be; so, however, that any such modification or annulment shall be without prejudice to the validity of anything previously done under that rule or regulation.

(2) Every rule made by a State Government under this Act shall be laid as soon as may be after it is made, before the State Legislature.

106. Power to remove difficulties. If any difficulty arises in giving effect to the provisions of this Act, the Central Government may, by order in the Official Gazette, make such provisions not inconsistent with the provisions of this Act as appear to it to be necessary or expedient for removing the difficulty:

Provided that no such order shall be made after the expiry of a period of two years from the commencement of this Act.

107. Repeal and savings. (1) The Consumer Protection Act, 1986 is hereby repealed.

(2) Notwithstanding such repeal, anything done or any action taken or purported to have been done or taken under the Act hereby repealed shall, in so far as it is not inconsistent with the provisions of this Act, be deemed to have been done or taken under the corresponding provisions of this Act.

(3) The mention of particular matters in sub-section (2) shall not be held to prejudice or affect the general application of section 6 of the General Clauses Act, 1897 (10 of 1897) with regard to the effect of repeal.

APPENDIX

3

The Fatal Accidents Act, 1855

(13 of 1855)

[27th March, 1855

1. Short title and extent. (1) This Act may be called The Fatal Accidents Act, 1855.

(2) It extends to the whole of India *[...].

1A. Suit for compensation to the family of a person for loss occasioned to it by his death by actionable wrong. Whenever the death of a person shall be caused by wrongful act, neglect or default, and the act, neglect or default is such as would (if death had not ensued) have entitled the party injured to maintain an action and recover damages in respect thereof, the party who would have been liable if death had not ensued shall be liable to an action or suit for damages, notwithstanding the death of the person injured, and although the death shall have been caused under such circumstances as amount in law to felony or other crime.

Every such action or suit shall be for the benefit of the wife, husband, parent and child, if any, of the person whose death shall have been so caused, and shall be brought by and in the name of the executor, administrator or representative of the person deceased.

And in every such action the Court may give such damages as it may think proportioned to the loss resulting from such death to the parties respectively, for whom and for whose benefit such action shall be brought; and the amount so recovered, after deducting all costs and expenses, including the costs not recovered from the defendant, shall

* The words "except the State of Jammu and Kashmir" are *omitted* by the Jammu and Kashmir Reorganisation Act, 2019 (w.e.f. 31.10.2019).

be divided amongst the before-mentioned parties, or any of them, in such shares as the Court by its judgment or decree shall direct.

2. Not more than one suit to be brought. Provided always that no more than one action or suit shall be brought for, and in respect of the same subject matter of complaint.

Claim for loss to estate may be added. Provided that, in any such action or suit, the executor, administrator or representative of the deceased may insert a claim for and recover any pecuniary loss to the estate of the deceased occasioned by such wrongful act, neglect or default, which sum, when recovered, shall be deemed part of the assets of the estate of the deceased.

3. Plaintiff shall deliver particulars etc. The plaint in any such action or suit shall give a full particular of the person or persons for whom, or on whose behalf, such action or suit shall be brought, and of the nature of the claim in respect of which damages shall be sought to be recovered.

4. Interpretation clause. The following words and expressions are intended to have the meaning hereby assigned to them respectively, so far as such meanings are not excluded by the context or by the nature of the subject matter; that is to say that word "person" shall apply to bodies politic and corporate; and the word "parent" shall include father and mother and grandfather and grandmother; and the word "child" shall include son and daughter and grandson and grand-daughter and step-son and step-daughter.

APPENDIX

4

The Majority Act, 1875

(9 of 1875)

[2nd March, 1875

1. Short title. This Act may be called the Majority Act, 1875.

Local extent. It extends to the whole of India *[........]:

Commencement and operation. and it shall come into force and have effect only on the expiration of three months from the passing thereof.

2. Savings. Nothing herein contained shall affect—

(*a*) the capacity of a person to act in the following matters (namely) —marriage, dower, divorce and adoption;

(*b*) the religion or religious rites and usages of any class of (citizens of India); or

(*c*) the capacity of any person who before this Act comes into force has attained majority under the law applicable to him.

3. Age of majority of persons domiciled in India. (1) Every person domiciled in India shall attain the age of majority on his completing the age of eighteen years and not before.

(2) In computing the age of any person, the day on which he was born is to be included as a whole day and he shall be deemed to have attained majority at the beginning of the eighteenth anniversary of that day.

---

* The words "except the State of Jammu and Kashmir" are *omitted* by the Jammu and Kashmir Reorganisation Act, 2019 (w.e.f. 31.10.2019).

APPENDIX

5

The Indian Medical Council Act, 1956

(102 of 1956)

[30th December, 1956

An Act to provide for the reconstitution of the Medical Council of India, and the maintenance of a Medical Register for India and for matters connected therewith.

Be it enacted by Parliament in the Seventh Year of the Republic of India as follows:

1. Short title, extent and commencement. (1) This Act may be called the Indian Medical Council Act, 1956.

(2) It extends to the whole of India.

(3) It shall come into force on such date as the Central Government may, by notification in the Official Gazette, appoint.

2. Definitions. In this Act, unless the context otherwise requires,—

(*a*) "approved institution" means a hospital, health centre or other such institution recognised by a University as an institution in which a person may undergo the training, if any, required by his course of study before the award of any medical qualification to him;

(*b*) "Council" means the Medical Council of India constituted under this Act;

(*c*) *Omitted* by Act 24 of 1964 (w.e.f. 16.6.1964).

(*d*) "Indian Medical Register" means the medical register maintained by the Council;

(*e*) "medical institution" means any institution, within or without India, which grants degrees, diplomas or licences in medicine;

(*f*) "medicine" means modern scientific medicine in all its branches and includes surgery and obstetrics, but does not include veterinary medicine and surgery;

(*g*) "prescribed" means prescribed by regulations;

(*h*) "recognised medical qualification" means any of the medical qualifications included in the Schedules;

(*i*) "regulation" means a regulation made under section 33;

(*j*) "State Medical Council" means a medical council constituted under any law for the time being in force in any State regulating the registration of practitioners of medicine;

(*k*) "State Medical Register" means a register maintained under any law for the time being in force in any State regulating the registration of practitioners of medicine;

(*l*) "University" means any University in India established by law and having a medical faculty.

3. Constitution and composition of the Council. (1) The Central Government shall cause to be constituted a Council consisting of the following members, namely:

(*a*) one member from each State other than a Union territory, to be nominated by the Central Government in consultation with the State Government concerned;

(*b*) one member from each University, to be elected from amongst the members of the medical faculty of the University by members of the Senate of the University or in case the University has no Senate by members of the court;

(*c*) one member from each State in which a State Medical Register is maintained, to be elected from amongst themselves by persons enrolled on such Register who possess the medical qualifications included in the First or the Second Schedule or in Part II of the Third Schedule;

(*d*) seven members to be elected from amongst themselves by persons enrolled on any of the State Medical Registers who possess the medical qualifications included in Part I of the Third Schedule;

(*e*) eight members to be nominated by the Central Government.

(2) The President and Vice-President of the Council shall be elected by the members of the Council from amongst themselves.

(3) No act done by the Council shall be questioned on the ground merely of the existence of any vacancy in, or any defect in the constitution of, the Council.

*[**3A. Power of Central Government to supersede the Council and to constitute a Board of Governors.** (1) On and from the date of commencement of the **[Indian Medical Council (Amendment) Act, 2019], the Council shall stand superseded and the President, Vice-President and other members of the Council shall vacate their offices and shall have no claim for any compensation, whatsoever.

(2) The Council shall be reconstituted in accordance with the provisions of section 3 within a period of **[two years] from the date of supersession of the Council under sub-section (1).

(3) Upon the supersession of the Council under sub-section (1) and until a new Council is constituted in accordance with section 3, the Board of Governors constituted under sub-section (4) shall exercise the powers and perform the functions of the Council under this Act.

(4) The Central Government shall, by notification in the Official Gazette, constitute the Board of Governors which shall consist of not more than ***[twelve persons] as its members, who shall be persons of eminence and of unimpeachable integrity in the fields of medicine **[and medical education or proven administrative capacity and experience], and who may be either nominated members or members, *ex officio*, to be appointed by the Central Government, one of whom shall be named by the Central Government as the Chairperson of the Board of Governors.

(5) The Chairperson and the other members, other than the members, *ex officio,* shall be entitled to such sitting fee and travelling and other allowances as may be determined by the Central Government.

(6) The Board of Governors shall meet at such time and places and shall observe such rules of procedure in regard to the transaction of business at its meetings as is applicable to the Council.

(7) Two-third of the members of the Board of Governors shall constitute the quorum for its meetings.

†[(7A) The Board of Governors shall be assisted by a Secretary General who shall be appointed by the Central Government on deputation or contract basis and he shall be the head of the secretariat in the Council.]

---

* *Inserted* by the Indian Medical Council (Amendment) Act 2010, w.e.f. 15.05.2010.

** *Substituted* by Indian Medical Council (Amendment) Act, 2019, w.e.f. 26.09.2018.

*** *Substituted* by Indian Medical Council (Amendment) Act, 2019, w.e.f. 12.01.2019.

† *Inserted* by Indian Medical Council (Amendment) Act, 2019, w.e.f. 26.09.2018.

(8) No act or proceedings of the Board of Governors shall be invalid merely by reason of—

(a) any vacancy in, or any defect in the constitution of, the Board of Governors; or

(b) any irregularity in the procedure of the Board of Governors not affecting the merits of the case.

(9) A member having any financial or other interest in any matter coming before the Board of Governors for decision shall disclose his interest in the matter before he may, if allowed by the Board of Governors, participate in such proceedings.

(10) The Chairperson and the other members of the Board of Governors shall hold office during the pleasure of the Central Government.

3B. Certain modifications of the Act. During the period when the Council stands superseded,—

(*a*) the provisions of this Act shall be construed as if for the word "Council", the words "Board of Governors" were substituted;

(*b*) the Board of Governors shall—

(*i*) exercise the powers and discharge the functions of the Council under this Act and for this purpose, the provisions of this Act shall have effect subject to the modification that references therein to the Council shall be construed as references to the Board of Governors;

(*ii*) grant independently permission for establishment of new medical colleges or opening a new or higher course of study or training or increase in admission capacity in any course of study or training referred to in section 10A or giving the person or college concerned a reasonable opportunity of being heard as provided under section 10A without prior permission of the Central Government under that section, including exercise of the power to finally approve or disapprove the same; and

(*iii*) dispose of the matters pending with the Central Government under section 10A upon receipt of the same from it.

3C. Power of Central Government to give directions. (1) Without prejudice to the provisions of this Act, the Board of Governors or the Council after its reconstitution shall, in exercise of its powers and in the performance of its functions under this Act, be bound by such directions on questions of policy, other than those relating to technical and administrative matters, as the Central Government may give in writing to it from time-to-time:

Provided that the Board of Governors or the Council after its reconstitution shall, as far as practicable, be given an opportunity to express its views before any direction is given under this sub-section.

(2) The decision of the Central Government whether a question is a matter of policy or not shall be final.]

4. Mode of election. (1) An election under clause (*b*), clause (*c*) or clause (*d*) of sub-section (1) of section 3 shall be conducted by the Central Government in accordance with such rules as may be made by it in this behalf, and any rules so made may provide that pending the preparation of the Indian Medical Register in accordance with the provisions of this Act, the members referred to in clause (*d*) of sub-section (1) of section 3 may be nominated by the Central Government instead of being elected as provided therein.

(2) Where any dispute arises regarding any election to the Council, it shall be referred to the Central Government whose decision shall be final.

5. Restrictions on nomination and membership. (1) No person shall be eligible for nomination under clause (*a*) of sub-section (1) of section 3 unless he possesses any of the medical qualifications included in the First and Second Schedules, resides in the State concerned, and, where a State Medical Register is maintained in that State is enrolled on that register.

(2) No person may at the same time serve as a member in more than one capacity.

6. Incorporation of the Council. The Council so constituted shall be body corporate by the name of the Medical Council of India, having perpetual succession and a common seal, with power to acquire and hold property, both movable and immovable, and to contract, and shall by the said name sue and be sued.

7. Term of office of President, Vice-President and members. (1) The President or Vice-President of the Council shall hold office for a term not exceeding five years and not extending beyond the expiry of his term as member of the Council.

(2) Subject to the provisions of this section, a member shall hold office for a term of five years from the date of his nomination or election or until his successor shall have been duly nominated or elected, whichever is longer.

(3) An elected or nominated member shall be deemed to have vacated his seat if he is absent without excuse, sufficient in the opinion of the Council, from three consecutive ordinary meetings of the Council or, in the case of a member elected under clause (*b*) of sub-section (1) of section 3, if he ceases to be a member of the medical faculty of the University

concerned, or in the case of a member elected under clause (*c*) or clause (*d*) of that sub-section, if he ceases to be a person enrolled on the State Medical Register concerned.

(4) A casual vacancy in the Council shall be filled by nomination or election, as the case may be, and the person nominated or elected to fill the vacancy shall hold office only for the remainder of the term for which the member whose place he takes was nominated or elected.

(5) Members of the Council shall be eligible for renomination or re-election.

(6) Where the said term of five years is about to expire in respect of any member, a successor may be nominated or elected at any time within three months before the said term expires but he shall not assume office until the said term has expired.

8. Meetings of the Council. (1) The Council shall meet at least once in each year at such time and place as may be appointed by the Council.

(2) Unless otherwise provided by regulations, fifteen members of the Council shall form a quorum, and all the acts of the Council shall be decided by a majority of the members present and voting.

9. Officers, Committees and servants of the Council. The Council shall—

(1) constitute from amongst its members an Executive Committee and such other Committees for general or special purposes as the Council deems necessary to carry out the purposes of this Act;

(2) appoint a Registrar who shall act as Secretary and who may also, if deemed expedient, act as Treasurer;

(3) employ such other persons as the Council deems necessary to carry out the purposes of this Act;

(4) require and take from the Registrar, or from any other employee, such security for the due performance of his duties as the Council deems necessary; and

(5) with the previous sanction of the Central Government, fix the remuneration and allowances to be paid to the President, Vice-President and members of the Council and determine the conditions of service of the employees of the Council.

10. The Executive Committee. (1) The Executive Committee, hereinafter referred to as the Committee, shall consist of the President and Vice-President, who shall be members *ex-officio*, and not less than seven and not more than ten other members who shall be elected by the Council from amongst its members.

(2) The President and Vice-President shall be the President and Vice-President respectively of the Committee.

(3) In addition to the powers and duties conferred and imposed upon it by this Act, the Committee shall exercise and discharge such powers and duties as the Council may confer or impose upon it by any regulations which may be made in this behalf.

*[**10A. Permission for establishment of new medical college, new course of study.** (1) Notwithstanding anything contained in this Act or any other law for the time being in force,—

(*a*) no person shall establish a medical college; or

(*b*) no medical college shall—

(*i*) open a new or higher course of study or training (including a post-graduate course of study or training) which would enable a student of such course or training to qualify himself for the award of any recognised medical qualification; or

(*ii*) increase its admission capacity in any course of study or training (including a post-graduate course of study or training),

except with the previous permission of the Central Government obtained in accordance with the provisions of this section.

Explanation 1. For the purposes of this section, "person" includes any University or a trust but does not include the Central Government.

Explanation 2. For the purposes of this section, "admission capacity", in relation to any course of study or training (including post-graduate course of study or training) in a medical college, means the maximum number of students that may be fixed by the Council from time to time for being admitted to such course or training.

(2)(*a*) Every person or medical college shall, for the purpose of obtaining permission under sub-section (1), submit to the Central Government a scheme in accordance with the provisions of clause (*b*) and the Central Government shall refer the scheme to the Council for its recommendations.

(*b*) The scheme referred to in clause (*a*) shall be in such form and contain such particulars and be preferred in such manner and be accompanied with such fee as may be prescribed.

(3) On receipt of a scheme by the Council under sub-section (2), the Council may obtain such other particulars as may be considered necessary

* *Inserted* by the Indian Medical Council (Amendment) Act, 1993, w.r.e.f. 27.8.1992.

by it from the person or the medical college concerned, and thereafter, it may,—

(*a*) if the scheme is defective and does not contain any necessary particulars, give a reasonable opportunity to the person or college concerned for making a written representation and it shall be open to such person or medical college to rectify the defects, if any, specified by the Council;

(*b*) consider the scheme, having regard to the factors referred to in sub-section (7), and submit the scheme together with its recommendations thereon to the Central Government.

(4) The Central Government may, after considering the scheme and the recommendations of the Council under sub-section (3) and after obtaining, where necessary, such other particulars as may be considered necessary by it from the person or college concerned, and having regard to the factors referred to in sub-section (7), either approve (with such conditions, if any, as it may consider necessary) or disapprove the scheme and any such approval shall be a permission under sub-section (1):

Provided that no scheme shall be disapproved by the Central Government except after giving the person or college concerned a reasonable opportunity of being heard:

Provided further that nothing in this sub-section shall prevent any person or medical college whose scheme has not been approved by the Central Government to submit a fresh scheme and the provisions of this section shall apply to such scheme, as if such scheme has been submitted for the first time under sub-section (2).

(5) Where, within a period of one year from the date of submission of the scheme to the Central Government under sub-section (2), no order passed by the Central Government has been communicated to the person or college submitting the scheme, such scheme shall be deemed to have been approved by the Central Government in the form in which it had been submitted, and, accordingly, the permission of the Central Government required under sub-section (1) shall also be deemed to have been granted.

(6) In computing the time-limit specified in sub-section (5), the time taken by the person or college concerned submitting the scheme, in furnishing any particulars called for by the Council, or by the Central Government, shall be excluded.

(7) The Council, while making its recommendations under clause (*b*) of sub-section (3) and the Central Government, while passing an order, either approving or disapproving the scheme under sub-section (4), shall have due regard to the following factors, namely:

(*a*) whether the proposed medical college or the existing medical college seeking to open a new or higher course of study or training, would be in a position to offer the minimum standards of medical education as prescribed by the Council under section 19A or, as the case may be, under section 20 in the case of post graduate medical education;

(*b*) whether the person seeking to establish a medical college or the existing medical college seeking to open a new or higher course of study or training or to increase its admission capacity has adequate financial resources;

(*c*) whether necessary facilities in respect of staff, equipment, accommodation, training and other facilities to ensure proper functioning of the medical college or conducting the new course of study or training or accommodating the increased admission capacity have been provided or would be provided within the time-limit specified in the scheme;

(*d*) whether adequate hospital facilities, having regard to the number of students likely to attend such medical college or course of study or training or as a result of the increased admission capacity, have been provided or would be provided within the time-limit specified in the scheme;

(*e*) whether any arrangement has been made or programme drawn to impart proper training to students likely to attend such medical college or course of study or training by persons having the recognised medical qualifications;

(*f*) the requirement of manpower in the field of practice of medicine; and

(*g*) any other factors as may be prescribed.

(8) Where the Central Government passes an order either approving or disapproving a scheme under this section, a copy of the order shall be communicated to the person or college concerned.

10B. Non-recognition of medical qualifications in certain cases. (1) Where any medical college is established except with the previous permission of the Central Government in accordance with the provisions of section 10A, no medical qualification granted to any student of such medical college shall be a recognised medical qualification for the purposes of this Act.

(2) Where any medical college opens a new or higher course of study or training (including a post-graduate course of study or training) except with the previous permission of the Central Government in accordance with the provisions of section 10A, no medical qualification granted to any student of such medical college on the basis of such study

or training shall be a recognised medical qualification for the purposes of this Act.

(3) Where any medical college increases its admission capacity in any course of study or training except with the previous permission of the Central Government in accordance with the provisions of section 10A, no medical qualification granted to any student of such medical college on the basis of the increase in its admission capacity shall be a recognised medical qualification for the purposes of this Act.

Explanation. For the purposes of this section, the certificate for identifying a student who has been granted to medical qualification on the basis of such increase in the admission capacity shall be such as may be prescribed.

10C. Time for seeking permission for certain existing medical college, etc. (1) If, after the 1st day of June, 1992 and on and before the commencement of the Indian Medical Council (Amendment) Act, 1993, any person has established a medical college or any medical college has opened a new or higher course of study or training or increased the admission capacity, such person or medical college, as the case may be, shall seek, within a period of one year from the commencement of the Indian Medical Council (Amendment) Act, 1993, the permission of the Central Government in accordance with the provisions of section 10A.

(2) If any person or medical college, as the case may be, fails to seek the permission under sub-section (1), the provisions of section 10B shall apply, so far as may be, as if, permission of the Central Government under section 10A has been refused.]

***[10D. Uniform entrance examination for undergraduate and postgraduate level.** There shall be conducted a uniform entrance examination to all medical educational institutions at the undergraduate level and post-graduate level through such designated authority in Hindi, English and such other languages and in such manner as may be prescribed and the designated authority shall ensure the conduct of uniform entrance examination in the aforesaid manner:

Provided that notwithstanding any judgment or order of any court, the provisions of this section shall not apply, in relation to the uniform entrance examination at the undergraduate level for the academic year 2016-17 conducted in accordance with any regulations made under this Act, in respect of the State Government seats (whether in Government Medical College or in a private Medical College) where such State has not opted for such examination.]

* *Inserted* vide the Indian Medical Council (Amendment) Act, 2016, w.e.f. 24.05.2016.

11. Recognition of medical qualifications granted by Universities or medical institutions in India. (1) The medical qualifications granted by any University or medical institution in India which are included in the First Schedule shall be recognised medical qualifications for the purposes of this Act.

(2) Any University or medical institution in India which grants a medical qualification not included in the First Schedule may apply to the Central Government to have such qualification recognised, and the Central Government, after consulting the Council, may, by notification in the Official Gazette, amend the First Schedule so as to include such qualification therein, and any such notification may also direct that an entry shall be made in the last column of the First Schedule against such medical qualification declaring that it shall be a recognised medical qualification only when granted after a specified date.

12. Recognition of medical qualifications granted by medical institutions in countries with which there is a scheme of reciprocity. (1) The medical qualifications granted by medical institutions outside India which are included in the Second Schedule shall be recognised medical qualifications for the purposes of this Act.

(2) The Council may enter into negotiations with the Authority in any country outside India which by the law of such country is entrusted with the maintenance of a register of medical practitioners, for the settling of a scheme of reciprocity for the recognition of medical qualifications, and in pursuance of any such scheme, the Central Government may, by notification in the Official Gazette, amend the Second Schedule so as to include therein the medical qualification which the Council has decided should be recognised, and any such notification may also direct that an entry shall be made in the last column of the Second Schedule against such medical qualification declaring that it shall be a recognised medical, qualification only when granted after a specified date.

(3) The Central Government, after consultation with the Council, may, by notification in the Official Gazette, amend the Second Schedule by direction that an entry be made therein in respect of any medical qualification declaring that it shall be a recognised medical qualification only when granted before a specified date.

(4) Where the Council has refused to recommend any medical qualification which has been proposed for recognition by any Authority referred to in sub-section (2) and that Authority applies to the Central Government in this behalf, the Central Government, after considering such application and after obtaining from the Council a report, if any, as to the reasons for any such refusal, may, by notification in the Official Gazette, amend the Second Schedule so as to include such

qualification therein and the provisions of sub-section (2) shall apply to such notification.

13. Recognition of medical qualifications granted by certain medical institutions whose qualifications are not included in the First or Second Schedule. (1) The medical qualifications granted by medical institutions in India which are not included in the First Schedule and which are included in Part I of the Third Schedule shall also be recognised medical qualifications for the purposes of this Act.

(2) The medical qualifications granted to a citizen of India—

(*a*) before the 15th day of August, 1947, by medical institutions in the territories now forming part of Pakistan, and

(*b*) before the 1st day of April, 1937, by medical institutions in the territories now forming part of Burma,

which are included in Part I of the Third Schedule shall also be recognised medical qualifications for the purposes of this Act.

(3) The medical qualifications granted by medical institutions outside India *[before such date as the Central Government may, by notification in the Official Gazette, specify] which are included in Part II of the Third Schedule shall also be recognised medical qualifications for the purposes of this Act, but no person possessing any such qualification shall be entitled to enrollment or on any State Medical Register unless he is a citizen of India and has undergone such practical training after obtaining that qualification as may be required by the rules or regulations in force in the country **[***] granting the qualification, or if he has not undergone any practical training in that country, **[***] he has undergone such practical training as may be prescribed.

(4) The Central Government, after consulting the Council, may, by notification in the Official Gazette, amend Part II of the Third Schedule so as to include therein any qualification granted by a medical institution outside India which is not included in the Second Schedule:

*Provided that after the commencement of the Indian Medical Council (Amendment) Act, 2001, no such amendment shall be made in Part II of the Third Schedule to include any primary medical qualification granted by any medical institution outside India:

Provided further that nothing contained in the first proviso shall apply to inclusion in Part II of the Third Schedule any primary medical qualification granted by any medical institution outside India to any person whose name is entered in the Indian Medical Register.

---

* *Inserted* by the Indian Medical Council (Amendment) Act, 2001, w.e.f. 3.9.2001.

** The words "or State" *omitted* by Act 24 of 1964.

Explanation. For the purposes of this sub-section, "primary medical qualification" means any minimum qualification sufficient for enrolment on any State Medical Register or for entering the name in the Indian Medical Register.

(4A) A person who is a citizen of India and obtains medical qualification granted by any medical institution in any country outside India recognised for enrolment as medical practitioner in that country after such date as may be specified by the Central Government under sub-section (3), shall not be entitled to be enrolled on any Medical Register maintained by a State Medical Council or to have his name entered in the Indian Medical Register unless he qualifies the screening test in India prescribed for such purpose and such foreign medical qualification after such person qualifies the said screening test shall be deemed to be the recognised medical qualification for the purposes of this Act for that person.

(4B) A person who is a citizen of India shall not, after such date as may be specified by the Central Government under sub-section (3), be eligible to get admission to obtain medical qualification granted by any medical institution in any foreign country without obtaining an eligibility certificate issued to him by the Council and in case any such person obtains such qualification without obtaining such eligibility certificate, he shall not be eligible to appear in the screening test referred to in sub-section (4A):

Provided that an Indian citizen who has acquired the medical qualification from foreign medical institution or has obtained admission in foreign medical institution before the commencement of the Indian Medical Council (Amendment) Act, 2001, shall not be required to obtain eligibility certificate under this sub-section but, if he is qualified for admission to any medical course for recognised medical qualification in any medical institution in India, he shall be required to qualify only the screening test prescribed for enrollment on any State Medical Register or for entering his name in the Indian Medical Register.

(4C) Nothing contained in sub-sections (4A) and (4B) shall apply to the medical qualifications referred to in section 14 for the purposes of that section.]

(5) Any medical institution in India which is desirous of getting a medical qualification granted by it included in Part I of the Third Schedule may apply to the Central Government to have such qualification recognised and the Central Government, after consulting the Council, may, by notification in the Official Gazette, amend Part I of the Third Schedule so as to include such qualification therein, and any such notification may also direct that an entry shall be made in

the last column of Part I of the Third Schedule against such medical qualification declaring that it shall be a recognised medical qualification only when granted after a specified date.

14. Special provision in certain cases for recognition of medical qualifications granted by medical institutions in countries with which there is no scheme of reciprocity. (1) The Central Government after consultation with the Council may, by notification in the Official Gazette, direct that medical qualifications granted by medical institutions in any country outside India in respect of which a scheme of reciprocity for the recognition of medical qualifications is not in force, shall be recognised medical qualifications for the purposes of this Act or shall be so only when granted after a specified date:

Provided that medical practice by persons possessing such qualifications—

(*a*) shall be permitted only if such persons are enrolled as medical practitioners in accordance with the law regulating the registration of medical practitioners for the time being in force in that country;

(*b*) shall be limited to the institution to which they are attached for the time being for the purposes of teaching, research or charitable work; and

(*c*) shall be limited to the period specified in this behalf by the Central Government by general or special order.

(2) In respect of any such medical qualification, the Central Government, after consultation with the Council, may, by notification in the Official Gazette, direct that it shall be a recognised medical qualification only when granted before a specified date.

15. Right of persons possessing qualifications in the Schedules to be enrolled. (1) Subject to the other provisions contained in this Act, the medical qualifications included in the Schedules shall be sufficient qualification for enrollment on any State Medical Register.

(2) Save as provided in section 25, no person other than a medical practitioner enrolled on a State Medical Register,—

(*a*) shall hold office as physician or surgeon or any other office (by whatever designation called) in Government or in any institution maintained by a local or other authority;

(*b*) shall practise medicine in any State;

(*c*) shall be entitled to sign or authenticate a medical or fitness certificate or any other certificate required by any law to be signed or authenticated by a duly qualified medical practitioner;

(*d*) shall be entitled to give evidence at any inquest or in any court of law as an expert under section 45 of the Indian Evidence Act, 1872 on any matter relating to medicine.

(3) Any person who acts in contravention of any provisions of sub-section (2) shall be punished with imprisonment for a term which may extend to one year, or with fine which may extend to one thousand rupees, or with both.

16. Power to require information as to courses of study and examinations. Every University or medical institution in India which grants a recognised medical qualification shall furnish such information as the Council may, from time to time, require as to the courses of study and examinations to be undergone in order to obtain such qualifications, as to the ages at which such courses of study and examinations are required to be undergone and such qualification is conferred and generally as to the requisites for obtaining such qualification.

17. Inspection of examinations. (1) The Committee shall appoint such number of medical inspectors as it may deem requisite to inspect any medical institution, college, hospital or other institution where medical education is given, or to attend any examination hold by any University or medical institution for the purpose of recommending to the Central Government recognition of medical qualifications granted by that University or medical institution.

(2) The medical inspectors shall not interfere with the conduct of any training or examination, but shall report to the Committee on the adequacy of the standards of medical education including staff, equipment, accommodation, training and other facilities prescribed for giving medical education or on the sufficiency of every examination which they attend.

(3) The Committee shall forward a copy of any such report to the University or medical institution concerned, and shall also forward a copy with the remarks of the University or institution thereon, to the Central Government.

18. Visitors at examinations. (1) The Council may appoint such number of visitors as it may deem requisite to inspect any medical institution, college, hospital or other institution where medical education is given or to attend any examination held by any University or medical institution for the purpose of granting recognised medical qualifications.

(2) Any person, whether he is a member of the Council or not, may be appointed as a visitor under this section but a person who is appointed as an inspector under section 17 for any inspection or examination shall not be appointed as a visitor for the same inspection or examination.

(3) The visitors shall not interfere with the conduct of any training or examination, but shall report to the President of the Council on the adequacy of the standards of medical education including staff, equipment, accommodation, training and other facilities prescribed for giving medical education or on the sufficiency of every examination which they attend.

(4) The report of a visitor shall be treated as confidential unless in any particular case the President of the Council otherwise directs:

Provided that if the Central Government requires a copy of the report of a visitor, the Council shall furnish the same.

19. Withdrawal of recognition. (1) When upon report by the Committee or the visitor, it appears to the Council—

(*a*) that the courses of study and examination to be undergone in, or the proficiency required from candidates at any examination, held by, any University or medical institution, or

(*b*) that the staff, equipment, accommodation, training and other facilities for instruction and training provided in such University or medical institution or in any college or other institution affiliated to that University, do not conform to the standards prescribed by the Council, the Council shall make a representation to that effect to the Central Government.

(2) After considering such representation, the Central Government may send it to the State Government of the State in which the University or medical institution is situated and the State Government shall forward it along with such remarks as it may choose to make to the University or medical institution, with an intimation of the period within which the University or medical institution may submit its explanation to the State Government.

(3) On the receipt of the explanation or, where no explanation is submitted within the period fixed, then on the expiry of that period, the State Government shall make its recommendations to the Central Government.

(4) The Central Government, after making such further inquiry, if any, as it may think fit, may, by notification in the Official Gazette, direct that an entry shall be made in the appropriate Schedule against the said medical qualification declaring that it shall be a recognised medical qualification only when granted before a specified date or that the said medical qualification if granted to students of a specified college or institution affiliated to any University shall be a recognised medical qualification only when granted before a specified date or, as the case

may be, that the said medical qualification shall be a recognised medical qualification in relation to a specified college or institution affiliated to any University only when granted after a specified date.

19A. Minimum standards of medical education. (1) The Council may prescribe the minimum standards of medical education required for granting recognised medical qualifications (other than post-graduate medical qualifications) by Universities or medical institutions in India.

(2) Copies of the draft regulations and of all subsequent amendments thereof shall be furnished by the Council to all State Governments and the Council shall, before submitting the regulations or any amendment thereof, as the case may be, to the Central Government for sanction, take into consideration the comments of any State Government received within three months from the furnishing of the copies as aforesaid.

(3) The Committee shall from time to time report to the Council on the efficacy of the regulations and may recommend to the Council such amendments thereof as it may think fit.

20. Post-graduate Medical Education Committee for assisting Council in matters relating to the post-graduate medical education. (1) The Council may prescribe standards of post-graduate medical education for the guidance of Universities, and may advise Universities in the matter of securing uniform standards for post-graduate medical education throughout India, and for this purpose the Central Government may constitute from among the members of the Council a Post-graduate Medical Education Committee (hereinafter referred to as the Post-graduate Committee).

(2) The Post-graduate Committee shall consist of nine members all of whom shall be persons possessing post-graduate medical qualifications and experience of teaching or examining post-graduate students of medicine.

(3) Six of the members of the Post-graduate Committee shall be nominated by the Central Government and the remaining three members shall be elected by the Council from amongst its members.

(4) For the purpose of considering post-graduate studies in a subject, the Post-graduate Committee may co-opt, as and when necessary, one or more members qualified to assist it in that subject.

(5) The views and recommendations of the Post-graduate Committee on all matters shall be placed before the Council, and if the Council does not agree with the views expressed or the recommendations made by the Post-graduate Committee on any matter, the Council shall forward them together with its observations to the Central Government for decision.

20A. Professional conduct. (1) The Council may prescribe standards of professional conduct and etiquette and a code of ethics for medical practitioners.

(2) Regulations made by the Council under sub-section (1) may specify which violations thereof shall constitute infamous conduct in any professional respect, that is to say, professional misconduct, and such provisions shall have effect notwithstanding anything contained in any law for the time being in force.

21. The Indian Medical Register. (1) The Council shall cause to be maintained, in the prescribed manner a register of medical practitioners to be known as the Indian Medical Register, which shall contain the names of all persons who are for the time being enrolled on any State Medical Register and who possess any of the recognised medical qualifications.

(2) It shall be the duty of the Register of the Council to keep the Indian Medical Register in accordance with the provisions of this Act and of any orders made by the Council, and from time to time to revise the register and publish it in the Gazette of India and in such other manner as may be prescribed.

(3) Such register shall be deemed to be a public document within the meaning of the Indian Evidence Act, 1872, and may be proved by a copy published in the Gazette of India.

22. Supply of copies of the State Medical Registers. Each State Medical Council shall supply to the Council six printed copies of the State Medical Register as soon as may be after the commencement of this Act and subsequently after the first day of April of each year, and each Register of a State Medical Council shall inform the Council without delay of all additions to and other amendments in the State Medical Register made from time to time.

23. Registration in the Indian Medical Register. The Registrar of the Council may, on receipt of the report of registration of a person in a State Medical Register or on application made in the prescribed manner by any such person, enter his name in the Indian Medical Register:

Provided that the Registrar is satisfied that the person concerned possesses a recognised medical qualification.

24. Removal of names from the Indian Medical Register. (1) If the name of any person enrolled on a State Medical Register is removed therefrom in pursuance of any power conferred by or under any law relating to registration of medical practitioners for the time being in force in any State, the Council shall direct the removal of the name of such person from the Indian Medical Register.

(2) Where the name of any person has been removed from a State Medical Register on the ground of professional misconduct or any other ground except that he is not possessed of the requisite medical qualifications or where any application made by the said person for restoration of his name to the State Medical Register has been rejected, he may appeal in the prescribed manner and subject to such conditions including conditions as to the payment of a fee as may be laid down in rules made by the Central Government in this behalf, to the Central Government, whose decision, which shall be given after consulting the Council, shall be binding on the State Government and on the authorities concerned with the preparation of the State Medical Register.

25. Provisional registration. (1) A citizen of India possessing a medical qualification granted by a medical institution outside India included in Part II of the Third Schedule, who is required to undergo practical training as prescribed under sub-section (3) of section 13, shall, on production of proper evidence that he has been selected for such practical training in an approved institution, be entitled to be registered provisionally in a State Medical Register and shall be entitled to practise medicine in the approved institution for the purposes of such training and for no other purpose.

(2) A person who has passed the qualifying examination of any University or medical institution in India for the grant of a recognised medical qualification shall be entitled to be registered provisionally in a State Medical Register for the purpose of enabling him to be engaged in employment in a resident medical capacity in any approved institution, or in the Medical Service of the Armed Forces of the Union, and for no other purpose, on production of proper evidence that he has been selected for such employment.

(3) The names of all persons provisionally registered under sub-section (1) or sub-section (2) in a State Medical Register shall be entered therein separately from the names of other persons registered therein.

(4) A person registered provisionally as aforesaid who has completed practical training referred to in sub-section (1) or who has been engaged for the prescribed period in employment in a resident medical capacity in any approved institution or in the Medical Service of the Armed Forces of the Union, as the case may be, shall be entitled to registration in the State Medical Register under section 15.

26. Registration of additional qualification. (1) If any person whose name is entered in the Indian Medical Register obtains any title, diploma or other qualification for proficiency in sanitary science, public health or medicine, which is a recognised medical qualification, he shall, on application made in this behalf in the prescribed manner, be entitled to have an entry stating such other title, diploma, or other qualification made against his name in the Indian Medical Register either in substitution for or in addition to any entry previously made.

(2) The entries in respect of any such person in a State Medical Register shall be altered in accordance with the alterations made in the Indian Medical Register.

27. Privileges of persons who are enrolled on the Indian Medical Register. Subject to the conditions and restrictions laid down in this Act regarding medical practice by persons possessing certain recognised medical qualifications, every person whose name is for the time being borne on the Indian Medical Register shall be entitled according to his qualifications to practise as a medical practitioner in any part of India and to recover in due course of law in respect of such practice any expenses, charges in respect of medicaments or other appliances, or any fees to which he may be entitled.

28. Person enrolled on the Indian Medical Register to notify change of place of residence or practice. Every person registered in the Indian Medical Register shall notify any transfer of the place of his residence or practice to the Council and to the State Medical Council concerned, within thirty days of such transfer, failing which his right to participate in the election of members to the Council or a State Medical Council shall be liable to be forfeited by order of the Central Government either permanently or for such period as may be specified therein.

29. Information to be furnished by the Council and publication thereof. (1) The Council shall furnish such reports, copies of its minutes, abstracts of its accounts, and other information to the Central Government as that Government may require.

(2) The Central Government may publish in such manner as it may think fit, any report, copy, abstract or other information furnished to it under this section or under sections 17 and 18.

30. Commissions of Inquiry. (1) Whenever it is made to appear to the Central Government that the Council is not complying with any of the provisions of this Act, the Central Government may refer the particulars of the complaint to a Commission of Inquiry consisting of three persons, two of whom shall be appointed by the Central Government, one being a Judge of a High Court, and one by the Council, and such Commission shall proceed to inquire in summary manner and to report to the Central Government as to the truth of the matters charged in the complaint, and in case of any charge of default or of improper action being found by the Commission to have been established, the Commission shall recommend the remedies, if any, which are in its opinion necessary.

(2) The Central Government may require the Council to adopt the remedies so recommended within such time as, having regard to the report of the Commission, it may think fit, and if the Council fails to comply with any such requirement, the Central Government may amend the regulations of the Council, or make such provision or order or take such other steps as may seem necessary to give effect to the recommendations of the Commission.

(3) A Commission of Inquiry shall have power to administer oaths, to enforce the attendance of witnesses and the production of documents, and shall have all such other necessary powers for the purpose of any inquiry conducted by it as are exercised by a civil court under the Code of Civil Procedure, 1908.

31. Protection of action taken in good faith. No suit, prosecution or other legal proceeding shall lie against the Government, the Council or a State Medical Council or any Committee thereof, or any officer or servant of the Government or Councils aforesaid for anything which is in good faith done or intended to be done under this Act.

32. Power to make rules. (1) The Central Government may, by notification in the Official Gazette, make rules to carry out the purposes of this Act.

*[(2) Every rule made by the Central Government under this Act shall be laid, as soon as may be after it is made, before each House of Parliament, while it is in session, for a total period of thirty days which may be comprised in one session or in two or more successive sessions, and if, before the expiry of the session immediately following the session or the successive sessions aforesaid, both Houses agree in making any modification in the rule or both Houses agree that the rule should not be made, the rule shall thereafter have effect only in such modified form or be of no effect, as the case may be; so, however, that any such modification or annulment shall be without prejudice to the validity of anything previously done under that rule].

33. Power to make regulations. The Council may, with the previous sanction of the Central Government, make regulations generally to carry out the purposes of this Act, and, without prejudice to the generality of this power, such regulations may provide for—

(*a*) the management of the property of the Council and the maintenance and audit of its accounts;

(*b*) the summoning and holding of meetings of the Council, the times and places where such meetings are to be held, the

* *Substituted* by Act 32 of 2010, section 2 (w.r.e.f. 15-5-2010).

conduct of business threat and the number of members necessary to constitute a quorum;

(*c*) the resignation of members of the Council;

(*d*) the powers and duties of the President and Vice-President;

(*e*) the mode of appointment of the Executive Committee and other Committees, the summoning and holding of meetings, and the conduct of business of such Committees;

(*f*) the tenure of office, and the powers and duties of the Registrar and other officers and servants of the Council;

*[(*fa*) the form of the scheme, the particulars to be given in such scheme, the manner in which the scheme is to be preferred and the fee payable with the scheme under clause (*b*) of sub-section (2) of section 10A;

(*fb*) any other factors under clause (*g*) of sub-section (7) of section 10A;

(*fc*) the criteria for identifying a student who has been granted a medical qualification referred to in the Explanation to sub-section (3) of section 10B];

(*g*) the particulars to be stated, and the proof of qualifications to be given in applications for registration under this Act;

(*h*) the fees to be paid on applications and appeals under this Act;

(*i*) the appointment, powers, duties and procedure of medical inspectors and visitors;

(*j*) the courses and period of study and of practical training to be undertaken, the subjects of examination and the standards of proficiency therein to be obtained, in Universities or medical institutions for grant of recognised medical qualifications;

(*k*) the standards of staff, equipment, accommodation, training and other facilities for medical education;

(*l*) the conduct of professional examinations, qualifications of examiners and the conditions of admission to such examinations;

(*m*) the standards of professional conduct and etiquette and code of ethics to be observed by medical practitioners; and

---

* *Inserted* by Indian Medical Council (Amendment) Act, 1993 (w.r.e.f. 27.8.1992).

*[(*ma*) the modalities for conducting screening tests under sub-section (4A), and under the proviso to sub-section (4B), and for issuing eligibility certificate under sub-section (4B) of section 13;]

**[(*mb*) the designated authority, other languages and the manner of conducting of uniform entrance examination to all medical educational institutions at the undergraduate level and post-graduate level;]

(*n*) any matter for which under this Act provision may be made by regulations.

34. Repeal of Act 27 of 1933. (1) The Indian Medical Council Act, 1993, is hereby repealed.

(2) Notwithstanding anything contained in this Act, until the Council is constituted in accordance with the provisions of this Act—

(*a*) the Medical Council of India as constituted immediately before the commencement of this Act under the Indian Medical Council Act, 1933, with the addition of seven members nominated thereto by the Central Government from amongst persons enrolled on any of the State Medical Registers who possess the medical qualifications included in Part I of the Third Schedule to this Act (hereinafter referred to as the said Medical Council) shall be deemed to be Council constituted under this Act and may exercise any of the powers conferred or perform any of the duties imposed on the Council; and any vacancy occurring in the said Medical Council may be filled up in such manner as the Central Government may think fit; and

(*b*) the Executive Committee and other Committees of the said Medical Council as constituted immediately before the commencement of this Act shall be deemed to be the Executive Committee and other Committees constituted under this Act.

---

* *Inserted* by Indian Medical Council (Amendment) Act, 2001 (w.e.f. 3.9.2001).

** *Inserted* vide the Indian Medical Council (Amendment) Act, 2016 (w.e.f. 24.05.2016).

APPENDIX

6

The National Medical Commission Act, 2019

(No. 30 of 2019)

[8th August, 2019

An Act to provide for a medical education system that improves access to quality and affordable medical education, ensures availability of adequate and high quality medical professionals in all parts of the country; that promotes equitable and universal healthcare that encourages community health perspective and makes services of medical professionals accessible to all the citizens; that promotes national health goals; that encourages medical professionals to adopt latest medical research in their work and to contribute to research; that has an objective periodic and transparent assessment of medical institutions and facilitates maintenance of a medical register for India and enforces high ethical standards in all aspects of medical services; that is flexible to adapt to changing needs and has an effective grievance redressal mechanism and for matters connected therewith or incidental thereto.

BE it enacted by Parliament in the Seventieth Year of the Republic of India as follows:—

Chapter I

PRELIMINARY

1. Short title, extent and commencement. (1) This Act may be called the National Medical Commission Act, 2019.

(2) It extends to the whole of India.

(3) It shall come into force on such date* as the Central Government may, by notification in the Official Gazette, appoint, and different dates may be appointed for different provisions of this Act and any reference in any such provision to the commencement of this Act shall be construed as a reference to the coming into force of that provision.

2. **Definitions**. In this Act, unless the context otherwise requires—

(*a*) "Autonomous Board" means any of the Autonomous Boards constituted under section 16;

(*b*) "Chairperson" means the Chairperson of the National Medical Commission appointed under section 5;

(*c*) "Commission" means the National Medical Commission constituted under section 3;

(*d*) "Council" means the Medical Advisory Council constituted under section 11;

(*e*) "Ethics and Medical Registration Board" means the Board constituted under section 16;

(*f*) "health University" means a University specialised in affiliating institutions engaged in teaching medicine, medical and health sciences and includes a medical University and University of health sciences;

(*g*) "licence" means a licence to practice medicine granted under sub-section (1) of section 33;

(*h*) "Medical Assessment and Rating Board" means the Board constituted under section 16;

(*i*) "medical institution" means any institution within or outside India which grants degrees, diplomas or licences in medicine and include affiliated colleges and deemed to be Universities;

(*j*) "medicine" means modern scientific medicine in all its branches and includes surgery and obstetrics, but does not include veterinary medicine and surgery;

(*k*) "Member" means a Member of the Commission appointed under section 5 and includes the Chairperson thereof;

(*l*) "National Board of Examination" means the body registered as such under the Societies Registration Act, 1860 (21 of

---

* 2nd September, 2019—Sections 3, 4, 5, 6, 8, 11, 16, 17, 18, 19, 56 and 57, *vide* Notification No. S.O. 3162(E), dated 2nd September, 2019, *see* Gazette of India, Extraordinary, Part II, sec. 3(*ii*).

25th September, 2020—all the remaining provisions, *vide* Notification No. S.O. 3262(E), dated 24th September, 2020, *see* Gazette of India, Extraordinary, Part II, sec. 3, sub-section (*ii*) .

1860) which grants broad-speciality and super-speciality qualifications referred to in the Schedule;

(*m*) "National Register" means a National Medical Register maintained by the Ethics and Medical Registration Board under section 31;

(*n*) "notification" means notification published in the Official Gazette and the expression "notify" shall be construed accordingly;

(*o*) "Post-Graduate Medical Education Board" means the Board constituted under section 16;

(*p*) "prescribed" means prescribed by rules made under this Act;

(*q*) "President" means the President of an Autonomous Board appointed under section 18;

(*r*) "recognised medical qualification" means a medical qualification recognised under section 35 or section 36 or section 37 or section 40, as the case may be;

(*s*) "regulations" means the regulations made by the Commission under this Act;

(*t*) "Schedule" means the Schedule to this Act;

(*u*) "State Medical Council" means a medical council constituted under any law for the time being in force in any State or Union territory for regulating the practice and registration of practitioners of medicine in that State or Union territory;

(*v*) "State Register" means a register maintained under any law for the time being in force in any State or Union territory for registration of practitioners of medicine;

(*w*) "Under-Graduate Medical Education Board" means the Board constituted under section 16;

(*x*) "University" shall have the same meaning as assigned to it in clause *(f)* of section 2 of the University Grants Commission Act, 1956 (3 of 1956) and includes a health University.

Chapter II

THE NATIONAL MEDICAL COMMISSION

3. Constitution of National Medical Commission. (1) The Central Government shall constitute a Commission, to be known as the National Medical Commission, to exercise the powers conferred upon, and to perform the functions assigned to it, under this Act.

(2) The Commission shall be a body corporate by the name aforesaid, having perpetual succession and a common seal, with power, subject

to the provisions of this Act, to acquire, hold and dispose of property, both movable and immovable, and to contract, and shall, by the said name, sue or be sued.

(3) The head office of the Commission shall be at New Delhi.

4. Composition of Commission. (1) The Commission shall consist of the following persons to be appointed by the Central Government, namely:—

(*a*) a Chairperson;

(*b*) ten *ex officio* Members; and

(*c*) twenty-two part-time Members.

(2) The Chairperson shall be a medical professional of outstanding ability, proven administrative capacity and integrity, possessing a postgraduate degree in any discipline of medical sciences from any University and having experience of not less than twenty years in the field of medical sciences, out of which at least ten years shall be as a leader in the area of medical education.

(3) The following persons shall be the *ex officio* Members of the Commission, namely:—

(*a*) the President of the Under-Graduate Medical Education Board;

(*b*) the President of the Post-Graduate Medical Education Board;

(*c*) the President of the Medical Assessment and Rating Board;

(*d*) the President of the Ethics and Medical Registration Board;

(*e*) the Director General of Health Services, Directorate General of Health Services, New Delhi;

(*f*) the Director General, Indian Council of Medical Research;

(*g*) a Director of any of the All India Institutes of Medical Sciences, to be nominated by the Central Government;

(*h*) two persons from amongst the Directors of Postgraduate Institute of Medical Education and Research, Chandigarh; Jawaharlal Institute of Postgraduate Medical Education and Research, Puducherry; Tata Memorial Hospital, Mumbai; North Eastern Indira Gandhi Regional Institute of Health and Medical Sciences, Shillong; and All India Institute of Hygiene and Public Health, Kolkata; to be nominated by the Central Government; and

(*i*) one person to represent the Ministry of the Central Government dealing with Health and Family Welfare, not below the rank of Additional Secretary to the Government of India, to be nominated by that Ministry.

(4) The following persons shall be appointed as part-time Members of the Commission, namely:—

(*a*) three Members to be appointed from amongst persons of ability, integrity and standing, who have special knowledge and professional experience in such areas including management, law, medical ethics, health research, consumer or patient rights advocacy, science and technology and economics;

(*b*) ten Members to be appointed on rotational basis from amongst the nominees of the States and Union territories, under clauses (*c*) and (*d*) of sub-section (2) of section 11, in the Medical Advisory Council for a term of two years in such manner as may be prescribed;

(*c*) nine members to be appointed from amongst the nominees of the States and Union territories, under clause (*e*) of sub-section (2) of section 11, in the Medical Advisory Council for a term of two years in such manner as may be prescribed.

Explanation.—For the purposes of this section and section 17, the term "leader" means the Head of a Department or the Head of an organisation.

5. Search Committee for appointment of Chairperson and Members. (1) The Central Government shall appoint the Chairperson, part-time Members referred to in clause *(a)* of sub-section (4) of section 4 and the Secretary referred to in section 8 on the recommendation of a Search Committee consisting of—

(*a*) the Cabinet Secretary—Chairperson;

(*b*) three experts, possessing outstanding qualifications and experience of not less than twenty-five years in the field of medical education, public health education and health research, to be nominated by the Central Government—Members;

(*c*) one expert, from amongst the part-time Members referred to in clause (*c*) of sub-section (4) of section 4, to be nominated by the Central Government in such manner as may be prescribed-Member;

(*d*) one person, possessing outstanding qualifications and experience of not less than twenty-five years in the field of management or law or economics or science and technology, to be nominated by the Central Government—Member; and

(*e*) the Secretary to the Government of India in charge of the Ministry of Health and Family Welfare, to be the Convenor—Member.

(2) The Central Government shall, within one month from the date of occurrence of any vacancy, including by reason of death, resignation or removal of the Chairperson or a Member, or within three months before the end of tenure of the Chairperson or Member, make a reference to the Search Committee for filling up of the vacancy.

(3) The Search Committee shall recommend a panel of at least three names for every vacancy referred to it.

(4) The Search Committee shall, before recommending any person for appointment as the Chairperson or a Member of the Commission, satisfy itself that such person does not have any financial or other interest which is likely to affect prejudicially his functions as such Chairperson or Member.

(5) No appointment of the Chairperson or Member shall be invalid merely by reason of any vacancy or absence of a Member in the Search Committee.

(6) Subject to the provisions of sub-sections (2) to (5), the Search Committee may regulate its own procedure.

6. Term of office and conditions of service of Chairperson and Members. (1) The Chairperson and the part-time Members, other than the part-time Members appointed under clauses *(b)* and *(c)* of sub-section (4) of section 4, shall hold office for a term not exceeding four years and shall not be eligible for any extension or re-appointment:

Provided that such person shall cease to hold office after attaining the age of seventy years.

(2) The term of office of an *ex officio* Member shall continue as long as he holds the office by virtue of which he is such Member.

(3) Where a Member, other than an *ex officio* Member, is absent from three consecutive ordinary meetings of the Commission and the cause of such absence is not attributable to any valid reason in the opinion of the Commission, such Member shall be deemed to have vacated the seat.

(4) The salaries and allowances payable to, and other terms and conditions of service of, the Chairperson and Member, other than an *ex officio* Member, shall be such as may be prescribed.

(5) The Chairperson or a Member may,—

(a) relinquish his office by giving in writing to the Central Government a notice of not less than three months; or

(b) be removed from his office in accordance with the provisions of section 7:

Provided that such person may be relieved from duties earlier than three months or be allowed to continue beyond three months until a successor is appointed, if the Central Government so decides.

(6) The Chairperson and every member of the Commission shall make declaration of his assets and his liabilities at the time of entering upon his office and at the time of demitting his office and also declare his professional and commercial engagement or involvement in such form and manner as may be prescribed, and such declaration shall be published on the website of the Commission.

(7) The Chairperson or a Member, ceasing to hold office as such, shall not accept, for a period of two years from the date of demitting such office, any employment, in any capacity, including as a consultant or an expert, in any private medical institution, whose matter has been dealt with by such Chairperson or Member, directly or indirectly:

Provided that nothing herein shall be construed as preventing such person from accepting an employment in a body or institution, including medical institution, controlled or maintained by the Central Government or a State Government:

Provided further that nothing herein shall prevent the Central Government from permitting the Chairperson or a Member to accept any employment in any capacity, including as a consultant or expert in any private medical institution whose matter has been dealt with by such Chairperson or Member.

7. Removal of Chairperson and Member of Commission. (1) The Central Government may, by order, remove from office the Chairperson or any other Member, who—

(*a*) has been adjudged an insolvent; or

(*b*) has been convicted of an offence which, in the opinion of the Central Government, involves moral turpitude; or

(*c*) has become physically or mentally incapable of acting as a Member; or

(*d*) is of unsound mind and stands so declared by a competent court; or

(*e*) has acquired such financial or other interest as is likely to affect prejudicially his functions as a Member; or

(*f*) has so abused his position as to render his continuance in office prejudicial to public interest.

(2) No Member shall be removed under clauses (*e*) and (*f*) of sub-section (1) unless he has been given a reasonable opportunity of being heard in the matter.

8. Appointment of Secretary, experts, professionals, officers and other employees of Commission. (1) There shall be a Secretariat for the Commission to be headed by a Secretary, to be appointed by the Central Government in accordance with the provisions of section 5.

(2) The Secretary of the Commission shall be a person of proven administrative capacity and integrity, possessing such qualifications and experience as may be prescribed.

(3) The Secretary shall be appointed by the Central Government for a term of four years and shall not be eligible for any extension or re-appointment.

(4) The Secretary shall discharge such functions of the Commission as are assigned to him by the Commission and as may be specified by regulations made under this Act.

(5) The Commission may, for the efficient discharge of its functions under this Act, appoint such officers and other employees, as it considers necessary, against the posts created by the Central Government.

(6) The salaries and allowances payable to, and other terms and conditions of service of, the Secretary, officers and other employees of the Commission shall be such as may be prescribed.

(7) The Commission may engage, in accordance with the procedure specified by regulations, such number of experts and professionals of integrity and outstanding ability, who have special knowledge of, and experience in such fields, including medical education, public health, management, health economics, quality assurance, patient advocacy, health research, science and technology, administration, finance, accounts and law, as it deems necessary, to assist the Commission in the discharge of its functions under this Act.

9. Meetings, etc., of Commission. (1) The Commission shall meet at least once every quarter at such time and place as may be appointed by the Chairperson.

(2) The Chairperson shall preside at the meeting of the Commission, and if, for any reason, the Chairperson is unable to attend a meeting of the Commission, any other Member, being the President of an Autonomous Board, nominated by the Chairperson, shall preside at the meeting.

(3) Unless the procedure to be followed at the meetings of the Commission is otherwise provided by regulations, one-half of the total number of Members of the Commission including the Chairperson shall constitute the quorum and all the acts of the Commission shall be decided by a majority of the members, present and voting and in the event of equality of votes, the Chairperson, or in his absence, the

President of the Autonomous Board nominated under sub-section (2), shall have the casting vote.

(4) The general superintendence, direction and control of the administration of the Commission shall vest in the Chairperson.

(5) No act done by the Commission shall be questioned on the ground of the existence of a vacancy in, or a defect in the constitution of, the Commission.

(6) A person who is aggrieved by any decision of the Commission except the decision rendered under sub-section (4) of section 30 may prefer an appeal to the Central Government against such decision within thirty days of the communication of such decision.

10. Powers and functions of Commission. (1) The Commission shall perform the following functions, namely:—

(*a*) lay down policies for maintaining a high quality and high standards in medical education and make necessary regulations in this behalf;

(*b*) lay down policies for regulating medical institutions, medical researches and medical professionals and make necessary regulations in this behalf;

(*c*) assess the requirements in healthcare, including human resources for health and healthcare infrastructure and develop a road map for meeting such requirements;

(*d*) promote, co-ordinate and frame guidelines and lay down policies by making necessary regulations for the proper functioning of the Commission, the Autonomous Boards and the State Medical Councils;

(*e*) ensure co-ordination among the Autonomous Boards;

(*f*) take such measures, as may be necessary, to ensure compliance by the State Medical Councils of the guidelines framed and regulations made under this Act for their effective functioning under this Act;

(*g*) exercise appellate jurisdiction with respect to the decisions of the Autonomous Boards;

(*h*) lay down policies and codes to ensure observance of professional ethics in medical profession and to promote ethical conduct during the provision of care by medical practitioners;

(*i*) frame guidelines for determination of fees and all other charges in respect of fifty per cent. of seats in private medical institutions and deemed to be universities which are governed under the provisions of this Act;

(*j*) exercise such other powers and perform such other functions as may be prescribed.

(2) All orders and decisions of the Commission shall be authenticated by the signature of the Secretary.

(3) The Commission may delegate such of its powers of administrative and financial matters, as it deems fit, to the Secretary.

(4) The Commission may constitute sub-committees and delegate such of its powers to such sub-committees as may be necessary to enable them to accomplish specific tasks.

Chapter III

THE MEDICAL ADVISORY COUNCIL

11. Constitution and composition of Medical Advisory Council. (1) The Central Government shall constitute an advisory body to be known as the Medical Advisory Council.

(2) The Council shall consist of a Chairperson and the following members, namely:—

(*a*) the Chairperson of the Commission shall be the *ex officio* Chairperson of the Council;

(*b*) every member of the Commission shall be the *ex officio* members of the Council;

(*c*) one member to represent each State, who is the Vice-Chancellor of a health University in that State, to be nominated by that State Government;

(*d*) one member to represent each Union territory, who is the Vice-Chancellor of a health University in that Union territory, to be nominated by the Ministry of Home Affairs in the Government of India;

(*e*) one member to represent each State and each Union territory from amongst elected members of the State Medical Council, to be nominated by that State Medical Council;

(*f*) the Chairman, University Grants Commission;

(*g*) the Director, National Assessment and Accreditation Council;

(*h*) four members to be nominated by the Central Government from amongst persons holding the post of Director in the Indian Institutes of Technology, Indian Institutes of Management and the Indian Institute of Science:

Provided that if there is no health University in any State or Union territory, the Vice-Chancellor of a University within that State or Union territory having the largest number of medical colleges affiliated to it shall be nominated by the State Government or by the Ministry of Home Affairs in the Government of India:

Provided further that if there is no University in any Union territory, the Ministry of Home Affairs shall nominate a member who possesses such medical qualification and experience as may be prescribed.

12. Functions of Medical Advisory Council. (1) The Council shall be the primary platform through which the States and Union territories may put forth their views and concerns before the Commission and help in shaping the overall agenda, policy and action relating to medical education and training.

(2) The Council shall advise the Commission on measures to determine and maintain, and to co-ordinate maintenance of, the minimum standards in all matters relating to medical education, training and research.

(3) The Council shall advise the Commission on measures to enhance equitable access to medical education.

13. Meetings of Medical Advisory Council. (1) The Council shall meet at least twice a year at such time and place as may be decided by the Chairperson.

(2) The Chairperson shall preside at the meeting of the Council and if for any reason the Chairperson is unable to attend a meeting of the Council, such other member as nominated by the Chairperson shall preside over the meeting.

(3) Unless the procedure is otherwise provided by regulations, fifty per cent. of the members of the Council including the Chairperson shall form the quorum and all acts of the Council shall be decided by a majority of the members present and voting.

Chapter IV

NATIONAL EXAMINATION

14. National Eligibility-cum-Entrance Test. (1) There shall be a uniform National Eligibility-cum-Entrance Test for admission to the undergraduate and postgraduate super-speciality medical education in all medical institutions which are governed by the provisions of this Act:

Provided that the uniform National Eligibility-cum-Entrance Test for admission to the undergraduate medical education shall also be applicable to all medical institutions governed under any other law for the time being in force.

(2) The Commission shall conduct the National Eligibility-cum-Entrance Test in English and in such other languages, through such designated authority and in such manner, as may be specified by regulations.

(3) The Commission shall specify by regulations the manner of conducting common counselling by the designated authority for admission to undergraduate and postgraduate super-speciality seats in all the medical institutions which are governed by the provisions of this Act:

Provided that the designated authority of the Central Government shall conduct the common counselling for all India seats and the designated authority of the State Government shall conduct the common counselling for the seats at the State level.

15. National Exit Test. (1) A common final year undergraduate medical examination, to be known as the National Exit Test shall be held for granting licence to practice medicine as medical practitioners and for enrolment in the State Register or the National Register, as the case may be.

(2) The Commission shall conduct the National Exit Test through such designated authority and in such manner as may be specified by regulations.

(3) The National Exit Test shall become operational on such date, within three years from the date of commencement of this Act, as may be appointed by the Central Government, by notification.

(4) Any person with a foreign medical qualification shall have to qualify National Exit Test for the purpose of obtaining licence to practice medicine as medical practitioner and for enrolment in the State Register or the National Register, as the case may be, in such manner as may be specified by regulations.

(5) The National Exit Test shall be the basis for admission to the postgraduate broad-speciality medical education in medical institutions which are governed under the provisions of this Act or under any other law for the time being in force and shall be done in such manner as may be specified by regulations.

(6) The Commission shall specify by regulations the manner of conducting common counselling by the designated authority for admission to the postgraduate broad-speciality seats in the medical institutions referred to in sub-section (5):

Provided that the designated authority of the Central Government shall conduct the common counselling for All India seats and the designated authority of the State Government shall conduct the common counselling for the seats at the State level.

Chapter V
AUTONOMOUS BOARDS

16. Constitution of Autonomous Boards. (1) The Central Government shall, by notification, constitute the following Autonomous Boards, under the overall supervision of the Commission, to perform the functions assigned to such Boards under this Act, namely:—

(a) the Under-Graduate Medical Education Board;

(b) the Post-Graduate Medical Education Board;

(c) the Medical Assessment and Rating Board; and

(d) the Ethics and Medical Registration Board.

(2) Each Board referred to in sub-section (1) shall be an autonomous body which shall carry out its functions under this Act subject to the regulations made by the Commission.

17. Composition of Autonomous Boards. (1) Each Autonomous Board shall consist of a President and two whole-time Members and two part-time Members.

(2) The President of each Autonomous Board, three Members (including one part-time Member) of the Under-Graduate Medical Education Board and the Post-Graduate Medical Education Board, and two Members (including one part-time Member) each of the Medical Assessment and Rating Board and the Ethics and Medical Registration Board shall be persons of outstanding ability, proven administrative capacity and integrity, possessing a postgraduate degree in any discipline of medical sciences from any University and having experience of not less than fifteen years in such field, out of which at least seven years shall be as a leader in the area of medical education, public health, community medicine or health research.

(3) The third Member of the Medical Assessment and Rating Board shall be a person of outstanding ability and integrity, possessing a postgraduate degree in any of the disciplines of management, quality assurance, law or science and technology from any University, having not less than fifteen years' experience in such field, out of which at least seven years shall be as a leader.

(4) The third Member of the Ethics and Medical Registration Board shall be a person of outstanding ability who has demonstrated public record of work on medical ethics or a person of outstanding ability possessing a postgraduate degree in any of the disciplines of quality

assurance, public health, law or patient advocacy from any University and having not less than fifteen years' experience in such field, out of which at least seven years shall be as a leader.

(5) The fourth Member of each Autonomous Boards, being a part-time Member, shall be chosen from amongst the elected Members of the State Medical Council in such manner as may be prescribed.

18. Search Committee for appointment of President and Members. The Central Government shall appoint the President and Members of the Autonomous Boards, except Members referred to in sub-section (5) of section 17, on the recommendations made by the Search Committee constituted under section 5 in accordance with the procedure specified in that section.

19. Term of office and conditions of service of President and Members. (1) The President and Members (other than part-time Members) of each Autonomous Board shall hold the office for a term not exceeding four years and shall not be eligible for any extension or re-appointment:

Provided that part-time Members of each Autonomous Board shall hold the office for a term of two years:

Provided further that a Member shall cease to hold office after attaining the age of seventy years.

(2) The salaries and allowances payable to, and other terms and conditions of service of the President and Members (other than part-time Members) of an Autonomous Board shall be such as may be prescribed:

Provided that part-time Members of each Autonomous Board shall be entitled for such allowances as may be prescribed.

(3) The provisions of sub-sections (3), (5), (6), (7) and (8) of section 6 relating to other terms and conditions of service of, and section 7 relating to removal from the office of, the Chairperson and Members of the Commission shall also be applicable to the President and Members of the Autonomous Boards.

20. Advisory committees of experts. (1) Each Autonomous Board, except the Ethics and Medical Registration Board, shall be assisted by such advisory committees of experts as may be constituted by the Commission for the efficient discharge of the functions of such Boards under this Act.

(2) The Ethics and Medical Registration Board shall be assisted by such ethics committees of experts as may be constituted by the Commission for the efficient discharge of the functions of that Board under this Act.

21. Staff of Autonomous Boards. The experts, professionals, officers and other employees appointed under section 8 shall be made available to the Autonomous Boards in such number, and in such manner, as may be specified by regulations by the Commission.

22. Meetings, etc., of Autonomous Boards. (1) Every Autonomous Board shall meet at least once a month at such time and place as it may appoint.

(2) All decisions of the Autonomous Boards shall be made by majority of votes of the President and Members.

(*3*) Subject to the provision of section 28, a person who is aggrieved by any decision of an Autonomous Board may prefer an appeal to the Commission against such decision within sixty days of the communication of such decision.

23. Powers of Autonomous Boards and delegation of powers. (1) The President of each Autonomous Board shall have such administrative and financial powers as may be delegated to it by the Commission to enable such Board to function efficiently.

(2) The President of an Autonomous Board may further delegate any of his powers to a Member or an officer of that Board.

24. Powers and functions of Under-Graduate Medical Education Board. (1) The Under-Graduate Medical Education Board shall perform the following functions, namely:—

(*a*) determine standards of medical education at undergraduate level and oversee all aspects relating thereto;

(*b*) develop competency based dynamic curriculum at undergraduate level in accordance with the regulations made under this Act;

(*c*) develop competency based dynamic curriculum for addressing the needs of primary health services, community medicine and family medicine to ensure healthcare in such areas, in accordance with the provisions of the regulations made under this Act;

(*d*) frame guidelines for setting up of medical institutions for imparting undergraduate courses, having regard to the needs of the country and the global norms, in accordance with the provisions of the regulations made under this Act;

(*e*) determine the minimum requirements and standards for conducting courses and examinations for undergraduates in medical institutions, having regard to the needs of creativity at local levels, including designing of some courses by individual institutions, in accordance with the provisions of the regulations made under this Act;

(*f*) determine standards and norms for infrastructure, faculty and quality of education in medical institutions providing undergraduate medical education in accordance with the provisions of the regulations made under this Act;

(*g*) facilitate development and training of faculty members teaching undergraduate courses;

(*h*) facilitate research and the international student and faculty exchange programmes relating to undergraduate medical education;

(*i*) specify norms for compulsory annual disclosures, electronically or otherwise, by medical institutions, in respect of their functions that has a bearing on the interest of all stakeholders including students, faculty, the Commission and the Central Government;

(*j*) grant recognition to a medical qualification at the undergraduate level.

(2) The Under-Graduate Medical Education Board may, in the discharge of its duties, make such recommendations to, and seek such directions from, the Commission, as it deems necessary.

25. Powers and functions of Post-Graduate Medical Education Board. (1) The Post-Graduate Medical Education Board shall perform the following functions, namely:—

(*a*) determine the standards of medical education at the postgraduate level and super-speciality level in accordance with the regulations made under this Act and oversee all aspects relating thereto;

(*b*) develop competency based dynamic curriculum at postgraduate level and super-speciality level in accordance with the regulations made under this Act, with a view to develop appropriate skill, knowledge, attitude, values and ethics among postgraduates and super-specialists to provide healthcare, impart medical education and conduct medical research;

(c) frame guidelines for setting up of medical institutions for imparting postgraduate and super-speciality courses, having regard to the needs of the country and global norms, in accordance with the regulations made under this Act;

(*d*) determine the minimum requirements and standards for conducting postgraduate and super-speciality courses and examinations in medical institution, in accordance with the regulations made under this Act;

(*e*) determine standards and norms for infrastructure, faculty and quality of education in medical institutions conducting postgraduate and super-speciality medical education, in accordance with the regulations made under this Act;

(*f*) facilitate development and training of the faculty members teaching postgraduate and super-speciality courses;

(*g*) facilitate research and the international student and faculty exchange programmes relating to postgraduate and super-speciality medical education;

(*h*) specify norms for compulsory annual disclosure, electronically or otherwise, by medical institutions in respect of their functions that has a bearing on the interest of all stakeholders including students, faculty, the Commission and the Central Government;

(*i*) grant recognition to the medical qualifications at the postgraduate level and super-speciality level;

(*j*) promote and facilitate postgraduate courses in family medicine.

(2) The Post-Graduate Medical Education Board may, in the discharge of its functions, make such recommendations to, and seek such directions from, the Commission, as it deems necessary.

26. Powers and functions of Medical Assessment and Rating Board. (1) The Medical Assessment and Rating Board shall perform the following functions, namely:

(*a*) determine the procedure for assessing and rating the medical institutions for their compliance with the standards laid down by the Under-Graduate Medical Education Board or the Post-Graduate Medical Education Board, as the case may be, in accordance with the regulations made under this Act;

(*b*) grant permission for establishment of a new medical institution, or to start any postgraduate course or to increase number of seats, in accordance with the provisions of section 28;

(*c*) carry out inspections of medical institutions for assessing and rating such institutions in accordance with the regulations made under this Act:

Provided that the Medical Assessment and Rating Board may, if it deems necessary, hire and authorise any other third party agency or persons for carrying out inspections of medical institutions for assessing and rating such institutions:

Provided further that where inspection of medical institutions is carried out by such third party agency or persons authorised by the Medical Assessment and Rating Board, it shall be obligatory on such institutions to provide access to such agency or person;

(*d*) conduct, or where it deems necessary, empanel independent rating agencies to conduct, assess and rate all medical institutions, within such period of their opening, and every year thereafter, at such time, and in such manner, as may be specified by the regulations;

(*e*) make available on its website or in public domain the assessment and ratings of medical institutions at regular intervals in accordance with the regulations made under this Act;

(*f*) take such measures, including issuing warning, imposition of monetary penalty, reducing intake or stoppage of admissions and recommending to the Commission for withdrawal of recognition, against a medical institution for failure to maintain the minimum essential standards specified by the Under-Graduate Medical Education Board or the Post-Graduate Medical Education Board, as the case may be, in accordance with the regulations made under this Act.

(2) The Medical Assessment and Rating Board may, in the discharge of its functions, make such recommendations to, and seek such directions from, the Commission, as it deems necessary.

27. Powers and functions of Ethics and Medical Registration Board. (1) The Ethics and Medical Registration Board shall perform the following functions, namely:—

(*a*) maintain National Registers of all licensed medical practitioners in accordance with the provisions of section 31;

(*b*) regulate professional conduct and promote medical ethics in accordance with the regulations made under this Act:

Provided that the Ethics and Medical Registration Board shall ensure compliance of the code of professional and ethical conduct through the State Medical Council in a case where such State Medical Council has been conferred power to take disciplinary actions in respect of professional or ethical misconduct by medical practitioners under respective State Acts;

(c) develop mechanisms to have continuous interaction with State Medical Councils to effectively promote and regulate the conduct of medical practitioners and professionals;

(d) exercise appellate jurisdiction with respect to the actions taken by a State Medical Council under section 30.

(2) The Ethics and Medical Registration Board may, in the discharge of its duties, make such recommendations to, and seek such directions from, the Commission, as it deems necessary.

28. Permission for establishment of new medical college. (1) No person shall establish a new medical college or start any postgraduate course or increase number of seats without obtaining prior permission of the Medical Assessment and Rating Board.

(2) For the purposes of obtaining permission under sub-section (1), a person may submit a scheme to the Medical Assessment and Rating Board in such form, containing such particulars, accompanied by such fee, and in such manner, as may be specified by the regulations.

(3) The Medical Assessment and Rating Board shall, having due regard to the criteria specified in section 29, consider the scheme received under sub-section (2) and either approve or disapprove such scheme within a period of six months from the date of such receipt:

Provided that before disapproving such scheme, an opportunity to rectify the defects, if any, shall be given to the person concerned.

(4) Where a scheme is approved under sub-section (3), such approval shall be the permission under sub-section (1) to establish new medical college.

(5) Where a scheme is disapproved under sub-section (3), or where no decision is taken within six months of submitting a scheme under sub-section (1), the person concerned may prefer an appeal to the Commission for approval of the scheme within fifteen days of such disapproval or, as the case may be, lapse of six months, in such manner as may be specified by the regulations.

(6) The Commission shall decide the appeal received under sub-section (5) within a period of forty-five days from the date of receipt of the appeal and in case the Commission approves the scheme, such approval shall be the permission under sub-section (1) to establish a new medical college and in case the Commission disapproves the scheme, or fails to give its decision within the specified period, the person concerned may prefer a second appeal to the Central Government within thirty days of communication of such disapproval or, as the case may be, lapse of specified period.

(7) The Medical Assessment and Rating Board may conduct evaluation and assessment of any medical institution at any time, either directly or through any other expert having integrity and experience of medical profession and without any prior notice and assess and evaluate the performance, standards and benchmarks of such medical institution.

Explanation. For the purposes of this section, the term "person" includes a University, trust or any other association of persons or body of individuals, but does not include the Central Government.

29. Criteria for approving or disapproving scheme. While approving or disapproving a scheme under section 28, the Medical Assessment and Rating Board, or the Commission, as the case may be, shall take into consideration the following criteria, namely:—

(*a*) adequacy of financial resources;

(*b*) whether adequate academic faculty and other necessary facilities have been provided to ensure proper functioning of medical college or would be provided within the time-limit specified in the scheme;

(*c*) whether adequate hospital facilities have been provided or would be provided within the time-limit specified in the scheme;

(*d*) such other factors as may be prescribed:

Provided that, subject to the previous approval of the Central Government, the criteria may be relaxed for the medical colleges which are set up in such areas as may be specified by the regulations.

30. State Medical Councils. (1) The State Government shall, within three years of the commencement of this Act, take necessary steps to establish a State Medical Council if no such Council exists in that State.

(2) Where a State Act confers power upon the State Medical Council to take disciplinary actions in respect of any professional or ethical misconduct by a registered medical practitioner or professional, the State Medical Council shall act in accordance with the regulations made, and the guidelines framed, under this Act:

Provided that till such time as a State Medical Council is established in a State, the Ethics and Medical Registration Board shall receive the complaints and grievances relating to any professional or ethical misconduct against a registered medical practitioner or professional in that State in accordance with such procedure as may be specified by the regulations:

Provided further that the Ethics and Medical Registration Board or, as the case may be, the State Medical Council shall give an opportunity of hearing to the medical practitioner or professional concerned before taking any action, including imposition of any monetary penalty against such person.

(3) A medical practitioner or professional who is aggrieved by any action taken by a State Medical Council under sub-section (2) may prefer an appeal to the Ethics and Medical Registration Board against such action, and the decision, if any, of the Ethics and Medical Registration Board thereupon shall be binding on the State Medical Council, unless a second appeal is preferred under sub-section (4).

(4) A medical practitioner or professional who is aggrieved by the decision of the Ethics and Medical Registration Board may prefer an appeal to the Commission within sixty days of communication of such decision.

Explanation.—For the purposes of this Act—

(*a*) "State" includes Union territory and the expressions "State Government" and "State Medical Council", in relation to a Union territory, shall respectively mean the "Central Government" and "Union territory Medical Council";

(*b*) the expression "professional or ethical misconduct" includes any act of commission or omission as may be specified by the regulations.

31. National Register and State Register. (1) The Ethics and Medical Registration Board shall maintain a National Register containing the name, address, all recognised qualifications possessed by a licensed medical practitioner and such other particulars as may be specified by the regulations.

(2) The National Register shall be maintained in such form, including electronic form, in such manner, as may be specified by the regulations.

(3) The manner in which a name or qualification may be added to, or removed from, the National Register and the grounds for removal thereof, shall be such as may be specified by the regulations.

(4) The National Register shall be a public document within the meaning of section 74 of the Indian Evidence Act, 1872 (1 of 1872).

(5) The National Register shall be made available to the public by placing it on the website of the Ethics and Medical Registration Board.

(6) Every State Medical Council shall maintain and regularly update the State Register in the specified electronic format and supply a physical copy of the same to the Ethics and Medical Registration Board within three months of the commencement of this Act.

(7) The Ethics and Medical Registration Board shall ensure electronic synchronisation of the National Register and the State Register in such a manner that any change in one register is automatically reflected in the other register.

(8) The Ethics and Medical Registration Board shall maintain a separate National Register in such form, containing such particulars, including the name, address and all recognised qualifications possessed by a Community Health Provider referred to in section 32 in such manner as may be specified by the regulations.

32. Community Health Provider. (1) The Commission may grant limited licence to practice medicine at mid-level as Community Health Provider to such person connected with modern scientific medical profession who qualify such criteria as may be specified by the regulations:

Provided that the number of limited licence to be granted under this sub-section shall not exceed one-third of the total number of licenced medical practitioners registered under sub-section (1) of section 31.

(2) The Community Health Provider who is granted limited licences under sub-section (1), may practice medicine to such extent, in such circumstances and for such period, as may be specified by the regulations.

(3) The Community Health Provider may prescribe specified medicine independently, only in primary and preventive healthcare, but in cases other than primary and preventive healthcare, he may prescribe medicine only under the supervision of medical practitioners registered under sub-section (1) of section 31.

33. Rights of persons to have licence to practice and to be enrolled in National Register or State Register and their obligations thereto. (1) Any person who qualifies the National Exit Test held under section 15 shall be granted a licence to practice medicine and shall have his name and qualifications enrolled in the National Register or a State Register, as the case may be:

Provided that a person who has been registered in the Indian Medical Register maintained under the Indian Medical Council Act, 1956 (102 of 1956) prior to the coming into force of this Act and before the National Exit Test becomes operational under sub-section (3) of section 15, shall be deemed to have been registered under this Act and be enrolled in the National Register maintained under this Act.

(2) No person who has obtained medical qualification from a medical institution established in any country outside India and is recognised as a medical practitioner in that country, shall, after the commencement of this Act and the National Exit Test becomes operational under sub-section (3) of section 15, be enrolled in the National Register unless he qualifies the National Exit Test.

(3) When a person whose name is entered in the State Register or the National Register, as the case may be, obtains any title, diploma or other qualification for proficiency in sciences or public health or medicine which is a recognised medical qualification under section 35 or section 36, as the case may be, he shall be entitled to have such title, diploma or qualification entered against his name in the State Register or the National Register, as the case may be, in such manner as may be specified by the regulations.

34. Bar to practice. (1) No person other than a person who is enrolled in the State Register or the National Register, as the case may be, shall—

(*a*) be allowed to practice medicine as a qualified medical practitioner;

(*b*) hold office as a physician or surgeon or any other office, by whatever name called, which is meant to be held by a physician or surgeon;

(*c*) be entitled to sign or authenticate a medical or fitness certificate or any other certificate required by any law to be signed or authenticated by a duly qualified medical practitioner;

(*d*) be entitled to give evidence at any inquest or in any court of law as an expert under section 45 of the Indian Evidence Act, 1872 (1 of 1872) on any matter relating to medicine:

Provided that the Commission shall submit a list of such medical professionals to the Central Government in such manner as may be prescribed:

Provided further that a foreign citizen who is enrolled in his country as a medical practitioner in accordance with the law regulating the registration of medical practitioners in that country may be permitted temporary registration in India for such period and in such manner as may be specified by the regulations.

(2) Any person who contravenes any of the provisions of this section shall be punished with imprisonment for a term which may extend to

one year, or with fine which may extend to five lakh rupees or with both.

Chapter VI
RECOGNITION OF MEDICAL QUALIFICATIONS

35. Recognition of medical qualifications granted by Universities or medical institutions in India.—(1) The medical qualification granted by any University or medical institution in India shall be listed and maintained by the Under-Graduate Medical Education Board or the Post-Graduate Medical Education Board, as the case may be, in such manner as may be specified by the regulations and such medical qualification shall be a recognised medical qualification for the purposes of this Act.

(2) Any University or medical institution in India which grants an undergraduate or postgraduate or super-speciality medical qualification not included in the list maintained by the Under-Graduate Medical Education Board or the Post-Graduate Medical Education Board, as the case may be, may apply to that Board for granting recognition to such qualification.

(3) The Under-Graduate Medical Education Board or the Post-Graduate Medical Education Board, as the case may be, shall examine the application for grant of recognition to a medical qualification within a period of six months in such manner as may be specified by the regulations.

(4) Where the Under-Graduate Medical Education Board or the Post-Graduate Medical Education Board, as the case may be, decides to grant recognition to a medical qualification, it shall include such medical qualification in the list maintained by it and also specify the date of effect of such recognition.

(5) Where the Under-Graduate Medical Education Board or the Post-Graduate Medical Education Board, as the case may be, decides not to grant recognition to a medical qualification, the University or the medical institution concerned may prefer an appeal to the Commission for grant of recognition within sixty days of the communication of such decision, in such manner as may be specified by the regulations.

(6) The Commission shall examine the appeal received under sub-section (5) within a period of two months and if it decides that recognition may be granted to such medical qualification, it may direct the Under-Graduate Medical Education Board or the Post-Graduate Medical Education Board, as the case may be, to include such medical

qualification in the list maintained by that Board, in such manner as may be specified by the regulations.

(7) Where the Commission decides not to grant recognition to the medical qualification, or fails to take a decision within the specified period, the University or the medical institution concerned may prefer a second appeal to the Central Government within thirty days of the communication of such decision or lapse of specified period, as the case may be.

(8) All medical qualifications which have been recognised before the date of commencement of this Act and are included in the First Schedule and Part I of the Third Schedule to the Indian Medical Council Act, 1956 (102 of 1956), shall also be recognised medical qualifications for the purposes of this Act, and shall be listed and maintained by the Under-Graduate Medical Education Board or the Post-Graduate Medical Education Board, as the case may be, in such manner as may be specified by the regulations.

36. Recognition of medical qualifications granted by medical institutions outside India. (1) Where an authority in any country outside India, which by the law of that country is entrusted with the recognition of medical qualifications in that country, makes an application to the Commission for granting recognition to such medical qualification in India, the Commission may, subject to such verification as it may deem necessary, either grant or refuse to grant recognition to that medical qualification:

Provided that the Commission shall give a reasonable opportunity of being heard to such authority before refusing to grant such recognition.

(2) A medical qualification which is granted recognition by the Commission under sub-section (1) shall be a recognised medical qualification for the purposes of this Act, and such qualification shall be listed and maintained by the Commission in such manner as may be specified by the regulations.

(3) Where the Commission refuses to grant recognition to the medical qualification under sub-section (1), the authority concerned may prefer an appeal to the Central Government against such decision within thirty days of communication thereof.

(4) All medical qualifications which have been recognised before the date of commencement of this Act and are included in the Second Schedule and Part II of the Third Schedule to the Indian Medical Council Act, 1956 (102 of 1956), shall also be recognised medical qualifications for the purposes of this Act, and shall be listed and

maintained by the Commission in such manner as may be specified by the regulations.

37. Recognition of medical qualifications granted by statutory or other body in India. (1) The medical qualifications granted by any statutory or other body in India which are covered by the categories listed in the Schedule shall be recognised medical qualifications for the purposes of this Act.

(2) The Diplomate of National Board in broad-speciality qualifications and superspeciality qualifications when granted in a medical institution with attached hospital or in a hospital with the strength of five hundred or more beds, by the National Board of Examinations, shall be equivalent in all respects to the corresponding postgraduate qualification and the super-speciality qualification granted under this Act, but in all other cases, senior residency in a medical college for an additional period of one year shall be required for such qualification to be equivalent for the purposes of teaching also.

(3) The Central Government may, on the recommendation of the Commission, and having regard to the objects of this Act, by notification, add to, or, as the case may be, omit from, the Schedule any categories of medical qualifications granted by a statutory or other body in India and on such addition, or as the case may be, omission, the medical qualifications granted by such statutory or other body in India shall be, or shall cease to be, recognised medical qualifications for the purposes of this Act.

38. Withdrawal of recognition granted to medical qualification granted by medical institutions in India. (1) Where, upon receiving a report from the Medical Assessment and Rating Board under section 26, or otherwise, if the Commission is of the opinion that—

(*a*) the courses of study and examination to be undergone in, or the proficiency required from candidates at any examination held by, a University or medical institution do not conform to the standards specified by the Under-Graduate Medical Education Board or the Post-Graduate Medical Education Board, as the case may be; or

(*b*) the standards and norms for infrastructure, faculty and quality of education in medical institution as determined by the Under-Graduate Medical Education Board or the Post-Graduate Medical Education Board, as the case may be, are not adhered to by any University or medical institution, and such University or medical institution has failed to take necessary corrective action to maintain specified minimum

standards, the Commission may initiate action in accordance with the provisions of sub-section (2):

Provided that the Commission shall, before taking any action for *suo motu* withdrawal of recognition granted to the medical qualification awarded by a University or medical institution, impose penalty in accordance with the provisions of clause *(f)* of sub-section (1) of section 26.

(2) The Commission shall, after making such further inquiry as it deems fit, and after holding consultations with the concerned State Government and the authority of the concerned University or medical institution, comes to the conclusion that the recognition granted to a medical qualification ought to be withdrawn, it may, by order, withdraw recognition granted to such medical qualification and direct the Under-Graduate Medical Education Board or the Post-Graduate Medical Education Board, as the case may be, to amend the entries against the University or medical institution concerned in the list maintained by that Board to the effect that the recognition granted to such medical qualification is withdrawn with effect from the date specified in that order.

39. Derecognition of medical qualifications granted by medical institutions outside India. Where, after verification with the authority in any country outside India, the Commission is of the opinion that a recognised medical qualification which is included in the list maintained by it is to be derecognised, it may, by order, derecognise such medical qualification and remove it from the list maintained by the Commission with effect from the date of such order.

40. Special provision in certain cases for recognition of medical qualifications. Where the Commission deems it necessary, it may, by an order published in the Official Gazette, direct that any medical qualification granted by a medical institution in a country outside India, after such date as may be specified in that notification, shall be a recognised medical qualification for the purposes of this Act:

Provided that medical practice by a person possessing such qualification shall be permitted only if such person qualifies National Exit Test.

Chapter VII

GRANTS, AUDIT AND ACCOUNTS

41. Grants by Central Government. The Central Government may, after due appropriation made by Parliament by law in this behalf, make to the Commission grants of such sums of money as the Central Government may think fit.

42. National Medical Commission Fund. (1) There shall be constituted a fund to be called "the National Medical Commission Fund" which shall form part of the public account of India and there shall be credited thereto—

(*a*) all Government grants, fees, penalties and charges received by the Commission and the Autonomous Boards;

(*b*) all sums received by the Commission from such other sources as may be decided by it.

(2) The Fund shall be applied for making payment towards—

(*a*) the salaries and allowances payable to the Chairperson and Members of the Commission, the Presidents and Members of the Autonomous Boards and the administrative expenses including the salaries and allowances payable to the officers and other employees of the Commission and Autonomous Boards;

(*b*) the expenses incurred in carrying out the provisions of this Act, including in connection with the discharge of the functions of the Commission and the Autonomous Boards.

43. Audit and accounts. (1) The Commission shall maintain proper accounts and other relevant records and prepare an annual statement of accounts in such form as may be prescribed, in consultation with the Comptroller and Auditor-General of India.

(2) The accounts of the Commission shall be audited by the Comptroller and Auditor-General of India at such intervals as may be specified by him and any expenditure incurred in connection with such audit shall be payable by the Commission to the Comptroller and Auditor-General of India.

(3) The Comptroller and Auditor-General of India and any other persons appointed by him in connection with the audit of the accounts of the Commission shall have the same rights and privileges and authority in connection with such audit as the Comptroller and Auditor-General generally has in connection with the audit of Government accounts and in particular, shall have the right to demand the production of, and complete access to, records, books, accounts, connected vouchers and other documents and papers and to inspect the office of the Commission.

(4) The accounts of the Commission as certified by the Comptroller and Auditor-General of India or any other person appointed by him in this behalf, together with the audit report thereon, shall be forwarded annually by the Commission to the Central Government which shall cause the same to be laid, as soon as may be after it is received, before each House of Parliament.

44. Furnishing of returns and reports to Central Government. (1) The Commission shall furnish to the Central Government, at such time, in such form and in such manner, as may be prescribed or as the Central Government may direct, such reports and statements, containing such particulars in regard to any matter under the jurisdiction of the Commission, as the Central Government may, from time to time, require.

(2) The Commission shall prepare, once every year, in such form and at such time as may be prescribed, an annual report, giving a summary of its activities during the previous year and copies of the report shall be forwarded to the Central Government.

(3) A copy of the report received under sub-section (2) shall be laid by the Central Government, as soon as may be after it is received, before each House of Parliament.

Chapter VIII

MISCELLANEOUS

45. Power of Central Government to give directions to Commission and Autonomous Boards. (1) Without prejudice to the foregoing provisions of this Act, the Commission and the Autonomous Boards shall, in exercise of their powers and discharge of their functions under this Act, be bound by such directions on questions of policy as the Central Government may give in writing to them from time to time:

Provided that the Commission and the Autonomous Boards shall, as far as practicable, be given an opportunity to express their views before any direction is given under this sub-section.

(2) The decision of the Central Government whether a question is one of policy or not shall be final.

46. Power of Central Government to give directions to State Governments. The Central Government may give such directions, as it may deem necessary, to a State Government for carrying out all or any of the provisions of this Act and the State Government shall comply with such directions.

47. Information to be furnished by Commission and publication thereof. (1) The Commission shall furnish such reports, copies of its minutes, abstracts of its accounts, and other information to the Central Government as that Government may require.

(2) The Central Government may publish, in such manner as it may think fit, the reports, minutes, abstracts of accounts and other information furnished to it under sub-section (1).

48. Obligation of universities and medical institutions. Every University and medical institution governed under this Act shall maintain a website at all times and display on its website all such information as may be required by the Commission or an Autonomous Board, as the case may be.

49. Completion of courses of studies in medical institutions. (1) Notwithstanding anything contained in this Act, any student who was studying for a degree, diploma or certificate in any medical institution immediately before the commencement of this Act shall continue to so study and complete his course for such degree, diploma or certificate, and such institution shall continue to provide instructions and examination for such student in accordance with the syllabus and studies as existed before such commencement, and such student shall be deemed to have completed his course of study under this Act and shall be awarded degree, diploma or certificate under this Act.

(2) Notwithstanding anything contained in this Act, where recognition granted to a medical institution has lapsed, whether by efflux of time or by its voluntary surrender or for any other reason whatsoever, such medical institution shall continue to maintain and provide the minimum standards required to be provided under this Act till such time as all candidates who are admitted in that medical institution complete their study.

50. Joint sittings of Commission, Central Councils of Homoeopathy and Indian medicine to enhance interface between their respective systems of medicine. (1) There shall be a joint sitting of the Commission, the Central Council of Homoeopathy and the Central Council of Indian Medicine at least once a year, at such time and place as they mutually appoint, to enhance the interface between Homoeopathy, Indian Systems of Medicine and modern systems of medicine.

(2) The agenda for the joint sitting may be prepared with mutual agreement between the Chairpersons of the Commission, the Central Council of Homoeopathy and the Central Council of Indian Medicine or be prepared separately by each of them.

(3) The joint sitting referred to in sub-section (1) may, by an affirmative vote of all members present and voting, decide on approving specific educational modules or programmes that may be introduced in the undergraduate course and the postgraduate course across medical systems and promote medical pluralism.

51. State Government to promote primary healthcare in rural areas. Every State Government may, for the purposes of addressing or promoting primary healthcare in rural area, take necessary measures to enhance the capacity of the healthcare professionals.

52. Chairperson, Members, officers of Commission and of Autonomous Boards to be public servants. The Chairperson, Members, officers and other employees of the Commission and the President, Members and officers and other employees of the Autonomous Boards shall be deemed, when acting or purporting to act in pursuance of any of the provisions of this Act, to be public servants within the meaning of section 21 of the Indian Penal Code, 1860 (45 of 1860).

53. Protection of action taken in good faith. No suit, prosecution or other legal proceeding shall lie against the Government, the Commission or any Autonomous Board or a State Medical Council or any Committee thereof, or any officer or other employee of the Government or of the Commission acting under this Act for anything which is in good faith done or intended to be done under this Act or the rules or regulations made thereunder.

54. Cognizance of offences. No court shall take cognizance of an offence punishable under this Act except upon a complaint in writing made in this behalf by an officer authorised by the Commission or the Ethics and Medical Registration Board or a State Medical Council, as the case may be.

55. Power of Central Government to supersede Commission. (1) If, at any time, the Central Government is of opinion that—

(*a*) the Commission is unable to discharge the functions and duties imposed on it by or under the provisions of this Act; or

(*b*) the Commission has persistently made default in complying with any direction issued by the Central Government under this Act or in the discharge of the functions and duties imposed on it by or under the provisions of this Act,

the Central Government may, by notification, supersede the Commission for such period, not exceeding six months, as may be specified in the notification:

Provided that before issuing a notification under this sub-section, the Central Government shall give a reasonable opportunity to the Commission to show cause as to why it should not be superseded and shall consider the explanations and objections, if any, of the Commission.

(2) Upon the publication of a notification under sub-section (1) superseding the Commission,—

(*a*) all the Members shall, as from the date of supersession, vacate their offices as such;

(*b*) all the powers, functions and duties which may, by or under the provisions of this Act, be exercised or discharged by or on behalf of the Commission, shall, until the Commission is re-constituted under sub-section (3), be exercised and discharged by such person or persons as the Central Government may direct;

(*c*) all property owned or controlled by the Commission shall, until the Commission is re-constituted under sub-section (3), vest in the Central Government.

(3) On the expiration of the period of supersession specified in the notification issued under sub-section (1), the Central Government may,—

(*a*) extend the period of supersession for such further term not exceeding six months, as it may consider necessary; or

(*b*) re-constitute the Commission by fresh appointment and in such case the Members who vacated their offices under clause (*a*) of sub-section (2) shall not be deemed disqualified for appointment:

Provided that the Central Government may, at any time before the expiration of the period of supersession, whether as originally specified under sub-section (1) or as extended under this sub-section, take action under clause (*b*) of this sub-section.

(4) The Central Government shall cause a notification issued under sub-section (1) and a full report of any action taken under this section and the circumstances leading to such action to be laid before both Houses of Parliament at the earliest opportunity.

56. Power to make rules. (1) The Central Government may, by notification, make rules to carry out the purposes of this Act.

(2) In particular, and without prejudice to the generality of the foregoing power, such rules may provide for all or any of the following matters, namely:—

(*a*) the manner of appointing ten Members of the Commission on rotational basis from amongst the nominees of the States and Union territories in the Medical Advisory Council under clause (*b*) of sub-section (4) of section 4;

(*b*) the manner of appointing nine members of the Commission under clause (c) of sub-section (4) of section 4;

(*c*) the manner of nominating one expert by the Central Government under clause (c) of sub-section (1) of section 5;

(*d*) the salary and allowances payable to, and other terms and conditions of service of the Chairperson and Members under sub-section (4) of section 6;

(*e*) the form and the manner of making declaration under sub-section (6) of section 6;

(*f*) the qualifications and experience to be possessed by the Secretary of the Commission under sub-section (2) of section 8;

(*g*) the salaries and allowances payable to, and other terms and conditions of service of the Secretary, officers and other employees of the Commission under sub-section (6) of section 8;

(*h*) the other powers and functions of the Commission under clause (*j*) of sub-section (1) of section 10;

(i) the medical qualification and experience to be possessed by a member under the second proviso to section 11;

(*j*) the manner of choosing part-time Members under sub-section (5) of section 17;

(*k*) the salary and allowances payable to, and other terms and conditions of service of the President and Members of an Autonomous Board under sub-section (2), and the allowances payable to part-time Members under the proviso thereunder, of section 19;

(*l*) the other factors under clause (*d*) of section 29;

(*m*) the manner of submitting a list of medical professionals under the first proviso to sub-section (1) of section 34;

(*n*) the form for preparing annual statement of accounts under sub-section (1) of section 43;

(*o*) the time within which, and the form and the manner in which, the reports and statements shall be furnished by the Commission and the particulars with regard to any matter as may be required by the Central Government under sub-section (1) of section 44;

(*p*) the form and the time for preparing annual report under sub-section (2) of section 44;

(*q*) any other matter in respect of which provision is to be made by rules.

57. Power to make regulations. (1) The Commission may, after previous publication, by notification, make regulations consistent with this Act and the rules made thereunder to carry out the provisions of this Act.

(2) In particular, and without prejudice to the generality of the foregoing power, such regulations may provide for all or any of the following matters, namely:—

(*a*) the functions to be discharged by the Secretary of the Commission under sub-section (4) of section 8;

(*b*) the procedure in accordance with which experts and professionals may be engaged and the number of such experts and professionals under sub-section (7) of section 8;

(*c*) the procedure to be followed at the meetings of Commission, including the quorum at its meetings under sub-section (3) of section 9;

(*d*) the quality and standards to be maintained in medical education under clause (*a*) of sub-section (1) of section 10;

(*e*) the manner of regulating medical institutions, medical researches and medical professionals under clause (*b*) of sub-section (1) of section 10;

(*f*) the manner of functioning of the Commission, the Autonomous Boards and the State Medical Councils under clause (*d*) of sub-section (1) of section 10;

(*g*) the procedure to be followed at the meetings of the Medical Advisory Council, including the quorum at its meetings under sub-section (3) of section 13;

(*h*) the other languages in which and the manner in which the National Eligibility-cum-Entrance Test shall be conducted under sub-section (2) of section 14;

(*i*) the manner of conducting common counselling by the designated authority for admission to the undergraduate and postgraduate super-speciality medical education under sub-section (3) of section 14;

(*j*) the designated authority, and the manner for conducting the National Exit Test under sub-section (2) of section 15;

(*k*) the manner in which a person with foreign medical qualification shall qualify National Exit Test under sub-section (4) of section 15;

(*l*) the manner in which admission to the postgraduate broad-speciality medical education shall be made on the basis of National Exit Test under sub-section (5) of section 15;

(*m*) the manner of conducting common counselling by the designated authority for admission to the postgraduate broad-speciality medical education under sub-section (6) of section 15;

(*n*) the number of, and the manner in which, the experts, professionals, officers and other employees shall be made available by the Commission to the Autonomous Boards under section 21;

(*o*) the curriculum at undergraduate level under clause (*b*) of sub-section (1) of section 24;

(*p*) the curriculum for primary medicine, community medicine and family medicine under clause (*c*) of sub-section (1) of section 24;

(*q*) the manner of imparting undergraduate courses by medical institutions under clause (*d*) of sub-section (1) of section 24;

(*r*) the minimum requirements and standards for conducting courses and examinations for undergraduates in medical institutions under clause (*e*) of sub-section (1) of section 24;

(*s*) the standards and norms for infrastructure, faculty and quality of education at undergraduate level in medical institutions under clause (*f*) of sub-section (1) of section 24;

(*t*) the standards of medical education at the postgraduate level and superspeciality level under clause (*a*) of sub-section (1) of section 25;

(*u*) the curriculum at postgraduate level and super-speciality level under clause (*b*) of sub-section (1) of section 25;

(*v*) the manner of imparting postgraduate and super-speciality courses by medical institutions under clause (*c*) of sub-section (1) of section 25;

(*w*) the minimum requirements and standards for conducting postgraduate and super-speciality courses and examinations in medical institutions under clause (*d*) of sub-section (1) of section 25;

(*x*) the standards and norms for infrastructure, faculty and quality of education in medical institutions conducting postgraduate and super-speciality medical education under clause (*e*) of sub-section (1) of section 25;

(*y*) the procedure for assessing and rating the medical institutions under clause (*a*) of sub-section (1) of section 26;

(*z*) the manner of carrying out inspections of medical institutions for assessing and rating such institutions under clause (*c*) of sub-section (1) of section 26;

(*za*) the manner of conducting, and the manner of empanelling independent rating agencies to conduct, assessment and rating of medical institutions under clause (*d*) of sub-section (1) of section 26;

(*zb*) the manner of making available on website or in public domain the assessment and ratings of medical institutions under clause (*e*) of sub-section (1) of section 26;

(*zc*) the measures to be taken against a medical institution for its failure to maintain the minimum essential standards under clause (*f*) of sub-section (1) of section 26;

(*zd*) the manner of regulating professional conduct and promoting medical ethics under clause (*b*) of sub-section (1) of section 27;

(*ze*) the form of scheme, the particulars thereof, the fee to be accompanied and the manner of submitting scheme for establishing a new medical college or for starting any postgraduate course or for increasing number of seats under sub-section (2) of section 28;

(*zf*) the manner of making an appeal to the Commission for approval of the scheme under sub-section (5) of section 28;

(*zg*) the areas in respect of which criteria may be relaxed under the proviso to section 29;

(*zh*) the manner of taking disciplinary action by a State Medical Council for professional or ethical misconduct of registered medical practitioner or professional and the procedure for receiving complaints and grievances by Ethics and Medical Registration Board, under sub-section (2) of section 30;

(*zi*) the act of commission or omission which amounts to professional or ethical misconduct under clause (*b*) of the Explanation to section 30;

(*zj*) other particulars to be contained in a National Register under sub-section (1) of section 31;

(*zk*) the form, including the electronic form and the manner of maintaining the National Register under sub-section (2) of section 31;

(*zl*) the manner in which any name or qualification may be added to, or removed from, the National Register and the grounds for removal thereof, under sub-section (3) of section 31;

(*zm*) the form and manner in which the National Register for registering Community Health Provider is to be maintained under sub-section (8) of section 31;

(*zn*) the criteria for granting limited licence to practice medicine under sub-section (1) of section 32;

(*zo*) the extent, the circumstances and the period under sub-section (2) of section 32;

(*zp*) the manner of listing and maintaining medical qualifications granted by a University or medical institution in India under sub-section (1) of section 35;

(*zq*) the manner of examining the application for grant of recognition under sub-section (*3*) of section 35;

(*zr*) the manner of preferring an appeal to the Commission for grant of recognition under sub-section (5) of section 35;

(*zs*) the manner of including a medical qualification in the list maintained by the Board under sub-section (6) of section 35;

(*zt*) the manner of listing and maintaining medical qualifications which have been granted recognition before the date of commencement of this Act under sub-section (8) of section 35.

58. Rules and regulations to be laid before Parliament. Every rule and every regulation made, and every notification issued, under this Act shall be laid, as soon as may be after it is made, before each House of Parliament, while it is in session, for a total period of thirty days which may be comprised in one session or in two or more successive sessions, and if, before the expiry of the session immediately following the session or the successive sessions aforesaid, both Houses agree in making any modification in the rule or regulation or notification; both Houses agree that the rule or regulation or notification should not be made, the rule or regulation or notification shall thereafter have effect only in such modified form or be of no effect, as the case may be; so, however, that any such modification or annulment shall be without prejudice to the validity of anything previously done under that rule or regulation or notification.

59. Power to remove difficulties. (1) If any difficulty arises in giving effect to the provisions of this Act, the Central Government may, by order published in the Official Gazette, make such provisions not inconsistent with the provisions of this Act, as may appear to it to be necessary, for removing the difficulty:

Provided that no order shall be made under this section after the expiry of a period of two years from the commencement of this Act.

(2) Every order made under this section shall be laid, as soon as may be after it is made, before each House of Parliament.

60. Repeal and saving. (1) With effect from such date as the Central Government may appoint in this behalf, the Indian Medical Council Act, 1956 (102 of 1956) shall stand repealed and the Medical Council of India constituted under sub-section (1) of section 3 of the said Act shall stand dissolved.

(2) Notwithstanding the repeal of the Act referred to in sub-section (1), it shall not affect,—

(*a*) the previous operation of the Act so repealed or anything duly done or suffered thereunder; or

(*b*) any right, privilege, obligation or liability acquired, accrued or incurred under the Act so repealed; or

(*c*) any penalty incurred in respect of any contravention under the Act so repealed; or

(*d*) any proceeding or remedy in respect of any such right, privilege, obligation, liability, penalty as aforesaid, and any such proceeding or remedy may be instituted, continued or enforced, and any such penalty may be imposed as if that Act had not been repealed.

(3) On the dissolution of the Medical Council of India, the person appointed as the Chairman of the Medical Council of India and every other person appointed as the Member and any officer and other employee of that Council and holding office as such immediately before such dissolution shall vacate their respective offices and such Chairman and other Members shall be entitled to claim compensation not exceeding three months' pay and allowances for the premature termination of term of their office or of any contract of service:

Provided that any officer or other employee who has been, immediately before the dissolution of the Medical Council of India appointed on deputation basis to the Medical Council of India, shall, on such dissolution, stand reverted to his parent cadre, Ministry or Department, as the case may be:

Provided further that any officer or other employee who has been, immediately before the dissolution of the Medical Council of India, employed on regular or contractual basis by the Medical Council of India, shall, on and from such dissolution, cease to be the officer or employee of the Medical Council of India and his employment in the Medical Council of India stand terminated with immediate effect:

Provided also that such officer or employee of the Medical Council of India shall be entitled to such compensation for the premature termination of his employment, which shall not be less than three months' pay and allowances, as may be prescribed.

(4) Notwithstanding the repeal of the aforesaid enactment, any order made, any licence to practice issued, any registration made, any permission to start new medical college or to start higher course of

studies or for increase in the admission capacity granted, any recognition of medical qualifications granted, under the Indian Medical Council Act, 1956 (102 of 1956), which are in force as on the date of commencement of this Act, shall continue to be in force till the date of their expiry for all purposes, as if they had been issued or granted under the provisions of this Act or the rules or regulations made thereunder.

61. Transitory provisions. (1) The Commission shall be the successor in interest to the Medical Council of India including its subsidiaries or owned trusts and all the assets and liabilities of the Medical Council of India shall be deemed to have been transferred to the Commission.

(2) Notwithstanding the repeal of the Indian Medical Council Act, 1956 (102 of 1956), the educational standards, requirements and other provisions of the Indian Medical Council Act, 1956 and the rules and regulations made thereunder shall continue to be in force and operate till new standards or requirements are specified under this Act or the rules and regulations made thereunder:

Provided that anything done or any action taken as regards the educational standards and requirements under the enactment under repeal and the rules and regulations made thereunder shall be deemed to have been done or taken under the corresponding provisions of this Act and shall continue in force accordingly unless and until superseded by anything done or by any action taken under this Act.

THE SCHEDULE

[*See* section 37]

List of Categories of Medical Qualifications Granted by Statutory Body or Other Body in India

Sl. No.	*Categories of medical qualifications*
1.	All medical qualifications granted by the Jawaharlal Institute of Postgraduate Medical Education and Research, Puducherry.
2.	All medical qualifications granted by All India Institutes of Medical Sciences.
3.	All medical qualifications granted by the Postgraduate Institute of Medical Education and Research, Chandigarh.
4.	All medical qualifications granted by the National Institute of Mental Health and Neuro-Sciences, Bangalore.
5.	All medical qualifications granted by the National Board of Examination.

APPENDIX

7

The Legal Representatives' Suits Act, 1855

1. Executors may sue and be sued in certain cases for wrongs committed in life time of deceased. An action may be maintained by the executors, administrators or representatives of any person deceased, for any wrong committed in the life time of such person, which has occasioned pecuniary loss to his estate, for which wrong an action might have been maintained by such person, so as such wrong shall have been committed within one year before his death; and the damages when recovered, shall be part of the personal estate of such person;

and further, an action may be maintained against the executors or administrators or heirs or representatives of any person deceased for any wrong committed by him in his lifetime for which he would have been subject to an action, so as such wrong shall have been committed within one year before such person's death; and the damages to be recovered in such action shall, if recovered against an executor or administrator bound to administer according to the English law, be payable in like order of administration as the simple contract debts of such person.

2. Death of either party not to abate suit: Proviso. No action commenced under the provisions of this Act shall abate by reason of the death of either party, but the same may be continued by or against the executors, administrators, or representatives of the party deceased: Provided that in any case in which any such action shall be continued against the executors, administrators or representatives of a deceased party, such executors, administrators, or representatives may set up a want of assets as a defence to the action, either wholly or in part, in the same manner as if the action had been originally commenced against them.

APPENDIX

8

The Medical Termination of Pregnancy Act, 1971

(34 of 1971)

[10th August, 1971

An Act to provide for the termination of certain pregnancies by registered medical practitioners and for matters connected therewith or incidental thereto.

Be it enacted by Parliament in the Twenty-second Year of the Republic of India as follows:

1. Short title, extent and commencement. (1) This Act may be called the Medical Termination of Pregnancy Act, 1971.

(2) It extends to the whole of India *[...........].

(3) It shall come into force on such dateas the Central Government may, by notification in the Official Gazette, appoint.

2. Definitions. In this Act, unless the context otherwise requires,

(*a*) "guardian" means a person having the care of the person of a minor or a *[mentally ill person];

**[(*b*) "mentally ill person" means a person who is in need for treatment by reason of any mental disorder other than mental retardation;]

(*c*) "minor" means a person who, under the provisions of the Indian Majority Act, 1875, is to be deemed not to have attained his majority;

---

* The words "except the State of Jammu and Kashmir" are *omitted* by the Jammu and Kashmir Reorganisation Act, 2019 (w.e.f. 31.10.2019).

** *Substituted* by the Medical Termination of Pregnancy Amendment Act 64 of 2002 (w.e.f. 18.6.2003).

(d) "registered medical practitioner" means a medical practitioner who possesses any recognised medical qualification as defined in clause (h) of section 2 of the Indian Medical Council Act, 1956, whose name has been entered in a State Medical Register and who has such experience or training in gynaecology and obstetrics as may be prescribed by rules made under this Act.

3. When pregnancies may be terminated by registered medical practitioners. (1) Notwithstanding anything contained in the Indian Penal Code (45 of 1860), a registered medical practitioner shall not be guilty of any offence under that Code or under any other law for the time being in force, if any pregnancy is terminated by him in accordance with the provisions of this Act.

(2) Subject to the provisions of sub-section (4), pregnancy may be terminated by a registered medical practitioner—

(a) where the length of the pregnancy does not exceed twelve weeks, if such medical practitioner is, or

(b) where the length of the pregnancy exceeds twelve weeks but does not exceed twenty weeks, if not less than two registered medical practitioners are,

of opinion, formed in good faith, that—

(i) the continuance of the pregnancy would involve a risk to the life of the pregnant woman or of grave injury to her physical or mental health; or

(ii) there is a substantial risk that if the children were born, it would suffer from such physical or mental abnormalities as to be seriously handicapped.

Explanation I. Where any pregnancy is alleged by the pregnant woman to have been caused by rape, the anguish caused by such pregnancy shall be presumed to constitute a grave injury to the mental health of the pregnant woman.

Explanation II. Where any pregnancy occurs as a result of failure of any device or method used by any married woman or her husband for the purpose of limiting the number of children, the anguish caused by such unwanted pregnancy may be presumed to constitute a grave injury to the mental health of the pregnant woman.

(3) In determining whether the continuance of a pregnancy would involve such risk of injury to the health as mentioned in sub-section (2), account may be taken of the pregnant woman's actual or reasonably foreseeable environment.

(4) (*a*) No pregnancy of a woman, who has not attained the age of eighteen years, or, who, having attained the age of eighteen years, is a *[mentally ill person], shall be terminated except with the consent in writing of her guardian.

(*b*) Save as otherwise provided in clause (*a*), no pregnancy shall be terminated except with the consent of the pregnant woman.

*[4. **Place where pregnancy may be terminated.** No termination of pregnancy shall be made in accordance with this Act at any place other than—

(*a*) a hospital established or maintained by Government, or

(*b*) a place for the time being approved for the purpose of this Act by Government or a District Level Committee constituted by that Government with the Chief Medical Officer or District Health Officer as the Chairperson of the said Committee:

Provided that the District Level Committee shall consist of not less than three and not more than five Members including the Chairperson, as the Government may specify from time-to time.]

5. **Sections 3 and 4 when not to apply.** (1) The provisions of section 4, and so much of the provisions of sub-section (2) of section 3 as relate to the length of the pregnancy and the opinion of not less than two registered medical practitioners, shall not apply to the termination of a pregnancy by a registered medical practitioner in a case where he is of opinion, formed in good faith, that the termination of such pregnancy is immediately necessary to save the life of the pregnant women.

*[(2) Notwithstanding anything contained in the Indian Penal Code, (45 of 1860) the termination of pregnancy by a person who is not a registered medical practitioner shall be an offence punishable with rigorous imprisonment for a term which shall not be less than two years but which may extend to seven years under that Code, and that Code shall, to this extent, stand modified.

(3) Whoever terminates any pregnancy in a place other than that mentioned in section 4, shall be punishable with rigorous imprisonment for a term which shall not be less than two years but which may extend to seven years.

(4) Any person being owner of a place which is not approved under clause (*b*) of section 4 shall be punishable with rigorous imprisonment for a term which shall not be less than two years but which may extend to seven years.

* *Substituted* by the Medical Termination of Pregnancy Amendment Act 64 of 2002 (w.e.f. 18.6.2003).

Explanation 1. For the purposes of this section, the expression "owner" in relation to a place means any person who is the administrative head or otherwise responsible for the working or maintenance of a hospital or place, by whatever name called, where the pregnancy may be terminated under this Act.

Explanation 2. For the purposes of this section, so much of the provisions of clause (*d*) of section 2 as relate to the possession, by registered medical practitioner, of experience or training in gynaecology and obstetrics shall not apply.]

6. Power to make rules. (1) The Central Government may, by notification in the Official Gazette, make rules to carry out the provisions of this Act.

(2) In particular, and without prejudice to the generality of the foregoing power, such rules may provide for all or any of the following matters, namely:

(*a*) the experience or training, or both, which a registered medical practitioner shall have if he intends to terminate any pregnancy under this Act; and

(*b*) such other matters as are required to be or may be, provided by rules made under this Act.

(3) Every rule made by the Central Government under this Act shall be laid, as soon as may be after it is made, before each House of Parliament while it is in session for a total period of thirty days which may be comprised in one session or in two successive sessions, and if, before the expiry of the session in which it is so laid or the session immediately following, both Houses agree in making any modification in the rule or both Houses agree that the rule should not be made, the rule shall thereafter have effect only in such modified form or be of no effect, as the case may be; so, however, that any such modification or annulment shall be without prejudice to the validity of anything previously done under that rule.

7. Power to make regulations. (1) The State Government may, by regulations—

(*a*) require any such opinion as is referred to in sub-section (2) of section 3 to be certified by a registered medical practitioner or practitioners concerned, in such form and at such time as may be specified in such regulations, and the preservation or disposal of such certificates;

(*b*) require any registered medical practitioner, who terminates a pregnancy, to give intimation of such termination and such other information relating to the termination as may be specified in such regulations;

(*c*) prohibit the disclosure, except to such persons and for such purposes as may be specified in such regulations, of intimations given or information furnished in pursuance of regulations.

(2) The intimation given and the information furnished in pursuance of regulations made by virtue of clause (*b*) of sub-section (1) shall be given or furnished, as the case may be, to the Chief Medical Officer of the State.

*[(2A) Every regulation made by the State Government under this Act shall be laid, as soon as may be after it is made, before the State Legislature.]

(3) Any person who wilfully contravenes or willfully fails to comply with the requirements of any regulation made under sub-section (1) shall be liable to be punished with the fine which may extend to one thousand rupees.

8. Protection of action taken in good faith. No suit or other legal proceeding shall lie against any registered medical practitioner for any damage caused or likely to be caused by anything which is in good faith done or intended to be done under this Act.

* *Inserted* by the Delegated Legislation Provisions (Amendment) Act 2004.

APPENDIX

9

The Mental Healthcare Act, 2017

(10 of 2017)

[7th April 2017

* * * *

2. Definitions. (1) In this Act, unless the context otherwise requires,–

* * * *

(*s*) "mental illness" means a substantial disorder of thinking, mood, perception, orientation or memory that grossly impairs judgment, behaviour, capacity to recognise reality or ability to meet the ordinary demands of life, mental conditions associated with the abuse of alcohol and drugs, but does not include mental retardation which is a condition of arrested or incomplete development of mind of a person, specially characterised by subnormality of intelligence.

* * * *

CHAPTER V

RIGHTS OF PERSONS WITH MENTAL ILLNESS

18. Right to access mental healthcare. (1) Every person shall have a right to access mental healthcare and treatment from mental health services run or funded by the appropriate Government.

(2) The right to access mental healthcare and treatment shall mean mental health services of affordable cost, of good quality, available in sufficient quantity, accessible geographically, without discrimination on the basis of gender, sex, sexual orientation, religion, culture, caste, social or political beliefs, class, disability or any other basis and provided

in a manner that is acceptable to persons with mental illness and their families and care-givers.

(3) The appropriate Government shall make sufficient provision as may be necessary, for a range of services required by persons with mental illness.

(4) Without prejudice to the generality of range of services under sub-section (3), such services shall include—

(*a*) provision of acute mental healthcare services such as outpatient and inpatient services;

(*b*) provision of half-way homes, sheltered accommodation, supported accommodation as may be prescribed;

(*c*) provision for mental health services to support family of person with mental illness or home based rehabilitation;

(*d*) hospital and community based rehabilitation establishments and services as may be prescribed;

(*e*) provision for child mental health services and old age mental health services.

(5) The appropriate Government shall,—

(*a*) integrate mental health services into general healthcare services at all levels of healthcare including primary, secondary and tertiary healthcare and in all health programmes run by the appropriate Government;

(*b*) provide treatment in a manner, which supports persons with mental illness to live in the community and with their families;

(*c*) ensure that the long term care in a mental health establishment for treatment of mental illness shall be used only in exceptional circumstances, for as short a duration as possible, and only as a last resort when appropriate community based treatment has been tried and shown to have failed;

(*d*) ensure that no person with mental illness (including children and older persons) shall be required to travel long distances to access mental health services and such services shall be available close to a place where a person with mental illness resides;

(*e*) ensure that as a minimum, mental health services run or funded by Government shall be available in each district;

(*f*) ensure, if minimum mental health services specified under sub-clause (*e*) of sub-section (4) are not available in the district where a person with mental illness resides, that the person with mental illness is entitled to access any other mental health service in the district and the costs of treatment at such establishments in that district will be borne by the appropriate Government:

Provided that till such time the services under this sub-section are made available in a health establishment run or funded by the appropriate Government, the appropriate Government shall make rules regarding reimbursement of costs of treatment at such mental health establishment.

(6) The appropriate Government shall make available a range of appropriate mental health services specified under sub-section (4) of section 18 at all general hospitals run or funded by such Government and basic and emergency mental healthcare services shall be available at all community health centres and upwards in the public health system run or funded by such Government.

(7) Persons with mental illness living below the poverty line whether or not in possession of a below poverty line card, or who are destitute or homeless shall be entitled to mental health treatment and services free of any charge and at no financial cost at all mental health establishments run or funded by the appropriate Government and at other mental health establishments designated by it.

(8) The appropriate Government shall ensure that the mental health services shall be of equal quality to other general health services and no discrimination be made in quality of services provided to persons with mental illness.

(9) The minimum quality standards of mental health services shall be as specified by regulations made by the State Authority.

(10) Without prejudice to the generality of range of services under sub-section (3) of section 18, the appropriate Government shall notify Essential Drug List and all medicines on the Essential Drug List shall be made available free of cost to all persons with mental illness at all times at health establishments run or funded by the appropriate Government starting from Community Health Centres and upwards in the public health system:

Provided that where the health professional of ayurveda, yoga, unani, siddha, homoeopathy or naturopathy systems recognised by the Central Government are available in any health establishment, the essential medicines from any similar list relating to the appropriate ayurvada, yoga, unani, siddha, homoeopathy or naturopathy systems shall also be made available free of cost to all persons with mental illness.

(11) The appropriate Government shall take measures to ensure that necessary budgetary provisions in terms of adequacy, priority, progress and equity are made for effective implementation of the provisions of this section.

Explanation.—For the purposes of sub-section (11), the expressions–

(*i*) "adequacy" means in terms of how much is enough to offset inflation;

(*ii*) "priority" means in terms of compared to other budget heads;

(*iii*) "equity" means in terms of fair allocation of resources taking into account the health, social and economic burden of mental illness on individuals, their families and care-givers;

(*iv*) "progress" means in terms of indicating an improvement in the State's response.

* * * *

23. Right to confidentiality. (1) A person with mental illness shall have the right to confidentiality in respect of his mental health, mental healthcare, treatment and physical healthcare.

(2) All health professionals providing care or treatment to a person with mental illness shall have a duty to keep all such information confidential which has been obtained during care or treatment with the following exceptions, namely:—

(*a*) release of information to the nominated representative to enable him to fulfil his duties under this Act;

(*b*) release of information to other mental health professionals and other health professionals to enable them to provide care and treatment to the person with mental illness;

(*c*) release of information if it is necessary to protect any other person from harm or violence;

(*d*) only such information that is necessary to protect against the harm identified shall be released;

(*e*) release only such information as is necessary to prevent threat to life;

(*f*) release of information upon an order by concerned Board or the Central Authority or High Court or Supreme Court or any other statutory authority competent to do so; and

(*g*) release of information in the interests of public safety and security.

* * * *

25. Right to access medical records. (1) All persons with mental illness shall have the right to access their basic medical records as may be prescribed.

(2) The mental health professional in charge of such records may withhold specific information in the medical records if disclosure would result in,—

(*a*) serious mental harm to the person with mental illness; or

(*b*) likelihood of harm to other persons.

(3) When any information in the medical records is withheld from the person, the mental health professional shall inform the person with mental illness of his right to apply to the concerned Board for an order to release such information.

APPENDIX

10

The Pre-conception and Pre-natal Diagnostic Techniques (Prohibition of Sex Selection) Act, 1994

(57 of 1994)

[20th September, 1994

*[An Act to provide for the prohibition of sex selection, before or after conception, and for regulation of pre-natal diagnostic techniques for the purposes of detecting genetic abnormalities or metabolic disorders or chromosomal abnormalities or certain congenital malformations or sex-linked disorders and for the prevention of their misuse of sex determination leading to female foeticide and for matters connected therewith or incidental thereto.]

BE it enacted by Parliament in the Forty-fifth Year of the Republic of India as follows:

CHAPTER I

Preliminary

1. Short title, extent and commencement. (1) This Act may be called *[the Pre-conception and Pre-natal Diagnostic Techniques (Prohibition of Sex Selection)] Act, 1994.

(2) It shall extend to the whole of India **[...].

(3) It shall come into force on such date as the Central Government may, by notification in the Official Gazette, appoint.

---

* *Substituted* by Act 14 of 2003 (w.e.f. 14.2.2003).

** The words "except the State of Jammu and Kashmir" are *omitted* by the Jammu and Kashmir Reorganisation Act, 2019 (w.e.f. 31.10.2019).

2. Definitions. In this Act, unless the context otherwise requires—

(*a*) "Appropriate Authority" means the Appropriate Authority appointed under section 17;

(*b*) "Board" means the Central Supervisory Board constituted under section 7;

*[(*ba*) "conceptus" means by product of conception at any stage of development from fertilisation until birth including extra embryonic membranes as well as the embryo or foetus;

(*bb*) "embryo" means a developing human organism after fertilization till the end of eight weeks (fifty-six days);

(*bc*) "foetus" means a human organism during the period of its development beginning on the fifty-seventh day following fertilization or creation (excluding any time in which its development has been suspended) and ending at the birth;]

(*c*) "Genetic Counselling Centre" means an institute, hospital, nursing home or any place, by whatever name called, which provides for genetic counselling to patients;

(*d*) "Genetic Clinic" means a clinic, institute, hospital, nursing home or any place, by whatever name called, which is used for conducting pre-natal diagnostic procedures;

*[*Explanation*. For the purposes of this clause, "Genetic Clinic" includes a vehicle, where ultrasound machine or imaging machine or scanner or other equipment capable of determining sex of the foetus or a portable equipment which has the potential for detection of sex during pregnancy or selection of sex before conception, is used;]

(*e*) "Genetic Laboratory" means a laboratory and includes a place where facilities are provided for conducting analysis or tests of samples received from Genetic Clinic for pre-natal diagnostic test;

*[*Explanation*. For the purposes of this clause, "Genetic Laboratory" includes a place where ultrasound machine or imaging machine or scanner or other equipment capable of determining sex of the foetus or a portable equipment which has the potential for detection of sex during pregnancy or selection of sex before conception, is used;]

(*f*) "gynaecologist" means a person who possesses a post-graduate qualification in gynaecology and obstetrics;

* *Inserted* by Act 14 of 2003 (w.e.f. 14.2.2003).

* [(*g*) "medical geneticist" includes a person who possesses a degree or diploma in genetic science in the fields of sex selection and pre-natal diagnostic techniques or has experience of not less than two years in any of these fields after obtaining—

(*i*) any one of the medical qualifications recognized under the Indian Medical Council Act, 1956 (102 of 1956); or

(*ii*) a post-graduate degree in biological sciences;]

(*h*) "paediatrician" means a person who possesses a post-graduate qualification in paediatrics;

*[(*i*) "pre-natal diagnostic procedures" means all gynaecological or obstetrical or medical procedures such as ultrasonography, foetoscopy, taking or removing samples of amniotic fluid, chorionic villi, embryo, blood or any other tissue or fluid of a man, or of a woman before or after conception, for being sent to a Genetic Laboratory or Genetic Clinic for conducting any type of analysis or pre-natal diagnostic tests for selection of sex before or after conception;]

(*j*) "pre-natal diagnostic techniques" includes all pre-natal diagnostic procedures and pre-natal diagnostic tests;

*[(*k*) "pre-natal diagnostic test" means ultrasonography or any test or analysis of amniotic fluid, chorionic villi, blood or any tissue or fluid of a pregnant woman or conceptus conducted to detect genetic or metabolic disorders or chromosomal abnormalities or congenital anomalies or haemoglobinopathies or sex-linked diseases;]

(*l*) "prescribed" means prescribed by rules made under this Act;

(*m*) "registered medical practitioner" means a medical practitioner who possesses any recognised medical qualification as defined in clause (*h*) of section 2 of the Indian Medical Council Act, 1956 (102 of 1956), and whose name has been entered in a State Medical Register;

(*n*) "regulations" means regulations framed by the Board under this Act;

*[(*o*) "sex selection" includes any procedure, technique, test or administration or prescription or provision of anything for the purpose of ensuring or increasing the probability that an embryo will be of a particular sex;

(*p*) "sonologist or imaging specialist" means a person who possesses any one of the medical qualifications recognized

---

* *Substituted* by Act 14 of 2003 (w.e.f. 14.2.2003).

under the Indian Medical Council Act, 1956 (102 of 1956) or who possesses a post-graduate qualification in ultrasonography or imaging techniques or radiology;

(*q*) "State Board" means a State Supervisory Board or a Union Territory Supervisory Board constituted under section 16A;

(*r*) "State Government" in relation to Union Territory with Legislature means the Administrator of the Union Territory appointed by the President under Article 239 of the Constitution.]

CHAPTER II

Regulation of genetic counselling centres, genetic laboratories and genetic clinics

3. Regulation of Genetic Counselling Centres, Genetic Laboratories and Genetic Clinics. On and form the commencement of this Act—

(1) no Genetic Counselling Centre, Genetic Laboratory or Genetic Clinic unless registered under this Act, shall conduct or associate with, or help in, conducting activities relating to pre-natal diagnostic techniques;

*[(2) no Genetic Counselling Centre or Genetic Laboratory or Genetic Clinic shall employ or cause to be employed or take services of any person, whether on honorary basis or on payment who does not possess the qualifications as may be prescribed;]

(3) no medical geneticist, gynaecologist, paediatrician, registered medical practitioner or any other person shall conduct or cause to be conducted or aid in conducting by himself or through any other person, any pre-natal diagnostic techniques at a place other than a place registered under this Act.

[3A. Prohibition of sex-selection. No person, including a specialist or a team of specialists in the field of infertility, shall conduct or cause to be conducted or aid in conducting by himself or by any other person, sex selection on a woman or a man or on both or on any tissue, embryo, conceptus, fluid or gametes derived from either or both of them.

3B. Prohibition on sale of ultrasound machine, etc., to persons, laboratories, clinics, etc., not registered under the Act. No person shall sell any ultrasound machine or imaging machine or scanner or any other equipment capable of detecting sex of foetus to any Genetic

* *Substituted* by Act 14 of 2003 (w.e.f. 14.2.2003).

** *Inserted* by Act 14 of 2003 (w.e.f. 14.2.2003).

Counselling Centre, Genetic Laboratory, Genetic Clinic or any other person not registered under the Act.]

CHAPTER III

Regulation of pre-natal diagnostic techniques

4. Regulation of pre-natal diagnostic techniques. On and from commencement of this Act—

(1) no place including a registered Genetic Counselling Centre or Genetic Laboratory or Genetic Clinic shall be used or caused to be used by any person for conducting pre-natal diagnostic techniques except for the purposes specified in clause (2) and after satisfying any of the conditions specified in clause (3);

(2) no pre-natal diagnostic techniques shall be conducted except for the purposes of detection of any of the following abnormalities, namely:

(*i*) chromosomal abnormalities;

(*ii*) genetic metabolic diseases;

(*iii*) haemoglobinopathies;

(*iv*) sex-linked genetic diseases;

(*v*) congenital anomalies;

(*vi*) any other abnormalities or diseases as may be specified by the Central Supervisory Board;*

**[(3) no pre-natal diagnostic techniques shall be used or conducted unless the person qualified to do so is satisfied for reasons to be recorded in writing that any of the following conditions are fulfilled, namely:—

(*i*) age of the pregnant woman is above thirty-five years;

(*ii*) the pregnant woman has undergone two or more spontaneous abortions or foetal loss;

(*iii*) the pregnant woman had been exposed to potentially teratogenic agents such as drugs, radiation, infection or chemicals;

(*iv*) the pregnant woman or her spouse has a family history of mental retardation or physical deformities such as; spasticity or any other genetic disease;

---

* Supervisory Board has specified as follows:–
"any other indication of possible genetic disease/anomaly in the foetus as sporadic genetic disease in the couple, a positive screening test for carrier status or positive screening test for genetic disease/congenital anomaly in pregnancy etc." [vide S.O. 189(E), dated 12th February 2004].

** *Substituted* by Act 14 of 2003 (w.e.f. 14.2.2003).

(*v*) any other condition as may be specified by the Board:

Provided that the person conducting ultrasonography on a pregnant woman shall keep complete record thereof in the clinic in such manner, as may be prescribed, and any deficiency or inaccuracy found therein shall amount to contravention of the provisions of section 5 or section 6 unless contrary is proved by the person conducting such ultrasonography;

(4) no person including a relative or husband of the pregnant woman shall seek or encourage the conduct of any pre-natal diagnostic techniques on her except for the purposes specified in clause (2);

(5) no person including a relative or husband of a woman shall seek or encourage the conduct of any sex-selection technique on her or him or both.]

5. Written consent of pregnant woman and prohibition of communicating the sex of foetus. (1) No person referred to in clause (2) of section 3 shall conduct the pre-natal diagnostic procedures unless—

(*a*) he has explained all known side and after effects of such procedures to the pregnant woman concerned;

(*b*) he has obtained in the prescribed form her written consent to undergo such procedures in the language which she understands; and

(*c*) a copy of her written consent obtained under clause (*b*) is given to the pregnant woman.

*[(2) No person including the person conducting pre-natal diagnostic procedures shall communicate to the pregnant woman concerned or her relatives or any other person the sex of the foetus by words, signs, or in any other manner.]

6. Determination of sex prohibited. On and from commencement of this Act—

(*a*) no Genetic Counselling Centre or Genetic Laboratory or Genetic Clinic shall conduct or cause to be conducted in its Centre, Laboratory or Clinic, pre-natal diagnostic techniques including ultrasonography, for the purpose of determining the sex of a foetus;

(*b*) no person shall conduct or cause to be conducted, any pre-natal diagnostic techniques including ultrasonography for the purpose of determining the sex of a foetus.

* *Substituted* by Act 14 of 2003 (w.e.f. 14.2.2003).

*[(*c*) no person shall, by whatever means, cause or allow to be caused selection of sex before or after conception.]

CHAPTER IV
Central Supervisory Board

7. Constitution of Central Supervisory Board. (1) The Central Government shall constitute a Board to be known as the Central Supervisory Board to exercise the powers and perform the functions conferred on the Board under this Act.

(2) The Board shall consist of—

(*a*) the Minister in charge of the Ministry or Department of Family Welfare, who shall be the Chairman, *ex officio*;

(*b*) the Secretary to the Government of India in charge of the Department of Family Welfare, who shall be the Vice-Chairman, *ex officio*;

**[(*c*) three members to be appointed by the Central Government to represent the Ministries of Central Government in charge of Women and Child Development, Department of Legal Affairs or Legislative Department in the Ministry of Law and Justice, and Indian System of Medicine and Homoeopathy, *ex officio*;]

(*d*) the Director General of Health Services of the Central Government, *ex officio*;

(*e*) ten members to be appointed by the Central Government, two each from amongst—

(*i*) eminent medical geneticists;

**[(*ii*) eminent gynaecologist and obstetrician or expert of *stri-roga* or *prasuti-tantra*;]

(*iii*) eminent paediatricians;

(*iv*) eminent social scientists; and

(*v*) representatives of women welfare organisations;

(*f*) three women Members of Parliament, of whom two shall be elected by the House of the People and one by the Council of States;

(*g*) four members to be appointed by the Central Government by rotation to represent the States and the Union territories, two in the alphabetical order and two in the reverse alphabetical order:

** *Inserted* by Act 14 of 2003 (w.e.f. 14.2.2003).

* *Substituted* by Act 14 of 2003 (w.e.f. 14.2.2003).

Provided that no appointment under this clause shall be made except on the recommendation of the State Government, or as the case may be, the Union territory;

(*h*) an officer, not below the rank of a Joint Secretary or equivalent of the Central Government, in charge of Family Welfare, who shall be the Member-Secretary, *ex officio*.

8. Term of office of members. (1) The term of office of a member, other than an *ex officio* member, shall be—

(*a*) in case of appointment under clause (*e*) or clause (*f*) of sub-section (2) of section 7, three years; *[***]

** [Provided that the term of office of a member elected under clause (*f*) of sub-section (2) of section 7 shall come to an end as soon as the member becomes a Minister or Minister of State or Deputy Minister, or the Speaker or the Deputy Speaker of the House of the People, or the Deputy Chairman of the Council of States or ceases to be a member of the House from which he was elected; and]

(*b*) in case of appointment under clause (*g*) of the said sub-section, one year.

(2) If a casual vacancy occurs in the office of any other members, whether by reason of his death, resignation or inability to discharge his functions owing to illness or other incapacity, such vacancy shall be filled by the Central Government by making a fresh appointment and the members so appointed shall hold office for the remainder of the term of office of the person in whose place he is so appointed.

(3) The Vice-Chairman shall perform such functions as may be assigned to him by the Chairman from time to time.

(4) The procedure to be followed by the members in the discharge of their functions shall be such as may be prescribed.

9. Meetings of the Board. (1) The Board shall meet at such time and place, and shall observe such rules of procedure in regard to the transaction of business at its meetings (including the quorum at such meetings) as may be provided by regulations:

Provided that the Board shall meet at least once in six months.

(2) The Chairman and in his absence the Vice-Chairman shall preside at the meetings of the Board.

---

* The word "and" *omitted* by Act 32 of 2001 (w.e.f. 3.9.2001).

** *Inserted* by Act 32 of 2001 (w.e.f. 3.9.2001).

(3) If for any reason the Chairman or the Vice-Chairman is unable to attend any meeting of the Board any other member chosen by the members present at the meeting shall preside at the meeting.

(4) All questions which come up before any meeting of the Board shall be decided by a majority of the votes of the members present at the voting, and in the event of an equality of votes, the Chairman, or in his absence, the person presiding, shall have and exercise a second or casting vote.

(5) Members other than *ex officio* members shall receive such allowances, if any, from the Board as may be prescribed.

10. Vacancies, etc., not to invalidate proceedings of the Board. No act or proceeding of the Board shall be invalid merely by reason of—

(*a*) any vacancy in, or any defect in the constitution of, the Board; or

(*b*) any defect in the appointment of a person acting as a member of the Board; or

(*c*) any irregularity in the procedure of the Board not affecting the merits of the case.

11. Temporary association of persons with the Board for particular purposes. (1) The Board may associate with itself, in such manner and for such purposes as may be determined by regulations, any person whose assistance or advice it may desire in carrying out any of the provisions of this Act.

(2) A person associated with it by the Board under sub-section (1) for any purpose shall have a right to take part in the discussions relevant to that purpose, but shall not have right to vote at a meeting of the Board and shall not be a member for any other purpose.

12. Appointment of officers and other employees of the Board. (1) For the purpose of enabling it efficiently to discharge its functions under this Act, the Board may, subject to such regulations as may be made in this behalf, appoint (whether on deputation or otherwise) such number of officers and other employees as it may consider necessary:

Provided that the appointment of such category of officers, as may be specified in such regulations, shall be subject to the approval of the Central Government.

(2) Every officer or other employee appointed by the Board shall be subject to such conditions of service and shall be entitled to such remuneration as may be specified in the regulations.

13. Authentication of orders and other instruments of the Board. All orders and decisions of the Board shall be authenticated by the signature of the Chairman or any other member authorised by the Board in this behalf, and all other instruments issued by the Board shall be authenticated by the signature of the Member-Secretary or any other officer of the Board authorised in like manner in this behalf.

14. Disqualifications for appointment as member. A person shall be disqualified for being appointed as a member if, he—

(*a*) has been convicted and sentenced to imprisonment for an offence which, in the opinion of the Central Government, involves moral turpitude; or

(*b*) is an undischarged insolvent; or

(*c*) is of unsound mind and stands so declared by a competent court; or

(*d*) has been removed or dismissed from the service of the Government or a Corporation owned or controlled by the Government; or

(*e*) has, in the opinion of the Central Government, such financial or other interest in the Board as is likely to affect prejudicially the discharge by him of his functions as a member; or

*[(*f*) has, in the opinion of the Central Government, been associated with the use or promotion of pre-natal diagnostic technique for determination of sex or with any sex selection technique.]

15. Eligibility of member for reappointment. Subject to the other terms and conditions of service as may be prescribed, any person ceasing to be a member shall be eligible for reappointment as such member:

**[Provided that no member other than an *ex officio* member shall be appointed for more than two consecutive terms.]

*[**16. Functions of the Board.** The Board shall have the following functions, namely:

(*i*) to advise the Central Government on policy matters relating to use of pre-natal diagnostic techniques, sex selection techniques and against their misuse;

(*ii*) to review and monitor implementation of the Act and rules made thereunder and recommend to the Central Government changes in the said Act and rules;

---

* *Substituted* by Act 14 of 2003 (w.e.f. 14.2.2003).

** *Inserted* by Act 14 of 2003 (w.e.f. 14.2.2003).

(iii) to create public awareness against the practice of pre-conception sex selection and pre-natal determination of sex of foetus leading to female foeticide;

(iv) to lay down code of conduct to be observed by persons working at Genetic Counselling Centres, Genetic Laboratories and Genetic Clinics;

(v) to oversee the performance of various bodies constituted under the Act and taken appropriate steps to ensure its proper and effective implementation;

(vi) any other functions as may be prescribed under the Act.]

*[**16A. Constitution of State Supervisory Board and Union territory Supervisory Board.** (1) Each State and Union territory having Legislature shall constitute a Board to be known as the State Supervisory Board or the Union Territory Supervisory Board, as the case may be, which shall have the following functions:

(i) to create public awareness against the practice of pre-conception sex selection and pre-natal determination of sex of foetus leading to female foeticide in the State;

(ii) to review the activities of the Appropriate Authorities functioning in the State and recommend appropriate action against them;

(iii) to monitor the implementation of provisions of the Act and the rules and make suitable recommendations relating thereto, to the Board;

(iv) to send such consolidated reports as may be prescribed in respect of the various activities undertaken in the State under the Act to the Board and the Central Government; and

(v) any other functions as may be prescribed under the Act.

(2) The State Board shall consist of,—

(a) the Minister in charge of Health and Family Welfare in the State, who shall be the Chairperson, *ex officio*;

(b) Secretary in charge of the Department of Health and Family Welfare who shall be the Vice-Chairperson, *ex officio*;

(c) Secretaries or Commissioners in charge of Departments of Women and Child Development, Social Welfare, Law and Indian System of Medicines and Homoeopathy, *ex officio*, or their representatives;

---

* *Inserted* by Act 14 of 2003 (w.e.f. 14.2.2003).

(*d*) Director of Health and Family Welfare or Indian System of Medicines and Homoeopathy of the State Government, *ex officio*;

(*e*) three women members of Legislative Assembly or Legislative Council;

(*f*) ten members to be appointed by the State Government out of which two each shall be from the following categories:

(*i*) eminent social scientists and legal experts;

(*ii*) eminent women activists from non-governmental organisations or otherwise;

(*iii*) eminent gynaecologists and obstetricians or experts of *stri-roga* or *prasuti-tantra*;

(*iv*) eminent paediatricians or medical geneticists;

(*v*) eminent radiologists or sonologists;

(g) an officer not below the rank of Joint Director in charge of Family Welfare, who shall be the Member Secretary, *ex officio*.

(3) The State Board shall meet at least once in four months.

(4) The term of office of a member, other than an *ex officio* member, shall be three years.

(5) If a vacancy occurs in the office of any member other than an *ex officio* member, it shall be filled by making fresh appointment.

(6) If a member of the Legislative Assembly or member of the Legislative Council who is a member of the State Board, becomes Minister or Speaker or Deputy Speaker of the Legislative Assembly or Chairperson or Deputy Chairperson of the Legislative Council, he shall cease to be a member of the State Board.

(7) One-third of the total number of members of the State Board shall constitute the quorum.

(8) The State Board may co-opt a member as and when required, provided that the number of co-opted members does not exceed one-third of the total strength of the State Board.

(9) The co-opted members shall have the same powers and functions as other members, except the right to vote and shall abide by the rules and regulations.

(10) In respect of matters not specified in this section, the State Board shall follow procedures and conditions as are applicable to the Board.]

CHAPTER V

Appropriate Authority and Advisory Committee

17. Appropriate Authority and Advisory Committee. (1) The Central Government shall appoint, by notification in the Official Gazette, one or more Appropriate Authorities for each of the Union Territories for the purposes of this Act.

(2) The State Government shall appoint, by notification in the Official Gazette, one or more Appropriate Authorities for the whole or part of the State for the purposes of this Act having regard to the intensity of the problem of pre-natal sex determination leading to female foeticide.

(3) The officers appointed as Appropriate Authorities under sub-section (1) or sub-section (2) shall be—

*[(*a*) when appointed for the whole of the State or the Union territory, consisting of the following three members—

(*i*) an officer of or above the rank of the Joint Director of Health and Family Welfare—Chairperson;

(*ii*) an eminent woman representing women's organisation; and

(*iii*) an officer of Law Department of the State or the Union territory concerned:

Provided that it shall be the duty of the State or the Union territory concerned to constitute multi-member State or Union territory level Appropriate Authority within three months of the coming into force of the Pre-natal Diagnostic Techniques (Regulation and Prevention of Misuse) Amendment Act, 2002:

Provided further that any vacancy occurring therein shall be filled within three months of the occurrence;]

(*b*) when appointed for any part of the State of the Union territory, of such other rank as the State Government or the Central Government, as the case may be, may deem fit.

(4) The Appropriate Authority shall have the following functions, namely:

(*a*) to grant, suspend or cancel registration of a Genetic Counselling Centre, Genetic Laboratory or Genetic Clinic;

(*b*) to enforce standards prescribed for the Genetic Counselling Centre, Genetic Laboratory and Genetic Clinic;

---

* *Substituted* by Act 14 of 2003 (w.e.f. 14.2.2003).

(c) to investigate complaints of breach of the provisions of this Act or the rules made thereunder and take immediate action; and

(d) to seek and consider the advice of the Advisory Committee, constituted under sub-section (5), on application for registration and on complaints for suspension or cancellation of registration;

*[(e) to take appropriate legal action against the use of any sex selection technique by any person at any place, *suo motu* or brought to its notice and also to initiate independent investigations in such matter;

(f) to create public awareness against the practice of sex selection or pre-natal determination of sex;

(g) to supervise the implementation of the provisions of the Act and rules;

(h) to recommend to the Board and State Boards modifications required in the rules in accordance with changes in technology or social conditions:

(i) to take action on the recommendations of the Advisory Committee made after investigation of complaint for suspension or cancellation of registration.]

(5) The Central Government or the State Government, as the case may be, shall constitute an Advisory Committee, for each Appropriate Authority to aid and advise the Appropriate Authority in the discharge of its functions, and shall appoint one of the members of the Advisory Committee to be its Chairman.

(6) The Advisory Committee shall consist of—

(a) three medical experts from amongst gynaecologists, obstetricians, paediatricians and medical geneticists;

(b) one legal expert;

(c) one officer to represent the department dealing with information and publicity of the State Government or the Union territory, as the case may be;

(d) three eminent social workers of whom not less than one shall be from amongst representatives of women's organisations.

**[(7) No person who has been associated with the use or promotion of pre-natal diagnostic techniques for determination of sex or sex selection shall be appointed as a member of the Advisory Committee.]

---

* *Inserted* by Act 14 of 2003 (w.e.f. 14.2.2003).

** *Substituted* by Act 14 of 2003 (w.e.f. 14.2.2003).

(8) The Advisory Committee may meet as and when it thinks fit or on the request of the Appropriate Authority for consideration of any application for registration or any complaint for suspension or cancellation of registration and to give advice thereon:

Provided that the period intervening between any two meetings shall not exceed the prescribed period.

(9) The terms and conditions subject to which a person may be appointed to the Advisory Committee and the procedure to be followed by such Committee in the discharge of its functions shall be such as may be prescribed.

*[**17A. Powers of Appropriate Authorities.** The Appropriate Authority shall have the powers in respect of the following matters, namely:

(*a*) summoning of any person who is in possession of any information relating to violation of the provisions of this Act or the rules made thereunder;

(*b*) production of any document or material object relating to clause (*a*);

(*c*) issuing search warrant for any place suspected to be indulging in sex selection techniques or pre-natal sex determination; and

(*d*) any other matter which may be prescribed.]

CHAPTER VI

Registration of Genetic Counselling Centres, Genetic Laboratories and Genetic Clinics

18. Registration of Genetic Counselling Centres, Genetic Laboratories and Genetic Clinics. **[(1) No person shall open any Genetic Counselling Centre, Genetic Laboratory or Genetic Clinic, including clinic, laboratory or centre having ultrasound or imaging machine or scanner or any other technology capable of undertaking determination of sex of foetus and sex selection, or render services to any of them, after the commencement of the Pre-natal Diagnostic Techniques (Regulation and Prevention of Misuse) Amendment Act, 2002 unless such Centre, Laboratory or Clinic is duly registered under the Act.]

(2) Every application for registration under sub-section (1), shall be made to the Appropriate Authority in such form and in such manner and shall be accompanied by such fees as may be prescribed.

* *Inserted* by Act 14 of 2003 (w.e.f. 14.2.2003).

** *Substituted* by Act 14 of 2003 (w.e.f. 14.2.2003).

(3) Every Genetic Counselling Centre, Genetic Laboratory or Genetic Clinic engaged, either partly or exclusively, in counselling or conducting pre-natal diagnostic techniques for any of the purposes mentioned in section 4, immediately before the commencement of this Act, shall apply for registration within sixty days from the date of such commencement.

(4) Subject to the provisions of section 6, every Genetic Counselling Centre, Genetic Laboratory or Genetic Clinic engaged in counselling or conducting pre-natal diagnostic techniques, shall cease to conduct any such counselling or technique on the expiry of six months from the date of commencement of this Act unless such Centre, Laboratory or Clinic has applied for registration and is so registered separately or jointly or till such application is disposed of, whichever is earlier.

(5) No Genetic Counselling Centre, Genetic Laboratory or Genetic Clinic shall be registered under this Act unless the Appropriate Authority is satisfied that such Centre, Laboratory or Clinic is in a position to provide such facilities, maintain such equipment and standards as may be prescribed.

19. Certificate of Registration. (1) The Appropriate Authority shall, after holding an inquiry and after satisfying itself that the applicant has complied with all the requirements of this Act and the rules made thereunder, and having regard to the advise of the Advisory Committee in this behalf, grant a Certificate of Registration in the prescribed form, jointly or separately to the Genetic Counselling Centre, Genetic Laboratory or Genetic Clinic, as the case may be.

(2) If, after the inquiry and after giving an opportunity of being heard to the applicant and having regard to the advice of the Advisory Committee, the Appropriate Authority is satisfied that the applicant has not complied with the requirements of this Act or the rules, it shall, for reasons to be recorded in writing, reject the application for registration.

(3) Every Certificate of Registration shall be renewed in such manner and after such period and on payment of such fees as may be prescribed.

(4) The Certificate of Registration shall be displayed by the registered Genetic Counselling Centre, Genetic Laboratory or Genetic Clinic in a conspicuous place at its place of business.

20. Cancellation or suspension of registration. (1) The Appropriate Authority may *suo moto*, or on complaint, issue a notice to the Genetic Counselling Centre, Genetic Laboratory or Genetic Clinic to show cause why its registration should not be suspended or cancelled for the reasons mentioned in the notice.

(2) If, after giving a reasonable opportunity of being heard to the Genetic Counselling Centre, Genetic Laboratory or Genetic Clinic and having regard to the advice of the Advisory Committee, the Appropriate Authority is satisfied that there has been a breach of the provisions of this Act or the rules, it may, without prejudice to any criminal action that it may take against such Centre, Laboratory or Clinic, suspend its registration for such period as it may think fit or cancel its registration, as the case may be.

(3) Notwithstanding anything contained in sub-sections (1), (2), if the Appropriate Authority is of the opinion that it is necessary or expedient to do so in the public interest, it may, for reasons to be recorded in writing, suspend the registration of any Genetic Counselling Centre, Genetic Laboratory or Genetic Clinic without issuing any such notice referred to in sub-section (1).

21. Appeal. The Genetic Counselling Centre, Genetic Laboratory or Genetic Clinic may, within thirty days from the date of receipt of the order of suspension or cancellation of registration passed by the Appropriate Authority under section 20, prefer an appeal against such order to—

(*i*) the Central Government, where the appeal is against the order of the Central Appropriate Authority; and

(*ii*) the State Government, where the appeal is against the orders of the State Appropriate Authority,

in the prescribed manner.

CHAPTER VII

Offences and Penalties

***[22. Prohibition of advertisement relating to pre-conception and pre-natal determination of sex and punishment for contravention.** (1) No person, organisation, Genetic Counselling Centre, Genetic Laboratory or Genetic Clinic, including Clinic, Laboratory or Centre having ultrasound machine or imaging machine or scanner or any other technology capable of undertaking determination of sex of foetus or sex selection shall issue, publish, distribute, communicate or cause to be issued, published, distributed or communicated any advertisement, in any form, including internet, regarding facilities of pre-natal determination of sex or sex selection before conception available at such Centre, Laboratory, Clinic or at any other place.

(2) No person or organisation including Genetic Counselling Centre, Genetic Laboratory or Genetic Clinic shall issue, publish, distribute,

* *Substituted* by Act 14 of 2003 (w.e.f. 14.2.2003).

communicate or cause to be issued, published, distributed or communicated any advertisement in any manner regarding pre-natal determination or pre-conception selection of sex by any means whatsoever, scientific or otherwise.

(3) Any person, who contravenes the provisions of sub-section (1) or sub-section (2) shall be punishable with imprisonment for a term which may extend to three years and with fine which may extend to ten thousand rupees.

Explanation. For the purposes of this section, "advertisement" includes any notice, circular, label, wrapper or any other document including advertisement through internet or any other media in electronic or print form and also includes any visible representation made by means of any hoarding, wall-painting, signal, light, sound, smoke or gas.]

23. Offences and penalties. (1) Any medical geneticist, gynaecologist, registered medical practitioner or any person who owns a Genetic Counselling Centre, a Genetic Laboratory or a Genetic Clinic or is employed in such a Centre, Laboratory or Genetic Clinic and renders his professional or technical services to or at such a Centre, Laboratory or Clinic, whether on an honorary basis or otherwise, and who contravenes any of the provisions of this Act or rules made thereunder, shall be punishable with imprisonment for a term which may extend to three years and with fine which may extend to ten thousand rupees and on any subsequent conviction, with imprisonment which may extend to five years and with fine which may extend to fifty thousand rupees.

*[(2) The name of the registered medical practitioner shall be reported by the Appropriate Authority to the State Medical Council concerned for taking necessary action including suspension of the registration if the charges are framed by the court and till the case is disposed of and on conviction for removal of his name from the register of the Council for a period of five years for the first offence and permanently for the subsequent offence.

(3) Any person who seeks the aid of any Genetic Counselling Centre, Genetic Laboratory, Genetic Clinic or ultrasound clinic or imaging clinic or of a medical geneticist, gynaecologist, sonologist or imaging specialist or registered medical practitioner or any other person for sex selection or for conducting pre-natal diagnostic techniques on any pregnant woman for the purposes other than those specified in sub-section (2) of section 4, he shall be punishable with imprisonment for a term which may extend to three years and with fine which may extend to fifty

* *Substituted* by Act 14 of 2003 (w.e.f. 14.2.2003).

thousand rupees for the first offence and for any subsequent offence with imprisonment which may extend to five years and with fine which may extend to one lakh rupees.

(4) For the removal of doubts, it is hereby provided, that the provisions of sub-section (3) shall not apply to the woman who was compelled to undergo such diagnostic techniques or such selection.]

*[24. **Presumption in the case of conduct of pre-natal diagnostic techniques.** Notwithstanding anything contained in the Indian Evidence Act, 1872 (1 of 1872), the court shall presume unless the contrary is proved that the pregnant woman was compelled by her husband or any other relative, as the case may be, to undergo pre-natal diagnostic technique for the purposes other than those specified in sub-section (2) of section 4 and such person shall be liable for abetment of offence under sub-section (3) of section 23 and shall be punishable for the offence specified under that section.]

25. Penalty for contravention of the provisions of the Act or rules for which no specific punishment is provided. Whoever contravenes any of the provisions of this Act or any rules made thereunder, for which no penalty has been elsewhere provided in this Act, shall be punishable with imprisonment for a term which may extend to three months or with fine, which may extend to one thousand rupees or with both and in the case of continuing contravention, with an additional fine which may extend to five hundred rupees for every day during which such contravention continues after conviction for the first such contravention.

26. Offences by companies. (1) Where any offence, punishable under this Act has been committed by a company, every person who, at the time the offence was committed was in charge of, and was responsible to, the company for the conduct of the business of the company, as well as the company, shall be deemed to be guilty of the offence and shall be liable to be proceeded against and punished accordingly:

Provided that nothing contained in this sub-section shall render any such person liable to any punishment, if he proves that the offence was committed without his knowledge or that he had exercised all due diligence to prevent the commission of such offence.

(2) Notwithstanding anything contained in sub-section (1), where any offence punishable under this Act has been committed by a company and it is proved that the offence has been committed with the consent or connivance of, or is attributable to any neglect on the part of, any director, manager, secretary or other officer of the company, such director, manager, secretary or other officer shall also be deemed to be

---

* *Substituted* by Act 14 of 2003 (w.e.f. 14.2.2003).

guilty of that offence and shall be liable to be proceeded against and punished accordingly.

Explanation. For the purposes of this section—

(*a*) "company" means any body corporate and includes a firm or other association of individuals; and

(*b*) "director," in relation to a firm, means a partner in the firm.

27. Offence to be cognizable, non-bailable and non-compoundable. Every offence under this Act shall be cognizable, non-bailable and non-compoundable.

28. Cognizance of offences. (1) No Court shall take cognizance of an offence under this Act except on a complaint made by—

(*a*) the Appropriate Authority concerned, or any officer authorised in this behalf by the Central Government or State Government, as the case may be, or the Appropriate Authority; or

(*b*) a person who has given notice of not less than *[fifteen days] in the manner prescribed, to the Appropriate Authority, of the alleged offence and of his intention to make a complaint to the Court.

Explanation. For the purpose of this clause, "person" includes a social organisation.

(2) No Court, other than that of a Metropolitan Magistrate or a Judicial Magistrate of the First Class, shall try any offence punishable under this Act.

(3) Where a complaint has been made under clause (*b*) of sub-section (1), the Court may, on demand by such person, direct the Appropriate Authority to make available copies of the relevant records in its possession to such person.

CHAPTER VIII

Miscellaneous

29. Maintenance of records. (1) All records, charts, forms, reports, consent letters and all other documents required to be maintained under this Act and the rules shall be preserved for a period of two years or for such period as may be prescribed:

Provided that, if any criminal or other proceedings are instituted against any Genetic Counselling Centre, Genetic Laboratory or Genetic Clinic, the records and all other documents of such Centre, Laboratory or Clinic shall be preserved till the final disposal of such proceedings.

(2) All such records shall, at all reasonable time, be made available for inspection to the Appropriate Authority or to any other person authorised by the Appropriate Authority in this behalf.

30. Power to search and seize records, etc. *[(1) If the Appropriate Authority has reason to believe that an offence under this Act has been or is being committed at any Genetic Counselling Centre, Genetic Laboratory, Genetic Clinic or any other place such Authority or any officer authorised in this behalf may, subject to such rules as may be prescribed, enter and search, at all reasonable times with such assistance, if any, as such Authority or officer considers necessary, such Genetic Counselling Centre, Genetic Laboratory, Genetic Clinic or any other place and examine any record, register, document, book, pamphlet, advertisement or any other material object found therein and seize and seal the same if such Authority or officer has reason to believe that it may furnish evidence of the commission of an offence punishable under this Act.]

(2) The provisions of the Code of Criminal Procedure, 1973 (2 of 1974) relating to searches and seizures shall, so far as may be, apply to every search or seizure made under this Act.

31. Protection of action taken in good faith. No suit, prosecution or other legal proceeding shall lie against the Central or State Government or the Appropriate Authority or any officer authorised by the Central or State Government or by the Authority for anything which is in good faith done or intended to be done in pursuance of the provisions of this Act.

[31A. Removal of difficulties. (1) If any difficulty arises in giving effect to the provisions of the Pre-natal Diagnostic Techniques (Regulation and Prevention of Misuse) Amendment Act, 2002, the Central Government may, by order published in the Official Gazette, make such provisions not inconsistent with the provisions of the said Act as appear to it to be necessary or expedient for removing the difficulty:

Provided that no order shall be made under this section after the expiry of a period of three years from the date of commencement of the Pre-natal Diagnostic Techniques (Regulation and Prevention of Misuse) Amendment Act, 2002.

(2) Every order made under this section shall be laid, as soon as may be after it is made, before each House of Parliament.]

---

* *Substituted* by Act 14 of 2003 (w.e.f. 14.2.2003).

** *Inserted* by Act 14 of 2003 (w.e.f. 14.2.2003).

32. Power to make rules. (1) The Central Government may make rules for carrying out the provisions of this Act.

(2) In particular and without prejudice to the generality of the foregoing power, such rules may provide for—

*[(*i*) the minimum qualifications for persons employed at a registered Genetic Counselling Centre, Genetic Laboratory or Genetic Clinic under clause (2) of section 3;

(*ia*) the manner in which the person conducting ultrasonography on a pregnant woman shall keep record thereof in the clinic under the proviso to sub-section (3) of section 4;]

(*ii*) the form in which consent of a pregnant woman has to be obtained under section 5;

(*iii*) the procedure to be followed by the members of the Central Supervisory Board in the discharge of their functions under sub-section (4) of section 8;

(*iv*) allowances for members other than *ex-officio* members, admissible under sub-section (5) of section 9;

**[(*iva*) code of conduct to be observed by persons working at Genetic Counselling Centres, Genetic Laboratories and Genetic Clinics to be laid down by the Central Supervisory Board under clause (*iv*) of section 16;

(*ivb*) the manner in which reposts shall be furnished by the State and Union Territory Supervisory Boards to the Board and the Central Government in respect of various activities undertaken in the State under the Act under clause (*iv*) of sub-section (1) of section 16A;

(*ivc*) empowering the Appropriate Authority in any other matter under clause (*d*) of section 17A;]

(*v*) the period intervening between any two meetings of the Advisory Committee under the proviso to sub-section (8) of section 17;

(*vi*) the terms and conditions subject to which a person may be appointed to the Advisory Committee and the procedure to be followed by such Committee under sub-section (9) of section 17;

(*vii*) the form and manner in which an application shall be made for registration and the fee payable thereof under sub-section (2) of section 18;

---

* *Substituted* by Act 14 of 2003 (w.e.f. 14.2.2003).

** *Inserted* by Act 14 of 2003 (w.e.f. 14.2.2003).

(*viii*) the facilities to be provided, equipment and other standards to be maintained by the Genetic Counselling Centre, Genetic Laboratory or Genetic Clinic under sub-section (5) of section 18;

(*ix*) the form in which a Certificate of Registration shall be issued under sub-section (1) of section 19;

(*x*) the manner in which and the period after which a Certificate of Registration shall be renewed and the fee payable for such renewal under sub-section (3) of section 19;

(*xi*) the manner in which an appeal may be preferred under section 21;

(*xii*) the period up to which records, charts, etc., shall be preserved under sub-section (1) of section 29;

(*xiii*) the manner in which the seizure of documents, records, objects, etc., shall be made and the manner in which seizure list shall be prepared and delivered to the person from whose custody such documents, records or objects were seized under sub-section (1) of section 30;

(*xiv*) any other matter that is required to be, or may be, prescribed.

33. Power to make regulations. The Board may, with the previous sanction of the Central Government, by notification in the Official Gazette, make regulations not inconsistent with the provisions of this Act and the rules made thereunder to provide for—

(*a*) the time and place of the meetings of the Board and the procedure to be followed for the transaction of business at such meetings and the number of members which shall form the quorum under sub-section (1) of section 9;

(*b*) the manner in which a person may be temporarily associated with the Board under sub-section (1) of section 11;

(*c*) the method of appointment, the conditions of service and the scales of pay and allowances of the officer and other employees of the Board appointed under section 12;

(*d*) generally for the efficient conduct of the affairs of the Board.

34. Rules and regulations to be laid before Parliament. Every rule and every regulation made under this Act shall be laid, as soon as may be after it is made, before each House of Parliament, while it is in session, for a total period of thirty days which may be comprised in one session or in two or more successive sessions, and if, before the expiry of the session immediately following the session or the successive sessions aforesaid, both Houses agree in making any modification in the rule or regulation or both Houses agree that the rule or regulation should not be made, the rule or regulation shall thereafter have effect only in such modified form or be of no effect, as the case may be; so, however, that any such modification or annulment shall be without prejudice to the validity of anything previously done under that rule or regulation.

APPENDIX

11

The Transplantation of Human Organs and Tissues Act, 1994

(42 of 1994)

[8th July, 1994

An Act to provide for the regulation of removal, storage and transplantation of *[human organs and tissues for the therapeutic purposes and for the prevention of commercial dealings in human organs and tissues] and for matters connected therewith or incidental thereto.

WHEREAS it is expedient to provide for the regulation of removal, storage and transplantation of *[human organs or tissues or both] for therapeutic purposes and for the prevention of commercial dealings in **[human organs or tissues or both];

AND WHEREAS in Parliament has no power to make laws for the States with respect to any of the matters aforesaid except as provided in Articles 249 and 250 of the Constitution;

AND WHEREAS in pursuance of clause (1) of Article 252 of the Constitution, resolutions have been passed by all the Houses of the Legislatures of the States of Goa, Himachal Pradesh and Maharashtra to the effect that the matters aforesaid should be regulated in those States by Parliament by law;

BE it enacted by Parliament in the Forty-fifth Year of the Republic of India as follows:—

---

* *Substituted* by the Transplantation of Human Organs (Amendment) Act, 2011 (w.e.f. 10.1.2014).

** *Substituted* by Act 16 of 2011 (w.e.f. 10.1.2014).

Chapter I

Preliminary

1. Short title, application and commencement. (1) This Act may be called the Transplantation of *[Human Organs and Tissues] Act, 1994.

(2) It applies, in the first instance, to the whole of the States of Goa, Himachal Pradesh and Maharashtra and to all the Union territories and it shall also apply to such other State which adopts this Act by resolution passed in that behalf under clause (1) of Article 252 of the Constitution.

(3) It shall come into force in the States of Goa, Himachal Pradesh and Maharashtra and in all the Union territories on such date** as the Central Government may, by notification, appoint and in any other State which adopts this Act under clause (1) of Article 252 of the Constitution, on the date of such adoption; and any reference in this Act to the commencement of this Act shall, in relation to any State or Union territory, means the date on which this Act comes into force in such State or Union territory.

2. Definitions. In this Act, unless the context otherwise requires,—

(*a*) "advertisement" includes any form of advertising whether to the public generally or to any section of the public or, individually to selected persons;

(*b*) "Appropriate Authority" means the Appropriate Authority appointed under section 13;

(*c*) "Authorisation Committee" means the committee constituted under clause (*a*) or clause (*b*) of sub-section (4) of section 9;

(*d*) "brain-stem death" means the stage at which all functions of the brain-stem have permanently and irreversibly ceased and is so certified under sub-section (6) of section 3;

(*e*) "deceased person" means a person in whom permanent disappearance of all evidence of life occurs, by reason of brain-stem death or in a cardio-pulmonary sense, at any time after live birth has taken place;

(*f*) "donor" means any person, not less than eighteen years of age, who voluntarily authorises the removal of any of his

* *Substituted* by Act 16 of 2011 (w.e.f. 10.1.2014).

** Came into force in the State of Goa, Himachal Pradesh and Maharashtra and in all Union Territories on 4.2.1995, *vide* Notification No. S.O. 80(E), dated 4.2.1995.

human organs for therapeutic purposes under sub-section (1) or sub-section (2) of section 3;

(*g*) "hospital" includes a nursing home, clinic, medical centre, medical or teaching institution for therapeutic purposes and other like institution;

(*h*) "human organ" means any part of a human body consisting of a structured arrangement of tissues which, if wholly, removed, cannot be replicated by the body;

*[(*ha*) "Human Organ Retrieval Centre" means a hospital,—

(*i*) which has adequate facilities for treating seriously ill patients who can be potential donours of organs in the event of death; and

(*ii*) which is registered under sub-section (1) of section 14 for retrieval of human organs;]

*[(*hb*) "minor" means a person who has not completed the age of eighteen years;]

**[(*i*) "near relative" means spouse, son, daughter, father, mother, brother, sister, grandfather, grandmother, grandson or granddaughter;]

(*j*) "notification" means a notification published in the Official Gazette;

(*k*) "payment" means payment in money or money's worth but does not include any payment for defraying or reimbursing—

(*i*) the cost of removing, transporting or preserving the *[human organ or tissue or both] to be supplied; or

(*ii*) any expenses or loss of earnings incurred by a person so far as reasonably and directly attributable to his supplying any *[human organ or tissue or both] from his body;

(*l*) "prescribed" means prescribed by rules made under this Act;

(*m*) "recipient" means a person into whom any *[human organ or tissue or both] is, or is proposed to be, transplanted;

(*n*) "registered medical practitioner" means a medical practitioner who possesses any recognised medical qualification as defined in clause (*h*) of section 2 of the Indian Medical Council Act, 1956 (102 of 1956), and who is enrolled on a State Medical Register as defined in clause (*k*) of that section;

---

* *Inserted* by Act 16 of 2011 (w.e.f. 10.1.2014).

** *Substituted* by Act 16 of 2011 (w.e.f. 10.1.2014).

(*o*) "therapeutic purposes" means systematic treatment of any disease or the measures to improve health according to any particular method or modality; *[***]

**[(*oa*) "tissue" means a group of cells, except blood, performing a particular function in the human body;]

**[(*ob*) "Tissue Bank", means a facility registered under section 14A for carrying out any activity relating to the recovery, screening, testing, processing, storage and distribution of tissues, but does not include a Blood Bank;]

(*p*) "transplantation" means the grafting of any †[human organ or tissue or both] from any living person or deceased person to some other living person for therapeutic purposes.

**[(*q*) "transplant co-ordinator" means a person appointed by the hospital for co-ordinating all matters relating to removal or transplantation of human organs or tissues or both and for assisting the authority for removal of human organs or tissues or both in accordance with the provisions of section 3.]

Chapter II

Authority for the Removal of †[Human Organs or Tissues or Both]

3. Authority for removal of †[human organs or tissues or both]. (1) Any donor may, in such manner and subject to such conditions as may be prescribed, authorise the removal, before his death, of any †[human organ or tissue or both] of his body for therapeutic purposes.

**[(1A) For the purpose of removal, storage or transplantation of such human organs or tissues or both, as may be prescribed, it shall be the duty of the registered medical practitioner working in a hospital, in consultation with transplant co-ordinator, if such transplant co-ordinator is available,—

(*i*) to ascertain from the person admitted to the Intensive Care Unit or from his near relative that such person had authorised at any time before his death the removal of any human organ or tissue or both of his body under sub-section (2), then the hospital shall proceed to obtain the documentation for such authorisation;

* *Omitted* by Act 16 of 2011 (w.e.f. 10.1.2014).

** *Inserted* by Act 16 of 2011 (w.e.f. 10.1.2014).

† *Substituted* by Act 16 of 2011 (w.e.f. 10.1.2014).

(*ii*) where no such authority as referred to in sub-section (2) was made by such person, to make aware to that person or near relative for option to authorise or decline for donation of human organs or tissues or both;

(*iii*) to require the hospital to inform in writing to the Human Organ Removal Centre for removal, storage or transplantation of human organs or tissues or both, of the donor identified in clauses (*i*) and (*ii*) in such manner as may be prescribed.]

*[(1B) The duties mentioned under clauses (*i*) to (*iii*) of sub-section (1A) from such date, as may be prescribed, shall also apply in the case of registered medical practitioner working in an Intensive Care Unit in a hospital which is not registered under this Act for the purpose of removal, storage or transplantation of human organs or tissues or both.]

(2) If any donor had, in writing and in the presence of two or more witnesses (at least one of whom is a near relative of such person), unequivocally authorised at any time before his death, the removal of any **[human organ or tissue or both] of his body, after his death, for therapeutic purposes, the person lawfully in possession of the dead body of the donor shall, unless he has any reason to believe that the donor had subsequently revoked the authority aforesaid, grant to a registered medical practitioner all reasonable facilities for the removal, for therapeutic purposes, of that **[human organ or tissue or both] from the dead body of the donor.

(3) Where no such authority as is referred to in sub-section (2), was made by any person before his death but no objection was also expressed by such person to any of his **[human organs or tissues or both] being used after his death for therapeutic purposes, the person lawfully in possession of the dead body of such person may, unless he has reason to believe that any near relative of the deceased person has objection to any of the deceased person's **[human organs or tissues or both] being used for therapeutic purposes, authorise the removal of any **[human organ or tissue or both] of the deceased person for its use for therapeutic purposes.

(4) The authority given under sub-section (1) or sub-section (2) or, as the case may be, sub-section (3) shall be sufficient warrant for the removal, for therapeutic purposes, of the **[human organ or tissue or

* *Inserted* by Act 16 of 2011 (w.e.f. 10.1.2014).

** *Substituted* by Act 16 of 2011 (w.e.f. 10.1.2014).

both] but no such removal shall be made by any person other than the registered medical practitioner:

*[Provided that a technician possessing such qualifications and experience, as may be prescribed, may enucleate a cornea.]

(5) Where any **[human organ or tissue or both] is to be removed from the body of a deceased person, the registered medical practitioner shall satisfy himself, before such removal, by a personal examination of the body from which any **[human organ or tissue or both] is to be removed, that life is extinct in such body or, where it appears to be a case of brain-stem death, that such death has been certified under sub-section (6).

(6) Where any **[human organ or tissue or both] is to be removed from the body of a person in the event of his brain-stem death, no such removal shall be undertaken unless such death is certified, in such form and in such manner and on satisfaction of such conditions and requirements as may be prescribed, by a Board of medical experts consisting of the following, namely:—

(*i*) the registered medical practitioner, in charge of the hospital in which brain-stem death has occurred;

(*ii*) an independent registered medical practitioner, being a specialist, to be nominated by the registered medical practitioner specified in clause (*i*), from the panel of names approved by the Appropriate Authority;

(*iii*) a neurologist or a neurosurgeon to be nominated by the registered medical practitioner specified in clause (*i*), from the panel of names approved by the Appropriate Authority; †[***].

*[Provided that where a neurologist or a neurosurgeon is not available, the registered medical practitioner may nominate an independent registered medical practitioner, being a surgeon or a physician and an anaesthetist or intensivist subject to the condition that they are not members of the transplantation team for the concerned recipient and to such conditions as may be prescribed;]

(*iv*) the registered medical practitioner treating the person whose brain-stem death has occurred.

(7) Notwithstanding anything contained in sub-section (3), where brain-stem death of any person, less than eighteen years of age, occurs

* *Inserted* by Act 16 of 2011 (w.e.f. 10.1.2014).
** *Substituted* by Act 16 of 2011 (w.e.f. 10.1.2014).
† *Omitted* by Act 16 of 2011 (w.e.f. 10.1.2014).

and is certified under sub-section (6), any of the parents of the deceased person may give authority, in such form and in such manner as may be prescribed, for the removal of any *[human organ or tissues or both] from the body of the deceased person.

4. Removal of *[human organs or tissues or both] not to be authorised in certain cases. (1) No facilities shall be granted under sub-section (2) of section 3 and no authority shall be given under sub-section (3) of that section for the removal of any *[human organ or tissue or both] from the body of a deceased person, if the person required to grant such facilities, or empowered to give such authority, has reason to believe that an inquest may be required to be held in relation to such body in pursuance of the provisions of any law for the time being in force.

(2) No authority for the removal of any *[human organ or tissue or both] from the body of a deceased person shall be given by a person to whom such body has been entrusted solely for the purpose of interment, cremation or other disposal.

5. Authority for removal of *[human organs or tissues or both] in case of unclaimed bodies in hospital or prison. (1) In the case of a dead body lying in a hospital or prison and not claimed by any of the near relatives of the deceased person within forty-eight hours from the time of the death of the concerned person, the authority for the removal of any *[human organ or tissue or both] from the dead body which so remains unclaimed may be given, in the prescribed form, by the person in charge, for the time being, of the management or control of the hospital or prison, or by an employee of such hospital or prison authorised in this behalf by the person in charge of the management or control thereof.

(2) No authority shall be given under sub-section (1) if the person empowered to give such authority has reason to believe that any near relative of the deceased person is likely to claim the dead body even though such near relative has not come forward to claim the body of the deceased person within the time specified in sub-section (1).

6. Authority for removal of *[human organs or tissues or both] from bodies sent for post-mortem examination for medico-legal or pathological purposes. Where the body of a person has been sent for post-mortem examination—

(*a*) for medico-legal purposes by reason of the death of such person having been caused by accident or any other unnatural cause; or

* *Substituted* by Act 16 of 2011 (w.e.f. 10.1.2014).

(*b*) for pathological purposes,

the person competent under this Act to give authority for the removal of any *[human organ or tissue or both] from such dead body may, if he has reason to believe that such *[human organ or tissue or both] will not be required for the purpose for which such body has been sent for post-mortem examination, authorise the removal, for therapeutic purposes, of that *[human organ or tissue or both] of the deceased person provided that he is satisfied that the deceased person had not expressed, before his death, any objection to any of his *[human organs or tissues or both] being used, for therapeutic purposes after his death or, where he had granted an authority for the use of any of his *[human organs or tissues or both] for therapeutic purposes, after his death, such authority had not been revoked by him before his death.

7. Preservation of *[human organs or tissues or both]. After the removal of any *[human organ or tissue or both] from the body of any person, the registered medical practitioner shall take such steps for the preservation of the *[human organ or tissue or both] so removed as may be prescribed.

8. Savings. (1) Nothing in the foregoing provisions of this Act shall be construed as rendering unlawful any dealing with the body or with any part of the body of a deceased person if such dealing would have been lawful if this Act had not been passed.

(2) Neither the grant of any facility or authority for the removal of any *[human organ or tissue or both] from the body of a deceased person in accordance with the provisions of this Act nor the removal of any *[human organ or tissue or both] from the body of a deceased person in pursuance of such authority shall be deemed to be an offence punishable under section 297 of the Indian Penal Code (45 of 1860).

9. Restrictions on removal and transplantation of *[human organs or tissues or both]. (1) Save as otherwise provided in sub-section (3), no *[human organ or tissue or both] removed from the body of a donor before his death shall be transplanted into a recipient unless the donor is a near relative of the recipient.

**[(1A) Where the donor or the recipient being near relative is a foreign national, prior approval of the Authorisation Committee shall be required before removing or transplanting human organ or tissue or both:

---

* *Substituted* by Act 16 of 2011 (w.e.f. 10.1.2014).

** *Inserted* by Act 16 of 2011 (w.e.f. 10.1.2014).

Provided that the Authorisation Committee shall not approve such removal or transplantation if the recipient is a foreign national and the donor is an Indian national unless they are near relatives.

(IB) No human organs or tissues or both shall be removed from the body of a minor before his death for the purpose of transplantation except in the manner as may be prescribed.

(1C) No human organs or tissues or both shall be removed from the body of a mentally challenged person before his death for the purpose of transplantation.

Explanation. For the purpose of this sub-section,—

(*i*) the expression "mentally challenged person" includes a person with mental illness or mental retardation, as the case may be;

(*ii*) the expression "mental illness" includes dementia, schizophrenia and such other mental condition that makes a person intellectually disabled;

(*iii*) the expression "mental retardation" shall have the same meaning as assigned to it in clause (*r*) of section 2 of the Persons With Disabilities (Equal Opportunities, Protection of Rights and Full Participation) Act, 1995 (1 of 1996).]

(2) Where any donor authorises the removal of any of his *[human organs or tissues or both] after his death under sub-section (2) of section 3 or any person competent or empowered to give authority for the removal of any *[human organ or tissue or both] from the body of any deceased person authorises such removal, the *[human organ or tissue or both] may be removed and transplanted into the body of any recipient who may be in need of such *[human organ or tissue or both].

(3) If any donor authorises the removal of any of his *[human organs or tissues or both] before his death under sub-section (1) of section 3 for transplantation into the body of such recipient, not being a near relative, as is specified by the donor by reason of affection or attachment towards the recipient or for any other special reasons, such *[human organ or tissue or both] shall not be removed and transplanted without the prior approval of the Authorisation Committee.

**[(3A) Notwithstanding anything contained in sub-section (3), where—

(*a*) any donor has agreed to make a donation of his human organ or tissue or both before his death to a recipient, who is his

---

* *Substituted* by Act 16 of 2011 (w.e.f. 10.1.2014).

** *Inserted* by Act 16 of 2011 (w.e.f. 10.1.2014).

near relative, but such donor is not compatible biologically as a donor for the recipient; and

(*b*) the second donor has agreed to make a donation of his human organ or tissue or both before his death to such recipient, who is his near relative, but such donor is not compatible biologically as a donor for such recipient; then

(*c*) the first donor who is compatible biologically as a donor for the second recipient and the second donor is compatible biologically as a donor of a human organ or tissue or both for the first recipient and both donors and both recipients in the aforesaid group of donor and recipient have entered into a single agreement to donate and receive such human organ or tissue or both according to such biological compatibility in the group,

the removal and transplantation of the human organ or tissue or both, as per the agreement referred to above, shall not be done without prior approval of the Authorisation Committee.]

*[(4)(*a*) The composition of the Authorisation Committee shall be such as may be prescribed by the Central Government from time to time.

(*b*) The State Government and the Union territories shall constitute, by notification, one or more Authorisation Committee consisting of such members as may be nominated by the State Government and the Union territories on such terms and conditions as may be specified in the notification for the purposes of this section.]

(5) On an application jointly made, in such form and in such manner as may be prescribed, by the donor and the recipient, the Authorisation Committee shall, after holding an inquiry and after satisfying itself that the applicants have complied with all the requirements of this Act and tile rules made thereunder, grant to the applicants approval for the removal and transplantation of the human organ.

(6) If, after the inquiry and after giving an opportunity to the applicants of being heard, the Authorisation Committee is satisfied that the applicants have not complied with the requirements of this Act and the rules made thereunder, it shall, for reasons to be recorded in writing, reject the application for approval.

* *Substituted* by Act 16 of 2011 (w.e.f. 10.1.2014).

Chapter III

Regulation of Hospitals

10. Regulation of hospitals conducting the removal, storage or transplantation of *[human organs or tissues or both]. (1) On and from the commencement of this Act,—

(*a*) no hospital, unless registered under this Act, shall conduct, or associate with, or help in, the removal, storage or transplantation of any *[human organ or tissue or both];

(*b*) no medical practitioner or any other person shall conduct, or cause to be conducted, or aid in conducting by himself or through any other person, any activity relating to the removal, storage or transplantation of any *[human organ or tissue or both] at a place other than a place registered under this Act; **[***]

(*c*) no place including a hospital registered under sub-section (1) of section 15 shall be used or cause to be used by any person for the removal, storage or transplantation of any *[human organ or tissue or both] except for therapeutic purposes; †[and]

†[(*d*) no Tissue Bank, unless registered under this Act, shall carry out any activity relating to the recovery, screening, testing, processing, storage and distribution of tissues.]

(2) Notwithstanding anything contained in sub-section (1), the eyes or the ears may be removed at any place from the dead body of any donor, for therapeutic purposes, by a registered medical practitioner.

Explanation. For the purposes of this sub-section, "ears" includes ear drums and ear bones.

11. Prohibition of removal or transplantation of *[human organs or tissues or both] for any purpose other than therapeutic purposes. No donor and no person empowered to give authority for the removal of any *[human organ or tissue or both] shall authorise the removal of any *[human organ or tissue or both] for any purpose other than therapeutic purposes.

12. Explaining effects, etc., to donor and recipient. No registered medical practitioner shall undertake the removal or transplantation of any *[human organ or tissue or both] unless he has explained, in such

* *Substituted* by Act 16 of 2011 (w.e.f. 10.1.2014).
** *Omitted* by Act 16 of 2011 (w.e.f. 10.1.2014).
† *Inserted* by Act 16 of 2011 (w.e.f. 10.1.2014).

manner as may be prescribed, all possible effects, complications and hazards connected with the removal and transplantation to the donor and the recipient respectively.

Chapter IV

Appropriate Authority

13. Appropriate Authority. (1) The Central Government shall appoint, by notification, one or more officers as Appropriate Authorities for each of the Union territories for the purposes of this Act.

(2) The State Government shall appoint, by notification, one or more officers as Appropriate Authorities for the purposes of this Act.

(3) The Appropriate Authority shall perform the following functions, namely:

(*i*) to grant registration under sub-section (1) of section 15 or renew registration under sub-section (3) of that section;

(*ii*) to suspend or cancel registration under sub-section (2) of section 16;

*[(*iii*) to enforce such standards, as may be prescribed,—

(A) for hospitals engaged in the removal, storage or transplantation of any human organ;

(B) for Tissue Banks engaged in recovery, screening, testing, processing, storage and distribution of tissues;]

(*iv*) to investigate any complaint of breach of any of the provisions of this Act or any of the rules made thereunder and take appropriate action;

**[(*iva*) to inspect Tissue Banks periodically;]

(*v*) to inspect hospitals periodically for examination of the quality of transplantation and the follow-up medical care to persons who have undergone transplantation and persons from whom organs are removed; and

(*vi*) to undertake such other measures as may be prescribed.

[13A. Advisory Committees to advise Appropriate Authority. (1) The Central Government and the State Governments, as the case may be, by notification, shall constitute an Advisory Committee for a period of two years to aid and advise the Appropriate Authority to discharge its functions.

* *Substituted* by Act 16 of 2011 (w.e.f. 10.1.2014).

** *Inserted* by Act 16 of 2011 (w.e.f. 10.1.2014).

(2) The Advisory Committee shall consist of—

(*a*) one administrative expert not below the rank of Secretary to the State Government, to be nominated as Chairperson of the Advisory Committee;

(*b*) two medical experts having such qualifications as may be prescribed;

(*c*) one officer not below the rank of a Joint Director to represent the Ministry or Department of Health and Family Welfare, to be designated as Member-Secretary;

(*d*) two eminent social workers of high social standing and integrity, one of whom shall be from amongst representatives of women's organisation;

(*e*) one legal expert who has held the position of an Additional District Judge or equivalent;

(*f*) one person to represent non-governmental organisations or associations which are working in the field of organ or tissue donations or human rights.

(*g*) one specialist in the field of human organ transplantation, provided he is not a member of the transplantation team.

(3) The terms and conditions for appointment to the Advisory Committee shall be such as may be prescribed by the Central Government].

***[13B. Powers of Appropriate Authority.** The Appropriate Authority shall for the purposes of this Act have all the powers of a civil court trying a suit under the Code of Civil Procedure, 1908 (5 of 1908) and, in particular, in respect of the following matters, namely:—

(*a*) summoning of any person who is in possession of any information relating to violation of the provisions of this Act or the rules made thereunder;

(*b*) discovery and production of any document or material object;

(*c*) issuing search warrant for any place suspected to be indulging in unauthorised removal, procurement or transplantation of human organs or tissues or both; and

(*d*) any other matter which may be prescribed.]

***[13C. National Human Organs and Tissues Removal and Storage Network.** The Central Government may, by notification, establish a National Human Organs and Tissues Removal and Storage Network at one or

* *Inserted* by Act 16 of 2011 (w.e.f. 10.1.2014).

more places and Regional Network is such manner and to perform such functions, as may be prescribed.]

*[**13D. National registry.** The Central Government shall maintain a national registry of the donors and recipients of human organs and tissues and such registry shall have such information as may be prescribed to an ongoing evaluation of the scientific and clinical status of human organs and tissues.]

Chapter V
Registration of Hospitals

14. Registration of hospitals engaged in removal, storage or transplantation of **[human organs or tissues or both]. (1) **[No hospital (including Human Organ Retrieval Centre)] shall commence any activity relating to the removal, storage or transplantation of any **[human organ or tissue or both] for therapeutic purposes after the commencement of this Act unless such hospital is duly registered under this Act:

Provided that every hospital engaged, either partly or exclusively, in any activity relating to the removal, storage or transplantation of any **[human organ or tissue or both] for therapeutic purposes immediately before the commencement of this Act, shall apply for registration within sixty days from the date of such commencement:

Provided further that every hospital engaged in any activity relating to the removal, storage or transplantation of any **[human organ or tissue or both] shall cease to engage in any such activity on the expiry of three months from the date of commencement of this Act unless such hospital has applied for registration and is so registered or till such application is disposed of, whichever is earlier.

(2) Every application for registration under sub-section (1) shall be made to the Appropriate Authority in such form and in such manner and shall be accompanied by such fees as may be prescribed.

(3) No hospital shall be registered under this Act unless the Appropriate Authority is satisfied that such hospital is in a position to provide such specialised services and facilities, possess such skilled manpower and equipments and maintain such standards as may be prescribed.

*[(4) No hospital shall be registered under this Act, unless the Appropriate Authority is satisfied that such hospital has appointed a

* *Inserted* by Act 16 of 2011 (w.e.f. 10.1.2014).

** *Substituted* by Act 16 of 2011 (w.e.f. 10.1.2014).

transplant co-ordinator having such qualifications and experience as may be prescribed.]

*[**14A. Registration of Tissue Bank.** (1) No Tissue Bank shall, after the commencement of the Transplantation of Human Organs (Amendment) Act, 2011, commence any activity relating to the recovery, screening, testing, processing, storage and distribution of tissues unless it is duly registered under this Act:

Provided that any facility engaged, either partly or exclusively, in any activity relating to the recovery, screening, testing, processing, storage and distribution of tissues immediately before the commencement of the Transplantation of Human Organs (Amendment) Act, 2011, shall apply for registration as Tissue Bank within sixty days from the date of such commencement:

Provided further that such facility shall case to engage in any such activity on the expiry of three months from the date of commencement of the Transplantation of Human Organs (Amendment) Act, 2011, unless such Tissue Bank has applied for registration and is so registered, or till such application is disposed of, whichever is earlier.

(2) Every application for registration under sub-section (1) shall be made to the Appropriate Authority in such form and in such manner and shall be accompanied by such fees as may be prescribed.

(3) No Tissue Bank shall be registered under this Act unless the Appropriate authority is satisfied that such Tissue Bank is in a position to provide such specialised services and facilities, possess such skilled manpower and equipments and maintain such standards as may be prescribed.]

15. Certificate of registration. (1) The Appropriate Authority shall, after holding an inquiry and after satisfying itself that the applicant has complied with all the requirements of this Act and the rules made thereunder, **[grant to the hospital or to the Tissue Bank, as the case may be,] a certificate of registration in such form, for such period and subject to such conditions as may be prescribed.

(2) If, after the inquiry and after giving an opportunity to the applicant of being heard, the Appropriate Authority is satisfied that the applicant has not complied with the requirements of this Act and the rules made thereunder, it shall, for reasons to be recorded in writing, reject the application for registration.

---

* *Inserted* by Act 16 of 2011 (w.e.f. 10.1.2014).

** *Substituted* by Act 16 of 2011 (w.e.f. 10.1.2014).

(3) Every certificate of registration shall be renewed in such manner and on payment of such fees as may be prescribed.

16. Suspension or cancellation of registration. (1) The Appropriate Authority may, *suo motu* or on complaint, issue a notice to any *[hospital or Tissue Bank, as the case may be], to show cause why its registration under this Act should not be suspended or cancelled for the reasons mentioned in the notice.

(2) If, after giving a reasonable opportunity of being heard to the *[hospital or Tissue Bank, as the case may be,] the Appropriate Authority is satisfied that there has been a breach of any of the provisions of this Act or the rules made thereunder, it may, without prejudice to any criminal action that it may take against such *[hospital or Tissue Bank, as the case may be,] suspend its registration for such period as it may think fit or cancel its registration:

Provided that where the Appropriate Authority is of the opinion that it is necessary or expedient so to do in the public interest, it may, for reasons to be recorded in writing, suspend the registration of any *[hospital or Tissue Bank, as the case may be,] without issuing any notice.

17. Appeals. Any person aggrieved by an order of the Authorisation Committee rejecting an application for approval under sub-section (6) of section 9, or any hospital **[or Tissue Bank, as the case may be,] aggrieved by an order of the Appropriate Authority rejecting an application for registration under sub-section (2) of section 15 or an order of suspension or cancellation of registration under sub-section (2) of section 16, may, within thirty days from the date of the receipt of the order, prefer an appeal, in such manner as may be prescribed, against such order to—

(*i*) the Central Government where the appeal is against the order of the Authorisation Committee constituted under clause (*a*) of sub-section (4) of section 9 or against the order of the Appropriate Authority appointed under sub-section (1) of section 13; or

(*ii*) the State Government, where the appeal is against the order of the Authorisation Committee constituted under clause (*b*) of sub-section (4) of section 9 or against the order of the Appropriate Authority appointed under sub-section (2) of section 13.

---

* *Substituted* by Act 16 of 2011 (w.e.f. 10.1.2014).

** *Inserted* by Act 16 of 2011 (w.e.f. 10.1.2014).

Chapter VI

Offences and Penalties

18. Punishment for removal of *[human organ or tissue or both] without authority. (1) Any person who renders his services to or at any hospital and who, for purposes of transplantation, conducts, associates with, or helps in any manner in, the removal of any human organ without authority, shall be punishable with imprisonment for a term which may extend to *[ten years and with fine which may extend to twenty lakh rupees].

(2) Where any person convicted under sub-section (1) is a registered medical practitioner, his name shall be reported by the Appropriate Authority to the respective State Medical Council for taking necessary action including the removal of his name from the register of the Council for a period of *[three years] for the first offence and permanently for the subsequent offence.

**[(3) Any person who renders his services to or at any hospital and who conducts, or associates with or helps in any manner in the removal of human tissues without authority, shall be punishable with imprisonment for a term which may extend to three years and with fine which may extend to five lakh rupees.]

19. Punishment for commercial dealings in human organs. Whoever—

(*a*) makes or receives any payment for the supply of, or for an offer to supply, any human organ;

(*b*) seeks to find a person willing to supply for payment any human organ;

(*c*) offers to supply any human organ for payment; or

(*d*) initiates or negotiates any arrangement involving the making of any payment for the supply of, or for an offer to supply, any human organ;

(*e*) takes part in the management or control of a body of persons, whether a society, firm or company, whose activities consist of or include the initiation or negotiation of any arrangement referred to in clause (*d*); or

(*f*) publishes or distributes or causes to be published or distributed any advertisement,—

(*a*) inviting persons to supply for payment of any human organ;

---

* *Substituted* by Act 16 of 2011 (w.e.f. 10.1.2014).

** *Inserted* by Act 16 of 2011 (w.e.f. 10.1.2014).

(b) offering to supply any human organ for payment; or

(c) indicating that the advertiser is willing to initiate or negotiate any arrangement referred to in clause (d);

*[(g) abets in the preparation or submission of false documents including giving false affidavits to establish that the donor is making the donation of the human organs, as a near relative or by reason of affection or attachment towards the recipient],

shall be punishable with imprisonment for a term which shall not be less than **[five years but which may extend to ten years and shall be liable to fine which shall not be less than twenty lakh rupees but may extend to one crore rupees.]

†[***].

*[**19A. Punishment for illegal dealings in human tissues.** Whoever—

(a) makes or receives any payment for the supply of, or for an offer to supply, any human tissue; or

(b) seeks to find a person willing to supply for payment and human tissue; or

(c) offers to supply any human tissue for payment; or

(d) initiates or negotiates any arrangement involving the making of any payment for the supply of, or for an offer to supply, any human tissue; or

(e) takes part in the management or control of a body of persons, whether a society, firm or company, whose activities consist of or include the initiation or negotiation of any arrangement referred to in clause (d); or

(f) publishes or distributes or causes to be published or distributed any advertisement—

(i) inviting persons to supply for payment of any human tissue; or

(ii) offering to supply any human tissue for payment; or

(iii) indicating that the advertiser is willing to initiate or negotiate any arrangement referred to in clause (d); or

(g) abets in the preparation or submission of false documents including giving false affidavits to establish that the donor

* *Inserted* by Act 16 of 2011 (w.e.f. 10.1.2014).
** *Substituted* by Act 16 of 2011 (w.e.f. 10.1.2014).
† *Omitted* by Act 16 of 2011 (w.e.f. 10.1.2014).

is making the donation of the human tissues as a near relative or by reason of affection or attachment towards the recipient,

shall be punishable with imprisonment for a term which shall not be less than one year but which may extend to three years and shall be liable to fine which shall not be less than five lakh rupees but which may extend to twenty-five lakh rupees.]

20. Punishment for contravention of any other provision of this Act. Whoever contravenes any provision of this Act or any rule made, or any condition of the registration granted, thereunder for which no punishment is separately provided in this Act, shall be punishable with imprisonment for a term which may extend to *[five years or with fine which may extend to twenty lakh rupees].

21. Offences by companies. (1) Where any offence punishable under this Act has been committed by a company, every person who, at the time the offence was committed was in charge of, and was responsible to, the company for the conduct of the business of the company, as well as the company, shall be deemed to be guilty of the offence and shall be liable to be proceeded against and punished accordingly:

Provided that nothing contained in this sub-section shall render any such person liable to any punishment, if he proves that the offence was committed without his knowledge or that he had exercised all due diligence to prevent the commission of such offence.

(2) Notwithstanding anything contained in sub-section (1), where any offence punishable under this Act has been committed by a company and it is proved that the offence has been committed with the consent or connivance of, or is attributable to any neglect on the part of, any director, manager, secretary or other officer of the company, such director, manager, secretary or other officer shall also be deemed to be guilty of that offence and shall be liable to be proceeded against and punished accordingly.

Explanation.—For the purposes of this section,—

(*a*) "company" means any body corporate and includes a firm or other association of individuals; and

(*b*) "director", in relation to a firm, means a partner in the firm.

22. Cognizance of offence. (1) No court shall take cognizance of an offence under this Act except on a complaint made by—

(*a*) the Appropriate Authority concerned, or any officer authorised in this behalf by the Central Government or the

---

* *Substituted* by Act 16 of 2011 (w.e.f. 10.1.2014).

State Government or, as the case may be, the Appropriate Authority; or

(b) a person who has given notice of not less than sixty days, in such manner as may be prescribed, to the Appropriate Authority concerned, of the alleged offence and of his intention to make a complaint to the court.

(2) No court other than that of a Metropolitan Magistrate or a Judicial Magistrate of the first class shall try any offence punishable under this Act.

(3) Where a complaint has been made under clause (b) of sub-section (1), the court may, on demand by such person, direct the Appropriate Authority to make available copies of the relevant records in its possession to such person.

Chapter VII

Miscellaneous

23. Protection of action taken in good faith. (1) No suit, prosecution or other legal proceeding shall lie against any person for anything which is in good faith done or intended to be done in pursuance of the provisions of this Act.

(2) No suit or other legal proceeding shall lie against the Central Government or the State Government for any damage caused or likely to be caused for anything which is in good faith done or intended to be done in pursuance of the provisions of this Act.

24. Power to make rules. (1) The Central Government may, by notification, make rules for carrying out the purposes of this Act.

(2) In particular, and without prejudice to the generality of the foregoing power, such rules may provide for all or any of the following matters, namely:

(a) the manner in which and the conditions subject to which any donor may authorise removal, before his death, of any *[human organ or tissue or both] of his body under sub-section (1A) of section 3;

**[(aa) the human organ or tissues or both in respect of which duty is cast on registered medical practitioner, the manner of obtaining documentation for authorisation under clause (i) of sub-section (1A) of section 3;]

* *Substituted* by Act 16 of 2011 (w.e.f. 10.1.2014).

** *Inserted* by Act 16 of 2011 (w.e.f. 10.1.2014).

*[(*ab*) the manner of informing the Human Organ Retrieval Centre under clause (*iii*) of sub-section (1A) of section 3;]

*[(*ac*) the date from which duties mentioned in sub-section (1A) are applicable to registered medical practitioner working in a unregistered hospital under sub-section (IB) of section 3;]

*[(*ae*) the qualification and experience of a technician under the proviso to sub-section (4) of section 3;]

(*b*) the form and the manner in which a brain-stem death is to be certified and the conditions and requirements which are to be satisfied for that purpose under sub-section (6) of section 3;

*[(*ba*) the conditions for nomination of a surgeon or a physician and an anaesthetist or intensivist to be included in the Board of medical experts under the proviso to clause (*iii*) of sub-section (6) of section 3;]

(*c*) the form and the manner in which any of the parents may give authority, in the case of brain-stem death of a minor, for the removal of any **[human organ or tissue or both] under sub-section (7) of section 3;

(*d*) the form in which authority for the removal of any **[human organ or tissue or both] from an unclaimed dead body may be given by the person in charge of the management or control of the hospital or prison under sub-section (1) of section 5;

(*e*) the steps to be taken for the preservation of the **[human organ or tissue or both] removed from the body of any person under section 7;

*[(*ea*) the manner of removal of human organs or tissues or both from the body of a minor before his death for transplantation under sub-section (IB) of section 9;]

*[(*eb*) the composition of the Authorisation Committees under sub-section (4) of section 9;]

(*f*) the form and the manner in which an application may be jointly made by the donor and the recipient under sub-section (5) of section 9;

(*g*) the manner in which all possible effects, complications and hazards connected with the removal and transplantation is to be explained by the registered medical practitioner to the donor and the recipient under section 12;

---

* *Inserted* by Act 16 of 2011 (w.e.f. 10.1.2014).

** *Substituted* by Act 16 of 2011 (w.e.f. 10.1.2014).

(*h*) the standards as are to be enforced by the Appropriate Authority for hospitals engaged in the removal, storage or transplantation of any *[human organ or tissue or both] under clause (*iii*) of sub-section (3) of section 13;

(*i*) the other measures as the Appropriate Authority shall undertake in performing its functions under clause (*vi*) of sub-section (3) of section 13;

**[(*ia*) the qualifications of medical experts and the terms and conditions for appointment to Advisory Committee under sub-sections (2) and (3) of section 13A;]

**[(*ib*) the power of the Appropriate authority in any other matter under clause (*d*) of section 13B;]

**[(*ic*) the manner of establishment of a National Human Organs and Tissues Removal and Storage Network and Regional Network and functions to be performed by them under section 13C;]

**[(*id*) the information in the national registry of the donors and recipients of human organs and tissues and all information under section 13D;]

(*j*) the form and the manner in which an application for registration shall be made and the fee which shall be accompanied, under sub-section (2) of section 14;

(*k*) the specialised services and the facilities to be provided, skilled manpower and the equipments to be possessed and the standards to be maintained by a hospital for registration, under sub-section (3) of section 14;

**[(*ka*) the qualifications and experience of a transplant co-ordinator under sub-section (4) of section 14;]

**[(*kb*) the form and the manner in which an application for registration shall be made, and the fee which shall be accompanied, under sub-section (2) of section 14A;]

**[(*kc*) the specialized services and the facilities to be provided, skilled manpower and the equipments to be possessed and the standards to be maintained by a Tissue Bank, under sub-section (3) of section 14A;]

(*l*) the form in which, the period for which and the conditions subject to which certificate of registration is to be granted

---

* *Substituted* by Act 16 of 2011 (w.e.f. 10.1.2014).

** *Inserted* by Act 16 of 2011 (w.e.f. 10.1.2014).

to a *[hospital or Tissue Bank], under sub-section (1) of section 15;

(*m*) the manner in which and the fee on payment of which certificate of registration is to be renewed under sub-section (3) of section 15;

(*n*) the manner in which an appeal may be preferred under section 17;

(*o*) the manner in which a person is required to give notice to the Appropriate Authority of the alleged offence and of his intention to make a complaint to the court, under clause (*b*) of sub-section (1) of section 22; and

(*p*) any other matter which is required to be, or may be, prescribed.

(3) Every rule made under this Act shall be laid, as soon as may be after it is made, before each House of Parliament, while it is in session, for a total period of thirty days which may be comprised in one session or in two or more successive sessions, and if, before the expiry of the session immediately following the session or the successive sessions aforesaid, both Houses agree in making any modification in the rule or both Houses agree that the rule should not be made, the rule shall thereafter have effect only in such modified form or be of no effect, as the case may be; so, however, that any such modification or annulment shall be without prejudice to the validity of anything previously done under that rule.

25. Repeal and savings. (1) The Ear Drums and Ear Bones (Authority for Use for Therapeutic Purposes) Act, 1982 (28 of 1982) and the Eyes (Authority for Use for Therapeutic Purposes) Act, 1982 (29 of 1982) are hereby repealed.

(2) The repeal shall, however, not affect the previous operation of the Acts so repealed or anything duly done or suffered thereunder.

---

* *Substituted* by Act 16 of 2011 (w.e.f. 10.1.2014).

Index